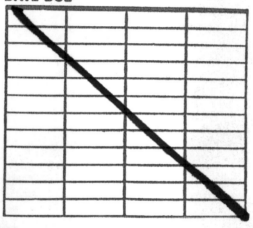

The Ways of Power

Patriae iuventuti
In memoriam S.F.C.L.
30.vi.1962 – 30.vi.1989

The Ways of Power

Pattern and Meaning in World Politics

GEORGE LISKA

Basil Blackwell

Copyright © George Liska 1990

First published 1990

Basil Blackwell Ltd
108 Cowley Road, Oxford, OX4 1JF, UK

Basil Blackwell, Inc.
3 Cambridge Center
Cambridge, Massachusetts 02142, USA

British Library Cataloguing in Publication Data

A CIP catalogue record for this book is available from the British Library.

Library of Congress Cataloging in Publication Data

Liska, George.
The ways of power: pattern and meaning in world politics
George Liska.
    p.   cm.
Includes bibliographical references.
ISBN 0–631–17188–6
    1. International relations – Research.   I. Title.
JX1291.L57 1990   89–29734
327'.072 – dc20   CIP

Typeset in 10 on 11pt Ehrhardt
by Hope Services (Abingdon) Ltd
Printed in Great Britain by
T.J. Press Ltd, Padstow

Contents

Prefatory Note
Writing about World Politics
in Light of Drama and Destiny

In the theater of classic tragedy, the actors' faces remained hidden behind masks to conceal their diverse individualities. Probing behind the many disguises that no less distracting events settle upon the physiognomy of world politics will inevitably retrace the Thucydidean search for the true face of politics behind the conflicting half-truths of a Cleon and a Diodotus, just as exposing the hypothesis of freedom that alone makes it possible for action to arbitrate between the half-truths to manifest constraints on choice is to re-enact the Machiavellian confrontation of *virtù* with necessity. Conveying such politics through the metaphors of a web (of tragedy), warp (of fate), and woof (of choice) suggests the interweaving of strands which, intriguing in themselves, achieve fuller meaning only when they have coalesced into the ways of power overall. If viewing the whole through a lens that lays bare the entanglement of parties to such politics in conflict and the desire to evade its hazards through dominance is to evoke the drama of politics, to view the latter in the perspective of growth and decay of the qualities that raise some of the parties briefly to the heights is to fathom the nearest thing to destiny. Finally, just as the dialectic between freedom and necessity draws the boundaries of choice, and the resistance of actuality to aspiration delimits the area of change, so to expose contemporary events to principles and patterns evidenced historically is to narrow the range of present options and future developments.

Whereas interlacing systematic exposition contrapuntually with speculative disquisitions has been chosen as a way of representing the intricate fabric of reality, the representation implies no judgment whether the result is one man's vision too convoluted to be of wider utility or is a coherent set of facets individually useful for further exploration; whether the product will increasingly take on the quality of a valedictory for a kind of politics about to disappear without trace (and, for most, regret) or will retain that of a diagnostic worth keeping in reserve for the next turn of the wheel. As the author was winding up the struggle with time for a chance to meld fragments scattered in earlier work into a final summation, it has become more important to him to note a similarity between the tragedy of a great state as it pursues supreme ambition at the cost of practicable ends and the lot of the arrogant believer in his ability to master, through understanding, the driven statesman's insurmountable plight. His risk is that he will pay with vain grief for the guilt of having presumed to confer life on phantasms of the mind at the cost of denying too much to the still living. It is then an insufficient apology to the dead, but also the one thought that offers some solace, that to anticipate their state in all-consuming labor is the desk-bound dreamer's only way to earn the consoling sweetness the ancients ascribed to letting go of the mere self for the sake of an ideal *patria*.

Confounded though the native land becomes over the years of separation with that *patria*, as something at once less and more, it is not unconcern which defers to the few lines devoted near the book's end to mine the suggestion that a weak country caught up often impotently in the drama of contests among greater powers can nonetheless remain inalienably in control of its moral destiny – so long as its conduct honors a difference: if adhering to permanent interests is for a great power the sufficient corrective to sentimentalizing friends and demonizing foes, the smaller people defending fewer choices against stricter necessity has the larger task of doing the same in ways that safeguard self-respect as a value above any interest.

Introduction
Beyond the Illusion of Progress

Whatever may be true for the conflict-centered interactions that represent the drama of world politics, the evolution of both states and interstate systems that encompasses their respective destinies has neither a single determinant nor a straight direction. It has no specific cause and sure conclusion outside a loosely cyclical rhythm enclosing gross sequences, despite some gradation in the levels of achieved development from one state and empire system to the next and the more definite gravitation of the centers of power and policy over time. Increases in the complexity of the arena as it crystallizes, and a less certain growth in the competence of state-like actors as part of their consolidation, do not result in fundamentally new kinds of either being or behaving any more than do changes in power configurations. Consequently, evolution as phased progression is not tantamount to anything like cumulative progress: where progression is focused on variably manageable process, the invariant core element of progress is perfectible product. Evolutionary outcomes do not automatically or materially alter the operations that mediate evolution; the aggregative consequence of ambiguities inherent in a competitive system is neither only antagonism, enacting *agon* before debouching in a state's or a system's agony, nor only accommodation, leading through particular appeasements to eternal and universal peace. "Facts" do not support a melioristic design that implements a steady increase in positive cooperation of societies which, overcoming the scarcity of both material and immaterial goods, would ascend jointly from the ordeal of recurrent conflict and crisis, denoting the fallen nature of man, to redemptive consummation of history in a pan-human community.

When secular progress in interstate relations has been severed from an eschatological vision of salvation, it will be equated with the defeat of the correspondingly desacralized sin of power-seeking pride. Such pride, served by instrumental and actuating strategic rationality, will be expected to yield before the virtue of prudent reasonableness: one that conduces to moderation because it combines practical or normative reason with ordinary common sense. However, to link progress to an indefinite increase of cooperation within the range of the modes of behavior that have grown out of evolution, is to interfere with the conflict mechanism that is most directly responsible for the evolution; it means pushing progression beyond its manifest bounds while loosening its vital hidden spring. The fallacy can produce only frustration when cooperative (or *sui generis* competitive) economic relations and consensual institutional frameworks or transactions are expected to function simultaneously in a dual role: as prime constraints on politico-military conflict, and as chief compensations for whatever either "growing" states or "evolving" systems might forgo as a result of lessened conflict and diminished role of conflict. In fact, institutionalization through the agency of rules-applying organization is little more than an unevenly moderating routinization of traditional modes of conflict and competition; and economic transactions are far from being discrete events separable from politico-strategic transactions, let alone capable of replacing them: to regard them otherwise can only very marginally supplement the traditional emphasis on the economic resource base of actor capabilities and the economy of force as a principle of costs and benefits-calculating conduct – the two main connecting links between economics and power politics and, relatedly, between material or organic givens and operational momentum.

Invoked in support of progress will be informal automatic laws of free competition or compelling interdependence in economics and freely observed formal dictates of compulsory self-restraint in international law-and-organization. An effective operation of either set of laws has been repeatedly held to enlarge the overall fund or provision of positive goods – material sustenance and psycho-political security – to be enjoyed by all simultaneously even if at first perhaps unequally. The enlargement would defeat the actuality, and discredit the quasi-mercantilistic assumption, of incorrigible scarcity spurring competition over mutually exclusive shares of either of the unevenly material goal values – an actuality that underlies, and an assumption that looms behind, the politico-military conflicts that implement the contrary and malignant "laws" of power and power politics. More extreme has been the progressivist assumption holding that the economic and legal-organizational principles and processes, being autonomous, can not only be differentiated from the power-political drives and dynamics but can also, if not wholly substitute for them, subsume them (i.e., come close to determining them): always in potentiality, and in practice under circumstances that make actors more receptive than they were traditionally. The extent of the requisite actor receptivity to the postulated corrective influence increases as the boundary of proposed progress expands beyond new diplomacy, to new politics for community-type world order.

The new diplomacy would only improve on the old, rooted alike in fear and confidence. The actual fears (of surprise by adversaries) and latent suspicions (of secession by allies) were paired with the widespread belief in a shared capacity to identify and assess – comprehend and calculate – each other's interests in ways sufficiently accurate to conceive strategies, contain anxieties, and conduct inherently unavoidable conflicts with a minimum of dislocation. By the time the old diplomacy reached the maximum of technical perfection (in eighteenth-century Europe), advocacy of its more "progressive" version began to reflect more faithfully the philosophical tenets of Enlightenment than the powerful tendencies responsible for diplomacy's rebirth (in fourteenth- to fifteenth-century Italy). Successive proposals of reform would invariably combine a program for implementing an essentially liberal economic theory with arguments in favor of tightening institutional procedures; the likewise persistent assumption was that the formalized procedures would lend a sufficient additional support to the material inducements if not impellents to the peaceful adjustment of conflicts, their composition being as necessary a condition of prosperity as it was the latter's probable consequence. One strand of opinion stressed wealth-creating economic competition or conflict-inhibiting economic interdependence; the other strand encompassed a range from literary peace plans to peace-promoting conferences and institutions. The strands were to meet eventually in a hypertrophy of international organizations devoted to shaping constructively the "interface" between material welfare and militancy leading to warfare. When accumulated experience had reduced expectations from punitive economic sanctions against unilaterally offending parties, institutionalized economic "regimes" took over the task of implementing the abiding trust in convergent economic sensitivities if not yet solidarities of mutually dependent parties.

Breaking with the classic Greek concept of an unchangingly cyclical movement of rising and falling power in history, ruling out existential progress and reducing ethical justification for penalizing conquest, the proponents of new diplomacy set out to replace constraints from highly specific configurations of power with restraints based on abstract norms of political behavior and concrete forms of economic conduct. The not always disinterestedly propounded or postulated improvements were at least as much part of efforts to hinder assaults on the authority as to soften the impact of one-sidedly advantageous major peace settlements beginning with Utrecht, continuing with Vienna, and so far culminating with Versailles. Thus, instead of aggregating into a widely assimilable if specifically Anglo-American "tradition" in conducting international relations, the innovative norms were flawed at their birth insofar as they (1) codified the peculiar material strengths or interests of the victors in the antecedent wars, and (2) collided in their thrust with the socio-political ideologies of the successive continental European losers, postulating a conflictually patterned behavior within and among societies. Rather than a new diplomacy actually muting conflict, the clash of the contrasting presumptions was mediated through real events arising out of actual ways of behaving on the part of unevenly evolved key powers. The resulting normative anarchy only helped escalate the operational level of crises in the twentieth-century installments of perennial struggles surrounding transfers of primacy at the summits of the power hierarchy, stoically endured hitherto by virtue of immemorial authentic tradition.

FACETS OF ILLUSORY PROGRESS

Supporting the new diplomacy in the enlightened liberal-progressive view is a reformed international politics, based on the weakening if not removal of material stimuli to military conflict. Conflict as the main occasion for gains from predation is henceforth discouraged by newly plentiful production, continuously fed by rising productivity and equally contingent on peace. The material is reinforced by a moral factor inasmuch as the victor or conqueror has become less capable of appropriating the productive surplus of the loser, which in an era of unceasing technological innovation depends increasingly on unenforceably spontaneous initiatives and inventions. The "post-industrial" setting revises thus both radically and beneficially the anterior relationships between predation and production, between war and welfare, and between surplus and security – in sum, between economic and politico-military factors. Ironically, the height of progress achievable in conditions of plenty is in these terms closest to the beginnings of a longest possible cycle, begun in the neolithic village's dependence for physical survival on utmost penury, likewise offering no meaningful reward from forcible conquest. The difference is that, while eternal peace of the future would go hand in hand with unbounded plenty, concord would expand from the smallest necessary to the widest possible community.

In a world economic "system" poised between incentives to conflict (competition between members of the industrialized "core" and among them over the less advanced sectors) and disincentives to militarily enacted and territorially focused contentions, progress would mean continuing to substitute indirect persuasive for directly coercive modes and instruments of influence or control. Just as a built-in net tendency of the world economy to go on expanding would shield industrial societies from the ancient woes of abrupt and irreversible material decline, so an accelerating diffusion of productive capacity from the core into the periphery would blunt the deleterious connotations of indirection in the former's sway over the latter. This being so, the benign effects of augmented productivity on both social and moral well-being in an ever-widening community would be only supplemented on the plane of developing institutions by a likewise auspicious nexus between societal pluralism and political stability. As an increasingly cooperative world order replaced the conflictual state system, the positive effects of exporting abroad the modes of competition precariously moderated at the center of the system would be completed by extending to relations among states the modes of integration, communication, and conflict resolution so far evolved within the most fully institutionalized polities.

From Athens via Venice to England and beyond, all trade-dependent powers were subject at all times to geostrategic imperatives conditioning their access to or control of routes or opportunities for commerce and propelling them into warlike continental involvements. By the same token, no major continental state had a real policy option to totally immerse itself in geostrategics, to the neglect of a separate or separable economic dimension. The most gladiatorial "wars of magnificence" of the early Louis XIV were conjugated with official (Colbertian) economic concerns, which underlay both specific wars (beginning with the Dutch) and the regime's enduring preoccupation with the allocation of mercantile-industrial assets (beginning with those to be extracted from Spain and her empire). To ignore such unevenly assorted overlaps leads to placing the real-political (or geostrategic) and economic (or mercantile-industrial) activities and domains next to one another as separate and equal. And doing this implies the possibility of one yielding to the other as solely determining. Yet whereas the ostensible purpose may be to rehabilitate the organizational patterns and operative processes of economics from appearing as irremediably subordinate to real-politics and its operational tenets, the consequence is to displace emphasis within the economic factor and distract attention from its primacy in the resource base of actors.

Material capability is part of the ultimately determinant givens, in conjunction with the geographic situation that itself conditions the economic surpluses and scarcities, assets and liabilities, of territorial actors. Conversely, particular economic concerns constitute only rarely the self-sufficient stake and stimulus of strategies; they are in the making of policy always subject to and mostly overlaid by the self-perpetuating operational momentum that highlights the more readily perceptible and at least seemingly more easily manipulable geostrategic factors. Hence, while material-economic and real-political factors and concerns are always interwoven, they influence policy at different levels of determination rather than each representing or affecting a different sector of significant activity. In the actually operative hierarchy of determinative influences, economic concerns will be or appear to be salient, and supposedly autonomous laws of free trade dominate, when a power superior both economically and geostrategically sets the tone for the politico-economic universe. They will cease being such when a more usual configuration of several powers includes some who rely on non-economic instruments for securing goals including economic access and standing. Normalcy is restored also whenever a systemic crisis focused on security-and-supremacy issues shifts any prior emphasis on economic back to geostrategic imperatives. It is then the temporary subsidence of the latter that will have created the vacuum of perceptions and motivations which, automatically filled by subsidiary considerations including economic alongside domestic and subjective-personal, had conduced to the normalcy-restoring crisis.

To hold otherwise requires reducing real-politics to a caricatural portrayal featuring territory as the sole stake and the use of military force as the sole instrument, just as to release economics for its role in a utopian vision of progress entails confining it to a uniquely propitious environment or system. Yet not even the capitalist world economic system, inseparable from conflicts among territorial states in its origins, was at any time designed or destined to progressively "economize" real-political relations any more than it has been responsible for creating the modern politico-military state system. Capitalism has at the most carried into deeper societal levels the role mercantilist policies had played in effecting a more fundamental evolutionary change – to wit, directing governmental functions from inter-actor competition to intra-unit consolidation, en route to inter-group conciliation, as a matching concern. However, even that shift was subject to alternations and did not guarantee progress toward more peaceful or stable international relations. Similarly, capitalism has been only one contributory factor in shifting emphasis from direct and coercive to more indirect and "persuasive" instruments and techniques of influence or control among states – another real, if not necessarily wholly progressive or permanent, change. Finally, softening and subsiding or not, the dominance of the world economy by the capitalistic core was no more indispensable in galvanizing the system's progression at the center than it was purely exploitative at the fringes. It merely reinforced for a time other factors – including military-technological, cultural, and resulting attitudinal – that combine in the dynamic which propels development and in the process changes the distribution of power and pressures between the center of the world political system and its periphery.

On balance and over time, primarily determinative will be the broadly defined "political" factor as it grows out of the more basic or inclusive, geohistorically conditioned structural and organic setting. The hierarchy of causal factors effective at any one time will be obscured by dialectical relationships militating against confident diagnoses as much as against authoritative prognoses. Crucially important will be the position of economic concerns within the system-structuring if not -controlling schisms, which succeed one another over longer periods of time than do changes in the location of control or crisis and place emphasis on subtle dualities within the core of the system rather than substantial discrepancies between its core and periphery. Thus, the economic concern will be fairly deeply hidden and only sporadically operative, also because it is unavowable, within the compass of the schism between sacral and secular powers and principles which tends to shape the earliest beginnings or most primitive conditions of an inter-unit system. Economic stakes will be conspicuously operative, but will be also conspicuously geopoliticized, in relations governed by the schism between land- and sea-oriented actors. And they will occupy an ambiguously intermediate position in the cleavage between East and West. Often complementary in tradable economic assets, the two have tended to be conflicted by virtue of ideo-cultural or value-institutional and geostrategic factors responsible for fundamentally different types of both political and economic organization.

In the case of any of the schisms, operationally predominant will be the politically defined ostensible issue or stake, one that can be openly avowed and intellectually mastered, meaningfully perceived and plausibly proclaimed as well as purposively pursued. This will be true even – or especially – when the economic factor appears to be clearly dominant, as it long was in the land–sea power schism. That which then determines policies is not economic conflict or asymmetric interdependence between materially differently endowed and specialized powers, but the presumption that the diverse resources are inseparable in upholding equal or paramount role and status in the power-political system. The inseparability will reinforce any prior stimulus implicit in physical contiguity as well as any surface frictions incidental to economic interdependence as such. By the same token, strategies of the two differently situated and endowed kinds of powers will be determined not by an easily conceivable division of productive economic labor, but by the difficulty to orchestrate a concertedly managed division of political labor for sustaining simultaneously the stability of the system and the dominant status of both parties in it. Nor will relations be often influenced primarily by the material price at least one of economically similar (maritime-mercantile) powers might eventually have to pay for political-military cooperation against the economically dissimilar one. Relations will respond instead to the incentives to politico-military conflict that are latent within a geostrategic triangle of disparately located (insular-to-continental) powers relating to one another through a finite range of diplomatic strategies. The conflict-stimulating incentives merely comprise the superior advantage the most competently mercantile actor does, or is suspected to, derive from the triangular pattern of trade (thus Britain from UK–Baltic–North America trade during the "first" British Empire and the UK–Indian–Euro-Atlantic trade in the "second" Empire, identifying the West Indies as the principal economic and geostrategic stake in the earlier and India in the later phase).

It merely dramatizes the inescapable interlocks – and, implicit in them, paradoxes – when politico-military conflict erupted over geostrategic stakes between each other's best customers – thus France and England and, subsequently, Britain and imperial Germany – in an atmosphere of rivalry that competition over trade with third parties had only helped inflect toward hostility. It confounds equally a simple single-factor assessment when some form of economic inferiority or weakness of major land powers is repeatedly matched by only partially compensating military forms of self-assertion in the geopolitical arena or when, as a counterpart to the resulting militarism, a compensatory economism permeates with differently disturbing judgmental criteria the foreign policies and differently lopsided values or societal mores of a maritime-mercantile power, not least when it is about to lose the economic foundation of its geostrategic superiority. In fact, policies seemingly softened by economism were no more apt to stabilize or pacify and qualitatively improve interstate relations than those tainted by militarism were uniquely responsible for regressions into destabilizing upheavals. And, no more than an example of self-denial offered from the position of undoubted politico-military strength would induce a mercantile society to forgo search for strategically significant assets could a leading maritime power buy off the geopolitical ambitions of an assertive land power by only economic gratuities with appeasing effect on a systemic crisis due to land–sea power contention.

There could be no incremental, either sustained or accelerating, progress toward the primacy of economic concerns, liable to promote peace while perfecting order so long as situational peculiarities of powers aggravated the consequences of their plurality in conditions of scarcity. For this reason alone, normative constraints and imperatives rather than material inducements and opportunities were repeatedly expected to replace power politics and root progress in developing international organization. However, the institutional sphere is even less inherently autonomous than the economic relative to the more change-resistant universe of *realpolitik*; and the interlock of norm with will is as strong as, if not stronger than, the link between politics and economics. It was the gradual discovery of this which has diverted the focus of international organization from concern with intractable politico-military security to economic issues as part of an evolution which, when it applies to the course of a particular international organization, inhibits anything like a cumulative increase in its authority and thus progress.

Nominally authoritative institutional norms will be subject to de facto "laws" – requisites, tendencies, and dynamics – of power politics inseparable from the averred purposes and actual procedures of international organization, attending its origination and operation. Newly established international organizations were repeatedly advertised as a means to instituting a new mode of relations among states. Beginning in the modern era with the institutionalized Concert of Powers (early nineteenth century), climaxing with the League of Nations (post-World War I), and continuing with only gradual diminution of expectations (post-World War II United Nations Organization and associated agencies), international organization was supposed to supplant "anarchic" self-help revolving around an adversarial balancing of capabilities and implemented by particularistic alliances. Yet the initially sustaining actual purpose, if eventually corrupting, was invariably more realistic or pragmatic. Its core was repeatedly the desire to establish control over the defeated major power through a barely disguised alliance of the victors, integrating only guardedly or partially the ex-enemy in an effort to prevent the wartime allies from courting the vanquished enemy competitively and divisively.

It will always be a problem whether to deal with actually or potentially disruptive powers by way of an adversary-type countervailing or a cooperative-type integrative form of containment. The integrative variety can be implemented within institutional frameworks ranging from general or "universal" to regional, with formats escalating from consultative through loosely confederal to more tightly communal or supranational ones. It can be directed with but minor adaptations also at a fellow-victor while the countervailing approach through adversary alliance will signal either failure or omission of an attempt to contain what typically is a rising power integratively in a wider association (thus tsarist Russia in the Quadruple Alliance, Germany by way of the League of Nations, or Soviet Russia by way of the UN). The highest community type of integration (thus of West Germany next to the ex-victors in the European Community) will mark the possibility to progress farther among not only fewer but also, typically, declining powers. In either case, the main underlying objects are two: (1) to spare the power to be contained through association the trauma of diplomatic isolation and the system the consequences of such trauma, while eliminating incentives for others to pre-emptively compete over its alignment (regardless of whether the power is rising or declining, formerly co-victorious or defeated); and (2) by voluntarily conceding the included power a legitimated role and status, to spare it the different trials of a unilateral drive for a greater if "illegitimately" acquired role (if the power is a rising one or still capable of reacting assertively to incipient decline).

The penalties of isolation and/or the questionable rewards of unilateral self-assertion govern, next to origination, also the operation of a political organization (of security) among the great powers. Whatever may be the constitutional norms, actually controlling great-power conduct will be considerations that do not differ fundamentally from those governing behavior outside the organization's precincts. Each great power will have to decide again and again whether to adjust its position on an issue so as to make joint great-power action possible, or face the equally unattractive alternatives of collective inaction or a unilateral action of its own or another major party's. The risk and cost of dealing with another power's unilateralism is then matched by the risks and costs of the effort to make one's own unilateral action effective. The action must be effective if the unilateralist is to secure a retroactive legitimation of the action and its results by the institutional collective, and avoid having to purchase at rising cost either the support of lesser powers or a full readmission into the greater-power fold. However camouflaged the operative blend may be in unevenly "legalistic" and "realistic" organizations, the crucial transactions will always consist of three components: consultation among great-power members prior to any one's committing itself to a course of conduct that temporarily at least forecloses conciliation; adversary-type containment of a disruptive or deviant major member; and a face-saving if no other compensation for the concessions that have been wrested from the thwarted member in the process of restoring great-power consensus.

The difference between following such a composite procedure in a real-political and in an institutional setting is not one between complying with the superior power of a politico-military adversary or coalition in the former instance and deferring to the superior authority of an impersonal institution or concept in the latter. The distinctive feature resides instead in the provisional deference a party thwarted in the institutional setting pays to the persuasive force of a superior politico-diplomatic alignment by accepting it as the preferred alternative to seeking the arbitrament of military force. Accepting the alternative will be conditional on compliance not being exacted too often from only one of the powers placed in automatic and permanent minority, and on sparing the complying power an uncompensated forfeiture of truly vital prestige or substantive interests. For the condition to obtain, the critical real-political background must not polarize the powers around a stake or schism in such a way as to overwhelm particular interests aligning them in different combinations on different issues; must not elevate the threat they pose to one another above either a third-party threat or the joint danger from instabilities originating within each or without; and must provide peripheral or other outlets for strains and stresses generated at the center of the system or internally. Implicit progress is thwarted when, instead of moderating conflict and fostering cooperation, a Concert of Powers or the great-power core of a "universal" organization is disrupted as a result of having to deal with contentions it has itself created: thus because a great power deviates from institutionally fostered norms of conduct that go beyond traditional rules of power politics, or claims to participate in "policing" or "pacifying" disturbances which, though outside its conventional sphere of interests or influence, are within the organization's formal mandate.

If international organization changes relations among major powers in no decisive way, neither will it alter the relative position of great and lesser powers. It will reverse the natural hierarchy of powers no more than it will substantially revise the requisites for equilibrium to result as it were spontaneously from parties abiding by their "vital" interests. However egalitarian may be the formal – constituent or procedural – norms, when lesser powers seek to translate equality in status into one of role, they will inevitably usurp a markedly greater influence than is the material capability they can deploy outside the organization, or in support of its aims and dispositions. They will drive major powers into taking decisive actions outside the organization, rendering it ineffective for small-state purposes as well. By the same token, the practicable institutional role of lesser powers will radically neither change nor differ from the fact that the smaller states always participate vicariously in international politics by virtue of the major states' desire for their support against one another whenever their tenuous status solidarity does not translate into convergence of concrete interests and actually implemented roles. Lesser powers will seek for ways of translating institutional membership into real influence by either dividing specific competencies with the greater states or infusing principle into greater-power pragmatism. They find out repeatedly that, little as an international organization will or can do to stabilize inter-great-power relations, its main benefit for the lesser (and, especially, newer) powers will be to socialize them into the routines of interstate relations without substantially enhancing their physical security or role-status standing. In fact, the more it projects them into materially unsustained and operationally unsustainable involvement, the more will a security organization expose its lesser members to powerful antagonisms against which it fails to provide assured protection.

In an international system that expands more easily in numbers than it evolves in the manner of conducting its business, the potential for socializing new or peripheral actors is a worthwhile residual function of international organization, itself subject to a species of evolutionary cycle. Successive international organizations will be repeatedly expected to develop continuously toward higher forms and more authoritative expressions of a collective interest. However, that initial stage will sooner rather than later give way to displacing their focus to politically less controversial and institutionally less exacting functions. Functional displacement from the originally central purpose, contrary to initially expected development, will terminate in either an only virtual or also formal demise of the organization as a major or only a significant factor in interstate relations – pending another organizational experiment of the same or different kind and subject to the same rhythm.

Continuous positive development was commonly thwarted by the primary mission of the organization being ambiguous to begin with, as well as aggravated by differences among members carried over from the real-political arena. Thus a very early organization, the Holy Roman Empire, was viewed by essentially "sovereign" and "independent" princes and potentates as a loose framework for managing relations among them and by the emperors as an organ for promoting centralization and consummating unity. An extraneously rooted conflict, between rival confessional camps over parity in representation and influence, made it even more difficult to distribute competencies between central (imperial) authority and regional (princely-territorial) autonomy. When the Germanic Confederation replaced the defunct Empire (at the Congress of Vienna), it could be viewed as nothing more than a standing diplomatic conference of particular states intending to remain sovereign and as an organ for fostering national unity. Its structural flaw lay in the emergent disparity between a relatively declining but institutionally dominant and entrenched power (Austria) and a relatively ascending and institutionally revisionist power (Prussia). The disparity translated into escalating tension between the alternatives of condominial parity and one-power predominance. The first of the "world" organizations, the post-Napoleonic Concert of Europe, could be seen as only an institutionalized alliance of, or a de facto government by, great powers. The conceptual was lodged in the situational cleavage between the maritime power (Britain), relatively liberal and overtly non-interventionist because pervasively (economically and navally) influential, and a range of continental states, increasingly conservative and authoritarian as their locus moved eastward as well as forcibly (i.e., militarily) interventionist in defense of the status quo against revolution.

The ambiguity in purpose persisted into the twentieth century, when the post-World War I League of Nations was conceived by some (mainly Britain) as a slightly updated consultative forum for traditional diplomacy and by others (mainly France) as a more authoritative agency for enforcing the observance of the territorial status quo by one particular power (Germany). The basic purpose of the succeeding United Nations Organization was more uniformly conceived by the victorious powers (as an organization for security against the ex-enemy Axis powers), but was sooner and more deeply than the League divided between rival (US and Soviet) conceptions of what constituted security and order in general and what should be the extent of great-power immunities and thus hierarchy in particular. Subsequent inter-superpower discords outside the institutional arena opened the door for the lesser states to reinterpret the organization as an agency for enforced decolonization and subsidized economic development of formerly colonial new states.

When Britain and France perpetuated in the League the dissension over intervention versus non-intervention between maritime-insular and military-continental members, previously manifest in the Concert, a secondary difference was that the "revolutionary" threat from Germany, as distinct from the earlier one from France, was viewed in its international dimensions only. When the UN reinstituted more overtly than had the League the principle of great-power government going back to the earlier Concert, it was near-instantly paralyzed by contest between two confessional-ideological camps reminiscent of the Holy Roman Empire, and two unevenly rising–declining major powers familiar from the Germanic Confederation, over the issue of parity as against one-party predominance. And whereas the UN was devoid of the thrust toward either the imperial or the communal type of unity under a central authority, peculiar to the two Germanic "regional" organizations, the North Atlantic Treaty Organization and the European Community resembled the latter in that they were poised between the end-goals of integrated community of either the hegemonial-imperial kind (NATO) or the supranational type (European

Community), and the methods of conventional military alliance of states or confederal association of governments.

Conventional dilemmas imported from the real world will foreclose incremental development in all institutions one way or another. They help debase institutional authority as they arrest its development and, by blocking the enforcement of normative constraints on self-help, rehabilitate the normal procedures of non-binding consultation within institutional frameworks that barely facilitate and frequently hinder such procedures. The same dilemmas foster a tendency for organizational functions to be displaced from essentially political ones dealing with security and status to economic or cultural functions, ostensibly keyed to deeper roots of longer-term stability. The trend to rationalize functional displacement as progressive innovation fed on the ambition for international organization to replicate, when not outdo, the liberal-constitutional tendencies operative within the modern state while wholly lacking their basis in societal consensus. The League declined from an authoritative to an optional regime of collective security and on to a predominantly socio-economic agenda; the displacement set the pattern for the initial distribution of tasks in the League's successor, destined to alternately de- and re-politicize the functional commitment and pass on much of its implementation to narrowly specialized particularistic agencies.

Since the sequence from one organization to the next has at best paralleled the sequence from one state system or its phase to another, the postulate of progress could be upheld only by reformulating the conception and the conditions of world order – and by doing this in ways that diminished the significance of formal institutions without automatically enhancing the status of the real-political arena. The difficulty of establishing a meaningful relationship between the two spheres has always grown out of a fundamental difference: The "laws" of the real-political world reflect near-equally attraction and recoil between unevenly forceful powers; institutions tend instead to dilute effective capability into forms of nominal authority and attributed function that exceed actual capacity to exercise the authority or implement the function. The consequent failure of international organization to grow in effective authority and role was in turn disclosed in two interrelated ways: (1) traditionally feasible functions such as diplomatic mediation, truce supervision, and negotiated accommodation, instead of multiplying in range or improving in efficacy to a point matching increases in institutional capacity, have only come to be performed by a vastly expanded bureaucratic apparatus taking over from feudal overlords or popes in medieval statecraft and from surrogate agents of classical diplomacy; and (2) the institutional hypertrophy has been matched by a spurious functional inflation, as a growing range of ephemeral because systemically unnecessary or practically infeasible functions could neither draw upon nor mobilize an enlarged and growing capacity of the organization to implement them. Instead of losing more of it as a result, international organization could enhance its authority only when functions that were intrinsically authentic (i.e., clearly necessary for routine operations and relatively stress-free restabilizations of the international system) actualized all of the organizational capacity to perform them latent in the system (confirming the functions as not only needed but also as feasible).

If a function is to give rise to real and enduring authority internationally no less than domestically, the appropriate institutional capacity to perform it must be present. If function is either unessential or infeasible, displacement will be to less onerous function; if institutional capacity is lacking, displacement may (provisionally) be to a different organ or organization. In either case, function and capacity will always "seek" and occasionally "find" one another, with the result depending on whether the function is necessary (in terms of system needs) and feasible (in terms of actor dispositions and inter-actor dilemmas), and whether institutional capacity is real (in terms of the potential to coordinate dispositions or attenuate dilemmas). Progress will be lacking so long as displacements show that formally instituted functions are not genuinely necessary nor practically feasible, and are thus unable to stimulate the emergence or growth of real capacity; it will be halting and intermittent when displacement discloses a search for the most suitable capacity (organ or organization) to perform a genuine function. An international organization will regress instead of progress when functions and capacity are related wholly negatively, with fatal effects on institutional authority. While its effective demise need not mean formal dissolution, it will always entail extensive functional displacement (to either politically neutral functions or barely perceptible diffuse functions such as socialization) and organizational devolution (to narrowly specialized agencies). In such a case, displacement and devolution may be the necessary condition of the organization surviving nominally as wholly un-threatening and discreetly serviceable to real or vital interests of key members. Whereas the League was dissolved in one kind of external setting, the UN had to outlive its originally intended self in order to survive on such terms in a differently constituted environment.

Instead of progressing in capacity and authority, international organization as such has survived because its focus receded from infeasible-to-fanciful to useful-and-feasible, but less system-modifying, functions. Neither feasible nor necessary for an orderly operation of the system were such functions as (general and universal) disarmament coupled with authoritative peaceful settlement of political disputes. Beginning with the so-called Hague Conferences, such functions went seeking one organizational forum after another without finding effective capacity to implement them. A potentially more genuine function, when it was not offered as instant substitute for the balance of power, inhered in the principle of collective security against unilateral use of force. It proved infeasible in practice after passing through several attempts to implement the principle in a manner decreasingly automatic (in the wake of the abortive League-related Geneva Protocol) and increasingly discretionary (within the UN compass), only to lapse into fictional warrants for traditional alliances (e.g., NATO, replicating those France had placed under the umbrella of the League). Any similarity in purpose between general collective security and system-wide balance-of-power mechanism as methods for aggregating compellingly deterrent or defensively countervailing capabilities, was massively overtopped by unsurpassable procedural difference. An essentially opportunistic, self-regarding response to an existential contingency of a power differential to be counterbalanced is one thing; an immediately disinterested obligatory compliance with a normative concept against any display of force is quite another – in fact, a contrary – thing. The procedural difference has proved too great to either reconcile or make inoperative the substantive difference in the targeted event, between "act" – aggression – and "fact" – imbalance, not to be undone by the ambiguity of each.

When functions were lowered to primarily economic-developmental and implicitly actors-socializing purposes, they were brought into equilibrium with institutional capacity on a low level of organizational authority thanks to concessions to realities such as unequal votes for unequally contribution-capable members in economic, and altered attributions of plenary organs in political, organizations. The depressant effect of prior institutional disequilibria achieved thus a viable ratio of individual members' organizational role and influence to their material capabilities (an issue of "structural equilibrium") and of stipulated to actually performed tasks (an issue of "functional equilibrium"), while a working distribution of functions between global-general and regional-particular organisms completed the requirement of minimal efficacy (an issue of "geo-functional equilibrium").*

The cost of approximating the overall institutional equilibrium was arrest in the institution's evolution amounting to growth, when not also a regression relative to expectations. The failure of the original conception to materialize meant that the intended institutional impact on the real-political dynamics was not calculated conservatively enough to keep in step with at best only incrementally improving or intermittently favorable preconditions. A more specific reason was that, just as mishandling the commercial- and the colonial-policy preliminaries to World War I defined the psychological environment in which the Anglo–German competition erupted into military confrontation, so mishandling the real-political preliminaries to institutional experimentation compromised the prospects of international organization after both of the twentieth-century world wars. The overcontainment of Germany after the first conflict by the territorial and economic clauses of the peace could not be sufficiently offset by the institutional compensations subsequently offered, in the formulae associated with the Locarno experiment; for inverse reasons equally ineffectual was to be the attempt to correct the failure to contain Soviet Russia on the ground in central Europe at the end of the second war by hemming in the co-victor inside the UN by an automatically pro-US majority, first illustrated on the Iranian issue. Both approaches differed inauspiciously from the British strategy at the Congress of Vienna preliminaries to the Concert of Europe, combining politico-military containment of Russia in association with allied Austria and defeated France without prejudicing Russia's central role in the conclave of the victors.

---

* The quoted concepts echo, while most of the discussion of international organization supplements, the author's *International Equilibrium: A Theoretical Essay on the Politics and Organization of Security* (Cambridge, MA: Harvard University Press, 1957).

Presumably progress-promoting economic and institutional features will heighten stress on the domestic arena. However, the much vaunted inter-penetration of domestic politics and foreign policy can be misconstrued, on whatever plane it may occur: the purposive, insofar as efforts to institutionalize interstate relations aim at matching the modes of moderating conflict in advanced societies; or the operational, inasmuch as inter-group political dynamics frequently stimulate interstate conflict. The interpenetration, despite its widely affirmed growth, has no definite and definitely positive implications for either the determinative primacy of domestic politics or its limiting effect on external contentions. It has them no more than the dual focus of the economics of resource formation on domestic welfare promotion and war-related outward power projection on the part of any one single actor or the dual, consolidative and frictional, effect of economic interdependence between actors, have for the primacy of economics or its bias in favor of conflict reduction. When a pacific posture is attributed to liberal domestic institutions on a par with free trade it will be commonly due to confusing the effects of liberal democracy with those of latent decline – a connection succeeding to that between climactic ascendancy and liberal economics. Especially where continental states are concerned, the fact that a link exists between liberal democracy and a far-progressed relative decline will be as bashfully concealed an aspect of progressivist thought as its key assumption: that an international system comprising only vigorous liberal states would radically depart – and depart for the better – from the conflictual real-political model of state behavior, is a confidently asserted one.

FOUNDATIONS OF REAL CHANGE

Much as the theses relying on either economic or institutional substitutes for power politics have been invigorated by the twentieth-century rationalistic bias to replace conflict as the engine of evolutionary progression with planning and social engineering as the way to progress, they reflect perennial aspirations. Following upon still earlier isolated efforts, the seventeenth-century religious and eighteenth-century mercantilistic wars gave a fresh impulse to ideas about "new" interstate relations (and related concepts of world order) and "new" diplomacy (and related peace plans). Since reformist notions were intellectual weapons against war, they centered fittingly on war as the principal regulator of system dynamics, while the practices that would validate the ethical or normative idea of progress were identified by critical reference to the theoretical or operative norm of a state system, one nearest to being actualized at the system's evolutionary climax when means–ends rationality in statecraft is most likely to prevail within a structurally well articulated conflict-prone setting. However, as a matter of recurrent fact, the practices most closely corresponding to the progressist post- and anti-war aspirations will characterize patterns of behavior in a later, regressive stage of the development of a system or "sub-system."

The tendency to substitute economic-welfare for real-political objectives had been manifest in fourth- to third-century BC Athens, conspicuous in sixteenth- to seventeenth-century AD Florence (by then the Grand Duchy of Tuscany), and replicated in eighteenth-century Netherlands before manifesting itself in mid-twentieth-century western Europe (now the European Community) in ever more elusive but unmistakable forms. In all cases both the actors and relative segments of the state system had by then been superseded by larger and more vital counterparts or analogues. *Realpolitik* could be only simulated, within the affected segment, inasmuch as the sure prospect of greater-power veto either ruled out expansionist policies altogether or confined them to marginal local gains (thus, anticipating on neither of the superpowers tolerating a resumption of the Franco–German conflict over Alsace–Lorraine as compared with competition over managerial leadership in the Community, when Spain blocked Tuscany's acquisition of Corsica while condoning the annexation of economically vital Siena nearby). In such circumstances, a prime object of foreign policy is only formal or nominal diplomatic independence, pursued by playing off the greater powers against one another while seeking to insulate as much as possible of the environing area from both (e.g. the Tuscan scheme for neutralizing the Tyrrhenian sea against Spanish and French inroads), and demonstrating one's economic and financial vitality implicitly useful to the dominant greater power. A major objective of efforts to expand the range of narrowly diplomatic options is to do better than merely exchange the material costs and risks of politico-military engagements for the economic penalties and other hazards of politico-institutional disestablishment (experienced by Milan and Naples, administered directly by Spain). Even a partial success will delay the moment when the domestic standing of the regime, as the henceforth all-absorbing concern of statecraft, will have been irreparably jeopardized by economic regression.

When formal-to-fictional status overtops effective role in the hierarchy of concerns, it will upgrade the significance of institutional devices and normative designs. The salience of interstate leagues of the Aetolian and Achaean variety in the receding Greek system is on a par with the institutionalized European communities of a later age; and if France's attachment to the League of Nations was comparable with Metternichian Austria's to first the Concert and then the Holy Alliance, it was outdone in the same and the subsequent forums by the institutional pacifism of the once militant members of Europe's warlike "northern system" adjoining the Baltic. French emphasis on independence after World War II has echoed the stepped-up diplomacy of the Tuscan Grand Dukes, itself reminiscent on a small scale of the defensively manipulative Byzantine statecraft, weakened politico-militarily but not abdicating. Such a diplomacy's general purpose is to create an aura around a declining power that safeguards it psychopolitically and holds off challenges liable to reveal its insufficient substance; it does not aim at optimizing conditions for effective resistance to an actually applied politico-military pressure. Moreover, displaying an independent posture on every comparatively cost-free occasion may also preserve the option of disengaging into neutrality in more stressful circumstances. Self-confinement to but token military engagement in collective enterprises (e.g. the Tuscan "volunteer" contingents in a campaign against the Turk no less than the prominent role of, say, the Swedish military in UN "peacekeeping" forces) confirms rather than contravenes the basic stance of opting out of power politics.

The most pragmatic exercises in institutionalized "new diplomacy" will be under the influence of world-order-centered aspirations predominating over *polis-* or state-centered attitudes and philosophies. Taking off from the monotheistic religions in late Mesopotamian–Near Eastern systems, the normative doctrines have covered a range from the Epicurean-Stoic in the late Greek system and mainly Stoic in the late Hellenistic era and neo-Platonic in late Roman Empire, through those of the Dutchman Grotius and the late ancien-regime Enlightenment, to the more recent western formulations of a liberal-cosmopolitan world order. All such doctrines substitute the affirmation of a higher reality for the mundane actualities of a political arena that no longer inspires the pursuit of either collective efficacity or personal excellence because it is no longer (seen as) manageable by traditional or conventional means. However, the particular conception of the "higher" reality has been progressively lowered from the religio-mythological or moral-philosophical through legal-institutional to rationalistic-functional if not also organic-physiological plane. The initial emphasis on individual self-fulfillment to be sought henceforth outside the moral-political framework of the *polis*, declined gradually to preoccupation with the effect war as a token of interstate anarchy was apt to have on civilization and to anxieties over the impact ultimate weaponry (or late-industrial pollution) would have on physical survival on or of the planet. Finally, although mirroring an acute crisis or actual decline in a particular state, the partially escapist world-order doctrines may also have denoted the commonly inadequate reception of previously generated values, institutions, or techniques in enlarged successor systems. As the alienation of more Hellenized, Italicized, or Europeanized policymaking and intellectual elites from culturally impervious nativist masses in the Hellenistic, European, and contemporary global system, respectively, translated into psychic and political insecurities, at least some of the elites would embrace the promise of leaving behind the dilemmas of political actuality for the dream world of a higher and safer reality on at least the "international" plane.

In a real world, however, the ideal of progress could not be safely founded on the psychopolitical pressures within a divided society any more than on the postulate of discrete spheres: the more progress-capable economic, institutional, or ideologically tinged domestic-political and the more progress-resistant real- or power-political ones. In lieu of discrete functional universes that coexist in ideal space and interpenetrate ever more benignly in actual systems, there are actually distinct evolutionary phases that overlap marginally over definite time spans. A more-than-rhetorically manifested or other-than-self-deluding shift in favor of the non-geostrategic determinants has been repeatedly a function of late evolutionary phase for a (superseded) system and late phase in the sequence of basic foreign-policy postures for the (declining) actors: it has not become over historic time a culminating expression of more enlightened values and more humane goals within an advancing civilization. Determinative potency of the various "spheres" will oscillate over time in function of the relative stress each occasions or is subject to – i.e., causal impact will follow the locus of crisis; and the degrees to which the elements that make up internationally relevant reality are most effectively determinant are distinct from the levels of causality that can be attributed to them. Thus the economic factor, decisive for resource endowment, and the domestic or societal factor, decisive for regime survival or stability, will be ultimately (and, thus, often un- or sub-consciously) determinative of action, much as they are themselves conditioned by or even derive from the state-like actor's position in geographic space and on the evolutionary time stream. They are among the basic givens of politics and lastingly indispensable supports of effective policy. However, by both subtle and substantial contrast, outward-directed strategic concerns of a more distinctly political character will be, along with their military-technological implications, the operationally more salient. They are the conscious proximate determinants whenever they have any bearing whatsoever on the dominant crisis. Insofar as the ultimate determinants are factors accounting for the intimate makeup of a society, they can be described as organic, distinct from the operational dimensions more germane to society's external face as an actor among actors.

Counterposing evolution and progress is not to deny development as either movement or accomplished change. It only means questioning linear cumulative transformation of a given state into one qualitatively superior as either process, product, or significant possibility. Real change becomes visible only when differences or discontinuities in organizational forms and organic features are discounted for continuing similarities in operations and objectives. To posit the particular organizational characteristics of, say, antique empires in general or the Assyrian Empire in particular as defining the entity called "empire" for all time leads through a preliminary finding – to the effect that more recent power and interest aggregations such as the British and the American were no empires at all – to the seemingly incontrovertible conclusion of radical or qualitative change having taken place over time. By the same token, treating the particular economic systems of the empires of antiquity as defining their organic essence *in toto* will likewise suggest radical discontinuity when the selective emphasis is employed to overshadow other, including operational, similarities with economically differently organized or sustained entities. Overall, the impression of a dramatic caesura in development is strongest when ostensibly new or different forms and instruments are not exposed to the test of functional equivalence. Arms or economic-growth competition cannot then be seen as functional substitutes for war, economic aid to other countries as equivalents of dynastic dowry or classical subsidies, domestic party politics as updating the role of court intrigue among individuals or cliques, international organization as performing the socializing function previously vested in the institutions of chivalry, and supranational communities (like pan-movements before) as having both the integrative function and the frictional effects of family ties in the dynastic era. When identity of function is not taken into account, radical novelty is imputed to merely rationalized – more elaborate or seemingly more efficient – instruments of policies and techniques or organs of competition, detaching them from the common ground in instrumental rationality they share with older analogues.

Stripped to its core, gradually emerging and lately accelerating real change could be located on several continua. Along one of them readily accomplished transformations have receded in favor of no more than corresponding tendencies; along another, organic substance and related development have gained in salience relative to operational skills and related dynamics. The degree of the change has depended on the extent the progressing expansion of internally feasible relative to externally performed governmental functions combined with the consequent growth of societal inhibitions to alter political mentality, with aid from changes in military technologies. Thus caused and constituted, real change has revolved around the timeless relationship of means to ends, in that reductions in the ends to be pursued abroad that were or appeared to be still desirable (in light of the expanded capacity of governments to achieve internal goals) were on a par or may even exceed limitations on objectives deemed still feasible (in light of the enhanced domestic checks and military-technological means).

Not least because it has been unevenly extensive in the more and the less evolved segments of the system, the change could modify the essence of inter-unit politics less substantially than it affected the exercise of statecraft. Whereas politics were traditionally focused on the actual incidence of empire as an alternative to failed equilibrium, and of hegemony as a radical consummation of hierarchy, it has increasingly revolved around corresponding tendencies reflecting the actual or imputed intentions to achieve – and ability to achieve – the critical transformations. At one historic extreme, vast goals coexisted with weak means in the form of resources and technologies for consolidating realized ends: primitive logistics alone made results depend on surprise, and concentrated force; at another, the means–ends reversal which expanded means beyond practicable ends has made even but remotely comparable results depend on a systematic application of diversified direct and indirect means. Complementing the effect of developments in the military means of destruction, the development of productive economic techniques has continued shifting the decisive effect on outcomes away from relatively short-term operational factors – purposefully active strategies and resulting interactions – to relatively long-term and in part at least spontaneous organic factors – sustained growth in capabilities and steady will.

If this has been the fairly manifest side of real change, its extent has been only relative since transactional tendencies preponderated over accomplished transformations at all times and organic substance and related stamina always proved more important than operational skills in the last resort. But the shift has been sufficient to expand, notably among major parties to the central system and extend thus to the core issues, the range of relations conducted more on the pretense than the presumption that traditional stakes were still practical (as to ends) and strategies effective (as to means). However, the more or less self-consciously "as-if" approach and attitude of salient powers remained as distinct from the simulation of procedures by declining "old" actors as they were from radical innovation introducing "new" international politics. They have not amounted to a distinctively novel mode of relations as either already in place or manifestly emergent, and would not introduce one so long as the territorial state

was the prime actor and the system of such states the critical arena. The scope of real change would remain limited and its nature elusive so long as short-term transactions (strategic modalities and diplomatic maneuvers backed by leverages extending to potential coercion) remained ostensibly the same, and longer-term trends and outcomes (variations in rankings as to role and status) were perceived as significant.

Change could not but be limited so long as the competitive dynamic stimulated perceptions and policies in the traditional manner and the stimulation surpassed the extent to which the traditional approaches were merely simulated by the competitors, out of inherent weakness or environmentally induced wariness, most of the time. And even the limited real change was precarious so long as policy might be at any time subjected again to diminishing constraints from either the military-technological or the sociopolitical sphere. This would happen when the way of enacting military conflict at the center of the system has gravitated back to conventional and thus feasible ways of waging war (by way of standoff in the "unusable" weapons, due to their escalating magnitude and a re-established balance between their "offensive" and "defensive" varieties), with the result of rehabilitating traditional practices (including "hegemonial") with the aid of political or environmental pressures increased sufficiently to make the renewed sense of possibility activate the feeling of necessity. Alternately or conjointly, societal restraints due to the character of industrial economy might collapse, conjointly with a return to crisis in that economy, into their opposites at the center and/or fail to spread from there evenly to the periphery.

Even as traditional modes of statecraft have continued to be reverted to from the extremes of change – one more persuasively implicit logically in than irreversibly secreted by military-technological revolution – both sets of constraints on pursuing the critical transformations by traditional modes of operation fell more severely on the major (industrial) than on the lesser ("industrializing") powers. It was even more paradoxical that whereas the tempo of role-and-status transfers was slowing down because it was tied more closely to incremental organic changes, the moderating effect on the operational context was nullified in crisis situations by foreshortened reaction time – in either conventional-military mobilizations or nuclear exchanges, and by virtue of instantly and visibly publicized communications between contestants. Moreover, while the timetable contracted in crises, the range and intensity of the crises were liable to increase whenever premature efforts to implement radical reform overtook the rate of possible actual change, and the inevitable reactions produced results contrary to those sought. The reacting parties revived traditional patterns regressively when they perceived liberal-utopian values as nothing but disguised defenses of status-quo conservatism by weakening incumbents of power and privilege. Thus German statecraft infused traditional norms of power politics with the mythology of a Third Reich, while in Soviet Russia the Third Rome mythology of nationalist-Slavophile derivation was ready and waiting to be transposed from samizdat pamphleteering into official policy making. On the Third World periphery, comparable consequences were dramatized by religious fundamentalism after being fomented by externally encouraged or imposed, premature or ill-conceived, attempts to foster not so much strategically rational procedures implementing the laws of power in incipiently crystallizing regional politics as socially reformist practices imitating advanced legal or industrial orders in precariously developing proto-national polities. Constraining inter-actor conflicts only contributed to repressing the conflicts inward sufficiently to deprive the new actors of the developmentally creative potential of both sustained and manageable rivalry. Somewhat similarly, injecting the rationalist secular temper of the Italian Renaissance prematurely into the north European periphery had helped exacerbate religiously rationalized reactions to weakening traditional modes, while attempts to transplant liberalism into unready societies of Germany and Russia have subsequently made it easier for totalitarianism to succeed to transitional chaos.

The common denominator was compounding the ambiguities of what will repeatedly be perceived as a transitional era with the anachronisms of either rushing ahead of or regressing behind the scope and rate of possible change. The consequent exposure of instrumental rationality to utopian reform at one extreme and to nostalgic reaction at the other, while both extremes rebel against the demands and consequences of strategic rationality, has mirrored the uncertain state of the evolution of the contemporary international system. The system's center in superpower behavior, one essentially rational (relating ends to disposable means) and responsible (adjusting ambition to sustainable consequences), has been suspended between differently non-responsible post- and pre-maturity patterns of behavior in the European west and the Third-World periphery. The tension of conflict between the two polar principals has kept the primitive global system from slipping into a chaos of the type endured at its post-Roman Empire beginnings. However, instrumentally rational statecraft for managing the conflict was also subject on both sides to an uncertain and varying awareness of the scope and the implications of a real change that was at once marginal and materially significant. Ultimate rationality and responsibleness were thus contingent on the sum of historical intelligence available to the two unequally history-conscious societies as they waged, with uneven results, an uneven battle against contrary rationalizations of self, the other, and the relationship between the two. Representing the progressist-utopian doctrine was, in the Soviet Union, a regime ideology of decreasing potency internally and virtually untraceable influence on major foreign policies; mediating it in the United States were more deeply internalized societal values and beliefs, surfaced by each periodic disenchantment with only superficially received rational *realpolitik*. The utopian strain has coexisted in both with a retrospective mythical element: crusading puritanical messianism in America (the "new" Jerusalem) and a millennially oriented religious orthodoxy in Russia (the "last" Rome). But whereas the irrational strain in Russian policy would be exacerbated by failure to achieve essentially traditional real-political goals, America's normatively phrased nostalgic myth fed the opposition to such goals for both self and alter in the name of an unreal past and unrealizable future - with the consequence of each polity mistaking the demoniac nature of power inhering in self for the diabolical character and intent of the other.

In such conditions, the potential for the international system to continue evolving on the global plane without recourse to major wars depended on meaningful progress assuming a novel and genuinely revolutionary form. This could happen only in the form of statecraft that orchestrated the elements of real change in international politics in support of enlarging the prospect for successfully implementing historically tried (and thus realistically validated) but unconsummated (and thus effectively untested) strategies – or strategy. Creating the basis for progress so defined would inevitably blend historical retrospection with anticipations about the future partaking of prophecy; doing so would entail, in conditions favoring radical doubts about the future's balance between promise and peril, placing the wager on the relevance as against gambling on the irreversible obsolescence of the structures, the strategies, and the stages of evolution bequeathed by the past.

Part I

The Web of Tragedy

I

Structured Systems and Shaping Schisms

When the objective is to explore relations among organized collectives in terms of the fundamental space-time dimension, the features to begin with are those revealed by the longest possible time perspective and unfolding in contiguous space over a traceable path from a distant point of departure. The temporal trajectory coincides with the full length of more or less known or recorded history; the physical path winds within an expanding scope from Mesopotamia to the eastern Mediterranean (centered successively on Egypt and Greece) and from there via the (Italy-centered) all-Mediterranean area to the Atlantic-abutting north-western Europe and beyond to the global *ecumene* enframed by the major oceans. If, thus located and mapped, a sequence of events is to be a process, the successive structures must be somehow connected in and through action; and for contiguity to mean more than what is implicit in the physical fact of space, the connecting path must become (if only figuratively) an axis around which a patterned development revolves, rotates, or spirals. Both process and pattern, centered on conflict, will be mediated by actor strategies that serve as links between conditioning structures and developmental stages. Thus, the interactions and the developments culminating in the Persian Empire link the Mesopotamian system to the eastern Mediterranean systems and the Roman Empire relates the eastern Mediterranean to the western and the all-Mediterranean systems in the empire's ascent period and, in its decline, mediates the transition from the latter systems to the future European and Eurocentric systems. Moreover, in order for there to be evolution, there must be some differences between the successive structures and stages; but there must also be sufficient similarities if there is to be meaningful recurrence in a development that is continuous. If, therefore, periodic recurrence neither must nor need be exact repetition, it is no less necessary for past events or phenomena to have relevance for possible-to-probable future. If analysis is to serve anticipation, whatever is non-recurrent is radically irrelevant even if otherwise revealing. By the same token, while development entails change, change is not only a logical counterpart of continuity but also a material ingredient in a continuity that is not fixed and unevolving constancy.

SIZES AND SHAPES OF "STATES" AND SYSTEMS

Before trying to discern patterns in evolution to complement those of interactions it is necessary to identify and assemble the possible elements thereof, beginning with the different (micro- or macro-) structures in the recurrent (proto- to meta-stage) sequences, along with the most readily discernible functional links or operational connections. It is they which bring sequences closer to being a continuous process, and separate structures to being also interlocking stages in the process. When the aim is no higher than to disarticulate an ostensibly formless flow into some of the shaping factors, forces, and functions, rigorously defining the constituent phenomena matters less than identifying their rudimentary relationships. These occur in, and to a large extent make up, a "system." The latter is present in a sufficiently developed condition when comparably constituted and motivated subjects of action ("actors") relate to one another more than accidentally. They do so then by virtue of a behavior that brings out innate drives which, responding to a finite range of possible environmental structures, are refined into competition over shared stakes. That is to say, actors-in-system pursue what are essentially the same goals by means that are qualitatively identical if unevenly efficient and must be at least minimally rational (in terms of means–end congruence) to keep the actor in the game. When the conditions are met in a full-blown system, activity is in principle predictable and the outward modes of conduct and intermediate outcomes conform to a discernible pattern; a parallel mobilization of resources for securing objectives and sustaining conflicts produces determinate configurations – distribution and hierarchy – of power which, in turn conditioning the contest, arbitrate the efficacy of alternative means (including strategies) in the last resort.

When such conditions are not yet realized, there is at best only a proto-system; when the definitional criteria of a system have been transcended in the direction of community-type formats, a meta-system has come into being. Within this sequence of time-bound stages, it will be a matter of the size of the space occupied by individual actors and the arena of their system-constitutive interactions whether the system is of the micro- or the macro- variety (a nomenclature which, though idiosyncratic, conforms to the dictionary meaning of the terms as small and large, mini- and mega-sized). The spatial dimension can appear also as one of location (as well as size) when, as often happens, a well crystallized micro-system is at the physical as well as the operational center of the total arena while the merely emergent (and at least partially still proto-systemic) complex of larger actors constitutes the arena's periphery.

Before attempting to intimate how the different system structures are related operationally, we must ask how they differ organically in terms of basic givens.

Compounding at least some of the salient traits of the Sumer-Mesopotamian, Greek, and Italian micro-systems, how do they differ from similarly evolved traits of the corresponding macro-systems: Near Eastern (or, as we shall identify it, Babylonic), eastern Mediterranean (or Hellenistic), and Mediterraneo-Atlantic European (or, again to anticipate, Italistic) ones?

The defining difference in size of both actors and arenas points to equally basic ratios, and their respective advantages and disadvantages. They are the ratios of size or scale to social energy and cohesion on the one hand and, on the other, of boundary circumference to intra-unit capability and inter-unit distance. Both ratios favor an earlier, because speedier, consolidation of the micro-actors and crystallization of the micro-systems, if typically at the cost of intense, volatile, and continuous conflicts. Power will be aggregated more quickly and effectively when smallness of a unit fosters the part-managed and part-spontaneous generation of surplus (moral) energy and (material) resource; and power will be more readily projected outward when, in a system of small units, closely adjacent boundaries are perceived as disproportionately long relative to the enclosed space and resource while distances between power centers are short, both features offering either the risk or the temptation of military surprise with irreversible political result. A likely consequence of warfare that inclines toward intensity and promotes instability will be a shorter life expectancy for micro-actors and -systems than is that of their larger analogues, not least because the latter's pertinent size–energy/cohesion and circumference–capability/distance ratios delay both actor and system crystallization. A major cost is greater liability of the bigger actors to dissolution for internal reasons and without coercion from the outside. But, insofar as the ratios also permit or facilitate defense in depth through either resistance or regeneration, while reducing the element of surprise, they also engender less pressure for politico-military conduct that is ambiguously precautionary-and-provocative and revolves around or ends in empire-type power aggregation.

The conditions and tendencies clearly apply to the Italian micro-system as against the European macro-system, to a system of city-states such as Milan, Florence, Venice, Padua, and Mantua and one of feudal monarchies of France, England, Castile or Aragon, the Germanic Empire, and, say, Poland-Lithuania. They make sense for the Greek city-state system consisting of a Sparta, Argos, Corinth, Athens, and Thebes and its Hellenistic macro-systemic successor comprising such kingdoms or empires as Macedon, Syria–Asia, Egypt in the eastern and Italy-dominating Rome and Spain-encompassing Carthage in the western Mediterranean. Nor are they without basis in, and irrelevant for, the less well-known conditions of the Sumer-Mesopotamian micro-system, with simultaneously or successively active city-states such as Umma, Lagash, Ur, Uruk, and Kish, as compared with the larger Egyptian, Babylonian, Hittite, Mitanni, and Assyrian empires of the Near Eastern macro-system.

It is still part of the spatial dimension that many or most of the city-states (often with mini-empires of their own) were located at or close to sea coasts and river deltas, while the larger territorial "states" or "empires" tended to evolve and expand out of the vaster hinterland. Their sheltered rear-continental location allowed for slower and longer gestation, while alternative (concentric or parallel) configurations of river beds fostered concentration or fragmentation, unity or disunity. By contrast, the close juxtaposition of population clusters in the obstacle-free alluvial plains of lower Mesopotamia allowed for mutually containing interaction of small units yielding in due course to conquest from within or without a region; the topography of a Greece criss-crossed with mountain ranges and valleys favored self-contained smallness, without excluding limited inter-valley expansion; and the intermediate state of Italy's physical environment combined the effects of plain (in Lombardy), river beds, and the principal mountain range in promoting smaller-sized entities to the north and a bigger one (Naples) to the south of the Apennines.

However otherwise different, small and big powers are equally part of a true system so long as they have the common denominator in a definite, expansible or contractable, territorial base. As such they will respond to fundamentally identical drives and concerns, follow an identifiable path of development, and share, due to a slow rate of innovations or their rapid diffusion, a qualitatively comparable technological (not least military) endowment. The territorially conditioned identity in basic makeup (or "constitution") and mind-set (or set of "concerns") will limit the operational significance of even apparently important variations, such as economic specialization and organization, informal political culture or formal political institutions, and related biases and orientations.

Within the bounds of territoriality shared by unevenly large actors, micro-actors have tended to be city-states oriented to commerce, and even to relatively long-distance trade, along waterways, with the socio-cultural consequence of being the seats of relatively advanced, urban, civilization. Thus, Umma and Lagash are more characteristic of the original Sumerian micro-system adjoining the Tigris-Euphrates delta than is the more inland situated Akkadian conqueror. And it is more than only symbolically significant that the supersession of the city-state systems in the delta by a power advancing from the hinterland coincided with the silting up of the river estuaries, removing the seminal trade centers from their natural outlets. Similarly, there is a sense in which the commercial cities of Attica and the Aegean are more typical of the Greek city-state system at its peak than the landlocked and agriculture-based ones in the Peloponnese or Boeotia: Athens more than Sparta. The same is true of Florence and Venice relative to Naples, the Romagna, and even (despite its industry) Milan once the Italian micro-system has absorbed, as had the Greek analogue, the stimulating initial impetus from the more military-continental and less mercantile-maritime *poleis* (Milan and Sparta, respectively – just as Umma in Sumer). Likewise, when the originally feudal-agricultural European macro-system, in large part conditioned by the distance of its core from the Mediterranean, will begin being dwarfed into a quasi-micro-systemic size relative to its emergent global setting, representative identity will have started shifting to actors (the Dutch and the English) of a more urban-commercial character than had been the civilization of the previously tone-setting actors.

Anticipating medieval Europe, typical of the "Babylonic" and the Hellenistic macro-systems of antiquity were empire-style actors of primarily continental character. They were based on agricultural (including slave) economies even when also exploiting traffic along trade routes and mineral resources for fiscal purposes and armaments. They opposed a rural-barbarian tenor to the urban-civilized character of the micro-states, beginning with the powers that successively triggered the macro-systemization of Mesopotamia: the Akkad of Sargon and the Babylonia of the Kassite conquerors, preceded by the empire of Hammurabi. If the Egyptian Empire turned intermittently seaward once it had emerged out of the Hyksos-barbarian invasion, it was, again characteristically, pulled into the Near Eastern macro-system by competing realms that expanded overland into the Syrian–Palestinian region in search of commercial-maritime outlets. The role the quest played in the formation and the fate, initial conquests and eventual collapse, of land empires such as that of the Mitanni and the Assyrians continued to apply to the Medan-to-Persian Empire, which brought to conclusion the first micro-to-macro- sequence, as well as to the Macedonian and Syrian (and, to lesser extent, Egyptian) post-Alexandrine kingdoms of the Hellenistic period – before coming to affect the early European monarchies emerging out of the wreckage of the Roman Empire.

Broadly parallel are related distinctions between the micro- and the macro-actors: (1) between freely-competitive and command-type economies (the former taking off from coastal traffic, the latter from inland canalization as their foundations); and (2) between dynamic finance and depressant fiscality as the monetary medium for economic activities and the material foundations of politico-military enterprises. The logic of the difference in size applies no less to the military tools of the micro- and the macro-actors (the former more often than not relatively western and the latter eastern). Thus the hoplite foot soldiers of the Greek city states is outsized by the armored elephants of the Hellenistic kingdoms on land just as the triremes of the former are by the unwieldy quinqueremes of the latter on the sea; a comparable difference in a later era will be that between the galleys (and mobile field artillery) of the Italian city-states and the galleons (and siege-cannons) of the European powers. Although the size factor in weaponry could not invariably favor the smaller political organizations when faced with the enlarged entities, gigantism defeated repeatedly its practitioners in the east, from the Hellenistic empires facing Rome to the Ottoman Empire borrowing from while confronting the West. To the extent that the military aspect of the dichotomy between micro- and macro-systems has also a socio-political dimension, it points to a mere tendency. Urban citizen militia in the service of oligarchy will tend to give way to and, in due course repeatedly, before the more easily extensible mercenary soldiery of the larger and more centralized-authoritarian type of power, if perhaps more consistently so in the antique Mediterranean than in the early-stage Italo-European system. There, too, successes of Lombard and Flemish urban militias against part-mercenary imperial or royal troops had been expunged (as they had been in the Graeco-Persian relationship) by the shift to mercenaries as a well-nigh universal phenomenon, before mass levies gave decisive advantage to the modern great powers.

The differences in military organization are of a piece with those in social mores and political culture, likewise rooted as much in the size as in the special character of the actors. In the decisive formative period if not later, the typically water-related micro-actors inclined toward socio-political spontaneity, while the macro-actors rooted in soil veered toward social hierarchization if not regimentation. Whereas the former shunned military or political professionals and ran the risks of amateurish performance, the latter embraced professionalism and courted the danger of seeing their moral or psychological foundation atrophy. Thus, there was no clearly defined warrior class in micro-systemic Sumer-Mesopotamia, while Hammurabi's Babylonian Empire introduced professional army supported by bureaucracy as a major innovation. Nor were the generals of the Greek city-states and other office-holders issuing from the public assembly in any way as career-professional as would be later the military and political managers of the Hellenistic kingdoms or empires. By the same token, it denoted the Italian micro-system's late maturity and initial deterioration when the transition from militias to the *condottieri* paralleled one from *popolist* communes to princely *signorie*. Finally, administrative as much as military professionalism, though initiated by the financially better-managed smaller insular or quasi-insular powers, would be perfected in Europe's continental-agricultural macro-actors.

Professionalization may not always connote decline in civic morale ultimately subverting public efficacy; and a micro-system only may tend to develop some of the attributes of a macro-system in its late maturity preceding decline, while at least some (coastal-to-insular) of the progressively differentiated members of a macro-system will in due course display traits characteristic of micro-actors. More certain is that, in their late decline phase, both systems will tend toward the meta-systemic opposite of the proto-systemic beginning on a spectrum that centers on a fully developed micro- or macro-system. The two extremes touch or overlap not only because a particular proto-system emerges out of a weakened or disintegrating meta-system; each also inverts in different degrees and ways the key characteristics of a crystallized system. Both proto- and meta-systems tend toward heterogeneity in structures where the system norm rests on actor homogeneity as to basic constitutions and concerns; and if differentiation as to key functions evolves with the crystallization of actors and systems, functional indifferentiation precedes as well as follows upon the developmental climax.

The most striking indifferentiation in proto-systems ranging from the earliest Mesopotamian to the European feudal sociopolitical orders is one between the sacral and the secular functions in a species of theocratic setting. It extends into an absence of sharp distinctions between the military, economic, and administrative functions inside an overarching political ensemble, as strikingly manifest in early Europe's manorial political economy as in the temple communities of Mesopotamia. Structure is radically heterogeneous in that it encompasses sociopolitical organizations both tied to a fixed territory to be exploited and transcending it by virtue of either physical mobility (e.g. steppe nomads and seafaring raiders) or qualitatively different (i.e., extra-mundane ecclesiastical) commitment. Nominally universal if actually finite empires rise and fall as vacuums of power in a discontinuous field of forces invite unconstrained expansion through unstructured violence, and turbulent peace is no more clearly differentiated from war on land than legitimate trade is from piracy at sea. One or another of such characteristics can be discerned in proto-systemic Mesopotamia's temple communities and in early Pharaonic Egypt, in Homeric Greece antecedent to the War with Persia as well as in Gothic-to-Frankish and Lombard Italy (in the peninsula's second proto-systemic phase, after the Etruscan–Phoenician or pre-Roman era), and in barbarian-to-feudal Europe.

Just as proto-systemic Italy and adjoining parts of Europe represent a regression from the degree of ordered unity achieved in the Roman Empire, so the latter displays (better still than the Persian Empire issuing out of the forceful unification of the Near Eastern macro-system) the characteristics of a meta-system in one, the imperial, of its varieties. The other (and more significant) variety of meta-systemization reflects a more partial or indirect submission of a multi-actor system in a single empire. It is illustrated by the late Sumerian-Mesopotamian city-state system in the period just preceding and attending its coercive unification by Hammurabi, as well as by the state of the Greek city-state system in transition to successively more effective overlordships from the outside: Persian after the Peloponnesian War, then Macedonian, and ultimately Roman, conjointly with the emergence of trans-*poleis* leagues and associations such as the Aetolian and Achaean. It denotes also the state of the Italian state system as it lapsed into deepening subordination, via the Franco-Spanish contest, to the victorious Habsburg (first Spanish and later Austrian) monarchies. Whereas the progressively tightening framework of republican Rome's hegemony had marked steps in the empire-type meta-systemization of the Greek micro- and the Hellenistic macro-system, the range from empire- to community-type was evidenced in Spain-dominated Italy across a spectrum from relatively most independent Venice via grand-ducal Tuscany (Florence) to directly ruled and administered Milan and Naples-Sicily – before a like spectrum has made its appearance in Europe after World War II.

In both sub-categories of the meta-system, the transition is from interactions based on conflict to patterns of behavior akin to a species of community, as a result of centralized authority or control in the starkly hierarchical empire-type variety or extraneously reduced incentives to conflict in the more egalitarian community-type variety. Both formats elevate economic and managerial over politico-military concerns while wholly subject polities differ from only dependent client states in the degrees of enjoyed or coveted autonomy in policy, and the ways they sublimate primeval power drives and simulate continuing concern with security and status, power and prestige. As semblance pushes out substance, it fosters interpenetration of "high" policy with and in favor of economics, of politics with and in favor of administration, and of external geopolitics with internal police in determining the role and organization of military or just coercive force – all this to a degree suggestive of, though different from, the functional indifferentiation typical of a proto-system.

In a proto-system, the primary givens are resource, situation, and skill, be it in Mesopotamia at the dawn of (broadly speaking) western civilization or post-Roman Italy at the beginning of European civilization. In pioneering Mesopotamia, the primary givens were implicit in the variety of terrain and were responsible for incipient differentiation of early actors. Alluvial plain and hilly country, river-bed or coast and hinterland, upstream and downstream location along rivers, are the respective soils in which were lodged the roots of functional differences between villages with settled agriculture, mobile-and-predatory hunters or pirates, and the intermediate half-sedentary and half-nomadic pastoralists. Such actor prototypes reappear, more fully developed, in a range of basic polarities. One recurrent dualism is the one between estates or "states" based on land and, likewise appearing in succession, commercial cities and entire countries oriented toward water, all the way from rivers through enclosed seas to vast oceans. Likewise reflecting the different situations and skills in a relatively primitive setting is the distinction, still firm at that stage, between productive and predatory activities: the former translating into defensive behavior of sedentary surplus-producing social organizations and the latter into offensive behavior of surplus-appropriating itinerant social organizations.

Another ingrained, and subsequently resurfacing, early polarity is between narrowly local and parochial and, at least in ambition, universal actors, each caught up in the search for a viable optimum size and scope under existing conditions. The prime structural alternative and operational tension in ancient Mesopotamia was between the overlarge empire and the too-small temple community or agricultural village. Both proved lastingly inviable despite the fact that, even before the empires, the temple community was among the first social organizations to intertwine the basic material and sacral-normative impulses to, and conditions of, actor formation and development. The more secular factor had to do with the production and management of a material surplus and the overcoming of scarcities; the sacral principle was incarnated in anthropomorphically conceived gods. The chief patron god of each temple community or city-state was seen as the owner of all land and chief protagonist in war; but the unrestrained competition implicit in thus exalted unilateralism was muted by the myth or fiction of a directing concert or *areopagus* of the parochial divinities under alternating directorship of one of them.

Projecting instinctual concerns and anxieties from the secular-pragmatic to the sacerdotal-providential plane stood then as it has since for the perennial tendency to rationalize hard-to-manage relationships within and among communities. Confounding locally focused material concerns with transcendental notions was in evidence also when the bishops governing the early communes in post-Roman Italy in competition with landed-aristocratic or urban-popularist elites, and the twin functions and allegiances of clerics in early feudal Europe, constituted miniature replicas of the interplays between armed Roman popes and anointed Byzantine, Frankish, and Germanic emperors. Each party compounded sacral and secular, this- and other-worldly, traits and tasks in uneven degrees and overlapping distributions. So long as divergent ideal outweighed shared mundane purposes, and propaganda was dominant over practice, the weight of experience was against identifying the stakes of competition as uniform for and thus shared by all actors. Reinforcing the effect of functionally lagging formation of actors, the result was to delay the system-crystallizing effects of centrally focused competitive interactions.

While emerging out of a decayed (Roman-imperial) meta-system, the Italian and the European proto-systems were shaped by interactions on two tiers, one consisting of survivors, successors, or simulators of the Roman-universal principle and the other of strictly local or particular, thinly Romanized or wholly barbaric, forces, peoples, or powers. Conjointly with impeding the functional differentiation critical for forming actors, a thus enhanced structural hetero-geneity made it difficult to differentiate intra- from inter-actor conflicts and develop a clear sense of strategic priorities. Both the Romanian and the barbarian tiers appear thus retrospectively as platforms for premature efforts at consolidation, while the false starts in actor formation illustrated by Lombard kingships in Italy and the Carolingian Empire in the European north were no more and no less untimely than efforts at system crystallization. Prominent among the latter was the quasi-balance-of-power cum concert system improvised in the barbarian west by an Ostrogothic king (Theodoric) from a transient power position in Italy, with the strategic purpose of keeping fellow-barbarian Franks out of Italy and away from the Mediterranean. Premature aggregations of "great powers" and precocious attempts at grand strategy added up to truly anarchic interactions. Scrambling quasi-systemic interactions and balance of power-specific impulses with nominally universalist rationales and nakedly personalist aspirations was then part and parcel of confounding secular geopolitical motivations with theologically tinted tribal concerns. A more effective systemization was possible in such conditions only within narrowly circumscribed boundaries of emergent actors-to-be, thus in the feudal micro-system inside France and its more urban analogue inside Burgundy.

The diffuse tendency to veritable anarchy that marks proto-systems is unlike the uniformly motivated and, consequently, essentially orderly competition among structurally homogeneous near-equal parties in a fully crystallized mature system, denoted as anarchical only by the absence of a conflicts-containing and/or -adjudicating central authority. Proto-systemic anarchy differs also from hierarchy in meta-systems exhibiting determinate patterns of unequal capabilities. Relatively straightforward is the role of the ordering power center relative to subordinates in the empire-type variety. The ordering function is enacted more indirectly by an extraneous balance of larger and newer powers in the more egalitarian community-type of meta-system delaying, in sharp contrast with effectively premature consolidations in a proto-system, the complete extinction therein of system-like interactions. Stalemate in the extraneous power balance acts then as a shelter for such interactions by reducing the risks of all-out imperial takeover by either of the outsiders, while these make overt conflict over traditional politico-military stakes among the "lesser" parties to the meta-system unrewarding because any individual gains illusory. One consequence is that the community-type is less vulnerable to failings internal to it than the imperial-type meta-system, so long as it retains or evolves the capacity to absorb shifts in sustaining vitality, including economic, from one of its members to another or others.

Both overlapping forms of a meta-system thrive on transforming armed conflicts among territorial units into unevenly competitive and consensual, either directly or indirectly induced, coordination of stakes, activities, and organs defined more functionally than power-politically. But the community-type variety can better combine that basic transformation with preserving residual identities of the parties as incumbents of autonomous energies and strategies. Moreover, so long as the extraneous power configuration holds, or is revised without giving rise to upsetting upheavals, the more egalitarian-communal variety will be less susceptible than the hierarchical-imperial type to diffusing positive attributes and overcentralizing control internally. Both diffusion and centralization will be eventually fatal to an empire-type meta-system as it degenerates into a top-heavy and uninnovative mega-actor, thus late republican Roman empire into last-stage Roman Empire.

The difficulty to adjust the needs of central authority, and the need for it, to a useful measure of spontaneity if not autonomy among dependents and clients beset both the Persian and the Roman empire-type meta-systems. They underwent in comparable ways the effects of long-term attrition as the aggregation of major capability from initially disparate skills, techniques, and energies gave way to their dispersion into economic and administrative localisms and, eventually, separatisms. Ultimate disintegration, following in the empire's life cycle upon aggregation and dispersion, was in turn a function of a three-sided relationship between the Empire, its civilized great-power rival (Alexander's Macedonia for Persia and a later, post-Parthian, Sassanid Persia for the Roman Empire), and either infiltrating or invading and alternately invigorating and enervating barbarians. The ultimate, empirically identifiable cause of empire dissolution will be typically economic, reducible to insufficient production and insufficiently innovative productivity relative to rising costs and consumption. The proximate cause is typically the moral one in terms of insufficient self-confidence on the part of elites and either disciplined obedience or spontaneous loyalty on that of the masses. Whichever may be the critical factor – the "cause" rather than the symptom – the empire will dissolve into a proto-system the more certainly the more concentrated and centralizing it was at its apogee – and the longer the civilization for which the empire had stood endured. Thus the Persian Empire dissolved at one point with unusual suddenness under the shock of conquest by a rival empire-builder (Alexander of Macedon). And the space it had controlled was near-instantly re-systemized with the benefit of energy inflows from successors partaking of the highly civilized, Hellenic, culture – a culture perfected in a microsystem whose final emergence from the proto-stage had been consummated by the need to resist the onslaught from an earlier and more vital Persia. These special circumstances were not those of the Roman Empire in decline when the onset of the so far most striking (western) instance of a long developmental cycle, a meta-system's lapse into a proto-system, was under way.

STRESSES AND SEQUENCES BETWEEN AND WITHIN SYSTEMS

The movement from proto- to meta-system via a matured micro- or macro-system, and from one to the other of these, constitutes an ideally continuous and coherent sequence, which operational transactions convert into trans-formations. Whereas each preceding phase prefigures somehow the next-following one, the operational links between the several formats and phases will vary. However, a proto-system will commonly tend toward the (micro- or macro-) systemic norm, and beyond, as erosion eliminates actors and actor-types incompatible with the special characteristics of a rationally conflictual interaction among territorially based parties. The turbulent events which mark the transition from a proto-system to a full-fledged system are punctuated by false starts due to premature efforts to aggregate power internally and project it abroad. The transition is accordingly a regression-prone incremental process culminating in a qualitative change, which then constitutes a distinct if likewise precarious developmental plateau. While the process can be fully analyzed in a particular system only in retrospect, each (except the first one) will be impinged upon by a more fully developed system. Thus impact from the Near Eastern sped up the crystallization of both member states and system dynamics in the Greek *ecumene*, while the interplay between unevenly articulated parties in "northern" Europe and in Italy stimulated recovery from the dissolution of the Roman Empire except when constraints on conflict dynamic emanating from one sector of the successor system delayed re-crystallization in other parts.

Before a proto-system can be galvanized by the dynamic impulses – or stymied by normative or operational inhibitions – flowing from a more fully developed system or segment of a system, it will be often latent in the structural or functional flaws of an antecedent meta-system of the empire type. It is thus latent immediately even if its constituent elements were assembling prenatally, as it were, over a very long period of the empire's life-span preceding its disintegration. Conversely, the meta-system of especially the community type will have been implicit in an earlier proto-system only ultimately via the intervening system crystallization. The latter will have suspended the salience of transterritorial or – "national" – unevenly institutionalized sacral or secular – authority structures and functional networks over territorially strictly delimited frameworks for managing and projecting power not yet sufficiently articulated in the proto- and no longer self-sufficient in the meta-stage. The circular linkages between developmental extremes differ from the connection between developed systems, which is typically one-directional in that the macro- is more likely to grow out of the micro-variety than vice versa, except when competition within a macro-system enlarges the total arena and upgrades peripheral actors to the point of dwarfing the previously self-sufficient system core. Moreover, whereas proto- and meta-systems are unevenly latent in one another as one succeeds to the other, a macro-system is immanent in the micro-system: it both supersedes and comprises the latter after growing out of it through the bigger actors' development-stimulating involvement in the smaller arena. What kind of macro-system comes into being, and the position of the smaller arena in it, will depend on one main factor: has the micro-system been unified – transformed into an empire or a great power – by a force and process from within, or did it remain divided and subject to competitive drives to unify it by actors intruding from outside even when invited from within its boundary?

Whereas the Sumer-Mesopotamian micro-system was unified from within and the Renaissance Italian was not, the Greek micro-system falls between the two extremes. It was not unified in its prime; was transiently unified in its late, close to meta-systemic, phase by a power, Macedon, which was itself part-outsider and part-insider; and was contended over in the post-Alexandrine phase by Hellenistic powers including Syria (of Antiochus the Great), pending terminal unification by the wholly extraneous Rome. In her late, micro-systemized, phase a Europe dwarfed in the global setting by marginal-to-outsider powers came close to being forcefully unified by (Nazi) Germany. She managed to avoid both the Akkadian-Babylonian and the Macedonian type of outcomes with the aid of outside power, with consequences for its subsequent role and status in the global arena. Whether the micro-system is or is not unified from within will determine not only its position within the macro-structure; it will also influence its being or not the military battleground of conflicts attending the transition to the macro-system.

Whether the decisive unification of the Mesopotamian micro-system was by Sargon (Akkad) or Hammurabi (Babylon), it was in both instances effected from within. Further stimulated in due course by contact and conflict with Egypt, the enlarged power aggregation set off reactions and adaptations to the new scale of things by a series of large-sized, invading or infiltrating, peripheral barbarians. The result was a Near Eastern macro-system, in which the older politico-cultural and -economic centers of Mesopotamia participated at least intermittently with a macro-actor of their own (e.g. Babylonia and, taking off from the Assur city-state, Assyria). A major side-effect of the direct line of descent from the Sumerian micro-system was the depth and persistence of the Babylonian culture's penetration of the enlarged arena. By contrast, the continuing divisions within the Renaissance Italian micro-system meant escalating involvement of relatively backward if bigger outside powers, in the end by invitation. This not only deepened the conflicts within Italy but also tended to polarize the emergent macro-actors as either competitors over the micro-systems (especially France and Aragon-Spain) or powers unevenly capable to engage in the competition.

Both kinds of polarization were eventually overcome, contributing in the process to diffusing power in the larger theater as parties previously left out (thus England) were drawn into and upgraded by the Franco-Hispanic conflict centered on Italy. But crystallization of the arena was consequently more turbulent and took longer than would probably have been the case if the northern monarchies had had to face a unified Italian macro-actor mobilizing superior political culture and disposing of superior functional techniques of various kinds. Instead, a delayed near-unification of Italy under the aegis of Spain reduced the effect of the correspondingly modified indigenous political culture on the macro-system. The link between the unevenly Spain-controlled (and, thus, meta-systemized) Italian actors and the crystallizing European macro-system and -actors was correspondingly limited to scattered and sporadic functional relationships, short of sustained systemic ones. Among these belonged, alongside the part Italian nobles played in administering the Spanish Empire, the role of Genoese financiers in the Spanish and Spanish-American economy, following upon that of Genoese naval contingents as an auxiliary ingredient in the capabilities of contesting European macro-actors. And if the relatively most independent Venetian Republic either had or only claimed a genuinely systemic, balance-of-power, role in and effect on the macro-system, the impact was limited in the extreme relative to what it might have been had Venice become a regional unifier at an earlier stage.

As for Greece, the role of outside powers in inter-Greek contests was at first (up to and including the longer first half of the Peloponnesian War) limited, though finally decisive (by virtue of the Persians' naval subsidy to Sparta and the frustration of the Athenians' amphibious onslaught by the Syracusans). But the role grew thereafter as the malfunctioning Greek city-state system lapsed into a succession of increasingly brittle Spartan, second Athenian, Theban, and Phocian pseudo-hegemonies. Before Macedonian muscle prevailed over Persian money, the conquering king's military-strategic apprenticeship in a Greek city to be subdued had constituted the most striking functional connection between the fading micro-system and the emergent macro-actor. In the still later, post-Alexander phase, the triangular contest among unevenly extraneous powers (Macedon, Syria, and Rome) being finally decided to the advantage of the remotest one meant that Greek opposition to unification under Macedon had also inhibited the latter's cooperation with Carthage in the west and policy toward Syria in the east of a kind sufficient to lastingly constrain Rome's expansion within a macro-systemic equilibrium.

In a foreshortened time span, the empire-type macro-systemization of the all-Mediterranean universe resembled a similar later process, inasmuch as the brief Roman–Syrian contest over Greece was the functional equivalent of the more protracted Franco–Spanish competition over Italy – while the ineffectual resistance of Macedon's later Philips and Perseus to Rome resembled the Papacy's to the "foreigners." Similarly, if the Hellenistic culture was exposed to the counter-thrust of the Roman imperial ethos after absorbing the Persian one, the impact of the Italian was to be blunted in Europe by the slow fading of indigenous northern feudal values before the onset of the mercantile-maritime ethos. In all instances, as in the case of Babylonic Mesopotamia, the dominant political culture synthesis registered a maturer culture's collision with greater force or efficacy, while Rome's contribution to the Mediterranean resembled most that by Spain to the early European synthesis.

In determining why the micro-system is or is not unified from within, the contextual structure is at least as important as the capabilities and the drive of a would-be unifier. The issue is clearest in Italy's oscillation between division and unity. An incipient micro-system centered on the Etruscan city-states was consolidated by Rome thanks also to Carthage, the Etruscans, and the local Greeks being distracted, within an equally but rudimentary macro-system, by a tripartite contest over southern Italy and Sicily. The distraction created a strategic sanctuary for Rome's southward progression that neither the Lombard kings or communes nor the Milanese dukes or the Venetian oligarchs were to enjoy in the later Italian micro-system. Following upon the Byzantine, first the Frankish and then the Germanic (Holy Roman) emperors did manage to exploit the contests between sets of more indigenous actors to the advantage of the (Rome-like) northern "barbarians" as the third, laughing, party. But their hegemony in Italy was too brittle for any resulting unity to resist opposition from rapidly crystallizing local micro-actors including the Lombard communes, acting as the seed-beds of the Renaissance period's city-state. By analogy, to-be-micro-systemized late Europe could have been rallied around France or, later, Germany only if the contest between British and Russian outsiders over the Near East and Asia had generated for the inner-core power the kind of sanctuary that had favored Rome's unifying drive.

Meanwhile, the fatal Renaissance-time polarization between pro- and anti-France elements was preceded in Italy by inter-city-state politics crystallizing into a five-power system. Anticipated in Sumerian Mesopotamia (e.g. Umma, Lagash, Ur, Uruk, Kish – with Akkad in the wings), the bias toward pentarchy was more reliably identifiable in the post-Roman Empire proto-system (Byzantine exarch, Lombardy, Papacy, Spoleto, and Benevento – with the Franks in the wings) and more fully articulated in the Greek city-state system (Sparta, Argos, Corinth, Athens, and Thebes) before re-emerging in Italy (Milan, Florence, Venice, Papacy, Naples–Sicily). Nor would five key powers be too few or too many in accounting for the essential dynamics of the European (proto-) system, with France, England, a Germanic center power, and one changing power aggregation in the south and another in the east constituting the essential actors. The five-power system emerged repeatedly in three movements: once an originally strongest actor (Umma, Sparta, the Lombard kingdom, Milan – and either Holy Roman Empire or France in early Europe) has been identified as the most challenging, it shocks a second key actor (Lagash, Athens, the Frankish monarchy, Florence or Venice – and either France or Holy Roman Empire), into opposition while the resulting two-power conflict generates or only activates as many as (and rarely more than) three more actors, sufficiently numerous for flexible balancing but not so many as to fragment a fixed pool of aggregate capabilities beyond its re-equilibration potential. Revolving around a dominant conflict, actor strategies will tend to configurate the five-power system into sets of interlocking three-cornered or triangular interplays whose thrust and tempo will materially co-determine the prospects of ultimate unification from within – or without.

So long as conflictual interplays within a micro-system avoid divisive polarization, the system has a better chance to escape unification from the outside. Thus, had Sparta and Athens managed Corinth's pretensions (relative to Corcyra) differently, they could have consolidated the Greek micro-system under their joint hegemony, and shut out Persia diplomatically and otherwise, with important consequences for an eastern Mediterranean macro-system; by contrast, the Papal presidency in the Italian Holy League was too nominal to offer even that much of a chance. Nor is it insignificant at what stage of their respective maturation a micro-system is integrated into the macro-system. Involving outside powers in the affairs of Italy was relatively safe so long as the outsiders were only emergent (thus the Franks) or already decaying (the Holy Roman Empire, following Byzantium); the immunity passed with the rise of the fifteenth-century despots in France and Aragon. Similarly, a micro-system that was unified from within while the macro-system is still only emerging or is in transition will have a greater impact. Arguably achieved at one time or another in the Mesopotamian context, the consequence only would have followed had Macedon, in the absence of wholly indigenous hegemony, unified Greece soon enough and effectively enough to arbitrate between Rome and Carthage in the western Mediterranean. The extreme instance of unification coming too late was that of Italy in the nineteenth-century by Piedmont, once more shielded by competition among three unevenly extraneous powers: France, Austria, and Prussia. As the nominal sixth, Italy could not be effective in a system of five powers highly crystallized by then – or avoid her efforts to make up for the delay being disruptive. The precedents were significant for a Europe resisting coordination around an indigenous unifier while outlines of a global macro-system were beginning to be drawn around her.

The role of tripartite contests in both the earliest and the latest unification of Italy highlights the importance of triangularity in shaping arenas – typically toward disunity when the triangle is internal to the affected system. That the earliest recorded polarities between Umma and Lagash or Isin and Larsa evolved into three-cornered contests in the Sumerian micro-system is supported by (1) evidence from later systems and (2) the finite range of practically possible strategic imagination and manipulative skills. The limitation hinders focusing on more than two other powers in any complex situation regardless of how many other actors secondary to the issue at hand may be involved at the margins of the strategist's awareness and calculations. In Greece, the polar Atheno–Spartan conflict was triangularized at different stages for different purposes – of only Peloponnesian regional or all-Greece maritime-continental balance – by either Argos (as a threat to Sparta's regional and domestic security and thus a potential accomplice for Athens), or Corinth (as the maritime-commercial rival of Athens and Sparta's conditional ally), or Thebes (as a possible hegemonial substitute for both major powers) – when not from the outside by Persia as the arbiter or balancer. In the post-Alexander period the triangle decisive for Greece consisted of a congeries of small cities (associated in the two principal leagues), residual (Antigonid) Macedon, and (Seleucid) Syria, while a formerly major actor such as Athens had been reduced to only economic role and cultural influence and Rome only loomed in the wings. Milan, Florence, and Venice were the essential three actors in Renaissance Italy, interacting in changing alignments according to whether Milan or Venice was the hegemonial aspirant to guard against, with the Papacy and Naples in the background. Similarly, in the earlier proto-systemic phase, the Ostrogothic–Frankish–Burgundian, Lombard–Byzantine–Papal, and Lombard–Papal–Frankish triangles had been in succession critical for the question whether and by whom Italy might be effectively reunified.

The third party was commonly strong enough to impede unification by the stronger of any two prime actors, without being threatening enough to propel them toward joint hegemony over the multi- (often five-) power micro-system: at any time or in time to fend off successively rising challengers. The situation was no different in Europe during the period when world-wide expansion and power dispersion was gradually turning her into the semblance of a micro-system. A succession of triangular interplays eventuated in Europe's partition between at least partially extra-systemic America and Russia, on the model of the provisional Franco–Spanish division of Italy and the fleeting Roman–Syrian division of the Eurasian Greek universe. Europe being thus transformed into a mere stage and stake of competition was in turn reminiscent of earlier instances, from the Syrian–Palestinian coastal cities in ancient Near East to the Italian and Burgundian microcosms in early modern Europe. Unlike the likewise triangular interplays among unification-resistant compact territorial powers or nation states in later Europe, those in both the Near Eastern Babylonic and the eastern Mediterranean Hellenistic macro-systems engaged empire-type aggregations of power. The forcible unifiers included Assyria, succeeding to an Egypto–Hitite–Mitanni triangle, and Persia, supplanting a Chaldean–Medan–Scythian "balance of power," in the earliest system – just as Rome was to roll up the Macedon–Egypt–Syria triangle and related interactions in the later one. Thus, like the peripheral powers that unified any of the micro-systems, the macro-systemic conquerors moved in from outside an eastern Mediterranean core that had been centered on Egypt as the pivot before the Pharaonic realm became the most valuable prey of the rear-continental conquerors.

The tension between the center of a system and its periphery is as elementary and recurrent a factor in articulating a system as are conflicts centrally engaging three parties. The tense relationship was characteristically one between powers and forces relatively civilized and differently barbarian. Only functionally barbarian are the typically fairly consolidated and territorially stable powers located outside a system of continuously interacting older powers, whose boundary they breach and enlarge in the process of being drawn in by central-systemic dynamics. Operating at a markedly different level of organization are the more literally barbarian elements, who typically invade or infiltrate settled social formations at the center of either a proto-system or a decaying system without necessarily enlarging its operative scope. Crucial for the scenario involving the only functional barbarians are the procedural norms or transactional styles that make up a formal diplomatic culture. Emanating from the systemic center, this particular culture is communicated to the outsider power as part of its assimilation. Critical in the scenario comprising authentic barbarians (culturally radically different and inferior in technological civilization) is their raw energy. It is infused into the new mix of a more broadly defined culture and of physical and moral energy that evolves out of a process of hybridization.

Thus, a macro-system is not only immanent in a micro-system operationally and structurally, as the emergent bigger outsiders react to and are involved in the smaller arena's configuration and balancing of power. Less determinate but no less shaping is the normative effect of the values and practices of typically smaller on the larger (and in the main functionally barbarian) actors and arenas. Operational concatenation through strategies is then infused with the results of diffusion: spreading next to the specifically "cultural" values of civilian life or civility comprising diplomacy are the administrative and technological means of generating and methods of managing power as the politically significant aspects of "civilization."

A common feature was present in the diffusion of the Babylonian Hammurabi's code of commercial law and diplomatic practices all the way to Assyria, the conventional prototype of a barbaric (if, in the main, but functionally barbarian) sociopolitical entity within the Near Eastern macro-system; in the spread of Greek culture and civilization via Macedon to especially the urban centers in the Hellenistic monarchies; and in the communication of the Renaissance Italians' norms, values, and practices to the early European macro-system by way of France and Spain in particular. In all these cases diffusion was mediated through major wars hinging on the issue of succession as the pull of an established – commonly also declining or dwarfed – power's culture combined with the physical push of only gradually integrated and civilized peripheral outsiders, evolving from literal to primarily but functional barbarians as they moved one after the other toward the center. The drama of succession to Hammurabi's and Kassite Babylonia as the preeminent major power (and, in the first-named incarnation, the last autochthonous local hegemon) was replayed in the Peloponnesian and the following wars over succession to Sparta as the uncontested hegemon prior to the Persian War, which helped diffuse Hellenic values and ways northward toward Macedon, westward toward Sicily, and eastward toward Persia. Nor were the climactic intra-Italian wars over who will succeed to Milan and Milan's Visconti dukes any different in their cultural consequences. And if not before then since the Italian wars, when major struggles in Europe were over succession to one preeminent power after another and, later, to Europe herself as the center of power in the world, the diffusion of the Italian modes in Europe was followed by the spread of European norms and methods world-wide.

Enlarging upon the acculturation of Akkad into the Sumerian value system under Sargon, and its effects, a major intangible in the shaping of the Near Eastern macro-system was the impact of Babylonian culture upon a long line of horse- or chariot-mounted barbarians. Similarly, the material ingredient in the winning Macedonian compound, next to indigenous *élan*, were the skills and techniques of phalanx warfare Philip II had learned in Thebes. But if the resulting syntheses fostered empire-type unification, this was not the case for the mercenary-type wars of position and the negotiating techniques spreading from commerce to diplomacy, acting as substitutes for unbridled military exertions, that were to be diffused northward out of Italy. Together, the innovations impeded forcible unification in early modern Europe, as they had inside Italy herself, while conditioning the struggle of the European powers for domination in and over the disunited peninsula.

To whichever structural consequences the diffusion and resulting hybridization might tend, an essential ambiguity characterized the Babylonization of the Near East, Hellenization of the eastern Mediterranean and all-Mediterranean, Italicization of early modern Europe – all the way to the Europeanization of the extra-European global (macro-)actors and global (proto-)system. As norms, values, and techniques radiated in one direction (toward the peripheral or marginal macro-actors) and effective mass inched or aggressive force swept forward in the opposite direction, culture blended with energy and values with vitality in different proportions and changing compounds. From the Assyrian interplay with Babylon if not before down the ages, impotent condescension of the overwhelmed cultural superior alternately resistant to and reliant on the barbarian was met on the part of the more dynamic cultural inferior with selective reception and equally qualified rejection of acculturation. The tension could be eased, and hybridization made less unsettling, as again prefigured by Babylonian high culture's impact on successive barbarians (including the empire-restoring Kassites), by substituting professionalized and institutionalized routines for the spontaneities of the original invention and creation. Similar operationally useful consequences followed from the infusion of increasingly secularized Hellenic culture into the largely theocratic value systems of the oriental regions or powers (institutionalized in due course by the implantation of Greek cities in oriental hinterlands), and of the Italian Renaissance mind-set into still medieval or feudal European culture (functionally completed by the settlement of Italian specialists in the northern monarchies).

However commingled the distinct features of functional and authentic, positional and cultural, barbarity might be in all outsiders or marginals, proportions and nuances mattered. The impact of the Kassite barbarians on a later Babylon – and of the so-called Sea Peoples on Mesopotamian social organization as a whole – differed from that of the Assyrian or Hittite or Mitanni empires on the early Babylonian culture area. Similarly, the influence of the "Germans" on a distressed and declining Roman Empire was unlike that of Macedon on the Hellenic and early Rome on the Hellenistic worlds. Although culture-or-civilization clashes and coalesces with energy-or-raw power in both kinds of hybridization, the operative emphasis in the first-named interactions is on the cultural intake by the to-be-civilized intruders over against diffusion out of the civilizing center, as the fresh barbarian energy strains toward the decayed or decaying center of a force field that is always fragmented and may be shrinking. In the second-named relationships, a new center of gravity aggregating civilization with energy will move from the core toward the periphery of an invariably expanding system, typically on a south–north before a west–east axis in Mesopotamia, the Mediterranean, and Europe.

Impulsion by literally barbarian forces may be carried by nothing more striking than insidious infiltration or be more dramatically imparted by massive invasion. In either case, the impact will be commonly mediated by agents in search of different kinds of material goods ranging from pastoral grounds to productive techniques or employment. Although such impacts will reform or reshape individual civilized actors as a matter of necessary consequence, the system – or, more typically, crystallizing proto- or decaying meta-system – need not be enlarged. System enlargement and consequent shift in the center of gravity is not among the defining characteristics of the first-named, as it is of the second-named, instances and kinds of hybridization. Thus the boundaries of the Romanized barbarian-Christian West fell short of the boundaries of the Roman imperial meta-system at its height – and when combined with the Islamic East did not as substantially exceed them as the Sumerian, Greek, and Italian city-state systems were outsized by the succeeding macro-systems.

In both of its forms and manifestations, the barbarian factor has been throughout a major connecting link between system forms. Accordingly, just as the antecedent micro-systems, so the European center of the emergent global system could either continue diffusing its culture and civilization from remaining vital strength to additional marginal if progressively integrated and assimilated (functionally barbarian) powers such as China and India in the wake of the United States and Japan. Or the Europe-centered and -derived center of the contemporary global system – however rated as to the stage of its crystallization and delimited as to its circumference – could be individually and collectively infiltrated materially and invaded psychologically by (authentically barbarian) influences and energies from the periphery. Either development would have significant consequences for the relationship of (former) core and (emergent) periphery in a world system engaged in the process of articulation and an international society engaged in the process of hybridization. In no instance could the center–periphery relationship be reduced to culturally or materially cost-free one-directional expansion and impact. It has always been the locus of a complex two-way interplay, not necessarily beneficial or harmful to either center or periphery.

In whatever form the marriage of raw power and energy with values and norms conducive to technically or institutionally improved management of resources took place, it proved repeatedly to be the winning formula. But it did so often at a cost and a risk: the cost was in creative spontaneity and originality of the elites; the risk that of a cleavage between acculturated elites and autochthonous masses. A successful mix or synthesis enabled a succession of macro-actors to supersede receding micro-systems and enlarge the arena in ways that combined a measure of temporal continuity in systemic evolution with physical contiguity along the pathway of power gravitation. Value diffusion established macro-systems as normatively descended from micro-systems, as both a part of and counterpart to the structural supersession of the smaller- by the larger-sized arena: a species of spiritual parentage compensated the smaller actors and arenas ideally for being at once dwarfed and demoted. And whereas micro-actors and -systems typically supplied much of the motion that impelled the transition and transformation, the macro-actors contributed the requisite mass for temporarily stabilizing the results. Finally, the barbarian factor served as a critical link: the functional barbarians *qua* provisional outsiders always linked micro- to macro-systems, with effect on scope and size; the more authentic barbarians *qua* cultural or civilizational inferiors often mediated the movement past crystallizing proto- or decaying meta-systems to a recrystallized system format, as a matter of developmental stage or phase.

PRIMITIVE DUALITIES AND PERENNIAL SCHISMS

Qualitatively different from the center–periphery dichotomy when overlapping with it are schisms which, rather than distinguishing more from less advanced and primitive actors, derive from and refine upon very elementary givens of physical nature or human perceptions. Either of the schisms can affect operations within any system, however structured, of any size (micro- or macro), its (civilized) core and (barbarian) periphery, at any stage of its development (from proto- to meta-stage), even if to an unequal degree or with unequal likelihood. The quasi-organic elements which the several schisms make operational are rationally manageable material and normatively biased propitiatory resources and competencies (the secular–sacral schism), either productive or predatory soil- and water-based or -related subsistence conditions and skills (the land–sea power schism), and geographic locations related to solar trajectory and affecting basic material and immaterial culture (mainly the East–West schism). Thus grounded, the three schisms exhaust the main possibilities for supplementing the size- and stage-related features of structure. Sufficient as to range, they must be included to complete the spectrum of dispositions that condition the action-reaction dynamics revealed in major events and phenomena. Moreover, they are pervasive also in the sense of being an evolutionary constant, insofar as each pair will undergo only inessential modifications whenever reappearing as either salient or subsidiary to one or both of the other two.

How are the pairs intrinsic to basic reality in its conditioning-physical or perceptual-psychological aspects? The secular-sacral cleavage denotes the distinction innate to perception between the here-now and the beyond, between "rational" knowledge or explanation and one kind of rationalization of the unknown or unknowable, the unexplained or inexplicable. It also bestrides the difference between pragmatic technique or transaction and some form of prophetic transcendence of proximate by an "ultimate" reality offering relief from or promising transformation of the actual. Both originally and quintessentially religious in concept and theological in representation, the sacral element can remain functionally such even if it has been highly secularized so long as it remains normative – is either myth-based in conception or myth-creative in function and is then meliorist in intention and/or escapist in purpose or motivation. The land–sea, continental–maritime, cleavage inheres in the contrasting nature elements of earth or soil and water: the finite and solid, and the fluid and seemingly unbounded, milieu. Each is and both are as critical for physical survival by the creation or collection of ever so elementary food and fuel as psychic balance rests on linking the visible or tangible to the invisible or intangible, so long as an ever so contingent mastery of the world depends on combining the satiating features of materiality with the reassuring facets of imagination. From the earliest inter-unit systems adjoining the Tigris-and-Euphrates and the Nile as much as the Indus and the Yellow rivers, differences between river bed-centered and rain-dependent plain or plateau and between life-supporting goods to be extracted from the conjunction of water and wind (transport, trade) and from the combination of soil and seed (agriculture) were intrinsic to laboriously developing civilization. Nor was ever the distribution of access to land (for plowing, planting, or pasture) or water (for fishing, irrigation, or navigation) alien to the causes or stakes of conflict among actors differentially favored or disadvantaged in regard to either element.

Finally, the East–West cleavage inhered not only and most obviously in the natural inclination to distinguish between the places where the sun rises and where it sets. It is also integral to the physical configuration of Eurasia, differentiating a territorially bounded western extremity from the seemingly limitless eastern expanse, even as the indented western peninsula projects toward an ocean along rivers that fan out toward it while most of the rivers of the eastern depths feed into inland or otherwise confined seas before some reach the other ocean. Thus, if one extremity suggests a bias toward mobility, the other connotes mass – and, when mobility, then mainly that of toil-free horse-riding steppe nomads careering across space and time as nature's noblemen and civilizational barbarians. One way or another, the center–periphery and civilization–barbary dualities, although neutral in principle also relative to the East–West cleavage, tended to coincide with the latter in separating civilizations even when the divide defined by culture followed that between south and north in geography within individual empires (thus in Egypt or China) or system segments (thus in Italy and between her and the European north). Thus, when the modern West came to connote the ostensibly higher civilization of outwardly free individuals in materially productive society, crystallizing first around the economic activities sponsored and symbolized by the sea- or ocean-going ship, the East has continued to militantly oppose to it the ostensibly unfree individual's unassailable inner freedom within a procedurally more sophisticated society. Nurtured by a close – including enforced – tie to the soil, in the larger setting of a more immediate or direct but not necessarily abject subjection to the authority of either God or state (or both), the Eastern culture product of the fusion between nature and nurture could then be regarded as superior to the West's artificially mechanical compound by its defenders.

For the several dualities to qualify as schisms, their constituents must be distinct, but not wholly disparate; differentiable, but not wholly separable most of the time: opposition must be qualified even as it is aggravated by an overlap of shared attributes generating convergent aspirations or ambitions. Differentiation spells contest over the dominance by one pair-constituent over the other; and, in function of the conflict, the very amount or degree of the overlap that objectively reduces the scope of differences enhances the psychological distance subjectively experienced by the parties to the schism. It does so as the ambiguity of identities that are both similar and dissimilar breeds reciprocal misperceptions which result in distorted attribution of goals and representation of means peculiar to the other.

In different ways and degrees, the ambiguities that foster ambivalence develop as each of the schisms evolves out of an original state or condition. One such condition is that of actual or perceptual, structural or functional, indifferentiation of the pair-constituents, typical of primitive actors in a proto-system and most pronounced in regard to the secular–sacral schism. Whereas the sacral tended to be fused with the secular in antiquity – all the way from the priests-administrators of the Mesopotamian temple communities to the deified rulers of Pharaonic Egypt, the Hellenistic Near East, and the late Roman Empire – the western Middle Ages perfected the formula of the differentiated-but-overlapping Church and State of Pope and Emperor while eastern caeasaro-papism maintained the sacral–secular distinction at least in regard to dogma under ultimate state authority. As the increasingly consolidated territorial state was sacralized in the West (witness "holy" France and Holy Roman Empire), the decreasingly other-worldly Church was territorialized (Church lands in Christian realms, Papal States in Italy). The resulting overlap could take the form of either an institutionalized Church–State or Pope–Emperor alliance (with condominial overtones, under the Gelasian doctrine) or of conflicting claims to authority also in or over the other party's domain (the Investiture conflict and beyond). And whereas the area of the overlap – involving identity, authority, and function – was fought over by partially identical (diplomatic) and partially divergent (doctrinaire) means, war itself partook of the ambiguity when it was conceived of as both an arena of chivalric prowess, an occasion for material gain, and the court of divine judgment. The diplomatic strategies of reciprocal encirclement, by Emperor of the Pope between northern and southern Italy, and of the Emperor by papal diplomacy opposing emergent northern and eastern as well as western European realms to the Empire, ended characteristically in mutual enfeeblement to the benefit of third parties.

Subsequent tendencies toward separation and secularization coexisted with their opposites, thus when priestly kings of high Middle Ages gave way to the secular monarchy by divine right and the other-worldly imperium of the pontiffs to the near-religious cult of the functional-administrative and professional-military territorial state. At a later stage, the deified state or nation was to be submerged in ostensibly transnational and reactively secular or pseudo-sacral sociopolitical dogmas, just as ungodly power politics was to be transcended with the help of pietistically inspired normative precepts, in defense of pragmatically rational propensities of one set of (matured or declining) societies against demonically irrational drives of their (late-developing) challengers. Each kind of intermingling the secularized sacral with the sacerdotally tinged secular elements entailed struggle over predominance, which surfaced the tension intrinsic to political power: between its connection to spirit, encompassing morale and morality without being accounted for by either, and embeddedness in structure as to its material constituents and operational compellents. The struggle was at its most intense when, at the recurring peaks of ideologically tinged conflict between actual powers, secular-pragmatic politics contended for primacy in motivation with pseudo-religious persuasion and propaganda: one which cast the rival territorial actor in the image of a false church spreading noxious doctrine so that the propagandist could more easily bring the New Jerusalem down from the celestial heights to his mundane habitat.

The sacral–secular cleavage became ever more controversial and the interpenetration of the pair-constituents more contentious as simple near-fusion (a tribe's or empire's god as the "real" ruler and effective rulers as "gods") gave way to overlaps in functions or values both within and between actors: the former as between kings-priests and priests-administrators, or between secular potentates as pretended defenders of the true faith and ecclesiastical would-be suzerains of territorial princes and powers; the latter as between ostensibly secular-pragmatic polities and political systems propagating quasi- or pseudo-sacral doctrines. By contrast, the relation of insular-maritime and continental-military powers denoted with increasing clarity the opposite to primitive indifferentiatiation (e.g. between river bed and surrounding plain and between fishing and farming as seasonally complementary or alternative source of nourishment): the contrast between radical differentiation and overlap, between polarity and schism.

The two types of actors can be differentiated to unequal degrees, thus when a both insular and maritime power such as Minoan Crete and a not yet maritime but insular England could insulate themselves from the adjoining mainland powers, until subdued by an exceptionally seaworthy invader. When, by contrast, insular-maritime and continental-military states have become engaged in sustained conflict, they may still continue to practice separation and postulate separability because they do not meet the conditions establishing the continental–maritime schism: a substantial degree of similarity between the unevenly situated and endowed contenders over primacy in a shared and in essence identically conceived universe. Thus, after these conditions had begun to emerge in the contests of maritime Egypt with the continental empires in ancient Near East, and before they evolved farther among the Hellenistic powers in the eastern Mediterranean, a full-fledged schism did not result from adding maritime Corinth to Sparta in the Peloponnesian alliance and finally adding naval to Sparta's military capability by virtue of outside (Persian) subsidy in the ensuing war. Nor was the preceding attempt of maritime-mercantile Athens at continental conquest closely and long enough interlocked with the power balance in the land arena, or the continental Persian Empire organically enough connected with the (Phoenician) naval capabilities at its disposal. Land–sea power bifurcation continued to be in evidence when Rome became and Carthage ceased being a prime sea power in the transition from the first to the second Punic War; it persisted even when the continentalization of the Mediterranean (as a Roman lake enclosed by Rome-controlled territory) yielded to segregation, between wholly land-oriented Gallo-Romans or Romanized Goths and the Byzantine naval monopolist anxious (and but for an emergency period able) to bar the North Africa-bound Vandals from mounting a naval challenge.

When land-bound Carolingian Franks were not able to meet either of the (Viking or Saracen) sea-borne invaders in their element in the ninth century, the inability had been as immediately significant as was to be that of the Germans at Frankfurt to finance a Confederate navy in the nineteenth. Disjunction continued to be in evidence when maritime Italian city-states, notably Genoa and Venice, fought one another on the seas – as had Byzantine and Moslem navies earlier – but not on or over land at the system's center; and when they hired out naval contingents to continental monarchs in the north for conflicts against one another or for joint crusades against the infidel. Thirteenth-century France of a Philip the Fair had been no more able to acquire and maintain a stable naval force than – at the dawn of the land–sea power overlap – the Portugal of Henry the Navigator was to match naval with land-military capability. Thus it was reserved for the European macro-system, markedly improving on the ancient Near East, to display the both sufficient and necessary – technological, geopolitical, and economic – conditions of a full-blown maritime–continental schism from late sixteenth century on.

A key requirement – or optimum condition – of the schism is that the sea power can affect warfare on land directly, so to say tactically, when opposing a land power that can fight on the seas. Consequently, the sea power must be capable of transporting troops in numbers across stretches of water to the battlefields in all fighting seasons and be able to effectively threaten, if not always maintain, a continuous blockade of the continental adversary. It must therefore possess the capability to destroy or neutralize enemy fleets by means that (unlike ramming and grappling) differ sufficiently from land warfare to call for special and rare skills in ship handling and maneuver (most conspicuously at a premium in line-ahead formations of the sailing-ship era). The implication is that it must be technologically and operationally possible for the sea power, as well as appear to be strategically necessary, to achieve and maintain a naval superiority sufficient to release the material and diplomatic resources required to stalemate the continental power on land and abort its capabilities and ambitions in the maritime arena. The land power in turn must possess the incentives and the instruments for contesting the rival's maritime near-monopoly, with a view to extending the struggle for a balance of power from land to the seas for the sake of a more equal bargaining over a more equitable distribution of coastal or overseas stakes and assets. The existence of such peripheral stakes – and their being viewed as vitally supplemental to the prizes worth fighting for and capable of being won in the heart of the continent – constitutes the geopolitical and related geo-economic conditions of a schism. The other economic or material, specifically financial or fiscal, precondition is the ability of both kinds of power – the dominant sea power and the navally ambitious leading land power – to mobilize resources adequate for militarily significant fighting capability on both land and sea: on two or more fronts and in both elements.

When the conditions – technological and operational, geopolitical and -economic, and material-financial – are present, the resulting pressures and opportunities for each kind of power to seek to penetrate the other's sphere in the given configuration of geographic space will engender a stable and predictable pattern of objectives and transactions within finite time intervals. Haphazard contentions over ostensibly theological (confessional) issues or genealogical (successional) stakes give way to authentic geopolitics within an ever-widening spatial compass. It is not of fundamental importance whether – as part of more or less closely coordinated or complementary military strategies, engagements, and outcomes – the "decisive" battles are fought (or are retrospectively thought to have been fought) on land or on the sea: at Breda or at the Downs, at Blenheim or La Hogue, at Waterloo or Trafalgar, on the Somme or in the Atlantic. What matters is the cardinal stake of world-wide conflicts. Can and will maritime or overseas and continental balances of power be combined into one all-encompassing equilibrium, annulling the situational advantage of the dominant (insular or near-insular) maritime power? Or will equilibrium and the struggle for equilibrium continue to be confined to the continental theater, perpetuating the handicap of the continentally preeminent and navally aspiring land power? No conflicts before those set off by the Dutch and English response to the existence of the Spanish overseas empire – not the Egypto–Hittite or -Assyrian conflicts, the Persian or Peloponnesian wars, the Punic or Syrian wars, not even the wars or conflicts swirling around Venice – fulfilled the conditions of a land–sea power schism, let alone on a global scale, however close either of the conflicts or situations may have come to realizing some of the conditions. The differences in situation and civilization, and the ensuing conflicts or competitions, between land-dependent and water-related societies or economies are perennial; but a conceptually and strategically accomplished land–sea power schism is a contingent as well as historically crucial and climactic event.

Whereas the overlap responsible for the sacral–secular schism is mainly in the normative or teleological area, and the land–sea power schism is mainly conditional on technological and operational conditions in the geostrategic and -economic sectors, the East and the West overlap is primarily in the cultural and social dimensions – and only derivatively in the other respects. An overlap is assured so long as there is no obvious geographical divide between East and West, and differently defined or constituted divides – including those which reflect aspirations to membership or developmental tendencies – do not coincide. Thus, ancient Byzantium (i.e., eastern Rome) in one setting, medieval and early modern Germany or Poland in another, and modern Russia in yet a different one, were alternately (or were alternately viewed as being) western or eastern in function of different – cultural, politico-religious, economic, diplomatic – standards. Much as the traits peculiar to each dimension might "objectively" vary in ways suggesting an internally coherent west-to-east spectrum, the several polities tended to be occidentalized or orientalized by changing situations and tendencies over time; and might "feel" western or anti-western – even if not altogether oriental – under different conditions and in response to different provocations or needs for protection.

Definitely oriental were only the states or societies to the east of the intermediate, ambiguously eastern-or-western, states or societies: a Persia or Islam relative to Byzantium, the Ottoman Empire at its height relative to Hungary and Austria or Poland, and the Mongol horde or China relative to Russia. The farther-eastern pushing the nearer-eastern party westward or pulling it eastward by different kinds of threats and opportunities would influence orientations in the East–West overlap zone; so would the gravitation of superior power westward or eastward: crystallization of superior concentrated power in the west would tend to relegate the state or society not unambiguously western to the east, while the center of gravity in the power balance shifting eastward would reverse the direction conjointly with the transfer of individual powers' role and status. A powerful Byzantium, capable of reconquest in the west, had been more "western" than was a weakened Byzantium at the mercy of western crusaders; much the same was true for a Russia facing a still weak Europe from Kiev and one languishing under the Mongol yoke, before moving again into a key role in the European balance of power. The opposite can also be true, but only formally: a decaying Ottoman Empire was more readily co-opted into the West-centered system – if only as ward or victim – than had been a conquering Ottoman Empire allied to France and subsidizing German and Dutch rebels against the Habsburg universal monarchy in the west. Nor is the configuration or distribution of power inside the West and the East neutral: a power needed for intra-western equilibrium will be westernized in strategic actuality and diplomatic fiction, if not otherwise: witness Russia and Prussia when mobilized against France by England. Conversely, the inability of western powers to sustain their interests and uphold the integrity of their allies farther to the east will push the latter eastward: witness Poland or the Czech lands when abandoned by one or both of the western protagonists.

The variants originating in the configuration of strengths and weaknesses, and in the patterns of cultural or economic propensities and products, are many and can be surprising. Thus, the societies or states situated in east-central Europe between Germany and Russia, and looking westward for support against one or the other of the stronger powers, will affect being more western in (liberal versus authoritarian) political culture or (Catholic versus Orthodox) religion than either great power: definitely a Russia geographically to the east of them, but on balance also a Germany historically ambivalent about the West and her appurtenance to the West. Thus, toward the end of the European state system as much as at its beginning east-central Europe came nearest to fixing in geopolitical space an East–West schism that was represented at all times more flexibly by cultural or institutional convergence coexisting with divergence, and economic or strategic complementarity with competition. Whereas competitively imposed or induced conversion (by western Roman Catholicism or eastern Greek Orthodoxy) was initially religious, the later bias was toward ideological indoctrination (by a more "western" fascism overwhelming islands of adopted liberalism and more "eastern" socialism displacing local-based fascism). Conjointly, the vehicles and instruments of overt politico-military conquest or pressure shifted to technologically more advanced analogues from horse-riding nomads or mounted knights, the Tartar horde from the east and the Teutonic Order from the west.

Whereas the several differences in identities, interests, or values defining the several schisms create the objective (or rational) basis for conflicts, the overlap between pair-constituents intensifies the subjective (or passional) incentives to the contest attending each of them. The area of a schism-defining overlap is one which each contestant will regard as his, to either control or have enforceable access to as a matter of right if not also duty. He will bring to the contest over the antagonistically shared stakes or sector radically different material and moral resources, shaped more thoroughly by his defining identity – as a primarily secular or sacerdotal, continental or maritime, and western or eastern, actor – than by the nature of the stakes themselves. Nor will the contention be eased by values-based motives or concerns overlapping with concrete stakes- or interests-related ones in all schisms, if somewhat differently. Thus a Papal–Imperial contest being formulated in doctrinal terms did not rule out its direct bearing on civilian-ecclesiastical administrative structures within the Empire, and the religious objectives of the crusades did not so much conceal as trigger, only to merge inextricably with, material and personal-dynastic considerations. The priorities are subtly changed when materially constituted differences between the parties shaping the land–sea power schism are distilled into ideatal contrasts, while in the East–West schism cultural and real-political factors and concerns are apt to be most evenly – or, at least, most consciously – balanced.

If both sets of overlaps invariably intensify conflictual interactions among actors, links between the several schisms cannot but affect the development of the multi-actor system. Will such links also fall into a logical pattern of sequences or combinations? First to surface will be secular–spiritual duality within primitive social units expanding from village to empire and lacking the elementary awareness of geography against which to project East–West value-institutional differences as well as the technology with which to implement the land–sea power disparity. Only when the original schism has extended to relations between radically separate actors (thus, the crusaders), will it combine with one of the other schisms intractable in narrowly rational-pragmatic terms and will impregnate the material stakes such a schism raises with immaterial values or principles. The next-following cleavage to fully surface was one between East and West, with the latter standing in succession for Greece (versus Persia), Alexander's Mecedon (versus Persia and India), Rome (versus Syria and subsequently Parthia), and the Romanized–Christianized barbarian kingdoms (versus Islam). Beginning with the Graeco–Persian interaction, the sacral–secular invaded the East–West duality in that the political orders became sacralized also in the West as the eastern mystery religions and ruler deification practices permeated essentially secular polytheistic cultures. However, it was reserved for the subsequent juxtaposition of Christianity and Islam to fuse the sacral–secular and the East–West schisms (and primitive elements of the continental–maritime disparity) into a multifaceted religio-cultural-geopolitical complex of contrasts and identities, antagonisms and alliances, antagonization and assimilation.

A climactic interlock of all three schisms occurred soon after in the two-sided contest pitting Spain against the Ottoman Empire along one (by then traditional East–West) axis, and against the Dutch and English maritime powers on the other (to-be-salient land–sea power) axis. And both contests were intensified by the doctrinal overlaps between the rival religious faiths (Christianity and Islam and Catholicism and Reform) and between the doctrinal and the real-political stakes (residually sacral–secular schism). Once the Ottoman threat had subsided on land and sea, West separated from East inside Europe and the previously interlocked segments of medieval Christendom turned their backs upon one another in geographically conditioned preoccupations and diverged in developmental momentum. In the west, the amplifying land–sea power schism continued to be affected by Protestantism's link with the Maritime Powers and Catholicism's with navally unevenly adept but essentially continental Spain and France. Only in the eighteenth century did the waning of the confessional issue and the only sporadically reactivated intra-European East–West issue isolate the meanwhile fully crystallized land–sea power issue, in ways constituting the high point of rational-pragmatic statecraft.

For this to happen, the land–sea power schism had to emerge from the receding association of confessional concerns with either irrational fears or dogmatic certainties, while concurrent innovations in means and adaptations in goals underwrote the progressing secularization of perceptions and attitudes. The henceforth critically diminished fear – after replacing the earlier terrors of the forest in the infernal nether circle of medieval demonology – was of the ocean, revalued from an unknown and quintessentially unknowable sphere into the pathway to actual worlds beyond the known one. The lost certainties were mainly those of naive faith, buttressed by credence in henceforth discredited Biblical geography. Innovative rationality produced simultaneously the tools for overseas travel and transport, conquest and commerce, ranging from compass through ocean-worthy ships to deck-emplaced cannon. As the goals embraced by the actual or aspiring voyager were being altered in tandem with the means, the unspoiled New World became ever more the place wherein to redeem the corruptions of the Old: a place where to regain lost paradise through works which, bringing material wealth, would also spread spiritual welfare, if only by imposing the formal observance of the true faith.

The concurrent tendency to secularization became fully manifest and a crucial link with the previously dominant schism was forged, only when England as the paramount insular-maritime state replaced the supreme spiritual power of the papacy in the pretension to arbitrate among earthbound actors as one not thus hampered. Nor did Great Britain play a lesser role in the re-emergent link between the land–sea power and the intra-European East–West schisms, growing out of economic conditions and culminating in strategic connections. Whereas an increasingly uneven economic integration had meant that the eastern form of primitive capitalism would assure seafaring west Europeans of cheap east European grain (next to requisite metals, before overseas supplies set the eastern region back materially further), the inequality stopped widening when first Russia and then Prussia–Germany got around to displaying maritime or colonial next to continental ambitions. The previously atrophied sacral–secular duality reinfused then the other two schisms, although the spiritual component pressed now from both sides against realistic power politics in the deceptively secular guise of socio-political ideologies and ethnic-cultural myths. Reuniting all three schisms re-enacted none the less their coexistence at the beginning of the land–sea power conflict cycle in the sixteenth to seventeenth centuries, and did so at the price of increased violence in fully globalized conflicts.

INTER-SCHISM DIALECTIC AND INTRA-ACTOR DYNAMICS

Thus variously represented by individual actors and variably interlinked within the structure of the arena, the schisms will have critical consequences for the dynamics of a state system. Just as each of the prime parties to a schism will sooner or later try to demote the other, so both will be responsible for projecting a third party to supremacy or also the next-dominant duality to salience as part of what eventually will be their reciprocal enfeeblement. This was as true of Athens and Sparta as of England and Germany on the land–sea power axis as it was for the Holy Roman Emperors and the Roman Popes in the context of the sacral–secular schism, and for seventh-century Byzantium and Persia and seventeenth-century Spain and Turkey on the East–West axis. Insofar as the shared deterioration attends the fading of a dominant schism, its terminal calamities become part of the no less turbulent surfacing of the next following one or ones – yet another instance of immanence or latency in the cyclically evolving system. Thus, the contest weakening both the Popes and the Emperors to the advantage of France and Spain set the stage for the Ottoman–Hispanic contention on the East–West axis to be extended beyond the Mediterranean (by way of Ottoman backing for Catholic France and German Protestants alike); and if the attendant economic decline of Germany relative to a West that was profitably opening up toward the Atlantic was co-responsible for the Protestant Reform, the conflict between the latter and reformed Catholicism helped ignite the land–sea power schism before being consumed in its fires – until the unevenly progressing erosion of the French and the British parties to the continental–maritime cleavage shifted its focus eastward, reactivating via the East–West a modified sacral–secular schism.

Just as interlocks between schisms, so conjunctions between them and radical scissions within actors will make for turbulent change – thus when the emergence of the land–sea power schism coincided with internal conflicts (echoing the sacral–secular schism) between divine-right monarchy supported by inland-located rural gentry and commercial profits-seeking oligarchies with links to ocean-adjoining areas and a stake in pragmatically adjusted, demythologized relations between state and society and ruler and ruled. Enlarging on the revolts of the Dutch against Spain and the Huguenots against Paris, the attendant revolutionary upheavals ranged from the two English revolutions to the French Revolution. Whereas the former released seventeenth-century England from the continental-absolutist associations and ambitions of the Stuarts fully for her naval destiny, the latter climaxed the failure of the French divine-right monarchy to forestall the rise of the updated English mercantile-maritime regime and then recoup its own backsliding behind it. Still later and more eastern upheavals marked the melding of the climactic stage of the land–sea power schism in the Euro-global setting with the re-emergence of the East–West cleavage, first within Europe alone. The second German quasi-revolution (in 1918–19) followed by reaction (in the 1930s) was then more consequential than the first such sequence (in 1848 and the 1860s respectively), because it alone was related to the dominant schism through a meaningful political or military confrontation with a maritime power. If containing the predominantly western-liberal first revolution by an authoritarian-conservative counterthrust out of Russia was part of the West–East cleavage, the second and greater Russian one (in 1917, following that of 1905 linked to regional Anglo-Russian contentions) was connected with critical aspects of more than one schism affecting the conflicted Russo-German relationship. The conflict combined a secondary variety of the East–West duality (between unevenly eastern parties) with the most critical question of all, as to which of the essentially non-western continental powers would become the prime challenger to Anglo-Saxon maritime supremacy.

Conflict-aggravating as the ostensibly schism-defining diversity in values or norms, principles or mind-sets, are, the latter are less an independent source of tension and conflict than they infuse either a higher rationale or a deeper emotion into routine stakes of contentions. However, both the ratio and the relationship between the two classes of determinants is not uniform for all schisms. Thus, however genuine and deep may be the beliefs of parties to the sacral–secular schism, they are unavoidably concerned with mundane causes and stakes of conflict. The tie-up was originally implicit in the indifferentiation of the sacral and secular reality from which the schism takes off. It has been perpetuated by the dual – sacerdotal and managerial or otherwise profane – functions of the priesthood over most of human history and consolidated, in social actuality, by the difficulty to separate transcendent from the transactional planes and normatively meliorative objectives from material reform. Regardless of whether the contention is between high priests and pharaohs or between princes and popes; divides Christians from Moslems or Calvinists from Catholics, and liberal polities or policies from conservative or (social-Darwinian) fascist from (Marxist-Leninist) communist ones, considerations of (individual or collective) creed and practical (group or national) concerns interpenetrate as much as does principle with power.

The more ideal of the determinants tend to become secondary as the contest extends in time and ramifies in space, when exposing differences in (quasi-) sacral or transcendental principles to secular or "real" stakes has deradicalized the contest and helped defuse the crisis at a relatively early stage. A more circuitous process will take longer when real or material issues are primary in the land versus sea power schism from the beginning. Once the schism's technological, economic, and geopolitical prerequisites have been met, structural incompatibilities and strategic dilemmas will dominate the definition of goals and the choice of means, to be only enhanced by the contest being rationalized in terms of values that are divergent because they originally derive from disparate physical locations. They will be secondary in their long-term consequences for outcomes, but be deeply felt and significantly impelling nonetheless as the conflict escalates.

Hardest to assess, because intermediate between the two extremes, is the ratio of pragmatic to propagandistic and real to rationalizing factors in regard to the East–West schism. East–West convergence coexists with divergence on the plane of values, principles, and practices just as integration does with polarization in terms of real- or power politics. Thus, East–West value divergence contributed to polarizing Graeco-Persian conflict on a par with situational (continental–maritime) disparity, but its impact was reduced by Persia's diplomatic–strategic role in resolving later intra-Greek conflicts (using Persian gold pieces in support of a King's Peace). Subsequently transforming Hellenic values into the Hellenistic occidental–oriental compound marked cultural and institutional convergence, which only half realized the Alexandrine utopia of universal concord but eased competition within the post-Alexander multi-power system. The utopia of East–West fusion was never – not even in the Near Eastern Latin kingdoms of the crusaders – applied to the medieval manifestations of the East–West cleavage and the draft of western humanists on Arab classical learning did not approximate the Hellenistic model of value convergence. But there was a considerable amount of politico-strategic interpenetration through mixed Christian–Moslem alliances which, when spanning the doctrinal chasm, alternately muted and aggravated the East–West conflict while complicating the definition of the real stakes.

Politically meaningful East–West interaction on a world-wide basis was long implicit in (western) strategies for immobilizing a more directly threatening nearer-eastern actor with the help of farther-eastern one or ones. Inside

Christian Europe the issue arose when the political and economic consequences of the eastern part's greater or longer exposure to incursions by steppe-nomadic forces had resurfaced the distinction between Romanized and non-Romanized Europe, previously muted by the decay of cities in the early medieval west and initial urbanization in the East. Only utopian designs could envisage thereafter, from tenth to the twentieth century, a prompt and easy East–West fusion inside Europe, whether by restoring the defunct Roman Empire (through the German Emperor Otto III's association with the ruler of Poland) or resuscitating a no longer viable continental hegemony (through France's alliances with resuscitated east European states including Poland). The crux of the issue was elsewhere. When would an ostensible or nominal convergence in values, techniques, and institutions begin to prevail over the disparate conditions of evolution producing a growing effective divergence? And how would the eastward diffusion of western values, techniques, and institutions that intensified politico-cultural divergence mesh with the East's diplomatico-strategic integration with the West and military-technological imitation of the West, so long as alliances and antagonisms were unevenly contributing to and synchronized with the gradual displacement of preponderant power eastward?

Originally, the disparities between western and eastern Europe were part and parcel of distinctive actor formation in the east, with large and unstable ensembles rising and falling in response to massive pressures emanating in too early a stage of development from still farther east (as compared with limited localized ones in the west). By no later than the sixteenth century, the first mainly politico-military and institutional difference had acquired a socio-economic dimension, as farther-eastern military invasions or impingements were replaced by western economic colonization of eastern Europe outside Russia with the assistance of a latifundist nobility hostile to developing the countryside into cities, the state toward centralization, and society toward diversity. The bastardization of feudalism in eastern Europe signalled the deformation that was to affect everything first developed in the West: from rational administration or bureaucracy through industrialization and nationalism to liberal representative government. Since innovations or impulses to innovate came either too soon or too late to be gradually absorbed and assimilated, the originally western value- or belief-systems and corresponding institutions were either radicalized or repressed: radicalized, as a way of overcompensating for the absence of sustaining conditions at the societal base internally; repressed, in ways consummating the vanity of resistance to transformations being imposed arbitrarily from above. On balance, the measure of East–West convergence was enhanced when the innovation was transmitted directly by an effective intermediary – ranging from the German peasants and urban settlers moving eastward in the earlier centuries to either western technicians or an ideologically and organizationally westernized political system in Russia later on. Conversely, the most eager elite receptivity to a western import was insufficient when the foreign source lacked in effective transmission capability: thus France for her capital and technology in pre-World War I Russia and – even more markedly – her culture, political ideas, and forms of capitalism in post-World War I eastern Europe outside Russia.

While divergent developments generated institutional and cultural sources of East–West conflict, the emergence of a major-power complex in eastern Europe exposed the value differences to a growing undertow from real-pragmatic stakes. Roughly a century after the trans-"national" or -regional religious conflicts had stopped interlocking the two parts of Europe to a degree, conventional feuding among the meanwhile strengthened eastern European powers helped involve them strategically in largely continental–maritime contests among the western European states. However, the brief period of flexible strategic integration – linking the increasingly Russia-centered northern and the intra-Germanic Austro-Prussian balances with the all-European and global balance centered on the Anglo-French competition – lasted only until one after the other economically decolonized eastern power would bid for access to the overseas commercial-colonial periphery: Habsburg Austria, when trying to deblock the outlets to overseas in the "Austrian" Netherlands; Russia, Prussia-Germany, and Russia again, attempting the same from the home base. Therefore, the eighteenth-century type of eastern Europe's strategic integration into the Euro-global system veered toward polarization on a global scale once the uncertain impact of the liberal–conservative dichotomy on East–West power alignments during the early nineteenth-century interlude having dissipated, the three effective great-power actors in eastern Europe were reduced to two (following Austria–Hungary's subordination to imperial Germany and subsequent disappearance) and eventually to only one (with the main part of divided Germany moving westward and out of world politics), even as the number of effective western sea powers had undergone a similar erosion beginning with the Portuguese and the Dutch.

Compounding the cultural-institutional East–West divergence with the politico-economic land–sea power schism, while interregional integration through diplomatic strategies yielded to polarization in Europe, was meanwhile a potent source of systemic crisis. While the grounds for conflict inherent in the two schisms were compounded with irritants due to the center of gravity shifting eastward on land, the tensions peculiar to the sacral–secular schism resurfaced due to the originally secular-pragmatic values and behavior forms peculiar to reason-of-state real-politics being exposed to a dual assault from the plane of transcendence: by the restraint-oriented norms of inter-state ethics promulgated by the (receding) western maritime political societies; and by the resurgence- or retribution-oriented dogmas peculiar to the (late-developing or also ascending) eastern continental powers.

As it took shape, the European inter-schism dialectic went far toward establishing the previously only intimated chronological sequence from sacral–secular via East–West to the land–sea power dichotomy (and back again) as one that was "natural" or, at least, optimal. In fact, the strategic integration of East and West in Europe might have proceeded more smoothly, and helped reduce gradually the evolutionary disparities, had it advanced farther before becoming involved in the contentious stakes and the societal conflicts characteristic of the land–sea power, continental–maritime, cleavage. Moreover, failure to come to terms with the East–West duality in the early crystallization phase of the European system aggravated the problem of dealing with the fluid

East–West overlap zone in the global setting, once the Russo-Japanese conflict had set off meaningfully systemic links between the western and the eastern hemispheres.

Acute or only latent, related problems comprised at all times and in all spatial settings an underlying two-part paradox. Firstly, since the land–sea power schism is the one most closely tied up with real-pragmatic stakes, it is most apt to help order inter-actor relations rationally once its geopolitical, economic, and technological requisites have been substantially met. However, the schism-supporting structural overlap – of maritime powers having a sufficient territorial base to inject themselves effectively into the continental balance of power with land powers disposing of sufficient resource base to permit effective action on the oceanic alongside the continental fronts – is equally apt to generate contrasting definitions of what constitutes an overall – continental-and-oceanic – equilibrium. The immediate consequence will be incompatible strategies tending to disrupt and in due course destroy the system itself. Secondly, existential or situational differences between insular-maritime and continental-military powers predominate over the largely derivative divergences in institutions and belief-systems. Yet as conditions sustaining the land–sea power schism erode, a moral-political vacuum will be filled by the comparatively less pragmatic stake definitions and ideological rationalizations peculiar to the other two schisms – meaning, in predominantly post-religious contexts, primarily the East–West cleavage with pseudo-creedal connotations. Thus, reducing conflicts along the land–sea power axis will diminish the sum total of contentiousness in the system only if principal actor strategies for dealing with immediate needs and interests have been directed to mitigating the impact of the other two schisms or schism-neutral power configurations.

Since the different schisms permeate other facets of structure, including the developmental stages of both actors and systems of different scope, a critical feature is the extent to which they shape intra-actor as distinct from inter-actor dynamics: impinge on the formation of actors as part of but also as distinct from the shaping of the system itself.

The secular–spiritual schism affected intra-actor developments earliest, when a key issue will be whether and how to liberate "State" from "Church" (the body politic from the *corpus mysticum*) or vice versa. To do either was to break up the primitive indifferentiation rooted in attributing a dual nature to both Man and God on one (the metaphysical) level and of both administrative and propitiatory functions to the clergy on another (the managerial) level. To the lesser extent that it affects inter-actor relations, as it did in the Papacy–Empire and Christianity–Islam setting, the schism will do so in the early, peculiarly ideology-saturated, proto-systemic stage – only to reappear, at a much later stage, duly modified and in association with the other schisms (e.g. by way of a spiritualized concept of the state and of politics in eastern land powers facing the western sea powers). By contrast, before the functionally specific land–sea power schism can be salient in the more fully crystallized norm-stage of a system, the center of political (and economic) gravity within particular actors will have to be first settled in contentions between inland-agricultural (or industrial) and coastal-mercantile sectors.

Compared with the other two schisms, the East–West schism is neutral relative to the evolutionary stage of both the system and the actors. And it will vie with north–south cleavages for primacy in affecting the formation of actors and the segmentation of systems in terms of unevenly civilized center–periphery dichotomy. At the same time, for an eastern power – say, the (late) Ottoman or Russian Empire – to be included eventually in the European system bears witness to a notable fact: to wit, that strategic-operational imperatives keyed to the land–sea power schism will attribute central-systemic status alone, or also "Western" identity, to parties situated conversely otherwise. The East–West distinction being thus malleable, only the sequence from the sacral–secular to the maritime–continental schism is "logical," because reflecting the ascendancy of rational-secular factors as the means grow to replace propitiation of supernatural forces with productivity-based protection from mundane powers. And just as the inter-schism sequence favoring the land–sea power cleavage only supplements or also stimulates the progression from a proto-system to a fully matured system, so the norm-stage will be propelled in due course toward the meta-stage by virtue of the dual paradox which, inherent in the most pragmatic of schisms, favors non-rational if not irrational impulses directing the system toward disruption.

To the extent that a schism intensifies intra-actor dynamics, it serves as a link to system crystallization by accelerating actor development. In ways replicating revolutions in ancient empires, the main European upheaval traceable to the sacral–secular schism was Germany's only genuine, pre-modern revolution, which intertwined in two stages – the struggle over Investiture and the Reformation – the relation between State and Church with that between central and local authorities. By delaying German unification, the upheavals had only an indirect if important impact on crystallization of the system and evolution of the land–sea power schism. By contrast, the English revolutions of the seventeenth century set the stage for the maturation and world-wide extension of the European system around the continental–maritime schism directly, by freeing the mercantile-maritime predispositions of the Stuarts from the functionally continental absolutist bias reflective of a rural political base. In France, the schism permeated the proto-revolutionary sixteenth- to seventeenth-century conflicts between interests and creeds entrenched in the inland core and the coastal rim areas. The outcome of the conflicts advanced internal consolidation more substantially than did the climactic Revolution via either the similarly conditioned Gironde–Jacobin feud within the Third Estate or the latter's challenge to the Second and First. However, the internal consequence of the ancien regime's failures against England helped trigger revolutionary transformations in the international system at large, which were to be accentuated by the next-following continental revolutions. Among these, the Russian upheaval was shaped primarily by the East–West schism insofar as the western values, alternately received and rejected by the radical intelligentsia (encompassing secular emphases), stood in opposition to the eastern values of the Autocracy (buttressed by the caesaro-papist emphases of Orthodoxy). Like the French earlier, the Russian Revolution was again only triggered by defeats in war. Arising out of a facet of the land–sea power schism (the Anglo-German) more directly responsible for the revolutionary convulsion in Germany, it was still one to which Russia was related as the critical third background party.

While all these revolutions marked a stage in either the formation or the development of major actors, they affected as powerfully the stratification of the system in that they raised and provisionally decided the issue as to which (type of) political class and which (type of) territorial polity would predominate in the following phase. In the process, the substantive values informing the both sequentially and circularly interlocked schisms, and instrumental in actuating the interlock, supplemented in regard to the performed function the more narrowly procedural-diplomatic norms which the antecedent micro-system had infused into the macro-system. Altogether different from both the values attending schisms and the norms mediating changes in system scope were to be the normatively formulated restraints on the use of force which, inspired by universalist considerations transcending both structure and scope of a system in fact or intent, were offered for application in the name of a development unlike any historically evident. They would signal not so much the special quality of a party to any particular schism (be it western, imitatively sacral, or maritime) or the immanence of an emergent (global) macro-system in a particularly enlightened micro-system (late European or Euro-Atlantic), as the precarious conditions and perceived needs of a particular, community-type, meta-system in being or hypothetical becoming.

2

Actor Formation and Schism-Related Differentiation

The process which underlies and actuates the transition from a proto-system to a full-fledged micro- or macro-system is one of the formation of actors as territorially-based units for aggregating and projecting power. By the same token, the alteration of a system into either the empire- or the community-type meta-system entails the *trans*formation of already formed actors. Formation implies growth: confluence and consolidation, via discernible procedures, of the essential attributes of effective actorhood (i.e., most commonly or generally, territorial statehood). Conversely, the actor transformation that antedates meta-systemization entails a deviation from the distinguishing attributes of territorial statehood which may, in the system-focused perspective, be equated with decline or decay. Pending transformation, actors uniform in their character as units of power fixed in space and subject to development and decline over time will differ qualitatively according to their position in the several schisms, not least as to their primary resource base (land-agricultural or maritime-commercial) and fundamental political culture (occidental or oriental).

FUNCTIONAL CLUSTERS IN CONTEXTUAL ARENA

It is part of the dialectic between the operational and the organic dimensions of inter-unit relations that, contrary to common sense, arena is functionally prior to actors – if not always, then at the early stage of their development; and if not absolutely, then relative to the general principle of reciprocal actor–arena conditioning. It has been suggested earlier that a macro-system is immanent in the specific configuration and the course of development (and decay) of the antecedent micro-system, while proto- and meta-stages are developmental extremes latent in one another. It can now be added that whereas actor transformation is implicit in actor formation (whatever makes for growth is subject to being inverted into the causes or symptoms of decline), actors in their earliest growth phase are implicit in the arena: not now in its particular configuration, but in its defining characteristics as competitively interacting plurality of actors, responding to the scarcity of material and immaterial assets to be distributed.

Arena comes before actors because, even at its most primitive and inchoate, it is fraught with inducements and constraints, rough rules of or guidelines for conduct, in excess of the resources which the primitive-inchoate actors, who "physically" make up the arena without constituting it operationally in full, can spontaneously generate. As a physically and functionally finite framework of scarce material (territory-based) and immaterial (security and status-related) assets, the arena compels competition over these assets among actors seeking survival through seizure or control of a vital minimum of such assets. In the process of competing over the survival-sufficient vital minimum, some entities will be forged into viable and differentiated from non-viable actors. However, if arena "comes before" actors, the actors have farther to go: the range of their possible development – in the guise of functional differentiation, institutionalization, rationalization, etc. – is more extensive than is the spectrum of essential attributes of the arena. The consequence will tend to be a shift in determinative salience from (an effective) one by arena over (developing) actors to (an attempted) one by (declining) actors over arena, as creation of states gives way to crisis of the system.

It is both "true" and "logical" that a perfect equilibrium or equivalence intervenes between the two boundary conditions. As a theoretical norm and a developmental mid-point, actor–arena equilibrium materializes when actors have in the main crystallized and elements of the eventual system crisis only begin to coalesce; when key actors are as effective in aggregating and projecting power as is the arena-wide mechanism for constraining superior and propping up inferior power. While an interactive or -stimulative actor–arena relationship denotes circularity in space, the distribution of reciprocal impact varies over time: the elementary dynamic of the interaction process (conditioned by basic structures while modifying the manifest configurations) is profoundly affected by the actors' developmental stage, even as their strategies are designed to manipulate – and are apt to mismanage – the interaction's particulars. But again, if the distribution varies over time, the constantly operative interplay of structure, (developmental) stage, and strategy rules out any neat dichotomization in principle and periodization in time – least of all as between actor formation and system crystallization (such as assigning the former in Europe to bureaucratic centralization of power prior to the Peace of Westphalia, and the later to balanced or balancing distribution of power up to the Congress of Vienna, with a system crisis beginning no later than the Versailles peace settlement).

The plural structure of the arena alone will stimulate inter-actor reflexes conducive to the search for supportive resources, in the absence of which both arena and actors would stagnate in conditions of underdevelopment. In addition, a particular arena will generate more specific infusions into the actor-formative process, in the guise of pressures to adapt to the arena's changing scope and dominant schism and of resources for implementing the techniques best suited to coping with the existing configuration of power through contemporaneously legitimate and effective ways of managing competition, composing quarrels, and compensating for specific actor setbacks or insufficiencies.

What the arena most significantly injects into the process of actor growth and selection will depend on how keenly actors are aware of and how deeply attuned to empirical causality, open-ended but divisible time, and articulated physical space – a condition as absent in the early European Middle Ages as at the earliest dawn of Mesopotamian civilization. The injected elements can be predominantly mythical or material and reflect a primarily genealogical or geopolitical bias. Mythical are divine sanctions and prohibitions, encouragements and mandates, mediated in one era by Egyptian and Mesopotamian priests and in another by Roman popes, while material assets and liabilities are processed by an economy centered on money or service or barter. When the genealogical principle obtains, actor initiatives are oriented toward lineages of blood in networks of more or less cognate dynastic or aristocratic families. The premium is on ruler longevity and fertility with implications for inheritance and succession, fragmentation and reaggregation of territories. By contrast, lines of force in a field defined by configuration of more or less contiguous territorial units are critical in the geopolitically biased setting. Either openings or constrictions release pressures toward contest (implicit in contiguity) and to alliance-type combinations (implicit in its unevenness), toward expansion or retrenchment (implicit in adjoining weakness or strength). The less settled is the experientially developed and pragmatically tested sense of why (causality) and when (temporality) to conceive, and whither (spatiality) to direct, action, the more influential will be the mythical and genealogical features of and emanations from the arena in imparting and maintaining the initial momentum of actor formation. Preponderant in proto-systemic settings, the features will reappear in the updated secularized or "democratized" forms of ideologies and pan-movements as the system approaches the meta-stage.

A significant impact from outside the ambit of the material resources primitive actors generate and control as they move beyond mythical and genealogical emphases will originate in elemental nature outside the emergent culture. When represented – next to climate or contagion, flood or fire – by the human factor, nature is most strikingly embodied in unfamiliar or alien (i.e., "barbarian") human types. The distribution of their physical impact "out of nowhere" or at least from the outside will be as important as is any qualitative aspect, including their readiness or capacity to assimilate. The near-continuous population migrations in antiquity established a heterogeneous range of proto-systemic actor types, from mere warrior bands through primitive monarchies or empires to decaying imperial residues or replicas. Thereafter, the Romanization of the "Germans" in their native realms coincided with the barbarization of Gallo-Roman sociopolitical organisms, before the two progressively faded as separate actors. Both differed from the revitalization-capable eastern Roman (Byzantine) Empire as much as, earlier, actors created by barbarian intrusion (e.g. Kassite

Babylonia) differed from actors propelled by barbarian impact from isolation into imperial expansion (post-Hyksos Egypt).

More significant were the two kinds of barbarian intrusion consequent upon the false dawn of initial actor and arena consolidation in early feudal (ninth-century AD) Europe. One kind of intrusion took the form of small-group raids (mainly from the north, the Vikings or Northmen, and less significantly from the south, the Islamic Saracens). They required and elicited the capacity for instant defense reaction on local basis; as a result, they fostered the nuclear type of actor aggregation: a gradual agglomeration – accidental or contrived, peaceable or forcible – of well integrated small defense units around a privileged-or-protected nucleus. Replicating (and improving upon?) the formation of Athens-dominated Attica and Rome-dominated Latium from a favorable socio-political and favored physical-material core, Capetian France as one of the offshoots of the prematurely aggregated Frankish-Carolingian realm was Europe's model of a viable actor to build up from a nucleus (royal Ile de France). The opposite to the nuclear is the nebular model of actor formation, embodied in the many ephemeral empires of antiquity and typified in Europe by the Germanic (eventually Holy Roman) Empire and transient agglomerates such as the Polish-Lithuanian and Serbian or Bulgarian "empires" to the east and south of it. Regardless of whether such large-scale, loosely organized, units were improvised around an exceptionally able ruler or a mere dynastic figurehead, they were so for defense against massive and coordinated barbarian invasions from the east (the Magyars in the ninth century followed by the Mongols and the Turks), wholly unlike the scattered raids in the west. Thus mandated, the scale of the primitive military aggregation was bound to exceed the range of feasible sociopolitical and -economic integration. So long as premature formation was then giving rise to de facto fragmentation underneath nominal coherence, and divergent real interests undermined personal unions, retrogressive evolution meant falling gradually behind the more slowly formed actors of the nuclear type.

However, even when impulses from the arena predominate, intra-actor ingredients and dynamics are necessary to mediate the conversion of arena-based challenges and resources into actor responses and performance. The scarcity of the assets to be divided among (potential) actors, ranging from territory via physical security or immunity to status or prestige, conditions the internal dimension of actor formation. It compels the development of the means for winning and retaining a share of the disposable assets that is sufficient for survival in reliably secured status and role. The core elements around which secondary functions and coordinating institutions of an organized polity take shape are an economic base and a military barrier. They can be severed from one another only temporarily, and be disjoined only arbitrarily from the sociopolitical processes that crystallize in institutions. The same is true for the formula of psychological reassurance. Vitally supplemental to material resources for physical security and satiety, it enables a mundane polity to relate all its works, constructive or coercive, to the plane of transcendence by conferring a necessary moral sanction on a territoriality rooted ultimately in force. The normative formula may be vested in local gods and temples of Mesopotamia and Egypt (thus the god Enlil at Nippur and the sacred city of Heliopolis in Egypt), the anthropomorphic pantheons of Greece and Rome, the sacerdotal anointment of kings or priest-kings of medieval and later France, and, in the wake of the divine-right conception of monarchy, in the cult of either the state or its basic law as standing above both ruler and ruled.

However secularized, when the quasi-religious beliefs and precepts effectively contain centrifugal and promote centripetal social forces and energies, minimal cohesion can help institutionalize a functional cluster of economic, military, and managerial-administrative means and ends. An increasingly intricate differentiation of functions or division of labor, shielded by and perfecting the means of destruction, will be materially supported from a progressively enlarged surplus of (agricultural and manufacturing) production over consumption sufficient for biological reproduction. And the resulting increases in efficacy will make it easier to reduce the psychological impact of a widening range of felt scarcities. Public action will initially be turned outward, where basic needs can in relatively primitive conditions be satisfied more easily, before turning inward (from warfare to welfare functions) in what is, past short-term fluctuations in concern with internal and external power and stability maintenance, one of the few altogether fundamental reversals in the making of and relations among sociopolitical organisms as they develop and "mature."

As the both necessary and sufficient primary givens in the formation, development, and decline of actors-in-arena, the paired economic and military factors will evolve from the military (or force) factor being the main or only means to securing economic goods such as booty, ransom, or territory – the latter for tilling, grazing, or generating taxes or tolls. The subsequent tendency will be toward an ever less straightforward relationship of the two activities, as the generation and maintenance of military power becomes only indirectly or ultimately related to the economic process while, more generally, each factor becomes (mainly or only) the prerequisite to either affirming or compensating for the other. A complete reversal, the near-complete substitution of economic for military power and instruments, will be achieved only as a facet of disengaging an actor or an arena segment politically, commonly attendant on decline. The vast middle ground, taking up most of evolutionary time, will be taken up by changeable techniques for implementing a well balanced, reciprocally supportive, circular relationship.

At bottom, economic resource *qua* wealth is the means for undertaking military exertions in war, and war the means for acquiring or the reason for developing economic resource and expanding collective wealth. At some point of actor development, the circular relationship becomes the more specific one of fiscal solvency becoming the condition of effective use of force, while effective enforcement (including military) of fiscal obligations is among the foremost conditions of healthy public finance. Moreover, whereas the economic and military components in the material-resource core are alternately the means and the proximate ends in a relationship that changes from direct to indirect within ever more complexly institutionalized interplays, critical surpluses and scarcities will alternate between material and immaterial as the actors themselves evolve, mature, and decay: the early material deficiencies in fiscally exploitable assets being made good by a surfeit of psychic energy (expressed in military control or conquest of toll- or other benefits-producing territory and trade routes) will give way to the expanding material surplus being eventually offset and operationally neutralized by a deficiency in psychopolitical energy (expressed in elite incapacity to make militarily or economically hazardous decisions and popular reluctance to endure the consequences of such decisions). As the system evolves, it will require an increasingly elaborate intra- and inter-actor dynamic to mediate between materially undersupplied temerity and oversupplied timidity. Just as actors are formed and grow when the critical factors and functions stimulate one another, so they will slide toward decadence when either force and fiscality or surpluses and scarcities have been paired off in ways that hinder projecting power effectively abroad for security or status in favor of perpetuating the stability of a political regime or social order. In the perspective of actor transformation, the shift from functional extra- to introversion is one from the arena injecting material and operational stimuli into the actor-formative process to matured or overmatured actors actually disseminating material goods or trying to diffuse immaterial values into the systemic arena.

Diffusing material assets among later-developing and initially weaker actors will create the power-political conditions for the relative decline of the farther evolved actor; attempting to diffuse outward, or infuse into the arena, the values of a mature polity, one that specializes in sidestepping or disguising the application of force and the exercise of power, will (in a systemic perspective) betoken the same polity's psychopolitical decay. The actor–arena relationship will be reversed in the process, as the initial stimulants from the arena are replaced by comparatively ineffective summons for more slowly- or later-developing actors to forsake unregulated or unrestrained competition for checks on the drives and the dynamics that formed the earlier actors even as they fueled competition. Sublimating the quest for power and the use of force within a mature polity will both signal and conceal the consolidation of power into authority and of force into the enforcement of authoritative rules and regulations of the social order; when materially viable actors issue or heed appeals to jettison the experientially ratified survival norms emanating from the structure of the arena in favor of contrary normative precepts and in support of undisturbed growth, they will conceal an insufficiency of either power or will to use power in its form as force. The intended mutation is from arena-induced activation of the basic means of self-supporting existence into actor-inspired promotion of a form of social organization which, though ostensibly higher, curtails the range of both means and ends implicit in the plural structure of the more primitive arena.

Just as a state system evolves past early heterogeneity in kinds of actors within largely but pseudo-hierarchical structure peculiar to the proto-systemic stage, so it does also develop past the initial plurality of operational norms (ranging from variably authoritative mediation to actually reflexive self-help and -assertion) toward the centrality of a dominant behavioral norm among qualitatively homogeneous parties. The norm will embody directives for pragmatic-rational balancing of power among uniformly territorial and status- if not role-equal actors. The actors will have meanwhile progressed toward a monopoly of legitimate internal authority to shape the policy and wield the force for implementing the operational norm, only to regress from the monopoly as part of declension into a condition peculiar to the meta-systemic stage denoting the actor's inability to sustain his part in the balancing of power.

The sequence from a system's proto- to its meta-stage, as it first assumes and then dissipates a self-sustaining determinate structure, corresponds thus to the developmental sequence from pre- to post-norm in the general behavioral dispositions of actors as they are formed and transformed. Coincidentally undergone are changes in the key functions to be performed: from their initial indifferentiation, through the key functions being isolated out and recoalescing in a mutually reinforcing interlock, to late-stage loosening of the connection between the economic-sustenance and military-coercion functions (as the latter ceases being the prime or only avenue to the former). The accompanying tendency is for the administrative-managerial function to be displaced from auxiliary means for coordinating the core (military and economic) functions into first a coequal role and eventually a nearly self-sufficient end. As this happens, the transition from behavioral or attitudinal pre-norm to post-norm is revealed most clearly in two interrelated tendencies. One surfaces as the relationship between external and internal functions of government evolving from an original imbalance in favor of the former to the opposite is reflected in a corresponding shift: from obligations to the public powers to assertions of individual rights against the state-like actor, even as the corporate right to self-help in nakedly conflictual inter-actor relations is subjected to affirmations of a duty to self-restraint within an ostensibly consensual pattern of interactions. The other tendency bears on the changing relationship between ends and means. The excess of attempted ends over disposable means which links the behavioral pre-norm to proto-systemic structure, will eventually settle into the mid-point condition of the means and ends being brought into rationally adjusted balance. From this high point, the balance will deteriorate into reducing politically or otherwise feasible foreign-policy goals below the level of actually or potentially available material and technological means – an inverted asymmetry or imbalance reflecting post-norm type of behavior peculiar to especially the community type of meta-system.

DIFFERENTIAL POWER AGGREGATION AND BASIC ACTOR TYPES

The social organization in the river-crossed plain of Mesopotamia, units smallest in space and remotest in time, highlights the role of specific geo-economic conditions in concretizing the dynamic of actor formation. Flat terrain without natural obstacles precluded isolation and induced conflict over scarce river-related emplacements suitable for collecting food from the surrounding countryside or establishing trade links farther afield. The converse pattern in the earliest European Middle Ages was that of impenetrable forests and widely scattered clearings, with nodes of population huddling together in fear of forest-inhabiting spirits or monsters. It illustrated the primeval psychopolitical bases of group cohesion for fearful self-protection. Both of the primitive conditions, but the open Mesopotamian terrain better than the relatively intractable medieval European, illustrated the ubiquitous actor-formative pressures to deal, in conditions of a but precarious surplus and pressing scarcities, with the key predicament: a vulnerable material-mythical nucleus facing others across a variable radius over which to project aggregated and preclude antagonistic "power." The predicament imposed the need for adequately responsive performance: a progressive institutionalization of a cluster of economic-military-administrative functions in geo-economically determined emplacements of minimally survival-capable material resource and both psychological and physical reassurance (priests and/or warriors).

The nuclei were initially close enough to one another to reduce the critical radius: one over which force or energy had to move before eliciting countervailing response and which an outside threat would have to obliterate if it was to compel precaution and test the efficacity of protection. In such conditions the need for managing and controlling the means of offense or defense becomes a function of contiguity, as the attendant danger of a surprise attack augments the sense of insecurity. Inducement and opportunity for the control mechanism to evolve toward concentration of authority grows as distance shrinks and interaction intensifies. Thus, for example, after Mesopotamia and Greece, oppressive tyrannies (*signorie*) evolved in Italy more readily out of feudal or communal antecedents in territorially confining and cities-studded Lombardy than in more spacious Tuscany, while republican oligarchy survived in sea-shielded Venice. When, conversely, insulation from outside as the "normal" condition will foster despotism in large empire-like units at safe distance from sustained (as against sporadic "barbarian") external threat, it is the interlock between political stability and economic survival needs that compels administrative centralization (e.g. to regulate the distribution of water from a river, thus Egypt; or an irrigation network, thus China and India).

Just as a short physical distance between potential power centers compresses the perceptual distance from a threat, so responding to it by producing a material surplus from which to support protection will attract predatory aggression. It is only when food- or other goods-producing techniques generate a resource margin great enough to be an exploitable asset, and its preemption does not reduce the producer of the margin to incapacity to sustain and reproduce himself, that there will be an incentive to conquest and coercion as distinct from non-repeatable raid and rapine. A momentum for conflict sets in when, in turn, even the smallest surplus permits the organization of defense by sustaining warriors and managers with functions justifying abstinence from manual and other productive labor. Nor will the relationship between surplus and scarcity lack circularity, thus whenever a deficiency (e.g. of regular and sufficient rainfall) indirectly generates a surplus (e.g. by way of irrigation as a remedy) as both cause and consequence of differentiating societal (including politico-administrative) functions further; and when the added differentiation, maximizing the productive surplus, multiplies perceived deficiencies.

Unlike primitive rural Mesopotamia which offers the best example of the agricultural land-based type of actor, Renaissance Italy illustrated a more complex, strikingly self-sustaining and self-correcting, relationship within the economic-military core. Then, mercantile activity and financial management provided the monetary basis for paying the mercenaries, whose purchasing power in turn stimulated production and commerce well beyond the potential of only local agriculture-related trade in either early medieval Europe or ancient China. If production and protection (just as export and expansion) could and did stimulate one another, any discrepancy between requisite armed men and available moneys could be corrected by shifting resources from the consumption to the coercion potential – which shift, except in the case of markedly weak cities doomed to absorption, was apt to foster stalemate-prone inter-city conflicts keeping Italy, as comparable conditions had kept Greece, from being transformed into a large-sized single actor. The material and operational (and, insofar as civic patriotism reinforced the tendency, mythical) factors upholding actor plurality were only helped by the physical factor, inasmuch as the valley of the river Po (and of any river in Greece) did not favor – unlike either the Nile or the Tigris and Euphrates rivers – upstream powers, able to enforce unity by interfering with water flow and exploiting either divisions or decadence on the part of downstream delta communities. Thus Venice could expand only so far along the Po on the terra firma before coming up against the resources of a strong Milan alone or a still stronger Milanese–Florentine combination. Neither had the more primitive Naples–Sicily any natural axis along which to roll up the divided north. And no more than did the Po river, could the wearers of the papal tiara, devoid of sufficiently persuasive mythical or compelling material force, foster unity because, celibate and mortal, they were unable to capitalize on the continuity peculiar to either institutionalized divinity (thus Marduk's in Babylon) or dynastic heredity (thus the Capetian kings' in France) to tip the balance from competition to cohesion.

Italy failed, where France succeeded, to combine men, money-generating material assets, and mystique – the need for protection, the means from production, and the instruments of propitiation – into an enlarged *patria*, built around individual insecurities and impersonal symbols of corporate immortality. Whereas Italy illustrated an atomized field of forces resistant to aggregation, France provided the classic example of a major actor cohering around a progressively firmed-up nucleus. A propitiously located central power (the royal domain) evolved into centralizing authority (the kingship) by converting its material and mystical assets into the capacity to either attract or coerce individually more substantial power units over a radius that was lengthening only as the requisite potential was increasing. The divergence between France's incremental growth from a nucleus and the delayed firming up of the invertebrate (nebular) Germanic political organism, likewise emerging out of the wholly prematurely assembled Carolingian realm, became a major factor behind the eventual crisis of the continental segment of the European state system – if only after a later-stage divergence in the capacity to project power overseas between at first parallelly developing France and England had produced an earlier and more protracted crisis. Neither purely nuclear nor nebular was the developmental model partaking at different stages of both. It corresponded in the formation of Russia (comparable in this respect with that of the United States) to the position of a vast peripheral entity, long impinging only intermittently on central systemic crises from afar.

Whereas France took off successfully only to founder later on some of the very features that had made for early success, Germany as a major actor was first assembled too soon and eventually reassembled too late (and, in both cases, too quickly): too soon relative to her potential for consolidation in the medieval period of her first (Ottonian and subsequent) empire phase; too late relative to the arena's capacity for absorbing her, in the period of her second (Hohenzollern and subsequent) empire phase. France could and did cohere around a nucleus that was sanctified (by the consecrated royal person and symbolism), steady (due to a long uninterrupted male succession in the Capetian line), and safe from total destruction (because shielded by mystic precept and feudal law from being absorbed by militarily more effective rivals inside the hexagon). The obverse was roughly true for Germany: her core was migratory (due to changing dynasties and an impermanent imperial seat), only occasionally and unreliably materially sufficient (due to one-element asset, such as silver mines, or fluctuating assets from an elective emperor's hereditary family domain), and safeguarded by an only problematic myth or mystique (due to the papal challenge to the emperor's sacerdotal attributes and fellow-rulers' denial of status primacy). Early Francia's feudal sub-entities found elementary stability in smallness before equally untidy balancing and unification processes attained the decisive "tipping point" in effective resistance to an external threat (from the Germanic Empire); the German complex was too large to begin with and too loosely centralized to avoid the converse process of dislocation. Among the reasons for, and compounding the effects of, these disparities were the divergent physical (geo-economic or -strategic) settings. Thus, a concentric disposition of river beds in France favored convergence around the Seine river, whereas their parallel course east of the Rhine fostered fragmentation also within the economic-military-administrative functional cluster. Extending imperial reach or just ambition southward toward Italy (even more than the more spontaneous movement eastward toward and beyond the Elbe river) could only reinforce the centrifugal thrust, inasmuch as military might (mounted knights and landsknecht infantry) was principally located in Germany while hard-to-integrate economic and much of administrative resource was in northern or, at a climactic point of decision, southernmost parts of Italy (including Sicily).

Within the arena, the tripartite contest involving Emperor, Pope, and an increasingly more assertive third force (German princes or Lombard communes) was as obstructive of unity as the interplay of king, nobility, and the urban or rural plebs in France was productive, generating the requisite military potential through the both growing and ever more regular ability of the fictionally continuous Crown to create, through taxation, the economic impetus to institutionalizing the functional interlock administratively. Nor did the actor–arena relationship point in a different direction once the dominant Papacy–Empire cleavage had placed France sufficiently at the periphery of the conflict map to provide her initial gestation with a protective sanctuary (while favoring the mediatory potential of the French Crown diplomatically). Stimulus was added to sanctuary when the secular contests with the German "imperialists" and the English "invaders" (or the Anglo-German alliance) helped consolidate the institutional framework around an aroused "national" feeling (the battle of Bouvines early in the thirteenth-, and the course and outcome of the Hundred Years' War up to mid-fifteenth, century). By contrast, the east-central European polities shielded the Empire long enough from eastern onslaughts to prevent it from building in time on the consolidating effect of the tenth-century triumph over the invading Magyars. And if the loose post-Ottonian Empire was too big for a European arena that had been constricted from the east to benefit from protracted competition with equals, the arena's initial crystallization occurred too soon: it was sufficient to prevent expansionists among the elective Emperors (culminating with the Hohenstaufens) from using an ever less resource-rich hereditary domain to serve as the springboard for coercive centralization or as a nucleus for organic aggregation.

Unlike the German realm and the even more insubstantial empires in east-central and south-eastern Europe, built around a single resource (thus silver in Premyslid Bohemia) or singularly auspicious individual (Dusan's Serbia or Jagellonid Lithuania), Russia settled down farther east increasingly into the fundamentally western (French and English) mode of actor consolidation around a nucleus. But she did so repeatedly with the aid of fundamentally eastern, oriental-despotic, methods of forcing the tempo of consolidation to counteract the disintegrative tendencies implicit in nebular-type features. Following the disintegration of a premature early Carolingian-like empire at the turn of the first into the second millennium, diversely resistant sub-units were aggregated around a geo-economic and -strategic core wherein a sacralized authority was simultaneously evolving from merely suzerain to fully sovereign status in both the pre-Mongol Kievan and the post-Mongol Muscovite phases. As consolidation proceeded along routes of interstimulating economic and politico-military expansion, well-distributed river flows impelled convergence by emptying into inland seas and facilitated expansion by being easily linked overland by fortified portages and canals. Struggles against first the Mongols and later the Polish–Lithuanian and Swedish neighbors were a parallel to France's exposures in fostering cohesion. But, though patterned on the forcible tax-gathering and force-mobilizing methods of the Mongolian overlord, the administrative corollaries to the link between force and fiscality were to materialize in Russia's case only at a later stage in spontaneous response to war-like crises.

To the extent that Russia followed more the lines of the western-nuclear than the east-central European nebular model, her formation differed from the extreme-oriental model of conquest and centralization by barbarian forces from the outside, the Ch'in and later analogies in China and the Indo-European charioteers or the Moguls prior to the British in India. However, just as Russia's size was among the reasons for deviating from the western model, so the coercive-despotic methods a succession of her rulers applied to consolidation were partly due to both the spatial and the temporal dimension of Russia's relationship to the arena. As crushing blow alternated with convergent squeeze and the latter gave way to urgent solicitation, likewise chaotic self-induced insulation or externally imposed isolation were precariously relieved by differently taxing involvement. All were the obverse of the segregation from and stimulation by arena-based pressures France had enjoyed at the right moments. Well into the late tsarist era, the dominant mode was thus not gradualness but gyrations between retardation by dull inertia and precipitation by either violent revolutions or failed ultra-liberal reforms from above, all responsible for chronic dependence on foreign resources invariably misapplied in the absence of an either self-sustaining or self-correcting economic-military-administrative functional circuit. The mystical nimbus surrounding an autocracy that was less profoundly militarized than bureaucratized as time passed, was an increasingly inadequate substitute for either an ingrained military and administrative ethos or an indigenous mercantile-industrial enterprise. As imperial Russia came increasingly to resemble "modern" China in key respects, she was forgoing the growth potential inherent in the agricultural version of the western nuclear model without sufficiently reviving the home-grown urban-mercantile (Kievan-cum-Novgorodian) tradition.

While Russia wavered between expansion and exhaustion, imperious coercion and imminent collapse, France was near-steadily regressing from a climactic mid-point. Among the reasons for the difference was Russia's relative immunity and France's acute vulnerability to the globalization of the arena, fully under way since the seventeenth century. Because the attendant changes reversed most or all of the key relationships in actor formation and development, before altering the hierarchy of effective actor types, France was pushed from being the key beneficiary of dominant trends to being (after or alongside Spain) their chief victim. As Europe expanded overseas, a territorial state had to extend itself also into hitherto unexplored reaches of society internally if it was to remain competitive in the henceforth dual environment. A major propellant was again war, or the exorbitantly rising cost of waging it in two concurrent as well as (fiscally and strategically) competing continental and maritime theaters. Critical for the balances and priorities within the military-economic-administrative cluster was henceforth this: Could bureaucratically enforced land tax-based fiscality hold its own against the more business-like principle of trade- or industry-based and privately capitalized (war loans-generating) public finance, advanced beyond the Italian urban prototype by first the Dutch and then the English oligarchies? And did or could the economic factor more than counterbalance the causal primacy of the military function by moving toward effective ascendancy within a relaxed administrative framework?

Chiefly peasants-taxing *taille* and a professional army had been sufficient as well as necessary to create the French state in the fifteenth century before, in the seventeenth, a standing army, state-sponsored mercantilism, and an expanded bureaucracy could lay the basis for dynastic absolutism challenging resistant (only to ally with residual) feudalism. In the decisive eighteenth century the question was thenceforth whether an alternately sponsored and neglected buildup, of ocean-going marine by a state wedded to the military ethos and of globally tradable manufactures by a commercial bourgeoisie aping the landed nobility, could make France's actor *trans*formation catch up with a changing arena that was resuming its determinitive influence. Innovations first in spinning techniques and sailing technologies, preceding the age of coal and internal combustion engines, would now do for the mainly Anglo-Dutch Atlantic beginnings of mercantile-financial capitalism that which the moldboard plow (suited to heavy soils) and the stirrup (seating the rider more firmly on heavier horses) had done to sustain the economic-military-managerial cluster of preeminently French extra-Mediterranean feudalism – and what the gunpowder-based fire-power of the siege cannon aimed at baronial fortresses was subsequently to do for dynastic centralization.

Overwhelming the ground swell of initial actor formation, the requirements of transformation turned the tide toward the fittingly called Maritime Powers. In the pre-global era, France could combine geostrategic marginality relative to the Papal–Imperial contest with a good measure of geo-economic centrality (relative to the prime north–south or German–Italian overland axis). Subsequently, she was as irremediably central in position (between the outer oceanic and the inner continental worlds) even when ceasing to be strategically encircled (by the Habsburg Austro/Spanish–Burgundian–Italian complex) as she became increasingly marginal and excentric economically (once the flows of seaborne commerce from the Mediterranean through Gibraltar to Flanders and the English Channel to the Baltic had expanded to comprise the Atlantic). Moreover, once built around a solid geo-economic and geostrategic core and coherently military-economic and sacral–secular nucleus, France became lopsidedly bi-focal between the mainly agriculture-based political core in the north-east, turned defensively or offensively to the continent and centered on Paris, and her maritime-mercantile coastal margins around the politically disenfranchised when not also rebellious Atlantic sea ports, typified by Bordeaux and La Rochelle.

Compounding the alternately retarding and distorting effects of the inter-functional and -regional derangement was an unsatisfactory surplus–scarcity relationship. It obtained so long as the surfeit of material resource internally (including the critical materials for ship-building and naval war-making, the domestic scarcity of which directed the rivals overseas) kept the enterpreneurial ethos at the middle ranges of the social hierarchy below levels necessary to galvanize sporadic official efforts to adjust an overcomplex fiscal system to the needs of unified industrial-commercial mercantilism as part of expanding domestic and diversifying external functions of government. Thus, the tripartite relationship of king, nobility, and bourgeoisie responsible for the rise of the absolutist state had ceased to work in support of a capitalist society. For the crown to preserve a special relationship to the nobility became even more critical for the regime's legitimizing mystique; but the reciprocally dependent aristocratic class's failure to make up for less of a role in the area of force with an enhanced one in fiscality erected a barrier to diversifying the monarchy's sociopolitical foundation at first the third-estate level of the pyramid. The prime casualty was the alliance of the crown with the bourgeoisie that had been shoring up royal mystique against feudal nostalgia whenever the nobility grew fractious because it felt physically safe from its peasantry, or was aligned with it confessionally.

The loss of the military function by the higher nobility, and the inadequate

performance of its economic function by the upper bourgeoisie, were matched by the regime's own failure to make up with manifestly useful internal service for growing deficits in self-legitimating successes abroad. Time for correction started running out once an insufficiently diversified and productive economy proved unable to keep in step with a suddenly enlarged politico-military and -economic global environment. The revolutionary response to the actor–arena discrepancy was at least half as much an effort to make the state more efficacious in the new medium as to revise social hierarchy or redress social justice in favor of the not-so-new middle or still older lowest (land-hungry but otherwise reactionary) stratum. Increasing state power so as to simultaneously revise and revive societal dynamism was the continental way to narrow the gap between expanding demands of world policy and a static national economy, avoided in maritime powers thanks to an inverse society–state dynamic. At bottom, the Revolution and its aftermath signaled the necessity to start reversing the pre-existing imbalance of governmental functions attendant on near-total extraversion, reflecting the incapacity of the medieval (or any other primitive) economy to produce more at home than could be obtained by military or diplomatic activity abroad. However, greater functional introversion reflected once again less, or less immediately, a newly pressing attention to social welfare than changing conditions and dimensions of warfare. An exponential growth in the size and cost of armies (alongside navies) between the Thirty Years War and the eighteenth-century's world wars had been more than any military-technological and -strategic innovation responsible for combining an administrative with a military "revolution" before the humanitarian revolution in favor of health care for combatants in mid-nineteenth century Crimean War would stimulate concern with social welfare for the civilians.

Whereas neither the revolutionary nor the Napoleonic (and successor) regimes managed to direct a rationalized state administration into reshaping society and economy fundamentally enough to halt France's backsliding, maritime England's ascension had started in the seventeenth century from an earlier development not fundamentally different and an economic position weaker rather than stronger than France's. Like Norman Sicily and French Normandy, pre-Conquest Anglo-Saxon England exhibited the advantages well managed smallness possessed in the conditions of the early Middle Ages. The foundation permitted transplanted Norman feudalism and, following its late-stage upheavals, Tudor dynasticism to develop public finance and administration on an increasingly "modern" basis. Subsequently, bringing in Scotland after Wales did more than continue the territorial aggregation around the geo-economically propitious core at the Thames estuary: by depriving France of the traditional Scottish alliance, it transformed the dynastically united kingdom into an island also geostrategically, and propelled the country on the road from vulnerable marginality *vis-à-vis* the continent to near-unassailable maritime primacy globally. And once a likewise two-faceted (landed-cum-manufacturing) ruling class had reduced the Crown in Parliament, it could safely preside over extending both power and prosperity by means of seemingly conflicting but actual benefits-cumulating continental and maritime strategic emphases identified with alternately predominating (Whig and Tory) oligarchical factions.

As a result, the English were able to profit from the conflict between France and Spain better and longer than the Dutch who had set the pattern, before becoming strong enough to exploit both of the contrasting principles: (continental) equilibrium and (maritime-mercantile) near-monopoly. Initiated by trade-related wars against the weaker-based and -armed Netherlands, the ascent was kept going with help from productive investments by the same Dutch in relative decline; innovative techniques in spinning and superior skills in sailing added economic to largely self-financing (naval) military enterprise and energy, as would later indigenous coal deposits and increasingly imitative steam-propelled and armored naval technology.

All in all, the British Isles' land mass and the empire builders' sea-borne momentum were sufficient to outdo contemporaneous France, in the enlarged two-elemental (continental–oceanic) arena, and overshadow the less solidly based nomadic or nebular continental empires carried afield in the past by a light steppe, or the heavier feudal, cavalry. Although mainly internally generated, England's success was as much a function of the continental powers' shortcomings in matters bearing equally on evolutionary time and environing space. This was not least true for Spain. Centered on Castile and forged by Catholicity after growing out of Visigothic mini-empires by way of the Islamic conquest and the post-*reconquista* multi-kingdom configuration, the accident of dynastic marriage had pulled the Iberian realm together for a world role in sufficient time but not in sufficient organic depth before it was strained and nearly torn apart by attempting too much too soon in too many directions. Germany, having missed early on the timing for unity, was to display thereafter consistently a mismatch between the European arena and her actual size and aspired-to role and coveted status. France's misalignment grew out of an evolutionary failure that occurred at developmental mid-point, causing a series of reactive convulsions but no lastingly reforming correction: even when she managed to win in real wars at the oceanic peripheries (e.g. briefly in India and more conclusively in the War of American Independence), France could not avoid losing the world to the secular arch-enemy. Her domestic failure spelled England's global success just as the still-birth of the medieval German Empire had been instrumental in permitting France's triumphs as a nation.

Only in the contest with a later – the "second" – German Empire was an England unable to underpin evolving sociopolitical norms with updated socio-economic structures at home and institutional arrangements for the empire to suffer shipwreck. Her inability to shield forever the fragility of her time-conditioned winning formula from the persistence of immemorial foreign-policy aims and means in the world at large was the context of the eventual American thrust forward. The erstwhile colony had meanwhile grown outward from a capability base aggregated around a nucleus even more favorably situated both economically and military-strategically than France's, and sheltered as well as stimulated for a longer spell by conflicts among a succession of stronger parties. Yet even before reaching its apex, America's trajectory was pointing toward a testing collision with the other power flanking historic Europe – a Russia ambiguously western-and-eastern in her spatial location and cultural persona and elusive in her temporal-evolutionary status: always behind but never too far for staging a bid to reduce the time lag; failing again and again but never sufficiently to fall and make her failure spell another power's safe ascendancy and effortless security.

Sequences in the ways the systemic arena is structured coincide more closely, or only more conspicuously, with changes in the states of development and behavioral dispositions of actors than with rhythms peculiar to the schisms that both divide and link actors. Each of these schisms is subject to its own internal history of progression in values-related attitudes. The sacral–secular and the East–West schisms are alike in that they evolve (through different paths) toward conceding behavior-determining primacy to the balance-of-power norm. This happens as the geo-cultural East–West cleavage incites extra-rational behavior before multiplying concrete issues and stakes compel inversion toward pragmatic modes; and it happens as the initial or intrinsic bias of the sacral–secular schism in favor of normatively formulated disguises of hierarchical pretensions gives way to the contrary egalitarian-pragmatic bias built into the balancing of material capabilities. Conversely, when attitudes linked to the land–sea power schism are abstracted from historically conditioned early associations (such as the religio-confessional ones in Europe), they will evolve in the opposing direction once the operational primacy of the dominant sea power is subsiding and the contrary bid of the continental state with different values has escalated (independently of any connection with one or the other of the alternative schisms).

On the whole and on balance, the continental-maritime schism is most closely tied up with real-pragmatic inter-unit politics and, as such, conducive to the most predictable and, in that limited sense orderly, behavior. However, this fundamental bias only augments the importance of strategy-relevant qualitative distinctions between parties to this schism that modify (instead of only mediating) inducements from schism-neutral structure, if they do not repress (rather than reflecting) these. A portrayal of the "typical" sea power (or empire) emerges from collating conspicuous with ideologically or otherwise concealed traits of historic maritime and land powers into contrasting ideal types. Thus schematized differences coexist with similarities due to the fact that actors of both kinds are anchored territorially and their characteristics must overlap as much as behavioral incentives do if there is to be a schism at all. Nor do the contrasts in identities and inclinations abolish more fundamental uniformities in all major actors' foreign-policy postures* and in schism-indifferent actor–arena interplays.

Nothing is more distinctive of wholly insular or insulated maritime-mercantile polities from ancient Egypt to modern England and beyond than a subjective attitude. It mirrors exemption from the predicament of spatially contiguous land-based actors, and imparts the sense of providential election,

* For such postures see discourses 4 and chapter 6, pp. 285–8.

based on a special situation or vocation; of lasting high privileges, carried over from beginnings amidst low environing pressures; and of exceptional license, flowing from an unusual latitude for initial self-definition and collective psychic as well as physical ego-expansion. Only when maturity approaches decline will the mystique of exceptionality lodged in the special nature of the polity be propped up by the myth of extraordinary sagacity or probity in policy. However, before this has become necessary for reassurance, the traits suggesting commonality with all territorial actors that contravene the distinctive self-image will be projected onto the main strategic adversary on the continent in the form of a "black legend" imputing to him an innately aggressive lack of shared humanity. The fundamental common denominator of the sense of uniqueness is natural or contrived insulation: of Old-Kingdom Egypt sheltered by the desert from outer barbarians prior to the Hyksos incursion; of early Athens ensconced in low-density demographic environment before a wall to the sea created the functional equivalent of insularity; of the quasi-insular Venetian and Dutch Republics shielded about equally by the sea and inter-land power stalemates; and of post-Norman Conquest England and the infant United States when guarded in addition by propitious naval technology. Even more uniformly in evidence were special economic assets or aptitudes for commerce; the long-enduring lower cost of seapower per unit of economic or military efficacy relative to the price of land-based power and prosperity; and the greater range and versatility of navally projected capabilities, near-automatically linked to both economic and politico-military proficiency.

The fact of insularity or insulation breeding the sense of moral superiority translated habitually at some point into the practice of free trade and advocacy of normatively constrained politics. Actual expansion generated meanwhile the claim for the extraordinary degree of physical protection and material prosperity being extended throughout three hierarchically ordered security–prosperity zones or areas. Priority could not but belong to the innermost circle of the core habitat: the Nile delta, the cities of Athens and Venice (distinct from their hinterlands), the province of Holland and city of Amsterdam, and the British Isles – and US-controlled territory in North America. Because the priority was as absolute as its object was only rarely placed in jeopardy, it was left to strategic contingency or stage of development to determine the immediate priority or relative value of the two outer arenas – the more adjacent and narrower mainland-continental or the commonly vaster and remoter maritime-commercial or -colonial one. In comparatively placid conditions concern with material prosperity favored overseas, while imperatives of political salience in support of physical security directed attention to the continent – an ambiguity that was rooted in its being increasingly difficult to segregate the balances of power from the balances of trade as the critical maritime-mercantile zone expanded, along "globally" mostly the west-to-east axis, past the core polity's location (Egypt's toward the Syrian or Palestinian coast; Athens' and Venice's toward the Black Sea, with secondary concerns located in the western Mediterranean; and, in the wake of the Dutch, Britain's and the United States' from the Atlantic to the Pacific and/or Indian Oceans). It was then no more possible to disentangle the objectives of commerce overseas and political access to the continent than to distinguish the requisites of economic prosperity in the core-habitat from the latter's physical security as alternately the immediate and ultimate purposes of diplomatic control or politico-military conquest abroad.

If pushing southward into Nubia (the Sudan) and westward into Libya was for Egypt primarily a matter of safety from overland barbarian intrusion, involvement in the Mesopotamian inter-empire balance of power was a way of either defending or regaining access to the vital Syrian coast and commercial city-state system. Similarly, the countryside outside Athens and the puny *contado* of Venice were only the mustering grounds for overland expansion: in the former's case, westward toward the Gulf of Corinth, northward in Boeotia, and eastward into Thrace; in the latter's, by way of the Paduan territory adjoining the Venetian gulf ever deeper into the Italian terra firma. Removing potential barriers to commerce turned readily into creating territorial springboards for further conquest, pending encounter with superior or effectively resistant power. When less costly or risky control could, or had to, do the work of conquest, England replaced earlier possessions in France, after they had shrunk from feudal holdings in the south to strategic strong points in the north, with nothing more than assured access to the Low Countries and Portugal in behalf of her Channel- and Gibraltar-centered maritime strategy, prefiguring America's entrenchment in western Europe.

The relationship of the wholly or nearly offshore-insular actor to the power equilibrium in the adjoining continental micro- or macro-system would commonly implement three always separable and often consecutive policy emphases. There would be, first, an expansionist movement into the mainland from early strength (acquired commercially in cases of Egypt, Athens, and Venice, and initially based on dynastic-feudal assets in Britain's case); second, a partial disengagement would coincide with assuming or aspiring to the role of a continental balancer or balancewheel (Egypt intermittently, Athens and Venice as well as the Dutch following major defeats or as part of declension, England at her peak); and third, possibly combined with the remnants of balancing but always marking a further retreat, an attempt to revert to a purely commercial career would be based on assets and aptitudes corresponding to a late – or the last – stage of economic and financial development (thus Egypt, whenever shut out of the overland routes, Athens and Venice when outmatched navally on the seas as well as on land by near-by or remote interlopers, and, as the Dutch earlier, Britain when attracted to combining unevenly splendid isolation from the continent with efforts to combine "free" with "fair" trade).

Tension between the strategic alternatives will reflect the tendency of the divergent pulls of the maritime and the mainland worlds to converge again and again. Short of strategic abdication, it will be impossible to opt irreversibly for any one approach, or evolve a lastingly coherent strategic whole of mutually reinforcing parts. The external will reflect the domestic aspect of a central dilemma, inasmuch as a strong territorial resource base will sooner or later prove essential for maintaining command and control in the maritime-mercantile arena, but concentrating on it will tend to divert the interests and the value-system of the dominant politico-economic class to unproductive areas. Two trends are relevant in this connection: (1) the size of the optimum in territorial base increased within each generation of sea power – from Crete via Egyptian or Greek mainland-based sea power to Italy-controlling Rome; from Venice or Genoa to the naval power of or associated with the Spanish and the Ottoman empires; and from Portugal or Holland to England and from Britain (and Japan) to North America; (2) the original ruling class was becoming increasingly land-bound, if not wholly feudal then functionless in commerce, even as the sea power itself was continentalized – directly in terms of the controlled domain or indirectly through diplomacy and strategic ties to continental outposts. The tendency will grow over the lifespan of a particular actor, even if in all instances not as strikingly as when the first-generation Venetian patriciate abandoned investments in trade for safer ones in the terrafirma, and exchanged open-ended economic competition for collective rule through a council closed to newcomers. However motivated and rationalized, the continentalization of an insular or quasi-insular sea power will unavoidably impinge upon the sphere of the dominant or aspiring land power – be it the prominent Mesopotamian land empire of the moment in the case of Egypt, Persia or Sparta to that of Athens, Milan or Florence in relation to a continuing Venetian push inland, or Spain when England's support for the Dutch revolt and France when English occupation of rebellious Egypt in effect continentalized the insular realm strategically.

The two-pronged expansion, across the sea and on land, will express a set of strengths and weaknesses unlikely to mitigate the conflict of interests and perceptions built into the relationship with the continental counterpart. The strengths and weaknesses are no more separable than the maritime and the continental spheres themselves because they are only different facets of the same identity, expressed in immunity to military containment and liability to economic crisis. The (quasi-) insular state will not arouse a concerted opposition by the mainland states so long as it does not (thus Athens and Venice) threaten directly the mainland balance of power or flagrantly abuse its advantages there (thus England in one instance). The reasons for the immunity are functional, in that the economic features of the sea power's ascendancy will be too indeterminate to be either directly threatening or readily imitable as part of counteracting them; and they are structural, in that the vast majority of the continental states will fear or resent another land power more than the insular state. Thus it will prove impossible for the continentals to compose rivalries and concert resources sufficiently to co-determine the incidental benefits flowing from the maritime near-monopolist's processing of trade and policing of the seas – the very performance which neutralizes hostility for the sea power's covert expansionism and jealousy of its vaunted exceptionalism.

The largely accidental – or accidentally combined – assets of the maritime-mercantile power cover a wide range, including superior naval technology (Athenian triremes, Venetian galleys, or British sailing wooden, and – despite corrigible backslidings – steam-propelled ironclad, ships); mineral resources (Egyptian copper, useful in the bronze age, but useless in that of iron, Athenian silver, or British coal); industrial or other skills and techniques (Athenian pottery, Venetian glass or textiles, and British draperies); and a location on or near trade-dominant routes or currents. Such assets are inherently cumulative at the outset and, for a time, individually self-sustaining as well as mutually reinforcing. Their combination converts economic assets into politico-military strengths and politico-military exploits into economic or financial advantages. However, they cannot be indefinitely confined to their possessors by reason of their nature as much as of their largely fortuitous acquisition or early nurture. Just as the sea power cannot elude the pitfalls of duplicating naval-commercial with military-strategic territorial involvement at its peak, so it will not be able to prevent the diffusion of its strength-creating assets as it descends from the summit. The wine and olive culture of Athens and her pottery-making skills had spread as surely across the Mediterranean as England borrowed from capital-richer Dutch and the United States profited from British investments.

Thus, the mutually reinforcing mechanisms responsible for the rise and ascendancy of the sea powers are offset by the implied liability of the advantages to self-liquidating diffusion or deterioration. The reverse side of the capacity to expand and grow at an unusual rate of speed is in consequence the more than common incapacity to stand still at the zenith of power and prosperity. The inability to stagnate without subsiding equals the impossibility for vessels to lie becalmed in port without deteriorating – in their wooden bottoms, mechanical maintenance, or personnel morale. The attendant strains will eventually consummate the results of the initial propensity for ostensibly contrasting strategic emphases on the oceanic and continental arenas to aggregate into a course toward overextension; their deepest source is the fact that the peculiar but, in a way, superficial strength is ultimately nullified by a likewise peculiar but, in its effects, substantial weakness. If strength flows from the structurally induced inertia of continent-wide opposition to the visible signs and symptoms of sea-power ascendancy, weakness lies only provisionally hidden in the volatile functional foundations of the sea power's favored position. It becomes manifest when the factors of winning productivity recombine in ways that redirect the highways of privileged commercial or financial exchanges, and the redirection does what counterbalancing realignment of powers and a consequent re-arrangement in the lines of force perform on the mainland.

Since the sea power will not commonly be the target of a coalition response unless it triggers one by deep overland penetration (such as that by Athens preceding the "first" Peloponnesian War and that by Venice antecedent to the opposing League of Cambrai), it will normally be in a position to pose as the guarantor of equilibrium. However, it will be a genuinely impartial arbiter only when decline has made it a less effectual one: thus (defeated) Athens between Sparta and Thebes or Venice between the Habsburgs and either France or the Ottomans, and Britain between France and Germany after World War I. The limited efficacy of impartiality in decline is matched by less than reliable coalition leadership when the insular power acts from strength. Whereas the weakened sea power is tempted to be the last to fight for its strategic interests (even though – thus for the Dutch – retreat into non-belligerent neutrality in the interest of wartime trade may have ceased being possible), its inclination when strong is to be the first to stop fighting in return for diplomatic or natural advantage (at the risk of triggering a rare joint reprisal, witness the Russia-sponsored "armed neutrality" prompted by eighteenth-century Britain's separate-peace practices). No less than the propensity to expand, precariousness of commitment reflects an external latitude and internal limitation – two more discrete facets of the same condition. A protected location confers the ability to alternately withdraw from involvement and resume it, to retrench or re-expand. However, the very leeway which reduces external constraints activates contentious domestic pluralism on issues of foreign policy.

When combined with external crises restoring foreign-policy primacy but intermittently, the contrary propensity, liable to increase the only distracting or also deranging impact of the very economic (including fiscal) interests and factors initially responsible for the rise to supremacy, will make a volatile foreign policy hostage to stressful relations among classes as well as within the ruling clans. Inter-class turbulence was conspicuous in Athens when the initial connection between sea empire and democratization gave way to mid-life crises for both the empire and the domestic political order. Empire and mass democracy rose together when shifting from hoplite infantry to sea-borne triremes required enfranchising more manpower; and, outdoing the Themisto-clean precedent, the material exigencies of the new property-less citizens inspired increasingly demagogic politicians (the Cleons, Cleophons, and Alcibiadeses) to complete under pressures of war the decay begun with the mid-course Periclean welfare state. The unquestioned trusteeship of the landed oligarchy (precariously prolonged by Cimon's machine politics) gave thus way to appeasing ever lower social elements by means of inter-class transactions liable to alter imperial expansion into imperialistic exploitation, pending an oligarchical reaction to anarchy in the traumatizing context of defeat* – a subsequent return to moderate democracy (after 403 BC) failing to create the basis for a foreign policy capable of preventing the Macedonian takeover.

A like sequence, contained in Venice at the cost of freezing the governing institution (*fermata concilii*), was to reappear muted in eighteeth- to twentieth-century British politics. A series of electoral reforms spawned by neo-conservative Tory demagoguery competing with Liberal-to-Labour radicalism eroded the political trusteeship of the traditional ruling class before the attendant transactions with the rising middle class would culminate in ruling-class trauma on the eve of World War I. Increasingly hollow victories in two world wars set thereafter the stage, not unlike the Athenian defeat, for political appeasement at home coinciding with strategic disengagement abroad.

More immediately disturbing than inter-class turbulence will be splits within the ruling oligarchy between advocates of accommodation (or "peace party") and proponents of denial (or "war party") *vis-à-vis* the continental rival. Led in Athens by Cimon, the accommodationist party was represented in eighteenth-century Britain by Bute and, in conditions nearer decline, by the *Vecchi* (the "old" ones) in seventeenth-century Venice. The contrary proponents of uncompromising self-assertion were in Athens the party of Pericles, in England

---

* The trusteeship–transaction–trauma triptych is borrowed from my *Career of Empire: American and Imperial Expansion over Land and Sea*. Baltimore: The Johns Hopkins University press, 1978, chapters 2 and 7.

that of Pitt, and in Venice that of the *Giovani* (the "young" ones). The differences on strategy mirrored polarization of material interests at least in part: if the expansionist (war) party represented the mercantile-financial, the party of (peaceful) accommodation responded more to the landed interests; the former's stake in forcibly extended or safeguarded profits was paralleled by the latter's in reducing war-induced fiscal charges. A trace of the split survived into later conditions whenever British Conservatives were more inclined to accommodate with imperial Germany before World War I than were the Liberals (or Liberal imperialists); ever more defense-oriented became simultaneously echoes of the early Tory versus Whig positions on overseas-imperial and continental priorities, keyed respectively to protecting investments for economic profit and acquiring diplomatic credit so as to avoid isolation.

The divisions in the class structure of the insular-maritime core polity's will extend into its imperial system when liberal pluralism is, albeit superficially or only conditionally, reproduced in relationships with clients and outright dependants. Overt constraint or coercion will be inopportune so long as basically complementary (even if unequally advantageous and "exploitative") economic interests combine with a comfortable margin of cultural attraction and strategic advantage – to wit, while the empire retains mastery of both the fluid maritime medium and the pathways of communication with and between fixed strong points: the equally critical areal and linear factors. The situation will change when the essentially opportunistic ties of interest have been overlaid with more organic tissues – thus when the empire of exploitation has become an empire of settlement or when alignment with free allies for mutual security has been integrated into a hegemonial association. Perpetuating liberal style and façade without jeopardizing substantial cohesion will then depend on the continuing credibility of an outside threat – such as that from Persia to the Athenian allies in the Aegean or from France-in-Canada to England's colonies in North America.

And even if external threat or just opposition continue, cohesion will not when the insular-maritime core power's margin of material superiority within its imperial system has shrunk or expansion beyond it has stalled. The need for constraint will then replace spontaneous consent and coercion may have to be called upon to maintain superficial consensus, while the new imperatives of a more "rational" or "equitable" distribution of costs and benefits from the (unequal) association will entail pressures for more extensive contributions from the lesser parties – trends manifest in the Athenian Empire prior to the Peloponnesian, and in the "first" British after the Seven Years, War. No more successful was to be in Britain's second, India-centered, empire the attempt to deal with the problem of cohesion through consensual devolution (to the "white" dominions) in lieu of timely intra-empire integration, while heeding the "self-governing" empire's opposition to timely accommodation with (imperial) Germany precipitated conditions responsible for the eventual defection of the dominions to a more effective English-speaking protector. Whatever the specific reasons for the imperial system's weakening, the easier part of a difficult adjustment will be to reaffirm or reformulate the external threat than to resume expansion, and the more tempting one to forge lastingly ineffectual tighter or milder new constraints than to forgo the residual tokens of cohesion.

Both the strengths and the weaknesses – the latitudes and the limitations – of the liberal-to-democratic sea-power-based insular polities will account for their variably accidental empires being inherently precarious after ceasing to be overtly predatory; being as impressive as they are fragile because as extensive in controlled space as they are relatively narrow in their home base. Taking long to surface from their long-invisible foundation inside the core polity's political economy and the environing actors' strategic stalemate, they will be relatively short-lived at their climax or, at least, be short on the capacity for regeneration in comparison with authoritarian-to-despotic continental empires. The exception, a near-endless series of reincarnations for the Egyptian empire, was due to Egypt's insularity being as qualified (by the implantation of the insulated Nile delta in a wider territorial setting) as was her maritime-commercial character (by the upper-Nile feudal-agricultural culture countervailing the lowerNile urban-commercial sector and society). Similarly, the longevity of Venice and, as it was shrinking, of the Venetian Empire itself was due to the gradual transfer of the politico-economic center of gravity to the terra firma – and of commercial enterprise to new social groups. Both transfers helped replace the "accidental" advantages behind the symbolic marriage of the lagoon-city with the sea with more modest but genuine assets. By contrast the no more than seventy five years (478–404 BC) of the prototypically maritime Athenian Empire made it the shortest recorded empire of antiquity, while the somewhat longer spell of Britain's (though not Holland's) commercial and imperial grandeur (even when not divided by two) shrinks in comparison with the self-renewing endurance of her continental antagonists. The British tenure is thus dwarfed even more markedly than the fragility of the Athenian Empire is highlighted by the greater adaptability to *its* special limitations of the Spartan hegemony.

The decline and dissolution of a sea-power empire may be due primarily to its failure to compensate by continuing innovation for the diffusion of its original economic-industrial and naval-technological, or the displacement elsewhere of its positional and related institutional, advantages. The regression may also merely register the declension of material benefits relative to the politico-military costs of upholding and defending an administratively integrated or institutionalized empire – a directly unproductive diversion of assets as distinct from their diffusion and displacement. In either case, the decline is no less real for being only relative to larger-based analogous or adversary powers and no less depressing for coinciding with absolute improvements: thus Venice had a bigger navy in the sixteenth century than she had possessed in the fifteenth; her political class was richer, and her overall economic base perhaps more solid or stable, in the seventeenth than it had been in the fourteenth century. Material well-being was more widely dispersed in late twentieth-century Britain than at the time of the Queen Empress's Jubilee, the smaller Royal Navy was technologically superior to Jellicoe's and the City, somewhat like late seventeenth-century Amsterdam and third-century BC Athens, continued to be prominent in the financial networks of the day.

At least three interrelated processes in three parts will cohere into a wholly negative configuration, triggering decline at a point hard to pin down. One involves the dynamics within and among the three security–prosperity zones of an insular power (the home base, the continental theater, and the maritime-colonial or mercantile sphere). Another has to do with the three stages in politico-military strategies toward the mainland (expansion into, balancing of, and attempted disengagement from, the continental field of forces). And still another bears upon the three phases in the economic growth and maturation (from industrial to commercial and on to financial and services-related preeminence). Disaster will not be far off when material assets from the last-phase form of economic strength have ceased being sufficiently self-perpetuating or -amplifying to underwrite the (simultaneously rising?) costs of politico-military continental involvement even when aimed at preemption of another rather than predominance for self, while erosive conflict with the land power has been interlaced with a trade-related feud with a rival or competing maritime-mercantile power – Athens with Corinth, Venice with Genoa, Holland with England, and Britain with the United States in the western hemisphere.

Just as it rose, the sea-power empire is also apt to fall in conjunction with major wars or, at least, in violent contexts. Thus, Egypt expanded first in the wake of the Hyksos "invasion" and faded temporarily in function of the comparable later inroads by the likewise barbarian "sea peoples"; Athens rose and fell in function of the Persian and the Peloponnesian wars; Venice in function of the offensive crusades against Arab Islam and defensive wars against Islamic Constantinople; and England in function of the Dutch and French wars and the two German wars – while the latter consummated the American succession begun with the war against Spain before a later and less splendid little war, now off the Philippine archipelago, would reveal symptoms normally associated with decline. One reason is that, no more than ascendancy, will descent engender either a strong incentive or an auspicious setting for an accommodation with the major continental state that would reapportion assets between the two parties while prolonging the salience of both. The most common scenario is instead that hegemony of the sea power has been eroded and maritime capabilities dispersed in the process of weakening or eliminating the rival land power. The mutual enfeeblement of the enduring Egyptians and their changing continental rivals to the advantage of chaotic multipolar interludes was followed by that of Athens and Sparta spawning a succession of pseudo-hegemonial drives and ascendancies. Nor was contention involving Venice with Milan resolved to the lasting profit of either Italian party, any more than the Anglo-French and Anglo-German contests were to ultimately benefit a European one when appropriate time lags are allowed for. After a shorter or longer interlude, possibly filled by inter-amphibian contentions, the land–sea power conflict will merely pass into the hands of other – initially less experienced if possibly bigger – powers, acting on a different – initially unstructured if possibly larger – stage.

When the replacement of a declining with a rising sea power does not substantially change either the structural make-up of the land–sea power configuration or the strategic options and preferences open to either party to the contest, it will be because the waning sea power preferred to pass into the orbit of a waxing maritime empire rather than pool its resources with the continental rival in time. An ever less maritime and commercial Egypt found refuge in a succession of larger sea-bestriding empires, beginning with the Persian–Phoenician, continuing with the Roman (and Byzantine) and Islamic ones, and ending with the British (and American). Athens fitted herself into the integrated trade-routes network accomplished briefly by Alexander and more lastingly by Augustus. And whereas the Venetians refused the chance for a new lease on life through a spice trade monopoly within the Spanish–Habsburg empire (perhaps because the arrangement was no longer commercially sufficient and economically vital for them by the latter part of the sixteenth century), the Netherlands merged practically into the more markedly maritime-mercantile system of the English shortly after the latter had declined union on the opposite basis and long before the British were to withdraw into the American fold. More or less forward and firm, but rarely or never timely enough to restore the lost economic or political advantages, were the receding maritime-mercantile polities' attendant attempts to disengage from the next round of land–sea power contests diplomatically or militarily, and make thus up for the failure to appease the earlier round of conflict with the land power from a position of still significant strength.

CONTINENTAL ARENA AND A DIFFERENT TYPE OF ACTOR

The fatality besetting the sea power, if it is one, is played out against the backdrop of the traits and attributes of the dominant land power which, when not symmetrically contrary, are perversely complementary in nearly all respects.

The fundamental difference from which many others follow lies in the formative environment. Whereas the maritime-mercantile ascendancy of an insular polity gathers force within a sheltered low-pressure environment before radiating out with relative ease, the nucleus of a continental power will be restrained by a high-pressure milieu of comparable or superior powers and will have to force its way out. As a result, just as external latitudes only permit or positively promote a measure of internal liberality, so the presence of outside constraints at birth will foster continuing prejudice in favor of authority. When the first necessity is to forge the weapons of survival, the wherewithals of material prosperity and the ideal goods deriving therefrom will come second to the conditions of physical preservation. Achieving such conditions, too, can awaken the sense of special election, although one that imparts comfort under stress where the sea power's crowns innate conceit; freely indulging the will to master necessity will be a way of denying the pretension to achieve and enjoy mastery in freedom.

When founding empire, land powers will experience a growth apt to be both enforced and forcible, in an environment that combines uniformly hostile military adversaries with one or another form of material adversity. So much is shared by Assyria as a counterpart to Egypt with Sparta in contrast with Athens and by both with Carolingia, a northern-continental opposite to seafaring

Byzantium. The situation was similar for the predecessors and successors to the Visconti dukes in Lombardy, the Habsburgs in the Ostmark, and the Osmanli Turks in Anatolia, before opposing and contrasting with Venice in one way or another; and it was such for Castile-Spain, France, Prussia-Germany, and Russia's Muscovy before or when engaged in contention with the British insular realm. As a group the land powers differ among themselves less than they do from the horse-mounted nomadic conquerors who, thus Genghis or Tamerlane, employ unmatched skills to surge out of the Asian sea of grass in an ocean-like tide in search of non-reproducible goods, before ebbing away just as suddenly. Whereas they are the land-based prototypes of the assets and ambitions of mercantile-maritime polities, it is the soil-exploiting sedentary agricultural communities exposed to mobile pastoralists who prefigure the polities tied to the land mass.

Beginning with the (biblically much maligned) Assyria, the land-power-based empire will expand from a core (the city of Assur) by virtue of superior organic strength more often than of spectacular originality: military-technological or any other invention, even when present, will typically count for less at points of decision than superior coordination, strategic exploitation, and psycho-political mobilization of widely available resources. The requirements of survival through modest initial expansion will be the same when the order of the day is to pull widely scattered territories together into a viable whole: thus medieval Burgundy and modern Prussia, and when to deal with are territorial outposts serving hostile aggression or alien oppression: thus Christian Spain and Russia, but also the Osmanlis in Asia Minor. Even when a power is itself conquering, thus Frankish Carolingia, it cannot develop momentum unless it first aggregates sufficient mass and will not survive if it does not learn quickly enough to fit the augmented resources into a coherent unity. Among propitious, but not in themselves sufficient, accidents have been a ruler's longevity (witness Charlemagne), an uninterrupted line of male heirs (the Capetian unifiers of France), or their absence in marriage-related houses (the dynastic ensemble of the Habsburgs). Likewise chancy will be the emergence of able rulers at critical points. Their emergence will be as unpredictable in an unregulated succession (the early Ottoman sultans) as in a regulated one (France's Salic Law), while the fragile personal unions in Eastern Europe show that dynastic accidents and opportunities will make ailing parts grow into a living social organism no more reliably than demonic challenge and threat from the outside. Raw power-based maneuvering consolidated by stern management had to supplement the ritualized mystique of inalienable territorial integrity so long as shaping the state as a work of art, through which a politics wielding force and fostering growth imitates nature, differed from putting together a social condition of prosperity as if it were a commercially exploitable industrial artifact. Having been born of greater stress only to be subject to lifelong strain, a major land power will equal the insular sea power when it seeks to reduce both by expanding. But, unlike the maritime-mercantile counterpart, it will act within limits rigorously set – rather than gradually relaxed – by the means through which it expands and the medium within which it pursues expansion: the processes related to capability and the structures related to conflict.

When the momentum of overland expansion is not backed by exceptionally strong drives facing unusually weak contrary defenses – thus republican Rome's and revolutionary-imperial France's – it will decrease rather sharply with every increase in the distance from its source or center. It does not matter what this declension is attributable to: the rising costs and growing difficulty of, or rising opposition to, first offensively and then also defensively projecting (or "transporting") the material or functional elements of power; or the diminishing marginal utility of (or declining economies of scale from) additional acquisitions. Either of the hard-to-perceive and -assess constraints will shift the balance of costs and benefits against continuing expansion beyond an optimum, one that can be determined only retrospectively and even then hypothetically. For the purpose of augmenting the directly controlled territorial area (as distinct from assembling conditionally reliable allies), the land power does not have the sea power's facility of overleaping or bypassing obstacles to expansion along flexible lines of communication in a fluid oceanic medium. Nor can it pick and choose freely which discontinuous material or strategic assets to conquer and concede, which to acquire only to abandon, and which to administer at cost or only indirectly control on the cheap, as part of gaining more in material benefits than expending in material resources or immaterial assets. The different costs of units of power or prosperity to be won and kept navally as against militarily is a function of such elasticities being present or absent, enjoyed or denied. Moreover, just as other powers' chances to contain a successful maritime-mercantile polity decrease as its sway expands, the fact that opposition to continuing overland expansion will soon begin to grow at a geometric rate will nullify the restraining effect of the parallel propensity for the costs of projecting power to grow at an arithmetic rate. Whereas containing the expanding sea power head-on ceases to be practical when it has become sufficient for the near-monopolist to practice indirect control, the tendency for opposition to the expanding land power to quickly become unappeasable will propel it into a bid for total domination. Thus the diminishing capability to husband available strength will have linked up with a combination of hindrances and impulsions inherent in the system's structure to thwart a land power's potential to grow incrementally in favor of frustrating it cumulatively.

The insular sea power's emplacement within three security-and-prosperity zones – the home base, the maritime sphere, and the continental sphere – will on balance stimulate expansion, either because the spheres are "necessarily" interdependent or because the power is "free" to alternately emphasize needs peculiar to each. By contrast, the corresponding three-zonal structure of a land-power empire has built into it definite constraints on expansion – directly in the continental sphere and indirectly in the commercial-oceanic sphere. Whereas Athens illustrates next to the dilemmas the latitudes of a sea power capable of expanding near-infinitely relative to the size of the home base, Sparta typifies the predicament of the land power for whom expansion abroad is the reverse side of constricting policies at home. For the same reason that Sparta's authoritarian domestic order needed protection against the majority-constituting helots at times of the freemen's absence for war abroad, her imperial system fanning out from the home base via the belt of wholly dependent satellite communities (the perioecs) to formally autonomous allies (the Peloponnesian League) was constructed so as to insulate the domestic order from any stimulus to or support for slave risings originating abroad. In order for the free outer-zone allies to remain fundamentally loyal, they had to continue rating the benefits of Spartan protection higher than the costs of subordination; keeping the bonds of subordination loose set a structurally decreed automatic limit on Sparta's territorial empire: it limited the range of free allies that could be reduced to the status of dependent satellites on pain of provoking defections to a rival alliance-building core power – Argos initially and Athens later. Thus, limitations on the size of the inner-zone dependent sector that was prudently practicable entailed restraint in the mode of dealing with the outer-zone allies; and the prime function of the inner and outer security zones, to safeguard domestic authority and order, limited the concern about how power and pressures were configured outside the Peloponnese. It was no more permissible to tolerate Athenian moves to divert a Megara from its allegiance than to deny support to Corinth in the last resort. But Athenian moves outside the League's boundaries could be countenanced so long as they did not go beyond neutralizing a potential challenger to Sparta's Peloponnesian hegemony – thus, the key city of central Greece, Thebes – and did not, by adding a Sparta-matching Athenian-controlled land mass to an unmatched and unmatchable maritime capability, manifestly threaten the all-Greece equilibrium.

The Spartan formula, one of trading off the scope of authority within the inner security sphere against access to friendly allied or neutral powers within the outer zone so as to shield the critical domestic order, contrived artfully the insulation maritime powers enjoy by favor of nature. The formula was tested in the Italo-European system in ways that progressively crystallized and clarified the associated key relationship, between a multi-state balance of power and one power's preeminence in role and status. Actual or apparent failure to limit control to a circumscribed inner security–superiority zone spelled isolation, the ultimate diplomatic liability fraught with imminent strategic peril, for a succession of continental core powers: beginning with Milan, even before the line of its conquering dukes became extinct, through the Spanish Habsburgs, but for frail links to an unstable England and a jealous Vienna, to the France of Louis XIV, forfeiting one-time allies against Spain one by one as she reached out into the Germanys and toward the lower Rhine. Nor was the pattern substantially altered when it was time for Russia and Prussia-Germany to incur adverse reactions to initiatives outside the east-central European inner security zone of either that seemed to make continental equilibrium incompatible with the Tsardom's massive power base or the Reich's mounting prominence.

Unless and until the dynamic of competition has subverted both reasons for self-restraint, factors pertaining to both capability and structure will limit either the ability or the utility for a land power to expand on the continent. At the same time, the incentive to expand past the continent into the maritime arena will be rooted in capability needs, but will not achieve its full global effect until the continental dynamic has cumulated with its overseas corollary, embodied in denial: the unwillingness of the insular power to abstain from interfering with even a narrowly defined, "legitimate" security zone of its continental counterpart; and its eagerness to foreclose the land power's diplomatic access to the outer zone of reliably inoffensive or potentially allied powers. A thus beset land power will feel impelled to complement its continental arrangements with access to the oceanic sphere as the outermost zone wherein to seek equal security and status by acquiring a countervailing ability to interfere with the offshore-insular power's own security and superiority zones. Thus to globalize the contest over henceforth overlapping interests and positions will impart the appearance of a drive for world domination to the more limited efforts to bargain militantly over the terms of a continental–maritime equilibrium; and it will obscure the fact that the continental power's maritimization, being both the obverse of and a response to the sea power's continentalization, was the only practical alternative to expanding its coercive dominion on the continent. Moreover, taking steps to protect the continental security orbit by action overseas will go readily hand in hand with attending outside the more proximate security zones to the relationship of power to prosperity and of security to sustenance by adding maritime-mercantile assets to land-agricultural and militarily relevant industrial resources. Reaching out beyond the intrinsically limited and incrementally diminishing ability to increase the supply of (farming and fighting) men and (fiscally extracted) money – or their analogues in more advanced economies – by overland expansion, and acquiring overseas a range of strategic leverages, will be the only way how to compete with the insular polity's no less ambiguously motivated and shaped urge to protect itself and to prosper.

The continental–maritime interlock was spectacularly manifest when Sparta, dependent on Corinth and Corinth's Corcyran colony for the maritime-mercantile supplement to the land-based military power of the League, was forced into the Peloponnesian War for fear of seeing the continental-military and the navally-capable parts of the alliance cleave apart and the alliance fragment also on land. Continuing access to the Sicilian granary was a related factor of material-economic capabilities, one even more directly at issue when the Assyrian and the Hellenistic Syrian and Macedonian land empires were unable to avoid some kind of contest with Egypt if they were to remain viable materially and, thus, strategically. No more could Rome confine herself to peninsular expansion once the line of her advance had cut across that of maritime-mercantile Carthage already implanted in the island of Sicily. At the beginning of the Atlantic and capitalist age, the strategic interdependence of the oceanic and the continental theaters was demonstrated whenever Spain resorted to variably efficacious naval and overland military strategies targeted at the commerce of the Dutch and the English. Neither could France renounce overseas activity and acquisitions if she was to deal with either a structurally conditioned internal liability (the inorganic juxtaposition of coastal-Atlantic maritime and the Paris-centered continental segments) or a strategic weakness (the growing English capacity to exert influence in and pressure on the French continental security zones). And the need for a retaliatory potential *vis-à-vis* a directly inaccessible England's commerce, colonies, and command of the sea grew as French wartime military gains on the continent proved insufficient to redeem wartime overseas losses when it came to making peace. Implementing naval-oceanic policies remained a valid imperative for Germany and Russia even as Britain's growing "continentalization" continued to extend the range of available pressure points on the insular realm from north-western Europe through the Near East (Egypt) to south Asia (India) in ways first intimated by Napoleon – and even as, near concurrently, the "normativization" of the policy environment exacerbated the always ambiguous issue of causation and responsibility for conflicts to be provisionally decided by military force.

The structure of all the successively premier continental powers was subject to potentially destabilizing polar divisions, suggesting a uniform need for compensating foreign policies even though the internal fissions were drawn along different lines: regional and ethnic or confessional (Spain, France), social-class and party-political (Germany, tsarist Russia). At the same time, the systemic environment was comparably structured with respect to an adversary displaying a different, plural rather than polar, sociopolitical structure. This conjunction of internal and external factors pointed throughout to an indeterminate circular interplay: between compensatory responses to domestic and reactively preemptive ones to external factors, with a tendency for the latter to become primary as systemic crisis escalated and expectation of warlike conflict shifted attention and emphasis from internal divisions to internal requirements for united action abroad. Even more ambiguous than causation was responsibility for the conflicts, revolving around the balance or balancing of power: balance, as to what constituted "equal" security and prosperity, and entitlement to enjoy both, for the two unlike powers; balancing, as to which of them was the "first" to interfere with the legitimate security, sustenance, or also superiority, requirements of the other.

However impressive the structure-related strategic rationale of the land power for extending itself overseas may be, it will only reinforce – and make operational – the incentives related to capabilities. So long as they were confined to the land mass, imperial states ranging from Mesopotamia to the Europe of the Middle Ages were only precariously viable. Moreover, their deficiency was to be as unaffected by later changes in the basic or material givens as the givens themselves were insufficient to control the less variable operational dynamics. When the center of gravity had moved from the Mediterranean northward on the strength of new technologies for working deeper soils and handling heavier horses, the Carolingian Empire suffered equally – and in the end fatally – from the anterior waning of economic contact with the southern Mediterranean world and the subsequent waxing of seaborne intrusions from the north. Thereafter, dependence on metals or trade routes could change to one on industry-supported balances of international payments, just as the problems of internal order to be dealt with by diversionary expansion could shift from baronial feuding to inter-sector diversity and inter-class dynamic. Still, the Carolingian experience was conclusive enough for both the French and the German offshoots of the Franks to make them sally forth, one after the other in the wake of the displaced Normans, into newly navigable oceans. Concerns with power, prestige, and prosperity were indistinguishable in releasing pressures for imitating the real or imagined – policy-determining whenever seemingly determinate – economic advantages of the insular, quasi-insular, or just coastal powers, beginning with Portugal.

The several desididerata were but the obverse of the gradually revealed requisites of a socio-economic and -political "national system" that would not be tributary to actors favored by the developing Atlantic and, eventually, world economy. And the resulting dilemmas were the reverse side of the lagging states' compulsion to seek many-faceted parity in defiance of the likewise multiple asymmetries between elementally insulated and territorially invested states, aggravated by the fact that parity could not mean an exact equality of assets and gains in both spheres for both types of power.

Rivaling the ever more closely linked external and domestic pressures to move overseas will be the land power's priority concern with continental security and defenses. But it will do so in ways that compound the overall effect. Since only limited resources could be released for costly naval construction and maintenance even when a two-front situation on the continent did not further complicate the two-elemental setting, the sea-centered efforts were typically the more stressful the more they were insufficient: they would be confined in space, to coastal defenses or the safeguarding of coastal trade; restricted in mode to types of ships and operations designed to hinder hostile commerce or communications by means of privateering, surface or sub-surface, vehicles and techniques; and finite or intermittent in time, as spurts of naval build-up alternated with longer periods of draw-down and neglect. The condition was illustrated in part or wholly by Persia and Sparta as much as by France and tsarist Russia under different regimes. It was liable to catch up with industrially and technologically superior imperial Germany had the fiscal implications of her naval build-up been exposed to changing parliamentary moods and majorities longer. And although the controversial Tirpitzian design keyed to capital ships rather than light cruisers differed from the norm, it still illustrated the habitual limitation as to purpose: military deterrence of the principal sea power's feared preemption and mainly political compellence of colonial concessions on its part.

The strategic implications of the continental priority will only augment the incentives to overseas forays implicit in the structure of the system by adding operational to the systemic structure- and organic capability-related constraints and compulsions. Since the overseas initiatives will be commonly perceived as exceeding the requirements of retaliatory leverage on the oceanic rival's continental involvements, they will induce the sea power to escalate conflict on the mainland in ways bound to increase its innate advantage in securing and keeping allies and sympathizers. The escalation, repeatedly exemplified due to Britain's extreme sensitivities on this account, will intensify the centrifugal tendencies that always beset the alliances of a major land power and *a fortiori* its continental empire, not least by jeopardizing the benefits accruing to dependants from access overseas. Sharing there in managerial or career opportunities even more than in material or commercial profits will be important for especially the dependent elites, as shown by the role the Italians played in the Spanish imperial system. The participation will impart to the empire some of the substance of an organic community distinct from the mere complementarity in factors of production and consumption that defines the prototypical maritime empire, held together by concentric lines of geostrategic and -economic communication and the outward diffusion of an opulent culture. The greater is a continental empire's propensity to coerce within the inner security zone that both reflects and augments internal regime strains, and is activated by the need to offset the divisive pressures or inducements to defections originating with the sea power, the more crucial will be the potential of the overseas arena to mitigate the empire's basically negative character: one increasingly manifest in modern times in the Russian and German empires as outlets overseas were blocked by sea-power imperialism and outlets within the continental empire were curtailed by ruling-nation nationalism.

The ambiguities surrounding both the capability- and the structure-related determinants of land-power policies will have their focus in domestic conditions. Much as regime prestige and wider prosperity or stability may seem to dictate extra-continental expansion, the dominant societal ethos and inter-group dynamics will tend to impede it. From Sparta through Spain to the successively preeminent continental-European powers, the ethos forged in the period of internal consolidation and overland expansion was not one best suited to foster initiative and enterprise in the maritime sphere. Whereas Sparta's societal matrix and social mores exemplified the militarism that had been adumbrated in Assyria and was to be perpetuated by Rome, Spain's already obsolete feudal-chivalric ethos, bred in the reconquest of the peninsula from Islam and surviving into the strengths and weaknesses of her imperial system, prefigured the continental European approach to overseas well into the twentieth century. Whereas France's colonial imperialism displaced abroad the values of aristocratic paternalism in military clothing, a more nakedly militarist Spartan–Roman type of ethos permeated Germany's overseas colonialism and world policy generally for reasons only partially due to financial limitations. The more the continental ethos of idealized statism contrasted with the materialist bias peculiar or attributed to the insular-mercantile society and confronted real conditions abroad, the more did maritime-imperial involvement appear as a source of moral corruption. The perception, amply vindicated by Sparta's experience in the periods immediately following both the Persian War and the Peloponnesian War, was far from nullified by the record of republican Rome. And whereas the sense of inflowing corruption was not to be everywhere as strong as it had come to be in Spain, and was to be echoed by the Prussian gentry, for the colonial sphere to be the refuge for aristocratic-authoritarian values would be perceived throughout the Republic in France and increasingly in pre-World War I England as a threat to the liberal-democratic domestic order – a threat all the more gratuitous in the French case for the empire failing to redress the demographic imbalance relative to Germany.

Increasing the strains due to taint of corruption or gaps in competence were stresses from the imperfect inter-group compromises, on or near the elite level, made more than commonly necessary by the intrusion of the maritime-mercantile factor. The brevity of Sparta's overseas involvement was a way of evading a problem Athens had managed in favor of landless city-bred sailors (the trireme rowers), to the detriment of the soldierly farmer (the hoplite) after the Persian War and in a way destructive of the landed aristocratic interest (when abandoning the countryside to devastation) during the Peloponnesian

War. For a grandee of Spain to nominally command the Armada instead of leading armies from horseback as the badge of caste superiority was, subsequently, a form of adjustment to the enlarged sphere of state- and war-craft inferior to the British (itself superior to the Athenian) model. It was also an improvised exception from the norm of relinquishing the operationally decisive naval and colonial sectors to the lesser nobility or the middle class under the Spanish as much as the French ancien regime and in imperial Germany and Russia. The attendant sociopolitical compromises – such as those between the Prussian Junkers (concerned with remaining viable as agricultural producers and, therefore, preoccupied with Russia) and the Ruhr-centered industrial and commercial class (concerned with augmenting profits from overseas trade and from naval construction and, therefore, focusing on Britain) – reached no deeper than their equivalents in post-revolutionary France or pre-revolutionary Russia. Equally futile in the last resort was the attempt of the German navalists to anchor the maritime surge in patriotic mass support, muting the appeal and complicating the message of social democracy. The effect of the contrived transactions was further eroded whenever the middle classes in France, Germany, and Russia emulated their country's traditional nobility rather than following the example of the British aristocracy. They were then trying to escape from the challenge of global modernity into time past somewhat like the Russian Old Believers when retreating ever deeper inland before Peter's reforms instead of venturing sea-ward along the path leading from Moscow to St Petersburg.

Still lower down on the social scale, the long overwhelmingly peasant and only recently urbanized masses were slow to establish a mental connection between maritime power and material prosperity. They would pull up their roots and overcome the inborn fear of flood and sea even less readily than their ancestors had mastered that of drought and fire. Cultivating the soil and growing land-derived produce was mutually supportive with trade and industry for the Dutch, the English, and the North Americans – and for a time for Venice; it was not the case by and large for continental Europeans beginning with post-reconquest Spain and ending with either pre- or post-revolutionary Russia. Similarly, the industrial base and potential of seventeenth-century France could be superior to England's (and an earlier Milan's may have been to that of Venice) without preventing subsequent reversal in trade and industry, and retrogression in naval and colonial enterprise. The fact that the ampler and intrinsically richer country possessed (thus in the crucial naval stores) that which England had to seek far afield (in the Baltic region and in North America) was only one of the reasons, but it illustrated amply the drawn-out consequences of resource sufficiency subverting incentives to resourceful risk-taking for others as well.

Inhibitions due to domestic class and value structures, to deficient material or psychological stimuli and functional skills, will necessarily multiply stresses to be managed simultaneously on domestic and external, continental and maritime, fronts. This will result in a certain incoherence in policies reflecting and affecting the land–sea power schism. An authoritarian-to-autocratic domestic regime will be tempted to enhance internal legitimacy and inner-zone security by successful activity in the most productive and prestigious, maritime-colonial-commerical, sphere. However, across a time span bounded by the Persian Empire (before it retreated into land-locked absolutism from its Phoenician–Carthaginian maritime connection) and imperial Germany's Prussian monarchy, a contrary tendency has been manifest. It surfaced when the ensuing functional differentiation, social-group pluralism, and pressures for political liberalism endangered the regime, causing it to hesitate before allowing the underlying cause of the loss of control to unfold too fast too far. The additional fact that, in continental states, the rise of liberal democracy tends to parallel the external decline of a state itself, even as the drama of overseas competition may overshadow conflicts on the continent but does not do away with their more deadly seriousness, may well strengthen the regime's reluctance to expand a narrow sociopolitical base sufficiently to match the global radius of socially vital requirements. Yet, managing the outreach abroad and evolution at home without sufficient authority and competence will repeatedly provoke a revolutionary effort to close the gap: to update the state machinery so as to create a firmer support for wider-ranging strategy; to establish a parity of means and instruments with the ascendant maritime-mercantile power as a preliminary to pursuing a parity of outcomes in satisfying newly vital interests.

The goal was truer or conscious sooner for the French than for the Russian Revolution, for the latter's liberal than its "socialist" phase, and in Germany for the rightist "revolution" preceding the Second World War than for the leftist upheavals ending and following the first. But all differed substantially from revolutions in England or revolts in the Netherlands and America, aimed at emancipating maritime-mercantile interests from the real or imagined fetters on the full exploitation of natural advantages supposedly forged by a superordinate power or authority. The continental revolutions disclosed the most salient among the strengths and weaknesses of the typical land power, different from the opposite type of actor. These same qualities will in turn delimit such a power's lifespan and encompass its eventual decline, be it in the metropole or in its continental security zones.

The greatest weakness – a ready exposure to containment from the outside – is due to the ease with which the insular rival can exploit third-party interest in confining the major land power's continental preeminence. It being liable to such a "defensive" coalition will make it impossible to concentrate either militant or pacific efforts on exploiting economic opportunity in the peripheries – a strategy more easily urged retrospectively than practiced. However, the same liability can become a source of strength if it helps prevent a too rapid or extensive territorial expansion, such as the sixteenth-century Habsburg conglomerate's, which fatally dispersed hard-to-rank priorities. Conversely, an innate strength such as a favorable ratio between the size and substance of the metropole and its dependencies (as a rule inversely proportioned for an insular core power) can become a weakness when it diminishes the stimulus to manage ample domestic resources optimally or seek qualitatively superior ones abroad. By the same token, the insular sea power's greatest strategic advantage – its customary immunity to concerted containment from the outside – becomes a liability if it fosters a feeling of effortless permanence, conducive to free-and-easy diffusion of the decisive original assets among imperial dependants and emergent competitors.

One-directional diffusion, and inversely routed "exploitation," peculiar to the political economy of a maritime-mercantile body politic, contrast with a land-power empire's more complex two-way interplay between core and periphery. Since the sedentary populace is commonly reluctant to settle in less civilized areas and the elites are averse to diversifying the dominant ethos along with critical skills, it will be difficult to either expand or extend abroad the foundations of overseas opportunities and commitments. A reinforcing weakness will spread from the periphery into the core-polity whenever the economic currents flow only sluggishly either way and military or administrative expenditures exceed economic gain. The Spanish Empire offered only the most dramatic example of the two-way frustrations when the metropole's failure to absorb the flow of specie from the colonies productively disrupted the central economy further, while the inability to generate the goods needed in the American dependencies helped break down order and security at the periphery and disrupt dynastic ties within the Iberian peninsula (following the Dutch assaults on Portugal's Brazilian dependency). A but embryonic German overseas imperial system suffered even more than the French when economic outlets were reduced further by inadequate population outflows, while the two-directional process acquired a political dimension when efforts to project the Reich's feudal-authoritarian patterns abroad coexisted with pressures to reshuffle functional and societal hierarchies internally so as to suit the newly diversified national-imperial environment. In the event, the German metropole had too little time, whereas the tsarist Russian Empire was too exclusively continental, to experience an impact that was manifest in France mainly by the colonial sphere draining off the atavistic remainders of the ancien regime. Neither could show whether the liberalizing effects of overseas engagement were sufficient to outweigh the despotizing influences from non-representative colonial administration, feared not least by the liberal opponents of Britain's imperialist ventures.

Much as it will be such in most cases, the (continental or overseas) empire of a land power will not be invariably more coercive than the empire of an insular state. Sparta's was less oppressive than was that of Athens, just as the early Roman was in comparison with the then Carthaginian; and England's controls in northern America provoked a more forceful revolt sooner than did Spain's, softened by co-optation, in the southern hemisphere and in Italy. The continental empire being more oppressive or only more centralized may actually be but the reverse side of its being a more closely integrated sociopolitical system on the level of elites imbued with shared interests, career oppportunities, and values that were dynastic-conservative in the mature Spanish imperial system, liberal-democratic in the late French – and "progressive" in the early and raw Soviet Russian. Treating the land-power-centered empire on the simplified Assyrian model as the only instance of authentic empire could be used to exonerate British or American-type systems of control or influence for power and profit. Actually, the land power's empire may be most coercive at its beginning, when it is being created and expands, and has a chance to redeem itself through co-optation if it lasts. Conversely, the insular sea power will be most tempted to increase constraints in its domain when, remaining tribally minded and thus co-optation-resistant in procedures, it has ceased being dynamically innovative in performance. Moreover, if managers of the continental empire will tighten the bonds to resist growing attraction from a "subversive" insular state, the latter will commonly have most reason to do likewise if and when diminishing threat from an "aggressive" land power has reduced its consolidating effect.

At bottom, the sea power will envisage most constraints as a method of equitably allocating the costs of maintaining and defending an empire expected to pay for itself. Because the constraints administered by the land power will reflect a wider range of security- and stability-related imperatives, they will relate only secondarily to the problem of funding a typically top-heavy bureaucratic and unproductive military machinery. Attempts to rationalize the distribution of maintenance costs in a sea-power empire will arouse elite responses escalating into resistance on mainly fiscal-economic grounds; the costs of maintaining a land-power empire are at least as likely to be increased, often beyond endurance, by resistance that originates in a wider range of deeper reasons. Thus, opposition to revising the cost–benefit equations of empire security had ignited the revolt of previously free-riding American colonists against the first British Empire, before this issue reappeared in different and milder (or better managed) forms in the second. Political disaffection rooted in historically evolved regionalism was basic to the reasons for the Catalan and Portuguese revolts, brought to the boiling point by war-induced fiscal exactions and economic distress. And although the French hexagon was integrated more closely than the multi-kingdom Iberian realm, regionally and ethnically caused disaffection (e.g. the Breton) was even less due to primarily fiscal reasons, just as the mixture of economic advantages and liabilities accruing to actual or prospective members of France's Rhenish complex, a German *Mitteleuropa*, or a tsarist Russian pan-Slav commonwealth did significantly either moderate or aggravate the ethnic or creedal motives of recoil from great-power domination.

Yet another – as always relative and often elusive – difference in the relative strengths and weaknesses has been that, whereas the sea power typically depends on accidental or transient advantages, the outlook for the land power will hinge more often on how severe are its inherent liabilities. The more agriculture-dependent is a continental economy, the more will it depend on a balance of nature that can oscillate even more, and can be even less influenced by human endeavor, than the balance of trade and payments. The greater importance of organic over contrived factors – including military-technological – was manifest in the late-consolidating empires of Habsburg "Austria" and Romanov Russia, as well as in the Prussian core of Germany and the briefly renascent Ottoman Empire. A significant increase in the agricultural surplus was necessary before the central authority could draw on it even but partially for financing improvements in administrative management and military enforcement. In the process, the ability to augment fiscal revenues from agriculture was more fundamental than the consequent ability to monopolize the field artillery essential for subduing sectional insubordination in the multi-ethnic east

European empires, replicating thus the much earlier promotion of strong territorial states in western Europe. The obverse of such states' subsequent diffusion-prone technological and organizational advantages overseas was the precariousness of industrial-commercial supremacy while the more sturdy, because primitive, continental economies were surviving from crisis to crisis.

The quality of its strengths and liabilities will mean that a major continental power will prosecute efforts at overseas expansion only fitfully and require then speedy results. A mercantile-maritime polity will grow stronger steadily and gradually before it surfaces with relative suddenness, only to subside eventually in the same manner. From Athens to Albion and beyond, the returns on and costs of relatively early wars will accordingly be critical for the rise, and those of late engagements for the decline, of a sea power. From Sparta to Spain and beyond, military confrontations will attend the entire trajectory of the continental state and will, even if they have produced, only rarely decisively destroy, the material foundations of power; they will be more likely to dramatize than to determine the operative ratios of costs and benefits from self-assertion and self-restraint over the longer – if only medium – run. The burden of a prolonged spell of simultaneous land and sea fighting on several fronts is as likely to affect the prospects and shape the fortunes of a land power negatively, as a single set of engagements is to reveal a sea power's latent strength with striking results. In partial compensation, the loss of the naval-commercial-colonial appendages will cut short the lifespan of the insular state as a major power factor, whereas international role or status and domestic material sufficiency are less contingent for a continental state. It may actually prosper from the loss of more costly than profitable overseas appendages, and recover from losses on the continent if it has learned in time to conciliate former subjects or inner-zone clients and integrate them into a broadened national community or regional economy. Sparta was unable to hold on to an overseas empire for any length of time and eventually lost also her hegemonic position in the Peloponnese; but the enslaved helots, who had necessitated much of the prior expansive effort, ended by fighting loyally in Sparta's armed ranks. Similarly, the Catalans not only recovered greater prosperity relative to Castile in the wake of the imperial Habsburg era, but resumed also a conditional allegiance to the succeeding Bourbon regime, not least in recoil from the self-interested French support for the earlier rebellious defection.

EAST–WEST SCHISM AND INTER-CULTURAL DIFFERENCES

All the factors that affected the material conditions and psychological dispositions of past sea and land powers influenced the way they dealt with – and intimate the conditions in which their eventual successors had to confront – the constant predicaments implicit in the land–sea power schism. Much the same applies for a peculiar kind of mostly land powers that occupy the farthest-eastern extremity on the variably expanding and contracting sector defined by the East–West spectrum and, intermittently, schism.

Whereas China is the "oriental" power that has survived into continuing involvement in the central system, it is the Ottoman empire that was the typical Asiatic political system which, traceable back to the Persian, was longest a party to East–West interactions in the Euro-global system. It also displayed characteristics most germane to a range of half-westernized and half-orientalizing land powers of eastern Europe, beginning with Byzantium and extending from tsarist Russia (as the fellow-claimant to Byzantine succession) to her Soviet reincarnation. The one characteristic distinguishing the oriental from nearer-eastern land powers was that it tended to eschew either far-reaching or continuous maritime involvements while intermittently impinging on the land–sea power schism and contest (by either impelling the nearer-eastern power toward the maritime sphere or attracting the farthest-western maritime power toward the rear-continental sphere for strategic relief).

Only special, and then transient, circumstances historically induced the power in the rear of the continent to deploy naval power – and then commonly through the agency of an alien or subordinate group. The precedent was set by ancient Assyria and Persia, both of which had to control the naval power of the Phoenician cities if they were to meet the externally set conditions of economic sufficiency and survival as major politico-military actors. Thus also China's relatively brief spell of naval proficiency between the late twelfth and mid-fifteenth century was largely contingent on Mongol interest and expertise. Similarly, Ottoman naval and mercantile competence rested on the skills of associated North African Moslems and other, non-Moslem as well as non-Turk, religio-ethnic groups. When it reached outside inland rivers, China's naval activity was more a matter of prestige than prosperity, a largely indirect compensation for than defense against Japanese piracy across the sea and barbarian overland pressures or territorial conquests in the north-west. The Ottomans' maritime involvement was due to more complex compulsions, ranging from the Persian Gulf–Indian Ocean area (to engage the Portuguese) and the Mediterranean (against the Venetians and the Spaniards) to the land areas north of the Black Sea (adjoining Muscovy-Russia), linked directly to the mere presence or actual pressure of militant Persia in the continental rear.

Heading the disincentives to substantial maritime exertions was the fact of geopolitical isolation (China's) or capacity for it (the Ottomans'), which made vast and costly naval deployments seem unnecessary. Among the conditions which made the deployment unattractive to initiate and difficult to sustain were the geophysical layout or topography (China's coast being unsuitable for good harbors except in the south-east matching the Straits' potential for both bottling up and shielding Ottoman sea power); the paucity of indigenous skills and external successes (China's failure in naval assaults on Japan, Indonesia, and Indochina equalling the Ottomans' mixed record against the Venetians and Spain, more symbolized than culminating at Lepanto); and, a most uniformly acting factor, either conflictual tension or just disjunction between the central authority and the social classes or groups with a stake in maritime commerce. In China, where state power rested on an essentially rural economy focused on inland market towns rather than on coastal cities plying long-distance trade, officialdom was suspicious of all activities that might augment social mobility and upset the established forms and methods of government. Although the demands of stability predominated over the requisites of either prosperity or security also in insular Japan until western sea-power imposed and the Meiji Restoration initiated imitation, China's major coastal cities such as Shanghai became politically significant only briefly in the twentieth century. And whereas trade was largely delegated to non-Turks in the Ottoman Empire even as economic policies favored Moslems over the Christians, official foreign-trade theory favored imports over exports while actual practice was subordinate to military-political or diplomatic conveniences (including special privileges for the French partner in the sixteenth-century quasi-alliance).

All such and similar predispositions were as certain to impede maritime-mercantile outreach as they were unlikely to create an integrated economic-military-administrative basis for foreign and imperial policies. The typical land power extrapolated into its empire an essentially idealistic statist bias which, centered on individual obligations over rights within a hierarchically authoritarian sociopolitical system, was vulnerable to coercion predominating over consent; and the typical western insular-sea power displayed an essentially materialistic societal bias centered on particular interests *qua* rights, while projecting the ethos into an ideally egalitarian imperial association was susceptible to generating unequal benefits. The typically despotic farther-eastern or oriental political system differed from both in that it would only superficially bridge the disjunction between state and society and, when trying to manage either preferred isolation from the outside world (China) or only sporadic involvement (Turkey), was prone to vitiating the regulatory instrumentalities of a command economy through a system of taxation that ranged from arbitrary to confiscatory. Sufficient revenues might flow from collection of tolls on transit trade (the Ottoman Empire) or from centrally maintained canal and irrigation networks (China). But the officialdom which dominated the state apparatus would only rarely and haphazardly support, and intermittently repress, private economic enterprise by ethnically or otherwise uncongenial middle-class, let alone foreign, elements. More often xenophobic than pragmatically imitative, the authorities could be distrustful also of their own military class in the last resort, even when leaning toward militarism more than mercantilism.

Such a political system was bound to inhibit – fail to generate if not positively obstruct – continuing technological innovations of a kind responsible for the rise of an industrial or capitalistic economy. By the time such an economy was developing and maturing in Europe under the impetus of a politically competitive state system, and was additionally stimulated there by the search for opportunities in the Ottoman and China markets, the eastern empires had conclusively failed to incorporate the socio-economic and functional differentiation mercantilism had fostered in the European sea powers and the need to remove retarding feudal-type inhibitions had encouraged, in a west-to-east progression, on the continent. Revolutions merely removed obsolete shackles from technological and managerial innovations for greater power and prosperity in the maritime West, while they would speed up administrative or technological modernization in the comparatively regressing land powers. In the farther-eastern empires, revolutionary upheavals were more likely to attend cultural disarrays following upon attempts to introduce military-technological and/or administrative novelties from the west: they stood for nativist-populist revulsions more than for political or economic reform, left to occasional initiatives from above.

The pervasive tendency in the eastern powers down the ages to favor size over efficacy and mass over mobility – not least in the caliber of (unwieldy) military or naval armaments and complexity of (top-heavy) bureaucracies – was but another facet of an inflexibility that underlay the propensity to crisis. However, the longevity of the eastern empires expressed their capacity to assign priority and resources to crucial strategic tasks, and to either mitigate the woes of an inorganic state–society relationship with the vitality of corporate groupings and patron–client relationships (Ottoman Empire) or offset decay with restoration and fragmentation with consolidation through assimilation-fostering inter-dynastic cycles (the Chinese Empire). Traditional China tended to stagnate when enjoying external safety and was restimulated when conquered by a succession of pre-western barbarians; stagnation in the less varied Ottoman career was a function of insufficient expansion rather than lagging exposure: as had been the case in the orientalized late Roman Empire, the outside threat subsiding provisionally was less damaging than the final arrest of forward thrust within a system of political economy dependent on conquest for land grants and on the latter for military and administrative service. Growing logistical constraints on long-distance military operations combined with near-simultaneous increases in socio-cultural (even before politico-military) forms of resistance from below to weaken the capacity of Ottoman institutions to absorb the multiplying administrative and other foreign improvements, with the result of lowering the entire system first to and then below the concurrently rising western levels.

No more than the Ottoman could the Chinese kind of debility be lastingly offset by an element of strength: the compatibility of a despotic system with disguises of authority and checks on coercion in the empire's peripheral regions. A system of tributes disguised as exchange of gifts with client states such as Korea was supported by, while mitigating any possible liability from, the shared perception of China as culturally superior – while the pretension to superiority underlay the perception of military engagements with insubordinate barbarians as nothing more than punishing expeditions. While it lasted, and for it to work, the combination of tributes and punishments depended on near-complete isolation from comparably civilized major powers (such as the European) and absence of competing regional imperialisms (such as the Vietnamese). It was then as effective in its results and as lenient in mode as was the Ottoman reliance on combining selective elite conversion with religious toleration for masking the face of a nakedly predatory imperialism and parasitic militarism. So long as inter-class discords within the subject Balkan communities and conflicts among the European powers performed for the Turks the function of China's isolation, assimilating religious converts into leading military-administrative roles at the center dovetailed effectively with devolving of authority to semi-autonomous dynastic clients (such as Transylvania) and confessional organisms when coping with competing (Habsburg and/or Turkoman–Persian) imperialisms.

As perfected in Byzantium, the indirect – alternately manipulative and managerial – mode of imperial control differed in either case from the practices of the European continental-military and insular-maritime empires when they either projected domestic authoritarianism or hesitantly exported internal liberalism, or just laxity, into imperial control modes. The divergent systems of control implied different causes of progressive erosion if not periodic collapse. Abetted or only surfaced by deterioration at the periphery, internally generated deterioration of the central institutions – the Sultanate and the regime of Christian converts (the *devshirma*) in Turkey or the dynastic-mandarinal equivalents in China – was critical for the oriental empires just as the obverse of inward seepage of decay, outward diffusion of assets, debilitated the western maritime empires and a two-way current between a core power and its inner security–superiority zone enfeebled the European land power-centered empires. occupying an intermediate position also in this regard.

One more difference was critical for the stability and predictability of external policies of the oriental-despotic political systems. Critical fluctuations in the farther-eastern empires depended less on impersonal organic factors (eventually critical for both of the other systems) and more on personal, even if institutionalized, factors. Ups and downs in the energies and talents of individual sultans and, increasingly, vizirs (or vizir dynasties) in the Ottoman regime were equalled in China by the shifts from able (often barbarian) initiators to inept (overly civilized) liquidators of imperial dynasties and their bureaucratic ethics. Overall, the eastern model of cyclical fluctuation-without-evolution within empires differed from the comparatively western model of the rise and decline of individual powers underpinning and actuating a discernible evolutionary trend: a difference that opposed discontinuity in particular policies in the former to a continuously unfolding pattern of policies in the latter case. Whereas dynasties rose and fell in China and authority was passed around from born Moslems to converts and partially back in the Ottoman realm, maritime-mercantile primacy was after Venice displaced from Portugal via the Dutch to England, before reaching North America, as navally backed technological and economic innovations in the rising polities and capital investments by declining in the future-dominating economies injected elements of material (if no other) progress into the attendant evolutionary progression. Although the improvements attending a parallel sequence among the land powers were procedural more than substantive, the preeminent European land powers displayed a capacity to regenerate themselves internally which was greater than that of failing sea powers even if, on balance, inferior to the better-shielded oriental powers'. However, the continentals' periodic attempts to reverse decline by acts of self-assertion reproducing earlier or essaying newer methods were unable to halt the continent-spanning gravitation of primarily military-political preponderance – a west-to-east path that (once the Byzantine and Ottoman bases for the superiority of the east had been broken in favor of Spain) paralleled the east-to-west path of power and prosperity migration on the maritime-mercantile plane.

In the three kinds of powers: (western) insular-maritime, (nearer-eastern or central) continental with overseas aspirations, and (farthest-eastern or oriental) rear-continental, the range from natural insulation through its strategically contrived approximation to preference for self-isolation was reflected in one from pluralist-societal through authoritarian-statist to autocratically headed despotic political systems. Insofar as the authoritarian land power displayed (quasi-) totalitarian features analogous to the oriental-despotic mode, these would make up for the (temporary) insufficiency of the authoritarian formula to deal with societal fragmentation or polarization while the state was contentiously engaged with politico-militarily or -economically equal or superior powers. Whereas the totalitarian deviation reflected then urgent pressures to prepare adequately for a belligerent engagement deemed imminent, such an engagement had to be already under way to instigate the technological or organizational imitations inherently inimical to oriental despotism – unless, as in China, the western innovations had to be imposed from the outside and then too late or too sporadically to be effectively stimulating.

Socially rootless and wholly state-dependent civilian and military bureaucracy (converted Christians including the janissaries in Turkey; eunuchs in both the Ottoman and the Chinese administrations) linked state to society only inorganically in both of the oriental despotisms. Similar in the totalitarian regimes were managerial methods, by a broadly comparable type of personnel (mass party-dependent and -conditioned functionaries, alienated from the wider society; elite military or para-military, including internal police, formations) recruited preferably from youthful converts; and so was leadership succession, favoring candidates with access to the means of, and support by the wielders of, violence in periods of dynamic growth, and individuals advanced in age as a guarantee of brief or inoffensive tenure and minimum consensus in periods of decline or mid-term disarray. Although oriental-despotic features were characteristically more pronounced in the totalitarian interludes of more markedly rear-continental Russia than in compartively more western Germany, the "occidental" totalitarians were alike in substituting pervasive sociopolitical ideologies and psychologically targeted techniques of terror for the formalized religio-imperial ethos of the typical oriental despotism (Islam and the ghazi-warrior ethos in the Ottoman Empire; the Mandate of Heaven and the Confucian-statesman ethos in China's). More importantly, the crisis-related and thus temporary or provisional nature of nearer-eastern land-power totalitarianism made it prone to reverting to the more germane authoritarian pattern, in contrast with the timeless quality of the despotisms of the oriental variety. Whereas the latter were ingrained both socio-culturally and organizationally and reinforced by isolation, Europe's totalitarian systems were twentieth-century adaptations of eighteenth century's enlightened despotisms to the conditions of mobilized mass society combining moral crisis with extraneous pressures for time-limited forced-draft development or single-minded use of material resources.

From this common basis, the ideologies of the continental European powers have rationalized distinctive handicaps and consequent requirements in one of two ways: the need for and dependence on authoritarian methods internally and coercive controls within the inner security zone, by glorifying authority and violence (a motif predominant in right-wing ideologies); the need for and dependence on centralized promotion and management of resources, by making a fetish of organizational and technological efficiencies and disciplines (a motif predominating in the applied tenets of left-wing ideologies). Either propensity would be intensified by interactions with the leading insular-maritime polity and culture, which will in turn engage in a two-pronged projection for a dual purpose: it propagates externally, as universally valid models, the liberal values and (political and economic) practices rooted in its natural advantages and (in large part accidental or temporary) assets; and it projects upon the outside, in the sense of attributing to the continental rival, its own darker side including expansionist drives and urges to dominate. The purpose of the attempt to universalize that which is inherently particular if not parochial will be to weaken external resistance to the liberal political system as one uniquely legitimate; the purpose of transferring and projecting the negative drives and urges on the adversary will be to galvanize an instinctively isolationist populace against a threat and to reassure the insular tribe that the to-be-exported positive values are safely ensconced within itself.

The oriental-despotic regime will be comparatively more ideology-free and the polity more confidently self-centered culturally. Seeking no deeper relationship to the other actor types, it will demonize the outside world (as the realm of infidels, white devils, or dark satans) and have as little desire to convert the outside world (contrary to the liberal sea power's universalism) as to coerce the insular power into a sense of community and identity-or-equality (contrary to the land power's ambivalence). The attitude of wholesale rejection is thus less ambiguous and more internally coherent (but, also, less externally flexible, except when dissimulated for immediately opportune reasons) than is either of the other tendencies: the two-sided projection of self-perceived positive-and-negative traits by the western insular-maritime polity, or the either explosion- or implosion-prone but also association-seeking and -capable ambivalence of the nearer-eastern continental-authoritarian power.

All in all, the factors that can be reduced to a common denominator form a continuum of internal structures, politically relevant functions, and related values of the crucial actor-types. The range from relatively liberal via increasingly authoritarian to despotic forms parallels a progressively decreasing capacity to administratively integrate the means of production and destruction (or "defense") with help from spontaneously operative secular-pragmatic values. The continuum reflects the actors' spatio-temporal situations, aggregating locations on the west-to-east topographically shaded geographic axis and positions in the stream of unevenly spaced long-term evolution. However, the interrelated traits and attributes pertaining to the basic givens will generate only diffuse predispositions, which only the degrees of closeness to other actors and the center of the system will translate into more specific precepts for strategic action. The same degrees of closeness will in turn determine not only how large a segment of the geographic (east–west) axis and geo-functional (maritime–continental) spectrum is activated by interplays of competing and cooperating policies, but also whether the distinguishable actor attributes are perceived to overlap sufficiently to give rise to conflict-intensifying schism or schisms. The least fixed position in these respects is that of the oriental despotisms, which relate to conflicts in adjoining space about as indeterminately as the East–West schism relates to the other two schisms. The farther-eastern a despotic power is, the more will it be only a background factor for the active sector of the East–West conflict axis and, thus China, the more remote from the Europe-centered land–sea power schism (as well as wholly extraneous to the enactment of the sacral–secular schism). Contrary to this aloofness, oriental-despotic features infiltrated the would-be amphibious European polities as their site moved eastward and the pressures on them grew at a rate proportionate to their developmental distance from the western-insular or geostrategic proximity to the rear-continental power.

As the three power types interact, the western insular sea power will resist relaxing its oceanic monopoly (and its conception of a "just" continental equilibrium) for the sake of accommodating differences with the preeminent continental power bent on a measure of maritime-mercantile access. The sea power will combine that propensity with pursuing access to the continent via alliances, and be tempted to temper the servitudes of the alliance option with flexible observance of individual alliance commitments. It will thus respond to the alternating attractions of, and intermittent availability of, either involvement in or disengagement from the continental balance of power – while exploiting its high degree of immunity to restrictive or punitive containment by continental coalitions. The contrary bias of the navally ambitious major continental state will be toward incoherence in its basic foreign-policy stance, reflecting the conflict of pressures from the continental sphere and pulls from the maritime sphere. Any inclination to accommodate with the insular state will be tempered by the insistence on this occurring on "fair" and "equal" terms. But just as the price of the achievable conditions of accommodation will be measured against the costs of a multi-front conflict, so will its rewards be weighed against the risks of exposure to a hostile coalition the sea power has merely inspired, actually headed, or also materially sustained. And finally, what about the farthest-eastern strategically significant, rear-continental even if not integrally oriental, power? Its capacity for self-isolation and preoccupation with cyclically endangered internal stability will translate into highly volatile-to-crudely opportunistic foreign policies apt to impact on the central system less predictably and more disturbingly even if less conspicuously than actions by the other two power types.

The typological differences among the major powers matter even when they only inflect or precipitate the course of competitive interactions among them *qua* uniformly territorial states; and when the operational significance of the differences has been muted by a primary impact, originating in structurally conditioned schism-neutral dynamic as to both style and substance. When a power participates in the dynamic on a sustained level, it will be confined to a finite range of practicable strategies; and it will disclose dispositions peculiar to one among the sequentially phased basic foreign-policy postures when reacting to the pressures, propensities, and resulting predicaments peculiar to its situation within the geostrategic setting. To the extent that powers were insulated from – or were less intimately engaged with – the (westward-moving) center of the state system, their external posture and foreign policies derived from the needs of internal authority more or more often than from external balance-of-power requirements. And if authority derived near-completely from the despotism-promoting vital functions of government and despotism-related cyclical regime fluctuations in the case of the farthest-eastern or oriental powers, and the priority from their isolation, domestic factors and related economic forces determined foreign policies of the insular sea powers more commonly than of the continental powers if mainly during external lulls. It was thus largely a matter of how the diverse powers were located on a west-to-east and insular–continental spectrum whether policy impulses would be propagated mainly through interstate or intra-state and -empire dynamics, and with what intensity. This fact was of particular importance in the modern Atlantic era during which, by an accident of geography enacted in history, the west-to-east axis has coincided with a spectrum of decreasingly maritime (pluralist-to-democratic) and increasingly rear-continental as well as physically larger (authoritarian-to-despotic) actors with the operationally long, but not permanently, insignificant exception of insular Japan at the Pacific extremity.

3
Inter-Actor Discords in Disparate Arenas

Reacting to structures of power and expected to either buttress or subvert them are strategies aimed at enhancing the position of an actor and only sporadically (and always secondarily) the stability of the system. Tied up with chronically lopsided structure, strategies are no less intimately linked to a balancing process that typically centers on crises and conflicts. And whereas structures crystallize the largely unintended resultants of prior strategies, the latter are commonly the product of deliberate calculations encompassing capabilities and intentions related to objectives. As for the attendant crises and conflicts, insofar as they arise out of a faulty match between structure and strategies that objectifies a misfit between capabilities and intentions, they occupy an intermediate ground between what is deliberate and what is determined.

TRIANGULARITY-PRONE STRUCTURES AND DUAL MODIFIERS

In a structure of two to five or more major powers, the original strategic relationship is one of two powers, related in conflict and confrontation or accommodation and collusion. In either case, a third power will enter the relationship as either a derivative, when conflict of two generates or enhances its standing and expands its options, or incentive, when two rivals are led to accommodate by shared concern over a rising third. As the number of major actors grows beyond three, so does the number of the three-cornered or tripartite conceptual universes into which strategic thought-experiments in effect decompose the system before the selected response resets it (by means of alliances) in a (provisional) configuration.

The tripartite perspective predominates even though a system of four powers will tend to polarize into a two-bloc structure, as the "first" actor fears that the "third" will join the "second" unless he does, thus forcing the "third" to join up with the "fourth"; and it predominates even though a system of five or more powers will tend to subdivide structurally and be managed strategically as a set of overlapping two-power balancing relationships. Each party to such a pair of either adversaries or, even, allies will seek to minimize the comparative advantage of the other in current or future relations with a third party – one of the attitudes that commonly produce the individually unintended result of a rough equilibrium for a multi-actor system when it lacks the all-overriding incentive of a conspicuous drive for hegemony. Moreover, the third-party factor will intrude into a system of more-than-three powers through strategic axioms requiring actors to seek inclusion in the relatively larger combination or coalition – most notably, to be one of three in a (historically recurrent) system of five major powers. On the other hand, it is less a structural than a functional phenomenon that, as the number of key actors approaches and exceeds five, one power will acquire a crucial role, as coordinator or reference point, in the balancing process and its concert-like institutional corollary, if any. How significant the impact of the additional parties is will depend on how weighty they are and how deeply and directly involved. They were marginal when the Rome–Carthage conflict, having unfolded during the First Punic War in relative independence from a third power once Pyrrhus of Syracuse had dropped out of the game, was briefly triangularized in the Second Punic War within the Rome–Carthage–Macedon configuration and thus tenuously linked to the larger-number structure including the lesser Greek and the major Hellenistic actors in the eastern Mediterranean. The Anglo–German–Russian triangle was much more fully integrated with the all-European system of five or six great powers in the late nineteenth and early twentieth century (comprising also France and Austria-Hungary, next to Italy), but the critical relationship for purposes of diplomatic strategy was still the tripartite one (covering the principals in the critical insular–continental and the subordinate West–East spectrum).

In any event, the alignment of any one party with another against a third (A cum B versus C, A cum C versus B, and B cum C versus A) exhausts the range of available basic strategies in a tripartite situation or perspective, while the strategic range encompasses – in the sense of reflecting and responding to – all the various interrelated "causes" of conflict: the "formal" cause is peculiar to the (desired or opposed) conditions of role-status parity or preeminence between any two parties and a range from (status) preeminence through (power) predominance to hegemony within a structure of more powers; closely related is the "material" cause inherent in actual or sought capabilities of actors more or less congruent with the distribution of roles or status; and if attaching to particular territorial or other issues at dispute is the "efficient" cause, the "final" one is embedded in the more fundamental dispositions of an actor ranging from early-phase spontaneous to late-phase compulsive urge to expand via a mid-term conservative stance. All of these distinctive "causes" contribute to the unfolding of a three-phase process reflective in one way or another of the tripartite setting: initial polarization (confrontation and conflict) between two parties as a function of converging expansionisms, which activates a third party;

mid-term exploration of the conditions of parity or equilibrium (in response to prior conflict-induced dispersion of power in favor of third party of parties); and some form of parallelism in post-maturity conditions (typically decline relative to third parties as background factors or reference points, when second-phase accommodation was aborted or set in train too late).

The number of major actors or "poles" denoting basic structure is in every respect anterior to the dynamic processes (of polarization, parity-exploration, and parallelization). However, when identifying the setting relevant for strategies, the structure defined quantitatively (in terms of mainly material actor capabilities) or numerically (in terms of the number of "poles") precedes only logically the actors' evolutionary (rise/decline-affecting) stages and their dominant schism-related peculiarities, which modify the structure qualitatively. Together, the quantitative and qualitative facets constitute the total dynamic structure of a system at any one time. The schism-related qualifiers or modifiers do not expand the range of available basic strategies, but they do affect the probability of one being chosen over another and its prospects. The result is a paradox: When a situation is compounded by schism-related diversities, the structure is more complex than when the actors are identical not only essentially, as territorial states, but also situationally, as secular, insular, or western and sacral, continental, or eastern, powers. However, the schism-related differences in situations, interests, and dispositions will simplify matters operationally insofar as they delimit the comparative appeals of the theoretically available basic strategic options and alignment alternatives.

Nor is this all. Athens being a sea power and Sparta a land power mattered, for military strategies even more than for diplomatic strategies, but it mattered less on either count than did the absence of a third fully coactive great power most of the time. The same was roughly the case when the Papacy and the (Holy Roman) Empire bestrode the sacral–secular schism, and the Ottoman and the Habsburg-Spanish empires alone represented mixes of continental and maritime attributes while bestriding the West–East dichotomy.

Yet again, the greater is the number of near-equal powers which interplay near-automatically in a mutually balancing fashion, the more will the crucial qualitative modifiers shift from schisms to the key actors' evolutionary stages and related foreign-policy postures. Since these only may be varied and complementary enough to facilitate the balancing interplay, their distribution will be most critical for the state of the system as a whole: What, and how much of, inter-actor conflict and conflict-related strategies the system can absorb before its potential for re-equilibration after disturbance has been eroded to the point that necessary adjustment of actor roles to actor capabilities requires the introduction of agents from outside the system's boundaries? In contrast from the effects of evolutionary stages, the schism-related differences will introduce rigidities into the balancing process when schism-related attributes make an alignment difficult-to-impossible. And they will raise the issue of functional equality or interchangeability among actors unevenly eligible for the role of balancer. Closely associated with the question of the role's functional utility is then its legitimacy and opportunity for performing it: thus, when the sacralized actor, from Mesopotamian high priest to medieval Papacy, or the relatively western insular-maritime one, from Egypt to England, proceeds to discredit the aspiration to role-status parity of its counterpart in the schism-related equations as being tantamount to equilibrium-upsetting hegemonial ambition.

The issue of legitimacy, associated with actual or attributed functional utility, completes the scope of strategy-affecting factors that are only superficially reducible (and may be analytically only provisionally reduced) to the mainly material capabilities-reflecting structure of the arena and intentions of actors. The greater is the range and complexity of the differentiating schism- and evolutionary stage-related modifiers that largely account for an actor's spirit in that they infuse interests with values and strategic rationality with passional stimuli, the more likely it is for a more narrowly focused reflexive-to-rational strategy to fit only poorly the total, quantitatively defined and qualitatively modified, structure; and the easier it is as a result for misfits between structure and strategy to cumulate perversely, and for particular crises to aggregate beyond what is necessary to propel the system's evolution, into a condition that threatens it with catastrophe.

CONFLICTING DYNAMICS OF ALIENATION AND ACCOMMODATION

When two major powers face one another in conditions of relative separation from third parties or salience over them, their choosing cooperation or conflict will engender strategies for accommodation or confinement through adversary alliances and actions: the first, for de facto collusion if not formal alliance and genuine solidarity in conditions of parity as fact or aim; the second, for either one-directional or mutual subversion in favor of one-party predominance. The many specific impediments to accommodation in a two-power setting will foster ideologically induced or, more often, formulated antagonisms. In compounding the underlying structural fact of polarity, the dichotomization in terms of some kind of values will draw on differences implicit in one or another kind of schism, while evolutionary disparities will absolutize these differences. The drawing of absolute contrasts in ideal or pseudo-ideal terms will be further nourished, and its consequences exacerbated, if one or both parties aim at containing the other by means of a tightly drawn encirclement. And just as the material factors prompting the strategy of containment-through-encirclement team up with ideal ones, the physical with propagandistic and the structural with spirit-related features, so the spatial dimension of the geopolitics of two-power confrontation will be inseparable from its temporal dimension. Not only will the rivals manifest an uneven readiness to accommodate at a particular time, but, if it occurs at all, movement toward a mostly unduly delayed accommodation will be tied up with the intrusion of later-emergent third parties. The rise of such parties is often a consequence in time of the enactment of the two-sided conflict at its peak, with effects in space that induce its subsequent composition or will be responsible for its supersession. Whichever way the conflict eventually subsides, moreover, it will have been interlaced with some features of prior convergence. Whereas the clash of two rival expansionisms has been blunted by mutual enfeeblement, polarization will have been eroded in favor of some parallelisms between the original contestants.

Any and all particular obstacles to timely accommodation between two powers (permitting their collusion relative to third parties) will be reducible to unresolved issues of priority among conflicting concerns and parity in concessions and compensations. The advantages of concerting reciprocal appeasement as a relief that is immediate in time and whose foundation is firmly localized in space will be at a discount when measured against the requirements of long-term strategy were the conflict to resume at some future time in the same or a larger geographic theater – an always possible contingency made probable by treating it as such. Conciliation risks breeding catastrophe if the hard-to-equalize assets that have been surrendered or forgone for the sake of appeasement turn into critical liabilities or deficiencies in the absence of a threat sufficiently shared and pressing to compel matching re-evaluations of strategic stakes and "vital" interests on both sides.

Compared with the fundamental impediment, specific obstacles to accommodation are both varied in kind and subsidiary in importance. Thus rivals may be unable to decide whether the primary threat is from the other major or civilized power or a common, if unevenly pressing, threat is from barbarian-peripheral or other lesser forces and factors: a recurrent issue vividly illustrated in the fluctuating contention of (first also western and subsequently only eastern) Rome with (first Parthian and then Sassanid) Persia between the second and the seventh centuries AD in an environment including changing sets of "barbarians." Or stakes that are substantively diverse may be functionally complementary and operationally interrelated, thus the unevenly ideal-transcendental and material-territorial concerns and ambitions of medieval Empire and Papacy or, among strictly territorial powers later, stakes in maritime or oceanic and continental arenas. Compounding the effects of such principled quandaries will be the practical ones of implementation. Timing is critical at a protracted conflict's mid-point lull when the likely difficulty is how to relate a shared need for respite to the divisive effect of unevenly successful provisional outcomes, how to square the contrary pulls of yet wholly unresolved past and only dimly recognized or crudely crystallizing emergent issues. Such dilemmas were in evidence at Cateau Cambrésis between (Valois) France and (Habsburg) Spain in mid-sixteenth century as well as between Athens and Sparta in 421 BC (the Peace of Nicias) and repeatedly between France and Britain. No less crucially, the factor of space is at issue when the question is how to allocate access to or control over secondary but supposedly crucial actors and assets located between spheres of influence: in the just-mentioned Atheno-Spartan accommodation effort and the Franco-Russian one prior to 1812.

Wherever the specific ambiguity may reside – in intermediate zones (of unassigned "neutrals"), interlocking (qualitatively unequal) threats, indeterminate (mid-course) outcomes, or intertwined (if qualitatively differentiable) stakes – the existential conditions will help absolutize the normative issue of real or imagined differences in values. Nor will dispassionate pragmatism be fostered when the salient rivals try to add sympathetic appeal to whatever self-interested support they may hope for from potentially like-minded if lower-ranking actors. The polarity in values and related ideologies can be phrased in terms of institutional differences between democracy and oligarchy in the Greek and republics and tyrannies in the Italian city-state system, and between absolute and constitutional monarchies or oligarchies in Europe from seventeenth century on; in terms of quasi-religious and cultural contrasts between western and eastern empires such as Rome and Persia and Spain and Turkey; in terms of still more transcendent claims to the possession of universal truth and (consequently) sway by rivals preceding and following the medieval Papacy and (Holy Roman) Empire and raising, in the twentieth century, to a new level the nineteenth-century opposition between liberal and authoritarian (cum western and eastern) political systems – an update of the Greek and Italian dichotomies and likewise related to the disparity between maritime societies and continental states.

In either case, the immediately operative object of the ideological formulation will be to rationalize pragmatically determined and conducted conflicts (not excluding those between the medieval or modern universalists) or to revitalize a recondite principle and its receding potency (thus, the medieval principle of universal empire by Charles V through opposition to Islam, prior to many a modern ism). As a source of moral reassurance and nervous energy, formulating a conflict ideologically will sustain it past any weakening of purpose when situational or strategic ambiguities accumulate. In fact, infusion of ideology is itself a strategy of sorts, to offset and if anything overcompensate for confusion: in adopted means or about actual (and not readily avowable) aims. It will prolong a conflict beyond its natural lifespan by making the issues at contention appear to be so fundamental as to require an outcome that is conclusive and final. Not for the first or last time, the ensuing deformation of actually finite and mundane stakes was at its highest in thirteenth-century Europe when the Papal-Imperial conflict reached a climactic phase while the conflict itself had already become anachronistic. Before fading in favor of its successors, the contention was kept alive by millenarian visions of its world-transforming or history-culminating resolution in favor of the forces of light defeating the agents of darkness.

Arising out of ambiguities which frustrate timely moves toward two-power accommodation, if more readily controllable than these, will repeatedly be the tendency to implement the strategy of containment by one-sided or mutual encirclement through adversary alliances. Although the policy will be motivated prudentially to begin with, its intensity and the encirclement's tightness will easily correlate with degrees of ideological radicalism between parties loath to blame the confrontation on spatially converging parallel (even when not temporally coincident) drives to expand. As a matter of fact, for territorially settled parties to clash in behalf of comparably (i.e., defensively) perceived comparable interests will not typically implement a one-sidedly aggressive simple motion, unprovoked by contrary strength and design or uninvited by negligent weakness or divisions. No more will the shared tendency to expand be reducible to the single motive of fear or ambition alone, one impelling preclusion of a real or hypothetical threat and the other predation of someone else's material or ideal goods. In such conditions, formulating a two-power conflict in ideological terms will be as much an ego-safeguarding as an equilibrium-supporting way of assuaging anxieties aroused by one's own and the rival's expansionisms. Ideology converts a shared predicament, the deepening insight into which might paralyze will, into matching stimuli to pugnaciousness armed with good conscience. Such a way of defining the stakes will be most pronounced at major transition points within or between systems, when inexperienced powers find it useful in an untested setting to melodramatize their conflict as one that pits right against wrong and good against evil.

The record of unevenly rigid containment strategies and unequally tight encirclements can be traced to the long-simmering competition between Athens and Corinth within the partially autonomous maritime-commercial sphere of the Greek state system. The contest triggered the Peloponnesian War when Corinth responded as she did to the threat of being invested within an Atheno-Corcyran naval ring and cut off from the vitally important western Mediterranean sphere. Henceforth, it became essential for Corinth to expand both the scope of conflict (by bringing in Sparta) and to absolutize it in ideological terms (as a crusade against Athenian democracy-cum-imperialism). Less specific and dramatic were the consequence of a later attempt by eastern Rome, early in the seventh century AD, to muster barbarian Avar power for a concentric attack on Sassanid Persia, although it served well neither of the civilized powers just before Islamic might erupted into the area of vital concern to both. Nor was either party decisively favored in early Europe when an ideologically defined contest over primacy was intensified by the Holy Roman Emperors trying to encircle the Roman Popes in Italy while being themselves subject to outflanking in Europe at large.

Decisively climaxing in the sixteenth and early seventeenth centuries, the protracted – multi-phase and pluri-regional – East–West conflict on land and sea between the Spanish and the Ottoman empires was one wherein more fully consolidated actors proved capable of discounting ideological rationalizations in favor of real, world-power, issues and strategic rationality. Intermittent attenuations and eventual appeasement contrasted then favorably not only with the reciprocal excommunications and depositions employed in the Papal–Imperial contest but also with the alternating thrusts of conquest and reconquest in crusades and counter-crusades which had punctuated an earlier Christian–Moslem confrontation along the West–East axis beginning with the eleventh century.

The expansive Habsburg power – centered on Spain and the Netherlands in the west and on Austria in the east – clashed with an Ottoman expansionism that had been initially propelled north-westward into Europe from Anatolia by the dynamics of the religio-political contest with (Shi'ite) Persia. When convergent expansions in space turned into strategic entanglement, Spain's priority concern with France in the west impeded the Habsburg forward defense in the Mediterranean while communal and social cleavages in central and south-eastern Europe were making the Ottomans' continuing expansion overland and implantation in the Balkans easier. Although the Spanish and, later, the Austrian Habsburgs experimented with an outflanking alliance with

Persia and the Ottomans responded with token gestures toward France and the Dutch rebels in the west and the German Protestants in the center, and each may have dreamt at one time or another of colluding with actual (Moriscos) or mythical (Christian) co-religionists in the other's midst or rear, neither side was either willing to incur the costs and risks or able to garner the rewards of a defensively–offensively motivated tight encirclement. It was at least as important that neither the maritime-Mediterranean nor the continental-Balkan halves of the Habsburg-sponsored arc of containment were either inflexible or designed to be impermeable. Instead, Spain's forward positions in Italy and in North Africa were part of a flexible defense strategy in depth, often spearheaded by an ambivalent Venice but always backed by the totality of Spanish power; nor was the Balkan land front conceived and constituted differently by the Austrian Habsburgs. Exposed positions in space were bartered against time when being yielded to the adversary in either the maritime sphere – thus Tunis next to Venetian Cyprus – or on the land front – thus parts of Hungary; at the same time, coastal strong points and reinforced towers in one arena and light fortifications in the other impeded too easy, while blunting too forward, Ottoman penetrations.

Intermittent fighting along porous boundaries fostered interpenetration conducive to the maturing of reciprocal perceptions. As superior Ottoman military efficacy began to be offset by superior western military technology, the alien eastern adversary appeared less demonic because more surely defeasible. Tactical and strategic flexibility within both theaters and principal fighting oscillating between them combined to erode the conflict before the main front shifted from the western maritime to the eastern continental sector in the aftermath of the more symbolic than strategically decisive Ottoman naval defeat at Lepanto. Promoting meanwhile the progressive subsidence in depth had been a stalemate again only symbolized by the successful defenses of Malta in the west and Vienna in the east and due about equally to growing logistical and technological inhibitions and sociopolitical weaknesses in the arrangements that had previously fueled and financed the Ottomans' *élan*. Even before this would happen, however, it mattered that the Hispano-Ottoman phase of the contentious East–West interplay had remained confined despite the fact that the initial gravity of the Ottoman threat to the forward defenses of Spain proper raised the geostrategic and -economic stakes materially, as did the deeply felt ideological (Christian–Moslem) cleavage. Allocating all resources to combating the other principal in the ever-widening peripheries was thwarted by Spanish preoccupations with the Dutch rebellion and the French reascendancy in the system's center and by the equally crucial Turkish ones with the religio-political enemy in Asia Minor. There was, as a result, neither a single catastrophic explosion between nor a revolutionary sociopolitical implosion within the contending parties – a consequence delayed, in Spain, to the climactic phase of conflict with France and the maritime powers.

The obverse development took place in the Papal–Imperial and the Habsburg–French conflicts – as well as, subsequently, within a more markedly triangular-to-pentagonal setting, in the Anglo-German even more than the Anglo-French contention.

Containment strategies in both of the earlier conflicts aimed at tighter encirclements than was the case in the Hispano-Ottoman context. Reciprocal outflanking efforts were in evidence when the Popes sought to invest the Empire or only individual Emperors strategically, and the Emperors the Papal States if not also the Papacy, in areas north and south of the other party's power center conjointly with fomenting dissension and dissidence within its domain. Newly christianized kingdoms breaking away from obedience to the Empire had been but the first to serve papal purposes in the north, to be followed by either independence-seeking territorial German dukes or conquest-bound amphibian Normans and Aragonese, with designs on either an emperor's hereditary domain in Germany or the Empire's strategic spearhead in southern Italy. The parallel imperial ambition, and the Popes' nightmare, was for the Papal States to be sandwiched between emperor-controlled Lombardy and Tuscany in the north and Naples-Sicily in the south. Whereas the triumph of one would make a papal ward out of the Empire's foremost warrior, the other's success would demote the Vicar of Christ to the Emperor's chaplain. Fractious Roman nobility and anti-popes on one side, rebellious German dukes and papally designated rival emperors on the other, together with rival (Guelph and Ghibelline) factions mirroring the larger schism locally across Italy and parts of Europe, were the prime instruments in the strategies of mutual subversion eventuating in the supersession of both.

The tighter encirclement of France by the Habsburg domains, beginning early in the sixteenth century, was due about equally to fragile outflanking alliances (including the matrimonially backed one with England) and precarious conquests (Italy), to chancy inheritance and "free" elections (to Roman Emperorship). Thus to aggregate territories around the French hexagon was no less unbalancing for being either accidental or wholly legitimate, and it did not illustrate any less the disruptive consequences of a strategy responding reflexively to the quantifiable and misjudging the qualitative facets of system structure.

Ideo-culturally disparate Hispanic and Ottoman parties progressed toward subsidence through a measure of pre-decline convergence, fostered by the mid-course perception of stakes as secular-hegemonial rather than religio-millennial. By contrast, the tighter mutual encirclements acted to polarize rivals issuing from a common spiritual or moral universe and inchoately constitutional order: broadly speaking Christian-hierarchical in the Papal–Imperial contest with a focal point in Rome, and imperial-Carolingian in the Habsburg–Valois (and, subsequently, –Bourbon) contest with its main battle line drawn along the ethnic Franco-German frontier. Both conflicts expanded in space, escalated as to stakes, and strained the spirits as the two heads of Christendom fought over predominance and as French statecraft tried to both loosen and counteract Habsburg encirclement by either diplomatic or military strategies in south (Italy) and north (Netherlands and – so long as the British Isles were a potential link in the encirclement chain – Scotland), east (allies in Holy Roman and Ottoman Empires) and west (Catalonia). And whereas the Papal–Imperial contest grew more absolute in doctrines and universal in claims even as revealing the rivals' real concerns legitimized wholly secular actors, the secular

French and Habsburg contestants were debased relative to the emergent mercantilist-capitalist powers when dynastic preeminence in Europe was overshadowed by more concrete overseas assets, including the domains of the defunct Spanish branch as the critical stake.

Even before conflicts between continental and maritime-commercial powers succeeded to the earlier kind of contests, the mode of waging the latter had proven inferior to the flexible strategies which, ranging across space, had extended the Ottoman–Habsburg conflict long enough in time for it to slacken through intermittent détentes and diversions into partial accommodations. Actual or threatening hostile encirclement engendered more than usual psychic stresses and material costs, regardless of how assertively self-induced it had been; it exacerbated physical and political energies next to exalting ideological or quasi-ideological convictions, regardless of whether coercion was actual, attempted, or imagined. The pressures could be relieved only when emotions and energies were released in violent explosions, in the guise of periodic clashes of arms between actors, or implosions, manifest in climactic convulsions within the parties. Then the forces behind the schisms internal to the Papacy and the Emperorship equaled in their effects those responsible for feudal-confessional or regional-separatist revolts, in that the disintegration of the universal Church under the impact of sectarian reform and of the universal Empire in favor of territorial particularism merely preceded the crisis of monarchical authority, in France at the hands of a largely heretical aristocratic Fronde and in Spain under the impact of fiscally resistant Catalan and Portuguese rebellions. And if both sets of crises merely prefigured in cause and context the French and German sociopolitical revolutions linked to struggles over world power, the more strictly secular one was secreted in large part by the ways of enacting the contentious Franco-Habsburg polarity.

The emergence of third parties is especially notable when their strengths are germane to stakes that reflect intervening changes in the arena. They will invariably disperse a two-power into a three-cornered conflict, but will not necessarily defuse it as both the conflict and the parties to it have been meanwhile demoted from salience. For such an event to appear imminent is the most reliable single impetus to a more than transient and superficial accommodation between two original contestants. However, the same conditions that make the accommodation possible are also unlikely to make it feasible in time sufficient to ensure a continuing preeminence of the (former) rivals.

Before the conflict has been dispersed into a tripartite one, the polar relationship will have made the gain of each party appear as a liability for the other; and so long as it is difficult to define and impossible to negotiate the conditions of parity in capabilities and access, role and status – and thus equal security or a matching share in supremacy – even but a partial or provisional accommodation will depend on the presence of objective conditions and subjective dispositions required for a more complete accord. The original basis and zest for the rivalry will begin to erode only when the parties' strategic interests and initiatives diverge sufficiently to offset the initial conflict-generating effect of converging thrusts, and when convergence in institutionalized methods and attitudes the continuing conflict has engendered modifies initial disparities. Yet when conditions favorable to accommodation finally do take shape, the fact that a simultaneously emerging third party which is strong enough to threaten both rivals is also sufficiently attractive to tempt either into cooperation or alliance against the other will tend to frustrate positive dispositions. This is serious because the greater is the discrepancy between conditions and dispositions at the critical juncture, and the more ambiguous becomes the relation between the different kinds of convergence and divergence in an indecisively protracted conflict, the more significantly will strategies toward the third party affect a process of accommodation that is as untidy as its product is likely to be precarious. It will matter decisively whether the strategy weakens or fortifies a simultaneous awareness of common perils, not least because it stimulates or mutes the tendency (and, if not tendency, temptation) to aggravate ideologically the last stages of a conflict over inherently finite, contingent, and composable stakes – a trap about as much eluded by Spain and Turkey in relation to third-party threats as fallen into by France and Spain relative to the Maritime Powers.

Insofar as readiness and reluctance to accommodate with the principal adversary alternate in function of momentary setbacks and successes, they are the tactically inspired operational expressions of all the other strategy-related paradoxes and structure-reflecting dilemmas that impede timely conflict resolution. They constitute the visible tip of the massive iceberg on which eventually founders more than one ship of state. For reasons such as these, Sparta's offer to Athens of joint hegemony in Greece while hurting from the strategic defeat at Pylos was as lastingly unproductive as was the mere truce achieved at mid-term in the wake of partial Athenian reverses in the same (Peloponnesian) war; nor was Sparta's offer to expansively democratic and imperialist Athens repeated to the more Sparta-like oligarchical Athenian regime which had emerged from the defeat of the imperial democracy. The impact of the actual or anticipated fortunes of war will be even more frustrating when accommodation with the foreign adversary becomes an issue in domestic power struggles. Thus, although the most traditional-conservative party in Sparta continued to favor composition of the issues making for the war even after the similarly disposed Athenian conservatives had fallen from power, it failed to prevail against its domestic rivals' backing for the radical demands on Athens put forward by Sparta's differently interested allies. In a later context, the question whether to compose in depth with France at the price of scaling down punitive peace terms was caught up in the more complex Tory–Whig rivalry in England, at key junctures (1713 and 1763) of the last major two-power contest free of extreme ideological overtones.

Sparta as the former hegemon in the Persian War was on balance more accommodation-prone than still-ascendant England in the eighteenth-century global wars, but not too differently from a later, twentieth-century Britain. This fact suggests that tactical motives for adjusting differences will be strengthened, albeit with uncertain results, by a more fundamental disposition to reduce the costs of ascendancy. The mature power has good reason to compose a rivalry before wasting its diminishing resources in a foredoomed effort to go on occupying the top in a state of superb exclusiveness if not also splendid isolation. Not the least reason is that its well established legitimacy translates for a time into the capacity to legitimate the aspiring adversary, and the conferral of prestige can translate into a relatively low cost of the composition. However, the equations will work out less neatly in the real world. Thus the ever-changing imbalances in immediate tactical advantages and uneven degrees of longer-term institutional maturation kept the Popes and Emperors in contentious ferment, contrary to the Gelasian doctrine of desirable condominium. Imperial ascendancy as fact (thus Charlemagne's) or fiction (Henry IV) differed as much from the norm as did papal supremacy as practicable pretension (Innocent III) or theoretical pretense (Gregory VII, Boniface VIII). No more prudently implemented than the vision of concord by the early medieval Pope had been the calls for a united Byzantine–Persian stand against the barbarians in late antiquity. It proved as impossible to have the papal and imperial wielders of the two swords combat in unison either the secular or the spiritual threats to both as it had been for the last surviving "two lighthouses" of ancient civilization to target the dimming beam of each so as to disclose the impending Islamic menace at their intersection.

The Popes and the Emperors achieved only temporary truces and opportunistic alignments even when faced jointly by threat to their moral credit, to the Christian religion (Islam), and to their universalist pretension ("national" and territorial actors). Much the same was true for France and Spain when, still in fighting trim, they shared challenges to their fiscal solvency (war costs), Catholic orthodoxy (Protestantism), and both status and role primacy (the Maritime Powers). By contrast, a still combat-capable as well as contentious Spain abstained from exploiting the naval victory at Lepanto (1571) by a move against Constantinople and veered instead seaward to combat the rising capability and threat of the Protestant north-west in the Channel and the Atlantic (pending resumed contest on land with resurgent France), while the Ottomans were turning south-east toward the Red Sea and the Indian Ocean and either north against coincidentally weakened Russia or east against still dangerous Persia.

As the Spaniards were adapting functionally to the enlarged naval arena and the Ottomans were being diverted inland from the maritime (Mediterranean) sphere, the divergence in strategic thrusts, more conspicuous on the Spanish side, was reinforced by converging development in mainly the Ottomans' politico-administrative structures – their apparent decline and decay being at first mainly a descent from a specifically oriental-despotic efficiency to contemporaneously conventional fiscal-administrative practices, accelerated by the gradual intrusion of the hereditary principle. Spanish Turcophobia and distorted perception of Islam were simultaneously being muted by the developing sense of shared dependence on strategic rationality for waging a protracted contention that fluctuated within a shrinking band of possible success – or failure. Finally the more aroused the Sunni Ottomans were against Shi'ite Persians and Catholic Spain against the Protestant maritime powers, the less keenly could either experience the idiosyncracies associated with the Christian–Moslem cleavage. A likewise favorable impact of third parties was due to the economic conditions which, although on balance expanding in the sixteenth and early seventeenth centuries, did not preclude mutual weakening of the contenders relative to the most spectacularly profiting third parties. When the several inducements to accommodation peaked coincidentally with the material decline and cultural flowering of both parties, world politics had already ceased being centered on the two oversized empires in favor of closer-knit middle-sized powers (typified by France and England) as the more authentic successors and enlarged analogues of the Italian city-states. Lesser powers can stimulate and perpetuate a two-power contest as part of promoting their particular interests and/or pursuing centrifugal drives under the safeguarding shelter of major-ally protection: witness the opposition of Sparta's smaller allies to the mid-course peace with Athens. Or, acting as a third force, they may foster temporary relaxation of major-power conflicts for fear of total victory by either contestant: witness the posture and influence of the still secondary kings of France and England in the thirteenth-century climax of the Papal–Imperial contest (and the later Venetian role in the Spanish–Ottoman contentions). Proto-nationalist societies in south-eastern Europe were for comparable reasons influential in impelling the Austrian Habsburgs and the Ottomans toward détente on the basis of status parity (expressed in reciprocal recognition of the rulers as emperors). However, whereas the conflict-moderating effect of a third major power may be strategically profound and lasting, witness Spain's concern over France when facing the Ottomans, that of lesser third-force elements will tend to be less so, witness the but temporary appeasement of the Franco-Habsburg contest over Italy (in mid-sixteenth century at Cateau Cambrésis) out of concern over then still inchoate Protestant forces abhorrent to both parties.

By the time the Austrian line had replaced the Spanish branch of the Habsburgs as France's chief continental adversary, the impact of Britain and Prussia as third major powers was equally frustrating for the till then hereditary enemies. It induced them to proceed over nearly half a century from tentative approaches (after 1713) to full alliance (in 1756), without eliminating reciprocal watchfulness over parity of profits from the "diplomatic revolution." However, whereas the earlier détente (at Cateau Cambrésis) responding to a diffuse threat had been from the start superficial and lasted too brief a time, the entente came typically too late to have its desired effect. Well before it materialized, the rise of the Maritime Powers in the aftermath of the Elizabethan consolidation had made France's contest with the Spanish Habsburgs (over the Anglo-Dutch sector) obsolete in a henceforth markedly multipolar situation. The effects of these changes made the accommodation between France and the Austrian Habsburgs as insufficient to reverse the intervening displacement of the center of gravity to outside the continent as to forestall its subsequent migration eastward on the mainland. By distracting and exhausting the chief contestants, the Franco-Habsburg contention had created once again the shelter under which the United Provinces and, with more marked effect and lasting consequence, the United Kingdom could undergo the revolutionary upheavals antecedent to their assuming a commanding position in the newly dynamic world economy with determining effect on national power. Just as the mutually destructive contest between parties to the sacral–secular schism had shifted the focus to the East–West (Turco-Spanish) cleavage, by removing the Holy Roman Empire as an effective buffer or moderator, so the moral and material exhaustion of Spain and France's failure to maximize her geo-economic assets by concentrating on more future-relevant pay-offs speeded up the transition to (increasingly uneven) contests between the non-mercantile autocratic and essentially continental powers and the chiefly maritime oligarchic-cum-capitalistic polities as the system-dominant conflict issue.

The fact that the Habsburg–Ottoman duel had engendered a less thorough and traumatizing transformation was at least as much due to the way it was conducted (elastically, without tight mutual encirclement, and intermittently, with lengthening interludes of deepening détentes) as to the direction in which it faded (toward peripheries in south-eastern Europe from a Mediterranean that was itself becoming eccentric). Conversely, the antiquity-terminating conflicts of western and eastern Rome with the "Germans" and Persia yielded the most catastrophic inheritance, and the correspondingly cosmic task of actually constructing an order-capable state system from overripe "civilized" and underdeveloped "barbarian" constituents. The mutual enfeeblement of Athens and Sparta produced an only seemingly lesser evil for an ongoing system on the verge of being superseded by larger outside forces. The outcome was not to be averted by either the immediate or the later third-party beneficiaries, the Persian Empire or the indigenous would-be hegemons such as Thebes, and could not be repaired by efforts of the somewhat revived initial contestants – a state of things not wholly unlike that in post-World War I Europe after the first Anglo-German hegemonial conflict. The later Italian micro-system – and, subsequently, the globally dwarfed nineteenth-century European macro-system polarized by rival alliances – displayed other system-perturbing consequences of the failure to accommodate a two-sided conflict when comparatively (if only potentially) stronger third powers loom outside the core-system. The threat from the outside power or powers to the position of the prime actors will commonly seem too remote to influence their conduct and compel their accommodation, just as pressures from strategically if not otherwise interposed lesser powers or forces will have been too unfocused and its source too peripheral to the main concerns of the principals to alter mutually self-destructive orientations – and self-demoting outcomes.

It follows that strategies will disrupt (and thus reshape) structures by failing to fit their qualitative (schism- and rise/decline stage-related) attributes (with the result of fostering a crises-propelled system evolution), just as the momentary state of narrowly quantitative structure (confined to the spatial distribution and configuration of material capabilities) will determine (i.e., shape) strategies more commonly than adequately (with the result of the strategies failing to maintain the "motivating" structure unchanged, and disrupting it instead in due course). Over the lifetime of the European system, the way of conducting the Papal–Imperial conflict was initially productive in that it secreted inchoate, and disengaged farther-developed, secular architects of a multi-power system-to-be, around a France physically best equipped to benefit from the dominant schism and institutionally best suited to fuse the overlapping sacral and secular facets of the schism in her ruling formula. Once the Spanish–

Ottoman conflict helped regenerate a factionally weakened later France, her conflict with the Habsburgs moved the system in two, Spanish and Austrian, phases past its initial secularization and multipolarization to mid-career institutionalization – as one not only routinely flexible but also open to a basic (in diplomatic terms revolutionary) reversal of traditional alignments. However, by advancing the relative standing of the Maritime Powers, the contest was instrumental in propelling the system past developing (multiple) structure to a radically expanded (global) scope as part of a qualitative redifferentiation (along the continental–maritime duality). Thus, the direct or immediate consequences of the failure of the temporarily preeminent would-be universal actors to retain a measure of joint control over the processes of change could be largely positive from the vantage point of the system's growth (as distinct from the combatant parties'). Only later and indirect negative effects (e.g. the religious wars) could be traced back to the decay of both the papal and the imperial universalisms and the opportunistic relations between a secularized-territorialized Papacy and the principal Catholic powers that followed. In the correspondingly affected later phase, the strategies applied to conflicts originating in the maritime–continental duality proved ever more costly as their continental fulcrum moved eastward. Value-laden East–West antagonisms infiltrated then essentially material-pragmatic stakes even before a partially consequent return to a denatured sacral–secular duality helped precipitate the very end of an autonomous European system.

Whatever the circumstances – thus, in seventeenth-century Europe, when the pattern of unevenly maritime and continental states of global reach or ambition began to replace only loosely interlinked two-power conflicts of mostly regional scope – the dispersion of significant capabilities to at least three major and continuously involved powers will have two direct consequences. One is to multiply the number of potential principal parties to either conflict or accommodation. This will facilitate accommodation by means of separate-peace transactions, but also intensify conflict when any two parties concert warlike pressures on a third party. The other consequence is that the schism-related qualitative differentiation will expand to include an intermediate condition or identity for the third party, one most conspicuously representative of the schism-constitutive overlap between the polar attributes. More graphically than the East–West and the sacral–secular schism, the land–sea power schism entails such a threefold differentiation when space is configured along a continuum from primarily insular-maritime via intermediate amphibious (or would-be amphibious) to wholly continental (or rear-continental) actors. When the structural makeup has been thus complicated, it will exhibit to the full the schism-related tendency to simplify strategic choices: it will affect the probability and prospects of alternative strategies insofar as the more unlikely becomes accommodation between the natural rivals, the insular and the amphibious power, the more (if unevenly) likely will be alignments between either of the two and the rear-continental state.

The determinative effect of the geo-functional spectrum and related schism on the probabilities and prospects of alternative strategies-implementing alignments reflects the peculiar character of the land–sea power schism. In its physical-geographical features it is closest to the material capability- and areal scope-centered character of the basic, schism-neutral, structure. Yet it alters the latter's effect on strategy most profoundly and distinctly. And it is so influential because, while radically distinct from the other two schisms, it also tends to comprehend or comprise them. This has been frequently the case before, during, and after the Eurocentric era, with significant and not necessarily positive consequences for the balancing process and the related balancer function, whenever the insular–continental spectrum coincided with the west-to-east spectrum geo-culturally and with the range from secular-societal to (quasi-) sacral-statist tendencies and propensities institutionally and normatively.

CRYSTALLIZING TRIANGLES AND PENTAGONAL BALANCE

The most continuously exerted, systemically critical, and operationally "legiti-mate," role within the triangularized insular–continental spectrum in modern European history has been Britain's. The role emerged out of a multi-phase crystallization of the first land–sea power triangle that reinforced the favorable basic givens accounting for Britain's growing preeminence in the system. A sheltered insular location shielded against critical early risks the extraordinary stimulus to systemic involvement which, deriving from dynastic links with the continental arena beginning with William III and continuity through the Hanoverian Georges, made protection of their familial domains into a domestically vital task for British statecraft and resources. A strong economic base made up of agricultural and mineral assets (coal), characteristic of ancient empires, combined with mechanisms for credit-supported commodity production and exchange, typical of modern maritime-mercantile empires. A thus buttressed growing naval strength originated in a triad of so-called Dutch wars that did for England all that the three-phase Punic and Syrian wars had done for Rome in projecting a peripheral power from localism to and past regional preeminence.

With the Franco–Spanish conflict acting as both a precondition and the precipitant of their near-parallel rise, England and Holland as the so-called Maritime Powers consummated the differentiation of actor types only initiated by a Portugal which, although naval-technologically innovative and prominent, was not involved in the larger system diplomatico-strategically and, while economically enterprising, was in no way engaged or eminent politico-militarily. Furthermore, rather than any peace settlement, including the Westphalian, it was the wars attending the distribution of the newly differentiated actor types along a geo-functional spectrum that determined the shape of the modern state system as to a structure persisting and the strategies near-automatically unfolding thereafter. The functionally crucial differentiation of territorial actors by types was more important than their secularization provisionally resolving an obsolete (sacral–secular) schism; extending equilibrium interplays in spatial scope and capabilities-related dimensions by wars was more significant than institutionalizing equilibrium formally in the language of the peace treaty.

In marking the end of an era and the beginning of a new, the earliest Spanish–Anglo/Dutch–French triangle was seminal and, as such, neither consummate nor typical when opposing the insurgent maritime ensemble and the comparatively rear-continental and "eastern" France to a centrally located and systemically predominant amphibian Spain. Before assuming a significant role in the developing triangle, the island state had first to graduate from a land-bound protégé of Spain to a maritime predator on the Hispanic empire, and from a procrastinating participant in French assaults on the Dutch to their patron and protector against France; the peripheral auxiliary of the world-dominating Habsburg Emperor (Charles V) pretending to be the system's balancewheel (Henry VIII) had first to become the indispensable backer of another Habsburg's (Emperor-to-be Charles VI) ambition to inherit the remnants of dying Spain's world power. Fostered by the protracted decline of Spain, the rise was parallel with the inconclusive leveling off and reorientation of French power, and with the initially faster ascent but shorter ascendancy of the Dutch pivot in a transitional triangle – one including the not yet integrally maritime and oligarchical Restoration England of the last Stuarts and the no longer only continental-military France of Louis XIV and Colbert. However, for the first structurally and strategically complete and aerially global (Anglo–French–"Germanic") triangle to subsequently take shape, the initially critical Hispano–Dutch–French interplays had first to create, against the backdrop of the Habsburg–Ottoman contest, the sanctuary for land-bound England's first unobserved and then unstoppable emergence into the sea-dominant power of the Atlantic era. Thus also the Etruscan–Syracusan–Carthaginian contentions had attended the rise of Rome to west Mediterranean hegemony, and two successive triangular contests spearheaded by England (and centered on France and, subsequently, Germany) were to shield her eventual successor's.

Even as England moved up in the vertical hierarchy of states, the attendant transactions served to order the future protagonists into a continuous geo-functional spectrum on the horizontal, insular–continental, plane. Reciprocal threats and conflicting ambitions became more determinate as a result and latitudes for choosing alignments narrower relative to what they had been while Spain was both the principal naval and land-military power devoid of a maritime-mercantile ethos, and economically predatory rather than diplomatico-strategically preemptive Dutch and English claimants to maritime primacy were located physically and/or strategically between a still farther western Spain and a France which, though "eastern" and "rear-continental" within the critical north-western sector, was exposed to an Austrian–Habsburg realm more meaningfully such in both respects. Attending the complex and protracted transition from loosely interlinked two-power (Spanish–Ottoman and Franco–Habsburg) conflicts to the first fully developed (Anglo–French–Austrian/ Habsburg or –Prussian, and thus in either case "Germanic") triangle was thus a correspondingly fluid mix of traditional military-strategic and updated mercantile-economic concerns and motivations. The more straightforward passage to the next-following (Anglo–German–Russian) triangle highlighted instead the structurally secondary but strategically significant intervening differentiation between a smaller (initially Anglo–Dutch–French) triangle of western actors keyed to politico-economic issues and the larger triangle interacting globally over essentially politico-military issues with an increasingly eastern-continental focus (as Russia and/or Prussia were surfacing as first but the complicating background factors to the tripartite dynamic on a multi-power plane).

Whereas the decline of the Spanish Empire had released forces to be channeled into the "first" global triangle, the simultaneous Anglo–Dutch contest over the balance of trade and naval preeminence exhibited traits reminiscent of the struggles of Athens with Corinth and Venice with Genoa: Spain being in full decline (after the Franco–Spanish Peace of the Pyrenees in 1659) and France not yet resurgent (under an adolescent Louis XIV), pressures from the major continental powers on either contestant slackened even as the difference between the relatively liberal economic policies on the part of the dominant (Dutch) and the comparatively protectionist ones of the ascending (English) mercantile power grew in intensity. The contest was briefer and more intensely fought than had been the Mediterranean predecessors' not least because the two northern maritime-mercantile rivals' spheres of interest were not as clearly segregated along an east-to-west axis. Nor did potentially more significant similarities in religious faith and sociopolitical structures prevail over the material reasons for conflict. Institutionalized association, on the basis of English predominance, became possible only when the Dutch had ceased being able to act as a neutralist balancer after becoming the key target for a France which, reascendant on land (thanks to Louvois- and Vauban-type militarism), sought to keep abreast of the maritime-mercantile island state by absorbing the Dutch (by means of Colbert-type mercantilism).

At that point, the system-regulatory function passed from the Netherlands acting from strength between the two unevenly ascendant, insular and continental, rivals to their role in more complexly interrelated interplays within and between the two triangles: the smaller regional and in its essence or enactment primarily politico-economic Anglo–Dutch–French triangle, no longer system-dominant politico-militarily, and the central-systemic or global Anglo–French–"Germanic" triangle, allocating politico-military impact on the Anglo–French conflict alternately to the Austrian Habsburgs and Hohenzollern Prussia (the former reduced from the coveted succession to the best of the Spanish Empire to the economically sterile and politico-militarily onerous possession of the Spanish Netherlands, the latter raised by the conflict over the Spanish succession an important inch toward near-parity with Austria inside Germany). Within the smaller triangle the economically matured Dutch, de facto losers in the Spanish Succession War after being the real winners in its thirty-years-long antecedent, were reduced to consolidating an unequal association by investing in the only maturing English economy while trying to combine an important trade with, with safety from, France on land. Their ambivalence, not unlike the earlier one of Venice between Spain and the Ottomans, made the Dutch lean toward the continental neighbor on grounds of economic prosperity (save the French trade and fight the English competition) and toward the insular neighbor on grounds of physical security (against overland pressures inspired by Colbertian mercantilism inextricably intertwined with the Sun King's sense of majesty). Trying to remain neutral in Anglo–French wars was a way of repaying the English for their profitable aloofness from the earlier Netherlands-centered conflicts, while this manner of trying to regain some of the lost commercial terrain would unwittingly and did only marginally contribute to the system's politico-military equilibrium.

When a declining power ceases being a prime actor in the central-systemic or global triangle – thus amphibious Spain and the maritime Netherlands – it does not automatically and immediately cease being active in system-wide balancing of politico-military power. Moreover, if, like the Dutch (and, in due course, France and Germany), such a power assumes a crucial role in the principally politico-economic regional triangle, it adds a functional link to the structural connection between triangularized patterns of land- and sea-based power and a multipolar balance of power tending to be pentagonal. Such a power is then not only a fourth party alongside the three principals in the (next) global triangle, a matter of structure; it will also tend to become the protected ally of the dominant insular sea power and as such a principal instigator of its involvement in the system-wide balance of power, a matter of function. That involvement is in turn likely to play a key role in activating an additional, fifth when not a sixth, major power (e.g. next to newly royal Prussia also newly imperial Russia in the British context) on its way to becoming either central-amphibious or rear-continental party in a next- or later-following global triangle.

The structural and functional links between the two kinds of triangle and of these with the five-power plus balance of power make operationally manifest a problematic connection: between politico-economic concerns and determinants (prominent within the smaller-western triangle) and the politico-military ones (salient in both the global triangle and the total balance of power system). The connection is inherent in the meshing of land-based and sea-based capabilities and of the balance of politico-military power, delimited aerially, with the balances of trade clustering along linear commercial flows. However, whereas the specific character of actor capabilities will depend on whether agriculture, manufactures-based trade, or trade-stimulating industry is the main economic constituent of state power, the attendant economic stakes will be intertwined with military-strategic ones whenever access to and role in the network of trade and other economic ties are significantly related to concerns implicit in the actors' territorially implanted positions. They will be so related indirectly, when the mercantile-maritime party relates to a dominant land power as strategic adversary or ally (without any specific territory being immediately at stake, e.g. Athens and Corinth, respectively, to Sparta); more directly, when the land mass is the disputed medium of economically crucial access (e.g. the adjoining Italian mainland extending to southern Germany for Venice's north-bound trade); and most directly when (prior) control or conquest of territory is a preliminary requisite to extending economic ties (e.g. France's in the Netherlands and, more successfully, Britain's overseas) or a provisional alternative to such extension (e.g. Germany's in Middle Europe, as a stepping stone to economic world power). The connection will be integral as well as inextricable when all three aspects are combined in a situation.

However related the balances of (overseas) trade may be to the balancing of military-political power on land, the latter will finally crystallize only when actors have become able to consolidate territorial or territory-related gains, and must therefore be checked to prevent an inordinate expansion from continuing. By contrast, the more fluid maritime-mercantile environment is adverse to anyone either consolidating or directly countervailing the assets and advantages peculiar to it. Moreover, the balance on land gains from the reduction of both physical and psychological distance between actors, inasmuch as friction-inducing proximity both permits and impels the projection of power to be offset. By contrast, a sea power's superiority that negates maritime equilibrium rests commonly (while it lasts) on the power's capacity to master great physical distances and open wide functional gaps in technology or skills relative to lower-ranking maritime powers. And whereas deliberate balancing shifts on land from instinctual reflex to intelligent and intelligible rationales as actors consolidate, confining or replacing a dominant mercantile-maritime power less prone to dissolve because of overextension in space or overdependence on an individual's longevity is different. It will be the result not so much of rationally conceived and implemented efforts or instinctual reflexes as of incrementally working productive and distributive routines. Therefore, a maritime-mercantile actor will be most vulnerable to its constituent skills or techniques being diffused as it exercises its superiority, while the diffusion-attending imitations will be commonly compounded by rival innovations in first narrowing and then eliminating the technological or functional gaps that had originally constituted the most pertinent species of distance.

The capacity to consolidate gains, resisted for fear they might cumulate to the point of becoming irresistible, replace dissolution-prone structures in fostering equilibrium and related expectations in a maturing territorial power field. The virtually self-liquidating devolution of assets and skills will, by contrast, only follow the otherwise hard-to-surmount superiority of the favored maritime actor being augmented by the benefits incidental to one-power sea control, sufficiently valued by parties other than the foremost rival to inhibit containment and promote the tendency to near-monopoly. Finally, the analytically distinguishable differences in operations breed differences in the normative assessments of the comparative legitimacy of one-actor superiority and inter-actor stalemate in the two arenas, rooted in the diversity of factors that make for the unevenness of the parties.

In the maritime-mercantile arena, the factors that differentiate actors comprise, next to geopolitically determined latitude and internal sociopolitical cohesion, the comparative advantage in naval techniques and economic transactions. Since the diversity of the positional, technological, and functional characteristics fosters volatility and competition, but not an automatically self-correcting inter-actor equilibrium, any measure of stability will tend to be shorter- rather than longer-range as bigger fish eat smaller fish and a nascent outcompetes an obsolescent economy. By contrast, the fundamental differences among parties to the territorial balance of politico-military power are broader-based organic rather than technological or functional in nature. They are disclosed less in specific skills than in the stage of evolution of the actors, manifest in foreign-policy postures keyed to expansion or conservation if not virtual withdrawal from competition. In a multi-power system, the rise–decline dynamics and the attendant distribution of waxing and waning powers at least equals in importance the impact of the disparities between land-military and maritime-mercantile powers, because both types are at bottom territorial actors. But the typological will become more critical than the evolutionary-stage factor in the core relationship of unevenly maritime and continental powers, insofar as all three will be typically if unequally rising when the triangle is being formed and be eventually if serially declining as it is being replaced by the next following one.

When self-consciously conservative powers counteract actors either spontaneously or defensively assertive in a matured system of several near-equal powers, a thus dovetailing pattern of actor dispositions will combine dynamism with stability. And the ensuing equilibrium will be best suited to shifting operational salience from military to diplomatic and economic transactions clustering around a power "liberally" prominent in both spheres. Such a rare condition prevailed in mid-nineteenth-century Europe. It differs not only from a volatile equilibrium containing forcible upheavals but also and principally from two extreme situations: (1) instability built into a system wherein most actors are declining and tend toward precluding the consequences of their decline by policies that either rigidly inhibit change or are themselves compulsively expansionist (late nineteenth to early twentieth century); and (2) an only accidentally deadlocked stalemate among actors most or all of whom are rising (up to seventeenth to eighteenth century) and as such incline toward either objectlessly expansive or wide-rangingly exuberant policies implementing an essentially predatory expansion.

A related difference between the two analytically, and oftentimes actually, distinct equilibrium arenas bears on transfers of primacy and changing pluralities. Unevenly deliberate operational checking and balancing fosters the organic rise of ever newer and retards the decline of comparatively longer-standing members of the overall system most of the time. When erosion or catastrophe has diminished the numbers all the way to two, this will restart the growth of numbers through competitive actor-generation, whereas intra-empire disintegration will achieve the same consequence. Conversely, the positional, technological, and functional bases of unevenness among actors peculiar to the maritime-mercantile arena make it more likely for superiority to rotate from actor to actor than for major-power status to be dispersed among several incumbents. But just as unavoidable diffusion of assets and capabilities over time does not generate dispersion of role-and-status at any one moment in time, so relative absence or inefficacy of deliberate containment does not guarantee conservation of primacy or near-monopoly.

Whether fought as irrelevant by the leading naval or fought for as equitable by the foremost continental power, a system-wide multi-functional equilibrium would comprise both territorial or continental and maritime or oceanic, politico-military and politico-economic, dimensions. The distinctive norms and tendencies peculiar to the two disparate arenas will always condition actual behavior and be often dramatized in declaratory policies. However, if it is critical for the way the balance of power operates whether and how the actors' unevenly phased foreign-policy postures dovetail, it is no less crucial whether and how the two disparate arenas overlap because action in one impinges on the other. Interpenetration occurs most strikingly when the requisites and stimulants of a sustained, deliberate or automatic, balancing process have been so fully met as to create a stalemate at the core of the continental arena, with the result that compensating stakes of competition and rewards of success have to be sought in the peripheral, including overseas, environment. At that point, the material capability factors which make land- and sea-based resources inseparable are reinforced by a transactional systemic factor. The material condition was met in Europe under the impetus of early or pre-mature capitalism and an expanding world economy; the systemic one was (as is habitual) met when late-maturation of both the system-founding actors and the system itself coincided with the operational if no other contraction of the system at its center.

Ongoing conflicts will complicate the connection between the two arenas when they do not reliably indicate the "real" or "ultimate" strategic object or concern for either type of actor: periphery-based prosperity or central system-related security. Does a thrust at the center aim at enhancing prosperity through gains at the periphery, or a periphery-related strategy indirectly aim at augmenting security at the center of the system? Such quandaries, and the resulting confusions, became increasingly dangerous for the Eurocentric system when late-entering powers were added to the dovetailing pattern of evolutionary states-related strategic postures among the original, or system-founding, members who had matured prior to the nineteenth century. As the number of stagnating or declining older major powers increased relative to the newly rising ones, and the margins of resource or resolution between them widened, the divergent trends compounded the destabilizing effect of disparities between the two arenas, under the influence of a weakening premier sea power (Britain) and an ascending preeminent continental power (Germany). Underlying the escalating Anglo–German conflict was then the habitual tension between two equally cardinal features or aspects of a multi-state balance-of-power system: quantitative near-equality of several principal actors as a matter of capabilities-reflecting structure, and the preeminence of one among them as a matter of role-implementing function. The only seeming contradiction will elicit all the more disruptive responses the more strenuously the dominant off-shore insular sea power protects its maritime superiority against the party preeminent in the territorial balance of politico-military power, and the more forcefully the latter bids for near-equality or parity in the all-systemic equilibrium comprising the maritime-mercantile plane.

A balance among several near-equal major powers can be the object of deliberate policies opposing a manifest would-be hegemony, but it will more frequently be the unintended consequence of policies incidental to waging particular lower-intensity conflicts. Coherence in such a conflictually enacted balancing and rebalancing of material capabilities will be enhanced when one of the players is foremost in capability and prestige and serves as the rallying focus of diplomatic interplays and the point of reference for the other actors: to wit, when one actor is preeminent in status and function, although not so markedly predominant or grossly preponderant as regards weight to qualify for coercive control. As a result, whereas dominance excludes recourse to actors outside the system boundary for redress of grievances in fact, preeminence does so in principle as a condition of preventing its degeneration into the opposite.

Seminal elements were present in the position of the kingly domain in France's early system of warring duchies, anticipated in the ritual-symbolic role of the Chou monarchy in China's system of warring states. On a larger scale, the institution and the related structural-functional compound took shape in Europe as the system evolved from the genealogical phase, with stress on status expressed in the matrimonial potential of a ruler within the extended family of dynastic lineages, to its geopolitical phase, making preeminence contingent on material capacity as the indispensable basis of role-related status. Serving as an intermediate evolutionary link, the Holy Roman Empire and Emperor were alternately preeminent in status only or also in role, and variably dependent for either or both on formal dignity only or material capability as well. The Empire thus pointed up a critical difference: between the position of a first among equals – a preeminent coequal – and an effective imperium over dependents; between hierarchy and hegemony – a difference illustrated in seventh-century BC China on the contrast between monarchical Chou and empire-founding Ch'in even better than by that between, say, Bohemia-based Charles IV and Charles V in fourteenth- to sixteenth-century Europe.

The superficial contrast between structurally (or quantitatively) crucial near-equality and functionally (or qualitatively) distinctive preeminence did not prevent the evolution toward both climaxing simultaneously in seventeenth-century Europe: even as equality was being approximated among several major powers, the France of Louis XIV could formally assert and be largely conceded preeminence as Spain's indisputable successor while the contrast between the two facets of equilibrium dynamics was almost simultaneously exacerbated into a conflict of principles between the disparate principals, France and England. The conflict polarized acutely the so far latent differences in rival conceptions of a legitimate, and perceptions of the requisites of an orderly, system of states. In regard to actors, the French (or Ludovician) principle and supporting policy were keyed to the concept of the "first monarch" and, thus, to vertical hierarchy encompassing *all* states. It contrasted and could not but clash with the English principle of the equality of the major *continental* states, aligned by position or policy along a horizontal spectrum of differentiated access and aspiration to maritime capability. With respect to the arena, the French principle and object of policy was one of homogeneity: it postulated as well as pretended to enforcing the identity of the continental and the maritime arenas as equally subject to the requirements of equilibrium. The English policy was keyed instead to heterogeneity being implicit in a fundamental difference between the two arenas: it postulated special needs and, thus, rights of the insular kingdom. The clash came to a head when the English insisted on command and control of the sea, tied directly and integrally to commerce and colonies by virtue of both material need and providentially conferred right; the rival French pretension was to wield the conductor's baton in the concert of powers, only contingently tied to overseas assets by virtue of the role's contemporaneously defined material requirements and attendant mercantilist-to-capitalist dynamics.

Rationalized by concern for the equality of continental powers as a value in itself, the insular sea power's opposition to the major land power's continental preeminence was in fact targeted at the anticipated effect of conceding the formal inequality on its own material superiority. A superiority sufficient to cope with safely established continental preeminence was at risk should the would-be amphibian be free to revise the allocation of national resources so as to translate continental preeminence into maritime equality (or, at least, a naval-mercantile capability sufficient to establish indisputable overall parity with the sea power). The premier insular-maritime and would-be amphibian continental powers may or may not have been always equally strong in their home base to permit movement toward a continental–maritime (or all-systemic) equilibrium to comprise parity overseas without producing a serious advantage for the land power. In any event, disparities in individual situations and related conceptions of the system were sufficient to make it more likely that each principal would target its strategies mainly against the asserted fact or feared prospect of the other's preponderance in his particular arena.

Under the circumstances, instead of fostering a unified equilibrium equally constraining for both types of actors, progressively more rigid and polarizing strategies pointed to "imperialism" in the maritime arena and "hegemonism" in the continental sphere while professedly guarding against either. On the face of it, the leading sea power's concern was to preserve its insular invulnerability by action on both land and sea in the face of the continental state's desire to either match the island's absolute security on land or else make the rival equally vulnerable on the seas and, consequently, in its insular fastness. But ultimately at issue was the question whether situational disparity or normative equivalence was to be operationally decisive between actors who, originating in an inordinate expansion of capability and control, remained nonetheless subject to the "laws" of competitive power dynamics. The answer to the query was being formulated while the premier insular-maritime power would, and Britain actually did, seek to constrain the capability or intention of the dominant land power, beginning with France, to consolidate its preeminence short of hegemony for the sake of pursuing overseas a compensation for the diminished gains to be won on land among stalemated near-equal actors.

The strategies of the two main parties to the land–sea power schism and global politico-military triangle will reflect the structural determinants, subject to the operationally crucial impact of the rear-continental state. But it will commonly be the declining third party to the smaller-western, only regional and mainly politico-economic, triangle that actually triggers the structurally conditioned conflict among the principals. Whereas defending such a party offers the sea power a legitimate occasion or legitimizing pretext for constraining the would-be amphibious land power, the protected party's commercial-naval-colonial assets present the continental aspirant with the option of winning material compensation for being stymied overseas on the mainland. And just as the major land power (first France, then Germany) will then have preferred the chance to assimilate critical assets ever so contentiously to combating the dominant sea power in its chosen element, so the cyclically recurring decline of a once key actor reduced to a place in the secondary triangle (first the Netherlands, then France) will have helped actualize latent disparities between the continental and maritime arenas into open conflicts between actors embodying the corresponding types of power. The decisive role of the Dutch in involving England in the European balance of power against France was subsequently the latter's in the Anglo–German setting, while either power's ambivalence toward the British had mirrored a two-sided role and performance: as a weak if not the weakest link in the two-dimensional (politico-economic and politico-military) tripartite configuration and the principal detonating agent in both the two- and the three-power interactions within the insular–continental geo-functional spectrum. The two facets would collapse into one strategic effect when the dominant sea power has refused to allow the maritime-mercantile resources of the declining party, critical for the naval and/or trade balance, to fall under the control of the ascendant would-be amphibian by default or otherwise.

The triggering effect of the least self-dependent party to the smaller triangle highlights the special problem declining capability poses for the stability of a balance-of-power system, wherein ascending power gives near-automatically rise to an intrinsically problem-free countervailing response. The problem is aggravated when the conflict-triggering party vacillates between the insular-sea and the continental power as it enters successive stages of decline. Thus, after vacillating between France and England also as part of internal power struggles between oligarchy and monarchy, the Dutch clung reluctantly to England – only to revert to France amidst internal upheavals just before the French Revolution. Similarly, the last-stage reaction to the Revolution's inheritance produced in the right-wing French "appeasers" and subsequently "collaborators" an attempt to revive the precedent of alignment with the principal Germanic power in traditional opposition to England globally, as an alternative to the intervening and increasingly unequal alliance ties with Britain against Germany. Although the temptation to derogate from alliance with the dominant sea power against the would-be amphibious continental state to alignment with it applied also to other powers, including Habsburg Austria, the tendency will be most destabilizing when it affects declining powers (including post-Habsburg Spain) situated in a key position between the premier maritime state and an assertive amphibious actor. It will then coexist with other reasons for variously assertive and defensive policies of unevenly rising and declining states to fail to dovetail into a propitious impact on the balance of power dynamics. Among them are the conditions of success peculiar to the maritime-mercantile arena. They are such as to accelerate the visible rise and fall of the insular actors and thus complicate the task of evaluation and response. Moreover, the maritime arena will seem to supply the preeminent continental state with alternatives to painful adjustments of its systemic role to a diminution in home-based resources. Whatever its origins, a malfunction in the organic and operational facets of the rise–decline dynamic will intensify the systemic disturbance as its part-cause and part-consequence. However, even when mediated through the declining power or powers, the main disturbance will be consequent on a very special conflict between principals that have been unevenly ascending before one declines relative to the other and both relative to the role-substitute for each: between the insular sea power as the acclaimed arbiter in the continental balance of power, and the would-be amphibious land power as the alleged expansionist and aggressor – the former the supposedly impartial balancer, the latter the severally indicted aspirant to hegemony.

PROVIDENTIAL BALANCER AND PROBLEMATIC BALANCING

In order to become the arbiter of the continental balance of power, England did not have to be a unique creation of the land–sea power schism and geo-functional spectrum. As a power insulated from a multi-power mainland, she stepped into the role desert-shielded Egypt had once occupied relative to the Mitanni, Hatti, Assyrian, neo-Babylonian and Medan or Persian land powers in succession. As a settled sociopolitical order embodying a mercantile-maritime civilization she reoccupied the position of Byzantium relative to the land-bound Goth, Frankish, Lombard and Hunnish barbarian war lords. And as a pretender to representing the transcendental principles of order and equilibrium (and, if only implicitly and contingently, peace) against the basely territorial and endemically contentious elements, England resumed the nominally arbitral role of the Papacy in relation to secular monarchies: sea power replaced spiritual power as both higher and more disinterested than its opposites. Collecting in her hands the different strands, England reproduced not only the aspirations and advantages of the antecedent arbiters and/or balancers, but also the ambiguities attached to the role even when she did not aggregate their separate failings.

Having risen to prominence conjointly with a successful revolt against the Papacy and its Catholic allies-antagonists, England reproduced the Holy See's immunity to total destruction by conquest. The secular strength of both lay more in finance than in force; where one could debar the transgressor from salvation by excommunication, the other could attack his solvency by exclusion from overseas trade. Strategically, both benefited from position at a nodal point: between south and north for the Papacy (continental Germany and semi-maritime Italy cum Sicily), east and west for Britain (continental Europe or Eurasia with adjoining seas and the Atlantic). And, like the British, so also papal influence stood highest when temporarily successful efforts to either sever or control the rival's connection between the two geographic sectors translated into dominance in the critical schism. Thus, if Pope Innocent III (and his immediate successors) broke the connection of the last Sicily-based Germanic Hohenstaufens (Frederick II and successors) with Germany, Britain uprooted France's implantation in both the western and the eastern hemispheres after successfully challenging the Dutch primacy in connecting one or both zones with the Baltic. However, the British consolidated their dominance in the mercantile-maritime sphere by military-political balancing only after shedding the results of an initial expansion onto the continent. The papacy compromised irreparably its standing as either secular arbiter or spiritual judge by becoming just one of the expansionist territorial princes in the Italian balance of power (and the technical aggressor in at least three out of seven warlike crises in its climactic late-fifteenth-century spell).

As alleged or aspiring balancers, the popes did not side with weaker against stronger powers at all times any more than did their secular counterparts among the maritime or insular powers: thus whereas Venice backed the conquering Charles VIII of France or England's Henry VIII sided with Charles V, and Elizabethan statesmen wavered between complex Spain and compact France, a later Britain vacillated repeatedly between France, Russia, and Germany as the actually or only potentially stronger or weaker parts. Like any other balancer facing distracting interests and ambiguous information, the British found it difficult to decide whom to counterbalance in behalf of whom or what, for how long, and at what acceptable cost to themselves and advantage to the assisted party or parties. The confusing variety of factors only includes, next to relative strength and weakness of powers or their combinations, the differently crude distinction between aggressor and defender, disturber and upholder of the balance, and the equally elusive indices of rise and decline as an immediate, imminent, or delayed event.

Nor will the balancer's dilemmas be eased when lesser or merely regional naval powers such as, from England's viewpoint, Sweden and Denmark in the Baltic theater in the seventeenth century, and France or Russia in the Mediterranean in the nineteenth, had to be not only differentiated from already manifest or only emergent major contestants such as the Netherlands and France or Russia in the earlier period and Germany and the United States or Japan in the later, but also aggregated with them as objects of concern. Inescapably intertwined with the numerical and the quantitative will then be the qualitative rise–decline dimensions fraught with a shifting distribution of assertive and conservative foreign policies. The major maritime-mercantile state will have reasons to hesitate whether to countervail the ascending (fellow-) insular or the challenging continental power in defense of economic prosperity or physical security, before assigning priority to the naval contingent and homeland security tips the balance in favor of checking the continental state preemptively – and thus, often, inordinately or prematurely. Moreover, in a multi- as compared with a bipolar setting, a would-be amphibian land power lacking in robust maritime and reliable continental allies will strenuously uphold any ally regardless of its state and degree of decline – and do so longer with more destabilizing consequences than had the conflict not been shaped by the land–sea power schism. Thus amphibian France would not have so persistently sought to uphold declining (Bourbon) Spain in the eighteenth century had not the global contest with England made even the decrepit Spanish maritime capability of value. Nor would Prussia–Germany have assumed a similarly onerous stance *vis-à-vis* Austria–Hungary when in France's place, had not the naval-colonial contest with Britain made continental isolation wholly unbearable.

Such derangements distort what otherwise would be a balancing process among near-equal homogeneous powers within a uniform arena, wherein both the rise and the decline of an actor act as a beneficial stimulant. Then, an ascendant power will activate the balancing process in that it creates the need for a countervailing response as an alternative to the snowballing effect of preponderance, liable to degenerate into a stampede toward the seemingly irresistible conquering power. Conversely, a material decline of an actor will engender the impetus to sustain the weakening party unilaterally or collectively lest its deterioration set off a vortex effect, liable to pull the system down into a bottomless void of irreversibly cumulative disequilibrium. Moreover, as a counterpart to such impulses from anticipated results of equilibrium dynamics, alliance policies will help regulate the rise–fall fluctuations. Thus, the institutional attributes and material assets associated with an alliance will be often compounded to accelerate the effect of the organic factors that had sustained the initial rise of a power: co-optation into role and status anticipates then upon actual or inherent capability. Alternately, alliance policy can constrain if not the momentum then the manifestations of continuing growth at a later stage of ascent: fellow-allies will then contain the too successful partner within a role and status they can live with and, incidentally, the system can absorb. And finally, alliance resources can compensate for initial decline of actor: the alliance tie will then at least provisionally conserve the weakening power in a formal status that exceeds the role feasible materially, even as it serves to inhibit adventurous reactions to the weakening.

When, conversely, continental and maritime powers are exposed unevenly to containment, ultimate (if indirect) control over the equilibrium dynamics will gravitate from the principals to mostly weakened and declining third parties with inhibiting effects. Either or both of the chief rivals will feel compelled, not least by the problematic relation between one power's maritime near-monopoly and other power's even but marginal naval capability, to conserve the receding states well beyond their capacity to regenerate themselves or the requisites for re-equilibrating the system. Thus, just as previously France had clung to Spain and eventually Britain to France, so imperial Germany held on to Austria–Hungary and would have backed the non-viable monarchy less stubbornly could she have assumed British support or neutrality relative to France and Russia individually or in encircling combination – and had the altered British stance reduced the probability of a major continental war. From the British viewpoint, for France and subsequently Germany to diplomatically control the declining allies strengthened the appearance of a quest for continental predominance and made even moderate maritime ambitions doubly suspect. Any move by the ascending to acquire the sea-borne or overseas resources of the receding amphibious powers (Bourbon Spain's by France, France's by Germany) became sufficiently intolerable to guarantee British backing for their autonomy.

The existence of a power determined to maintain its naval superiority against a state intent on extending continental equilibrium to the seas will thus be at least partially responsible for the conditions on the mainland the self-same power has ostensibly set out to correct or contain. The insular power acts then as a balancer which, though located within the geo-functional spectrum, is functionally poised not so much between as above two individual actors or bloc of actors: the would-be amphibious state and its allies or clients as alleged unbalancers, and their opposition, typically consisting of the previously dominant maritime or amphibious power or powers and the not yet fully either ascendant or assertive rear-continental power. Conversely, when the less conspicuous struggle over the maritime sphere is between two mercantile parties, there will be no third-power balancer to arbitrate the issue between them on the seas or in the world's markets.

It is factors such as these that interfere, within a deliberately manipulated balance of power involving three crudely differentiated actors or actor categories, with the subtle schism-neutral tripartite interplays which near-automatically equilibrate an ideal-type system, distorting or delaying the interplays' effect in an actual one. When the structure of the system-wide balance of power divides in fact – or is analytically divisible – into a set of two-power relations between direct rivals, the state of equilibrium is typically the not so much accidental as unintended result of each party in the pairs having two concerns: not only to match or outdo the other party, but also to achieve the result without resorting to actions that would either markedly benefit or fatally alienate a third party in ways that would cancel, and to an extent that would exceed, the gain secured relative to the main second-party rival. Whether the third party to consider is a potential future adversary or a present ally, in neither case must it be inordinately aggrandized or unnecessarily antagonized in the process of dealing with the immediate threat; parity (or better) of gains (and liabilities) arising out of a successfully enacted conflict is as important with respect to third powers as is equality (or better) of capabilities with respect to the immediate adversary to be deterred or defeated.

Conscious concerns and apprehensions about third parties establish an otherwise missing link between actors' perceptions and policies and equilibrium-type arena product. They overcome the vast gap between actor response and ostensibly unintended system result in conditions that preclude a rational estimation of the "objective" requirements of equilibrium. The system would work ideally, if at specific costs, were the plural network of a variable number of two-sided (dyadic) structural patterns and capability ratios (two-power conflicts and balances), operating within tripartite (triadic) contexts of strategic reasonings and rationales (triangular conflict relationships), allowed to operate free of extraneous frictions. This will be the case least when the operation has been distorted by a relationship polarized, along the geo-functional spectrum, between an insular balancer and to-be-balanced continental party or parties, expansionist aggressor(s) and defender(s) of stability, while normative discrimination is foisted upon functional differentiation. Were this not so, the would-be amphibious continental party in the center would be better able and thus more likely to moderate its goals relative to both the previously dominant maritime or amphibious state, undergoing the first stage of decline, and the rear-continental state, engaged on an initial phase of ascent. It would have every reason not to create in relation to either a situation advantageous for the other, either by provoking an erosive and distracting conflict or by making the third party more receptive to joining an encircling alliance, under the auspices of the insular balancer.

Thus, had France and imperial Germany not had to anticipate an automatic

British opposition to their overseas ambitions, each had reason to avoid doing anything in relations with the other (receding or advancing) continental powers liable to expand the diplomatic options of the insular balancer after activating his involvement in the politics of the mainland. When the obverse occurred, it was also because the propensities and prejudices of the dominant sea power propelled the premier continental state into reactive or preemptive policies contrary to self-restraint. After an interlude of violent conflict, the destabilizing effect of the resulting immoderation could be only partially offset by the insular power actualizing its latent capacity to reduce either the gains or the leverages of its (continental) allies by entering into bilateral accommodation, including separate peace-making, with the continental challenger – an *ex post* corrective available to still-strong Britain *vis-à-vis* ancien-regime France but not to a weakening one relative to Germany. In this manner, the basic posture and the implementing activities of the insular-maritime state will have subverted the self-equilibrating potential of the multi-tripartite pattern of system dynamics, creating the need for its services as the ostensibly impartial balancer between warring continental factions.

The sea power's predilection for equating even but moderate continental preeminence with hegemonic drive, in preemptive defense of its own maritime superiority and as a means to mobilizing allies in the continental balance of power, is only one – subjectively strategy-relevant – basis for the resulting ironies. The other basis is objective and structural, and has more to do with the discrepancies between the two hard-to-separate arenas than with any independent dissonance or disequilibrium between any two continental actors or combinations of actors. Notably if the insular state's territorial resource base being inferior to the continental power's augments opposition to parity overseas further, the intrinsically weaker party will have little alternative but to dampen one and escalate another set of the constantly (even if latently) present two-sided conflicts within the multi-tripartite pattern in ways that focus attention on a one-actor threat from hegemony-bound aggression or expansion. Contrary to the resulting impressions is the fact that few continental states have aspired to hegemony as willful and unprovoked aggressors, and still fewer achieved it.

When overlarge power concentrations had ceased dissolving under their own weight, the presence of preemption in motivating expansive self-assertion made impulses such as those of France under Louis XIV and Germany under William II less than purely aggressive and boundless. For an insular-maritime balancer to ignore this and confuse assertion of diplomatic preeminence with militarily aggressive pursuit of dominance will be plausible in only two situations: one applies when the amphibious party impinges directly on a receding micro-system, as Assyria did in relation to Sumer, Macedon to Greece, and Spain to Italy. However, no balancer was in being, let alone effective, in those circumstances. The other is when all parties to a triangle are members of a multi-power macro-system, and the first-phase drive of an amphibian power to combine preeminence on the continent with oceanic or overall parity has been frustrated by the sea power. This was the situation in Europe between the seventeenth- and twentieth-century world wars, when Spain under Olivares, France under Napoleon, and Germany under Hitler, reached out for continental as a prelude to world-wide hegemony in the wake of their predecessors' failure to achieve the lesser objective.

If the insular sea power is to tolerate a land power's preeminence on the continent, that power will have to do better than merely renounce significant maritime ambitions, and will have to directly or indirectly subserve the sea power's stake in maritime near-monopoly. And it will have to do more than abstain from interfering with the mercantile power's commercial access to the continent, and apply its diplomatic weight there on the insular state's behalf. The latter will then cease to balance and will actually lean upon the preeminent land power in an effort to combine a dominant role in system-wide equilibrium with subdelegation of continental management: it will lower the continental sword supplied by secondary allies as it elevates the premier continental state to a diplomatic surrogate on the mainland. Thus Byzantium leaned on Theodoric's Ostrogothic realm within a roughly five-power barbarian proto-system (the Ostrogoths, the Visigoths, the Franks, the Burgundians, and the Vandals), and Britain was to draw on post-Utrecht France for support in the early eighteenth century (with respect to revisionist Bourbon Spain, Habsburg Austria, Russia, and Sweden) and lean on Bismarckian Germany within a later five-power continental system (France, Germany, Austria–Hungary, Russia, Italy). Just as Theodoric abjured all ambitions in the Mediterranean while keeping the ascendant Franks away from it, so defeated France under the Orleanist Regency renounced naval ambitions while seconding British interests in both north (mediating the Northern War) and south (against the Spanish Bourbons in Italy). As for Bismarck, he disclaimed designs on the Mediterranean-abutting Balkans and the Near East while long discouraging all acquisitions in the farther oceanic-colonial sphere, even as he pinned down France and Russia on the continent in ways limiting the scope of their maritime forays. The situation changed back to the norm of containment only when Byzantium transferred its favors from heretic Ostrogoths to the Franks, and first France's Cardinal Fleury and then Germany's Kaiser William abandoned their predecessors' naval abstention.

If the major land power's multiple self-denial will always be a condition of toleration for its continental preeminence, the sea power will restrain itself in the pursuit of all-out oceanic-colonial monopoly only occasionally. Its prime purpose will then be to remain effective in the continental balance of power, thus when Britain restituted some of her wartime conquests to allies in the wake of the Napoleonic wars.

Ideally, self-denial by the preeminent land power and self-restraint by the superior sea power would mesh into managing an all-systemic equilibrium in (unequal) association. More commonly, the sea power's actual attitudes and policies will invest it with a special kind of hegemony over a polarized continent. Only when the (quasi-) insular power – Athens in Greece, Venice in Italy, or Japan in Asia – has raised its aims on land beyond manipulation to domination will it itself become the object of countervailing. The sea power's more typical hegemony will be less effective than phantom-like because it is both unavowed and largely invisible; and the insular will be largely an absentee hegemon because his involvement in the continental balance will be always intermittent and for long periods unreliable (witness both ancient Egypt and modern England), a fact that makes him more tolerable. The hegemony will be intrinsically precarious and contingent inasmuch as the sea power's resources will be such as to typically require activating reserve power not only from within itself but also from within or without the system's boundary. If such a power is the rear-continental one, it will be sporadically tempted to join the would-be amphibian in an effort to expel the sea power from the continent; if it is a previously extra-systemic state, it will tend to displace the insular balancer functionally within a correspondingly enlarged system. Such displacement will expand the results of the maritime-mercantile power's liability to diffusion and dissipation as to resource, and offset somewhat the inherently more resilient land power's handicaps as to strategy.

Underlying the difficulty to coordinate actor goals and gains in the two disparate arenas in ways that derange routine balancing processes least was historically the near-impossibility to evolve a parity in land- and sea-based resources so long as equality on the seas spelled overall inequality. Whereas the equality would favor a land power possessed of a stronger or more readily expandable home base, the difficulty to define parity has tended to favor the sea power by legitimizing its stake in confining the balancing process to the continent. Consequent dilemmas have been aggravated by two additional circumstances. One is the seeming incompatibility between quantitative near-equality of several major powers and one-actor functional preeminence. How to orchestrate the two aspects will be especially problematic when the sea power's tendency to equate preeminence with hegemony reactively impels the preeminent land power to cross the line between the two degrees of ascendancy. The other is the but seeming congruence of two practical inabilities: of the sea power to achieve complete maritime monopoly, and of the land power to secure full maritime equality. Whereas falling short of naval monopoly weakens the sea power's insulation and immunity and impels it toward continental involvement, the inability to achieve naval equality makes it impossible for the land power to either bar the sea power from continental access or transfer the contest to the seas only. Despite fundamental disparities between the two arenas, neither actor can then avoid entanglement in both.

Land- and sea-based capabilities being inseparable prevents the potentially positive fact of either power type being invulnerable to conventional modes of conquest by the other taking full effect. So long as they apply, facts as well as fears will militate against anchoring the stability of the maritime cum continental system in the complementary character of the two actor types' actual resources and potential roles and functions. Before a concerted division of labor could implement a joint preeminence, the resource–role complementarity will have been defeated by the insulated and the exposed actor's contrasting situations. The dialectic between potential complementarily and actual contrasts will result in strategic options unlikely to fit the structure of actors-in-arena sufficiently to satisfy the desideratum of either equal security through maritime–continental parity or a uniformly structured and served system-wide equilibrium.

At bottom, it will prove impossible to satisfy either of the requisites of stable equilibrium: (1) for basic foreign-policy orientations to dovetail within a narrow band of deviation from the equilibrium-oriented or -fostering conservative policy norm; and (2) for the motivating impulses peculiar to the global politico-military triangle (and, secondarily, the politico-economic regional triangle) to be subordinated to the disciplines of rational cost-benefit calculations implicit in the multi-tripartite pattern of relations and perceptions – the very calculations that tend to produce an unintended equilibrium among homogeneous near-equal powers. By contrast, pervasive misfit between (qualitatively diversified) total structure and (more narrowly focused) grand strategies in a heterogeneous system is the source of high crisis potential, because misperceptions of the reasons for and implications of the mismatch will make the three principal powers along the geo-functional spectrum of insular, amphibian, and rear-continental actors experiment too soon, or proceed too far, with one of the available alliance combinations. Or else the powers will vacillate indecisively between any two or all three of the combinations in response to their immediate concrete means and needs or in pursuit of more basic and enduring, but also more elusive, objectives. Either mode of trying to overcome the dilemmas will periodically actualize the system's crisis potential in major convulsions.

The land–sea power interplays will intensify and the attendant convulsions deepen according to the rate at which the discrete traits constituting the relevant schism and spectrum aggregate into the classic triangular pattern in terms of both actor capabilities and system configuration. Thus, beginning with the seventeenth century, the Euro–global system progressed from aggregation of traits through intensification of tensions to its collapse and supersession. In the process, the theater was expanding spatially even as the time spans available to resolve the successive installments of the key conflict tended to shrink. The world economy grew simultaneously more complex, even as the growing inclination to define the underlying issues ideologically simplified the perception of issues, polarizing the politico-military stakes further. The progressively revealed tendency for the near-identical conflicts to unfold virtually automatically along comparable lines, if with rising intensity, ran counter to the presumption of increasing control over events. The earliest major, so-called hegemonic, wars were either preliminary to or instrumental in enacting the contention over the succession to the Spanish Empire; continued through the mid-eighteenth century to the Napoleonic wars; and climaxed in the two twentieth-century world wars. The level of violence kept rising once the English incumbent of maritime-mercantile primacy had begun to contend from a narrowing margin of advantage with continental claimants ever bigger in size or power potential, and increasingly anxious to accelerate the pace of advance so as to make up for delays in fully organizing and utilizing long-latent resources.

Although only France had been economically ahead of England at the outset, she, like the late-developing Russia and Germany, confronted Britain under two successive pre- and post-revolutionary regimes; and the two continental late-comers challenged Britain near-simultaneously with the United States and Japan, the potential insular-maritime supplanters of the more European island state. The continental late-comers – and, in the case of Japan, also the insular-maritime late entrant – were exposed to increasing internal strains acting as incentives and decreasing external opportunities and outlets. Both of the contrary trends urged them to speed up the pace of their self-affirmation and shorten the period of conflict resolution while, paradoxically, specific variations in their sociopolitical structures and domestic dynamics served to corroborate the continuity in fundamental systemic structures, perceived stakes, and available strategies over against any affirmed changes in the norms governing the system. The attendant politico-military crises either mediated shifts in economic primacy or actually implemented its transfers from the Italian via the Portuguese and Spanish to the Dutch and English industrial-commercial-financial centers. But the cycles of the centers' emergence, maturity and dominance, and decay and decline were no less a function of changing capacity to innovate and produce, trade in and transport, the most valued goods of an age at a viable margin of profit.

The fact that to the costs of production had to be added those of military-political protection meant throughout that world politics was not only distinct from but also broader than world economy. Although role transfers on the politico-military and the economic planes would commonly not be simultaneous between, any more than on the part of, individual actors, the time lags have not impeded the attendant crises from interlocking as part of the engine that propels a system's evolutionary dynamics. Between actors, the lack of synchronization merely reflected differences in the causal determinants of the rise and decline of maritime-mercantile and continental-military powers resulting in uneven lengths of ascendancy. It was no more preordained that before Britain's life cycle as the major economic power came to a close, it would have lasted longer than did the acute challenge from France, let alone from Germany, and encompassed the still briefer time-gap separating the two, than that Rome's longevity as essentially a military power would reduce that of Carthage, let alone Rhodes, to but episodic significance.

4
Strategies for Conflict along a Three-Part Spectrum

The ever-present quandary as to what caused crises and who was individually responsible for conflicts highlights the heavy burden that rests on foreign-policy strategy as the precarious combination of (rational) thought and (passional) will, relating more or less appropriate means to unevenly feasible ends. A strategy's effectiveness depends on how aptly it adjusts action to the power factors that constitute and the tendencies that pervade the environing configuration, and balances the adjustment with mastery over the resulting process, within a total structure that is a function of mind and matter operating in space and time. Disparate actor perceptions representing mind, and tinged by association with the various key schisms, are susceptible to constraints from distinctive material or technological capability factors standing in for matter. By the same token, mind-sets reflecting the evolutionary stages of actors in time interact with influences due to the location within the physical (continental versus oceanic) or systemic (core versus peripheral) settings that represent space. Misconceived or misapplied strategies are a hard-to-avoid consequence of the complexity and resulting ambiguity most of the time in most places.

TRIPARTITE CONFIGURATIONS AND STRATEGIES ACROSS THE AGES

Just as the basic strategic orientation will be prudently tripartite – the action of power A relative to B being affected by concern over its consequences in relation to C – so the range of options will logically comprise three main diplomatic strategies. And the strategies will have assumed a specific expression insofar as the arena has approximated, let alone achieved, the configuration of three salient powers of unevenly insular and continental character arrayed along a geophysical and -functional spectrum – as happened historically while the center of gravity shifted first westward and then eastward.

The foremost strategy adapts and expands the basic, schism-indifferent, instinct to outflank and thus counterbalance a prime rival with the assistance of a less immediately threatening and, as such, in one way or another more distant, power. In the triangular land–sea power context, this instinct assumes the form of the (westernmost) insular sea power initiating and heading, in association with the relatively (farthest-eastern) rear-continental flanking power, a continental coalition against the topologically intermediate and positionally central amphibious (navally equipped or ambitious land-based) power. The other two strategies are adaptations to the continental–oceanic setting of alternatives logically available in any three-power setting. One (or second possible) strategy is the alliance of the two major (central-amphibious and rear-continental) land powers, as part of a duopolistic approach to either only the continental or also the all-systemic equilibrium. It reduces the offshore insular power to seeking counterpoise, if such is available, outside the core system in what is then an oceanic alliance with a matching, if mostly (still) inferior, insular-maritime power at the other extremity of the geophysical spectrum. Another (or third possible) strategy is an alliance of the insular sea power with the premier continental (actually or would-be amphibious) state for a species of condominial ordering role within the system. It reduces any other, continental or maritime, state to either only a secondary role or also the status of primary target.

Each of the strategies will somehow polarize the actors. In the continental-coalition strategy of the sea power, the polarity will be between the central-amphibious and the two (insular and rear-continental) wing powers; in the land powers' duopolistic (matched or not by the sea power's oceanic) strategy, between the two major land powers and the offshore insular actor (or actors); and in the condominium strategy, between the two (navally and continentally) preeminent states and third parties. The range of, and tactical interplays among, the three strategies cumulated the prerequisites in Europe by the seventeenth century, when the rise of a model insular sea power (England) attended the consummation of the land–sea power schism by means of the appropriate functional cum technological cluster, geographic inter-actor spectrum, and actor–arena scale. In the earlier Babylonic, Hellenistic, and post-Roman barbarian macro-systems, also-maritime Egypt and (first "western" and then "eastern") Rome had interacted with likewise ambiguously circumstanced (central-amphibian and rear-continental) continental powers – an advance over the very earliest juxtaposition, without a traceable systemic (as distinct from trading) interplay, of insular-maritime Crete, continental–maritime or amphibious Egypt, and in their rear a Babylonia that had been in effect continentalized by the silting up of its sea outlets.

The strategy of an only quasi-insular maritime Egypt to ally with a succession of powers located behind the most immediately assertive, actually or would-be amphibious, continental power did more for aggrandizing the rear power (most notably Assyria) than safeguarding the interests and, eventually, the independence of Egypt. This was so even at the time when the latter admitted the previously contained, and henceforth diminished, central power belatedly to either parity (the Mitanni) or a formally sealed farther-reaching condominial alliance (the Hittites). Nor would several centuries after the latter signal event (i.e., in late seventh century BC) an ineffectual conservative (near-condominial?) alliance of an again navally-capable (Saite) Egypt with by-then declining Assyria fare better. It did not frustrate a re-expanding neo-Babylonia, precariously allied with the Medan Empire in a semblance of continental duopoly, nor did it prevent ethnic Persians from taking over the Medan Empire and rolling up the entire Near East, including Egypt. It would thus seem that Egypt managed the Egyptian–neo-Babylonian–Medan triangle, centered in the post-Assyrian phase on the conflict over sea and land routes to India, no better than she had managed the earlier triangles centered on the Syria–Palestine and the Black Sea area trade routes. A standing feature was the tendency for a succession of initially rear-continental powers, from before Assyria all the way to Persia, to assume the central amphibian position as they forced their way toward the sea coast and the control of the crucial east Mediterranean–Persian Gulf axis under pressure from the next generation of farthest-eastern barbarian migrants. Before consolidating into settled land powers, such populations were no better suited for a stable alliance with either the central continental or the western maritime empire than the former's overland drive would incline either of the two pre-established actors to explore common interests relative to the newcomers in time.

After the demise of the Persian Empire, the post-Alexandrine Hellenistic system consisted of three major powers, the relatively most maritime (Ptolemaic) Egypt and two unevenly amphibian (but near-equally "eastern") land powers, Macedonia and Syria. Apart from Indo–Scythian migrant populations moving in from North China under Hun pressure, there was no comparably consolidated rear-continental party for the Ptolemies to bring into containing alliance against the other two when they combined around 200 BC to establish a species of duopoly in the eastern Mediterranean on the ruins of navally decayed Egypt even as a new imperial power with military, and lately also naval, capabilities was rising in the west: a Rome readied by the victory over Carthage to contest Illyria and the Adriatic coast with Macedon as well as Asia Minor and the eastern Mediterranean seaboard with Syria–Asia. The failure of the two Hellenistic powers to mount joint opposition divested Rome's oceanic alliance with the island of Rhodes among others of a compelling rationale after exempting Rome from the need to seek an even but temporary (condominal) association with either of the amphibian powers. When Syria–Asia followed the more Greek-European Macedon into the position of Rome's principal adversary to be "encircled" in alliance with the eastern Mediterranean Greeks, the still inchoate land–sea power cleavage and spectrum became intertwined with the better-defined West–East schism, prefigured in the transplanted mercantile Greek cities representing the West inside the eastern-theocratic rural hinterlands of the post-Alexandrine successor empires of Egypt and Syria.

The imperfect status of both the tripartite configuration of maritime–amphibious–(rear-) continental actors and the basic strategy of the wing powers against the (would-be) amphibious center reflected the insufficient realization of most or all prerequisites of a full-fledged land–sea power schism. Whereas the maritime-mercantile factor was represented by at best only quasi-insular parties exposed to overland assault, maritime capability was neither sufficiently salient as a distinct category over, nor dominant in relation to, land-based power so long as it failed to meet a set of technological and related conditions. These conditions were not present so long as ship-building and -steering technology put a premium on the size of vessels (for ramming and grappling) rather than on less easy to match skills in the handling of (sailing) ships in maneuver. Even a navally superior actor such as Egypt was not capable of sustaining effective blockade of land masses and exercising sea control and command in all seasons, while failing to enjoy the full advantage of integral insularity. This reduced the both military- and diplomatic-strategic premium from naval superiority while material gains from the control of sea routes could be, if not wholly matched, then approximated by means of mastering overland routes and land-based assets (from life-giving foodstuffs to economically or militarily vital metals or minerals). Only when navally backed mercantile-maritime activities and assets became sufficiently hard to match, and sufficiently superior operationally to create the possibility – and the incidental threat – of virtual monopoly, forcing the preeminent land power to seek access to the seas and overseas as a condition of overall parity, would two consequences follow: (1) the two arenas and the capabilities germane to each will be inseparable for both material and political (role-status) reasons; and (2) the completed interlock will have full-fledged consequences for strategy, centering on responses to the disparate actor strengths and weaknesses and shared immunity to direct assault by the other.

In the pre-existing conditions, the major continental states could and did press toward the coasts in order to enlarge the sphere of their commercial operations, whether or not also to overwhelm the principal trading sea power; and the latter was typically weighted down by a rural hinterland and by militaristic traditions engendered in prior overland expansion of its own unless, like Crete, exceptionally an island (but then one still vulnerable to assault from the adjacent land mass). Finally, the actual alignment of active powers on a west–east or south–north geographic axis coincided in only a few instances with the optimum geo-functional spectrum locating the would-be amphibious actor in the middle between the maritime and the rear-continental wing powers.

The essential prerequisites and attributes of a land–sea power schism and spectrum being only partially realized prior to early modern Europe showed in the strategic interplays falling short of a settled hierarchy of military-strategic and economic-commercial priorities in a fundamentally predictable setting of actor types and strategy alternatives. Even rarer than sustained implementation was a dynamic relation of any one strategy to the alternative strategic options, which could slow down when not prevent the standing of powers being abruptly altered by unhindered conquering force. When land-based power was strong, it found it relatively easy to absorb not only coastal maritime cities (e.g. alternately the Babylonian and the Phoenician cities by Assyria), but also an adjoining major sea power such as Egypt; when the adjoining land power was weak, even territorially thin-based maritime-mercantile actors (such as the Phoenician cities) could enjoy seaward expansion without having to shield themselves strategically from the rudimentary dynamic in their rear.

Even fewer conditions for sustained land–sea power tripartism obtained at first after the unevenly spaced decline of the two parts of a Roman Empire. The cleavage between seaworthy Gallo-Roman and Italic west and Byzantine east on one side and the land-rooted populations on the other was more meaningfully one between (civilized) center and a (barbarian) periphery than between sea and land powers. Before a reconstituted geo-functional spectrum could evolve into a schism, the European proto-system (and the Italian micro-system) had been segmented in substantially discrete land- and sea-based or -oriented compartments. There was little or no interconnection between conflicts engaging the sea powers (e.g. Byzantium against Islam in the Mediterranean) and conflicts among land powers (the Lombards against the Franks in the Gallo–Germano–Italic heartland). A radical split between land- and sea-based entities continued well into the ninth century, delaying the emergence of significant overlaps so long as local naval superiority did no more than engender isolated raids from north or south into helpless hinterlands. Among the original causes of the bifurcation had been Constantinople's determination to enforce its sea-power monopoly in defense of vital North African coasts and agricultural resources after recovering control from its brief breach by the Vandals. The fact that, before the rise of Islam's naval arm, the recovery had been more effective and lasting than Justinian's reconquests on land was just another aspect of the two arenas being separable in the then existing conditions of not only geostrategic but, increasingly, geo-economic segmentation.

Before eastern Rome's contest with Persia had opened the path of conquest to Islam, strategy in the west could therefore display only elements of two of the three major options. One was the tentative quasi-condominial arrangement of the more civilized (and maritime) Roman party with the Goths (not yet replaced by the Franks in that party's favor). It was repeatedly qualified by collusions with the prime targets of the strategy, the most eastern or rear-continental Huns and/or Lombards, aimed at containing the centric Goths in a subordinate position to the Roman wire-pullers. This semblance of a continental-coalition strategy was prompted less by ideological considerations (the revulsion of Catholicized eastern Romans against the Arian heresy of the Goths) than by a practical concern (the local Gallo–Roman aristocracy's desire to limit Gothic takeover of arable land). But the ideal and the material incentives combined to intimate enduring obstacle to condominial alliance between value-differentiated land and sea powers: the maritime party's determination to allocate the "proper" shares of control or influence, while remaining supreme in the maritime and normative realms, ruling out genuine parity with the more continental party. Another precedent was set by the unanticipated character of the outcome, in the form of a gradual rollback of Byzantine hold on Italy, of saving the Huns from total defeat, using them and the Lombards as auxiliaries in the reconquest of Italy, and promoting the Catholicized Franks previously kept off the Mediterranean by the Goths-centered inter-barbarian "balance-of-power" and "concert" system linking Italy to Germany. The outcome's beneficiaries were, typically, ever less manageable local actors including the land-oriented Lombards, the initially Byzantium-dependent maritime-mercantile Venetians, and a succession of seafaring conquerors of southern Italy and Sicily. And just as the northern continental heartland's economic links with the Mediterranean were fading, the Franks' growing military near-monopoly had made a "duopolistic" alliance with another major land power unnecessary even before Charlemagne was ready to substitute status parity for Byzantine pretensions to system-wide preeminence as a key "third" in the Frankish–Byzantine–Islamic configuration.

When the dynamics of the "European" proto-system on macro-scale were resumed in the better-crystallized Italian microcosm, the prolonged maritime-mercantile contest between Venice and Genoa (analogous to the Byzantine–Islamic) had again no settled counterpart along the inchoate land–sea power geo-functional spectrum comprising land-oriented Milan, near-amphibious Florence, and maritime Venice, except for the latter's brief encircling alliance with Florence against expansionist Milan. The subsequent realignment of Florence to the domestically troubled Milan against continentally expansive Venice reflected continuing concern about the territorial balance of power among the Big Three, with the Papal States and Naples completing the five-power structure. So long as it was a threat from Venetian designs on the Milanese that triggered reactive strategies, no significant impetus was lodged in the land–sea power dichotomy – to wit, specifically, in the concern of Venice over the finite trading and maritime ambitions of either Milan or Florence (in any case turned toward the western Mediterranean, of greater concern to a Genoa not significantly involved in the continental interplays). As the controlling environment of strategy, continental–maritime segmentation began to yield to land–sea power spectrum (i.e., evolve into schism) only when Venice had subsided into a balancing "neutralist" between the greater amphibious powers (Habsburg and Ottoman or French) contending in the Mediterranean. Concurrently healed began to be another Italian deficiency, having to do with the scale of actors relative to the scope of the arena and affecting the autonomy of the system. Insofar as actor–arena congruence is the ultimate requisite of a fully operative land–sea power complex, it mattered that neither maritime Venice (or Genoa or Naples) nor continental Milan (or Florence or the Papacy) had either the commercial or the military reach appropriate to the scope of the all-Mediterranean arena into which the Italian micro-system was being increasingly absorbed. After reducing materially the significance of locally contested stakes, size disparaties undermined the finality of results achieved by local contestants once these impinged on the interests of the larger powers in the total system. It was then but another aspect of the consequent demotion when the larger northern (land) powers valued the maritime Italian actors – the Genoese or the Neapolitans – most as the actual or potential suppliers of auxiliary naval facilities.

The shortcomings of the Italian being similar to the earlier ones of the Greek micro-system confirmed their implications for strategies, unaffected by a difference: whereas the former emerged out of a larger-scale land-centered European proto-system only to be subsumed to it in function of Europe's crystallization and continental–maritime differentiation, the latter's career was traced by the early Cretan–Egyptian–Babylonian maritime–continental configuration having evolved into a unified Persian–Phoenician land–sea power complex (or empire-type meta-system) before the complex would impinge on the Hellenic micro-system in its climactic phase preceding immersion in the Hellenistic macro-system. In the Greek microcosm, the objective conditions consequent upon the collapse of Athenian overland expansionism fostered the perception of land- and sea-based capabilities and roles as separate and separable. Whereas this perception had prompted the fleeting bids for a division of labor between Athens and Sparta that would implement a hegemonial condominium, the accelerating conflict between equally maritime-mercantile Athens and Corinth along an east–west axis of prime thrust and orientation confounded the neat structural segmentation. This counteracted the related scenarios when, in the ensuing conflict (the Peloponnesian War), the geo-functional spectrum was extended in the west to Sicily, along the maritime axis, and in the east to Persia, along the navally significant overland axis. In the strategic rationale for the Athenian expedition, Syracuse was a prospective party to a species of (enforced) oceanic alliance encircling the amphibian (Spartan–Corinthian) Peloponnesian center. And when Persia underwrote Sparta's end-of-war acquisition of naval capability, she acted as the rear-continental power intent upon arbitrating a central-systemic conflict to its advantage.

The ensuing merger of preeminent land-military and sufficient if not superior maritime capability under single (Spartan) command proved to be a formula for victory in war. It did not equal the potential of a land–sea power condominium as a formula for stable order and orderly evolution in peacetime. If the merger has been the recurrent aim and its realization the rare accomplishment of the preeminent land power in contests with a preponderant sea power, the latter was no less determined to frustrate the accomplishment with varying degrees of consistency or clarity of purpose and continuity in execution – all of which qualities have been contingent on first realizing the full range of the naval-technological and the geo-functional prerequisites of a tripartite land–sea power schism.

Before the pre-conditions were at long last realized in the European macro-system, the primitive interlock of the continental and the oceanic dimensions and factors had passed through their being combined in the amphibian Spanish and Ottoman Empires. While those were close to the Hellenistic great powers in kind, their situation was differentiated operationally by the absence of a continually engaged equivalent third power. This limited the range of available strategies to one-sidedly or reciprocally outflanking alliance with relatively minor and only intermittently involved secondary powers. More like previously, the absence of a fully developed land–sea power differentiation in regard to theaters, actor tendencies, and applied technologies shifted the critical spectrum from the geo-functional (insular–continental) to one more markedly geo-cultural (West–East) albeit without reducing the former to irrelevance.

The outflanking strategies were illustrated by the amphibian Spain-centered western side seeking alliance with the wholly continental farthest-eastern Turkomans or Persians against the fellow-amphibian nearer-eastern Ottoman Empire. Exposed to two fronts, the latter courted alternately the wholly continent-bound German Protestants, (proto-amphibian) French, and (maritime) Dutch for relief or support against the two-wing Habsburg realm within either the Mediterranean maritime or the continental theater. Meanwhile, the land–sea power dimension related to the spectrum's west-to-east direction in the form of temporarily relaxing or rerouting rather than continuously radicalizing the conflict. Thus the stalemate that had set in in the eighth decade of the sixteenth century redirected Spain toward (or liberated her for) a sea-borne assault on England in the west while propelling the Turks into an overland assault on Persia as a complement to a resumed advance into south-eastern Europe against the Austrian Habsburgs. And although the Ottomans' increased capacity or reasserted intention to interfere with or exploit overland routes to the east may have had a marginal role in diverting the western powers toward the Atlantic, Portugal's maritime bypass of Turk-controlled routes had stimulated the Ottomans' interest in expanding northward on land to supplement ineffective counteraction in the Indian Ocean area. On a smaller scale, the standoffs between the Ottomans and the Venetians in the eastern Mediterranean and the Black Sea areas helped impel the city of St Mark westward into the Italian terra firma, while a later Austro–Turkish stalemate on land helped awaken the interest of the Viennese Hofburg in the northern sea or seas, in opposition to the maritime–mercantile Dutch fanning out from the west.

When the basic pattern of either alternating or competing propulsions land- and sea-ward was perpetuated in the later conflicts between unevenly eastern land powers such as Germany and Russia, this confirmed the tendency for such a conflict to do one of two things: propel the nearer-eastern power westward, and thus seaward, in a mode that is both strategically and tactically offensive on the face of it (even if ultimately defensively preemptive of adverse long-term developments and outcomes); or else, draw and pull that power farther eastward, away from critical sea outlets as part of strategic offense aimed at eliminating the danger of distraction in its rear, or as part of tactical defense designed to buy time in periods of relative weakness or involvement in the west. A thrust westward was commonly hampered by the more intricate countervailing dynamics of a developed system segment, and the move seaward by the inadequate naval deployments of an essentially continental state; the thrust eastward was hampered by combinations of overland distance, intractability of terrain, and the elasticity if not impregnability in defense of the farther-eastern adversary. For such reasons, the Turks when interacting with Persia repeated, before they prefigured, the experiences of comparably situated powers when they, too, proved unable to free themselves in the continental depths for decisive action against the maritime west – a fact that was compensated in part by the limitations incurred by the western powers when pursuing outflanking alliances in the east.

Despite any such limitations, it will be common for the farthest-western power to neutralize the nearer-eastern party's propensity to move westward and seaward by only activating the farthest-eastern one or aligning with it outright. When Spanish diplomacy sought to use the Turkish–Persian rivalry so as to present the Ottomans' inflexible one-front army with a two-front situation on the continent, and relieve thus the maritime front in the Mediterranean, it re-enacted the strategy of ancient Egypt against the successive nearer-eastern continental empires as well as one by Carthage (in alliance with Macedon) against Rome. And it refurbished the grand design of the medieval Popes to arouse and align with farther-eastern Mongols, before they converted to Islam, against the Turk. Inverting the same strategic reasoning, the French sought the Ottoman alliance as a defensive counterweight to the design of the Spanish Habsburgs to consummate the encirclement of France with the assistance or the resources of the Holy Roman (Germanic) Empire, just as Britain was to only support or also stimulate the same Empire (under the Austrian Habsburgs) against France before backing the declining Ottoman Empire against both Austria and Russia.

On its part, the still ascendant Ottoman Empire showed that such strategic interactions along the west–east (cum sea–land) spectrum could have major incidental effects, thus when its physical and ideological pressure on the Habsburg conglomerate intensified the efforts of Charles V to centralize the Holy Roman Empire into a medieval-type institutional and religious unity while, at a later date, military contentions with the same (if weaker) Ottomans instigated the Austria-based Habsburgs to modernize their imperial domain in a wholly secular manner. On a different plane, when the medieval West proved less antagonistic toward the religiously wholly alien farther-eastern Mongols than toward the ambiguously cognate-and-contrary Turks, it set the pattern for the role values-related dispositions were to play on the West–East spectrum. Conversely, if the nearer-eastern power was commonly closer to western standards than the farther-eastern one in organization and efficiency, this was not least because it found (when it did not seek) in actively militant competition with the western powers the surest mechanism for insuring transmission of technologies to be used against the principal overland rival in the east.

By the time the West had decisively outstripped the East, the dynamics of conflict-spawned technological transmission and differentiation was at work not only between the Ottomans and Persia but also post-Mongol Russia and the Crimean Tartars (pending China). When the Turks and the Muscovites gained thus repeatedly some advantage even from disastrous military engagements with parties located to the west of them, encircling the nearer-eastern power strategically from the west invigorated the former technologically and organizationally, if not always and necessarily organically. No more intentional will be the likewise two-sided impact of the eastern power in the west when it contributes to stabilizing the central or western segment of the system operationally while destabilizing or subverting it on a deeper, structural and capability-related organic level. Thus, the Ottoman quasi-alliance with France helped contain the imperial Habsburgs, despite its being tactically limited and strategically unreliable on both sides. But its religio-ideological impropriety weakened France's position as an internationally legitimate and internally cohesive counterpoise. Similarly, the Turks' involvement in the intra-German confessional conflicts was on balance subversive of the established European order, even if consequently prolonged German disunity related at first as positively to maintaining the European balance of power as the French alliance had done to propping it up.

It required the near-simultaneous rise of insular England to maritime supremacy and the maturation of a key nautical innovation in the form of ocean-going sailing ships – wind-propelled, skills-dependent, and cannon-carrying – to pull together the several prerequisites of land–sea power schism and activate the corresponding geo-functional spectrum into strategic tri-angularization. Britain was better protected from the European land mass by the channel than insular Crete had been in relation to the Greek mainland; she was more integrally insular than had been quasi-insular Athens (behind the wall) or Venice (amidst the lagoons) or the (self-inundation-capable) Netherlands; and her location to the west of decreasingly sea-abutting and -worthy land-military powers extending eastward completed a geo-functionally differentiated spectrum of hierarchically stratified powers. And just as the scale requisite was satisfied so long as the island state's expanding material resources kept abreast of a progressively globalized arena, so England's naval capability was growing sufficiently long enough to permeate all critical local or regional (including Baltic and Mediterranean) theaters to an unprecedented degree. Finally, only few feudal survivals had impeded timely revolutions creating a sociopolitical base and a governing elite favorable to maritime-mercantile development at home and abroad. This made an increasingly conservative – i.e., more strategically defensive than tactically assertive – stance sufficient to implement Britain's leadership in defining the legitimate shape of equilibrium in quasi-oligopolistic competition with the primarily continental major powers.

Having assembled the elements of its supremacy on the seas beginning with the late sixteenth century, the island state experienced the initial fading of its supremacy – and of any leading sea power's relative advantage overall – in the nineteenth century, in parallel with the transition from the Anglo–French to the Anglo–German contest as the dominant one in the system. The concurrent movement was past the crystallization of the individual components of the schism and their aggregation, coincident with articulating the related strategic options, toward the land–sea power conflict escalating and intensifying in a manner that was to encompass the collapse of the European or Eurocentric system. The interplay between the economic or fiscal and the military or force factors which had been critical in the forming of actors and the shaping of their identities – not least by determining the outcome of rivalry between coastal-commercial and heartland-rural sectors – had been meanwhile instrumental in consummating the continental–maritime dynamics, only fragmentarily adumbrated in earlier micro- or macro-systems, world-wide. While this was happening, the scales of the principal maritime and continental actors were congruent enough with the scope of the global arena to make the strategic outcomes conclusive for the entire system and Britain's role therein appear consistent with the needs of most of its members. However, actually implementing the role was increasingly subject to the system-deranging effect of the growing disparity between the scales of the strictly metropolitan (home-based) resources of the insular kingdom and the successive continental adversaries, even as the latter incurred a comparable trend relative to the rear-continental power when France's exposure to the divided Germanic powers was followed by unified Germany's to Russia.

TECHNOLOGICAL AND OTHER PRECONDITIONS OF SCHISM-RELATED STRATEGIES

When geo-functional spectrum, actor–arena congruence as to scale, and the insular sea power's systemic role or function conspired to augment England's position, they also actualized the main strategy options. One condition on which the options feed is the salience of the naval category of actor capabilities and the mercantile category of actor concerns; another, a setting in which land- and sea-based factors of power are objectively inseparable and the leading maritime and continental actors are close to invulnerable to one another in isolation from either supports or impediments introduced by a third party or parties. Sea-based will be salient over land-based capability whenever naval technology makes the former less costly and more productive for both military and economic purposes. That condition was conspicuously met by the technology of sailing ships capable of navigating the big oceans and combining the economy of wind-propelled mobility with the potential for continuous operations in all seasons, including a close blockade of an economic or politico-military rival. Moreover, such advantages were at a premium in the economic environment of an early capitalism keyed to long-distance trade implementing a growing – if unevenly balanced – complementarity of resources and performances between the core of the system and the peripheries. The growing advantage of oceanic commerce over both land cultivation and overland trading highlighted the mutually reinforcing link between accumulation of national wealth and control over the world's waters, between successful maritime warfare and domestic welfare, at a time when arms and armed contentions on land were becoming ever more certain to expend physical and financial resources than expand either wealth or welfare.

In the presence of the technological, geopolitical, and economic preconditions of a land–sea power schism, no major continental power could jeopardize its internal stability and external status by abstaining from the pursuit of overseas access. And in response to the premier continental state's peculiar mix of instrumentalities for fighting war and either promoting its own or impeding the insulars' trade, the latter neither could nor would neglect a countervailing involvement on the continent with the support of *their* mix of capabilities and resources. Before the interlock was fully demonstrated in the Anglo–French contention, England had intimated it in the mid-seventeenth century when, after challenging amphibious Spain's monopoly, she mobilized a larger and richer land base for naval challenge to the more one-sidedly maritime-mercantile Netherlands. Toward the close of the era, the reasons for continental–maritime entanglement had withstood the dual shift from overseas (carrying) trade to home-based industry in the foundations of economic power, and from sail to steam in the naval-technological dimension of military prowess. The change increased the importance of both overseas raw materials and naval facilities (coaling stations) not least for the continental powers anxious to export manufactures as a corrective to an insufficiently integrated interregional domestic market in France and, in Germany, to an unbalanced inter-group income distribution. A productivity in excess of internal purchasing power encouraged expansion abroad as less costly than internal restructuration of one kind or another.

Anything that gives maritime-mercantile capability an advantage salient over land-military capabilities will matter all the more as the maritime state's naval superiority over a would-be amphibian increases, not least because whatever makes sea-power as such salient also propels naval superiority into supremacy while the contrary propensity of continental-military advantages is toward engendering stalemate. Sustaining England's superiority in the age of sail were the premium conferred on nautical skills by a stable naval technology, and the reduction of the cost burden due to the actor and arena scales being congruent. Supporting both advantages was a hard to imitate and inculcate matured socio-cultural and professional ethos. Skills were at a premium when, sail having replaced oars as key propellant, mobility and maneuver supplanted muscular energy and mass; when earlier times' confused ramming and boarding in line-abreast formations gave way to coordinated artillery duels in line-ahead formations as centrality passed from the Mediterranean to the Atlantic and Indian oceans. Not even more frequent technological innovations by the continentals could compensate for the island people's superior expertise, nurtured by merchant marine and fisheries and refined through a long spell of largely static technology from the sixteenth through the first third of the nineteenth century. When emphasis shifted from the bulk of ships to their number in a fleet in the size category, not only the value of manipulative skills was enhanced but also the burdens of building and maintenance for states suffering equally from the absence of continuously compelling motivation and from a constant drain on resources in the continental arena of contention.

In terms of the same factors, built-in maritime superiority of the favored actor will increase – or conditions for it improve – when the operational radius of navies expands and so does the range at which they engage in direct combat. The same is true if the scale of needed resources and related costs exceeds (in importance) the rate of technological change i.e., quantitative predominates over qualitative arms race. Whether these conditions be defined in terms of skills, stability, size, and sustainability of costs, or formulated in terms of radius, range, resource requirements, and arms race criteria, the consequences are the same: the would-be amphibious challenger finds it not necessarily less pressing, but certainly more difficult, to contest the superior with an inferior navy, and to rebuild its navy fast enough when it was destroyed by decisive defeat or had deteriorated from protracted non-use and neglect. The premier sea power will then be at least as invulnerable in its element as the strongest continental power is likely to be in its habitat to the sea power acting alone.

Although the advantages of superior naval capability continued past the age of sail to that of steam and diesel engine-propelled and externally-armored battleship, they were diminished in proportion to the disparity in skills being easier to contain in regard to both cruising and combat, maneuver and missile targeting. The critical gap in expertise and ethos could be narrowed further, even when not fully closed, by the accelerating rate of technological innovation favoring the navally inferior continental power with a smaller psychological stake in established traditions and lesser financial investment in obsolete or obsolescent craft. Relative to England's, the propensity to innovate was greater for France in the 1850s and (to a lesser or less easy-to-establish extent) for Germany in the early 1900s in regard to either offensive thrust (guns) or defensive parry (armor). With the factor of size regressing again partially from numbers toward magnitudes of individual ships, and the requisite materials changing from timber and tar to coal and iron or steel, the newly critical advantages became easier to replicate and disadvantages to compensate for. And if costs were rising absolutely, they were declining relative to the expanded resource base of mass-producing economies that, emerging out of an industrial revolution, had meanwhile spread to the continent. By the time of the Anglo–German naval race, the fiscal burdens weighed near-equally on the social capital and the societal tolerance of both parties to it.

Most significant for operations was the increased dependence of engine-propelled ships on stationary land-based facilities for resupplies and repairs. It made the leading sea power more likely to overextend itself globally and the land power to develop an at least regionally effective naval capability. And if fixed support bases made travel paths more predictable than dependence on prevailing winds had done, bigger ships became more vulnerable to tech-nologically innovative faster small boats (from torpedo boats to submersibles) than comparable vessels had been to the hit-and-run tactics of an inferior navy in the *guerre de course*. Finally, it being harder to stay afloat without resupply in a torpedoes- and mines-infested environment made also a close blockade harder to sustain. The local effects of overall naval superiority became thus as uncertain as command of the sea was difficult to approximate and exploit worldwide. However, anything liable to reduce the gap in naval capabilities without closing it could act to intensify the rivalry between premier maritime and continental powers and enhance correspondingly the importance of diplomatic strategies. In the absence of accommodation, the increased dangers for the sea power encouraged it to augment, and the enhanced overseas opportunities for the land power prompted it to reduce, the weight and scope of conflicts on the continent. Whereas the sea power's physical invulnerability to the premier land power will make it safe to embrace an alliance strategy for maximizing overseas advantages, even but partial or hypothetical vulnerability will intensify diplomatic efforts in behalf of homeland security – and disclose concern for the immunity as ultimately strategy-controlling.

Competition will wax and wane depending on the extent to which the leading maritime power views near-monopoly in naval capability as either necessary or possible, and so does the would-be amphibious continental party its capacity to contain the superiority short of supremacy. What the maritime state deems necessary will be a function of its physical or economic vulnerability to the rival's naval capability in and of itself, and when combined with his land-based potential; the continental state's sense of necessity will depend on how important it deems naval capability to be as either deterrent to sea-borne assault or leverage for bargaining over formal (role-status) or substantive (security-sustenance) stakes of competition. Technological, fiscal, and operational conditions of feasibility will set the simpler criteria of capability perceived as possible. The tension is least when both sides proceed on the premise of possibility (are motivated by opportunity), and highest when both act on the premise of necessity (respond to pressures) while at least one side's actual possibilities have been on the wane. Contest will fluctuate around middle levels of intensity when the superior sea power's necessity is confronted with the land power's possibility only, or vice versa. After the British had established naval superiority between the late 1680s and 1715, France met their unwavering sense of necessity to retain the headstart with fluctuating assessments of how possible or necessary it was to curtail the advantage, as military perspectives improved by technological progress combined perversely with fear of the political consequences of economic stagnation. So long as neither free nor fair trade was felt to be reliably independent of navally secured access, protection, or control, an acute status- and role-consciousness of the challenger could only enhance his sense of urgency further – and the incumbent's sense of peril.

In the widest systemic scope and in the last resort, the way superior relates to inferior naval capability – near-monopoly to the capacity to contest it – will engage the issue of the two actor-types' reciprocal vulnerability. The issue is the politico-military and geostrategic counterpart to the economic and geo-economic factors critical for the issue of separability of land- and sea-based capabilities and concerns. If the superior sea power is an island, the nature-given potential of an invulnerable location will have to be actualized by technologically and operationally infallible naval armament. In order to generate and free the resources for challenging the insular state, the would-be amphibious land power will seek to approximate the latter's geostrategic invulnerability by means of an inner-zone security–superiority belt. So long as the continental balance of power-related constraints last in full, they will not only drain the resources of the land power; they also supply the insular state with strategic opportunities for enhancing the vulnerability of the continental rival to fellow-continentals and, through them, to the insular state. Since the land–sea power relationship revolves around the degree either type of actor is vulnerable or invulnerable relative to the other as a contingent fact or the stake of contest, the way how the ratios of superior to inferior naval capabilities relate to only the continental or the system-wide balance of power is as critical for any state system comprising both types of actor as the attendant contest is endemic to it. However, the resulting conflict will be all the more intense and the strategies for implementing it more predictable, the more fully the requisites of a land–sea power schism-cum-spectrum are realized.

The contest will escalate when the insular sea power's initiatives have made the would-be amphibian more vulnerable to continental interactions than is normal. The climax is reached when an effective blockade has extended the issue of vulnerability beyond the strategic advantage or disadvantage of the state-like parties to the physical substance of the combatant peoples. Thus, when the two-sided blockading operations at the Napoleonic peak of the Anglo–French conflict era matured in World War I, they emotionalized further the Anglo–German conflict already subject to East–West value differences. In both contests the inferior capacity of the land power to inhibit the rival's supply strengthened its desire to circumvent the immunity of the insular state to sea- (or air-) borne assault by transferring the struggle to the more readily conquest-prone continental hinterland. In invading Russia, Napoleonic France and both Wilhelmine and Hitlerite Germany pursued with increasing thoroughness the substantive goal of an autarkic wartime and post-war economy, resting on the control of critical overland routes and vital commodities to a degree that permitted an at least provisional separation of the continental from the maritime domain. A partial reversion to the condition of a major ancient empire such as Assyria went finally hand in hand with approximating its methods of conquest and rule. The other strategic objective was to frustrate the alliance option of the insular state relative to the continental wing power in favor of a coercive substitute for consensually concerted duopoly of the two continental powers. Ideally, continental mastery would augment the strategic leverage for a future condominium with the insular sea power, to rest on the provisionally evened out reciprocal invulnerability and forestalling a mutually enfeebling contest.

Unless associated with emotions-arousing creedal issues such as the Catholic–Protestant or the East–West schism, land–sea power contests were much less ideologically motivated and exacerbated than had been either the Papal–Imperial or even the Spanish–Ottoman conflict. And the more salient were the pragmatic (including vulnerability-related) imperatives, the more did preferred military-strategic theaters of operations influence the choice of diplomatic strategies.

Thus, before England achieved naval primacy, it had been a plausible military strategy for Spain to opt for a maritime assault on the island state (in 1588) as a means of subduing the Dutch rebels through the elimination of their English backer. Only later was Spain reduced to primarily overland "German" strategy of conquest or attrition (in the Thirty Years War), consigning maritime operations against the Dutch and their interests in the Baltic and continental trade to a supporting (if not insignificant) tactic. Whereas for a cross-Channel assault to succeed a quasi-duopolistic alliance with France's Catholics had to neutralize French interference, the overland strategy inclined an internally reconsolidated France to ally with the maritime Dutch and fight Spain directly – so as to make good earlier failures to best Spain directly on land in Italy and impede Spanish communications with the Netherlands by sea via diplomatic control (through Mary Stuart) over English policy. Even after France had become navally capable, her military-strategic emphasis continued to be continental with the aim of imposing on the navally supreme English a land frontier to defend (in Germany, and eventually, via Egypt in India). Attempts for the supporting maritime strategy to do more than interfere with England's commercial and colonial activities and assets (*guerre de course*, naval support for rebellious American colonies), and target the insular fastness itself (naval preparations for cross-Channel invasion by both Louis XIV and Napoleon), required diplomatic strategy to do better than secure one major ally on the continent. By the same token, when the French military options, including the alternate maritime (light commerce-raiding versus heavy battle ships) ones, resurfaced for Germany in the next conflict series, they continued to shape German diplomatic options, notably relative to Austria and Russia.

Contemplating a direct sea-borne assault (or its equivalent, a continental "blockade") against the insular power will incline the amphibian to seek a duopolistic alliance with the rear-continental state. By contrast, an overland strategy culminating in a coercive approach to neutralizing the easternmost power will facilitate the sea power's encircling grand coalition. More ambiguously strategy-related than either of the two military scenarios will be the capacity and disposition to embarrass – but no more than embarrass – the maritime power on the seas and overseas, combined with the willingness to use politico-military preeminence on the continent in ways consistent with the insular state's interests. The stance will incline the latter toward (condominial) accommodation, attractive to the land power as a less costly and risky avenue to rough parity and system-wide equilibrium than either military strategy is likely to prove to be in the best of circumstances.

So long as the continental and the maritime spheres appeared separable, the preponderating preference of the conservative majority in Sparta's councils was for a virtual condominium with Athens, leaving each hegemon predominant and undisturbed in his special sphere. When the two spheres have become manifestly inseparable and the two powers' interests overlap as a result, the form of possible accommodation is less clear, and its extent is apt to be less far-reaching. Critical is then the balance of either structure- or capability-related incentives to and restraints on the land power's oceanic outreach, and the insular power's attitude to any such outreach. On the one side, the built-in strategic and technological limitations on the land power's productive overseas outreach are offset by its stake in internally stabilizing economic performance, backed by international role and status embracing an appropriate assortment of both mainland and maritime assets and interests. On the other side, counteracting the insular-mercantile state's stake in political stability overall will be its inclination to deny the land power's overseas initiatives wholesale, in the interest of total homeland security and virtual oceanic monopoly. Given the conflicting needs and dilemmas reflecting disparate situations, asymmetries in capabilities and dispositions could be reconciled, ideally, only in an equilibrium that both mirrored and materially sustained the two powers' respective – offshore insular and continental – bases of security, while allowing each to reinforce its security and prosperity to a comparable extent in the environment more closely associated with the other party and more vitally indispensable to it.

Once the continental–naval Spanish giant had been slowly brought down by the Maritime Powers' assault on the Hispanic monopolies, successive major continental European powers inclined toward accommodation with the dominant sea power. Were it not for actual or suspected insistence on virtual monopoly, they might have adhered to the policy all the time. At the very least, there were prolonged spells of French foreign policy that could be so described under both pre- and post-revolutionary regimes, and there is no conclusive evidence to the contrary with respect to the pre-revolutionary German and Russian regimes. It was then for British statecraft to correctly assess, and by measured concessions ease, the limitations on the actually feasible ambitions of the land power outside the continent or at its periphery – provided (and the proviso is crucial) that it was prudent to discount the risks implicit in the relatively greater resource and population base of the continental states. In fact, whether or not due to that particular impediment, there was little prolonged accommodation when the preeminent continental state sought to extend from strength an access that, though limited, would not be subject to arbitrary restrictions by the dominant sea power – i.e., when the continental party was not willing to accept a subordinate status consequent on defeat or domestic upheaval.

The contrasting views of what was the legitimate scope of the balance of power – only continental or all-systemic – pitted throughout the principle of equity between differently constituted actors against the implications of structural disparity between the corresponding arenas. Looming behind the contrasts were throughout two material concerns: the major maritime-mercantile power's about its land-based resource strength as more or less sufficient to compensate for diffusing naval capabilities and related access and assets; the major continental state's about its capacity to deal with the maritime-mercantile dimension halfway satisfactorily before being disqualified by a hostile coalition or superseded by a still stronger power on the continent.

CERTAIN RISKS AND ELUSIVE REWARDS OF ALTERNATIVE STRATEGIES

From the latter part of the seventeenth century, when the land–sea power schism crystallized conjointly with the corresponding triangles, to the mid-twentieth century, when the schism-related conflicts provisionally climaxed, it was the "grand" or continental coalition that was the principal institutional device implementing the preferred strategy of the dominant sea power. The successive coalitions comprised three key actors: the dominant insular-maritime state (England), the formerly dominant but since declining sea or amphibian power (the Netherlands and, eventually, France), and the rear-continental power (Austria or Prussia and, eventually, Russia). Underneath the averred concern for continental equilibrium, the prime purpose of the insular power was to safeguard itself within all three of its own security zones and resource bases: the insular home base, the central-systemic continental balance-of-power system, and the maritime-colonial global periphery. While the security zones were concentric and the resource bases complementary throughout, the strategic priority would move from the periphery toward the metropole as the intensity of the continental challenge rose. And whereas the dominant sea power would initiate, lead, and materially sustain the coaliton, and although the declining sea-or-amphibious power supplied the triggering pretext or impulse as the coalition's weakest and most immediately or directly exposed link, it was actually – if often inconspicuously – the rear-continental state that played the crucial role. It not only complemented the off-shore insular party in the effective armature of the alliance by virtue of its military resources; it was also the ultimate regulator in the processes and perceptions leading to the coalition.

The rear-continental state in effect regulates the strategic response by being weak or strong: when it is strong, it attracts the sea power to the continental-coalition response as a materially feasible one, while it intensifies the compulsion on the central would-be amphibian power to act in preemptive ways that can be construed as provocative; when it is weak, it will encourage a defensive sea power response as necessary, because the weakness will increase the margin of resources the central power can release for overseas-related (naval or other) efforts and decrease its incentive to accommodate with the dominant sea power on a basis of less than parity. The tendency to conflict may be greatest when the two principal rivals evaluate the rear-continental state differently: the would-be amphibious central power as strong, rising, and threatening; the offshore insular power as weak or weakening.

Either side's perception will foreshorten the period available for a successful conflict resolution and reduce its likelihood. The sea power's will set the stage for attributing only hegemonial or also world-domination goals to the so far only continentally preeminent state, and engender preemptive measures tending to impel the target state toward policies vindicating the imputation of the farther-reaching aspirations. Thus, in addition to being actually regulative as a major resource factor, the rear-continental actor will be potentially disruptive as a major – immediate and deferred – risk factor. It is the latter insofar as the coalition strategy does more than integrate the rear-continental state prematurely into the international system, but also projects it into the vacuum the defeat of the so far preeminent continental state will have created at the center of the system. When the defeated central power was farther evolved institutionally as well as weaker in material potential than the ascendant rear-continental state, relatively flexible balancing around the issue of one-actor preeminence will be in greater danger than before of lapsing into the statics of forcible unification around a single pole of power. And although the central power overreacting under pressure will seemingly justify the strategy, the strategy will actually defeat the coalition's limited objective of containing the central power within bounds compatible with continental equilibrium and the sea power's oceanic superiority. Moreover, instead of achieving the objective without serious detriment to system stability, the strategy will disruptively overstimulate actors along both slopes of the rise–decline curve: the ones in decline who trigger the conflict and the ascendant one who regulates the competition.

While the attendant exertions will undermine the dominance of the sea power only in the longer run, the precariousness of its seeming control over the strategy and its objectives, and the implementing coalition itself, will be disclosed sooner. Thus, in some circumstances, embracing the strategy may help remove prior constraint on the rival's overseas goals. One such constraint was the awareness in Germany that an early dissolution of the British Empire would benefit Germany less than France and Russia – and the United States. Subsequently, the pattern of the conflict being intensified by a strategy keyed to containment was most clearly in evidence in the period preceding World War I. Since Germany was then a late-entering as well as an upthrusting power, England was in a position to deny her parity in both role and resource endowment more stringently, and with more galling effect, than she had been either disposed or able to do with respect to France in the eighteenth century – whether it was in the Far East in favor of the Japanese (the 1902 alliance), in North and Central Africa in favor of the French (the 1904 accommodation), and in the Near East and Asia Minor to the advantage of Russia (the 1907 accommodation). Moreover, Russia as the rear-continental power loomed larger in terms of both strengths and weaknesses for imperial (and subsequently Nazi) Germany than had either of the Germanic powers, Austria or Prussia, for ancien-regime France. Finally, the German late-comer's domestic socio-political strains and stresses were more pressing, and the value-ideological diversity between the continental and the insular polity more intensely polarizing, than either had been in the contention between the more organically evolving and equally western England and France.

The risks and costs attaching to the grand coalition-type of continental strategy are thus considerable. On one side they comprise central-systemic disruption, attendant on the explosive reaction of the central state to pressures from oceanic denial and continental encirclement. And they include on the other side the operational displacement of the rear-continental power toward the system's center, threatening to set off the system's implosion upon itself. Aimed at constraining one power's inherently finite ambition to expand, the strategy amplifies a multi-state conflict beyond anyone's control. Despite its risks, the most reflexively driven of the strategies will be common also because of the limitations besetting the main alternatives to it.

One alternative is an association or alliance of the two principal land powers aimed at instituting a species of collusive duopoly for insulating the continental balance of power from sea-power interference. The central power would thus avoid encirclement and the rear-continental power entrapment into unsheathing its sword to defend another's trident. The strategy was essayed by the French when trying to reconstitute the position once held by Habsburg Spain, first in association with Habsburg Austria as part of the but slowly maturing project of a humbled Louis XIV realized in the mid-eighteenth century "diplomatic revolution," and later in league with Russia at Tilsit (the Continental System, based on the Berlin decrees) when a triumphant Napoleon had virtually eliminated Austria and Prussia as great powers. Louis-Philippe and Napoleon III replayed the scenario from growing weakness with either Austria or Russia in the wake of disappointments over a "liberal" alliance with England. Russia was subsequently the sole potential fellow-duopolist for both imperial and Nazi Germany, as either an alternative to or a leverage for accommodation with Britain on the basis of equality. In one form or another, all moves toward active solidarity expressed the continental parties' shared grievance against either specific policies or the general posture of the insular-maritime power (reflecting the disparities between the two arenas) and the sense of their identity as to internal orders and external predicaments (reflecting the special characteristics of the continental arena).

In actuality, the strategy for duopoly broke down again and again under the weight of built-in limitations. Closely interrelated, these comprised divergence of more specific objectives, the difficulty to divide spoils equally, and disparity in stages of evolution. The prime objective of the central power will be to neutralize balance-of-power contests in the continental core at a point of its clear advantage, in order to release resources for enforcing parity-or-equilibrium in the oceanic peripheries. The rear-continental power's contrary prime objective will be to materially improve its position closer to the center of the continental equilibrium. Thus Austria would partition or otherwise demote Prussia (in the Kaunitzian scheme) and successive Russian regimes would control or conquer next to the Baltic littoral also the areas adjoining the Straits. Whereas the would-be amphibian central power sought to match the insular state's advantages overseas from an impregnable continental position, notably in the west, the rear-continental power felt obligated to compensate for any resulting gains of the central power, more commonly in the east. The scheme for duopoly tended to falter, or the duopoly itself collapse, whenever revealing the impossibility of dividing the potential spoils of collusion equitably in terms of both space and timing disclosed a fertile ground for the divisive tactics of the insular state.

A larger or earlier gain of either party to the continental combine would make it less needful of support by the partner and potentially threatening to him. The near-insoluble problem was thus how to share gains in a manner that would make the contiguous continental states mutually supportive in the present as well as individually secure relative to the other into an indefinite future. In particular the rear-continental state would tend to keep open the wire to the maritime wing power as the guarantor of last resort against the actual or potential partner's manifest strength and suspected ambitions, while the continentally preeminent state would be from the start preemptively on its guard against such eventuality. If one could not envisage with equanimity that peripheral-oceanic be added to the core-continental strengths of the would-be amphibian, the other would forestall the suspect ally's overland gains in lower-pressure hinterlands pending equivalent acquisitions of its own. More even than Austria's designs on Prussia for Louis XV, Russia's probings and aspirations in the Ottoman Empire and beyond created the last-mentioned problem for Napoleon's France and, subsequently, for Germany. Nor was it ever likely that, in conditions precariously poised between tentative concord and prospective conflict, the security systems of major land powers extending from the metropole through an inner belt of clients to the outer zone of potential allies would not disturbingly overlap between closely adjoining actors. In ways complicating the security strategy of each party and jeopardizing stability in its orbit, Poland and Prussia illustrated the problem in the Franco–Russian, and the Balkans and the Middle East in the Russo-German, transactions and could not but facilitate the task of the insular power within the continental balance-of-power sector of *its* three concentric areas of security and prosperity.

Divisive in themselves, the stakes and stimulants introduced by the land–sea power schism will only aggravate the impediments to accommodation always present between juxtaposed territorial powers, at a loss whether to risk demonstrations of solidarity by sharing control in intervening areas or seek safety by contentiously subverting there one another's position. One such impediment consists of divergent evolutionary stages along the entire rise–

decline range. In the nature of things, the globally ambitious would–be amphibian power will be climactically ascendant while the rear–continental state, typically occupying a more indeterminate stage, may waver between incipient decline and tokens of resurgence (Austria), or be only initially rising (Prussia, Russia). In such circumstances the rear-continental state will be unable to identify with the overseas concerns or priorities of the potential partner in duopoly. It will have been either navally frustrated by then if declining, thus Austria, or if ascendant, be two steps short of entering upon its own future bid in the global maritime arena: eighteenth–century Prussia through Bismarckian to Wilhelmine Germany, and early nineteenth–century Russia through late Tsardom and the Stalinist phase to Khrushchevite and subsequent Soviet policy. Such a power will be unwilling to allow duopoly to consecrate a second–ranking position on the continent before encompassing its full evolutionary trajectory. Thus, rather than make lastingly common cause with either (Napoleonic) France or (Wilhelmine) Germany as a lever or battering ram against England, Russia would first replace Austria and Prussia as Britain's main continental ballast.

The incentive will be even stronger for the once dominant (coastal) maritime or preeminent amphibian power, entering upon the second stage of decline, not to expand a duopoly into a continental bloc before exhausting the one remaining alternative to strategic irrelevance. Thus, just as Russia replaced Austria and Prussia as the continental ballast of Britain, France will take the place of the Dutch as Britain's chief overland bridge to the mainland. Only a self-denying moderation of the would-be amphibious central power in the territorial sphere could persuade the diminished party to renounce strategic protection by the dominant sea power, with its prospect of war, for the promise of peace and prosperity under the fellow-continentals' diplomatic protectorate. Such moderation was always apt to be impeded by the would–be amphibian's need for access to coastal bases in the west and for territorial gains in the east to counterpoise the larger-based rear-continental party's organic growth. Thus, in the Kaunitzian "system," France's contractually secured compensation in the by-then Austrian Netherlands (today's Belgium) for Austria's reinvigoration in Germany (at Prussia's expense) was bound to alienate the Dutch. And if a later France was reacting similarly to imperial Germany's urge to offset (at cost to herself and the Low Countries) the growth of Russia and break through Britain's naval stranglehold on Germany's coasts and maritime exits into the Atlantic, the continental–maritime configuration was identical to that which a later Russia would confront (and Western Europe guard against) in the enlarged oceanic gap between north-western Europe and the Greenland–Iceland complex. Just as in the later, so in the historical instances the greater fears neutralized the diminished "third" mainland power's grievances against the age's principal sea power, which to surface and exploit was the standing interest, intermittent policy, and rarest achievement of the would-be amphibian.

In view of such impediments, prospects for a continental duopoly or bloc will be as implausible as have commonly been the apprehensions of one-power hegemony. Britain's fears of a Franco- or German–Russian dominance of the heartland were, when not simulated, no more warranted than had been Rome's pretended alarms over a Macedonian–Syrian bloc replicating the world empire of Alexander in the third century BC. The deeply divided Hellenistic realms would no more block growing Latin power in the Mediterranean than a solid alliance with Persia freed the Ottomans for a decisive bid in the same area centuries later. There are, thus, only weak grounds for the sea power's prime strategic response to the prospect of continental duopoly. An encircling – but, now, oceanic rather than continental – coalition with the maritime power or powers in the rear of the continental combine represents only a secondary constraint on the latter when compared with the hindrances intrinsic to the formula. And it will be but a second-best short-term safeguard for the insular-maritime actor when the alliance turns into a hard-to-steer vehicle for sharing maritime superiority. Where alliance with the much weaker island of Rhodes had extended Rome's Mediterranean sway at little or no cost, Great Britain took a first step toward renouncing naval supremacy globally when allying with Japan to preempt a Germano–Russian combination. Thus to "turn the tables" on Britain was then a but remotely possible consummation of the Germans' diplomatic retaliation for having been spurned by the British; and, by setting the stage for Russia's defeat by Japan, the oceanic alliance made the continental duopoly appear more plausible than it had been before.

When added to risks flowing from the continental grand coalition, limitations on the strategy for continental duopoly or bloc will increase the preeminent land power's interest in accommodating with the dominant sea power. A conservative alliance potentially extending all the way to a condominium would shift division within the geo-functional spectrum to the heart of the continent; and it would defuse the land–sea power schism as sharing role and status system-wide with the insular state simultaneously compounded and could be used to contain the continental preeminence of the central power. As the otherwise irreconcilably asymmetric resources of the two kinds of powers became complementary in cooperation, the alliance would institutionalize the inseparability of the two arenas and the reciprocal invulnerability of the two types of power, instead of both features instigating involvement in opposing alliances.

As an incentive to the accommodation, the insular-maritime power can look forward to preserving the essentials of its favorable situation at a lessened cost and for the indefinite future. The land power will expect to exchange restraint on the continent for globally expanded role and resource even as it registers a decrease in the risks implicit in challenging the sea power and realizes a prompt substantive return on its extant capacity to defy the sea power militantly. Since the anticipated savings of the sea power will be principally material, in regard to the costs of a contested naval supremacy and contingent military preparedness, the economies will be especially precious for a societal order and political regime typically dependent on assured prosperity. The land power's dividend will be more of the ideal than the material kind insofar as association with the premier world power enhances the internal legitimacy of a regime typically anxious to garner prestige externally. An immediate price to pay by the land power will be integration into the "liberal" modalities of the world economy favored by the maritime-mercantile state. But it will be difficult to measure the immaterial cost of relaxing the illiberal – protectionist and/or statist –

management of the economy (a likely objective of the sea power) against either eventual material gains or immediate easements in military expenditures. Nor will the sea power's gains be without costs in geopolitical and -economic assets. But such costs have to be assessed against the price of contesting a transfer of primacy which, the more assertively if not violently it is sought by the land power, will all the more insidiously unfold peacefully in favor of other parties including the mercantile-maritime ally-competitor.

Potential advantages will inevitably run up against actual constraints. Thus, the land power will normally be inferior to the sea power in diplomatic prestige and options even when equal or superior to it in material capabilities. For a Louis XIV to offer virtual condominium to a questionably legitimate ruler (William III) of still inferior England, to follow on an agreed-upon partition of the Spanish Empire, was an exception confirming the rule applied thereafter to all other French regimes: after a defeat (the post-Louis XIV regency and its immediate aftermath) but also following major victories (to the debatable extent that either side viewed the 1802 Peace of Amiens as a platform for accommodation); after an English-type liberal revolution in France (under the Orleanist dynasty) and in the course of Anglo–French co-belligerency (under a neo-Bonapartist regime). The disjunction between material power and diplomatic prestige translating into only deceptively real options became even more pronounced in Anglo–German relations. The power–prestige gap instrumental in thwarting either tentative cooperation or hesitant mutual courtships in the Bismarckian and the Wilhelmine eras widened as the Second yielded to the Third German Reich. And for the gap to widen compounded the effects of a growing because related discrepancy, between the long-term German condominial objective and short–term coercive pressure tactics for gaining British acquiescence.

Just as the asymmetry in tangible and intangible assets will aggravate impediments due to the conflict between principal objectives (when the sea power's aim to disable the land power as a candidate for maritime equality clashes with the land power's demand for legitimized continental preeminence plus significant advantages from oceanic parity), so the divergent fundamental purposes will encompass contrasting particulars. The continental regime will typically favor the condominial formula in order to enhance internal stability, as either a flagrant object of policy (thus the illegitimate Orleanist and Bonapartist regimes in two installments each) or a valued side effect (thus the socially embattled imperial German regime). By contrast, so long as the insular polity is at or near the apex of its power and prosperity, its more stable or legitimate ruling elite will pursue primarily strategic objectives, tied in the official mind's "unspoken assumptions" only loosely to longer-range economic and immediate political domestic implications. In consequence, judged by the islanders' criteria, the continental state's foreign policies will often appear as erratic, opportunist, or adventurist, and will cast doubt on its readiness for accommodation. The policies of the sea power will in turn appear as insensitive to the pressing domestic needs (tied to legitimate external aspirations) of even a well-disposed continental regime.

The diversity in specific stakes will thwart any identity, be it only conditional or temporary, of interests in the stability of an international system on balance propitious to both of the relatively favored and in the last resort more conservative than revisionist powers. Thus, Franco–British accommodation might have stabilized the world and foreclosed a chain of the global wars that began in 1701, while a comparable opportunity arose in Anglo–German relations from 1890 to about 1901. However, Anglo–Dutch interests would not willingly permit the French crown to inherit fragments of the Spanish Empire in the Mediterranean just as Britain acting alone would no more condone the thrust of a later friendly and pacific French regime (of Louis-Philippe) than the push of alienated Germany, either in Belgium toward the Channel and the Atlantic or in the Middle East in the hypothetical direction of the Indian Ocean. The more or less subtle reasoning against a different strategic choice comprised the fear lest a mere prospect of a far-reaching accommodation with the second-named power induce first the Dutch to accept diplomatic subservience to France, and then the French to submit to Germany, foreclosing Britain's access to the continent in case the preemptive third-party moves made the condominial alliance less necessary or attractive for the continental rival. The apprehension, bound to escalate into acute anxiety as war on the continent became imminent as a result, undermined appeasement of the schism independently of the would-be amphibian's actual or projected maritime-mercantile activities and naval capabilities. Moreover, the British reasoning, focused on France as the key third party to include in diplomatic calculations concerning Germany, meshed well enough with the Germans', focused mainly on Russia, to keep the conflict-prone land–sea power triangle intact. Whereas matching those of a Salisbury or Lansdowne regarding a German connection were Bülow's fears lest rushing into duopoly with Russia impel Britain toward preemptive accommodation with the Tsardom before Germany could capitalize on a warlike escalation of Anglo–Russian competition, lost in the new was Bismarck's earlier concern that a German-fostered Anglo–Russian crisis would induce St Petersburg to forsake the German in favor of an English connection.

If the potential for combining efforts at control in behalf of the general ends of order faltered again and again before either conflict over concrete stakes or similarly hypothetical diplomatic-strategic worst-case projections, it was because the realistic presumption of the inseparability of land- and sea-based capabilities, propelling the land power sea-ward and the sea power land-ward, prevailed over the ideal postulate of their functional complementarity. The possibility of basing joint order-maintenance on a functioning division of labor (reflecting complementary capabilities) would repeatedly break down over the difficulty to concert a "fair" division of spheres (reserving individual control or influence). If realizing a quasi-condominial association was contingent on the land power upholding the British peace in general and British interests in particular in areas tradition or geography opened wide to that power's diplomatic influence or material impact, this meant for the continental state to forgo overseas rewards adequately compensating increases in security risks and diminished diplomtic credit on the continent: to acquiesce in the denial of oceanic partnership without being assured additional profit or protection on land. In the event, Bourbon France would not lastingly act for Britain in the

Great Northern War centered on Russia in the early eighteenth century, any more than neo-Bonapartist France would go on antagonizing Russia after doing most of the fighting in the Crimea or Hohenzollern Germany defy her at the risk of having to do so in China. Whereas the late French regimes had first to enhance the country's security on the Rhine frontier against the Germanys, unified Germany had to win first or simultaneously greater control and security in Middle Europe against Russia; nor would either of the continental regimes be compliantly cooperative on the continent unless the British condoned their combining self-affirmation overseas with improvements in naval capabilities – be it through restoration to past levels (Fleury, Choiseul), technological modernization (Napoleon III), or rigidly planned and graduated build-up (Tirpitz), as either a basis for "equal" alliance or a safeguard against the consequences of cooperation failing to materialize or endure.

By the time it became commonplace for the continentals to impute only a double standard or also outright perfidy to the British, they themselves had failed to appreciate the inhibitions on the island state implicit in both space-determined structures of its domestic authority and national capabilities and time-related stages in the evolution of the contending polities and policies. The conundrum how to combine inequalities in land- or home-based resources (favoring the leading continental power relative to the insular and/or the contiguous continental states) with maritime parity or near-parity, and fit the discrete capability aggregates into an all-systemic equilibrium that would leave the British Isles with a comfortable margin of security and prosperity, defeated even the best of intentions to appease the conflict: in mid-eighteenth century, when a pro-peace British ministry would settle the first truly global war (the Seven Years War) by leaving defeated France with a supposedly adequate base for naval power and overseas empire in the western hemisphere, at a cost (sacrificing Britain's alliance with Prussia without the certainty of recovering one with Austria) of great benefit to France's much eroded diplomatic preeminence on the continent; and in late nineteenth century and beyond, when, in hopes perhaps of forestalling a still larger conflict, one set of British colonial policy-makers inclined toward conceding to Germany overseas outlets in Africa as a counter to the Foreign Office's determination to limit Germany's rise and sustain faltering France in Europe.

Prussia and/or Austria as rear-continental, and France like the Netherlands earlier as formerly major western and maritime or amphibious, powers illustrate (as do their later role-substitutes) the negative impact "third" continental powers will have on the prospect of land–sea power condominial alliance. When the rear-continental power is strong, the sea power will abstain from paying the price of accommodation on the seas in anticipation of a distracting conflict between the two major land powers; and, if the farther-eastern will often gamble on, if not incite, dissension between the more western parties, the nearer-eastern actor will speculate along similar lines when the receding maritime or amphibious power he is about to supplant as the main challenger is still in a position to engage the sea power in competition. Conversely, when the "third" powers are weak, the insular state will feel the need to shield them from any inclination to submit to the preeminent continental power in the absence of such protection, while their weakness diminishes the pressures on the would-be amphibian to compromise with the sea power. In either case, deciding against intimate land–sea power accommodation will undo any existing opportunity for substantially advancing politico-economic integration within the smaller-western regional triangle (comprising next to the insular incumbent and the continental claimant the declining predecessor of either) under the condominial auspicies of the two principals; the makers of the decision will shift the gears instead to accelerating the course toward global politico-military triangularization (favoring the grand coalition approach to conflict), as part of which the critical role in inhibiting condominium will migrate from the declining (and more western) to the ascending (and more eastern) third party.

Radically diminished in either case is the possibility of the third continental parties encouraging the cooperation of the dominant land and sea powers by being either so strong and ambitious or so weak and unpredictable as to endanger both of the more stable or stabilizable and saturated or satisfiable powers. Instead, and regardless of the specific character of the third party, if the perceivable threat flows from its strengths, the condominial response may well appear as no longer sufficient and the threat invite efforts at unilateral appeasement; if the threat flows from third-party weakness, a cooperative response may well appear as unnecessary, because the threat to stability is too remote or too difficult to deal with to warrant the costs of a condominial arrangement and forgo the gains from co-opting the third party into one's sphere of influence.

Further augmenting the hindrances from structurally conditioned disparities in short- and long-term costs and advantages will be expectations and apprehensions linked to disparities in evolutionary stages. A land power will find a junior partnership less attractive when it is ascending, lest the unequal association hamper its organic growth or curtail its operational freedom; a maritime power will resist a condominium even when lopsided in its favor if it is past its peak and approaches the initial stages of decline, lest the formula accelerate the fall while disguising it on the surface. The land power's reluctance is based on distate for the condominium preempting open-ended hypothetical developments; the sea power's, for it projecting the land power into a future more assured for one than reassuring for the other partner. Even an unequal condominium under such circumstances would place the continental preeminence of the land power under constraints that are flexible at best and at worst fragile; nor would it foreclose longer-term changes in capabilities and intentions militating against both denials and self-denials of expanding access to naval or oceanic resources.

One or another of the several limitations will make it near-impossible to divine the right timing for the rare attempts at land–sea power condominium, resulting in its even rarer transient realizations. Ancient Egypt, after weakening the successive would-be amphibian powers through outflanking coalition, essayed a condominial alliance with the Mitanni and entered one with the Hittite central power too late to forestall an ultimately fatal Assyrian expansion. Conversely, in the period between the Persian and the Peloponnesian Wars, Sparta and Athens may have made an attempt prematurely, before their feasible goals and effective capabilities had been sufficiently clarified: a conservative association in support of Sparta's internal order (against insurgent or unreliable helots) and nominal system-wide hegemony would come too soon for a rising Athens yet uncertain whether she could not add a continental empire to maritime supremacy, as well as too late for a Sparta manifestly receding from the hegemonic role in all of Hellas and uncertain that she could safely relinquish the maritime arena to Athens. The larger quandary was only illustrated by specific events, thus when during the Peloponnesian War a Sparta militarily set back (at Pylos) sought peace too soon, and the Athenians, after losing the military advantage, too late.

The time factor was no more propitious in the European setting, when the Anglo–French accommodation subsequent to a peace (of Utrecht, 1713) ending the Ludovician wars came too late. Neither of the two parties could control one set of resentful and resurgent allies (Habsburg Austria and Bourbon Spain, respectively) any longer, and would be soon unable to check either individually or jointly the rising power of those same or different allies' enemies (Prussia's in regard to Austria any more than Russia's in regard to Sweden and Poland). From a different perspective, the accommodation may also have been attempted too soon, because its terms could not be settled so long as the relative decline of France was no more certain than was the relative rise of England. Once a new administration in France had recovered from the War of Spanish Succession and its sequelae, it would not regard as either timely or lastingly tolerable a markedly unequal alliance with England if it meant forgoing the restoration of preeminent status on the continent and an important naval capability on the seas. Allowing for specific differences, France's situation after the major wars of Louis XIV and Napoleon prefigured Germany's before the major wars of William II and Hitler closely enough to discount the particulars.

Moreover, the diversely evolving parties' divergent time-frames will not necessarily fit the time clock of the system itself. If a timely Atheno–Spartan concord would have prolonged the autonomy of the Greek state system, an Anglo–French accord would have perpetuated the global centrality of the European system even more reliably than a later Anglo–German entente. By the time Britain had first become ready and then anxious to accommodate with Germany, a truncated European system could no longer be stabilized around an enlarged central power without others reaching outside its boundary for countervailing resources contrary to the requisites of continental preeminence if not also oceanic parity. The requirements of system stability are thus not necessarily congruent with the role-status exigencies of its major actors and their readiness to consent to the necessary adjustments to changing capabilities. And if the timing is rarely if ever quite right, it will be wholly wrong when both sides face decline: not only the dominant sea power, at long last ready to consider accommodation, but also the would-be amphibian, by then determined to foreclose prospective regression on the continent by consolidating preeminence into hegemony as a prelude to reaching out for world power. Such had not yet been the case when still ascendant Britain was facing a second-phase bid by France under Napoleon, consequent on the more moderate self-assertion of the ancien regime in both the continental and maritime arenas simultaneously. But the situation was markedly in evidence when Britain came up against the second-phase German bid by the Third Reich after weakening herself in contention with the more moderate "mixed" (continental–maritime) initiatives of the Second.

Even if the policy of appeasement in the late 1930s was either consciously aimed, or could be rationalized as aiming, at doing no more than integrate a satisfied Nazi Germany into a revised four-to-five member European balance of power, its unavoidably implicit thrust was toward an Anglo–German co-guarantee of a revised European and, through eventual colonial rectifications, global order. In that perspective the policy of Joseph Chamberlain's son took up again, in less favorable conditions, the short-lived initiative of the father. By the later time, however, even a far-reaching recasting of oceanic-colonial assets in Germany's favor could not reliably keep German gains on the continent from doing more than redress the imbalance between capabilities and roles inherited from World War I. An altogether unlikely self-restraint was required in an overly mature system susceptible to one-power hegemony by virtue of a sharp decline on the part of the two co-victorious western powers and the uncertain growth–decline status of a severely ambivalent rear-continental state, while a differently ambiguous detachment from the central system was shared by competing (US and Japanese) candidates for succession to sea-power dominance. In these conditions, for the central power (Germany) to draw the rear-continental one (Soviet Russia) into a duopolistic partnership on the continent was no longer a maneuver for coaxing the sea power into a condominial arrangement world-wide on the basis of equality; it became a preliminary to eliminating the rear-continental party as a possible ally for the insular state (and instigator of a mutually frustrating conflict between the challenger and that state) in order to coerce the latter into an inversely unequal accommodation. Understandably, the prospect of thus reversing post-Versailles positions in favor of Germany was even less likely to appeal to a Britain confident of support by a more congenial successor than mere equalization of positions with France had appealed to the still-ascendant Britain in the hundred years between Utrecht and Vienna.

If degrees of weakness or strength of the rear-continental power are at least as critical for the strategy keyed to condominium as for strategies directed at continental coalition or duopoly, degrees and timing of accommodation between the leading land and sea powers are just as crucial for system stability. This raises the question whether reshuffling tactical emphases on priorities can replace a farther-reaching revision of the controlling mind-sets, on the part of the sea power in particular.

Conditions for taking steps toward limited accommodation were present in the periods just before the French Revolution and before World War I: in the first case following France's effective but financially ruinous overseas revanche in North America, and the demonstration of the impotence of both western powers in the east attending the partition of Poland; in the second case, in the face of Germany's real but faltering and financially onerous advances in the naval sphere and in the Ottoman Empire, and of rising social pressures in both countries and disorders in the Balkans. However, a mainly procedural détente could not compensate the central power for its position weakening substantially on the continent: relative to the growth of Prussia and Russia and resurgence of Austria as the eastern powers from the viewpoint of France, and the renewed surge of tsarist Russia backed by revanchist France from the German viewpoint. Whereas the full extent of the threat from the east was to materialize for France only during the death throes of the *ancien* regime, a growing fixation on it in Germany gave rise to a mentality that became fatal to the established order. The perceived threat made the central continental power adopt an all-or-nothing attitude to cooperation with the insular state, more so in the German than in the French case and, in the last analysis, in the case of the Third than of the Second Reich. A "nothing-rather-than-everything" response was all the more assured from the insulars' standpoint if choosing otherwise would mean alienating or sacrificing the rear-continental power or powers. Britain would no more collaborate unreservedly with imperial France in the difficult task of safeguarding the fragile bases of the Peace of Amiens so long as Russia stood firm at the back of Prussia and Austria than she would let cooperation with imperial Germany in appeasing the Balkan Wars or settling disputes over the Berlin–Baghdad railway escalate into a pledge of unconditional neutrality on the continent that would stand in the way of vetoeing any German action susceptible of humiliating Russia again in the Balkans to the point of neutralizing her as a willing and valuable ally alongside France.

DILEMMAS AND DESIGNS IN THE CHOICE OF STRATEGIES

The price of failure to choose a "correct" strategy – one fitting the "total" structure – includes the costs attached to adopting the seemingly most realistic strategies of the ostensibly principal two parties: the sea power's grand continental or oceanic coalition for containment and the central power's for continental duopoly and naval standoff. Both encompass the continental and the maritime arenas, give rise to purely operational dilemmas, and occasion problematic choices and trade-offs in the material, capability-related under-pinnings of strategy.

Formally identical are the costs and risks accruing to the sea power from the continental grand coalition against land-power hegemony and from the oceanic alliance against land-power duopoly (or joint hegemony). Just as a successful continental coalition promotes the rear-continental state and risks projecting it into the center of the international system politico-militarily on land (thus recreating the central-power problem), so an oceanic alliance (when geo-graphically feasible) replaces the displacement of a politico-military center of gravity with fostering the devolution of only maritime or also mercantile parity or primacy to an upcoming peripheral insular state. Thus, Britain's continental coalition strategy made it easier for a Germanic power to succeed France as the continental challenger, and upgraded Russia against first France and then Germany. And the British were to lose much of their position in Asia to the Japanese partner in an oceanic alliance concluded as a counter to a still possible Germano–Russian duopoly and an alternative to a no longer or not yet attractive Anglo–German accommodation. Britain's overseas strategic assets going even more conclusively or immediately to the United States in the wake of two wartime associations consummated the consequences of the same kind of preference. The transfer completed the reversal in the Anglo–American balance which, only latent in the armed conflict over a different British oceanic strategy *vis-à-vis* a Franco–Russian "continental system" (in 1812), had been decisively advanced once Britain recoiled from using the French alliance against Russia in the Crimea for a more than casual joint effort to contain the United States in the western hemisphere. Finally, when defeat of the preeminent central power has made the conflict-triggering ex-dominant maritime-mercantile or amphibious power less insecure, this will propel it into another round of competition with the insular power. Thus, the temporary removal of pressure on France in the period between the two Anglo–American comradeships-in-arms (matching a reprieve for the Dutch in the French setting and its consequences) revived Anglo–French competition overseas even more acutely than it did the two "allied" powers' differences over strategy in Europe.

The dominant sea power's dilemma regarding whom to lose to and when is replicated in the quandary of the would-be amphibian whether to elect cooperation or conflict as the way to winning concessions from the sea power, and then how much to seek at what rate and cost or risk. The Hobson's choice of the maritime-insular state is between division of labor (and of rewards from joint control, with the central power), diplacement (of the still less congenial rear-continental state's power and policy toward the center of the stage), and devolution (of maritime-mercantile assets to an ascendant fellow-insular ally-competitor). As for the central power's polar options, they are equally unpalatable: it can forswear pride and prestige and seek peace and prosperity at the cost of acting as a continental surrogate for the dominant sea power, or it can invest all power and passion in the effort of becoming the latter's imperial successor and risk submission to a neighboring empire on the mainland.

A way to sidestep the choice is to seek continental duopoly before or after the decisive bid for an "equal" condominium, employing the former as an incentive to being conceded the latter in the first case or an alternative to realizing it in the second case. Louis XIV had offered condominium to England before redirecting the diplomatic process toward duopoly with Austria, while the continental alliance materialized (under Louis XV) only after an unequal condominial alliance (during the latter's minority) had broken down. Napoleon courted Alexander of Russia only after failing to either conquer England (by way of the Egyptian route to India or in a cross-Channel invasion) or compose with her (Peace of Amiens), while both Louis-Philippe and Napoleon III looked eastward to either Vienna or St Petersburg for conservative union when disappointed with the liberal liaison across the English Channel. Once unified, Germany started out with a bias toward duopoly (Bismarck's Russian orientation), renounced it (after Bismarck's fall) for a new course of entente with England, only to fluctuate thereafter between hopes of securing a place for herself on the seas and in the world at large on a moderate scale in alliance with Britain (von Holstein and, differently nuanced, the Kaiser) and the conviction that the objective could be achieved only on a larger scale against Britain on the seas (von Tirpitz) in cooperation with Russia on land (von Bülow and, with modifications, the Kaiser). As also in Britain, the clearest difference was between policy-makers believing that a definite rational choice between radical alternatives was both possible and necessary (von Holstein, Joseph Chamberlain) and those persuaded that a choice could and had to be finessed (Bismarck, Lord Salisbury), with still others wavering between the two positions (the Kaiser, Lord Lansdowne). The more dogmatic position prevailed only when a more singly policy-controlling emperor-substitute in the more radical Reich preferred throughout a condominium with Britain (under the formula of guaranteeing the British Empire) to duopoly with Russia (favored by von Bülow's clone in the Wilhelmstrasse), and employed a simulacrum of the latter only as a tactical transition to bidding one last time for the former.

Notably a maturing central power will more often than not prefer equal condominium to all-out conflict. When the regime is primarily interested in domestic stability (Napoleon III), it may hope to both compensate for its internal weaknesses and put them to use by alternately stressing condominium (before the Crimea) and duopoly (after the Crimea). When the regime is more self-confident, it will vacillate between courting the insular sea power and trying to coerce it into association by militant diplomacy (the Second Reich) or military force (The Third Reich). On balance, the central power will approach duopoly – by mutual consent (Louis XIV, William II) or by unilateral coercion (Napoleon, Hitler) – more often as a leverage for producing a compromise than as an alternative to composition with the sea power: will aim at uniting the continent under its leadership as an incentive to the maritime power agreeing to share global role and status (in effect, if unevenly, Napoleon, both William II and Hitler) rather than as a means of turning the tables on the sea power and setting the stage for forcibly acquiring or dividing its assets (Napoleon on and off while trying to detach Austria to begin with, von Bülow and von Ribbentrop when courting Russia).

Regardless of whether duopoly is sought through consent or coercion, it will be part of the central power's effort to achieve a strategic breakthrough: only diplomatic, when the continental aggregation is sought as an inducement to land–sea power condominium; politico-military and physical, when it is an immediate alternative to such concert. Insofar as implementing the inducement option successfully pointed to a reduction of tensions on the continent, the would-be amphibian might be advantaged also tactically by an attendant estrangement between the currently and the formerly principal farther-western and more closely sea-adjoining powers. Conversely, for the land power to implement duopoly as a coercive approach or alternative to condominium is the counterpart of the insular state forcing the would-be amphibian into an attempt to break out of military-strategic encirclement by violent means. Whereas the attempted breakout will consolidate the sea power-led grand coalition around the rear-continental ballast, the additional tactical advantage will come from the once-dominant maritime or amphibious power performing wholeheartedly as the insular state's live wire and solid bridge to the continent.

Since a diplomatic strategy always risks leading to military conflict on land or sea, the effect of strategic choices on capabilities will be critical for decisions on strategy. The key trade-off for the insular sea power is between immediately positive and eventually adverse consequences. A coalition strategy for containment will entail immediate savings on land-based military capabilities that are either direct (resources of continental allies or "swords") or indirect (if an oceanic alliance distracts the rival's capabilities), permitting the concentration of resources on the more productive (trade-promoting or -protecting) naval capabilities. However, there is a deferred cost if and when naval resources have been diffused and the maritime-mercantile role devolved (consequence of the oceanic alliance), and the next-in-line land-military power to be faced is enlarged (consequence of the continental coalition), while the pool of potential continental allies has been depleted. The rub is that the land–sea power condominium may entail still greater erosion of potential allies as the long-term obverse of immediate savings. The quandary of the central power is more concentrated in time, and presses as such more heavily on the choices of strategy. While subtracting from the resources available to the sea power, duopoly will release commensurate central-power resources for a naval build up. But it will not necessarily reduce substantially the land-military capability required for maintaining an even balance with the partner in consensual duopoly, as a safeguard against concert deteriorating into conflict. Hence the attraction of coercive duopoly, despite its immediately greater capability costs and medium-term risks. Conversely, the lesser cost and risk of a more limited naval build-up implicit in condominium will realize enough savings in resource to provide for comparatively stress-free maintenance of a land-military capability sufficient to uphold continental preeminence within the narrowed bounds compatible with, and under relaxed constraints consequent on, the condominium. Hence the would-be amphibians' re-emergent interest in the condominial arrangement, despite its costs in either role or status and (possibly) material substance.

Both the allure and the difficulty of achieving the association with the sea power raise the question of the purpose of the would-be amphibian's naval build-up, the counterpart to the sea power's links to the continent. Is the build-up intended as a lever to induce or compel admission to condominium on the basis of naval near-parity (also by increasing the value of the central power as ally for other continental states)? Or is it a weapon not only usable but actually intended for use in a climactic assault on the insular state or its overseas empire? Both purposes are likely to coexist, and be alternately dominant, so long as the sea power's responses are contingent on the amphibian's averred or assumed intentions, co-determining the prospects for breaking out of the resulting vicious circle. Because, as a quandary, the persuasive or coercive purpose of the naval build-up is the equivalent of the operative objectives behind the amphibian's strategy for continental duopoly, the two crucial issues introduce similar ambiguities into the land–sea power relationship and instability into the international system. Moreover, they surface the subjacent link between economic (including fiscal) and politico-military capabilities and concerns – a relationship that is equally key if differently structured in the insular powers' oceanic alliance.

Even when competition centered on economics is initially secondary, it will easily compound political rivalry. This will be equally so when a duopolistic alliance works to exclude the insular sea power from trading with the continent as when the naval build-up of the central causes the insular power to incur economic stress directly (by serving or being intended to serve the amphibian's competitive trade) or indirectly (by distorting the allocation of productive resources in an arms race). Whether the material consequences are direct or indirect, they will add a domestic to the interstate dimension of the land–sea power relationship. Reciprocally hostile sets of public opinion may then be the result of, or a device for sustaining tolerance for, the costs of the naval-commercial competition. In either case, the resulting emotions will help a mature-to-declining sea power resist the temptations of a geopolitically costly compromise, just when an insufficiently stable or confident continental regime may have to decide whether to improve its domestic position by entering upon a legitimacy-enhancing association or by denouncing an equity-denying antagonist.

Neither of the principals is likely to have an easy time of it. The central power will have little effective choice between strategies and have ready access to none that is safe. Condominium entails renunciations due to junior status, and risks provoking other continental parties into moves calculated to disclose the contrary interests and preoccupations of the partners. Duopoly places the central power in a no more comfortable senior-ally position relative to a materially and institutionally less developed, but more actively restless or potentially resource-rich, associate. Long before (Soviet) Russia's with China, France's experiences with both Austria and Prussia and Germany's with Russia revealed the more eastern continental powers' tendency to turn up eventually on the side of a materially more attractive and physically distant (western-insular) sponsor. Thus, if condominium invites renunciations that are not rewarded by instant satisfaction of scaled-down or subtly altered goals, duopoly will tend to entail immediate material reinforcement of another party that risks being unrequited strategically in the longer run. Whereas a condominial alliance harbors the possibility of irreversible regression from a high point in bargaining power, alliance for duopoly conceals the prospect of unmanageable reversal in relative brute power.

As for the sea power, it can choose any of the strategies but one, and will be commonly able to frustrate duopoly as the one association it cannot join. However, the advantage of greater operational control over strategy will be offset by a psychological disadvantage as to the stakes of conflict. If the insular realm can better choose, it has more to lose; if it can limit costs and defer risks, it cannot refight a decisively lost naval engagement and recoup broadly based economic decline. Its stake in stability is at odds with the febrile search for complete safety of possessions, ever-expanding prosperity, and unassailable home security, to be perpetuated in fact because apparently enjoyed as of right. The insular state can decide more effectively with whom to share, when, and how much, than it can prevent having to eventually share and ultimately losing all of everything it held or claimed before. A thus both enlarged and confined capacity to choose is not insignificant. But it is not one a dominant power can regard as sufficient when confronted with the central power's feeling of necessity and the insular/maritime-mercantile ally-competitor's moment of opportunity: the first to move at long last into the maritime arena at any risk and all costs, the second to reap first only material profits at little risk and less cost. The dominant sea power can henceforth only lose what it has where the would-be amphibious central power had first to gain what it wanted before it could defend what it won. If to place in the scales against the long odds and ultimate risks the latter has only resilience in overcoming setbacks and surviving catastrophe, the sea power can deny sharing its rich substance peacefully only at the incrementally rising cost of irreversibly accelerating its developmental cycle as a lead-economy. It does so as it freely diffuses assets to succession-bound (fellow-insular) surrogates while foreshortening its own career as effective balancer or phantom-hegemon by displacing the focus of rivalry and devolving role and influence to (continental) rivals-to-be.

Comparatively best and safest is the position of the rear-continental power. It is vital to both principals, as either the lever for securing an association that excludes it (condominium) or as the key to an alternative combination (continental coalition, and duopoly). And although it is primarily valued and sought as a diplomatically passive and only on demand militarily active resource, and is a material asset more potential than actual, it ultimately regulates which strategy, first diplomatic and then military, will materialize because that strategy has come to be viewed as the only available even if not ideal. The risks the rear-continental power incurs in or from ill-chosen or ill-fated strategies will be muted by the material and psychological reserves implicit in its comparatively least advanced development and largest physical (territorial or demographic) potential. The pertinent gaps relative to the principal two powers have been growing as the role's incumbency migrated from Prussia or Austria to Germany, from Germany to Russia, and beyond, with the spatially anchored advantage exceeding even the offshore insular power's from either strategic latitude, contingent on fickle responses by other parties, or physical invulnerability, conditioned by fail-proof control over the insulating moat. For the rear-continental's advantage to be abridged, his own rear would have to be exposed to hostile and effective offshore-insular power (an aggressive Japan or Anglo–Japanese alliance in the rear of Russia; similarly disposed Japan or US–Japanese Pacific partnership in the rear of a Russo–Chinese duopoly or of China alone).

So long as the rear-continental is freer than any other power to defer or reverse the choice of strategy while absorbing intermediate setbacks, an advantageous time factor follows from favorable situation in space. The advantage is not insignificant when built-in discrepancies and attendant dilemmas foster misjudgments, encourage indecision, and multiply risks to actors as well as to systemic structure, polarized by the alliances that institutionalize either of the several strategies. The continental coalition of the two (maritime and continental) wing powers polarizes the system against the central (would-be amphibious) power; the alliance of the central and rear-continental powers for duopoly polarizes the system against the offshore insular state or states; and the conservative (land and sea power) alliance for condominium or mere accommodation polarizes the system against potentially or actually disruptive forces in either the central system or at its fringes.

Whereas applying constraint to contain one power or group of powers will entail accommodation with another in the correspondingly fragmented geo-functional spectrum, the priority assigned to one or the other objective or outcome may marginally differ from one strategy to another. It is only possible, but not unlikely, that containment of the central-power adversary will be the primary object, and accommodation with its neighbors only the secondary means, in the continental coalition and the oceanic alliance, while priorities in the means–ends relationship are reversed in favor of accommodation with the partner in the condominium and the duopolistic formulas. However, in neither case will there be two-power accommodation without there being some (increase in) inter-power competition or conflict, acting as both inducement to the cooperative relationship or posture and a potentially deranging or distorting consequence.

The relationship of antagonism to accommodation, of conflict to containment and coalescence, is replicated – and to some extent mirrored – in the most fundamental purposes behind the several strategies. Thus the insular power will employ the continental coalition to divide and control the continent so as to facilitate desired and confine hostile acquisitions overseas; the associates for continental duopoly would avoid being controlled (as to goals or means of policy) and divided (between adversary blocs) in order to conquer at the continental or oceanic peripheries; and the continental party to a condominium would co-rule the international system and eventually succeed to the maritime empire without incurring the stresses of conquest. The mutually exclusive drives and designs are less likely to be checked, and extreme aims thwarted, by voluntary self-restraint than by unintended effects of the several strategies and alliance formats. Thus, the continental coalition will tend to intensify the land–sea power conflict into a mutually damaging stalemate or create a serious imbalance if not vacuum of power at the center of the system. The duopolistic alliance is more likely to shift hostilities to the periphery, and expand the area of conflict to include one more major overseas actor, than it is to deter or favorably resolve conflict at the center of the system. And the odds are about even that the land–sea power condominium will realize the conservative object of orderly stability and that it will merely realign the pattern or revise the level of conflict by impelling the forces of revolutionary disorder into assaulting the barrier raised against any but evolutionary change.

If the relationship between the risks attached to the different strategies and the probability of their being adopted were an inverse one, it would be possible to discount the adverse effects on the stability of the system. However, not only are the risks uneven, but the more risky strategies are more frequent, because more readily feasible. Thus, the continental coalition has been most common as well as most commonly dangerous for both the rival states and the system of states. Historically, it was only the habit of the insular power to make a separate peace with a politically fading or militarily losing continental challenger that reduced the risks inherent in the coalition strategy while setting the stage for more far-reaching accommodation after a war. The strategy for continental duopoly has a lesser risk potential and is also less likely to materialize in the face of the divisive tactics of the targeted party, the inherent difficulty for the potential partners to divide actual or prospective gains, and the tendency of both of them to employ the strategy mainly as a tactic to make themselves more attractive or indispensable for association with the extra-continental protagonist. The land–sea power condominium is least risky for either party and the system, but also least likely because its fit is not with the system's most commonly envisaged, but with the ideally pertinent, structure: one expanded beyond the configuration of quantitatively defined poles of power in undifferentiated space to comprise the schism-related qualitative and time-related evolutionary features of the contending powers. For this reason alone, the low risk potential will be matched by the option's being but a passing strategic temptation.

The greater are the risks attaching to the more plausible strategies, the more will all three categories of actors be frustrated in their search for an optimum strategy – one that is safe, enhances security, and helps stabilize the system through a better fit with its total structure. The impasse will foster an excess of tactical volatility across the entire range of strategies. Each of the strategic options will be as often employed to promote or forestall one of the other strategies as it will be embraced with a view to fostering substantively positive ends. Inter-strategy dialectic will fail to enhance security of actors and stability of system, while the agitation attending the search for a strategy that would accommodate any two actors more than it antagonized a third one will impede overall appeasement. There is no assured or easy solution to the predicament ensuing from any two competing states being inescapably caught up in – and, therefore, preoccupied with – the effect their actions have on third parties. The dilemmas engendered by a ubiquitous multiple tripartism become only more determinate, and their forms manifest, within the specialized kind of triangularity into which the land–sea power schism arrays parties to an insular–continental spectrum. The competing actors are exposed to a greater–than–normal stress, and the system to more acute crises, inasmuch as the schism introduces both the contrasts between, and the heightened need to coordinate, two disparate physical arenas (continental and maritime) and more than two overlapping conceptual referents of strategy (the global politico-military and the narrower politico-economic triangles within conventional balance of power among more than three actors, all comprising unevenly rising and declining parties). How autonomously these structure-differentiating factors determine the inherently (if unevenly) predictable shorter- and longer-term outcomes of rationally devised strategies is revealed best in escalating crises, when such factors have overridden influences peculiar to particular domestic structures or claimed for transcendent systems of belief.

WAR-GENERATING PERCEPTIONS AND SHARED RESPONSIBILITIES

Crises relating to the land–sea power schism that assume the form of major wars are flanked by two limiting cases of appeasement of conflict or its resolution: an ideal norm and a primitive historical model. The ideal norm is appeasement within a land–sea power condominium, making the partners unassailable and stabilizing both them and the system. A major war between the two kinds of powers raises instead the question who was the prime assailant that exploited or deepened system instability – and set off the revolutionary upheavals problematically related to the war. The primitive historical model is the contiguity between coastal-maritime cities and a land empire pressing against them from continental depth – e.g. Assyria and Persia against Syrian–Palestinian or Phoenician (or Babylonian) cities. It is dealt with by the cities being either conquered from the hinterland or allowed to face away from it toward the seas and commerce. When, instead, land- and sea-based power potential becomes inseparable and each kind of actors invulnerable to single-handed assault by the other, protracted conflicts and attendant social and systemic upheavals replace both separation and unilateral absorption.

The high crisis potential of the land–sea power schism is actualized by actors investing real capabilities in their strategic impulses and becoming thus responsible for what they do and seek to accomplish; and it is actualized in major wars when the crises-generating factors obstruct efforts to keep readjusting the role-status hierarchy of actors to their uneven and unevenly changing capabilities by peaceful means such as realignment and rearmament within a more-than-mechanical equilibrium. Accounting for the wars-engendering crises are disparities in the structures of the (inseparable) arenas and asymmetries in the capabilities and concerns of the typologically discrete actors, exacerbated by strategies that are not providently keyed to counteracting either. The disparities between maritime-mercantile and continental-military arenas induce each of the differently situated principal powers to seek a safe and safeguarding access to the other's natural habitat, but for the same reasons of military security or economic welfare make both unwilling-to-seemingly-unable to even but briefly allow (let alone lastingly tolerate) the other's substantial (let alone equal) penetration. As this happens, the ideal complementarity of the distinctive capabilities translates into the actual incompatibility of needs and requirements the two kinds of states seek competitively in both arenas. The leading land power's safeguarding continental preeminence by means of parity-approximating access to the seas or overseas will be no more easily compatible with the equality of the two powers in the overall system than will the sea power's promotion of maritime near-monopoly (and insular immunity) by means of anti-hegemony balancing on the continent.

The discrepancies and incompatibilities will hamper statecraft's object of relating rationally feasible ends to appropriate means, within strategies that address the attendant paradoxes as more the makings of a shared predicament than the products of the rival's predation or perfidy. It is part of the predicament that, if the land power will seek duopoly mainly in order to secure condominium, it must also probe for gains overseas for no other reason than to shield its position in the central system, on the assumption that more leverage in the periphery will increase the sea power's self-restraint on the continent. On its part, if the insular actor resorts to continental coalition-type containment so as to forestall land-power duopoly, its involvement in the central system will perforce have no reason more important than to protect its home security and position overseas, on the rationale that anything that compels the chief rival to divert resources inland will constrain him in the more critical maritime spheres.

Uncertainties in differentiating and weighting the other party's proximate and ultimate goals will activate the more deeply rooted reasons for divergent calculations of one's own short- and long-term gains and liabilities from accommodation or conflict. The aspiring land power will lean toward accommodation only if the prospective short-term gains or savings do not exceed the costs or risks from immediate renunciations and indefinite postponements that can be discounted only if the latter do not compromise longer-term opportunities in relations with third (rising continental) powers. The possessing sea power will tend on its part to compound the short- and the long-term costs of accommodations in the coin of assets to be conceded to the challenging and the alienation to ensue on the part of the declining-defensive land powers. These can be discounted only by rating as very high and growing the costs of conflict with the would-be amphibian.

When such calculations are seemingly accurate because short-term and narrowly focused, but in fact erroneous because they are willed to be impossibly precise, they partake of the actors' liability to misperceptions and misjudgments. Being the subjective counterpart of the structurally conditioned and operationally manifest disparities between the arenas, the critical perceptions focus on these and are fostered by them. One is the sea power's view of the continental state as aggressive in intention and oppressive in purpose: intent spontaneously (as a matter of uninduced willful act) upon, and (unless resolutely checked) irresistibly engaged in, transforming preeminence on the continent into a hegemony liable to transfer competition wholesale to the periphery. The other is the would-be amphibian's image of the insular-maritime power as selfish in motivation and sanctimonious in the manner of disguising it, using the posture of a disinterested balancer to exacerbate power fluctuations at the center of the system into polarized confrontations so as to keep competition away from the oceanic sphere. Underlying the one-sidedly exaggerated perceptions of distinguishing attributes and attitudes will be an underestimation of one's own and overestimation of the other's existing potential, or likely future capabilities, tending to enhance the probability of the most feared event occurring in the worst conceivable circumstances.

The pessimistic presumption will prompt both sides to adopt preemptive precautions apt to precipitate the feared event. In the process, the sea power will not take adequately into account any existing discrepancy between the land power's military capabilities in being and its less impressive material or institutional resource base, any more than it will weigh its own part in making the land power overreach itself in response to being overcontained. Conversely, the would-be amphibious power will readily fail to assess at its full worth the discrepancy between the superior role-status of the maritime opponent in the system at large and the different frailties inherent in its sociopolitical pluralism and economic performance, with the result of overestimating its capacity for concessions.

The time factor contributes when the land power overrates the insular sea power's latitude for concessions at any one time, especially if the latter's margin of maritime-mercantile superiority is lessening relative to third parties; and when the sea power exaggerates the length of time the would-be amphibious power can wait for even but initial moves toward conceded sharing, especially if its margin of preeminence on the continent shrinks faster than the leeway for escaping forward into the larger beyond expands. Over the longest term, the sea power risks misjudging the odds that displacing the defeated continental challenge to a power both stronger and less congenial or manageable will convert the thwarted opponent into a willing vital partner in a future continental coalition against his successor. The would-be amphibious challenger misjudges typically the possibility to gain in due course, if not the insular's neutral detachment from the continent, then the active support or passive toleration of the other continentals for defying the sea power's abusive phantom hegemony. It is a mistake certain to give rise, by way of compensatory overreactions, to developments apt to depress the frustrated challenger to a role and status below the previously scorned one of a junior partner in prolonging the insulars' dominion.

If skewed perceptions of so fundamental space-time factors generate the potential for crises, specific strategies of actors unevenly but jointly responsible for the result will be foremost among the operative mechanisms for actualizing the potential in wars or revolutions. It is strategies that transmute misperceptions into misjudgments and sporadic incidents into the incidence of war; strategies that link ingrained propensities of actors to preemptive precautions closely enough to engender precipitants of conflict and make compulsively generated tendencies surface as ostensibly culpable transactions. All this happens as actors seek to defend or achieve a satisfying role and status by assuming risks; and as the risks, implicit in the configuration of capabilities within the system's structure, are allocated among or freely assumed by the several parties in degrees inversely proportional to the disposable resources of each.

In subtly varying ways, the structural–perceptual grounds for major conflicts and the actualizing mechanisms will repeatedly come together in wars which neither side patently desired but both sides came to regard as eventually inevitable. Such were the climactic land–sea power wars of the matured Greek state system (the "second" more than the "first" Atheno–Spartan or Peloponnesian War) and European state system (the First World War as contrasted with the Second). Conversely, close to the mid-point of the concerned state system's development, the resumption of the Hispano–Dutch 80-year war (in 1619, as distinct from its origins in the Dutch rebellion) and, later, the Anglo-Dutch and Anglo–Spanish/French wars were belligerent encounters which, hard to avoid, were at least half-desired (as had been the Atheno–Spartan conflict preceding the peace of 446 BC) on one or both sides. The instances cover the range of evolutionary stages and related behavior patterns of the sea power in particular, from rising aggressively (early fifth-century BC Athens, sixteenth- to early seventeenth-century Holland, and seventeenth- to eighteenth-century England) to being incipiently defensive (mid-fifth-century Athens and mid-seventeenth-century Holland) and incrementally declining (late nineteenth-to twentieth-century Britain).

The changing propensity to growth and decline, aggression and defense, self-aggrandizement and self-preservation, will introduce variations into the causal and conditioning factors responsible for major land–sea power wars even when they do not fundamentally alter their identities, thrust, and range of effects. However, the conceptual norm and the classic exemplar of the unwanted–unavoidable conflict will remain the war between a defensively minded dominant sea power determined to push back an adverse tide and an assertively disposed continental power intent on moving beyond a narrowly territorial habitat. Such a war marks the developmentally crucial transition (and both operationally and normatively critical departure) from wars engaged upon in response to opportunities, in search of the fruits of victory, to wars incurred in response to pressures, in an effort to exhaust the possibilities of defense or offense before incurring the penalties of decline or defeat. It is only when the premier continental power, too, faces diminution on the mainland without having satisfied its felt needs and professed claims outside the land mass, that it moves war back again along the continuum from one undesired but unavoidable to that only provoked or also preferred. The resulting clash of arms will be all the more desperate and the war total when the continental state challenging the insular power has not only moved beyond the first moderate to the second climactic phase of its quest for world power (Napoleonic France) but engages (Nazi Germany) a declining sea power equally forced back onto a compulsively offensive–defensive posture of last-ditch resistance to retreat from world power.

Whether ostensibly a challenger to a pre-established hegemon (such as Athens to Sparta and the Anglo-Dutch pair to Spain) or a defender of the status quo (such as later Britain) the principal sea power has its share in instigating warlike conflict. It does so not only directly, by contesting or denyig the land power's parity or insisting on its own near-monopoly in the maritime sphere, but also and more pervasively indirectly by being what it is rather than by behaving as it does. It exhibits a high degree of security and generates a new kind or an augmented range of resources for prosperity that invite contentious imitation of the major continental state, disadvantaged by the changed stakes and means of competition when not also by altered norms of conduct. The maritime-mercantile power becomes thus the unmoved mover, the *causa causans*, behind contrary initiatives to be resolved by war. Moreover, since the physically (quasi-) insular sea power is less subject to the constraints and compulsions that beset territorially contiguous land powers, its policies will be more exposed to the influence of domestic and economic factors and interests: witness the role the Piraeus merchants (competiting with Corinth in the western Mediterranean) and the Periclean *clientelae* (dependent on mercantile-maritime empire for employment on food and leverage against the traditional land-owning ruling class) had played in the origins of the Peloponnesian War. If that role was replicated in the eighteenth-century wars by the English stake in commercial profits and the Protestant–parliamentary settlement, only the antecedents to World War I would reveal how vulnerable the British sociopolitical-economic system had progressively become to escalating costs of naval armaments, and how dependent on negotiating the transition from British-dominated free trade to a species of "fair trade" competitive with Germany's and the United States' in the western hemisphere and elsewhere. Such special features, or emphases, only increase the difficulty to assimilate the sea power into a conventional system of territorial states in that they make its foreign policies more than commonly fickle-to-unpredictable (reflecting pluralism) or inflexible-to-rigid (reflecting economic priorities while invoking principle).

The likewise special kind of sea-power responsibility for warlike conflicts that ensues is as problematic with respect to the ultimate causation of major wars as is the control either principal can exert over such wars' more proximate precipitants in the actions and apprehensions of the ostensibly indispensable lesser partners of each. Sparta could not avoid backing Corinth and imperial Germany could not afford abandoning Austria–Hungary lest they transform indispensable major ally into an unpredictable actor on the lookout for compensating policies or alignments, with dire consequences for regional security and internal stability. By the same token, if Athens would not forgo the naval contingent of Corcyra, neither would Britain forfeit France's to Germany, lest they be compelled to neutralize the pivotal naval capability forcibly for fear of it shifting the balance of navally significant assets to a hostile amalgamation. When a Bourbon Spain despoiled of Gibraltar by the British assumed a comparable significance for France in the eighteenth century, she only confirmed the rule: at the heart of the residually seaworthy powers' triggering role was throughout the issue of their continuance as great powers. For either of the principal rivals to play upon or adopt as his own the weaker state's particular grievances at the risk or cost of war, was the price to pay for the alliance and, through it, either continental preeminence or naval superiority. The threat to peace lurking in unconditional loyalty to an ally surfaced as the immediate cause of war when a prior partial accommodation or détente between the main adversaries, Athens and Sparta or Britain and imperial Germany, had made more plausible a last-minute miscalculation: Corinth's, that Athens would not back Corcyra's defection and defiance at the cost of a breach with Sparta; and Germany's that Britain would not back Russia (and France) at the cost of a major war over minuscule Serbia.

While the secondary powers – typically once-dominant and henceforth declining – act as conspicuous precipitating triggers, compounding their role will be the major rear-continental states acting as the virtually imperceptible background regulators of the actions and aims of the principals. Thus Persia was directly or indirectly responsible for both the outbreak and the outcome, the timing of the onset and the end, of the Peloponnesian War. It was Athens' part in the Persian War that had set her off on the career of imperial expansion as a matter of right and capability, and the failure of the later assault on Persia in Egypt that redirected her expansive energies back to Greece, before Persia's wealth and residual prestige would help end the war by financing Sparta's navy and legitimizing the peace. Similarly, Russia's weakness after 1905 both allowed and compelled Britain to identify Germany as the henceforth principal threat and rival, while Russia's subsequent recovery forced an increasingly fearful Germany into precautions against the implications of the 1907 Anglo–Russian entente, deepening the crisis further. Russia differed from Persia in that she determined the outcome of the war less directly than its outbreak, when the rate of her recovery and the tempo of her strategic railway building set a time limit for Germany's war fighting scenario (the Schlieffen Plan). Moreover, as the role of a Russia perceived as the backward and barbarous link in Germany's pre-war encirclement grew, so did the Germans' sense of the kind of right and justice the Athenians had derived from saving Greek civilization from the Persian "barbarian." Comparable if less compelling had been the roles of then rear-continental Austria or Prussia in the world wars of the eighteenth century, less unwanted than the later one but for different reasons (of conflicting expansionist drives and ambitions) likewise unavoidable. Neither the French nor the English felt they could manage without cornering the military resources of one of the two Germanic powers for service in the continental sector of the total war theater. And whereas the precautionary peacetime moves to make sure of one or the other added to the proximate causes of the wars, the wars themselves grew in scope and length so long as the two unevenly strong-and-weak rear-continental powers exceeded the two world powers in the intensity of their mutual rivalry, the precision with which they evaluated its stakes, and the purposefulness of their strategies.

However incalculable may have been its weight and thrust, being crucial in fighting the war will have made any particular rear-continental power critical for decisions leading to the outbreak of hostilities. It will be all the more critical, the more asymmetric are the capabilities and indeterminate the comparative rise–decline trends on the part of the principal maritime and continental rivals. The impact of the rear-continental state as the major operational cause – through its actual or anticipated actions supported by available or prospective capabilities – is thus the counterpart of the sea power's impact as the real structural cause – through its effect on the identity of the main stakes of competition and the system's principally contested arena. Although the wing powers combining the two kinds of ultimate "causes" of war will be obscured by the spectacular initiatives of the central power qualifying as the proximiate ostensible cause, it is the former that will inflect the net thrust of uniformly ambiguous trends and tendencies toward a deepening sense of that war's inevitability. As for the war's timing, it will be as much a function of sheer material weight of the rear-continental state as of the capacity, reserved to the sea power, to control the rate of appeasing concessions to the would-be amphibian; together they will decide when the war has ceased to be hard to avoid and becomes unavoidable for all, if in any real sense unsurvivable only for the two principals.

Adding up the roles of the two wing powers in ultimate causation with the immediately precipitating trigger effect of the declining secondary powers delimits correspondingly the responsiblity of the central power. The would-be amphibian is always the challenger when facing a superior sea power and will often be technically the aggressor when it initiates the war or supplies the occasion or pretext for its outbreak. However, its formal responsibility will be offset by the degree of objective plausibility for the felt necessity to react assertively-to-aggressively to prior or parallel acts of adversaries. The compulsions are not necessarily such as to manifestly transform offense into self-defense – a concept as ambiguous as aggression and likewise inseparable from provocation, itself more often than not the negatively perceived obverse of a measure adopted for another's self-protection. Without doing away with his share in overall responsibility, existential necessity will reduce the weight of the alleged (hegemonial) aggressor's formal accountability. And it will do so all the more materially the more receptive he has previously shown himself to be to a condominial form of land–sea power accommodation on terms (objectively) consistent with an evolving equilibrium.

In such a perspective, Bourbon France and Wilhelmine Germany were not more responsible for the respective world wars when challenging Britain as the presumptive aggressors than a Sparta defending the status quo had been when challenged by maritime Athens. By the same token, maritime Britain incurred a roughly equal measure of somewhat differently constituted responsibility when defending her maritime superiority and upholding her unavowed hegemony overall as had maritime Athens when challenging Sparta's nominal hegemony. The ratios of responsibilty for war will move against the central power only in the second and wholly continental phase of its self-assertion (escalating from the fourth Philip's Spain through the first French to the third German Empire), when a domestically repressive and systemically revolutionary reaction to the impending onset or accelerating tempo of decline will have gone far toward abrogating the redemptive effect of felt necessity on formal responsibility. But, while assigning war guilt dogmatically, even the inordinate ambition at the root of the climactic confrontation – a root planted in the soil of a reaction to prior frustration of more limited and diversified objectives – will remain in such a case distinct in morality from excesses wrought in preparing for and enduring this ultimate ordeal by war. Regardless of whether the tested polity's search was for religious or racial, social-class or ideological, uniformity and cohesion, at the expense of the Moriscos as before of the Jews in Spain, old-regime favorites in the wake of Old Testament faithful in France, and the Jews again following the Marxists in Germany; regardless of whether to be violently excised from the body politic were its most enterprising members with a view to thus perversely regalvanizing the society's flagging energies, or the expulsion was aimed at the most heterodox rationalist dissenters from the society's inherited myths in vain hope of recalling the tribe to critically unexamined life, they were as separate then as they are judgmentally separable in the longest perspective from the causal nexus behind the attendant wars: the brief chain of proximate events entangled in the longer sequence of developments preceding the catastrophe. Only at the deepest level do all these filaments come together in the web of guilt and error spun by polities unevenly strong but equally self-righteous, the unintended consequences of whose actions constitute the outer face of world politics.

Discourses 1–2
The Inner Economy of World Politics

The economy of world politics – like that of a treaty or a statute – consists of discrete, but internally coherent and reciprocally consistent, parts – rules or stipulations – which, though subject to interpretation in particular contingencies, set the framework within which the interpretation can proceed in an intellectually disciplined manner and arrive at conclusions capable of being adjudicated in terms of right and wrong, truth and falsehood, plausibility and fallacy. At its most abstract but also most inward, a thus understood economy of world politics is made up of approximations of physical and adaptations of moral laws construed and applied by essentially rational, if differently practical and politic, intelligence.

Discourse 1   On Force Fields and Finalities in Political Physics

If interstate relations are subject to recurrent patterns, this is so not least because they are subject to "laws" of power and conflict dynamics constituting a species of political physics, by analogy from classical physics to begin with. There is little room for categorical change in a universe wherein bodies politic as masses of matter and energy revolve interactively around a center of gravity located nearest the greatest mass.

The analogy survives the caveat that the mutual attraction held responsible for the motion of physical bodies applies only loosely among bodies politic. Between equal powers, it stands for the convergent movement of two to three actors toward a territorial or immaterial stake of interaction to be apportioned, or into an interposed vacuum of power to be filled, competitively because preemptively. Mutual attraction operates less simply or directly between unequal parties. A client state revolves around a larger core power in reaction against a repugnant adjacent, just as a satellite regime adheres to it against a rival internal, force of equally small scale. More common for the smaller corporate entity intent on autonomy is resistance to and recoil from the larger mass that impacts, or the stronger force that is impressed, upon it. Such resistance will translate into attraction toward a larger mass located at safer because greater distance from the impacting force, and will exert a matching attraction on the former as part of equalizing the originally uneven contrary forces within an automatically materializing equilibrium. Impulsions from either direct or circuitously encompassed attraction produce in the real world the agitation that deflects bodies politic from an inertial position or course, in keeping with laws that are easiest to formulate for a quasi-Newtonian triangular structure of states replicating the model of the three celestial bodies within the solar system.

Although modifiable by specific frictions, the laws of motion are not subject to fundamental alteration. For one, the sum total of motion and momentum, matter and energy, in the systemic universe are held constant. In consequence, any one actor's retrogression or decline in the amount of momentum will automatically entail a compensating increase in another or others. For another, the principle of equivalence in action and reaction, force and counterforce, ensures a balancing response of defensive to offensive actions and actors. The consequent tendency to conflict and equilibrium is sufficiently pervasive and permanent to agitate the system coherently around its center of gravity. No actor is free to reform the system dynamics in an effort to evade its impress. Only the way energy, motion, and momentum are allocated among a smaller or larger number of clusters in a bi- or multi-polar system can vary, while combinations of masses or forces alternately aggregate and disaggregate in changing coalitions of bodies politic. The formation of such bodies is broadly analogous to that of heavenly bodies, postulated by classical physics, in the guise of corpuscles or particles aggregating by virtue of both attraction and repulsion operative internally. Thus also initially centralization-resistant particular groups and group interests coalesce into viable state-like actors by virtue of centripetal attraction emanating from the requisites of common defense or shared prosperity, around a core of basic (force-related military, fiscality-related economic, and managerial-administrative) functions within a territorial nucleus. Flowing along the lines of force delineated by the most usable means of communication, formative energies aggregate into areal complexes best suited to crystallize previously latent social affinities and political loyalties around material surpluses and scarcities.

It changes the perspective, but expands usefully the compass of the metaphor, when the analogy with discrete if not necessarily contiguous bodies interacting across distance in space is supplemented by the analogy with continuous fields of force lines or waves. The focus is then not on revolutions of bodies but on radiation and refraction pertaining to waves and wave-like particles, while law-like regularity in attraction and repulsion is replaced with randomness. Transposed onto politics, actors assimilated to hard and ponderable bodies deflect one another at the center of forces with effects that are predictable in principle; to be added is the equivalent of waves that are detached from ponderable matter and capable of interpenetrating without fatally impeding one another. The equivalent in policy, distinct from force-generated coercive impacts, is wave-like influence or competitively inter-penetrating and overlapping influences brought to bear upon and among actors and refracted through their perceptions. The refracting perceptual medium can be more or less complex and distorting. When it becomes more so – thus as a consequence of increasingly potent and diversified isms and ideologies – the political physics undergirding classic-rational statecraft of the kind characteriz-ing seventeenth- to eighteenth-century Europe becomes less adequately des-criptive of interstate politics such as that of the nineteenth to twentieth centuries. It becomes more necessary to expand the analogue with classical physics in the direction of post-classical physics' allowance for decomposition, dematerialization, and relativization.

When space has been dissolving into relations, all matter is transformable into energy or is identical with it, and there is no particle that cannot be decomposed into sub-particles or converted into radiation, the political analogue will move from conflictual interactions in a system of states toward integration of societal elements and relations in a world community. To the extent that international politics evolves toward disaggregation, an indefinitely augmenting plurality of actors generates tension between the infinitesimal size of components and the indefinite scope of the network of multiple lines of force and paths of influence; this same trend fosters one for up-to-date technological means of communication and power projection to superimpose increasingly variable linear on relatively stable areal modes of integration as crucial. An intervening increase in indeterminate or unconsummated tendencies favors only statistical probabilities as to outcomes; but it, too, will not have changed the international system and politics suddenly – nor has anything succeeded yet to change it fundamentally. Although tendencies manifest themselves within less definite ranges of effects, the dispersion of impacts and impulsions does not prevent interstate relations from being conducted *as if* traditional outcomes remained wholly achievable by political or politico-military activities. But the amplified range of existentially or normatively constituted frictions will, when not attenuate, hamper the operation of the laws of classical mechanics in world politics without ruling out their periodic reassertion if not accentuation in reaction to the inhibiting frictions.

If changes such as these (toward decomposition and dematerialization) do not abolish the inherently conservative because self-perpetuating thrust of the classical-mechanics equivalents, even less does a break follow from the substitution of relativized time-space for absolute simultaneous time and undifferentiated space. In "pure" power politics as in classical physics, not only do events that externalize the operation of the "laws" peculiar to either universe occupy simultaneous time in undifferentiated space; space (or, by analogy, spatial location of actors) and time (their rate and stage of evolution) are also presumed identical for the critically interacting bodies politic. In the altered and more realistic view, both the temporal and the spatial dimensions become relative to the particular reference system of the perceiving actor within the total situation. The equivalent of the physicist's "reference system" in politics is determined by the actor's position relative to the principal dominant schism, such as maritime–continental and East–West, and is conditioned by his location at the center or the periphery of the system and his early or late entry into it as fully participating member. The (situational) factors of space and (evolutionary) ones of time are in all instances variously but indissolubly commingled in constituting actor perspectives.

In most systems, not least the continental among the late-entering powers, commonly situated farther from the center of the arena, will have taken longer from their primitive inception – but may also take less time at a later stage of their evolution – to cover an evolutionary distance already traversed by the system-founding, includng the insular-maritime, powers located at the core of the system. As a result, the time–distance coordinates of the two kinds of actors will be not only non-identical but, more importantly, non-comparable. Although the world-historical time clock runs at its set speed, the manner in which individual actors subjectively measure or perceive time in relation to their evolutionary speeds and states will be different. The later, slower, or unevenly developing peripheral-continental states will wish to accelerate their rate of evolution to fit the system's pre-established norm of developmental climax once they have qualified for the effort to catch up. Conversely, when the sooner or initially faster developing powers have reached their specific optimum in development, and find it difficult to perpetuate their role and status at peak level, they will wish to slow down the tempo (if they cannot alter the thrust) of evolution in the system, which the previously lagging actors would perpetuate through their self-assertion.

Accomplished evolution has run its course through anterior phases of a perceptually foreshortened past, perennially subject to being extinguished by some as irrelevant; yet-to-be realized evolution lies in a future others would bring about at the greatest possible speed. Just as the manner of perceiving and measuring past and future time is relative to the location of the actor-observer in differentiated space, so location in such space conditions time as it is expressed in the actual or accomplished rate, speed, and stage of evolution. Accordingly, the late-coming and increasingly eastern continental states, Germany and Russia, were at different points in the twentieth century the contemporaries in terms of action-relevant time of the earlier-formed western (quasi-) insular-maritime Netherlands and Britain in the seventeenth to eighteenth – and, with corrective adjustments for its remoteness from the system center, of nineteenth-century United States. They have been such in the fundamentals of both the domestic political orders and the concept of power and attitude to the use of force in territorially focused policies for expansion and control abroad. In its impact on actual interactions of the same actors, the discrepancy in rates of evolution and consequent modes of perception will modify significantly the influence a shared basic conception of time unfolding in the abstract or "objectively" in history can have on the making of policies. The conception has become one which, as distinct from other periods or cultures (such as the early medieval one in Europe), postulates an indefinite future and incorporates a known past as the source of familiar (if not uniformly evaluated) precedents; and one that does so in a setting wherein action-relevant time is compressed by speedy ways of communicating and projecting power, but is also subject to a more complex and time consuming mode of making decisions.

In the classic model of (political) physics ignoring the spatio-temporal modifiers, homogeneous structures vary in terms of requisite and/or available reaction times within a balance-of-power universe operating mechanically like clockwork. Spatio-temporal relativism highlights instead variations in the modes of action and reaction, reflecting spatially conditioned differentials in rates of evolution. And again, the classic model is one of near-equal powers interacting around an equilibrium point or norm in conformity with laws that are universally applicable within a field of forces characterized equally by uniformity as to spatially conditioned dynamic and temporal–evolutionary simultaneity or contemporaneity. Conversely, the model biased toward relativity modifies the classic pattern in favor of unique actor perspectives that are essentially equivalent while existentially deriving from different individual reference systems. Consequent on the analytic refinement is the incentive to adjoin differentiated principles of behavior to uniform laws of motion and to invest the simplicity of abstracted reality with the motley garb of actuality. The model of space-time relativity compensates for lost parsimony through grater verisimilitude and by offering a wider scope for informed intuition. It only follows that cost will attach to conceiving and conducting interstate relations as if the space-time modifiers were immaterial for shaping conduct or irrelevant for evaluating and responding to conduct. Ignoring them will intensify conflicts by counteracting the obverse effect of frictions that impede or attenuate the operation of the laws of power and momentum of conflict dynamics highlighted by classical (political) mechanics.

A physics biased to relativity encourages its analogue concerned with politics to inject insights from historical evolution (time) into considerations of geopolitics (space); it corrects the limitations of instrumental strategic rationality relating specific means to determinate ends, which is peculiarly germane to the classic model. To the extent that this happens, the world-view grossly assimilable to Einsteinian physics is closer to the image of the state system analogous to the physics of Aristotle than it is to the chronologically intervening Newtonian mechanics. Developmental extremes touch insofar as the structure of both the proto-system (closed-hierarchical or quasi-Aristotelian) and the meta-system (dissolved-indefinite or post-classical) deviate from the strict compliance with the cause–effect or action–reaction type of nexus, germane to the intervening (finite-crystallized and articulated or quasi-Newtonian) system norm.

Aristotelian physics points to shifts in determining influence on motion and momentum that correspond to changes in evolving interstate relations, but do so without replacing the cyclical pattern (dear to the Greeks) with qualitative progression in one direction. Just as objects are held to move in response to tendencies that are implanted in them, so can bodies politic be viewed in the same manner by analogy. The shift is then from externally impacting force (Newton's *vis impressa*) to the innate urge or drive (Aristotle's *hormē*); tendency *qua* final cause predominates over impulsion which, operating *qua* efficient cause only between contiguous bodies, does no more than release the potentiality inherent in the object to be moved. Yet again, although the urges or desires for and aversions to something or other are innate, they are influenced in the ways they manifest themselves by the structure of order sufficiently intelligible theoretically as well as practically to permit reasoned and realistic choices. In the analogy, Aristotelian finalities can stand for tendencies in political actors directed to traditional results or outcomes of statecraft, regardless of whether they can be achieved by coercive impacts of a superior force that may be either unavailable or unusable because the ends exceed the means or vice versa. Implicit in the model is an increase in the importance of organic growth–decline factors over outcomes achieved operationally, corresponding to Aristotle's concept of the nature – as distinct from the source – of motion. It consists of actualizing internal power *qua* potentiality rather than of altering position in space. Motion connotes thus less revolutions in a more or less circular orbit than more or less cyclical fluctuations in the vitality of bodies politic. And inasmuch as motion *qua* organic change is impelled from within, it can be no more than conditioned by the object's environment. In the real world of power politics the environment includes powers other than the actor, to be viewed in the Newton-like terms of forces and leverages as well as Aristotle-like in the light of developmental potentials they have realized in themselevs and affect in others.

Like Aristotle's nature, the quasi-Aristotelian interstate system and politics are not only dynamic; they are also productive in that they generate and assimilate into an operative system new values or institutions or actors that manifest the arena's character as an evolving system. However, although the state system may tend nature-like toward some kind of inner coherence standing for harmony, it will not realize its *telos* by means of the individual actors' finalities converging spontaneously. Still, the emphasis is on becoming, rather than on being as in Newtonian physics. The stage for this becoming is a universe that is teleological or purposive – has a meaning of sorts – rather than mechanistic and, confined to its own terms, purposeless; and its structure is qualitatively hierarchical rather than uniform even if not wholly egalitarian. The implied potential for change is likewise circumscribed, by the fundamental philosophical postulate of a cyclical pattern of evolution that can be validated empirically. The cyclical pattern in evolution is analytically something different from circular motion. But the two complement one another in the historical reality of politics insofar as (1) circular motion is as much a deviation from unilinear inertial motion as the cyclical pattern is a variation on evolution proceeding in a particular and identifiable direction; and (2) evolution actually grows out of the orbital gravitation of actors of unequal mass with respect to one another in the dynamics of the state system, which analogically equates the push of centrifugal and the pull of centripetal forces in classical mechanics.

The Aristotelian view of nature contributes plausibly to the geo-historical view of interstate politics and system as combining the dynamics of equilibrium with evolution and operational mechanics with organic maturation. With features pointing forward to Darwinian–Spencerian classical evolutionary (socio-) biology, the Aristotelian imagery supplements the tenets of classical and post-classical, including Einsteinian, physics. It adds to the awareness of perceptual divergences between actors differently situated in physical space and in evolutionary time-stream a sharpened appreciation of the role organically maturing idiosyncratic desires have, as "unmoved movers," in affecting the rational core and inflecting the routine course of actor strategies.

When transposed to politics, the Einsteinian and Aristotelian modifiers of Newtonian physics alter the simple picture of reciprocally impacting and mutually countervailing powers representing unequal mass while manifesting invariably operative uniform laws of motion. But the principle of relativity abolishes the essential validity of the classical model and its "laws" no more than does the concept of finalities. Even when interstate relations only approximate the classic model, the latter will circumscribe the range of events attending conflict and suggest procedures susceptible of encompassing catastrophe. The continuity that ensues is sufficient to permit the projection of persistent trends and provisional transformations from the past into both the present and a prospective future.

Political physics elucidates the dynamics arising out of the basic structure of the universe of interstate relations. But the strategies through which actors seek to fit their objectives to the structure constitute also, if less consciously, the mostly unsuccessful efforts to loosen the bonds of tragic entanglement. First dissected in Aristotle's *Poetics*, the tragic nexus compounds the necessitarian implications of quasi-Newtonian political physics while confirming the relativistic bias of its quasi-Einsteinian variety. It adds to the interplay of force with opposing force the collision of value with contrary value. And it does so without the lopsided balance between choice and necessity changing significantly because the exercise of will being refined into purpose on the plane of norms has converged with the refinement of instinctual reflex into instrumental rationality with respect to interests. Nor is there less of an interpenetration between the drama of entanglement and the dynamics of equilibrium when passion has invaded purpose in informing perception and directing the thrust of power. Whenever the perception of more-than-routine crisis infuses heightened spirit into structure, just as heat increases the kinetic energy of molecules with the effect of expanding a given volume of gas, so the crisis-attending increase in frictions or pressures inflames a polity into expressing expansively its innate urge to self-preservation.

In propelling action, routinely interests-promoting and power-optimizing purpose is intimately linked to values-upholding passion that exacerbates the purpose, much as each of the two assorts material with immaterial factors and rational with non-rational elements differently. Similarly, whereas force in physics is no less closely akin to fate in poetics when it comes to enduring, resisting, or overcoming either, political physics and likewise modified poetics diverge significantly when sheer mechanics confronts the differently constituted issue of meaning. The more completely purposive aim has disappeared from the physical universe in the transition from Aristotelian physics to Newtonian mechanics, the more unequivocally does the analogously construed power-political process depend on the tragic predicament for the infusion of meaning. This is so even if the meaning, construed restrictively and as it were procedurally, is confined to purposeful striving (the "endeavor" of pre-

Newtonian physics) conducive to suffering (the "terror" of Aristotelian poetics). Taken together, the striving and the suffering impart an intrinsic dignity to an interstellar-like dynamics among states that is senseless when abstracted from the substantive interests and values engaged in actual conflict.

Discourse 2   On Collisions and Conceit in Politicized Poetics

Two kinds of entanglement are central to tragedy in politics: rivalry between two near-equally powerful actors and an over-mighty one's revolt against the existing order. A two-power conflict is genuinely tragic when each of the clashing parties embodies a value and both share in the guilt of asserting the value absolutely. The confrontation of cognate opposites in precarious balance that is basic to the tragic form releases tensions that elude satisfying resolution and leave the central problem unresolved. A positive value is defeated by another positive value, without being thus judged unworthy, in a clash of rights and interests righteously construed, while tendencies innate to the confrontation clash with institutionalized constraints and tend to defeat them. Promoting the values entails their destruction in a collision that lacks a patent villain because each opposite contains or represents some good while much of the good is wasted in casting out imagined or exaggerated evil. Wrong leads to wrong as part of exacting revenge, a motif that permeates tragic drama and is implemented in politics by reprisal or retaliation. Since each protagonist hates in the adversary the pride or pretension (to total security through assured superiority) he loves in himself, animosity represses the least recognition of affinity. The conflict warrants thus a feeling of detached irony before its outcome can arouse redeeming grief.

Comprising the minor ambiguities and crowning them is a major one, due to the essence of tragic action as a compound of guilt and innocence. Guilt is implicit in desire and choice, and entails responsibility; necessity minimizes the accountability inherent in experienced freedom by drawing attention to endured fate. The resulting events are neither strictly predictable nor wholly fortuitous, because they record the acting out of a medley of compulsion and conceit in a conflict that absolves adversaries of guilt to the extent that it is unavoidable. Whereas the minor and major ambiguities are essential for a tragic equilibrium, a deeper repose is achieved only when the curse that rested upon the parties from the outset has worked itself out. The fundamental vanity of their *agon* is then revealed in the conflict being resolved by the instant and simultaneous defeat or unevenly deferred destruction of both parties, the conquered Trojans as well as the Argives returning from conquest in triumph, whether or not also to the benefit of a third party.

It follows that neither war nor defeat are by and of themselves automatically tragic, any more than is the attendant suffering. They can be instead routine events in nature, commanding stoic acceptance, or epic feats of Homeric legend, inviting admiration before arousing disbelief. A warlike conflict is not tragic if the parties to it represent no significant values or when one party's guilt and the contentious stakes are unambiguous and the conflict has been resolved without engendering still more intractable controversy. Few if any major conflicts will qualify as thus untragic upon closer inspection. However, plausibly diminished in their tragic quality will be conflicts that have been sought or accepted as a relief from internal strains and tensions (that is, are cathartic in originating intention rather than in unintended consequence), or conflicts that, acting out a crusading zeal in support of a just" cause or "true" faith, reflect a naive view of the world springing from a youthful culture's overflow of unspent energies.

The place of compassion for both parties to a tragic collision is taken by compassionate sympathy for – or only sympathetic understanding of – only one actor when the mantle of tragedy descends upon the rebel against an existing order. Such an order embodies, in politics, the very dilemmas that, impaling two or more powers on their horns, impel them toward conflict. The aspirant to hegemony who defies the system and seeks release from its rules and restraints, imperatives and inhibitions, is the tragic hero in interstate relations. Like his dramatic analogue, he tests all norms of the existing order at total risk. His arrogance of pride lies only secondarily in the quest for immortality through fame at a cost in violence that abridges lives; the hubris resides primarily in the attempt to defeat and then abrogate the laws of the relevant nature by escaping not only the chain of conflicts with equal powers but also and mainly the next turn in the cycle of rise and decline deputizing for birth and death among mortal states. Instead of sharing the mundane lot of his species, the state-like actor aspiring to hegemony sins by excess of god-like ambition: he would convert a transient advantage into the assurance of unchallengeable existence at the pinnacle of power. The tragic flaw in the striving is disclosed when the hero defeats himself by acting in character – is destroyed by the driving will-to-power that made him powerful to being with – and his defeat is encompassed by the operation of the very laws of the system dynamics he set out to suspend in relation to himself if not abolish forever.

Like the tragic hero he is, the hegemonial aspirant gathers in himself the ambiguities dispersed between near-equal parties to conflict and within the ordering principles of the system. He is both free and constrained; percipient of opportunities and blind to consequences; a bearer of a divine spark and the performer of demoniac acts; would-be destroyer of the established order and the doomed pathfinder for the next. In the latter capacity he is a both unwitting and unwilling agent as the same features of the order he has set out to overcome – decentralized competitiveness, rooted in actor autonomy as the central value; invitation to self-help and its arbitrary confinement – finally thwart his undertaking. In that he forces those free to resist his bid into defending the system's imperfections, the would-be hegemon imparts to initially weaker opponents his own qualifying moral and material strengths. He must now match overweening ambition with superhuman effort and step up excess to fight off terminal exhaustion. Having set out to reshape the cosmic order he ends up perverting his communal order, since being ever more repressive internally will have become a condition of taking the ever greater risks necessary to compensate for waning resources.

The outline of tragedy is filled out as it becomes clearer that the gradually surfacing "dreadful act" intended to resolve the actor's predicament has not been so much a crime as an error regarding what was feasible as against what is fated: *hamartia* as much as or before hubris. The tragic hero of politics mistakes for an attainable fair reward of exceptional courage and capability the fickle chance offered by a transient configuration of less potent or resolute parties: while he sees himself as relying on *virtù*, he courts *fortuna*. Pride and error become one – and can be explained so that they may be excused – when the would-be hegemon, acting as if he were free, forgets the role of constraining structures in prompting also his responses and portending their consequence.

For his effort to be tragic also because it is exemplary of a general condition, a rebelling state-like actor who is as much representative of his kind of being as he is exceptional in his daring, must not seek supreme power for reasons of physical security and spiritual pride only. He must also serve a purpose transcending self. Caught up as he is in the impersonal net of circumstances through which the dynamics of the system implement the decrees of fate, the rebel's attempt to rise above the common norm will unwittingly test the health of the larger body politic. The testing may prove to have been necessary when it has revealed patent flaws and released latent forces in a system that had to be defied before it could be defended, and be defended in its particulars if it was to be upheld in its principles. Since the challenger's obvious guilt is thus offset by a hidden merit, the tragic hero's punishment as he is being reduced to a diminished place in a restored order is not necessarily proportional to his crime. The critical relationship is between his character and the circumstances that have activated in and through him more widely distributed predispositions.

In a tragic drama, crime breeds crime while each protagonist would stop the concatenation at a moment and with a deed that marks the success of his revenge. Similarly, although each hegemonial assault on the order of a plural system of states is the direct or indirect consequence of previous such challenges and their outcomes, the subduers of the latest aspirant to hegemony will seek to enjoy the fruits of ascendancy even as they denounce the folly of seeking supremacy. It is one of the victors' serviceable fictions that the thwarted tragic hero has been rightfully subdued before being sacrificed as a ritual scapegoat. He is brought low as part of a vicarious purging of the communal guilt prior to restoring a semblance of order or raising the level of insight into the conditions of a superior order. Whereas the kingly hero is killed in tragic drama, the defeated greatest power is dismembered by conventional diplomacy: it is an object of supposedly redemptive peacemaking before it can, diminished, be brought back to life by pragmatic statecraft in the interest of the system's post-revolutionary restoration.

Since the fabric of order in a system of states is fragile, the political arena is a proper stage for tragedy even if the dreadful acts of a would-be hegemon fall comparably short of the ideal standard and so does the expiatory suffering of the thwarted polity, the resultant learning by and realized knowledge of all, and the reaffirmed order itself. However, the lowering of acceptable standards does not mean that tragedy is present in international relations when the protagonist lacks all or most of the defining traits of tragic heroism. They are lacking when the rebel feels no connection to the existing order and his purpose is only destructive; or when, rather than being nihilistic, he is naively unaware of the surrounding ambiguities and of the certain cost attaching to all efforts to transcend them; or finally, when the hero is an epic hero who joyfully combats manifest dangers instead of coping with arcane dilemmas as a last resort. Tragedy is thus a characteristic of maturing or matured states and systems, whereas romance and epic are paramount in their early or primitive stages and nihilistic rebellion denotes overmature decay. Nor is tragedy present or even possible in either pre- or post-mature systems or segments of system where natural-reflexive power drives, institutionalized constraints, and internalized principles of statecraft are very unevenly developed and active.

Thus delimited, tragedy is not confined to plural systems of near-equal states. Instead of being banished, it is transposed to a different plane when success has propelled a hegemonial drive into an imperial climax. Just as hubris stands for too great an ambition, so nemesis announces the fated failure of the grandest of accomplishments. The empire succeeds where the thwarted hegemonial aspirant has failed, and overcomes the contradictions and incoherences in a plural system. Yet it succeeds only at the price of repressing the flaws deep into its own structure. By transcending the contentious system in the area of its sway, the empire opens itself to subversion by the forces it has subdued and encompassed within itself.

The would-be hegemon falters because he has communicated his strengths to adversaries as part of the *agon*; the empire begins to prepare its demise when it achieves apotheosis by diffusing skills and resources to its dependants in the initially successful and increasingly necessary effort to enlarge the bases of its stability within and salience without. The hegemonial aspirant revitalizes a fractured or failing system of states by empowering previously flagging or marginal resisters; for an empire to erode its monopolies in favor of subjects prepares its decomposition into a primitive plural system by devitalizing the center. The society striving for hegemony will be overpoliticized at the commanding heights during the climactic phase of a bid; in particular its elites will be progressively de-politicized as the empire enters twilight. The empire incurs tragedy when it expresses its nature by applying the principles of hierarchy and control in behalf of universality, but unwittingly fosters equality and autonomy in the framework of particularized plurality. And when the empire's only deferrable fall surfaces the incurable contradiction between ecumenical pretense and actual dependence on uniquely specific moral and material resources, its fate reveals the mere humanity of man himself, unable to hold on to his highest political achievement.

The tragic knot can be tied by two major powers in mutually destructive conflict, by the hegemonial aspirant achieving self-destruction through an attempt to transcend a frustrating order, or by the triumphant empire that falls because it can rise no higher and must spread itself wider. In either case the grief tragedy elicits is commingled with tragic irony by virtue of the antinomies that pervade the systemic universe. The competitive system encourages the striving for individual grandeur out of which it grows, and the system's operation depends for a measure of order on self-assertion by especially the greater powers. Yet the order of things is also implacably hostile to, and sets up provocative constraints on, the natural tendency of players to extend potency into presumption. If the legitimate goal of measured mastery is often perverted in the megalomaniacal loss of control over self, this is also because the way the system works raises the sights of daring spirits above the golden mean only to reaffirm the equation of stable structure with drab mediocrity. As a result, whereas the system's operation is ultimately shaped by the tragic form, it is most of the time replete with routine trivia. Yet if the apparent futility of most human efforts intimates the vanity of the most ambitious among them, it also excites the urge to wrest some measure of dignity from the least promising of enterprises.

Just as tragic form imposes an aesthetically satisfying shape on the fatally futile endeavors of the more heroic among the protagonists, so the incidental trivia supply everyman with the stuff of the intervening comedy of petty errors and mistaken identities. The dramatic cast of interstate politics at its moments of climax favors contemplating its processes from the vantage point of spirit that infuses the structures of power with morale while it contends with different forms and layers of conventional morality; the more frequently commonplace actuality is part of the prosaic fact that the dramatic cast is more distinctive of high politics than descriptive of policies most of the time. If this is part of the irony of things, it only heightens the sense of terror and pity evoked by the genuinely tragic event. The rare event that discloses reality will be often lost in the confusing complexity of the tragicomic plot, with peripheral incidents blocking the avenues to central insight. Yet, underneath the complexity, the austere simplicity and constancy of the forces and principles constitutive of the state system go on acting as the secret cause of the political animal's enduring condition and the hidden spring behind his ennobling predicament.

The tragic grief that is inspired by feelings of fear and pity without extinguishing the feeling of pride in the contemplation of tragedy suggests implicitly what tragedy is not. The acts that constitute tragedy are terrible in the sense of inspiring awe, but they are not horrible in the sense of being monstrous. They do not offend moral sensitivities any more than they can leave one indifferent, because their absence implies a vacuum. A system of states risks dissolving into a condition of chaos when the tragic tension implicit in two-power conflict or one-power drive for conquest subsides without opening up other sources of elementary disciplines. While tragedy has thus a determinate relationship to elementary order, and has next to an emotional impact also an ethical dimension, it does not perform a judicial function: although it itself issues out of misjudgments, completed tragedy does not leave behind a verdict. Neither pure righteousness nor markedly greater or lesser right does or can reside in any one protagonist or cause, because all of justice dwells in the expiatory suffering to be shared by all if order is to be restored and raised to a higher plane in due course. The tragic plot is as different from the morality play as tragedy is from melodrama. Good does not battle and cannot vanquish evil so long as the two are commingled in beast-like predators aspiring to god-like powers; meet and merge in protagonists whose crucial encounter is as much with their own limitations that shape their fate as with the strengths that inhere in a rival force.

Grasping the essence of tragedy opens up vistas on how to attenuate, rather than abolish, the predicament attendant on actual conflict or attempted conquests. And since awareness of tragedy informs, but cannot transform the plight lying in wait for future as it did for past protagonists, it matters little whether in dealing with the predicament the actor-observer imitates tragic theater (Thucydides) or it is the drama on the stage that imitates life (Aeschylus, Sophocles) – so long as the life is one that the striving and struggling of state-like moral personalities has raised to the heights. Lessons follow from insight independently of whether Athens is a model for *Oedipus Tyrannus* or the Oedipus myth is the paradigm for the tyrant-city: the hubris of each is rooted in a prior exemplary act destined to grow into a defiance of the limits that are the soul of order. Much the same is true for the contest of equally valid if differently rooted values of an Antigone and a Creon, and the mutually annihilating orders of battle between two brothers-enemies at a gate to Thebes: each intimates the dilemmas of struggling Athens and Sparta while the plight of the cities writes large the predicament of citizens. Like political physics, politicized poetics abstracts meaningful facets of reality, if with a different slant and focus, from a history that moves forward from its origins in myth. As either the model or a replica, matured Athens' hegemonial ambition is inseparable from the contest with Sparta: it springs from the confrontation, is meant to provide an escape from the contention, and will be contained before collapsing. So was among the moderns Germany's in relation to her contest with Britain near the end of a later chain of tragic embroilments.

The attendant tragedy is confirmed as universal by the culpable tragic hero-state being in one case a maritime empire of a western cast, in the other a power both continental and, relative to the main adversary, eastern. The arrogant pride of Athens sprang from her part in the defeat of Persia (and seeming capacity to challenge Sparta on land), imperial Germany's from her triumph over France (and seeming capacity to challenge England on the sea). Both of the defeated-to-be "older kings," Persia and France, had themselves been caught up in the web of necessity: both compelled in the past as primarily land powers to become efficient at sea, the Asian power had at the critical juncture to act so as to become also European if it was to achieve universal sway, and the European state, firmly established as global power, to fight lengthening odds if it was to retain continental preeminence. As for their immediate supplanters, hubris was the offspring of *hamartia* when error born of arrogance concealed the questionable feasibility of hegemonial designs from bases in resource too slender relative to the size of the theater to be mastered: all-Mediterranean for the Hellenic and global for the Germanic realm. However, the Athenian error was as fated as was the German inasmuch as a misjudgment encouraged by the fluctuating structures of power and conditions of prosperity in the respective arenas was only ideally avoidable, had the two protagonists been not only willing but also demonstrably able to rely indefinitely on the silently subversive effect of their precariously based economic strengths on the less-than-reassuring general state of things.

The element of choice implicit in the notion of misjudgment was outweighed in both instances by factors that easily took on the appearance of compelling necessity: to face up to an unavoidable conflict sooner rather than incurring the cumulating cost of deferring it further. Accordingly, Athens could no more lastingly appease Sparta than she would Persia before or after without jeopardizing both her domestic and her imperial orders: the inner increasingly dependent on public hostility for Sparta and the highly popular gains from empire, the outward contingent on the allies-clients' continuing fear of Persia. The apparent choice was thus between continuing to grow by war while risking defeat, and coveting peace at the cost of accepting stagnation as a prelude to certain decay. The attendant anxiety reflected genuine dilemmas, inherent in both the narrower and the larger setting: the former shaped by either a dissolution-prone alliance of equals or precariously domination-based empire; the latter consisting of a system of states formally autonomous and actually subject to either Athenian or Spartan hegemony. Similarly, Germany's position in a two-front external and a sociopolitically cleft domestic setting pointed powerfully to the choice between expansion into a world power and extinction as a great European power; between pushing forward to stabilized ascendancy and being pulled down by growing dependence on a self-servingly assertive decadent ally.

Neither did either Sparta or Britain feel able to endanger the layers of interests tied to concentrically arrayed alliances, associations, and affinities by doing less than confront the adversary; their choice was between retreat toward a downslide and leap into the unknown. The tragedy-defining equivalence of the contestants' values was implicit in the very ambiguities that made it difficult to distinguish their application from aspiration or affirmation: essential equivalence was manifest in the combinations of Athens' internally free polity with externally tyrannical power and Sparta's oppressive regime with only moderate hegemony; it was only latent in the differing allocation of and balance between social reformism and ingrained conservatism, hierarchical practice and egalitarian propensities and professions, in "authoritarian-militarist" Germany and "liberal-pacifist" Britain, with neither side willing or able to compromise the values mix springing from the different continental or maritime habitat any more than to disengage strategically from its counterpart's.

Whatever role third parties as agents of impersonal fate may have had in tying the tragic knot around the protagonists, the main agency of fatality resided in the absence of "acceptable" alternatives to conflict. All seemed convincingly to entail loss of control over critical assets, only including the capacity to maintain either the imperial or the domestic order in being indefinitely. In the complex plots preceding or attending the outbreak of war, fatality assumed the mask of tragicomic futilities attending attempts at conciliation. Sparta's hard-to-fathom expulsion of the Athenian contingent sent to help suppress a helot rising as a token of conservative solidarity matches the even harder-to-penetrate intricacies of the Anglo–German negotiations for outright alliance or more limited understanding. Failure of conciliation attempts marked the "fatal" moment past which the narrowed range of choices translated into an accelerating onrush of events toward calamity. Fear lest adverse organic developments outstrip operational options blocked insights which might have deferred conflict and thus helped avoid it altogether. Pericles would not withdraw the Megarian Decree in the face of a Spartan ultimatum any more than Bethmann–Hollweg would default on the blank check to Austria–Hungary despite a premonition of catastrophe, because both were convinced that to defer battle would only bring defeat nearer by reducing the chance of victory. Nor did either Sparta or Britain feel confident enough about long-term trends to let the rival grow incrementally by means short of major war.

Both of the two-power conflicts caused, more than they had been caused by, escalating bids for ever more total hegemony by one of the parties. The passional excess in executing the bid surpassed in both instances the extent of the underlying purpose, reducible to anxiety as much as to ambition. It was yet another element in the unfolding of tragedy that when a timely perception of the portents menacing both sides might have had a chance to moderate the belligerents, a strategic gamble stood for the attempt to find a shortcut out of catastrophe. The Sicilian expedition and, after the failure of the Schlieffen Plan, an unrestricted U-boat campaign outdid in this regard the laying waste of Attica on land and the naval blockade of Germany by sea. They were the arguably necessary "last" or "only" recourses for swaying fate, before they would be condemned as frivolous attempts to court fortune. Strategic desperation was the external side of demagogic-to-dictatorial abuses, in an Athens about to forfeit imperial in favor of internal tyranny and in a Germany poised to descend from military to totalitarian dictatorship. And it was only a faint echo from lost pre-war opportunities that the final strategic wager became necessary only when Athens had neglected to conclude a favorable peace after humbling Sparta at Pylos and both later belligerents neglected occasions to negotiate a peace of compromise in the first two years of the First World War before the struggle became genuinely "total."

As passions rose further in the second and climactic installment of the Anglo–German conflict and the German bid, it was a defeated Third Reich that was to suffer the most drastic dismemberment as the sacrificial scapegoat for the flaws of the system as much as for its own crimes. The immolation was all the more in keeping with the tragic form the more the rise, the brief triumph, and the fall of Nazi Germany was the form's border case. The ritual announced more clearly in the German than it had in the Athenian case the impending end of an entire system. Whereas the European was capable of arousing only nihilistic rebellion, the rebel's sacrificial quartering was but the most dramatic evidence of the short-lived continental German imperium representing the imperfections of the system in an even more extreme fashion and on a grander scale than the Athenian maritime empire had done. The would-be hegemon's striving, and the attendant wider suffering, were inherent in the continental–maritime schism cleaving apart first the Greek and then the European arena. As a result, the misdeeds attributed to each expansionist individually – be they against peace in both cases or against humanity in one – were, even when in themselves horrendous, formally extraneous to the tragic character of the entanglements. When the victors held themselves innocent of contributions to the ultimately culpable clash of interests, their sense of righteousness did not rule out their being indictable of the venial sin of hypocrisy when disguising self-serving interests as universally beneficial needs and rights. Nor could the essential equivalence be fully abrogated by the values of the defeated having been progressively deformed, as the prior denials of equal benefits of peace or the ensuing ordeal of battle helped corrupt the best in them and convert it into the worst.

As in the progressively debased scenarios of the Greek city-state system, so also in the European system of states, the horrors of the continent's final agony paled in time before the terror inspired by its long-hatched fatality and the grief occasioned by the long-term consequences of the indigenous parties' mutual self-destruction. The fear and pity could once again be redeemed only by remembering that, while war's horrors are readily forgotten, tragedy survives through the demise of its subjects. The thwarted hegemonial bid by Athens emerging out of the Atheno–Spartan competition was followed in the chain of events by the successful hegemonial bid by Rome emerging out of conflict with Carthage. The victor, before being vanquished by the dilemmas of empire, had first been weakened by the corruption of his qualifying constituent virtues. Since these were deployed most fully but also for the last time in the Second Punic War, Carthage won in her defeat a delayed victory over Rome by disappearing as the prime source of the fears sustaining the Roman virtues.

The compatibility of triumph with tragedy signalled once more the difficulty of triumphing over tragedy. For any present time only history could grant insights, and only viewing the future in terms of history could profit from insights, into the lineaments of tragedy. As between America and Russia, it was yet impossible to decree who if either was the future's tragic hero or the posthumously avenged victim in a struggle wavering between the dominance of hubris and *hamartia* – of arrogance and misjudgment; impossible to foresee whose brief triumph, if anyone's, would be merely a prelude to tragedy. In any case, so long as tragedy rules because the system of states endures, the hegemonial challenger pitted against the precarious order wrested from anarchy will occupy a position doubly central to the wider predicament.

Firstly, the aspirant to hegemony is flanked at both ends of the continuum of fallible ambitions capable of only partial realization. At one end is the territorial state in its defining attributes, designed to shield as much as to harness individual spontaneities but apt to repress them as it struggles with like states for survival through growth. At the other end is the territorial state in its most triumphant accomplishment, exceeding in both power and purpose the common lot. Then, in the shape of empire, it is repeatedly propelled toward demise by the tendency for continuing growth to generate overextension, for deliberate concentration of resources to trigger their uncontrollable diffusion, and for the formative coherence of culture and ethos to be fatally diluted through deceptively regenerative co-optation. Accountable for the shifting boundaries between state and empire is a process, as part of which individual strategies achieve the opposite of intended objectives when they rationally respond to the ostensible (quantitative) at the cost of harder-to-intuit hidden (qualitative) attributes of the structure of power – and the repeated subversion of goals ends by inverting the factors and features responsible for the formation and growth of actors into causes and conditions of their finally debilitating transformation.

And secondly, the hegemonial aspirant stands at the operational focus of the system-defining tension between orderliness and anarchy which to challenge, in the guise of the balance of power, bestows upon the key protagonist a heroic stature and burdens the process with the dilemmas peculiar to the operationally crucial feature of tragedy: the one trait in the universe of power balancing that distinguishes states *qua* actors functionally interchangeable in all other respects because uniformly situated is the distinction between offense and defense. The moral absolutism inhering in the distinction when superficially applied is fundamentally at variance with the ethical relativism grounded in the spatially and temporally diversified situations of actors that make both the distinction and the dialectic between offense and defense highly ambiguous. It is this ambiguity which corroborates on the plane of actual operations the essential equivalence of contending values responsible for the occurrence of tragedy, just as conceding it is preconditional to the awareness of tragedy in world politics.

An attempt to transpose the offense–defense ambiguity from the plane of military or politico-diplomatic tactics and strategy onto that of ethical judgment will compel falling back on the murky realm of averred or imputed intentions. Yet the correct determination of an act's intrinsic quality will remain precariously suspended in the grey area delimited by past and future. Representing the past is the regressive causal chain of anterior acts, controversially intended for self-protection and perceived as constituting denial- or demand-based provocation. While the acts may stand for either defense or offense in conclusively established fact or only in convenient fiction, the incrementally cumulating consequences of the action–reaction series will indisputably culminate in a balance-of-power setting that can be only superficially addressed in terms of "offensive" or "defensive" forms of conduct. Representing the future will, at a critical juncture, be the anticipation of impending contingencies in arbitrarily delimited space and deferred time, to be promoted or prevented in the present after being more or less plausibly projected from speculatively discounted existing trends so as to reveal the immediate implications and determine corresponding requirements.

Where past antecedents typically justify initiatives for corrective revision of the status quo, future-related anxieties can arguably warrant action of offensively-defensive or defensively-offensive kind for either upholding or challenging the existing state of the balance. Thus questionably founded claims and counter-claims will, together with likewise deterioration-prone and negation-inviting institutional or instrumental innovations, invariably generate the major crises which release the extra motor energy that converts systemic interactions into a system's evolution. These same crises will in due course contribute to a system's salience devolving to its successor when the conflicts concealing tragic collisions have acted out their part as the progression's mechanism. They will by then also have ceased permeating evolution's matrix while serving as the operational façade for the normative dilemmas spawned by the ambiguously offensive–defensive interactions centered on equilibrium.

In the process, the evolution-propelling crises will have aggregated the similarities with the differences between equilibrium-centered interactions and tragic entanglement-implementing collisions. Most basically, the interactions implement the potential of a reflexive drive to be institutionalized in an objectively positive norm of order-promoting behavior; the collisions externalize the tendency for designs driven by values next to interests to encompass an objectively negative inversion and/or self-destruction of these same values. The unequal outcomes materialize as, in both instances, presumptive or effective choice is in secret contention with inevitability and the degree of necessity is revealed by the extent individual intentions have been modified into, when not overwhelmed by, unintended results or consequences. It will be for the balancing of power, whether deliberate or incidental to other purposes, to restore, by virtue of the clash among uneven forces, the stability activating tragedy through the collision between equivalent values has temporarily upset. Moreover, if the equilibrium-centered interplay has restored or reapproximated equality among major players in the very act of protecting or promoting lesser ones, and does so repeatedly enough in actual fact to be anticipated with confidence, a retrospective awareness of tragedy having been consummated must intervene again and again before equanimity can be restored through grieving acceptance of the greater actor having been struck down by a lesser, and noble values by no higher ones.

Despite the differences, order is eventually restored in both cases with the same inevitability it was upset; and it is so renewed through a chain of action and reaction that has mediated progression toward greater maturity, attended by deepened insight into motivations. Moreover, in the process of thus helping actors achieve catharsis, the drama of their interactions in a vain search for the catalyst susceptible of arresting inconclusive drift will have in both instances only surfaced the deeper tension between a consuming desire for choice and its abridgement by countervailing necessity. As the drama discloses the central dilemma, the destiny of actors will be enacted through decline's being implicit in earlier development; and it will be so encompassed in ways that match the destruction of values being latent in the very power, purpose, or process responsible for their generation.

Yet again, and finally, if balancing of power protects the lesser parties in the name of rights and these are invoked by greater powers as a matter of choice in behalf of practical expediency, tragedy at its truest is present when high value is destroyed or self-destructs in the performance of an inescapable duty necessarily assumed as a matter of fundamental and fundamentally self-sufficient principle. However, this difference also matters less so long as both expediency and principle are the mutually reinforcing imperatives sustaining a coherent reason of state. And it matters less so long as application of the balancing principle grounded in reflexive instinct and conducive to equilibrium, and intuitive awareness of the entanglement constitutive of tragedy, both have a moderating effect on the behavior of states and the operation of the system of states. Balancing of power has such an effect as it mutes the consequences of relative (or also absolute) growth and decline of states; the awareness of tragedy, as it militates against the ethical dogmatism forged in zealous defense of ostensibly absolute good against inveterate evil.

Part II

The Warp of Fate

Discourses 3–4
Manifest Forms of World Politics

The principal dimensions shaping – and keys to understanding – world politics correspond to the duality of drama and destiny that links active operations at any one time to evolutionary progression over time. If a rational management of the equilibrium mechanism encompassing the physics and poetics of inter-actor relations is critical for the operations, the way these are linked to progression is opened up by larger intelligence revealing the organic growth, maturity, and decline of actors caught up in the resulting imbroglios.

Discourse 3   On Strategic Rationality and Historical Intelligence

The inner economy of world politics derives its coherence from two facts. One such "fact" is that the balance-of-power or equilibrium mechanics, which implements the action–reaction/attraction–revulsion interplays in political physics, is linked to the poetics of tragic entanglement no less closely for being so linked clandestinely through differences as well as similarities. Whereas the entanglement permeates the moral sphere and the equilibrium shapes much of the operational sphere, the former affects the latter at a deeper level than do the formally institutionalized norms designed to contain and control it. The other "fact" is that while the balancing process is mediated through a rationality best described as strategic, it requires an intelligence comprising the historic dimension if a fuller awareness of the tragic entanglement, correcting for the limitations of the rationality, is to humanize the mechanics. Historical intelligence adds a temporal dimension to the spatial determinant of behavior. The two must be combined to produce a relativistic perspective on competing actors which, essential for affirming the normative equivalence of their fundamental values, is as indispensable to the tragic character as actually reoccurring differentials in locations and stages of development are to the geo-historical constitution of world politics.

In as much as equilibrium and entanglement give equally rise to the predicament that excludes both final remedies and facile judgments, tragedy-conscious geo-historicism differs fundamentally from a pragmatism which, keyed to solving particular problems through the balancing of capabilities and adjusting of interests, is normatively focused on a superficial distinction between acts offensively disrupting and defensively upholding the status quo. The narrower approach reflects correctly the self-imposed limitation of a conventional diplomacy adequately equipped to deal, and properly applied to dealing, with the last emergent product of an antecedent chain of causal and a subjacent hierarchy of determinant factors. But it does and can do so only at the hidden cost of foreclosing valid moral judgments which, when hazarded nonetheless, can do no better than buttress apparently reasonable rationalizations of ostensibly efficient conduct.

More problematic than the relation of equilibrium to entanglement and of rationality to intelligence is the relationship of the inner economy of world politics to international aspects of political economy. Elusively underlying the various operative connections between the two is the ultimately critical distinction with a difference between politics in its pristine form, implementing the reason-of-state principle, and economics, focused practically on managing socially significant resources. The statist principle and perspective are driven by the presumption that role- or status-related requirements do and will constrain, in the last resort, an expediency routinely sufficient to support particular second-order interests. The implied decisional hierarchy reflects the graduated structure of priorities and risks attendant on an inescapable scarcity of security and its immaterial (role-status) supports or attributes, all of which can be allocated only conflictually. This being so, the statist perspective differs critically from the individualist-and-societal one on two grounds: (1) the latter is shaped by expedient-to-opportunistic modes of either competition or collaboration with a view to actualizing the potentially infinite expansibility of material goods; and (2) whereas some at least of individual or group claims on such goods depend for justification on a morality extraneous to the process of production and distribution, no transcendent morality can be invoked to make up for a state-like collective's failure to wrest a share of security from its ideally fixed and chronically inadequate sum.

To the extent that the societal prevails over the statist perspective, it erodes the grounding of tragedy in the enactment of a duty or duties implementing an uncompromisable principle, ultimately regulatory of conduct. When this happens, the locus of tragedy has passed or is about to pass on beyond state-like entities constrained in the last resort both operationally and normatively to abide by principles reflecting their essence when acting in defense of their existence, after having migrated there from the realm of high-born heroes empowered materially and obligated normatively to observe canons of behavior fitting to implement an exceptional role and vindicate a privileged status. Tragedy's last and precarious refuge can then be nothing more closely attuned to its defining attributes than the more neurosis- than nemesis-prone psychic universe of the apolitical individual released from the bonds of the classic territorial state when the atrophy of its basic function, to stand guard over corporate autonomy while draining into itself individual anxieties, had altered its nature from the most comprehensive among authority structures into but the largest of limited-liability corporations. The idea of the state as an institution for harmonizing rights and obligations of citizens and governors is then over-shadowed by the fact of society being reduced to a mechanism for allocating material rewards and penalties among consumers and between them and producers, with consequences fatal to community as an organism equally dependent on the state to elevate society and on society to sustain the state.

Insofar as such a transformation corresponds to real changes in the environment rather than only tentative postulates about ongoing or impending ones, the ensuing disarray in the formulation and implementation of high policy or grand strategy marks more than a temporary, only restful or also regenerative, interlude in the cycles of war and peace. The pause turns instead into an uncontrolled descent from tragic heights into an uncharted sea of troubles yet unknown – unknown because, when decay of principle has relaxed the predicaments immanent in its application, the familiar patterns of action and of its results dissipate into inherently structure- and purpose-less drift. Two consequences would follow from a shift away from the political and toward the economic component within political economy, and the attendant one from the centrality of the inner to that of a but residually political economy within world politics. The demise of tragedy as it was extinguished under the weight of societally focused economics in the West – the home of classic tragedy and the distinctive terrain of its presence in state-centered politics uniquely keyed to managing the contrasting demands of principle and expediency – would properly coincide with the center of material wealth creation and diffusion gravitating from Euro-Atlantic to the Asian–Pacific basin. And, as the displacements evolved beyond tentative hypotheses predicated on inconclusive trends, and gave way to actual transformations, they and the related predictions would challenge the validity of both present analysis and prophetic anticipation drawing primarily on the constituents of world politics' inner economy.

As cyclically unfolding processes, equilibrium-centered interaction and crises-absorbing evolution congeal into discernible surfaces the norms of behavior that implement instrumental rationality within structures of unevenly consolidated actors and differentially crystallized system. By contrast, the idea of progress hinges on the affirmation of a normative utopia which, embodying an ethical desideratum, is the product of some kind of rationalization. The way instrumental rationality – one that relates or seeks to relate means to ends – works will inhibit when not altogether thwart progress toward the utopia designed to correct the effects of that same rationality; reaction to both pragmatic rationality and rationalizing utopia will foster a regressively irrationalizing mythology of interstate politics – the chimera of mytho-normative statecraft as the inverse facet of the utopian-progressivist fallacy.

Whereas instrumental rationality translated into deliberately power-balancing strategies is central to political physics, both the utopian- and the mytho-normative rationalization relate to tragedy. The search for utopia is a way of escaping from the terrifying consequences of hubris and *hamartia* into harmony; it will be stepped up all the more eagerly, the deeper was the enforced descent into pity and fear. But if the arrogance of the tragic hero is spiritual, the utopian reformer's is cerebral; whereas the former's is linked to well-conceived ambition or ill-founded anxiety instigating action, the latter's consists of intellectual pride in conceiving a perfect design founded on just desire. However, the utopist is too self-satisfied and risks too little in failure to be either heroic or tragic. His ambition to resolve ambiguities by rational analysis, and vanquish fate by constraining power through institutions or de-politicizing functions, is based on an error still greater than the tragic hero's; as such, his striving forms a link in the tragic chain of futile endeavors with unforeseen consequences that permeate interstate politics. The connection of mytho-normative statecraft to tragedy goes deeper and reaches farther back. It points to the relation of tragedy to myth as the nostalgic recreation of the origins of the world and the species. In politics, the return is to unrestrained force as the primordial essence of power. The mythomaniac escalates, where the utopist would escape, the tragic motif of collision and rebellion. He treats both as not so much the regrettable consequence of ambiguities, to be abstracted from confusing actuality, as the full and sufficient depiction of the actual, evoking satisfaction rather than sympathy. Conflict is then seen as enhancing man's existence rather than redeeming his errors, and as offering an opportunity for quickened evolution and moral growth.

Instrumental rationality as a norm against which to measure strategic behavior and judge its results develops with the capacity to construe reality objectively. In enhancing control over the subjective urges of an actor, in the interest of action capable of constraining the behavior of others, it manifests the crucial ability to relate (i.e., significantly intend to relate) appropriate (i.e., plausibly sufficient and necessary) means to inherently feasible ends. The requisite systemic setting will be one that has reached a corresponding mix of complexity and crystallization that both permits and compels the exercise of such rationality. The progression is then from (typically) reflexive to (habitually) reflective behavior: from instinctive to informed responses, reacting less to seemingly unique present stimuli than anticipating alternative future sequelae to alternative kinds of behavior. The propensity and capacity to relate means to ends as the conscious criterion and intended form of rational action will parallel thought patterns imbued with a critical awareness of cause–effect chains in a reality which, being rationally articulated, is rationally apprehensible. This ingredient of rationality in strategic behavior will grow *pari passu* with the evolving structure of a system. It will do so inasmuch as the conflict-related mechanism of evolution promotes the development, and the manifestations of achieved evolution compel the application, of instrumental rationality as a condition of actor efficacy or outright survival.

It is in and through conflict that means–ends disparities will be revealed and eventually corrected to the advantage of some and detriment of other actors, that comparatively most efficient (i.e., instrumentally rational) foreign-policy elites will be selected, and the most manageable actor optima (as to size, situation, and skills) be identified. As actors and systems evolve, increasingly sophisticated enactment of conflicts will automatically raise the standards of instrumental to the level of strategic rationality. This will happen not least by extending the ranges of both competition and compensation past mainly physical or tangible assets (slaves, territory, booty) to stakes less easy to grasp instinctively and operationally manage. And if means–ends rationality is promoted by the conflictual mechanism of evolution, it will be at a growing premium as progressing evolution is manifested through actors increasingly identical, because territorial, but also differentiated in other respects, becoming ever more closely contiguous through physical contact or direct communication. The parallel developments will both intensify and diversify hostile pressures to be identified and met ever more rapidly in order to avoid ill-conceived action among decreasingly dissolution-prone and ever more consolidation-capable power aggregations.

Two more reasons will tend to refine further the requisite strategic rationality. For one, developing actors will expand less as a result of drives that are easy to discern and (at least in principle) deal with, and will act more or equally as a result of being drawn into risky enterprises by a combination of pulls (from vacuums or upheavals of power: opportunities) and pushes (from adverse power concentrations: threats). For another, the countervailing responses to expansion will be ever less unilateral, as alternately resistance-capable actors substitute for one another, and ever more collective, calling for rational coordination. Acceleration on the temporal plane, expansion in the spatial domain, and differentiation in several spheres are the main impellents to rationality. They enhance the need for deliberate, strategic or tactical, invention to supplement near-accidental innovations occurring outside the system boundary strictly defined.

A dispassionately utilitarian rationality will be necessary for, but also sufficient in, a statecraft that acknowledges no higher standard or rationale of action than the reason of state. In fifth-century BC Greek, fifteenth-century Italian, or eighteenth-century European, system the instrumental approach to a finite secular actuality is then manifest in morally neutral concepts of desirable individual quality and conduct (the Greek *arete*, closer to Italian *virtù* than either is to Christian virtue) and societal or systemic condition (the Greek *dike*, a matter of proportion closer to *balancia* than to abstract justice). If the former acts then as impulse behind, the latter does as constraint on, conflict. It is no accident that a rationality free of both utopian desiderata and mythological delusions will repeatedly crest in a system of close to five powers. The pentagonal pattern implies a compelling rational rule for each (to be included in the stronger majority of three) as well as a realistic goal for all (to transcend the 3:2 division in a concert of five, or pentarchy). Adding the differentiation between land- and sea-oriented powers stimulates means–ends rationality further. It not only introduces the ethos of the mercantile-maritime powers peculiarly prone to calculate costs and benefits; it also raises reactively on the part of the continental-military powers the need for perfecting the clusters of functions centering on force and fiscality that form actors capable of not only conceiving but also implementing action rationally.

Likewise helping to support (and define) the norm of instrumentally rational behavior will be rough equality or balance between external (power- and security-promoting) and internal (prosperity- and stability-serving) functions of government. It is such a balance that fosters, but also depends on, individual claims on the corporate society being matched by a sense of social obligation within a territorial state that has remained an ideal value as it perfected its functioning apparatus. And although any one state stands for the particular, to do so effectively it will have to hold its own within that which is nearest to being universal system-wide. The latter is practically expressed best or only in the balance of power (as the mostly unintended result of individual self-assertions) and intermittently in the concert of powers (as the rare consequence of a fortuitous convergence of requisite conditioning and contributory factors). When the balances are right, the state will be equipped to channel any extant surplus of social energy away from inter-factional or -personal conflicts into coordinated efforts, and apply these to utilize available material surpluses for developing capabilities and strategies that can reduce critical material or other scarcities by effective action abroad.

Inasmuch as the norm of instrumentally rational behavior marks the peak of evolution, it implies a pre-norm and, since the evolution is apt to be cyclical, also a post-norm, which sets the stage for the next beginning. The behavioral pre-norm is dominated by instinctual urges within an inchoate (proto-) systemic setting. In that it intimates the deep-seated non-rational sources of statecraft, the pre-norm signals limits to qualitative progress; but by pointing to the statecraft's potential for becoming increasingly rational it implies an evolutionary range. In terms of the basics, the pre-norm is marked by an excess of unrealizable goals over inadequate means. The primary imbalance extends to secondary ones. Thus efforts to project power abroad predominate over functions that are or can be performed internally by what then passes for government; and universalism as an insubstantial myth towers over, more than it actually threatens, the emergent particular-territorial state. Any and all energetic or material surpluses tend to be turned inward, into factional conflicts when not fanciful institutional constructions, or outward into military distractions lacking specific object. The consequence is a highly fluid situation of both abruptly and in most cases accidentally aggregating and disintegrating actors. The sustaining ethos and its implementing mentality compound elementary power-political modes inextricably with exalted (quasi-) religious moods while displaying a crude opposition between transcendental aims, reflecting world-denying aspirations, and mundanely opportunistic impulses, wedded to tactically devious methods.

The early European Middle Ages illustrate the starting point out of which must evolve a primitive (proto-) system if it is to pass through the behavioral pre-norm to the norm-stage. A radical deficiency in relation to space was one key element in the failure to relate means to ends pragmatically in rationally conceived and realistically conducted conflict. Ignorance of geography conspired with cult of the grandiose to favor pursuing limitless ambitions in undifferentiated space by military engagements difficult to distinguish from peace. The failure to apprehend space and apply to it practically feasible political or military strategies fostered a personalized and familistic statecraft, one informed by genealogical calculations rather than geopolitical considerations. So long as the matrimonial potential of rulers mattered more than the material potency of their realms, status related to blood-lines predominated over administratively implemented functions. Implicit in the familistic bias was the more speculative than reliably calculable diplomacy of the marriage market, producing rivalries that would decay into mere feuds before dying out in abortive forays. Neither procedure was suited to forming either state-like actors or system-like arenas – that is, was designed to establish effective control within manageable territorial scope capable of eventuating in a moderately stable configuration among contiguous units of spatially circumscribed capabilities. Since a slow rate of military-technological or any other innovations neutralized the effect of their irregular diffusion, no one actor could gain a decisive advantage for long enough to consolidate gains and begin shifting the functional focus from predation abroad to fostering prosperity at home. In sum, accidental aggregations of power prevailed over contrived ones as the main agent of change other than elemental irruptions of conquering energies from an unknown and unknowable periphery.

Ignorance of space went hand in hand with misconceptions about time, matching uncharted physical vastness with a compressed timetable in impelling a restless but strategically aimless activism. The sense of time running out soon with the impending end of the world was both the analogue to and an allegory for man's brief and uncertain lifespan, both imparting the quality of impermanence to human achievement and justifying any lack of continuity in either personal or group efforts. To polarize time between instant present and unbounded eternity meant overleaping the intermediate dimension of an open-ended mundane future, critical for rational planning; the stress on "now" entailed fixation on valorous-glorious acts, epitomized by the crusades, to be performed "here" as stepping stones to salvation in a realm beyond the here and now. Thus any continuity could be only mystical, such as that of a Christian ruler with the sacred stock of Charlemagne, the prototypical emperor, before the (Aristotelian) notion of open-ended indefinite time reasserting itself over the (Augustinian) polarity made it again possible for continuity to comprise the development of an impersonal body politic as an ongoing moral personality. Only when the concept of an indefinite future had re-emerged enough to engender the awareness of an ever-lengthier past could a growing fund of precedental guidance supplement static resources in backing strategies. And only as governmental functions grew conjointly with taxation as the means to provide against future emergencies would the evolution of strategic conduct be supported by a widening range of instrumentalities. Finally, only as instrumentally supported interpretations of the historical past took root could reasons from cause and effect begin to displace anecdotal rationales and mythological rationalizations in explaining current events and guessing at future eventualities.

Before a better grasp of space and time stirred instrumental rationality conflict had done little to advance evolution. Wars served the political order primarily as a remedy against tedium of functionless elites issuing into turmoil in the body politic, and secondarily as a device for recruiting ever new additions to feuding elites engaged in systematic self-destruction. So long as man's muscular impact on man could barely make up for his being unable to leave a significant impress upon the world of either nature or its institutional nurture, the best a display of piety in the right cause through strength could do was to wash off some of the taint from sinful man's insufficient goodness. Such primordial, confusedly symbolic and substantive, secular and spiritual, functions of military contest meshed well enough with the primitive but crucial economic-material function of conflict as a source of booty or ransom. So long as they did this, and before the scope of warfare could be expanded instrumentally while its imputed significance was being rationally curtailed in real-political statecraft, knightly tournaments as symbolic rituals with fixed procedural routines would do much of the duty for purposeful prosecution of substantively significant outcomes. They regulated violence by siphoning off its surplus, rationalized its display by virtue of firm rules designed to diminish fatalities, and socialized the participants by bringing together in regulated interplays otherwise isolated and widely dispersed participants.

As a rationalized ritual, the knightly tournament prefigured the conventions of formal diplomacy and stylized warfare in matured systems; as a device for socializing immature actors, it performed a function transferred in still farther-evolved systems to international institutions. By contrast, the elementary economic function of military conflict in materially primitive conditions intimated a connection that seemed ready to be reversed when, as an alternative to institutionally framed utopia, self-supporting economic agenda would be expected to replace war-centered or -threatening activities as the prime vehicle for qualitative progress taking over from evolutionary progression.

Closer to reality was the fact that, as part of inverting most of the features of the behavioral pre-norm, available material and military-technological means have in an overmature system tended to exceed the feasible goals of statecraft on the part of governments increasingly absorbed in domestic (welfare) functions over against external (warfare) functions. Just as the armed horde could best employ limited resource through unrestrained violence in a mêlée, so the many-sided expansion of resources was now invoked to sharply reduce the use of organized force when not repudiating it altogether. The new extreme has been a reaction to the prior degeneration of rationally measured employment of force, typical of the norm-stage, into what struck contemporaries as wars that were total in terms of either available or utilizable resources. The tendency for pre-norm to be altered into obverse post-norm features of behavior will be confirmed whenever a renascent actor-transcending universalism changes its formerly religio-political into material-economic form of expression, without for all that becoming more effectual in containing particular interests. And if continuing fragmentation retreats then into sectarian substitutes for the state-centered patriotism and institutionalized religiosity dominant in the intermediate phase of maturity, it is because the territorial state has weakened by virtue of a decaying political mentality being polarized between petty materialism on the elite and ersatz spirituality on the mass level. As the increasingly socio-economic bias of reformist utopianism evokes variously regressive political reactions, only intermittent foreign-policy initiatives are clung to as largely but symbolic tokens of the formal attributes of statehood. They have lost their vital basis in a viable reason of state as leadership preoccupations with domestic maladjustments reflect a critical shift: of surpluses to the side of material resources, and of scarcities to the plane of morale and motivation.

As spirit oozes out of the structure of power, policy is emptied of passion. The tendency is for politically ineffectual solidarity of participants in a defensively slanted culture – be it late Greek, Italian, or (west) European – to displace the schisms that governed the system and ordered statecraft as each was evolving toward and reached maturity. A system of states is replaced by political forms and institutional façades combining the community- with the empire-type variety of meta-system, wherein the lesser parties depend for the last remnants of diplomatic independence and strategic importance on the changing status of the stalemate-prone contest between two hegemonic powers: the Greek on Rome's contention with Macedon and then Syria, the Italian on France's with Spain, and the west European on America's with Russia. The only nominally still ruling political class is busy orchestrating the latitudes won from the stalemate between, with the comforts derived from being sponsored by the more congenial among, the system-dominant rivals. If it clings to the residues of power in the outside world, it is mainly as one of the means for upholding a fading domestic authority unsupported henceforth by a manifestly necessary security function.

The attendant declension reverses the antecedent progression toward the rigors of conduct necessary to link the security of states to individual self-help in the last resort. In system after system the emergence of instrumental means–ends rationality paralleled evolution that differentiated actors and ranked them hierarchically by virtue of their unequal capacity to pursue conflicting strategic goals. It was this concurrence that has impeded progress construed as movement toward uniform compliance with institutional norms implementing legal equality and forms of organization implementing equally mutual material dependence. Where the progressist utopia would subdue the deep-seated drives and urges defining man as a political animal, strategic rationality leans upon these while refining and restraining them. However, if the greater psychological realism behind such rationality thwarts radical reform, the pragmatic-utilitarian bias which rationality introduces into secularized statecraft as it reaches and passes beyond the norm-stage will also invigorate regressive reactions biased toward irrationality.

Unlike the progressist utopia, which extrapolates into normative doctrine any tendency for behavior to depart from the maturity norm in ways denoting a meta-system, the opposing mytho-normative reaction is a revivalist throwback to the earliest, behaviorally pre-norm proto-systemic stage. Its fundamental quality reflects the aspiration to restore to politics a measure of the indifferentiation between the secular-political and religio-ideological universes attending the mythical origins of all or most and shaping the actual practices of early or young civilizations. More specifically, the regressive outlook reaffirms hierarchy if not also empire, conflict in general and war in particular, and the absolute primacy of politico-military and (via the primacy of foreign policy) structural-systemic determinants of action. It contrasts thus item by item with the prospectively future-oriented utopia's stress on equality, peace, community, and the primacy of economic and domestic determinants in radically secularized and routinely institutionalized politics. While the utopian stress on reformed procedures is consistent with the primacy of the operational factor provided it affects all parties evenly, an equal or higher standing for the organic factor is implicit in the nostalgic emphasis on differences among unevenly vital players. And just as the former bias may be peculiar to mature-to-declining maritime-mercantile (and liberal-democratic) powers, so the latter is more common to continental (and conservative-authoritarian) states all the more arduously ascending when they are late-entering. Whether thus constituted continental polities revive in superficially secularized garb the medieval dominance of rationally compelling transcendent dogma (early Soviet Russia) or corrupt the medieval ideal of unquestioning faith to be exhibited by an unflinchingly leader-following chivalry (Nazi Germany), they will have one trait in common: be fighting off the prospect, if they have not been already caught up in the trauma, of a compulsively expansionist response to the incipient decline threatening to precede and thus forever prevent role-status equality with the other type of power.

It follows that both the utopian and the mytho-normative modes are idealistic rationalizations of vulnerable positions. They differ most from, and are intended to supplant, the perception and practice of statecraft as a matter of prudently enhanced efficacy relating growing means to scaled-down ends. In sharply opposed ways, both of the idealistic varieties would validate or justify actual or advocated conduct by elevating it above the empirical realm "as is," while injecting into that realm a superficially plausible rationale for what ought to be.

In a progressist utopia instinctual power drives would give way to policies more reasonable (in the sense of conforming with humane common sense) as to the ends, and more in keeping with the precepts of (scientific or abstract) rationalism in regard to means, adjusted to the tenets of economic theory and only organizational or also military-technological planning. Mythologically influenced statecraft would not so much eliminate pragmatic *realpolitik* as render it emotionally or spiritually more satisfying by formulating correspondingly the stakes and the sustaining values of conflict. Common to both kinds of deviation from the norm of instrumental rationality is their tendency to displace the means of statecraft, conciliation through compromise or reciprocity, coercion by war or revolution, into its ends. Neither can thus serve usefully as a bridge between rational statecraft and the evolving variations on its traditional virtues and vices. Both are more effective as a barrier to deepening rationality through association with historical intelligence.

Such intelligence assigns its proper – crucial but contingent – place and role to strategic rationality in the evolutionary stream. It delimits the conceptually steady place, and the actually changing contexts and efficacy, of rational strategy as the central – both intermediate and mediatory – operational link between the nether layer of basic or organic givens, accounting for primitive urges and pristine impediments, and the uppermost plane of the normative (either utopian or mythological) rationalizations of either. As a result, historical intelligence permits a largely intuitive identification of real changes and root continuities as the coequal precipitates of a progression unfolding in phases and cycles of unequal length in time. By enhancing the analytic grasp of the scope of evolutionary change and persistence, historical intelligence also lays the groundwork for delimiting the scope of genuine progress that is possible and has become necessary. Its true form is a synthesizing policy, one that self-consciously relates past precedents to existing conditions and both to intended outcomes on issues with different maturation spans, not least by paying attention to temporally conditioned differences among actors occupying disparate situations in space.

The nexus of capabilities, conflicts, and strategies is the permanent nucleus of any system's configuration. However, concurrently with the crystallization of structure and codification of perceptions – with the growth of the actors' sense of place in space and position in time – will change also the quality of required strategic responses to (diminishing) opportunities for rewards and (increasingly determinant) risks from threats and pressures. The climb toward ever "higher" rationality starts out from responses rooted in the instinct of self-preservation, translated into the drive for self-aggrandizement as a means to survival in a fluid environment; it evolves by way of instrumental rationality, which relates consciously finite means to feasible ends by processing instincts through prudential judgments objectified in institutionalized management, into strategic rationality objectified in shared diplomatic conventions and individual foreign policy traditions; and it climaxes in historic intelligence responsive to accumulated precedents from protracted conflicts that have bequeathed warnings in the form of unintended consequences and untoward outcomes.

Strategic rationality comprises the instrumental variety's task of adjusting means to ends so as to better apply internalized rules for meeting thrust with counterthrust and opposing force to force. And historical intelligence refines primitively reflexive responses to conspicuously manifest structures further in that it enlarges and diversifies the range of conditions assigned relevance. Although strategic rationality is perfected by abstracting guidelines to action from a historical experience that illustrates the workings of instinct, its efficacy is contingent on not overwhelming the instinct or weakening it to the point of atrophy. By the same token, whereas historical intelligence can control instinct only with insights inferred from a more self-consciously conceptualized record, it must not dry up the vital roots of past politics for the sake of formal rigor if it is to engender practical remedies for future politics.

Even when routinely precedents-absorbing, strategic rationality will not reliably suffice to reconcile the defense of spatially determined vital interests of territorial actors with a due regard for the actors' temporally conditioned states of being and – becoming. And it will reconcile even less certainly the requisites of an actor's success or survival with the requirement of a system being shielded from extinction as an autonomous and focal theater of action. Performing either of the more demanding tasks requires transcending a strategic rationality that is attuned to actors-centered equilibrium mechanics with insights encompassing the actors-affecting organic and systemen-aggregating dynamic elements pertaining to evolution. A thus armed historical intelligence will be rarely applied successfully, because, multi-faceted evolution being more amorphous than is interactional equilibrium and long-term system-related concerns more ambiguous than short-term actor-related ones, the intelligence itself cannot be reduced to a simple formula any more than it points to straightforward progress or supplies a self-evident imperative for strategy. Moreover, even when the implications of evolution for equilibrium have been intuited correctly, extending the speculative insight into instruction for strategy will be operationally impeded by the more immediate priority not to incidentally prejudice interests affecting the state-like actor's corporate autonomy. It will not suffice as a deterrent to paralyzing caution that, notably as its declining members reach outside an overmature system's boundary for help in redressing imbalances that seem to threaten the supreme value, routinely conceived strategies will have ceased crystallizing the structure of a system in favor of expanding its scope and will bring nearer, if not bring about, the system's demise as a self-dependent aggregate. Calling in powers from the outside may first only reduce the eroding system to the status of a micro-system. But the eventual consequence will be unfailingly to consign the abdicating constitutent members to the post-norm type of behavior, characteristic of a system's meta-stage, while the expanded macro-system embarks on its own evolutionary course. The question then left open will be whether the superseded system core has been lifted to the condition of conflict-free community or its members were debased to the position of effectively stateless clients in an empire-type association.

Discourse 4   On Intelligible History and Rational Strategies

Fundamental to historical intelligence is a sense of evolutionary progression and the capacity to locate specific present and prospective future tendencies and events in an articulated time-space continuum. A key sequence is that of basic foreign-policy postures of major actors or historic powers arising out of and bringing to the surface a plethora of conditioning factors. Among such factors are the clusters of military, economic, and administrative functions attuned to material and immaterial surpluses and scarcities which, critical for both the formation of actors and their behavior, are more or less aptly coordinated in regime efforts directed externally. The way actors relate to the outside through the medium of foreign policies mirrors not only their evolutionary stage but also and more immediately the dynamic condition of the arena. However, the latter fact allows for the basic – assertive and self-protective – foreign-policy modes to contribute, as they alternate without being each time around identical and strictly repetitive in either underlying impulse or outward thrust, to the overall environment of particular strategies in a way that transcends particular stimuli.

The initial foreign-policy posture, implementing the most essential prime requirement of delineating a sustainable physical habitat of a social group, falls into two times: undirected expansiveness in the direction of least resistance, followed by the effort to consolidate the consequently enlarged habitat into a lastingly defensible and viable one. Efforts to escape a too narrow initial confinement and to consolidate the enlargement are stimulated by the alternative, that of succumbing to a stronger party. Whereas the basic stimulus is the plural competitive dynamic innate to a multi-unit system, the expansive first movement is also facilitated by the structure being not only plural but also loosely articulated, making the arena in a general way permissive even if farther-evolved than the actors themselves. So long as plentiful vacuums of power coexist with easy-to-secure sources of material goods in excess of any existing barriers to expansion, the arena will be typically close to a proto-system; it is not yet of the constraining kind, replete with inhibitions that mark the transition from a congeries of dissolution-prone actors to a configuration of defense-capable and strategy-conscious actors negotiating the tension between their drives and arena-wrought deterrents to easy expansion.

In the initial aggressive-expansive stage, force, expressing the society's intrinsic nature, is mainly the means of securing adequate energy-sustaining nurture – food, fuel, and fodder (and whatever else can substitute for acquisitions from fiscal revenues), pending a more elaborate approach to enhancing the society's acquisitive powers and resulting prowess. It is equally probable that the accumulated surplus, permitting a rudimentary differentiation of the functions of warrior and either manager or propitiator from those of the producer, is of lesser size than the perceived material scarcities that imperatively demand satiation. And it is even more likely that only such individual ruler or collective ruling group will be tolerated (but, when tolerated, enjoy unrestricted command and confidence) whom the opening struggle for survival has shown able to direct elementary governmental functions outward as part of an essentially predatory policy, compensating for an insufficiently productive domestic economy immune to deliberate intervention. The primordial thrust and its underpinning will be subtly changed when the main purpose of policy has become to consolidate the initially expanded habitat on the strength of regularly collected public revenue. Coincident with progressing institution-alization of differentiated functions including a primitively bureaucratic-administrative one, that development draws on the previously enlarged material surplus without substantially altering the mainly outward slant of the government's orientation. However, foreign policy initiatives are restricted to areas closer to home than was the case previously, and any previous means–ends imbalance is substantially redressed in the process.

Functions and competencies remain fundamentally unaltered for the next turn in the expansion–consolidation–re-expansion cycle, when expansion has been resumed with support from the previously ensured basic stability and solvency. Expansion is no longer blindly instinctual as a response to an elementary survival need, an apparent opportunity offered by adjoining weakness, or transcendentally defined injunctions from a divinely ordained or dynastic purpose. Foreign policy can now be placed under the auspices of a self-confident mood that is positively exuberant even if the implementing method is pragmatically experimental. The surplus peculiar to the exuberant posture is clearly one of energy and enterprise even more than of hoarded up treasure; it is the product of the still raw social forces and individual drives constrained at home by the mounting inhibitions implicit in the most elementary regulation and management. The attendant scarcity is the new one of deficient domestic outlets for personally satisfying and internally stabilizing activity, as much as the continuing one of scarce material assets for the collective as a whole and of immaterial prestige for its main corporate bodies.

In keeping with what is a natural state and normal sequence in articulating the arena, the surrounding power configuration has by then become more tightly crystallized, and thus constraining, at the center than in the periphery that is emergent or newly manageable. Actual or prospective gains at the borderline of the center or in the periphery are well in excess of the material resources to be mobilized and expended for securing the coveted pay-offs. War is still a key means to wealth and wealth the prime anticipated consequence of war. However, since trade rather than raids or rapine implement henceforth the dependence of military resource on economic rewards and vice versa, the more complicated relationship's military and economic components are now more evenly matched in requisite efficacy and each can be invoked to rationalize the other's promotion and pursuit. Like any other orderly economic activity such as sedentary agriculture capable of generating a surplus where hunt or grazing consumes it, trade – and especially long-distance or overseas trade – will need authoritative protection and/or support more than does predatory raiding. In consequence, the functional balance will have begun to turn, although not yet to a degree that would significantly redirect the bulk of public or official concerns inward from those reserved for the outside.

Ensuing next is the evolutionary mid-point that is also the analytic norm around which the antecedent and subsequent postures and phases cluster. It is reached when maintaining the previously achieved standing of the actor in the coincident distribution of power in the arena becomes an object of policy, even if not necessarily and at all times its priority. At that stage both the norms that reflect and the forms of conduct that sustain the competitive character of the arena, and the values that reveal the maturity of a satiated actor, are biased toward the preservation of established positions and the moderation of conflict. The consequent, conservative foreign-policy posture is in keeping with the perception that constraints on expansionist initiatives will checkmate any remaining inducement to advance further at the center of the arena, and that opportunities at a widely penetrated periphery are in rough balance with obstacles to easy gains. An incrementally achieved central control over policy has, in the matured major actor, encountered growing pressures to complement differentiation of functions with diffusion of authority. First to benefit are sociopolitical groups that have contributed most to maximizing material surpluses and augmenting fiscal solvency, and reduced thus the most keenly perceived deficiencies immune to remedy from a judicious application of armed force or diplomatic finesse. Constraining insurgent and compensating accommodating social forces will require a continuing success in foreign policy. This, however, will not prevent temporary stalemates from degenerating into a static form of stability inviting challenge from more slowly developing actors, moving up from behind in the evolutionary procession or from outside the spatial proscenium. Consequently, the conservative posture attuned to the balance of power or equilibrium is not likely to be any more restful for a major actor than a settled equilibrium is enduring for the arena.

In its ideal perfection, equipoise is more often but a figment of the theoretical imagination: an ideal norm not yet fully realized when it seems to be in being, a potentiality already fading when its actualization appears to be imminent. Inside the sources of brief contentment for putative beneficiaries of outward calm will already germinate the conditions of decay surfacing in due course as past winners' manifest decline. Earlier attainments do not guarantee immunity for the weaknesses of the mature actor about to be diminished, any more than they ensure his abstention from efforts to fend off the prospect of accelerated retrogression. But such an actor's aggressive quest for more territory or enhanced role differs now as much from aimless gropings for power voids, typical of initial expansion, as it does from the self-confident expressions of superabundant confidence and energy in the later outreach of a just consolidated actor. Replacing both are compulsively intensified attempts to overcome the temptations of repose and avoid the penalties for voluntary retreat. However, such efforts are henceforth sufficiently out of tune with ebbing vigor to signify nothing more than a prudent refusal to rely on supporting structures of the arena as a whole, one at best accidentally configurated by the drives and energies of other parties in such a way as to provisionally shelter some of the positions and privileges the waning actor acquired forcibly in its prime.

The key trait of this next-to-last, the compulsive foreign policy posture is the refusal to translate the altered relationship of weakening factors into a policy of undisguised weakness. By now, deteriorating economic structures, once again less independent of military supports than they were at their peak, will have failed to perpetuate the fiscal foundation for a sustained but moderate display of force. They will be further undermined by ultimately futile military exertions keyed to only peripheral enterprises or to despairing demonstrations of resolve at the center. As governmental functions continue to grow, their marked surplus over deficiencies in spontaneous initiatives and innovations dispirits to the point of traumatizing a political class unable to live indefinitely off past achievements while fending off multiplying rival claimants to authority who offer greater efficiency or only éclat abroad and seek wider justice or only more perquisites of power at home. Superficially assertive or ostensibly aggressive actions abroad will in consequence be even more markedly preemptive in the compulsive than they were in the conservative phase. Unlike the still earlier predatory bias toward concrete acquisitions, the preclusive urge will react to hypothesized dangers: expansionism will represent not so much a relentless advance toward predetermined targets as a headlong flight forward from often but preconceived threats. What matters now in regard to the arena is less its permissive or constraining structure at the center and the periphery and more the assortment of varied stages in the growth, decline, and actual or threatening dissolution of individual actors: will still more decadent and sharply declining actors offer an opportunity for aggressively acquisitive action? Or else, will more recently ascendant actors, engaged in anterior facets and phases of expansionist policy, embody the agonizing necessity to take aggressively defensive precautions? Least reassuring will be to take refuge amongst or behind the precariously "balancing" (or only vacillating) policies of mature actors of conservative dispositions.

To fully surface the posture's unevenly latent or suppressed features is reserved for more or less complete withdrawal from self-reliance, in favor of dependence on another power or the protective sanctuary contrived by configuration of active powers if not also prevailing norms. A graduated recession into strategic passivity precedes surrender to multiple derangements: in an economy in danger of being uninnovative or becoming uncompetitive; in a military establishment used and usable for mainly internal political or residual status-related prestige purposes, as part of largely token or secondary participation in plural alliances acting as a substitute for more independent action in wider settings; and in the making of public policy, dispersed among either sub- or trans-"national" entities. The benefits of successful war will be typically sought through sagacious investments of wealth in countries or areas that either offer better economic prospects or promise an easy acquisition of politically useful goodwill. And while trade and investments gravitate outward, the functions of governmental institutions are displaced in the opposite direction at an accelerating rate. They veer inward by default, when filling a vacuum of regime legitimacy previously due to triumphs accomplished abroad or tribulations mastered at home; or by design, when functional introversion is tolerated or encouraged so as to extract from a more widely diffused prosperity the kind of internal stability that earlier or more primitive social arrangements sought and often achieved by action outside the collective habitat from a more lopsided as well as narrower basis in prosperity and power.

Thus, the key surplus consists henceforth of a hypertrophy of societal demands over civic-minded willingness to deal with hitherto ignored deficiencies in ways entailing individual or group sacrifice. Just as the earliest foreign-policy modes are likely to denote exit from a proto-systemic setting, so withdrawal will tend to connote the acceptance of only local or more widely extending meta-systemization. Submission to a major-power protector or a multi-power pattern of protection will be the operative facet of subsiding into sublimated-to-simulated forms of competition within imperial- or community-type associations. Either of these will implement the primacy of welfare economics over warfare-related strategics more effectively than any single actor could in isolation, or at least reassuringly postulate such primacy as the gravamen of progress.

Developmentally the obverse of the last-phase withdrawal by an overmature actor is overassertion by a late-entering one, whose developmental cycle either began later or unfolded more slowly than that of the parties who, fully present at the beginning, evolved concurrently and more or less symmetrically with the systemic arena. Even a full congruence between an actor's phased foreign-policy posture and the system's structure and stage of evolution does not rule out retrogressions by system-founding powers, signalling an effort to retrace the evolutionary pathway and revert to behavior characteristic of an earlier and more dynamic phase, most likely under the impetus of internal regime needs or change. However, the ensuing crisis (more serious than any due to the less frequent attempt to overleap a phase and have foreign posture anticipate on domestic potential or propensity) is likely to affect mainly the recidivist actor, its regime or society: brief and partial revivals are no more evidence of recovered vitality than recurrence equals exact repetition. Conversely, it will be the system as a whole that experiences crisis when a major late-entering state behaves in ways out of phase with the system's own developmental stage – or, more precisely, acts at variance with the norms propounded, attitudes preferred, and alignments practiced by earlier evolving and farther developed parties. The late entrant will try to return the arena to a condition of sufficient permissiveness to allow for a new cycle of development. He may break instead at the system's remaining capacity to resist retrogression at the requisite (and substantial) risk, including the system's tendency to self-destruct as the final price of its most representative members' immediate self-preservation. Either of the courses and outcomes are among the most dramatic in the many-sided actor–arena interplays; they will at the very least propel the system from one system or scope to another as the terminal ordeal of actors engaged in being transformed fuses with the growing pains of actors that are still being formed.

Always contingent on a prolonged evolutionary career of an actor relatively autonomous because major, the phased sequence of foreign-policy postures is least manifest in the longest-lived of ancient actors, one which realized to a high degree the obsessive aspiration to afterlife of the individuals composing it. The perennial Egyptian Empire achieved a species of hard-to-articulate immortality for itself, despite its several apparent demises extending from the Pharaonic era through the Saite dynasty to the Ptolemies, punctuated by successive conquests by the Hyksos, the Assyrians, the Persians and the Romans, in antiquity alone. Once the Hyksos experience had removed the presumption of safe insulation from the outside world, repeated spells of imperial expansion, each time less instinctual or exuberant, alternated with periods of consolidation and retrenchment. One conservative or balance-of-power midpoint transpired before the Assyrian conquest in the guise of a condominial arrangement with the Hittites (thirteenth century BC); another following the Assyrian collapse in the period of indigenous restoration under the Saite dynasty (seventh century BC). The several periods of decline and near-dissolution were either caused by internal religio-political upheavals or only coincided with them promoting actual or attempted conquests or partitions, including an attempt at conquest by Athens in the period between the Persian and the Peloponnesian Wars.

The life-path of the premier Greek city had begun with an expansive response to the pressures from overpopulation. When the previously inviting empty spaces had been filled, overseas colonization gave way to a policy of consolidation in Attica until the energies released by the successful resistance to Persia and the conversion of the Delian League into an Athenian Empire impelled attempts to expand over both land (into central Greece) and sea (into the Black Sea area and Egypt). The strains attendant on the ensuing setbacks compounded those due to events that aborted the brief spell of conservative foreign policy (associated with the leadership of Cimon and aiming at an all-Greek equilibrium through Atheno–Spartan co-hegemony), which in turn set off the Periclean strategy for forestalling decline by bidding for sole hegemony (the Peloponnesian War). When prolonged stand-off in the war deepened the prospect of internal decay and relative decline externally, the effort to break the strategic stalemate through the Syracusan expedition marked a self-destructive climax in the psychopolitically plausible phenomenon of compulsive late-phase expansionism. All this time, the environing arena was changing from an initially permissive one – underpopulation and primitive economic development in both East (Ionia) and west (Sicily and southern Italy, or Magna Graecia) – into one ever more constraining throughout the Mediterranean-centered arena. An initially orderly diffusion of internal authority and influence on policy in response to the expanding demands on personnel implicit in the changing military technologies and strategies shifting from land and sea, concurrently with productive assets and activities, degenerated into a radical displacement of both authority and influence: beginning with the fall of the conservative aristocrat Cimon and continuing through the ascendancy of Periclean aristo-demagogy the process debouched at the war's peak into blatantly demagogic excesses of a Cleon and Alcibiades, only to finally give way to reactionary-tyrannical usurpations after the defeat.

When a failed attempt to reverse the evolutionary dynamic and recover empire after a Sparta-dominated interlude set the stage for withdrawal from politico-military activism, an accelerating diversion of Athenian resources from the requirements of warfare to those of welfare signalled the abandonment of military preparedness for cultural-intellectual prominence and economic prosperity. It prepared the ground for submission to Macedon. The efficacy of the late-entering intruder from the margins combined with ineffectual Greek resistance to foreshorten the terminal crisis of the Hellenic system, if only in favor of the protracted agony of phased absorption into an empire risen out of the Roman city-state in a comparable sequence of early expansiveness, brief consolidation, and resumed expansion. It had meanwhile been part of the crisis-attenuating background that, contrary to progressivist and reformist exhortations (by men like Isocrates), the receding Hellenic actors were neither willing nor able to generate norms of politico-military self-restraint substantially different from the early formative and mid-term conduct of the Greek city-states themselves. Such norms alone would have set the ways and means of transferring primacy to the Macedonian marginal and on to the Roman outsider disturbingly apart from the natural order of things viewed by the Greeks in terms of the cyclical rise and decline of states as they inverted formative virtues into fatal vices.

In consequence, the long evolutionary progression toward a revolutionary perception of the actor–arena interplay – one viewing the exercise of raw power as incompatible with humane progress – was deferred to an era that began with the end of the long-lived empire that had replaced the brief Athenian one. In the aftermath of the failed Carolingian effort to take over the heritage of Rome, the henceforth standards-setting French realm proceeded, according to the pattern, from a diffusely expansive phase (in the thirteenth century's politico-cultural "hegemony" associated with the crusades) to the foreign policy of consolidation attendant on the successful conclusion of the Hundred Years War (and reaching its acme in the reign of Louis XI). Thereupon, the Italian wars represented the post-consolidation release of enhanced public and internally contained private energies into an exuberance that continued through the vagaries of alternate fragmentation and reconsolidation of central authority – until the restoration following late Valois confessional–conspirational disorders under the Bourbon dynasty set the course toward an essentially conservative foreign policy posture. This mid-point phase unfolded consistently with the both timeless and peculiarly continental European interlock of drives for preeminence and for (self-) preservation in a balance-of-power policy. It did so as the more assertive initial stance (from Henry IV to Louis XIV) evolved into the more defensive or preclusive later policies (Louis XV and XVI). The English wars of the mid- and late eighteenth century bore increasingly the stigmata of a compulsive effort to stem and reverse decline relative to the new kind of power in the maritime west and the old kind (Austria, Prussia, Russia) in the continental east, an effort that was to peak in the revolutionary climax and produce the Napoleonic cataclysm.

Napoleon's final defeat ought to have introduced – and in the initial concept of the second restoration (now *of* the Bourbons as well as *under* them) did intimate – a foreign policy of retrenchment and relative self-effacement, short of total withdrawal into last-stage Portugal-like inertia and obscurity. Instead, beginning with the final days of the Restoration, it was the instability of the successive regimes more than either Gallic vanity in diplomacy or French furor for war-making that accounted for over-ambitious efforts to recover past power and prestige by way of regressive relapses into foreign policies typical of earlier phases. The series of failures climaxed in the traumatic defeat of Napoleon III in the European theater by Prussia–Germany in the wake of Crimean, Italian, and Mexican adventures (a replay of those of Louis-Philippe in the Near East), before resuming under republican auspices in the colonial peripheries (defying Britain in Egypt and Fashoda) and gravitating back to Europe (to encompass the last French attempt at "hegemonism" in the Ruhr and through east-central European alliances). Throughout the late period, an intermittently manifest impulse to withdraw spelled submission to the English ally, just as resistance to final resignation was part of the refusal to settle for Anglo–Saxon protection in the period between the two world wars and after the second.

Alongside internal transformations in both countries, the Anglo–French clashes in the colonial peripheries corresponded to the terminal state of the Eurocentric arena. Following the rollback of ninth-century barbarian inroads, the arena had evolved in rough correspondence with major-actor policies. When the eastern periphery, which the weakening of Islam and Byzantium had made briefly accessible, congealed into a power potential made manifest in the Islamic counter-crusades and culminating in Ottoman expansion, the contraction of the theater spelled intensified conflicts. Consolidating the core-area actors, the conflicts first confined arena crystallization to its systemic center including when not focusing on Italy. Thereafter, new navigable oceans reopened the outer world to a more lasting and thoroughgoing movement, now west- as well as eastward, powered by the urge to trade and conquer and sustained by an equally strong recoil from constraints on large-scale (or, under the practice of bartering oceanic against continental conquests, significant net) gains to be won on the continent outside eastern Europe.

Toward the close of Europe's expansionist cycle, Britain's late nineteenth-century imperialism was an instance of policy compulsively fighting off decline relative to the rising power of America, Japan, and Germany. It was such even more than the rival overseas expansionism of France, compensating psychologically for the loss of Alsace–Lorraine. The weakening, concealed behind diplomatic ascendancy in the period between the two twentieth-century German wars, was followed more readily than in the French case by abdication. Withdrawal from empire into the fiction of a commonwealth, and retreat from the mature policy of equilibrium into the fantasy of an enduring tutorial guidance of immature American power, was then the terminus of "normal" evolution.

At its outset, following upon the expansive feudal-dynastic forays into France in the fourteenth to fifteenth centuries, the foreign-policy posture keyed to consolidation marked a predictable reaction to premature overextension and its internal causes and consequences. Re-ordering priorities favored integrating Wales and Scotland with the English core, next to safeguarding on the north-western fringes of the continent a few crucial outposts for a habitat the internal consolidation had rendered also diplomatico-strategically insular. Under late Tudor Elizabethan and early Stuart auspices, an effective containment of threats to the revamped politico-religious establishment set off a period of exuberance in the form of overseas enterprise and expansion, sustained by both witting and unwitting cooperation of crown, colonists, and trading companies. Subversion of the would-be monopoly of Spain overseas combined then with opposing France's succession to Spain to generate first the resource and then the rationale for substituting effective policy for a fanciful claim (by Henry VIII to arbitrate the European balance of power): a policy of conservative support for equilibrium. Initially either imported by, or prosecuted in the interests of, transplanted continental dynasts (from William III to the Hanoverian Georges), the conservative posture adjusted the classic continental mix of concern for self-preservation and tendency to preeminence to the peculiar facility of an insular state anxious to have continental deadlock underwrite overseas dominion.

The policy's viability well into the nineteenth century had first been assisted by the migration of power eastward on the continent to the disadvantage of the French adversary, and subsequently shielded by the only initially emerging configuration of new powers at the global periphery. Accelerating British decline in due course was the convergence of America's post-Civil War exuberance – expressed in the war with Spain and overseas Pacific and Caribbean imperialism – and the "world policy" of the Second German Empire manifesting *its* exuberance in the aftermath of (and in reaction to) Bismarckian policy of consolidation. Successorial ambitions of the friend- and the foe-to-be alike interfered with the stately unfolding of the older Anglo–Russian conflict, reflecting Britain's essentially conservative predispositions world-wide and the ambiguously nationalist-cum-imperialist Russian urge to consolidate a continental habitat regionally.

In the case of Germany, the first (and "holy") German Empire had never evolved from early expansiveness (toward Italy and eastern Europe) into a consolidation (last attempted by Charles V) sustained by a successful foreign policy. It could not experience the normally succeeding foreign-policy phases as a result. A relapse into the first expansively formative phase by the liberal-nationalist parliamentary forces at Frankfurt was, by 1848, inherently obsolete in its retrospective *grossdeutsch*-imperialist goals and motivations. It was also ineffectual as to means when projected against the greater-German realizations of the 1930s and 1940s. The compulsive features marking that foreign policy phase reflected growing fears of decline relative to eastern continental (Russian) and both western and eastern maritime powers (US and Japan). It was these same powers that had been responsible for the failure of the Wilhelmine regime to evolve past initial exuberance to a mature conservative policy of equilibrium from manifest strength (a failure that burdened the luckless Weimar successor with the task of achieving this from but latent strength). It was the fatal consequence of the artificially compressed development of modern Germany that, in the wake of prior developmental arrest and following Bismarckian consolidation and early Wilhelmine exuberance, she did not experience a lengthy – sustained because properly sequential – conservative balance-of-power phase, despite the over-elaborate (because premature) post–1870 efforts by Bismarck in that direction. By the time the Bonn-based second Republic displayed pro-equilibrium western orthodoxy in an attempt to recapture the missed phase, the effort seemed to be more promising than had been Weimar's, although it followed rather than preceded the climactic-compulsive expansionism of the Third Reich. The needs and conditions of both internal and systemic stability could now conspire to gradually introduce elements of balancing between the western and eastern superpower into an initially too radical policy of withdrawal into conformist Atlanticism.

If modern Germany displayed traits of compression and acceleration as well as distortion relative to the developmental norm, Russia's characteristic has been retardation as well as, following radical regime change, repetition. In both instances, abnormality was due to the absence of fit in the developments of actor and arena, peculiar to either only operationally or also positionally marginal if not peripheral late-entering powers. For the same reasons, symptoms of later-phase foreign-policy postures have tended in Russia's case to be deceptive when projected against the basic fact of a developmental arrest, or slow-down, in a relatively early phase: not now, as in the case of traditional Germany prior to, but at the point of, territorial and political consolidation in a securely viable scope. Still in both instances, but even more markedly in Russia's case, the difficulty surrounding "consolidation" – achieving it or unambiguously moving beyond it – has resided fundamentally in the impossibility to distinguish clearly between "nation" or state" and "empire" in the case of a multi-ethnic or -regional political entity of geographically contiguous parts.

Efforts to consolidate a viable Russian state began in earnest under Ivans III and IV and Peter the Great, building on the largely spontaneous prior expansionism from Muscovy outward, including into Siberia. A foreign policy (and, relatedly, war policy) directed henceforth mainly toward the Baltic, and either secondarily or later toward the Black Sea, created from the mid-

eighteenth century on the narrowest requisite basis for a farther-flung and
more self-confident diplomacy in Europe and expansionism also outside her
(Tsaritsas Elisabeth and Catherine; Alexander I). Just as the attendant internal
turmoils would in mid-nineteenth century prompt a pseudo-conservative
response to revolutionary upheavals in central Europe (Nicholas I), so
subsequently an economic backwardness most irksome relative to England and
(eventually) Japan in the Far East provoked (from Alexander II to Nicholas II)
reactions which, although as superficially compulsive as the responses to initial
territorial consolidation had been exuberant, in turn set off developments
leading in two revolutionary installments to the terminal crisis of the regime.

The ideologically formulated and conspirationally pursued diffuse
expansiveness by the Soviet successor yielded soon to the foreign policy of
consolidation under Stalin, of ostensible exuberance under Khrushchev, and of
territorial if no other conservatism in Europe but not outside her under
Brezhnev, in the interest of regime stability as much as of national security.
However, just as the anticipatory tsarist evolution so the accelerated Soviet
replay were epiphenomenal relative to the persisting concern with and
commitment to consolidation. The apparent evolutionary momentum was in
both instances incongruent with both domestic and systemic structures: in
regard to the domestic order, no sufficiently developing domestic pluralism was
there to fuel a genuinely exuberant and sustain a full-fledged balance-of-power
policy; in regard to the international system, the peripheral position of late-
entering tsarist Russia had been as inhibiting as the primitive condition of the
global system co-founded by Soviet Russia in contention with a United States
that was farther advanced in its foreign-policy orientation as well as domestic
structures was to prove complicating. Measured against the prototypical
European actor, France, the United States could be said to have emulated the
latter in some of the key conditions of a favorable early development, but was
not immune to later deformations connected with the difficulty to negotiate
transition to the conservative pro-equilibrium posture. As for Soviet Russia, she
could hope to avoid the post-revolutionary maladjustments of a (by then)
farther-evolved France without being certain of eschewing premature decline.

Late-phase attempts of declining actors to revert to post-consolidation
exuberance or resist last-stage withdrawal in favor of an overly active role in
maintaining the balance of power will engender crises whose severity may
exceed that provoked by compulsively expansionist resistance to the first signs
of decline. A recidivist policy will complicate the otherwise routinely conflictual
mechanism of role-and-status transfer most when a so far preeminent power
resists being relegated to the sidelines. Thus post-Bourbon (i.e., Bonapartist to
republican) France refused to emulate post-Habsburg (i.e., Bourbon) Spain in
reducing efforts to resist organic decline to a level of ambition and enterprise
that caused only local or regional – and in either case containable – disturbance
in the system (e.g. dynastic intrigues of early eighteenth-century Bourbon Spain
in Italy). The larger-scale tremors in the system caused by France's strategic
relapses posing as substantive resurgence originated in large part in the flawed
legitimacy of the post-revolutionary French regimes before aggravating its
consequences. The resulting ferment linked up eventually with the other

causative factor in the larger crisis of the arena when the agonizingly prolonged French ordeal merged explosively with the time-compressed ascent of the renewed German Empire, no less abnormally retarded than the French decline was artificially prolonged. In the end, German attempts to overleap inhibitions to the formal recognition of upgraded status and tangible representation of enhanced role (with a view to consolidating a differently precarious regime) differed more in style than in substantive consequence from France's efforts to raise ever new barriers to her diminished power and receding status becoming manifest.

The inversely developing continental opponents being thus entangled was not made insignificant by the fact that this operational reason for the system's malaise depended for full effect on a structural determinant illustrated by the Anglo–German relationship. Whereas the Franco–German rivalry was reminiscent of past inter-tribal passions going back (in that particular case) to the Middle Ages, the Anglo–German contest betokened an updated version of a polarity between maritime and continental polities traceable back to the remotest antiquity. When she claimed a place in the sun from an empire constantly enveloped in its rays, unified Germany typified both of the key (structural as well as evolutionary) aspects of an arena crisis. She did so as an actor too big for an only routinely contentious integration into the extant arena – an arena too small both as delimited by the denial of access and role to the claimant on the part of the dominant (British) incumbent and as defined by the still mobilizable power potentials of the system's original constituent members. In this respect the situation was the obverse of that obtaining when the likewise essentially continental-military late Bourbon France had proven too small in requisite resources relative to the opportunities and demands of a radically expanded global arena open to the superior capacity of maritime-mercantile England to mobilize and exploit new-type assets.

The translation of divergent trajectories of unevenly developing actors into a central-systemic trauma occurred even as the shrinking center to the European system was on its way to being dwarfed from the periphery – reduced from a macro- to a micro-systemic status. That crisis-intensifying feature was compounded by the fact that the self-assertion of a slower-developing late-entrant marked a transition between distinct generations of actors – and actor-types. As a result, a routine collision of conflicting interests and converging security strategies was infused with clashing sociopolitical ideologies, stimulated by efforts to resist (inevitable) decline or compensate for (artificial) delays along the normal evolutionary pathway. While the distinction between originally constituent and late-entering members of a system only points to the existence of distinct generations of actors and dominant or representative actor-types, the generational issue is an integral part of the sequence of cleavages or schisms that differentiate actors and tend to polarize arenas. These differences and divisions are no less significant for being less conspicuous than those between micro- and macro-systems and their proto- and meta-systemic boundary states or those between center and periphery within an arena or system and between actor and arena. All are linked by a combination of interaction and reciprocal immanence over unequal time spans. Just as the total process of relations among armed sociopolitical organisms displays a wider range of surface traits than of the more basic givens, so reducing its operations to few and simple rules and precepts offers but a foreshortened view of the collective drama enacting individual destinies.

5
Motor and Mechanism of Evolution

Surfacing in wars or revolutions, more or less violent crises attend the system's turbulent re-equilibration (and thus maintenance) over the short runs. The same crises perform an even more creative function in the long term when they propel an inter-actor system into evolutionary progression. Basic to the evolution are the motor that energizes change and the mechanism through which infusions of energy are transmuted into outcomes. Both contribute to shaping the matrix within which the in-part cyclical process of adaptation and alteration takes place, and are co-responsible for the manifestations of real, as distinct from superficial, change. The individually complex facets are not reducible to a single factor as to causal determination any more than the overlaps among and circular relationships between them are to a simply conceptualized descriptive formula. Through its effect on the practice of statecraft, this fact helps bring about the crises responsible for changes in the makeup of the complexities, inasmuch as evolutionary transformations are part of the structural environment which the several strategic options fit unevenly and mostly inadequately at any time and over time. Thus, although the mechanical checking and balancing among parties to the interplay of strategies, and the same operational dynamic's relationship to the organic rise and decline of individual actors, are salient as both propellants and products of the evolutionary process, they do not for all that fully account for the process's protean character and problematic implications.

STRUCTURAL ROOTS OF CRISES IN ACTOR–ARENA SETTING

For a system to escape the tendency for energy to disperse or dissipate unproductively in developmentally inconclusive low-level disorders spelling evolutionary stagnation and structureless drift, it must periodically receive infusions of extraneous energy generated by major crises typically but not solely related to one or another schism. Inasmuch as the crises generating the infusion cause disruptions, they compel more or less revolutionary and innovative adaptations giving rise to new levels and standards of fitness, of strategies relative to structure and of states for survival, as a matter of the natural selection of viable actors and agendas.

A major source of energy released by crises and fueling the motor of evolution are individual power drives or urges, harnessed to the basic value of a political collective, its autonomy. Psychopolitical self-assertion, whether implemented expansively or defensively, will be tied to both material and immaterial factors. Among the material factors, existing surpluses and deficiencies are related to the survival minimum (i.e., supply of vital food and fuel) in the last resort. Whereas surplus permits initial, scarcity compels continuing, development of diversified functions within a collective. Among the immaterial factors, communal authority must justify itself by acceptable performance in matters of the collective's physical security, material subsistence, and social stability, and either status- or role-based self-confidence or -respect, if it is to enjoy the degree of legitimacy necessary to avoid enforcing obedience most of the time. When focusing the basic drives and urges on the elementary needs and functions becomes operationally manifest in crises, the incidence of such crises will augment the amount and realign the impact of energy available in the system as a remedy to its antecedent depletion and an alternative to deterioration in actors, system, or both. Once disruption of the pre-existing equilibrium has occasioned the release of previously dormant energy, a thus triggered movement toward restoring equilibrium will revitalize the system on its existing or push it toward the next-higher level of evolution, unless the lack of fit between actor capabilities and roles or between system structure and strategies is such as to exceed the system's re-equilibration potential and triggers evolutionary regression (toward a meta- or next-in-line proto-systemic phase).

A condition for infusing motor energy into system evolution which, being fundamental, is only elusively operative, pertains to the structure of the inter-unit system in regard to both individual actors and the arena. Whenever the impetus comes from disproportions between actors and arena, states and system, flows of energy will be released by either individual adaptations to the disparities or by the re-equilibration consequent on disruptions resulting from the asymmetries. A most fundamental disparity over the longest time-span bears on the differential rates and ranges of development of state-like actors on the one hand and of the systemic arena on the other hand. Since the development of state-like actors in terms of organized resources and of the systemic arena in terms of operative stimuli condition one another over the long pull, no point in time can be fixed when the development of the "powers" ends and the articulation of the "balance of power" begins. All that does change are net margins of shaping impact by the arena on the actors and by (major) actors on the arena, as a proto-system evolves into and past a fully crystallized system norm. The reason is that the minimum of essential supports for patterned interactions over shared (and, therefore, divisive) stakes materializes faster than do the attributes of fully consolidated actors, but do so within a narrower range of possible development: if the actual rate of development favors initially the system, its potential range favors the states.

Even but haphazard interactions will help the arena engender constituent resources (e.g. inherited or conquered assets), constraints (e.g. reflexive countervailing reactions), and compellents (pressures and threats) among primitive actors. But whereas the adaptations required for actor survival will gradually foster the functional (military-economic-administrative) coherence and the societal cohesion of the surviving polities, augmenting their capacity to project power externally, the ongoing development of the principal actors will progressively impinge ever more significantly upon the modes, techniques, or formal norms, of the interplays constituting the system. The structure of the system will always determine the operational setting of major policies. But the internal development of some actors will have progressed at some point so far as to be at variance with the relatively less malleable basic norms and rules of the system. This will give rise to some kind of crises, although the internally generated actor biases will predominate over the external constraints implicit in routinized balancing only when the internal changes have become sufficiently widespread to transpose the system (or system segment) itself into a post-mature meta-stage. However much the internal needs and limitations of the overmature members may then influence their relations, these will always be highly circumscribed from the outside: when the late meta-systemic phase assumes the form of empire-type unification, the decisive impact will come from the imperial center; when it expresses itself through the sublimation or mere simulation of traditional actor drives and goals within community-type integration, the dynamics of the superseding larger arena will be controlling also for the demoted sector in the last resort.

Within the European state system, the evolution-propelling salience of the arena over the actors in the early medieval period was gradually reversed, via actor–arena equality and congruence at (say) the eighteenth-century climax and divide, into the multiplying incidence of impact from major actors whose internal evolution made them unfit or unwilling to abide by the strict norms of the system and satisfy the requirements of efficacy in the system. When this happened, just as the initial bias of primitive power aggregations to dissolve intermittently from within had become insufficient earlier to maintain and regulate the system in the face of system-induced increases in the capacity of actors to stabilize gains, so now the consequently perfected balance-of-power or countervailing mechanism could do no better. It proved unable to maintain and regulate the system within its original boundaries in the face of the uneven development of the founding and the late-entering, the declining (over-) matured and the rising and only maturing, actors. Meanwhile, alternating expansion and contraction of the arena will have complemented the evolution-inducing stresses and strains due to the changing balance of actor and arena salience and impact.

If what is crucial for the long-term interplay between actors and arena is their differential rates and ranges of development, that which matters over a comparatively shorter time span is the relationship between the changing scope of the system and the scale of actor resources, testing individual aptitudes to readapt actor energy to arena space. When the systemic arena contracts as a result of some kind of widespread deficiency – e.g. contraction due to the decay of the Roman, rather than the dynamism of the Islamic, Empires in Europe – the initial depressant effect upon all sectors will be more uniform than the eventual corrective responses; especially when arena shrinkage occurs at an early developmental stage, the dissolution-prone actors (e.g. the early ninth-century Carolingian realm, lacking a solid fiscal-economic base) will lose out to better-integrated smaller actors capable of projecting a complex of mutually supportive material, military, and managerial resources abroad (e.g. the French realm after the ninth and, for different reasons, the fourteenth century). By contrast, a system that expands in accessible physical space or in usable assets and instruments will generate new surplus or surplus potential; especially when expansion occurs at a later stage, the tendency for the surplus to be allocated unevenly will not so much threaten the existence of some actors at the center of the system as re-rank all according to their ability to exploit the new opportunities. Moreover, when expansion has been into virtually empty spaces thus out of seventh-century BC Greece, the critical transition to functional differentiation (e.g. of agriculture and trade-related activities and actors) will only follow upon arena expansion rather than precede and propel it, witness sixteenth-century Europe until exhausting the finite new latitudes will have reactivated the sense of compression (e.g. in response to a worsening land-population or production-consumption ratio). Intensifying thus inter- and intra-actor conflict will then have helped reconcentrate power internally and redistribute it externally.

Whether alternation between system scopes has compelled the generation of energies instrumental in identifying viable actors (in the case of shrinkage) or induced energy increases by segregating differently specialized or enterprising actors (in the case of expansion), either reaction will advance the system's articulation and diversification. When system contraction is due to elemental factors such as demographic decline and either antecedent or consequent economic depletion, this may in turn be due to either "natural" causes (e.g. plagues in eighth- and fourteenth-century Europe) or man-made causes (e.g. the seventeenth-century Thirty Years War). Demographic regression and economic depressions will in either case augment the need for remedial improvements in the mobilization, utilization, and management of shrunken resources, likely to intensify intra-actor tensions and inter-actor conflict. Meeting the resulting demands will eventuate, thus in post-fourteenth-century Europe, in the creation of an efficient bureaucratic state and correspondingly rationalized inter-actor relations. Alternately, the arena may be constricted by the preemption of space or the curtailment of strategic options by outside (peripheral or barbarian) forces or actors, as it was in the early and again the later Islamic centuries. Reducing thus the sociopolitical units of organization to the most resistance-capable scale is likely to be most invigorating in the early stage of the system's evolution by marking the end of a period of false developmental starts by too-large power aggregations. Conversely, any positive effect will be gradually exceeded by a degenerative one in a maturing system increasingly responsive to cyclically alternating economic expansion and contraction and subject to growing differentiation between declining and ascending members of successive generations of actors. Either liability will first expose the system to and eventually invite impingements by extra-systemic parties – by Rome in second-century BC Greece as well as France and Aragon–Spain in late fifteenth-century Italy and, following on Russia, by the United States and Japan in early twentieth-century Europe. This is especially the case when the system has also become too "small" in terms of the energy available for either containing or assimilating outsized actors, from Macedon in Greece through Venice in Italy to Germany in Europe, within arena boundaries. Evolution will then be advanced only within an enlarged arena in favor of previously peripheral actors disposing of a commensurate scale of resources.

When, instead, the core-system remains at the center of an expanding area, the bracing effect will be confined to actors ready to move out into new areas or arenas of opportunity. Such were the only just consolidated northern monarchies beginning with the 1490s and, on a wider basis, the Protestant maritime powers a century or two later. By the same token, arena expansion will produce a stressful actor–arena disproportion for unready parties, and will tend to demote, if not decompose, them. Following upon the eighth-century Carolingian Empire in north-western Europe, the adverse consequence befell the Holy Roman Empire or Emperors in the Italo–Germanic complex in the twelfth, the crusading "Franks" in the Near East in the thirteenth, and on balance ancien-regime France globally in the eighteenth century. In addition to only suspending or also distorting the evolution of the overstrained actor, the attendant stresses may help revolutionize the system itself. Nor will energies be channeled into a smooth and even evolution if the critical disproportion is between the shrinking margin of newly allocable space in a still expanding system and the increased number of unevenly satiated expansion-ready and -able actors, anxious to preempt a fair share – a situation peculiar to the late nineteenth-century late imperialist era. Finally, a special kind of major crisis will arise when one kind of expansion (e.g. spatial) coincides or closely overlaps with another kind of contraction (e.g. economic). Such was the case in late seventeenth-century Europe and, to some extent, in the period between the two twentieth-century world wars. Cross-cutting tensions will then release both positively expansive and remedially reactive energies as part of testing the continued viability and proficiency of actors amidst contracting resources and the efficacy of inducements or pressures to exploit enlarged outlets. By reinforcing or contradicting one another, the results of such testing will determine the course of the international system in a prolonged ensuing phase.

When the disproportion between a major actor or the scale of a typical actor and the arena is extensive and more than transient, it will engender a crisis of adaptation keyed to re-establishing proportionality. When the arena has expanded suddenly as well as substantially, adjustments in the dominant actor norm (favoring the fifteenth-century "new monarchies" and the seventeenth- to eighteenth-century oligarchical proto-capitalist polities) or in the standards of performance of only the lagging major actor (producing the French Revolution) will be all the more radical. Alternately, it is the arena that will have to be enlarged in proportion to the increased strength of efficient and expansive actors (e.g. late sixteenth-century overseas expansion of Europe, compensating for Ottoman pressures against her south-to-north Italo–German dorsal spine). In either case, general crises *of* the international system originating in deranged actor–arena ratios and centering on proportionality are different from the more frequent particular crises *in* the international system originating in inter-actor conflicts and centering on parity or primacy. The latter produce at the most crises of structure, inasmuch as the distribution of the intangible role-status assets is part of a system's structural makeup. However, consequent adjustments or adaptations may well be part and parcel of yet another – third and final – kind of structurally conditioned crisis of the system. It compounds crises due to disparities in (developmental rates-related) salience and (expansion- or contraction-related) sizes of actors and arena and attends shifts in the number of major poles of power whenever the system's re-equilibration entails its repolarization.

Transmission of energy as well as transfers of role and status are involved as cause or effect in a system being transformed along a range from uni- through bi- or tri- to multi-polarity, each pattern exhibiting its particular mix of stability and instability. Whereas especially the bipolar structure will promptly promote the rise of additional poles, and notably the multipolar pattern will exhibit a protracted tendency to erode existing centers of power, all structural patterns generate, while persisting or changing from one into another, strains and stresses sufficient to energize the system. They do so because each kind of polarity will engender – within the framework of either an ideal and corruptible norm (empire-type unity under one pole of power) or a largely pragmatic self-generating and -perpetuating norm (bi- to multi-polar equilibrium) – different and hard to conciliate basic attitudes or expectations and more specific behavior patterns on the part of the major and of the lesser, superior and subordinate, actors. Thus crises-related and -generating structural transformations punctuated the evolution of the European system, out of a Roman Empire that had completed the erosion of an anterior multipolar one, via ever less neatly bipolar Papal–Imperial, Habsburg–Ottoman, and Franco–Habsburg, contests. Each projected other major actors into significant roles in a multipolar structure strained by the pursuit of unattainable unity and modified by actually operative tripartite strategic calculations until, multipolarity having attained its most finished state in the eighteenth century, it began to erode in the nineteenth to twentieth centuries in favor of an eventually restored bipolarity.

EVOLUTION-PROPELLING INNOVATIONS AND STABILITY-RESTORING DIFFUSION

The crises induced structurally will coincide with – be mediated and made operative by – more narrowly delimited sources and channeled flows of energy. These are inherent in instrumental devices, constitute major innovations, and implement functional revolutions. And they transmute strains and stresses occasioned structurally into institutionalized outcomes, by means and in settings that will often partake of a values-related sociopolitical revolution.

The extra energy latent in any major functional innovation is injected into the system by way of the initial disruption an innovation brings about, and it permeates the system en route to updated stability as actors adapt to the innovation and assimilate it within an adjusted posture or policy. A primary, including technological, innovation will typically originate independently of the functioning and outside the analytic boundary of the system, being thus an emergent as well as extraneous factor. But the process of adaptation itself is intrinsic to the operation of the system and so are the secondary innovations spawned by the adaptation. By the same token, an innovation can markedly increase the supply of raw energy – thus when the horse-drawn plow or war chariot adds animal to human muscular energy and wind-, steam-, or nuclear-propelled vessel adds inanimate to animate energy source. But the instrumental multipliers of energy will merely initiate the critical effect which the psycho-political energy generated by the attendant disruption and adaptation will have on evolution. The same is true for innovations that may actually save "physical" energy, such as efficiency-augmenting rationalization of administrative routines.

The most potent impulse will come from a cluster of interlocking innovations. By both stimulating the onset and constraining the effects of one another, these constitute jointly a functional revolution subject to the usual rhythm of status-quo disruption, initial radicalization and ensuing confusion, and eventual absorption apt to scale down sustainable change to a condition somewhere between its climactic peak and the anterior state of things. Typically inter-connected military-technological, material-economic, and administrative-managerial innovations bear, respectively, on the means of destruction, production, and coordination or control. They impinge on actor interplays with decreasingly direct (or directly traceable) effect as they relate in one way or another to existing surpluses to be increased or allocated and to scarcities to be compensated for or neutralized. It will matter less or least which of the categories of innovations is primary in that it generates the other or others as part of the readjustment process or influences the related operations most directly or potently. The impact on evolution will be greatest and easiest to trace when the linked innovations cluster over a not too long time span.

Since the number of individual innovations over time is near-infinite, the range of the functional clusters susceptible to innovation is correspondingly great. Among the salient ones have been those centered on war: cavalry-centered and infantry-focused types of land warfare, and naval warfare. All three have been recurrent and alternately dominant, each being subject to satisfying in one way or another, if mostly unevenly, the basic requisites of (offensively impacting) thrust and (defensively protective) parry, with emphasis on either mass or mobility in efforts to nullify (neutralize) actual impact or magnify (actualize) contingent immunity.

In a European state system that drew and improved upon Near Eastern innovations, the prototypical calvary-focused cluster consisted of a military-technological device (the stirrup, both permitting and compelling the use of heavy armor as protection against intensified thrust) and an agro-economic device (the moldboard plow, producing fodder for the heavy horse carrying the armored knight). Each innovation generated in its fashion the material surplus – the extra bounty – that in turn generated the public revenues necessary to sustain the transition from man- and land-centered feudal to money-based proto-capitalist political economy and, increasingly, warfare characteristic of the early modern administrative state. The latter reached its apogee when a later cluster combined armored tank, as a substitute for the mail-coated horseman, with motorized infantry, both drawing for efficiency on technologically innovative industrial productivity and managerially specialized technocratic trends in administration. The still vital role of infantry in tank warfare highlighted meanwhile the centrality of innovations focusing on the foot soldier, extending backward and forward from the Greek hoplites. Their helmet, spear, and shield were individually financed from the new surplus released by the transition from grain- to wine- and olive-growing agriculture within the political-administrative framework of "democratic" or oligarchical" poleis – a political order dependent on seasonal rhythms of key economic activity for citizen participation in peace as in war, wherein the phalanx added the necessary minimum of mobility and maximum of mass to the spear's thrust and the shield's parrying potential.

A different combination of military column, primarily agricultural economic base, and authoritative-to-authoritarian management, had evolved first in the despotic empires of the ancient Near East. It was to reappear in east-central and eastern Europe as a basis for the infantry-based proficiency of the modern land powers. The resulting eastward shift of critical power potential on the continent was supported by improved agricultural and locally also early industrial productivity, capable of sustaining a specially trained professional bureaucracy. The two together generated the capital – and fostered the confidence of foreign capital – required for financing networks of strategic roads and, eventually, railways capable of converting internal aggregation of resources into enhanced capacity to project militarily relevant capabilities, defensively or offensively, along interior lines. As the rail began to readjust the previously lopsided balance of military-economic-administrative potential of (western European) sea power and (eastern European) land power, it did for system evolution that which technologically revolutionized construction of wind-propelled ocean-going and gun-carrying sailing ships had done earlier by replacing the manually propelled vessels of the Mediterranean era.

The nautical were then more than accidentally combined with the first stirrings of the mechanical innovations that undergirded the later Industrial Revolution, itself building upon the commercial revolution (unfolding from the thirteenth century on) and stimulated by the preceding (seventeenth-century) inflationary price revolution. The naval–commercial–industrial aggregate was the substantive content poured into a coactive institutional framework made up of the oligarchical-capitalistic state and its administration, typical of the polities dominating the Atlantic age when mining of silver (Spain) yielded to spinning of cotton (England) as the fiscal or economic fundament soon after replacing the galley with the bigger galleon had propelled the north-westward migration of power centers, initiated by the larger horse and heavier plow, beyond the land arena to the seas. It was then left to the progression from galleons to bigger sailing ships and from cruisers to dreadnoughts and on to aircraft carriers to re-enact the degenerative effect of gigantism previously manifest in the expansion of Hellenic three-deckers (the triremes) into Hellenistic four- to five-deckers. It increased decisively the bigger and slower ships' vulnerability to faster-moving mobile attack vessels and air-borne projectiles, even as a growing bureaucracy became harder to sustain by slower-expanding economies. However, prior to its erosion, the cluster supporting the superiority of naval powers fostered evolutionary change in that it stimulated the unevenly industrial and amphibious land powers' ambition to restore role-status parity.

Intervening fluctuations in the technologically effected comparative advantage of land and sea powers and, in land warfare alone, of horse-drawn chariot or mounted cavalry and foot infantry, influenced systemic interactions and evolution more fundamentally than parallel variations in military strategies. This does not mean that, conjointly with corrective instrumental counter-innovations, the strategies were not an integral part of functional revolutions as a key element in the process of adaptation to and absorption of the more original innovations. However, being both adaptative and experimental, the strategies underwent a sudden major change only rarely. On the seas, this happened when maritime warfare ceased being assimilated to fighting on land by means of grappling for the sake of killing men in hand-to-hand combat and shifted to mobility and maneuver for the sake of sinking ships with the aid of long-distance gunshot or missile; on land, when, supplanting the mêlée, close formations for stylized maneuver and massed fire power (reflective of enlightened despotism) gave way to dispersal for mobility and individual initiative (reflective of passional patriotism) or when tank-supported infantry warfare across plains and deserts became seemingly assimilable to naval strategies on the oceans and to cavalry-type tactics originated on the Iranian plateau and the central Asian steppe.

Military strategies amplify changes in the comparative advantages and liabilities attaching to different technologies and techniques by externalizing them in actual operations. Military-technological innovations themselves are constrained by their cost relative to the available material surplus permitting their development, even as they respond to an external strategic threat or opportunity. Who funds the military equipment, from what kind and scale of surplus resources, and in strategic response to what kind of threat or opportunity, are elements that will interlock in the total political, or politico-military, economy of an actor. And if the triad of cost, surplus-based funding, and strategic employment influences the location of central authority within actors directly as part of differentiating social groups functionally, it will also have some effect on the geographic scope of the critical arena and the position of competing parties within it.

So long as costs are borne primarily by individual fighting men – thus the Greek hoplites, antique charioteers and feudal knights, or modern-age privateers or trading companies and predatorily self-supporting guerrillas – the prime effect will be on sociopolitical stratification. The internal hierarchy will favor the actual wielders of force, reflecting the uneven individual capacity to appropriate economic surplus and convert it into military sinew. That same hierarchy will determine next to aggregation also the projection of military power in and for organized inter-city warfare (the hoplites), surprise raids (charioteers) or localized self-defense (feudal knights) as well as attacks on enemy shipping (privateers) or assaults on political adversaries or adverse political systems (guerrillas or terrorists). When costs of adequate military capability on land or sea rose – e.g. with the onset of massive fire-power or capital ships – barter-type politico-military economy expressed in the truck of pivotal military performance for privileged political role tended to be replaced by monetary purchase-type economy. A centrally appropriated economic surplus will then fund progressively regularized warfare waged wholly or in part by professionals in pursuit of centrally designated goals by conventional military means. The critical stratification or hierarchy moves concurrently from within actors to ranking among them within an enlarged arena. Greater powers or units of power are differentiated from lesser ones, and transferring costs to the public purse expands next to the scope of the central authorities also their capacity to deploy military capabilities expansively with sustainable effect.

As part of the recurrent transition, money was both the medium for and a major regulator of an organized projection of substantial, and substantively conventional, capabilities by institutionalizing the role of spatially unevenly distributed metals (such as bronze, tin, or copper, less widely and evenly diffused than iron), needed equally for forging weapons and minting coinage. The distribution of either minerals or money influenced then not only the direction of trade routes and the location of markets but also, and more significantly for inter-unit politics, the optimum size of adequately funded actors and the practical scope of the related arena. And whereas centrally paid mercenaries and professional armies or navies were more readily usable for expansionist policy on a grander scale than either (quasi-) feudal levies or civic militias in ancient or modern democracies, typically (if not always actually) confined to time- and space-limited employment for defensive purposes, rising material costs of military equipment and human ones in military operations had less determinate effect. Thus, they were but unevenly reflected in the extent of civic participation in the shaping of public policy when, before compelling its eventual dispersion, the increased costs entailed a tightened control over military formations and operations. More than the Spartan phalanx, the Frederician square carried over into concentrating (high) policy-making in function of a development reinforced by a danger. The former comprised the rationalization of state bureaucracies needed to raise the necessary resource and assure a productive return on (fiscal) revenue; the latter beset the administratively rationalized restraint on the employment of the magnified means of destruction, in both the ancient and the modern variety of the bureaucratic state, whenever agents of some kind of anarchy disposed of unofficially funded means of violence.

The triad comprising costs of military equipment, variably produced and appropriated economic surplus for funding the costs, and strategic threats or opportunities determining the employment of military force, disaggregates naturally into sets of paired relationships. Centered on the economic surplus, the variations relate to the two basic (barter- and purchase-type) modes of relating military activity to politico-administrative management, while the interlock of innovation-prone military, economic, and managerial factors will be periodically coherent enough to amount to a comprehensive functional revolution.

Economic surplus relates most basically to the employment of military force in the form of a trade-off, between economic productivity and military preparedness. A political system is in basic equilibrium when it assures adequate production while releasing sufficient manpower for service in military self-protection – or, alternatively, provides for adequate consumption while setting aside sufficient assets for military capability – to insure preparedness congruent with the scale and kind of either threat or opportunity in the environment. Thus the Greek *poleis* (and, with due differences, the early Roman body politic) were capable of coordinating war-making and agricultural production in situations of low surplus: the hoplite-type farmer-warrior could both train and fight during leisure periods made sufficiently long by the nature of cultivation as determined by climate, and by distances between power centers as determined by the terrain; and he would contend with adversaries subject to comparable timetables and involved in the pursuit of identically space-related stakes (territory for cultivation and trade routes) pertinent for the issue of "hegemony." It was consequently not necessary to set aside a separate professional warrior group for a standing army, a fact that made the barter-type politico-military economy (exchange of military performance for political participation) possible. The possibility was actualized by the next relevant relationship, between economic surplus and cost of military equipment bearing on control over it and the degree of centralization of policy-making authority. The cost of hoplite equipment, being moderate though not negligible, could be borne by the propertied farmer (and, in Rome, by the propertied plebeian, relinquishing the expensive cavalry equipment to the patrician), but not by members of the propertyless rural or urban proletariat. The resulting tendency was toward qualified democracy within a comparatively mildly graduated sociopolitical hierarchy.

The situation is comparable when strategic opportunities predominate over threats, and can be exploited by enterprising individuals. Existing in seventh-century BC Greece and in the peasant–pirate economy of ninth-century AD Norsemen, the conditions began to change, thus in post-ninth-century Europe, when it was no longer feasible to combine agriculture and seafaring. Piracy and trade began then to be more clearly differentiated, and privateering entre-preneurs were superseded by officially chartered and gradually étatized trading companies. However, so long as a supporting relationship between (relatively low) military costs, (individually produced and appropriated) economic surplus, and employment of force (for limited ends) fosters the barter approach to politico-military economy, the equilibrium will hold: an essentially consensual and functionally limited central authority will reflect, within a mildly graduated social hierarchy, the actual allocation of (private and public) control over military equipment. It will set limits to rationally purposeful aggregation of collective power as well as to its projection in both diplomatic and military strategies.

The production of the economic surplus and its relation to the employment of force was changed in a model that, differing from the ancient democratic-to-oligarchical, characterized early feudal (western) Europe. A reduced surplus of production over subsistence needs required constant labor within a tech-nologically primitive system of agriculture and animal husbandry, while military force was employed primarily against locally dispersed predatory raids requiring constant preparedness by small but mobile cavalry forces capable of instant reaction to surprise attacks. The expense of supplying the horseman with heavy armor resistant to the offensive thrust magnified by the stirrup and of maintaining a correspondingly heavy horse costly to feed and unsuited for labor in the fields, exceeded by far the cost of equipping the foot soldier of antiquity. Only a small number of individuals could be allowed to preempt a share of the small aggregate surplus sufficient to equip themselves, while the problem of assembling and transporting the main energy-generating fuel (bulky horse fodder) was sufficient to preclude provisions being procured any more than arms by an only re-emergent central authority. The resulting strict specialization of functions between mounted warrior and rural worker entailed sharpened sociopolitical hierarchization within a correspondingly adjusted barter-type politico-military economy, just as locally decentralized threats constituted the military-strategic counterpart to a highly fragmented, manorial, economy. All these factors were reflected in a deconcentration of political power within any larger unit. A coherent mobilization and administration of resources and coordination of foreign-policy strategies could occur only intermittently, under the impression of an unusually strong overlord, within a political system prone to dissolution under peasant-like rules of contentiously divisive succession.

The situation was again different when beginning with early modern Europe technological innovations increased the cost of armaments above those typical of either the ancient *polis* or the feudal polity, while a growing economic surplus had risen less sharply. In such a situation the relationship between economic productivity (surplus) and military preparedness (employment of force) could still resemble the feudal-polity more closely than the ancient-*polis* pattern insofar as conditions fostered specialization between producer and protector (thus in the non-Mediterranean northern climate and type of economy which made warfare near-coincident with peak seasons for agriculture). However, when the combatant as the main consumer depends on fiscally generated public revenues to fund individually unsustainable expenditure for the force-in-being, money-based politico-military economy is apt to do more than only replace barter of auto-financed military service against privileged political status. It will also depress the personal status of the centrally funded fighting man within a standing army relative to public authority, to a greater or lesser degree in unevenly mobile societies. The development will be similar when opportunities for maritime-mercantile gains have expanded beyond a scope that could be exploited at a cost and risk assumed individually, while improved naval technology came to require, and consequent prolongation of the navigational season placed a premium on, uninterrupted service of specialized naval personnel. Even when anachronistic institutions – thus privately equipped and owned regiments in lieu of ships – perpetuate forms of feudal-type sociopolitical stratification for a time, hierarchy will have lost its basis in politico-military and -economic functions. It will degenerate into an obsolescent caste system of formal privilege devoid equally of justifying performance and correlative power or influence.

Once substituting purchase for barter has conclusively limited access to policy-making decisions in absolutist land-power and narrowly oligarchical sea-power regimes, the barter economy will reappear only with the employment of military force at material and human costs that reflect a substantial increase in strategic threats and their growing salience over strategic opportunities. "Total" threats to a self-consciously "national" community will predominate under technological-cum-tactical conditions evolving from formalized maneuver dependent on drill and discipline to flexible operations dependent on *élan* and *esprit*. However, the increased military costs and intensified deployment of force will also make for centralizing managerial functions to the detriment of consensual policy determination, replacing direct with representative democracy consistent with high-level bureaucratization. Whereas the bureaucratic con-solidation of actors – intervening between the onset of the money-based and the qualified reversion to barter-type politico-military economy – will have reflected the high cost and frequent incidence of warfare, improved control over equipment and more concentrated authority will rationalize the manage-ment of both resources and policy within a systemic environment that has become correspondingly more constraining – more tightly structured and necessitating prompt reactions.

If a political system is in rough equilibrium when economic productivity meets the requirements of military preparedness for dealing with the existing mix of strategic threats and opportunities, while control over funding armaments and the making and implementing of policy are centralized about equally, it will have faltered when at least one of the key relationships has been upset. One such contingency arises when the dispersion of decision- or policy-making in a mass-democratic kind of barter-type politico-military economy has lowered readiness to employ force below the existing level of threats or opportunities. Insofar as the imbalance is apt to favor reversion to purchase-type politico-military economy in the form of a formally professional and actually mercenary armed force, the political participation may remain diffused only nominally or provisionally while some at least of the lost latitude for policy and flexibility for the military is being recovered under pressure from a crisis-prone system of unevenly rising and declining actors. Or, the cost of armaments may decline relative to either opportunity or perceived necessity for force-employing operations by private individuals or groups hostile to the established order. Rebels of conventional or non-conventional (i.e., terrorist) makeup – rural or urban guerrillas – reproduce then the medieval "free companies" of marauders, subverting established domestic authority whether or not receiving or soliciting subsidy from a foreign power. Such private units of force become effective in a military-strategic universe that favors the dispersion of wielders, and the depression of kinds, of violence most common in conditions of military stalemate between state-like organisms and (consequent) political paralysis within them.

If the first-mentioned evolutionary regression fits into alternations between barter- and money-based politico-military economies, the second-mentioned one marks the oscillation between conventional and "barbarian" types of military challenges. In one fairly continuous historical sequence, early-state barter economy had evolved into mid-term professional and terminal-stage mercenary Roman military establishment, itself superseded by the politico-military barter economy of the feudal polity, the latter to be followed by the money- and purchase-based fiscal-bureaucratic cum professional-military formula of the modern authoritarian territorial state, itself due to be supplanted by a mass-democratized reincarnation of the ancient *polis* in the early-type nation state. By the time the latter exchanged participation in mass levy for defense against participation in expanding political rights, an industrial economy had been sufficiently enlarged and growing to translate adequate productivity into preparedness in appropriately spaced total wars, replacing near-continuous lower-level warfare of the earlier eras. Meanwhile, the socio-economic and -political ramifications of the military revolution focused on the stirrup, amalgamated within a personalistic feudal order based on land tenure, had been reproduced around military transformations due to either gun- or cannon-encompassed escalation of fire-power or skyrocketing numbers of fielded military personnel. Both underpinned trends toward the progressively regularized fiscal orderliness of the ostensibly dynastic but actually ever more impersonally administrative state.

By the same token, the built-in elitism and dynamically thrusting force of tank-centered mechanized warfare seemed for a time to reinforce the tendencies responsible for the emergence of the (right-wing) totalitarian state, before the nuclear revolution reopened the question of the corresponding optimum in sociopolitical order. Its only superficially modified requisite was to generate public policy best suited to contain technocratic impulses toward continuing-to-aimless functional, including military-technological, innovations of an alternately offensive and defensive character. In addition, it had to bring the innovations into balance with societal disposition to fund and employ force in increasingly ambiguous strategic and socio-economic conditions, delimited by extremes of wealth and poverty on the one hand and nuclear-type terror and semi-private terrorism on the other.

As military-technological, productive-economic, and administrative-managerial innovations ramify within political societies and coalesce into functional revolutions, their impact on the system will be reduced and the system restabilized from time to time by the effects of a twin tendency: for functional innovations to be diffused among as well as ramify within actors, and to generate counter-innovations of an adaptive or corrective character. An endlessly repeatable cyclical process of innovation–diffusion–counter-innovation will then be liable to add, via the attendant disruptions, a sociopolitical to the structurally conditioned and functionally induced kind of revolutionary crisis.

Any major innovation will differentiate actors more or less effectual in making use of the novelty for self-aggrandizement. In the opportunities it represents and the unevenly positive immediate effects it has, such an innovation resembles the expansion of the systemic arena, which it is likely to foster. Conversely, inter-actor diffusion and functional counter-innovations will augment the overall tension as part of a stalemate that tends to match the general effects of system contraction. In the end, however, diffusion and counter-innovation will both intensify conflict and consolidate actors who have assimilated the interlocking changes best. Thus, when horse-centered innovations with thrust-improving military and surplus-magnifying economic effects had ended by favoring monarchical unifiers against feuding magnates in both the ancient Near East and medieval Europe, the counter-innovation to the ascendancy of cavalry in the form of reorganized (missiles- or guns-wielding) infantry mattered even more than diffusion of the horse-related innovations. However, both were responsible for restabilizing the arena around less extensive but more compact or coherent, internally somewhat more egalitarian units of power. Similarly, intensified fire-power favored first the innovators, be it the Byzantine employers of the "Greek fire" against Moslem navies, cannon-equipped centralizing monarchies against unruly feudal lords, and colonizers with the Maxim gun against unarmed peripherals – or the superpower so long as it monopolized nuclear missiles or precision-guided munitions. In each case, however, the situation was returned at least partially to antecedent conditions by the novelty being diffused through either imitation or (in the case of Greek fire if not also of nuclear fission) illicit transmission. Reinforcing the tendency, either technological or strategic counter-innovations would range from tactical dispersal or orderly drill of infantrymen and improved techniques of fortification against conventional fire-power to hardening of missile sites or dispersal of mobile missiles and deployments of inner- or outer-space defenses against nuclear-tipped projectiles.

Occasionally it was possible or even profitable to delay diffusion-fostering imitation, thus when England waited until the end of the sixteenth century before replacing the crossbow wholesale with by then more reliable musketry and other implements of fire-power, laying thus one of the bases for the gradual pace in the country's sociopolitical transformations. But diffusion could not be blocked permanently, thus when in the early nineteenth century the British tried to outlaw the flow of industrial technology and expertise to the continent with no greater success than had accrued to late Roman/Byzantine efforts to forestall the diffusion of either naval expertise (to the Vandals) or sea-borne fire-power (to the Moslems). More important than the effects from briefly delaying diffusion were the consequences of a widening disparity: between the quickening rate of either technological or organizational innovations to-be-diffused and the comparatively ever more sluggish politico-administratively counter-innovative societal adaptation. If this gap was co-responsible for the evolutionary failure of the European state system, it was also because, beginning with Spain, each of the successive major innovators in war-related functional spheres was able to detain continental preeminence for less of the time usable for the wider adaptation before being challenged by a more effective imitator and succeeded by the next-following innovator. The accelerating rate and widening gap were in sharp contrast with the evenly slow-moving and indecisively fluctuating innovations and adaptations on the part of both the earlier universal actors, the Empire and the Papacy, and the not yet consolidated particular actors such as thirteenth-century French, fourteenth-century Anglo–Norman, and fifteenth-century Aragonese, monarchies.

The net result of the completed cycle of diffusion and adaptation may be nothing more striking than the re-ranking of powers within the hierarchy component of restored equilibrium. Such a re-ranking took place when, for instance, France's early advantage in feudal cavalry had first been neutralized by the deployment of missile-throwing English yeomanry. It reoccurred when the later French advance in artillery or Spain's in infantry were minimized by a next round of innovations, favoring powers such as Sweden and Prussia capable of building upon the revolutionary integration of arms in regularly paid and vastly increased standing armies initiated in the Netherlands. As the rate of diffusion and counter-innovation accelerated in the evolving European state system, the system coud be nonetheless repeatedly restabilized in a strategic stalemate that frustrated the successive bids to root enforced unity in a transient monopoly of innovative military technology, organization, and strategy – and their material and managerial supports. As a motor of evolution, the militantly encompassed standoffs contrasted positively with stagnation due to a unified empire suspending if not suppressing innovations in either the pre-European era or extra-European arena, without preventing speed-ups from alternating with slow-downs also in the European system subject, like any other, to peak-and-trough alternations in crisis intensity.

If time lags in diffusing new techniques, modes of organization, or strategies within Europe and from Europe outward were not sufficient to foster evolutionary stagnation across the system, they did tend to provisionally segment the arena while periodically restratifying actors vertically. Uneven fitness of soils for the key productive-economic innovation (the moldboard plow) eventually lifted the "western" over the "eastern" empire(s). In a later phase, innovative administrative techniques and psychopolitical attitudes such as nationalism spreading eastward relaxed earlier inhibitions on the diffusion of the means of both production and destruction originating in western Europe. When this happened, the gunpowder revolution could be brought to bear fully on so far unstable personalist aggregations of potential power in eastern Europe. The ensembles could then be transformed into institutionally centralized empires, pending subsequent migration of centers of gravity still farther east toward the Pacific Ocean arena. In a similar fashion the conjunction of radically novel naval technology and techniques of navigation with previously unattainable overseas material assets had imparted an additional impetus to the westward migration of power centers past the Mediterranean to the Atlantic.

The most direct influence on the size of the total arena and the way it is segmented will flow from innovations in transport, extending from travel of persons to transport of economic goods and military implements. When successive improvements in navigational instruments and ship construction increased the long-standing advantage of water-borne over land-bound carriers in regard to range, cost, and safety, local trade yielded to long-distance commerce within the expanded arena, and handicraft manufactures merged gradually into mechanized industry. The arena was resegmented whenever retooling entailed rerouting, thus when the magnetic needle made it possible to navigate the Red Sea and better-constructed ships to circumnavigate Africa, deflecting the paths of power migration and flows of wealth away from Constantinople with results that could be contained only temporarily at best. And since not even the configuration of continents and oceans was immune to technologically wrought interference with nature, realigning access routes and force fields through the construction of the major intercontinental canals, Suez and Panama, improved the strategic position of some major powers (Britain and the United States respectively) to the detriment of other powers (Russia and Japan), while speeding up the economic development and exploitation of relevant peripheries.

Whereas segmentations of geopolitical space reflect the (vertical) fluctuation and reveal the (horizontal) gravitation of power clearly enough, the picture is hazier when to be subdivided is the lifespan of an evolving system in function of the lengths of time during which this or that function or factor enjoyed relative salience or advantage. One such pair pits offensive against defensive military technology, the former conducing to warfare that is tactically or strategically decisive and the latter liable to provoke encounters that are only politico-diplomatically inconclusive or also militarily indecisive. The technological primacy of offensive and defensive weaponry alternates typically within the offensive–defensive mix, as a result of automatic technological or strategic counter-innovations. However, this has not nullified the tendency for periods of politico-military stalemates to predominate over spells marked by the capacity of the victor to decisively subdue the defeated party politically because smashing it militarily. Operationally related are oscillations of big, empire-like, actors with middle-sized compact territorial states or, secondarily, altogether small city-centered units. But, again, if the different formats, too, alternate in function of changing organizational aptitudes to harmonize the scales of divisible space and disposable energy, there is no clear trend over a long span that would disclose a comparative advantage for bigger over smaller size any more than for centralized over decentralized or pluralistic political structures – or vice versa.

Other things being equal, big-sized actors will be favored when offense predominates over defense in technology and strategy, and be optimal when men and mass matter in the era's politico-military economy more than do money and mobility in maneuver. This means that sheer size and mass prevailed over magnitudes scaled to fit the needs of cohesion and mobility (*qua* flexibility) no more reliably than offensive predominated lastingly over defensive military advantage. If the dual failure points to the size-related oscillation around middling actor size being a reflection of the tendency to military (or military-political) stalemate, the fluctuations suggest that continuous redistribution of accumulated matches the intermittent generation of novel energy in stimulating the evolutionary process. Redistribution is in evidence not least when the task of qualitatively counter-innovative correction of novelties apt to aggrandize an individual actor to the detriment of system stability is performed by the tendency for an innovation to neutralize itself through quantitative excess. Thus bigness and consequent loss of mobility and maneuverability neutralized in due course the overly armored feudal knight as much as the oversized Hellenistic ship, unmovable Ottoman cannon, or top-heavy tank or missile, in favor of smaller and more numerous counterparts. Similarly, a succession of power aggregations fell prey to integration-resistant accumulation of component parts and coordination-eluding allocation of control. The bias to bigness in scale may have been strongest in the east, but size has ultimately defeated itself everywhere when growth atrophied the spirit of innovation and its results stifled the capacity for adaptation. In the social universe of natural selection, bigger has not been necessarily better because more survival-capable, any more than in the physical realm.

Comparatively less related to size than adaptability will be the nature of controlling authority. It is more likely to reflect the situation of the actor in his relation to the insular–continental and/or East–West duality. Both small and large land powers, the eastern more or longer than the western, have tended toward despotic authority while the mostly relatively western sea powers have displayed an ambiguity. They depended increasingly on money economy to defray the rising cost of building and keeping up ships; but their resulting need for an authoritative allocation of resources will not entail pressures for authoritarian control over both men and money equal to the more man-dependent land powers' even when these are not more resource-poor or technologically backward. The ambiguous pattern began to be set when the democratic character of the Athenian polity suffered in the passage from self-supporting hoplites to state-subsidized urban-proletarian trireme rowers as the representative military manpower type. Yet Athens had not suffered as much in the transition from the barter of military service for political privilege to its purchase by pecuniary rewards as the larger and less markedly maritime Roman republic was to suffer from a comparable transformation. And the drift to demagogy eventuated in neither polity in the degree of internal despotism characteristic of the essentially continental, alternately conquest- and self-isolation-prone, Assyrian or Persian Empires – and the late Roman Empire after it had completed the control of the entire Mediterranean littoral and became quasi-continental in consequence.

EVOLUTIONARY-TO-REVOLUTIONARY DYNAMICS OF SUCCESSION

When crises originating in structures and functions coalesce, they will climax in contentions centering on the hierarchical re-ranking of social groups or state-like actors as an aspect of inter-group or -state succession. The issue will have to be resolved before a destabilized political system can regain equilibrium by recovering the lost congruence between intrinsic capability (power) and systemic role (authority) of either class-like groups or state-like actors. The attendant upheaval is apt to escalate internally to the plane of sociopolitical revolution and externally to that of a major (revolutionary) war. And the ensuing crisis will be keyed to revising the administrative machinery into one that can fit antecedent military-technological or -strategic and productive-economic innovations into an updated relationship between internally generated economic surplus and requisite strategic responses to external threats or opportunities, and do this at socially bearable material costs.

When it brings structural (including actor–arena) disparities and changing functional clusters into a common (socio-revolutionary and/or warlike) focus, the succession-related vertical dimension of hierarchical ranking differs from the horizontal segmentation of geopolitical space in ways that include discrete temporal rhythms. The retrogression and/or advancement of a particular area relative to others, responsible for segmentation, will normally unfold over a long time, as will its reversal. Conversely, a severe disjunction between the several economic, military, and administrative functional spheres within individual actors will act more rapidly to set off the radical-to-revolutionary pressures for making the spheres congruent again and the actor well functioning. It is when the two different timetables of the two discrete processes intersect that a major if not also terminal systemic crisis is apt to erupt – such as the one implicit in the chain of wars and revolutions punctuating the westward gravitation of power in the Mediterranean from the fifth century BC on, its north-west migration in and from Italy peaking in the fifteenth century, and its eastward shift in Europe accelerating in the eighteenth.

The climactic adjustments that determine the outcome of a successional crisis will be commonly compressed within a short time, creating an opportunity hard to recover by a candidate to succession when missed. When the succession issue is between territorial units, its resolution will be confined within a still more fixed and finite amount of geopolitical space, difficult to ignore even if the succession issue is not directly linked to the possession of such space. The time and space constraints will account for the intensity with which crises surrounding the succession issue infuse extraordinary amounts of energy into the system. So will additional circumstances. In any bid for succession, the negative goal of weakening and dispossessing the incumbent is motivationally prior to any desire for possession, entailing a newly uneven distribution of scarce resources to be repeatedly reallocated in contentious operations. Thus the intensified generation and flow of energy into a dissolving order will engender the urge to rationalize – disguise or legitimate – succession bids by reference to apparently transcendent objective values. This is liable to further exacerbate the conflict until such time as the temporary resolution of the interlocked structural–functional–sociopolitical crises has coincided with institutionalizing the subsidence of energy flows in revised or only restored operative norms of conduct within the affected system.

Such routinized rules of the game concern the use of and restraint on force in pursuing superiority and promoting stability while, secondarily, reconciling formal equality (of status) with actual hierarchy (in role and function). Unlike the emphatically asserted values that rationalize bids for succession, the norms that institutionalize the outcomes are less compelling – will be more certain in regard to the intentions behind them than to their actual incidence and future effects. Yet in regard to both the values and the norms the successorial crises differ from crises set off by functional innovations. Since the latter channel energy into essentially pragmatic responses to instrumentally conditioned concerns, they are keyed to efficacy, where the ideological rationalizations are at least ostensibly concerned with validity, while the operative norms would ideally span the two poles. The difference complements one between the more concrete focus of the functionally and the more diffuse one of the structurally rooted or triggered crises.

However, the more the three types of crises differ, the more they complement and reinforce one another in stimulating evolution of actors and systems alike. The same element of paradox applies to the fact that although the impulse behind the crises is negative (i.e., disruption and dispossession) and their enactment, averred objectives, or both, are radical-to-revolutionary, the hidden purpose and the most conspicuous outcome of the crises of succession within and between actors are essentially conservative and constructive. Within actors, they are constructive in that they tend toward identifying, and conservative because they aim at restoring, managerial-to-"constitutional" arrangements and distributive techniques and processes within actors; among them, because they promote regulatory-to-institutional arrangements best suited to narrow the disparities between goal-related drives and sustaining capabilities – with the effect of reconciling (normative) constraints and rules with (environmental) incentives and latitudes in both actors and arenas.

Not at all paradoxical is the parallel course of the general dynamic of evolutionary change and the changing specifics of the issues that have or are assigned priority in the process of equilibration and its results. Thus the question whether there will be a settled administration, arising concurrently with the initial formation of actors, evolves by way of the question as to where rudimentary administrative functions are to be located to the salience of the always latent issue of the key functions' particular beneficiary or beneficiaries. The latter issue highlights the potential of the state to grow into an autonomous entity by developing organs and functions capable of transcending particular interests. The corollary for the interstate system is the movement toward conceding to likewise transcendent objective norms of external behavior a legitimacy, if not always efficacy, comparable to those vested in drives and interests continually asserted by individual parties and climaxing in hegemonial contests over major-power succession. Finally, the priority issue in an evolving system can revert to an initial one as between core-systemic "civilized" and peripheral "barbarian" actors. Salience if not outright primacy is then retroceded to the latter after an intervening period wherein the succession issue was confined to core powers equally or comparably developed technologically and organizationally, and only differently specialized and differentiated in specific attributes as time passed and evolution progressed.

Some such trends informed the various (proto-) systems inching up toward and then extending beyond the Mediterranean coastlands, beginning with the successorial contests between functionally indifferentiated transient centers and peripheries and climaxing in contests over preeminence or hegemony among more firmly structured and better-equipped land- and sea-oriented actors. The contentious interplays would be punctuated by schisms-related social or political revolutions as priestly administrators-managers were initially defied by ritually sacralized but essentially secular monarchs; and as the latter were challenged in turn, decreasingly by warlike aristocratic and increasingly by commerce-oriented "middle" classes if not plebeian collectivities, themselves subject to reactionary tyrannical usurpations. Sequences such as these, and their transient derangements or derailments, marked the successional struggles within the several imperial phases or incarnations of Egypt (different in this respect from the more static and shorter-lived continental Near Eastern empires), in many a Greek *polis* (of the Athenian more than the Spartan variety, as distinct from the Hellenistic monarchies), and in the Roman republic (as distinct from the Roman Empire). However modified in time and place, the patterns anticipated the upheavals marking the Italian and European state systems, as they evolved out of the late- and post-Roman "barbarian west."

Toward the end of each sequence it was a modified variety of the earliest priority issue, whether any settled administration could survive or be effectively revamped, that became acute for the relatively mature-civilized power caught up in the severe-to-terminal ordeal. High and rising costs of defense would typically test and strain the capacity of an economic surplus depleted by arrest in technological innovation and imbalance in external trade and payments, and of an overgrown administrative bureaucracy, to meet an ambiguously external and internal challenge. The growing, if often but diffuse, threat would typically emanate from barbarian peoples marginally favored militarily as to thrust (e.g. type of sword in the late Roman setting) and mobility rather than numerical mass, and served more decisively by a favorable ratio of low charges for military procurement and administration to an elastic (including predatory) economic surplus. The dominant question was then whether civilized institutions would be diffused fast and penetrate deep enough among the barbarians to counteract and contain the impress of their moral or physical energy on the civilized-sedentary society – and at what cost in reallocated material (mainly landed) wealth and social status. The issue was critical when, in early Europe to a greater extent than was to be the case in revolutions that mediated succession between more firmly articulated parties, the successor to the late "Romans" was a hybrid comprising attributes of both sets of actors rather than a new hegemon only superficially imitating the values or just the mores of the supplanted predecessor. Subsequently, eighth-century Frankish–Carolingian synthesis blended Gallo-Roman and Germanic features more organically than the cultural-political preeminence of Capetian France assembled indigenous-particular and Holy Roman Empire-type universalist traits in the thirteenth century. And the politico-militarily preeminent Bourbon France incorporated the Spanish–Habsburg ceremonial traits even more superficially in the seventeenth century.

In a fragmented setting succession will tend to revolve around managerial forms and functions that are universal (or universalist), if only normatively or nominally so. Thus the struggle between (Holy Roman) Emperors and the Papacy was waged ostensibly over hierarchical primacy within the inextricably terrestrial-and-transcendental Christian universe and symbolically over succession to the unifying Roman Empire, although it was actually fought also or primarily over more concrete and mundane stakes. Only when contention had ensured the succession of more internally coherent and manageable territorial powers of smaller size to both of the pretenders to universal dominion, could the next critical successional struggles take place. They did so in the sixteenth to seventeenth centuries, in a reactively exacerbated religious atmosphere, over the primacy not so much of particular traditional actors (the Habsburg and French monarchies) as of sub-types of the secular territorial actor (the Protestant Maritime Powers versus Counter-Reformation Spain). The oligarchical maritime-mercantile polity replaced as a result the sacralized monarchical-military type of actors in setting the tone and defining the prizes of world politics no later than in the late seventeenth and early eighteenth century. That ascendancy was followed by the Eurocentric state system's last, multi-phase crisis of succession involving successive French, Russian, and German challenges to the primacy of maritime Britain, initially overlapping with secondary conflicts over a different, dynastic succession (in Austria and France herself, next to Poland and Bavaria) that had marked the twilight of Europe's ancien regimes. To an uneven and as they shifted eastward growing degree, the continental challengers were meanwhile reverting to the original – universalist and sacral monarchical – actor type. They combined re-emphasis on physical-military power with at least partially transferring the aspirational world beyond the known and given one from the material sphere of tangible overseas values (distinctive for the second-generational type) to one of futuristic collective utopias, replacing the otherworldly individual salvation of the earlier era (dominated by the first).

It was part of the in-depth foundation of the continuities linking the three distinct eras that the crises of succession between state-like actors coincided with crises of inter-group succession within them, each projecting to prominence a new class or social group. Thus the Investiture Contest promoted the shift from ecclesiastical to secular administrative personnel and the rise, in Germany proper, of knights and, in Italy, of the burgher-patricians (even if not, immediately, the *popolo*) at the expense of previously dominant prelates of the Church. In the next crisis, the Italian formula prevailed over the Germanic whenever a proto-capitalist cum proto-industrial mercantile oligarchy challenged and eventually dispossessed land-holding warrior nobility, at rates reflecting local conditions more or less favorable to social change. Finally, as the third crisis series unfolded, inter-group contention spread eastward and escalated in intensity conjointly with the upthrust of successively lower classes, from the lower middle class or bourgeoisie to the urban proletariat. In all eras and at all stages, the role and the rise – and, specifically, the rebellious risings – of rural peasantry, were part of an ambiguous, alternately para-revolutionary and wholly reactionary, factor, impacting on the evolutionary process mainly by way of more crucial groups aligning with transiently activated peasant elements or engaging in repressive reactions to rural upheavals.

As the succession crises followed one another – coincidentally lowering the social rank of the key challenger group – the effective weight or only a full recognition shifted from value-ideological rationales to real-political stakes and concerns. In the political culture of inchoate actors and system, relatively most compelling were the elaborately formulated doctrinal claims of the papal (Guelph) and the "imperialist" (Ghibelline) parties within an overarching

Christian cosmogony. The nominal overlaid heavily the real stakes revolving around such issues as to who, and to what extent, would control administration and thus landed property in Germany and commercial assets of Italy. Whereas the Emperors were anxious to consummate the essential territoriality of the Holy Roman Empire by means of securing for themselves an effective and effectively hereditary imperial domain, the Papacy was equally eager to ground its spiritual authority in a solid territorial foundation. By the time of the next succession crisis, sufficiently crystallized territorial actors recognized even more readily the prevalence of the economic or military stakes of power politics over religious rationales whenever the requirements of confessional solidarity were at odds with the stakes implicit in hegemonial succession between or within actors. Just as the support of popes for Catholic rulers was always contingent on its effects on the autonomy of the Papacy, the Protestant Anglo–Dutch alliance withstood divisive pressures from maritime competition only so long as Spain remained strong enough to serve as the unifying target. And neither of the Catholic powers, Spain or France, placed restoration of religious unity above either retaining (Spain) politico-military primacy or recovering (France) diplomatic autonomy. Similarly, within any one confessionally divided country, such as France, the religious preference of major sociopolitical groups, such as the rural gentry and the coastal oligarchies, reflected largely the strategic requirements of alliance with one and struggle with another group. Thus adjusting to the Calvinism of the peasantry was opportune or even necessary for the gentry, and to religiously cognate overseas counterparts for the commercial oligarchies, if they were to contend successfully for either control over, or autonomy from, the established central authority in Paris, Catholic and hinterland-oriented.

Insofar as doctrinal convictions played a role, it was to help define the overall environment in terms broad enough to help rationalize the strategic options and priorities of actors caught up in the more than usual uncertainties of a major turning-point in the development and differentiation of only the actors or also the arena. Even the limited motivational autonomy of the dominant ideological issue was curtailed in the last revolutions- and wars-attended series of successional crises, marked by dichotomies of liberal and conservative, democratic and authoritarian, and free-enterprise capitalist and planned socialist or state-capitalist principles and institutions. The crises were developmentally climactic because they aggregated features of all fundamentally motivating schisms. The always primarily intra-actor sacral–secular schism had been updated in the tension between secularized transcendent and more immediately tangible values and concerns (henceforth represented by state and community on the conservative side and embodied in individuals and their societal aggregates on the liberal side); and the attendant institutional refinement of the by then well-defined conditioning cleavages between insular-maritime and continental-military powers had been progressively compounded with a deepening cleavage between west and east European powers (displacing emphasis from traditional-communal to transformational-collectivist values). When the growing intrusion of factors peculiar to the last-mentioned schism came fully into play in the twentieth-century contests between right- or left-wing totalitarian-despotic and pluralist-democratic principles and powers, ideologies reasserted themselves increasingly in their immemorial capacity and role: to orient more than motivate ever more newly dominant actors, emerging to prominence in a cumulatively revolutionized technological environment better suited to provisionally obscure real- and geo-political patterns and guideposts than to lastingly efface and replace them.

As the major successional crises followed upon one another, not only the weight but also the character of the ideological rationalizations changed. Thus the cosmologically formulated conflict of values between unevenly spiritual and secular parties replaced the (late Roman) conflict of anthropologically definable cultures of unevenly settled-civilized and migratory-barbarian parties, only to be itself supplanted by contentions between socio-economic and -political ideologies focusing on relations between social classes or groups and between individuals-in-society and the state. It was inevitable for the intra-actor issues to be carried over into the concurrent tug of war in inter-actor relations between progressive-internationalist and traditional-statist doctrines. As this happened, the escalating reaction of either doctrine to the challenge posed by the other reinfused the previously secularized approaches to 'real' issues with tribally romanticized pseudo-religious myths or permeated the previously pragmatized rationalizations of issues and approaches with pseudo-scientific motifs.

Operationally more significant than, if roughly parallel with, changes in the normative sphere was the transition from structurally significant consequences of contests over succession to structurally generated constraints on such contests. Thus while the principal consequences of the Papal-Imperial (and subsequent quasi-bipolar) contests was to project lesser territorial powers into existence or salience, the main effect of resulting multipolarity and contiguity was to confine the range of options effectively available to later contenders. A more structured competition was gradually superimposed on inherently competitive primitive relations, rooted in both unformed and uninformed instincts of self-preservation through self-aggrandizement; and reflexes were replaced with increasingly routinized and rational efforts to relate means to ends by actors made aware of the "objective" world in terms of its space and time dimensions, as well as more self-aware as to their motives and proximate objectives. Concentrating previously diffuse and near-continuous violence in both space (conflict theaters) and time (fighting seasons) as a result meant narrowing the channels through which energy flowed into the system and enhancing thus the intensity with which the energy flow actuated the evolutionary process.

As the structure of the system evolves from one that is inchoate and as such permissive to one more determinate and constraining, it becomes increasingly likely that failures to adapt to changes in either the structural or the functional sphere will link inter-actor succession due to conclusive defeats in major wars with inter-class succession implemented internally through revolutions closely related to such wars. Just as proximate differs from ultimate causation, without one invalidating the other, so especially defeat in war as the immediate consequence of maladaptation of goals to capabilities or strategies to structure can reinforce the effect of inadequate internal adaptation to change without materially detracting from the latter's (ultimately primary) causal impact. The revolutionary reaction to domestic failings will be all the more radical when adaptation has been blocked or delayed in peacetime out of regard for the costs, in the coin of achieved stability or status, of updating either the makeup of or the control over the interdependent instruments of production, destruction, and coordination.

The connection between the intensity of sociopolitical revolution and the degree of constraint from system structure became manifested when radical upheavals appeared first in the earliest-crystallizing micro-systems of north-western Europe (Low Countries–Burgundy) and Italy, closely resembling the revolution-prone Greek city-state system at its apogee. The militant self-assertion of the Flemish and Lombard patrician and/or plebeian urban elements, against the feudal and ecclesiastical forces associated respectively with rural France and Empire, was successful in adjusting the management of resources to the local ascendancy of commerce and manufacture over agriculture – and of the properly armed and motivated foot soldier over the mounted nobleman. However, the absolutist princely reaction that followed in both regions institutionalized the insufficiently enduring capacity of the civic elements to assert themselves over against the increased potential of the autonomous state externally and transcend competing group interests internally. The sequence illustrated meanwhile the full range from rebellion, essentially for political independence, through social revolution from below, to statist reform or revolution from above.

Only several centuries later were these varieties of upheaval fully manifest in the European macro-system, beginning with the successive rebellions of the mercantile-maritime Dutch, Catalans, and Portuguese in the sixteenth to seventeenth centuries. Underlying them was the failure of imperial Spain to meet growing outlays in decreasingly successful wars and an increasingly inflationary setting without resorting to fiscal and administrative measures culminating in a flawed effort at a revolution from above: Olivares's "union of arms" as the failed substitute for converting overseas silver into a domestic surplus sufficient to fund wars on land and sea and forge links between metropolitan and colonial economies. The scope of the failure was highlighted by the successful revolutions from above in future major powers, Prussia and Russia, where debasing the landed nobility from quasi-feudal barter of free service for privilege to enforced service in return for direct or indirect monetary renumeration raised a state made transcendent over class to institutional efficacy. The bravura of the self-supplying calvaryman hacking his way through the mêlée was doomed to give way to the disciplines drilled into publicly funded infantry formations. Thus to update the barter-type in favor of money-based politico-military economy could in both unevenly eastern countries be sustained to a degree (greater in Prussia than Russia) by state-subsidized improvements in estate management and state-promoted implantation of manufacturers. However, much as internal adaptations dovetailed with the diffusion of functional innovations from a similarly revolutionized nearest-western neighbor (Sweden), neither land power was sufficiently transformed to meet the longer-term challenge from maritime Britain, any more than was better-endowed ancien-regime France in the absence of more effective comparable initiatives from above.

The ensuing sequence of the (1789) French, the (1918–19) German, and the (1905 and 1917) Russian Revolutions shared the common denominator of militarily unsuccessful and economically ruinous wars fought against Britain or, in Russia's case, either against Britain's ally (Japan) or in support of Britain's world position (World War I). Critical in ancien-regime France was the growing disjunction between responsibility for public revenues, performance of socially vital functions, and enjoyment of class prestige and privilege on the part of traditionally crucial combatant and more recently critical commercial upper strata. The result was a both inefficient and inadequate funding of the costs of both the productive and the destructive technologies, associated with the just barely beginning industrial and the not yet fully assimilated military (including naval) revolutions – the former taking off in England as the remote consequence of a successful challenge to the Spanish hegemony and the latter initiated in the Netherlands as its direct concomitant. When the greatest of the French was followed by the two-stage Russian Revolution, shortcomings in civilian and military administrations had become relatively more important than failures to adjust the traditional status hierarchy in favor of the only emerging modernist socio-economic groups. But it was the latter kind of maladjustment between status and role in an altered world environment that was to be again critical in imperial Germany, although more for the style than for the substance of the geopolitically and economically motivated policies ending in war and revolution.

However, beyond any other particular differences, administrative inflexibility and social rigidities reinforced one another, albeit in different ways and to different degrees, in all three instances. They did so not less when the time came to orchestrate military and economic performances in wartime than when the crucial peacetime task had been to generate the material and moral underpinnings for battlefield performance. Just as the ruling classes had expected a military victory to contain societal stresses within the social hierarchy, one to be at worst amended authoritatively no more than necessary to take into account wartime sacrifices, military setbacks made thus augmented stresses elude the least chance of pacific adjustment. The disruptions in the continental states were consequently more severe by far than had been the earlier and more timely sociopolitical and administrative transformations in the maritime powers, which, preparing them to bid for inter-actor succession rather than being reactions to failures, had barely deserved the label of bona fide revolutions. If the Dutch (as later, the American) "revolution" was primarily a rebellion for national independence, the two English seventeenth-century revolutions were more constitutional revisions from above than compellingly spontaneous risings from below, a fact that delayed their social implications to the "reform" bills of the nineteenth century.

In an essentially continental power, the revolution could assume the moderate form of a palace revolt, thus when overthrowing the pacific Lerma in favor of the bellicist Olivares regime in Spain, or the more radical guise of full-scale revolution reacting to the unrequited costs of the equilibristic diplomacy of a Vergennes in France, or finally the disparate shapes of the ambiguous German upheavals of 1919 and 1933 feeding on reactions to failures associated with Versailles and Weimar. In either case the agitation did repeatedly precede the second and decisive revolt of the land power against sea-power ascendancy or dominance – a fact that consigned the Russian Revolution of 1917 as much as its predecessor of 1905 and the German "revolution" of 1919 to the category of an internally preliminary and internationally uncompleted upheaval. In keeping with this fact, the continental type of radical perturbation will be in many key respects different from revolutions – thus the Themistoclean in sixth-century Athens as much as the later Dutch, English, and American ones – that equip the insular-maritime community for its initial rise and prominence. Since the land-power revolutions were the consequence of defeats in the first and relatively moderate round of inter-empire contest, their object was to compensate for and correct the deficiencies the defeat had revealed, not least by a reorganization suited to narrowing the gap between the actor's (waning) capabilities and the scope of the (expanding) arena. By contrast, the quasi-revolution typical of a maritime-mercantile polity will be a response to opportunities offered by a fluctuating contest between rival land powers (be it Sparta and Persia in the case of the Athenian or, still more markedly, France and Spain in that of the Dutch and English revolutions) and the contrasts between the two disparate (continental and oceanic) arenas.

Thus whereas the revolution in a land power is in essence compensatory, for initial decline, and in aspiration preclusive, of continuing decline, the sea power's is preparatory to realizing predatory ambitions. And whereas the former is predominantly social and ideological, and is keyed to improving the administration of domestic resources, the latter is more narrowly political or institutional, and bears on enhancing further the capacity to exploit opportunities outside the country. As a result the former will be more violent, but its consequences in the systemic arena be more dramatic than durable; the latter will entail less internal upheaval, but will have a deeper and more lasting impact on the interstate system, its hierarchy-determining assets, geographic scope, and functional range.

There are other, more specific, nuances that vary within the bounds of the broad differences. Thus the sea-power revolution sets the stage for integrating a rising mercantile or industrial (urban) middle class into the political system by displacing an autocratic in favor of an oligarchical regime. Conversely, the more negative as well as urgent object in the land-power revolution is to dispossess a henceforth non- if not dysfunctional aristocratic-military (landed) upper class. Accordingly, the sea-power revolution is aimed at reallocating public expenditures from conspicuous statist outlays (for royal court or imperial overhead, internal police through foreign warfare) to commercially productive and socially mobilizing outlays (including the navy); as for the architects of land-power revolution, they would expand total public revenues in order to cover combined expenditures for (militarily upheld) power, (navally promoted) plenty, and (psychopolitically satisfying) prestige, in deference to previously repeatedly demonstrated impossibility to insulate productive maritime-mercantile from distracting continental-military contentions. Consistently with these differences, the land-power revolutions attended the linking up of the land–sea power with the reviving East–West schism insofar as the French Revolution aroused German, and the German revival Russian, national feeling in self-conscious opposition to the West. By contrast, the sea-power type of revolution accelerated the passage from the previously dominant sacral–secular to the continental–maritime schism (and the former's transposition into a secularized variety) as the triumph of Dutch and English Protestantism over the Catholic Madrid–Rome–Vienna axis consummated the transition from the age of faith into the age of finance.

As part of their role in system evolution, the antecedents and the anatomies peculiar to each of the forceful eruptions – rebellion or revolt, revolution from above and from below – highlight the different causes or courses of the other, while all share the strengthening of the state as their more or less direct, deliberate, and durable consequence. And, as they strengthen the state at its administrative summit, the scope and foundation of the system of states is being expanded in the number of significant players and the range of mobilized domestic participants. However, the full significance of forceful internal upheavals for the evolution of the system will depend not only on the successional crisis extending to inter-actor conflict but also on the upheaval relating to a dominant schism. Thus, unlike the significant revolts and revolutions, the revolution of 1848, although transnational in character, was neither directly nor unequivocally related to either a principal schism (and only indirectly to the liberal–conservative secularization of the secular–sacral schism) or a preeminence-focused struggle. As a result, its value-ideological content wasdnot tied clearly to, nor was it made operational by, the real interests of any of the major powers (including "revolutionary" France and "reactionary" Russia), whatever may have been the relation of ideal aspirations to practicable ambitions on the part of the spearheading liberal-nationalist intelligentsia. The Spring of the Peoples was, therefore, unable to leave a significant imprint on the autumnal phase of the European system of states except insofar as it could be subsequently used to justify the procedures and legitimate the product of the Prussia-centered statist revolution from above, when anachronisms born of the intervening systemic stagnation had given birth to a more vital force with a viable program.

The Frankfurt mismatch between ideals and realities merely highlighted the fact that, as the factions-transcending state gathered the strength necessary to dynamize interstate relations, an equal vigor did not flow into norms that, although differing materially from precipitates of habitual routines, would nonetheless constrain either the tribal mores or the instinctual power drives of state-like actors. Especially when attempts are made to push declaratory norms of conduct beyond the range of their possible efficacy, it will be the late-entering major powers that ignite a systemic revolution by reasserting the more traditional actor- and system-formative modes and rules of conduct. They will do so as part of pressing toward center-stage out of a segment of the system the lagging development of which had provoked the internal upheaval energizing the late entry. In contrast from the barbarians who bid for succession to receding civilized actors at the beginning or close to the terminus of a system, the powers entering the latter at or immediately past its mid-term represent the latest wave or generation within a family of states with fundamentally identical if situationally or developmentally modified basic values. That is to say, the goals and means Russia and Germany as the successive late entrants in the European system would oppose to formal norms tending to inhibit a continuous adjustment of roles to resources were not, as were those of previously peripheral powers such as Japan and the United States, peculiar to distinctive cultures or politico-military economies. They implemented drives and mores original to the system and prevailing universally so long as favored by the organic conditions or opportunistic considerations of the system's founding members. Changes in such organic conditions and related social institutions and societal norms reflect the wider range of transformations possible within actors as compared with changes in either the arena or inter-actor relations; the opportunistic considerations reflect the progressively extending range within which older members of a system can and do decline from the peak of collectively mobilizable energy and acquire a corresponding stake in peaceably retaining once militantly appropriated assets, role and status. Especially when clashing with the galvanizing effects of revolutionary upheavals within the late entrants, the emphasis on self-protection through a revolution in values will only stimulate the infusion of energy into the system by provoking the challengers into overasserting the traditional modes.

Attempts to revolutionize procedural norms might compensate for the erosion of vital energies in declining actors, or the revision be intended to extend to the arena newly progressive societal values of developing actors. In either case, the upgraded norms will only fail to acquire efficacy or will also forfeit moral authority when constraints intended to regularize conflict are replaced by restraints aimed at repressing assertive drives. The crisis will be all the more pronounced when the environment of the later-wave actors' full participation in the system has shrunk in terms of both space and time: when much of the geopolitical space has been preempted by earlier-developing actors, and the time scale within which heirs presumptive and holders of prescriptive rights confront one another has been foreshortened in a matured system by a speed-up in the rate of change. Conflicts over parity-or-preeminence do then more than reveal contrasting disparities between resources and roles on the part of unevenly evolving incumbents and challengers, as they did in the European system until the late nineteenth century; successional bids will be exacerbated, as they were thereafter well into the twentieth century, by being impugned as a culpable deviation from and infraction of the achievements of universally beneficial progress.

Before this can happen, a system responding to the more or less genuinely revolutionary sources and effectively revolutionizing infusions of energy, augmented directly or reactively, will have to have evolved at least part of the way through phases of unevenly manifest evolution, linking its proto-to its meta-stage. As the evolution takes off from the decaying remnants of the preceding system being exposed to so far peripheral forces, the assault of the latter will be favored by social stresses within and inconclusively contentious stalemate among the established actors while only functional stagnation or also structural (actor–arena) asymmetry pervades the receding core. Besetting the settled actors, migrant invaders or just intruders performed the same role in the ancient Near East and in the decaying Roman imperial and incipient European systems – ranging, in the latter, from the "Germans" up to and including (Arabic) Islam and ending with the Ottomans in the south-east. The contest over succession is typically disorderly at this stage, the unevenly territory-fixed parties to it are radically heterogeneous, and the net result tends to be a hybrid political culture of hard to identify or trace victors and victims. As evolution advances toward its mid-point, actors become more homogeneous as to basic type and so do systemic norms keyed to regularized or routinized but essentially unrestricted balancing of power; the contest over preeminence if not hegemony becomes relatively orderly and predictable, more so because effective means have become more congruent with feasible ends and scales of actors with the size of the arena than because authoritative rules of contention and succession are being implicitly complied with; and, finally, crucial revolutions take place within actors as innovations and their diffusion among actors accelerate while individual actors adapt to both processes unevenly in environments that are themselves increasingly differentiated both functionally (innovating versus imitative, commerce- versus agriculture-centered, segments) and structurally (more or less firmly articulated and thus operationally constraining).

Specialization among actors that have become generically homogeneous, because equally territorially implanted and impelled, will take place along function- rather than norm- or culture-specific lines of differentiation that reflect a corresponding schism. Military and mercantile, land-focused and maritime factors were initially intermixed in "medieval" Greece, so long as Minoan Crete differed little from Mycaenean Peloponnese, as well as in medieval Europe or antique Mesopotamia, when river-based cities were being only gradually differentiated from their agricultural-pastoral hinterland. A subsequent specialization will in turn be revealed as a mere prelude to the resurgence of more fundamental heterogeneity in a system's late phase, as late-entering have only preceded substantively still harder-to-assimilate and more peripheral powers. Assyria or Persia had been such relative to (neo-) Babylonia just as Rome was relative to Macedon and America has been relative to Russia, bidding for parity if not preeminence either individually or as a category. When, as a result, a growing divergence between system-inherent and -shaping original norms and putatively system-transforming or only -institutionalizing reformist norms has eventuated in a transitional normative anarchy, inter-actor relations will be deranged if not debased rather than lifted to new levels and system evolution will be derailed or distorted rather than actuated or accelerated. This will continue until such time as ensuing contests will have produced a viable (Babylonic–Sumerian, Graeco–Hellenistic, Romano–Germanic, Italo–Europeanist or Euro–Atlantic) hybrid or synthesis of old and new modes of action and molds of actors.

Sociopolitical revolutions within countries become more violent in manner, if less promptly constructive in their effects, as they migrate to retrograde segments of a developing system. In the process they tend to combine, on a lowered plane of feasible purpose, the prepatory function of revolutions in maritime core powers and, on a lowered level of genuine impulse, the reactively compensatory and would-be reparatory function of revolutions in continental core powers. Whether they originated from above or below, and whether they coincided in time with the decline of the Athenian or Macedonian, the Egyptian or the Persian, Empires well before the twilight of French preeminence, the in-part-imitative revolutions made up in intensity for diminishing spontaneity as socially reforming and/or administratively reshaping upheavals. The degradation of the prototypes will take place against the background of an all-systemic or grand-political revolution springing from the confluence of structurally, functionally, and sociopolitically engendered or enacted particular revolutions and uniting internal upheavals with external conflicts.

Exteriorizing the dominant schism, the escalating intensity of accompanying violence will denote the passage through stages typical of any full-fledged revolution: from beginnings in increasingly space- and time-compressed but still comparatively low-level competition (e.g. pre-fifth-century AD Greek and pre-fifteenth-century Italian wars and seventeenth- and eighteenth-century European wars) to a climactic series of increasingly total wars (the Peloponnesian, Milan-centered peninsular, and twentieth-century world, wars). Whereas the milder conflicts are analogous to pre-revolutionary reform efforts, the terminal ones implement the terror stage pending a thermidorian scaling down of goals and expectations in a still unstable new equilibrium. Since actors will be unevenly capable and willing to absorb the lessons and conform to the limitations revealed by the just-preceding revolutionary experience, the modifications attendant on the eventual system restoration may not be limitable to the style of inter-actor relations and require the arena's scope to be expanded as well.

Such a grand-political revolution was centered on the land–sea power schism in all of the successive systems, although more clearly delineated in the Greek than the Mesopotamian and in the European than in the Italian system. But anything like a post-revolutionary system restoration could be achieved in either case only at a cost of the most radical of transformations for the founding and previously ruling members: in favor of kinds of activities (more welfare- than warfare-oriented and correspondingly costs-burdened) and competition (over stakes and by methods more simulated or sublimated than substantive) characteristic of a meta-system, intimating the supersession of a comparatively smaller or micro-system by one a macro-systemic scale if not also the former's subversion during the latter's proto-evolutionary phase.

MANIFOLD CONFLICTS AND MAJOR WARS IN ALLIANCE SETTING

Although the more or less severe inter-actor conflicts that punctuate the life cycle of a system take place in conjunction with the severally occasioned crises, crises are no more identical with conflicts than energy-generating motor is with the mechanism of evolution. In that the conflict-centered mechanism channels the inflows of energy and focalizes the latter's outflow in strategically significant action, it gradually articulates a system of state-like actors with developing capabilities capable of being effectively projected abroad and organs susceptible of constraining if not arbitrating inter-group conflicts.

However motivated specifically, conflicts express the urge of state-like actors to achieve the greatest possible autonomy or self-direction in regard to comparable actors. Whenever this prime value of politically organized societies is in conflict with the realization of other values, including that of individual or group autonomy, it will have to outrank them if the state is to continue being effectual and the system of states to operate at its best. Corporate autonomy implies subjection to the will of no other power outside the laws of power instituting the requisites of communal survival. Yet if these "laws" affect all parties equally, they also make operative the differences in actor capabilities through the medium of the basic tendencies of attraction (exerted by lesser power or power's absence on greater power) and repulsion (making lesser recoil from superior power). Unlike what is true for consciously formulated normative rules of conduct, which receive only contingent compliance, actors are subject absolutely to the imperatives implicit in the natural tendencies. They are so subject because the laws governing the resulting interactions are only the objective expression and the systematic aggregation of the subjective and random individual impulses that propel such interactions in a setting defined by plurality (of actors) and scarcity (of assets).

Conflicts that implement the general laws of political nature contingently qualified by the norms of a particular political culture are the prime mechanism for translating evolution-propelling energy into evolutionary outcomes. In this perspective, the several kinds of crises that generate unfocused energy convert basic givens into secondary effects. The primary given consists of the many different disparities (structural, functional, succession-related sociopolitical) that create the potential for crises, while conflicts actualize the pressures for adjusting or removing the disparities. However, although the extent of the several disparities will determine the volume of energy released by unevenly severe crises, such energy's amplitude will not by itself determine how and with what effect it is channeled or focused: it may be diffused in the system with no definite or an adversely disruptive effect on its evolution when embodied in unstructured or objectless violence. And although functional innovations will focalize somewhat the flow of energy induced by actor- or arena-related disparities in structure, the flow's direction will be subject to the technological or administrative novelties being unevenly diffusion-prone. Moreover, any consequent realignment of sociopolitical hierarchy within actors will begin by directing energy toward societal dislocation, while crises attending the adjustment of the hierarchy between actors point initially to enhanced social cohesion on the part of the challenger. Nor are the level at which energy flows and the location where it coalesces either constant or indifferent, as atrophy alternates with hypertrophy and the site of main contention varies between intra- and inter-actor or intra- and inter-civilizational theaters. Finally, there are degrees of immediacy with which different disparities and processes of adaptation impact on the system. A disparity and reactions to disparity between the part a group plays in the production and the share it receives in the distribution of the economic surplus, or between the group's political status and its functional utility and performance in the politico-military arena, will have a less direct impact than have responses to a disparity between an actor's national resources and his systemic role.

It takes overt conflicts openly waged to bring the competitive nature of the system to the surface, and for the system to process the disparate flows of energy into their precipitates in the form of ostensible changes in, or even of, the system. Inter-actor conflicts do this as they conciliate divergences in structures and capabilities in the interest of maintaining or restoring congruence between role and resource, compel functional innovations and inter-functional adjustments in the interest of actor efficacy, and concentrate aimless drives in successional bids. In that they result in individual setbacks or successes, conflicts act as the medium of selection in a process of evolution which is as destructive in its procedures as it is one way or another productive in its immediate or eventual results. It is through conflicts that specific conditions present as a given become operative as compellents to actions centering generically on coercion; that structures are more vividly experienced as stakes; and that individual (including individually trivial) motives are transmuted into the transactional momentum that breeds its own motivation, while divergent objectives are processed into outcomes that are universally pertinent even if not uniformly relevant for all.

Finally, while focalizing diffuse and actualizing latent energy, inter-state conflicts also distribute the total flow of energy between intra- and inter-actor arenas, in keeping with the tendency for the two arenas to alternate as salient within the bounds of a constant sum of conflict in being within the system over not too long periods of time. Initially manifest when perpetual and inextricably internal–external contentions become at once rarer and more concentrated, the sum remains constant as acute inter-state conflict only dampens or wholly represses inter-group struggle, while inconclusively stalemated or long-suspended conflict between states will cause strife to devolve to the inter-group level. This happens as frustrations experienced on the higher level release the stresses that accumulated internally, after the severity of the external conflict had previously served to diminish attention and tame contentious responses to internal problems. Thus, internal conflicts were resurgent in the wake of inter-state appeasement after, say, 1559 (Peace of Cateau Cambrésis) in the modern European system, if mainly in France, and after 1815 and 1919 throughout Europe (and beginning with the late 1960s also outside her), while conflicts between major powers became again acute after 1632 (a restored France's entry into the Thirty Years War), beginning with the 1850s (Crimean War and the wars of Italian and German unification), and the mid–1930s (while interstate tensions resurfaced in the 1970s).

Although the basic effect of conflicts on evolution is constant and pervasive, this does not mean that changing intensities of overt conflicts and the underlying crises do not affect the rate of evolution, accelerating it (in function of hegemonial conflicts and authentic revolutions) or decelerating its course (in periods between either). Throughout, moreover, just as the relationship between intra- and inter-actor conflicts, so the relation between inter-actor conflicts and constituents of crises, will be reciprocal: the impact is no more one-directional than is that between military costs and economic surplus or among components of the functional clusters. Conflicts make the constituents and immediate consequences of crises fully operative in generating evolutionary outcomes. But the constituents of crises influence and may even control the ways the conflicts originate, are waged, and may be terminated. Circularity extends to a still wider compass in the cause–effect interplays of the factors that make up, next to the energizing motor and the energy-converting mechanism of evolution, its conditioning matrix and resulting manifestations. And, although such circularities are distinct from any cyclical patterns of phases or stages that an ostensibly shapeless (if not chaotic) evolution may reveal in retrospect, they do underlie such patterns even when they are linked to them most ambiguously.

Since conflict, though not omnipresent, is the distinctive characteristic of interstate relations, and because the phenomena responsible for crises encompass the full range of significant determinants of action, it is inevitable that the crisis constituents influence conflicts in all of their facets and stages. Thus, in determining the readiness of actors to engage in conflict, specific technological or organizational innovations clustering (or not) in functional revolutions will affect material capabilities more directly than they do psychopolitical dispositions; and the latter will depend to a larger extent than the former on the state of the sociopolitical frameworks and value-institutional features that bear on inter-class even more than inter-actor successional crises and, through them, on the distribution and hierarchy of roles in relation to the resources to be allocated more or less authoritatively. The next step in the incidence of conflicts is their actual generation or origination, as distinct from anterior readiness to engage in them. It can be due primarily to frictions and pressures induced by near-physical contacts between territorially contiguous actors or primarily to clashes of meta-rational concepts, embodied in belief systems or ideologies. When contact matters most, disparity in structural and functional factors will be primarily determining; when concepts, value-institutional factors matter more and routinely give way to revolutionary conflicts. Territorial contiguity between fully formed actors typically only follows upon a more primitive condition, when tribal-ethnic groups or feudal-type and other ties or obligations interpenetrate within wide frontier zones. Contacts being thus blunted or confused will confound strategic rationality, responsive to the territorial imperative amplified by the antagonisms and alignments which implement the balancing of power. However, the concepts that rationalize disparate "real" concerns and intensify conflict more than they instigate it will have an impact on rational strategy that is not only more adverse but also extends unevenly through all evolutionary phases.

A similar configuration of incentives and determinants will obtain when a conflict, after originating, is enacted or managed in ways conforming to the underlying purpose. When conflict is engaged in mainly to reduce internal pressures for relieving accumulated stress or tension, a militant posture or token military effort will aim at no more than (and may suffice) to give a new lease on life to the policy-making group while keeping an internationally significant desideratum or claim alive: it is no more expected to achieve full satisfaction than it is likely to propel evolution materially. The essentially cathartic object of the ensuing conflict, denoting its character, will be to sidestep an immediately unmanageable link between the available material or immaterial surplus for funding a conflict and the military costs and risks of waging it effectively. To the extent that the conflict exhibits then a functional disparity, say one between the managerial authority of a ruling group and its capacity to achieve deeply felt goals of the larger collective, it will differ from one lodged more intimately in disparities primarily structural, such as those between an actor's systemic role and his resource or actor capabilities and arena scope. Such a conflict will be conducted less with an eye on purging emotional stress with temporarily appeasing effects and more with the intention to redistribute concrete assets and role-status attributes: be catalytic rather than cathartic in purpose and function, although equally if not more prone to eventuate in a stalemate as to outcome. No more assuredly conclusive than the military will be the diplomatic methods of enacting conflict – thus when a structurally induced crisis is due to an exceptionally big actor asserting himself in an arena too small to comprise adequate countervailing forces. A way to manage the resulting conflict will be to enlarge the arena either in scope – by co-opting hitherto peripheral and uninvolved actors – or depth – by mobilizing hitherto passive population strata or latent resources. Conversely, the object may be to adjust actor–arena disparity by reducing the actually mobilized or invested actor potential to the actual or desired contraction of the relevant arena. Strategies will then aim at localizing or limiting military conflict with a view to avoiding disruption or radical imbalance at the system's core.

Although the more narrowly military method of enacting conflict will militate against truly decisive subduance of one of the belligerents, which outcome prevails in a specific case will depend on the state and shape of military-technological or -strategic defensive or offensive innovations and counter-innovative adaptations, amounting periodically to a military revolution. Drawing for material support on comparably configurated commercial or industrial and administrative revolutions, the supporting morale will be commonly due to some form of prior or attendant sociopolitical revolution. The ways in which conflicts originate and are managed affect thus the course of evolution more as to style than substance, pattern more than product, denoting no clearly discernible evolutionary tendency in and of themselves. At the very most, as actors mature and system crystallizes, there will be a trend from psychopolitical disposition to material capability as the more important factor in making parties ready to engage in conflict, from concept to contact in actually generating conflict, and from cathartic to catalytic conflicts in terms of the underlying incentive or unavowed objective. By the same token, the direction or trend will be reversed when actors decline and the system decays as part of either or both ageing. Finally no more discernible – either over the full lifespan of a system or its identifiable phases – is any trend toward enlarging or contracting the arena of conflicts as part of managing them politically or diplomatically.

Alternations that do not fall into a neatly sequential or cyclical longer-term pattern will predominate also among modes of resolving or terminating conflicts: through negotiating transactions or mediatory strategies on the one hand and with the help of devices and conditions of an essentially structural character on the other. When the latter prevail, the dispersion of a two-sided into a three-cornered conflict will invite any two of the parties to enter preemptively into a separate peace at the immediate expense of the third party with the result of defusing the conflict. Or the more serious the conflict, the more likely it becomes for it to be terminated by a change in structure combining with one in evolutionary stage. The conflict subsides then as it is being supplanted by a conflict more relevant to altered conditions and/or updated concerns of unevenly developing parties; it is "resolved" when its motivating causes and transactional momentum have been resorbed in transformations – an instability or an equilibrium – centering on the next-dominant conflict. The anterior conflict's resolution-through-supersession may, but need not, mark a step toward system restoration to follow from the completed course of any one or several of the conflict-inducing revolutions. Although there is, again, no conspicuous evolutionary trend in the modalities for terminating conflicts, the supersession of one conflict by displacing the focus of rivalry to another will, like military stalemates that prepare the ground for this form of conflict resolution, be the most frequent as well as most fundamental mode of disposing of conflicts that qualify as "hegemonial" in a system of major states no longer prone to near-continuous warfare and periodic dissolution of actors from within.

Major or hegemonial, unlike lesser or routine, conflicts are directly related to significant transformations in the system as both cause and effect. They are closely linked to the uneven rise and decline of the greater powers, occur at intersections of divergent trends, and implement transfers of primacy from a declining incumbent to a rising challenger. In such conflicts, the element of capability within the category of actor readiness to engage in conflict is not a matter of actually available resources only. It is also, and primarily, a matter of perceived or anticipated capability trends that strongly affect psychopolitical dispositions: will capability increase or decrease over time relative to the other critical actor or actors individually and to the fluctuating fund of capabilities they constitute in the aggregate? And will they do either by virtue of what kind of functional innovations and strategic or instrumental counter-innovations are susceptible of more or less speedy diffusion away from the innovating party (most likely to be the challenger)?

A prospectively continuing actual growth in capabilities will fuel an expansionism on the part of an aspirant to preeminence that is essentially offensive. The thrust from an unstable base can then be only diffusely expansive (e.g. south- or eastward by the Germanic Emperors and Frankish crusaders); or a just–accomplished consolidation of the actor may release consequent exuberance into more precisely targeted and firmly sustained expansion (e.g. by the continental French and maritime Dutch and English powers relative to Spain and, initially, by Wilhelmine Germany relative to Great Britain). The object is in either case to translate either only latent or already realized power potential into only parity (when facing a still strong incumbent) or outright preeminence (when the lesser objective is resisted or no such impediment obtains), as existing assets in being are parlayed into effective access and activated resource into acknowledged role or also rule.

When growth decelerates and veers toward decline relative to either median capability in the pertinent arena or the principal target party (or, most likely, both), defensive begins to predominate over offensive, preclusive over predatory, components within the offensive–defensive mix that shapes most impulses to self-assertion. Then, instead of embracing the conservative bias toward maintaining the existing distribution of power and positions in the system from a posture of role-status inferiority to the nominal incumbent, the challenger, typically frustrated when he has manifested (exuberantly) the still unquestionably rising strength in an earlier attempt, will resort to compulsively overassertive (would-be preemptive) reactions to an anticipated weakening. Whereas the challenger, unsuccessful in his heyday, is running out of both steam and time for more effective challenge (e.g. late eighteenth- to early nineteenth-century France and twentieth-century Germany *vis-à-vis* the leading Anglo–Saxon insular power), the defender will continue being unwilling to concede assets and share influence in hopes of prolonging a diminished advantage in capabilities by tightening up the structure of constraints (still strong Britain less markedly relative to revolutionary–Napoleonic France than France on land and Britain globally relative to Germany). When they assert themselves compulsively from weakness, both challenger and defender are no more resisting one another than the loss of control over events. They resist a regression from the contest over primacy accelerating into premature withdrawal from active self-help, apt to terminate in actual or virtual dependence on the ratios of capabilities and relationships of conflict among other, the most likely successor, parties for safeguarding a drastically curtailed position.

If relative rise infuses additional energy into hegemonial wars, relative decline injects augmented intensity into them. Thus capability-related trends increase readiness to engage in conflict, if differently. Major increases in capability will denote extraordinary propensity to innovate in technology or strategy, adding up to leadership in a military revolution for more effective destruction (thus the seventeenth-century Dutch and later French–Napoleonic one), an economic revolution for sharply increased production (thus the British industrial one), or a combination of the two (thus late nineteenth- and early twentieth-century German innovations in both technological-and-strategic military and industrial-economic areas). Moreover, an increase in capability owing to innovation will normally coincide with enhanced social mobility that stimulates the psychopolitical disposition to engage in competition leading to conflict either directly or indirectly. The effect is direct when ascending groups push to extend the actor's external scope or sway in hopes of re-ordering a domestic political arena that expansion abroad had made more easily if differently enlargeable; it is indirect (and may actually complement the direct effect even when apparently conflicting with its cause) when the ruling group pursues the same external objectives as an alternative to and defense against domestic transformations that would only undermine or immediately threaten its position.

So long as the relative capability of the challenger either grows or seems poised for growth, the concern of his ruling regime or class will predominate and a revolution from above will be the more likely instrument of the initial bid for ascendancy. This was the case for the Dutch, the "glorious" English, and Colbert's mercantilist French "revolutions" as much as for the social and economic policies or programs associated with the Bismarck and early William II periods in Germany and with a Witte or Stolypin in tsarist (and Stalin in Soviet) Russia. The situation is reversed when a relative slow-down or less-than-anticipated growth has compelled, often conjointly with a military defeat, a galvanizing internal shake-up as the preliminary to one more, final because in all probability non-repeatable, bid for parity or preeminence. Then regime- or elit-einstituted measures will tend to yield to more radical transformations wrought by sub-governmental forces such as those responsible for the French Revolution, the National-Socialist German "revolution," and, in the fore-shortened time-frame of only tsarist Russia, the Marxist–Leninist revolution.

A more or less genuine revolution is (again) apt to proceed from above when it is the incumbent hegemon or quasi-hegemon that is threatened by decline and the ruling group seeks to restrain growing pressures from lower social strata or peripheral ethnic groups to reallocate shares in the stagnating or diminishing fund of the socio-economic capital. Here belong measures and objectives behind Olivares's attempt to fiscally unify the Spain of Philip IV and the policies of the French Second Empire in especially its "liberal" phase prior to 1870 and of either the Conservative or Liberal government in Britain before World War I. The regime's task is then made easier when, as is possible, the lower classes find a momentary reprieve from domestic frustrations in militant nationalism or imperialism, enhancing the utility of military crisis as a tactical diversion. When, conversely, the preeminent power is poised at the peak of its power curve, it will be engaged typically in less strenuous wars such as those of the sixteenth-century Spain of Charles V and Philip II in Italy and the Mediterranean, the France of the young Louis XIV on the Rhine, and the British at the rims of their first (North America-centered) and second (India-centered) Empires. The conditions of ascendancy favor then a controlled ascent of safely cooptable social or nationality groups into positions of authority in empire administration or metropolitan management. Italian or Flemish aristocrats or (upper) middle-class financiers-merchants in the Spanish Empire are in this respect the equivalents of non-noble ministers and financiers in Ludovician France and Scottish or lower middle-class members in the British Empire, with corresponding (rationalizing or routinizing) effects on administrative set-ups within and interactions between actors.

The twin aspects of readiness to engage in conflict, comprising actual capacity and attitudinal disposition, conjoin thus the advantages to accrue from functional innovation and from sociopolitical activation of succession-capable groups. Incentives to conflicts rooted in structures made up of uneven capabilities intensify when, the scales of the main actors and the arena having ceased to be congruent and the territorial contiguity among actors having evolved from a prerequisite to sustained interaction into a precipitant of acute conflict, the relatively oversized challenger acts on a particular assumption: the belief that neither the central arena nor its periphery contain an adequate countervailing power to conjure up and coalesce by the reigning "hegemon" as he passes from prudently resolute via hesitantly vacillating to high risk-taking diplomatic strategies in an effort to only conceal resource deficiencies or also compensate for them. When, as a result, structural factors as they relate to capabilitites are mutually reinforcing with psychopolitical dispositions tied to unevenly revolutionary internal contests over power distribution or foreign-policy directions, readiness to engage in conflict is apt to issue into conflict being generated on a vast scale. And when divergence in the growth rates of capabilities is added to existing derangements in the distribution of resources and roles, longer-term anticipatory-to-alarmist perspectives will compound reflexive short-term perceptions and escalate routine balancing of power into ostensibly reckless bidding for predominance.

Intensified balancing of power in the central system tends to actualize power potentials at the system's periphery, just as the dovetailing of moderately assertive and conservative foreign-policy dispositions facilitates stabilizing balance-of-power interplays and suspends contests over primacy. The latter was the case in the decades following 1715 and 1815, while, as happened both before and after these periods, acceleration in contrasting growth and decline trends will widen the band within which capabilities and policies fluctuate, shortening the time available for effective reactions within an exacerbated balance-of-power dynamic. Since this will hinder parties from considering the costs and benefits of alternative strategies for the structure and scope of the system at large, both a too rigid, because declining, defender and the too pressing, because precariously poised, challenger will discount the implications of alternative strategies for the developmental tempo and trends in the periphery. As immediate pressures blot out longer-term prognoses and militant propensities overwhelm predisposition to prudence, the offensive strategy of the challenger will be keyed to mobilizing forces internally and colluding with dissatisfied forces abroad; and the incumbent will apply no other standards than those of containing and countervailing the challenger when soliciting the cooperation of all and sundry. As the system expands and the center of gravity is about to shift farther afield, the heightened crisis narrows the range of practically available strategies while increasing the probability and widening the extent of their mismatch with the structure of the system "as is" or has been until lately, to the detriment of only gradual and moderate adaptative change.

The propensity to major war will be increased to a maximum when the adopted strategy is one of encirclement that expands the area of frictional contact even as it aims at enhancing coercive pressures. The strategy-motivating intentions and its explosive consequences link the alternating encirclements and counter-encirclements engaged in by Empire and Papacy in Germany and Italy to the investment of France by the Habsburg complex, and the latter to France's and England's eastern alliances against the Germanic center. The area of frictional contact is liable to expand in space when extending beyond the encircled party's metropolitan core-area, and to become multi-faceted when more widely felt economic pressures and privations are added to the diplomatic and politico-military stress confined to the elites. The

resulting strains will make the stimulants of major conflict spill over from
contact to concept, sublimating real into ideal stakes and absolutizing the
situationally conditioned relative value differences. A vertical deepening of the
system's dynamics as to mode is then added to any horizontal enlargement at
the margins. Thus both the Franco–Germanic and the Anglo–French conflict
became more intense and ideological as it ceased being a matter of frontal
confrontation between equally territorial and relatively static powers, only
intermittently subject to loose mutual encirclements by alliances such as the
Anglo-Imperial (aimed at France) or Franco-Scottish and -Polish (aimed at
England and the Empire, respectively). Similarly, the relatively ideology-free
Franco-Spanish contest over preeminence heated up only when the effects of
France's encirclement penetrated her innards by way of a politicized
confessional (Catholic–Huguenot) schism.

Actual evolution emerges from inflows of energy that have been molded into
manifest outcomes by conflicts in general and their hegemonial variety in
particular; potential evolution is one that would have taken place in the absence
of actually transpired conflicts, if not necessarily of any and all other conflicts.
The implicit paradox is that while major conflicts determine the main lines of
evolution, as actors and systems change, the conflicts themselves arise
increasingly out of concern to prevent feared or undesired developments rather
than produce desired or coveted outcomes: to be both rational and responsible,
policies must and will be aimed at preempting or preventing the consequences
of alternative, spontaneous or otherwise directed, occurrences. The urge to
prevent undesired transformations is then at the root of actual evolution being
the unintended resultant of individual aspirations. Whereas the dominating
impulse of the ascending challenger is to employ his functional or strategic and
organizational innovations before their being diffused in the system has
nullified the advantage, it is near-avoidable that the ensuing military conflict
will actually accelerate the diffusion among imitative, or surpass its effect
among counter-innovative, members of the adversary coalition, with the result
of frustrating the challenger. Similarly, in relation to regime concerns, when the
challenger's dominant political class bids militantly for more prestige abroad as
a safeguard against the peacetime effects of materially stimulated social mobility
dispossessing it internally, the mostly or ultimately self-defeating urge is to
avoid sharing material innovation with outside and immaterial assets with
internal rivals. This ambition will have a counterpart in the declining defender's
when he refuses to peaceably accept, in the shape of the challenger's role-status
increase, the consequence of the already completed diffusion of the innovations
originally responsible for his ascent. The incumbent's ruling class hopes then to
find in resolute foreign-policy leadership a safeguard against being displaced
also from this, its last, defensive redoubt by upthrusting sociopolitical strata.
Neither side will heed, under stress, the probability that the ensuing war – more
brutally and quicker if lost, but eventually also if won – will effectively bring
about the most feared and primarily resisted internal development.

Before incumbent and challenger are thus thwarted, their matching impulses
exhibit differences ranging from different emphases to inverted priorities. If the
challenger's ruling class is immediately intent on self-affirmation, the

defender's is on self-preservation: the former would prevent a process of internal power dispersion from getting under way prematurely, whereas the latter seeks to preempt the ultimate consummation of an already ongoing process. And if the challenger would preclude future diffusion of his qualifying innovations in the system at large by means of a deliberate interposition, the incumbent would prevent the incrementally surfacing natural consequences of a consummated dispersal to be irreversibly formalized; while the former would delay possible or probable counter-innovations, the latter would gain the time to assimilate already existing correctives to prior innovation. Whereas the challenger's priority is on balance to forestall premature diffusion of innovative assets abroad, the defending elite's fears focus on the terminal dispersion of domestic authority and functions.

It follows that the challenger's operative impetus is predominantly catalytic: he will act to achieve decisive outcomes abroad rather than allow a possibly non-repeatable occasion to slip (e.g. imperial Germany in 1914 after missing it in 1906); the guiding object of the defending incumbent will gravitate toward the cathartic pole: he will assert an increasingly but nominal international leadership to purge himself of self-doubt and prevent inaction from legitimating a "peaceful" transfer of primacy (Great Britain in 1939, after starting the process in 1914). The underlying state of mind was disclosed formally when first the Spanish and later the Austrian branch of the one-time Habsburg family tree insisted on incurring, when not actually inviting, military defeat so that being coerced into territorial or other concessions left the legitimacy of surviving authority intact. Only in desperate last resort would they gamble on the remote chance of military success as the only remaining remedy against creeping degeneration (Spain) or disintegration (Austria–Hungary). Accordingly, if the challenger's urge to preempt diffusion of his assets by initiating military action will instigate counter-innovations liable to harm him materially if not also physically, the declining incumbent's last stand will signal a suicidal determination to redeem himself morally at least as much as politically.

If the dialectic between actual and potential evolution – realizing one outcome because resisting another – amplifies conflict, so do disparate efforts to consolidate one set of achievements in space and perpetuate another set in time. After being formed to the point of consolidating a viable territorial habitat, actors will commonly continue developing as they reach out for additional spatial and/or strategic gains that range from seemingly essential to inherently redundant. The indispensable first stage will bring viable habitats into a close contact amounting to territorial contiguity, while the habitual second stage will compel routinely competitive balancing to contain one-directional or conciliate converging territorial thrusts that have become unlikely to dissipate spontaneously. Whereas the balancing reflects a rudimentary ability to retain acquisitions in space, only to improve on the ability when making the territorial gains finite in scope, the opposite will be true for the growing aspiration to perpetuate support from more elusive role-status gains in time. It is this larger aspiration of an incumbent – and its denial by the challenger intent on eluding the systemic constraints it symbolizes – that will transform routine contentions over space-anchored balance of power into hegemonial confrontations. Stakes will escalate not only because they are high to begin with and the players major; they will grow also because the actors have been caught up in an unequal struggle to do more than defeat the present adversary by dominating space. They will aspire to master time itself by controlling its erosive effect on either the pillars that support, or the tools that were and might again be instrumental in acquiring, preeminence. As the incumbent would arrest the rush and the challenger outstrip the pace of time, the contest is as much against feared fate as it is with a detestable foe. And if conflict intensifies whenever the prevailing rate of innovations and their diffusion among (or the tempo of erosion and its spread within) actors has seemed to accelerate the flow of time, it will grow even more intense when the disposable space shrinks simultaneously because the incumbent, having preempted much by prior appropriation, would substitute norms for arms in protecting it all against redistribution.

Affecting the incidence and intensity of conflicts more tangibly, but less uniformly for all (continental and maritime) types of actors than does either the space-and-time factor or the actor-to-arena proportion, is the economic dimension, likewise subject to expansion and contraction. This happens as the more narrowly gauged economic transactions and processes condition the more broadly defined frameworks of politico-strategic perceptions and responses substantively, although with a less determinate impact than the longer-hatched material capability foundations of particular actors and deterioration-prone conditions in the actors-encompassing "world" economy.

An expansionist phase of an economic cycle within a country or the system-wide economy, or only an initial movement out of economic contraction, ought logically to end political depression and may well in particular instances actually translate into offensive politico-military initiatives, if only thanks to the functional-technological innovations associated with the economic recovery. Alternately, economic contraction can increase the time-related pressure on exploiting a waning capacity and translate gradually into hard-to-resist domestic pressures for hacking one's way out of the tightening material enmeshment, especially if attended by geostrategic encirclement. The state of the expansion–contraction cycle is less likely to be knowingly perceived in time by the directing or policy-making personnel than be merely filtered through diffuse moods affecting domestic group dynamics, with inevitable if variable time lags. In neither case will economic conditions inducing optimism or dejection, adventurousness or restraint, in and of themselves cause hegemonial conflicts. The conditioning role of a fluctuating economic ambience in deepening or easing psychopolitical pressures, and of economic conjunctures in augmenting or curtailing militarily usable resources, will translate into the sense of greater possibility to act decisively or necessity to act preventively. But such factors are more likely to influence the timing of climactic encounters than determine their incidence between parties disposed to conflict by more basic or more varied – including ostensibly trivial – considerations. The economic conjuncture, including commercial rivalry and industrial competition, will influence the ways actors interpret and evaluate structurally induced and functionally or sociopolitically intensified crises and resulting contingencies. Only when economic pressures have become sufficiently acute to threaten internal stability, without undercutting regime capacity to act forcefully abroad, will economic factors do more. They will stop shaping the preliminaries to conflict by affecting actor predispositions and actually surface as the precipitant of conflict by converting general dispositions into specific decisions. However, even then will the economic dimension figure in the evolution of the international system only as a factor in fueling the crises mediated through conflicts, and one apt to determine less often or visibly the onset than the outcome of a conflict through the effect it will have had on military performance.

For the longer or shorter cycles of economic expansion or contraction and the attendant conjunctures to be causally related to a hegemonial conflict, they must be operationally related to a readily perceptible structure of power and its configuration. One such situation involved seventeenth-century Netherlands as the former leader in world economy and nineteenth-century France as a power receding from continental preeminence. Both were parties to the small or regional western politico-economic triangle, including next to England also France in the first and Germany in the second case. It was their economic preoccupations, compensating for political decline, that affected the contests between the two main parties to the coincident politico-military global triangle most, if indirectly and unevenly, while each acted as the actual or potential junior ally of the (British) incumbent. The latter, in adjusting his militant involvement with the challenger (first France, subsequently Germany), had to continually monitor the junior party's assessments of the often conflicting requirements of economic prosperity and physical security. On his part, if more markedly so for the Dutch than for the politically revisionist French, the junior partner would be tempted to constrain the senior ally by engaging him in economic competition in disregard of longer-term security needs, hold him back from military engagement for fear of the economic gains the lesser ally would make by remaining neutral, or even propel him toward embracing military conflict as an alternative to deepening economic maladjustments removing the junior party wholly as a viable partner. In either case, the direct operational impact of economic conditions and considerations by way of a secondary actor (the junior-ally party to the lesser triangle) within the key politico-military relationship was but one example of the ultimately conditioning material given being overtly causative only at second remove or on issues of secondary importance.

In its limitations, the role of the economic has paralleled that of institutional and narrowly diplomatic factors materializing in alliances and alignments. They too, rather than determine anything, derive from more fundamental conditions and tendencies, regardless of whether they are formally offensive or defensive and their purpose is to aggregate capabilities against an ascendant rival or restrain an ally's adventurous reactions to decline.* Alliances cause conflict least when they precede a conflict that is viewed as impending, because desirable or unavoidable; nor do they necessarily prevent a conflict when deferring its onset,

---

* For more on this and alliances generally, see my *Nations in Alliance: The Limits of Interdependence* (Baltimore: The Johns Hopkins University Press, 1962, 1968).

if postponement merely accumulates pressures by polarizing adversaries. Thus (somewhat like economic contingencies) alliances do commonly no more than shape the circumstances under which, and the intervals at which, competitive relationships erupt – and, then, on what scale of intensity as near-continuous yields to intermittent but intensified violence as part of the system itself evolving. The but narrowly autonomous momentum of alignments will influence more the actual course of a conflict, toward its being expanded or limited; and intra-alliance dynamics will help determine whether a conflict continues too long or ceases in time to favor the chances of post-conflict re-equilibration.

All this applied in the hegemonial contexts to alliances designed to be offensive and alliances designated as defensive: in the first group France's with Cromwellian England against a Spain about to forfeit the last vestiges of preeminence preceded one with Prussia (or Austria) and Bourbon Spain against ascendant England allied with Austria (or Prussia); in the other, France's alliance with Russia prefigured Britain's ententes with both. Although nominally defensive coalitions came to be gradually preferred as normatively superior to offensive combinations, they proved equally provocative of conflict when they inhibited rising capability from being deployed so as to bring in adequate dividends. Consequently, while tempting opportunities were yielding to immediate pressures or deferred predicaments as key incentives to alliances and stimuli of conflict, the implied evolution has at the most increased the gap between extant capabilities and corrective concessions that was required to trigger a conflagration.

6
Matrix and Manifestations of Progression

Conflicts in general and hegemonial conflicts in particular transpose energy flows originating in crises into more determinate outcomes. The mechanism which processes energy is itself conditioned by the overall environment within which it takes place. The total matrix has a less directly determining effect on behavior than do perceptions of vital geostrategic interests, manifest capability trends, or even discernible economic pressures or opportunities. However, all these are reflected or comprised in a matrix which, in its fictional entirety, is only derivative and its effect merely conditioning. It engenders an atmosphere and inflects attitudes and propensities rather than distilling imperatives for action because it represents a moment in the ongoing crystallization of disparately impacting tendencies. Being all this, so much and so little, just as crises feed into conflicts and conflicts exacerbate crises, so the fact that the matrix is only the more active and differently articulated side of evolution's manifestations completes the interlocking relationship of the facets which constitute, together, the evolutionary dynamic in its complex totality.

Just as it is difficult-to-impossible to clearly differentiate factors that constitute the setting of evolution and which denote the latter's course, so it is futile to sharply differentiate factors that inhere in the actors and those pertaining to the arena. The former will, in one way or another, impinge on or denote the actors' rise and decline as part of their evolutionary progression (or regression); the latter's corresponding movement will occur in terms of different kinds of expansion and contraction, attended by either the fact or the mere impression of qualitative progress (or relapse). As for the rise and decline of actors, they display long-term (evolutionary) features with organic characteristics, outwardly manifest in sequences of foreign-policy postures of the major actors and of salient actor-types over the lifetime of a system; and they exhibit short-term (interactional) features of an operational character, which encompass beyond factors that make up the vertical rise–decline axis also and more directly those that constitute the horizontal plane of action and reaction as part of power-balancing. And, just as the actor-related features and facets interplay among themselves, so do they with the arena-related ones (responsible for expansion and contraction) in a process of reciprocal conditioning. Too complex to dissect and delineate more than suggestively, the process is, however, too intrinsic to the environing matrix of evolution and its outward manifestations to be ignored in favor of either superficially only-operational or one-factor organic features, be the former procedural or the latter material, institutional, or normative.

ACTOR GENERATIONS AND PHASED ACTION IN THE BALANCE OF POWER

Phased foreign policy postures of key actors punctuate their rise (from expansive through the consolidative to the exuberant posture), their maturity (conservative posture) and eventual decline (compulsive self-assertion, recidivist regression, and withdrawal). Conjointly, any specific configuration of such postures – their composition and uneven incidence – constitutes a significant facet of the matrix within which the system evolves while denoting the stage of evolution it has reached. The mediating link between actor- and arena-related stages of development are competitive interactions associated with the balance of power, the core dynamic of interstate relations which is itself subject to development as a progressively rationalized mode of operations. Over time, finally, the operations are in turn paralleled not only by the parties' progressive consolidation but also, if less conspicuously, by a succession of distinctive types of actors as individual states advance to tone-setting function and representational position concurrently with passing through a foreign-policy phase and posture broadly suggestive of the ascendant power's distinctive peculiarity.

Thus, France began her ascent to the position of typological primacy, as distinct from (though potentially connected with) role-status paramountcy, while still in the expansive foreign-policy phase. The actor dispositions and systemic setting associated with that phase coincided closely with the characteristics of the sacral–military monarchy, the first-generation actor-type in Europe as, before, in other systems. The relatively objectless expansionism the policy posture implements was in no way contrary to the non-rational and myth-saturated approach to existence fostered by rain-dependent agriculture, one conducive to anxieties engendered equally by nature's unpredictable effect on the fertility of the soil and universe's mysterious hierarchy extending beyond the earth to heavenly supernature. The condition favored fluidly ranked roles of priesthood and kingship to overlap in the propitiatory function as the sacral component of the medieval monarchy's basic constitution, while the alternately protective and predatory performance of the warrior in relation to agriculturally exploitable territory accounted for its military component.

Thus even better than the Holy Roman Empire, increasingly oriented toward its territorial foundation, did France's essence and existence illustrate through her holy kings the attempt to overcome the deepening schism between the sacral and the secular, well before England as the next tone-setting power type would *qua* balancer pretend to the arbitral function once claimed by the Papacy. For the essentially secular, naval-maritime and mercantile-colonial, power to become the prominent actor-type reflected the shift from soil to a wider basis of sustenance and from nature to active nurture; from religio-political mystique to the rational character of commercial exchanges as they expanded from local to long-distance and shifted from overland to transoceanic routes. The need to give free rein to individual initiatives in support of such exchanges coincided with the characteristics of the exuberant foreign-policy posture, which in fact propelled England to typological primacy; nor was the need to both implement and constrain the attendant functional differentiation and consequent socio-political pluralism less accurately expressed in an oligarchical form of government, ideally suited to manage the country's transition to a conservatively power-balancing posture and implement it through coalition diplomacy.

Having replaced the alliance of throne and altar with that of landed with mercantile interests at home, England's oligarchy had next to confront a recombination of the traditional factors abroad. This happened when the effort to telescope a foreign-policy posture directed to territorial consolidation with an atypically state-backed exuberance abroad, prematurely displaying compulsively expansionist features, become typical of late-entering powers. The combination became manifest in the third generation actor-type: one intent on synthesizing the characteristics of the two preceding types in an ideologically (i.e., quasi-sacrally) supported fusion of land-based military and ocean-related naval and mercantile orientation. When the powers of the first generation were staging their second and terminal, compulsively expansionist, bid for hegemony in an effort to retain (Spain of Philip IV) or reacquire (Napoleonic France) primacy, they had prefigured this type whose main characteristics (late tsarist) Russia began developing and (Wilhelmine) Germany began assuming conjointly with an initially more moderate challenge. Reflecting the attempted synthesis in the war-related sphere was then a combination of radically augmented fire-power for increasingly mobile-motorized (replacing horse-mounted or -driven) land-based force with technologically upgraded commerce-supporting and/or -raiding naval capability. Backing the two branches was an authoritarian management of the economy that stopped at first short of the oriental-despotic system's tendency to neglect when not penalizing foreign trade, and to substitute for both hierarchy and oligarchy a polarity separating slave-like agents and enslaved subjects from the effectively tyrannical or only titular despot. Some of these traits, responsible for the tendency to alternate between degeneration and attempted renovation, centralized coercion and deconcentrated conflict, in lieu of converting periodic dissolution into continuous development, were to impinge on the European scene only marginally in terms of both space (from the east) and time (as a transitional phenomenon) in Nazi and Soviet totalitarianisms when they denatured the third-generational power type by exacerbating its defining traits.

By contrast, oriental-despotic attributes had been prominent in earlier state systems as they underwent the generational sequence. It first unfolded from the quasi-feudal charioteer-based monarchy of the Iranian plateau and theocratic polities in early Mesopotamia and Old-Kingdom Egypt, by way of the typological ascendancy of commercial sea powers in places such as Crete and Syria–Palestine (with offshoots in Carthage and links to later imperial Egypt), to the third-generation would-be synthesis in the guise of amphibian "totalitarians" in Mesopotamia (thus Assyria, Persia). Thereafter, more than any other single power's, Rome's development telescoped the inter-generational transition from beginnings in religio-political kingship (Pontifex Maximus), through Carthage-imitating and -subduing maritimized republic, to the orientalized continental-naval and authoritarian-to-totalitarian empire (deified Emperors). However, the pattern to become fully manifest in Europe had by then been anticipated also in the Greek system's evolution from the Homeric kingship, through seafaring Hellenic city-state, to Hellenistic monarchy, and was to be resumed in the post-Roman Italian micro-system as the Lombard or Frankish model of kingship was superseded by the Florence- and Venice-type oligarchical city-state before the two actor-types were synthesized in the Spain-dominated parts of Italy.

Just as the successive power types organized internal power relationships in ways peculiar to them, so they influenced the development of the inter-actor balance of power over the lifetime of a state system. In the European instance, salience of the increasingly secular (if residually theocratic) and mainly land-based (if in position or function peripherally naval) first-generation actors coincided with consolidating the innermost core of the balance of power dynamic, as one primitively enacted through one principal party opposing defensively one overassertive party (thus France, England, and France again, checkmating imperialist Habsburg universalism in succession). Thereafter, the second-generation actor-type was decisive in introducing a more deliberately manipulative mode into a plural coalition-type response to balance-disruptive behavior on the continent. The final impetus, in response to the implied effort to segment the system into operationally discrete continental and oceanic sectors, originated with the third-generation power type. Its key incumbents contributed to globalizing the balance of power system, as part of a bid to assimilate the oceanic to the continental theater, and to homogenizing the system within Europe, in function of the incumbents' relatively eastern identity. The inter-generational succession was, thus, only coincident with, or also responsible for, the expansion of the balance of power dynamic: in terms of the range of simultaneously involved major players, encompassed theaters and resources, and the range and variety of transactional techniques and ideocultural values subject to rationalization – all these compounding an expanding scope with heightening intensity.

In registering this effect, the inter-generational sequence mirrored the more direct impact of sequentially ordered basic foreign-policy postures. Thus, a widespread incidence of the expansive variety of early-formative posture was consistent with a relatively low intensity of near-continuous conflicts. This was liable to expand the territorial sphere of largely nominal control by dissolution-prone actors more certainly than increase the rates of conclusive inter-actor transactions in the (proto-) system. A subsequent prevalence of the next-in-line posture, aimed at consolidating a viable habitat, tended to augment the number of effective players at the core through high-intensity conflicts more certainly than enlarge the physical expanse of the system. Conversely, peripherally manifest exuberant posture would reduce intensity to an intermediate level between the preceding extremes and enlarge once more the system's physical-spatial arena rather than augmenting actor plurality. The conservative posture is apt to become widespread conjointly with late entry of new and the incipient decline of initial actors, both events tending to restructure the hierarchy in the central system. Whether the system boundary expands and in function of what degree of conflict intensity will depend on whether the conservatively stability-related constraining, or the compulsively descent-resistant galvanizing, features predominate in a situation that displays a maximum variety of postures and is fraught with terminal bids for hegemony. Withdrawal of previously key actors would in and of itself constrict the system territorially as well as contract it transactionally. But it will add new to earlier incentives for previously peripheral actors to enter the system, even as intense conflicts tend to concentrate in areas subject to the decline-wrought vortex effect before spreading and escalating into end-of-system convulsion.

Much as the way the balance of power operates at any one time is conditioned by the manner in which the sequential foreign-policy postures of the salient types of actors are configured in space, it is no less the case that any one particular posture will more or less coherently aggregate strategic intentions that respond to more immediately perceivable specific interests reflecting the material capabilities of individual actors. Although capabilities can and do rise or decline absolutely, in comparison with their antecedent state, it is their standing and the trends relative to only comparable or also competing powers that matter more. In a situation characterized by flux, hardest to assess and maintain is a safely stable, stationary condition. The condition nearest to it is realized when growth has slowed down, but is still sufficient to preclude significant backsliding. However, inasmuch as power is relative, such a "stationary" condition is apt to be the product of delayed perception or outright misperception of ongoing trends. In either case, the operationally significant facet of material, managerial, and moral rise-and-decline will be the reflection of either in specific strategies. Coalescing into a foreign-policy posture broadly consonant with the actor's position in the rise–decline trajectory, such strategies are intended to relate essentially constant general objectives of security, internal stability, and status to more particular but likewise traditional goals affecting critical antagonists and vital assets.

Reflecting capability-related states or conditions will be approaches that are more or less direct or indirect, unilaterally coercive or oriented toward suasion within multi-actor diplomatic constellations or cooperative frameworks. Thus France's constant aim of security on her eastern (or Rhine) frontier was approached at various times by bids to detach and annex cis-Rhenish areas, attempts to dominate trans-Rhenish parts of Germany by means of unequal associations against farther-eastern German parties, and initiatives favoring close institutional cooperation or functional integration with all or most of Germany. Similarly evolving in mode while constant in basic motive was

England's approach to the control of or only access to the Low Countries, beginning with economic devices (the wool staple), escalating to politico-military methods, and finally subsiding again to (free-market) economic techniques and institutions.

The relatively more coercive modes denote upward trends on the rise–decline curve while revealing foreign-policy propensities keyed to expansively effected consolidation; the more cooperative modes suggest relative decline and reveal concern with conserving essentials at lowered cost when not also camouflaging regression short of withdrawal. If, in the process, the specific policies produce the more conspicuous events, the phased foreign-policy postures they implement disclose more conclusively some of the subjacent givens of interstate relations. The situation harbors a paradox. The organic growth of a power from within is not a legitimate ground for mechanical counterbalancing responses in the classic theory of the balance of power; yet no explanation of state behavior is complete if it ignores, and no such behavior is successful if it mismanages, the interplay of the organic properties with the mechanical process. And again, although the interplay is constant and fundamental, the relationship is not altogether equal. Organic rise-and-decline dynamic is the more original or independent factor and impels balance-of-power operations materially in the last resort; mechanical checking and balancing tends merely to marginally foster rise or ease decline, tempering the consequences of one or the other.

As shown by the reactions to the growth of, say, Milan in Italy and of France in Europe impinging on Italy, the balancing response is most automatic and effective when addressing the spectacular rise of an actor in the segment of the system that immediately surrounds it, if not necessarily beyond. Less straightforward, instinctive and effective, are responses to a steep or abrupt decline of one or more powers. They will nonetheless repeatedly entail either a major realignment within the immediately affected orbit or the mobilization of capabilities previously outside it, lest a severe and uncompensated erosion of power create greater dangers than its hypertrophy can. However, the fact that the capacity of balancing realignments to reduce and retard a subsiding actor's losses in role and status does not extend to precluding the inescapable material consequences of decline was demonstrated again and again – thus, in modern Europe, to Spain and the Dutch when they joined anti-French coalitions. By the same token, the balancing mechanism could only facilitate, and did not generate, the material ascent of an actor when implemented through allocating subsidies to a marginally most useful lesser ally and conceding war gains to a least threatening fellow-victor. Prussia was thus enhanced beyond what her rulers were able to do for themselves, first by the grace of the king of France and subsequently at his expense. But she also exemplified the fact that conferral of enhanced status may but need not translate into a corresponding role. Whereas the bestowal of kingship as a reward for joining the enemies of Louis XIV (in the War of Spanish Succession) was a milestone on Prussia's road to effective greatness, Italy's progression to greatpower status that had begun with Savoy joining Russia's foes (in the Crimean War) was destined to stall midway. Finally, misguided balancing will commonly do no more than accelerate or consummate a decline that was already well advanced – thus when an Anglo–French alliance speeded up in the 1650s the decline of Spain only marginally; when beginning with the 1770s the western powers failed to countervail the eastern European powers' license to adjust the balance among themselves at the cost of a Poland already decisively weakened within; or when in the 1920s and early 1930s France pursued a lastingly impractical and immediately unnecessary balancing of power strategy against Weimar Germany.

Comparatively more independent, if potentially distorting, will be the effects of power-balancing responses to rise and decline that are premature or obsolete. Anticipating on either development will trigger excessive preemptive reactions, thus when, prior to 1914, Germany feared the irreversible rise of Russia and Britain exaggerated the consequences of France's weakening, as if either were imminent. By the same token, tradition-bred habits of mind, originating in an earlier period, will risk perpetuating once valid policies beyond their *raison d'être* and prove likewise unsettling. Such was the case when Britain continued to frustrate French ambitions in the Low Countries (and the Near East) in the 1830s and beyond, although France had definitely ceased to seriously threaten the continental equilibrium. For Britain to condone within more flexible limits the changing French regime's compulsive efforts to continue asserting itself was then needed to uphold the balance against powers, such as Prussia and Russia, waiting in the wings. More positive is the effect of the balance-of-power mechanism when it reduces stresses from rise and decline by helping expand the systemic arena's pool of reserve power or powers. This happens when cross-regional alliances link conflicts that were before only parallel, and integrate thus a so far peripheral regional into the central or overall system. Thus, beginning with the 1630s, alliances between or, alternately, centering on Sweden and France integrated the long autonomous "northern system" finally with the central or all-European arena. Or central-systemic powers can look for compensating reinforcements beyond so far peripheral actors to likewise situated material or demographic resources. Thus the assets that had stimulated Anglo–French overseas competition, which in turn helped contain the ascendancy of France in Europe, were eventually called upon to cushion France's decline relative to Germany.

When the balance-of-power mechanism is directly responsible for expanding the system, it comes closest to causing the rise of some and comparative decline of other individual actors, if only in role. As for the rise–decline dynamic itself, it may merely encourage institutionalizing (instead of actually impelling) the operation of equilibrium. This will happen when stationary powers in transition from relative rise to relative decline – thus Austria in early and Britain in later nineteenth century – have been moved to propagate the ideology of the balance of power (as "just equilibrium") and the related institutions ("concert of powers") as if they were policies-legitimating values independent of specific interests and objectives of the parties. When, instead, some kind of rigidity – thus at the height of religious ferment in the sixteenth century, nationalistic fanaticism in the nineteenth, and ideological zealotry in the twentieth – inhibits power-balancing because certain alliances appear more intolerable than the hypothetical consequences of their exclusion, the ensuing operational contraction of the system will augment stresses from both rise and decline.

In any event, organic rise-and-decline interacting with the action–reaction mechanics of the balancing process adds up to an inherently dynamic matrix. It prevents the system from being ever wholly static while impelling its being periodically restabilized after major disruptions, insofar as action–reaction transactions contain the extent (or only the effects) of relative growth and decline trends within margins sufficiently narrow to preclude any one power being aggrandized to the point of dwarfing all other powers. Stabilization will be smoothest when the relatively strongest power enjoys sufficient preeminence in role and status to serve as a focus for interactions, but is restrained in employing its capabilities aggressively, as are other, quantitatively near-equal, powers, when most of them deviate but moderately in either direction from the conservative foreign-policy posture characteristic of maturity.

Whereas hegemony signifies irresistible military capacity to coerce of an extraordinarily strong (preponderant or paramount) state, preeminence reflects the comparative inferiority, temporary infirmity, or progressing decline of other powers in resource-backed diplomatic role more than it conveys the surge of driving energy in what is but a quasi- or pseudo-hegemonial actor. Thus the French drive for a position to replace Spain's up to about the mid-point in the reign of Louis XIV was neither intended to translate nor capable of translating into continental, let alone combined continental–maritime, hegemony. So long as it lasted, mere preeminence rested on the war-weariness and exhaustion of both Spain and the Dutch, the Habsburg hereditary domains and the Empire, and on internal disorders in England, as much as it revealed the recovery of the French monarchy from the confessional feuds and the aristocratic Fronde. Conditions were similar when England wrested maritime supremacy from Spain and the Netherlands (after the latter had benefited by the transition from Spanish to French ascendancy) and combined it with a key role in the continental balance of power into European near- or phantom-hegemony. Notable among the weaknesses elsewhere were, next to the abrupt shrinkage of the Dutch maritime-mercantile range to fit its narrow territorial and naval-military base, France's continuing industrial and commercial backsliding and erratically fluctuating investment in naval proficiency, and the long absence of alternative challengers to the east or west.

Containing weaknesses such as these by a combination of one-power role-status preeminence and an approximate balance of activated and latent material capabilites will account more often and more reliably for periods of enduring peace than one-power preponderance by and of itself. However, even if quasi-hegemonial, preeminence will avoid eliciting disruptive challenge only so long as it is exercised moderately from adequate strength. Anything else will arouse the always latent reluctance of territorial actors to allow the prestige of another state to long outlive its power, or themselves to depend on another's revocable self-restraint for an irreducible measure of autonomy. As a result, no particular stability-sustaining preeminence will endure past its own support in bases that are both vitalistic (organic rise–decline) and behavioral or normative (operative practice in keeping with the imperatives of self-restraint and self-dependence).

Yet just as one actor's preeminence was erected on (or only highlighted by) the weaknesses of others, so the same weaknesses will prompt actions apt to provoke a bid for coercive dominance when, implementing the natural reluctance of states to see one power's effective role primacy depreciate their formal status equality into a legal fiction of little practical significance, they propel the preeminent power into offensively defensive reactions. Only when the preeminent power is also the superior maritime actor and can as such plausibly pose as rendering useful service on the seas, will the advantage be endured by others – and if by all except the continental challenger, in large part also because of the others' still stronger suspicion of the latter. This was Britain's long-lasting advantage over France to begin with, except for an interlude the French were able to exploit but briefly, and then on behalf of Britain's eventual successor.

When, reinforcing or replacing one-power preeminence, stability is on both behavioral and vitalistic grounds rooted in the phased foreign policy postures clustering within a narrow band around the conservative norm betokening maturity, enough effective capability will be dispersed in the system. This will prevent the system's disintegration by virtue of any one abruptly declining power pulling also other states into the turbulence set off by uncompensated erosion of capabilities, let alone permit an openly hegemonial drive by an ascending power. More than the eclipse of the Holy Roman Empire, because within a more firmly structured system, the decline of the Spanish Empire triggered such a turbulence in the form of major wars among would-be successors extending from the seventeenth to the eighteenth century. No such radical watershed was to be in evidence again before the uncompensated decadence of the western European democracies in the early twentieth century propelled a range of likewise abruptly rising powers into competition over shares in filling a widening vacuum of effective power.

During the period intervening between the two cataclysmic periods, the basic foreign policy dispositions of the great European powers were repeatedly diverse and complementary enough, within a sufficiently narrow band of divergence, to eschew both extremes: high-tension deadlock from converging drives of equally expansionist emergent powers, and high-turbulence dynamics of confrontation between unevenly declining "older" and ascendant "younger" powers, the former resisting withdrawal and the latter resenting denial. A major intermediate lull around the middle of the nineteenth century witnessed instead low-tension equilibrium interplays. Conservative foreign-policy tendencies, routinized in Britain and intermittently re-emerging in volatile France, dovetailed with the sequentially antecedent foreign-policy posture of the lagging Russian mass and sufficed to contain, separately or in combination, declining Austria's propensity to compulsive self-assertion. Concurrently, Prussia continued to oscillate between wider (European) and narrower (Germanic) frameworks within which to pursue a foreign policy that was latent with the prospect of consolidation setting off its more widely upsetting, exuberant, sequel later in the century.

Further easing the situation was the not unrelated fact of the continental–maritime schism being provisionally suspended while France was fading as the continental challenger and neither Russia nor Prussia–Germany was ready to replace her. In part as a result, the more flexible mid-nineteenth century equilibrium differed favorably from the tendency toward deadlock in the late eighteenth century, when neither of the expansionist global contestants, France and England, could bring both Austria and Prussia, aggressive rivals in and over the Germanic power balance, into the same alliance while an unpredictable Russia and unstable Spain were the only disposable significant weightmakers. Reinforcing the greater flexibility was the fact that neither the main geopolitical issue (over the Near Eastern Question) nor the ideological issue (liberalism versus conservatism; revolution versus reaction) nor any residual or artificially revived religious issue (intra-Catholic or Catholic–Protestant), could propel more than three out of the by then more unevenly matured principal powers into alignment against the remaining two powers. Moreover, the effect of any numerical or quantitative inequality between contrary alliances would be offset by the larger bloc's continuing cohesion being even more than the smaller one's dependent on keeping both goals and gains limited. Finally, the perennial dynamic of inter-allied relations that, supplemental to countervailing actions among adversaries, revolves around allies preventing each other from making disproportionate gains, was more than ever certain to continue operating in favor of balanced power distribution so long as powers were not rigidly polarized by a dominant, schism-related conflict.

ALTERNATING POLICY POSTURES AND FLUCTUATING POWER POTENTIALS

Unlike a more stressful balance of power, low-tension stability constitutes a matrix that temporarily slows down evolution because it dampens crises and limits conflicts. However, détente is also likely to foment instrumental innovations as actors search for (relatively unprovocative) advantage, and is liable to give rise to psychopolitical moods favorable to the discharge of replenished energies in the next evolutionary speed-up. Thus the lull starting in the 1820s began to erode and yielded to renewed intensity in the 1850s. Alternations in developmental tempo due to changes in the balancing process demarcate thus comparatively brief periods within the complete evolutionary process. This enhances the importance for the longer term of the more basic discontinuities in successive foreign-policy postures and actor-type generations. These disclose, against the background of conditions obtaining at the outset of a (proto-) system, changes over the full range of more particular factors, including material capabilities and domestic structures.

Prior to their consolidation all major actors-to-be experience in their initial formative phase the objectlessly expansive moment. Thus, the policies of the early (Ottonian and Hohenstaufen) Holy Roman Emperors, the medieval English kings pursuing feudal-dynastic aims in France, or the French rulers and their retinue propelled by a fusion of ideal and pragmatic motives into the Holy Land were, on more limited local bases, replicated by the Kievan or Novgorodian forces fanning out in pre-Mongol Rus' or the Iberian ones in pre-conquest Spain. The fact that they all – and, *mutatis mutandis*, actors in other times and places – pursued far-reaching ends with inadequate and fragile means produced false starts for both the actors and the system. And since the domestic orders lack structure at that point, and implementing agents lack resources, a transcendently rooted sanction will be commonly called upon to sustain mundane authority more effectively than either an effective control machinery can from the center or a balanced sociopolitical pluralism does at the base. Norms of behavior are often conflicting for the same reason, thus when feudal associations compete with geopolitically prompted alignments, a barely emerging instrumental rationality of the "laws of power" is challenged by the normative rationality of "natural law," and confessional imperatives rival those rooted in a nascent sense of distinctive nationality. If each and all of the stimuli are little apt to guide – impel or constrain – behavior unequivocally, so is the still uncrystallized configuration of significant capabilities (power) and dominant conflicts (polarities). The consequence is an inter-actor structure that is porous in kind and permissive in effect. Goals of foreign policy are far-fetched also because the prizes are typically remote from the home base while internally dissolvent effects of overexertion or overextension, more than countervailing responses to concentrated threats, safeguard the autonomy of (lesser) actors or the elementary stability of the (proto-) system. With confusion causing convulsions, and vice versa, disparity between ends and means must achieve the nearest equivalent of what parity between force and counter-force does in farther-evolved settings, and mostly will protect the proto-system from premature extinction by the strongest actor.

Largely lacking in concrete or lasting achievement, the early agitation was nonetheless a potent source of energy inflows in, first, western Europe after the ninth-century inroads from the peripheries. Crises and conflicts propelled future actors toward an evolutionary takeoff from elements left behind by anterior false starts, ranging from the fifth-century Theodorician five-power "system" to the Carolingian imperial realm. The urge to consolidate viable habitats by targeting achievable goals close to the home base was succeeding by the late fifteenth century in response to escalating troubles of one kind or another. Just as the early Tudors were emerging in England out of the combined effects of continental forays and the Wars of the Roses, so Louis XI in France was consummating prior efforts interspersed with crusades and interrupted by the Hundred Years War, and Ferdinand and Isabella in Spain were concluding the reconquest from Islam. Eastern Europe had been long held back by the need for dynastically improvised ensembles in responses to more massive invasions. But, there too, Russia was starting under Ivans III and IV on the long road from under the Mongol sway to consolidation, while Charles V resumed in the west for the last time in earnest the vain effort to extend to the shadowy Holy Roman Empire the benefits and costs of consolidation, before the mixed blessing finally settled on the Empire's constituent parts.

By the time consolidation has become the main object of foreign policy, a both centralized and centralizing authority strains perforce toward internal monopoly from a moral-political basis resting on former competitors having been subdued while the only emerging future domestic challengers can be manipulatively contained. The authority's material basis is its capacity, no longer shared or to be shared, to secure the funds necessary for combining essential internal performance with inherently feasible urgent external tasks. The power to tax combines with access to credit from abroad (witness the "international" bankers financing Charles V) while periodic bankruptcies slow down and occasionally becalm the ship of state, but are no longer sufficient to sink it for good. Legal doctrines or fictions that supplement the still but narrow sociopolitical foundation of stability, and the checks on excess implicit in a still slender material base, are now matched by an emerging doctrine and practice of the reason of state. The latter gradually supplants residual admixtures of transcendent ideal norms, be they particularist-feudal or either sacrally or temporally universalist, even if not yet eliminating in all places the transnationally dynastic ones. The structure of the system tends simultaneously to reinforce the other grounds for the "normal" scope of foreign-policy objectives being limited and their site proximate. Weaknesses within the immediate orbit of the consolidating actor, susceptible of exploration if not exploitation, coincide with inhibitions due to the advancing crystallization in the system's inner core (a function of the major actor not being the only one to consolidate), just as consolidation being yet incomplete has diminished the attractiveness of remote or peripheral prizes. A contentious polarity between two relatively most powerful actors had by then typically evolved out of an effective, crystallization-triggering, response to the prior emergence of one of them. It will offer limited opportunities while implying additional constraints for any third power or powers (e.g. the Franco–Habsburg contest's on the England of Henry VIII), reducing their vaster pretensions to only declaratory significance.

The posture keyed to consolidation shapes the major territorial blocks for constructing a balanced hierarchy of powers, after the phase of undirected expansiveness revealed the impossibility to stabilize a larger order on the basis of sporadic one-actor resistance to transiently inflated power or by virtue of the liability of oversized power to self-dissolve. The balance-of-power mechanism takes off into self-sustaining development only when the accumulated capability and compressed energy of consolidated major actors are channeled into the next, the exuberant variety of expansionism, motivated and modulated differently from the initially formative one. It will galvanize the so far crystallized core system and expand its scope directly, as well as indirectly by virtue of counterbalancing responses that will gradually link the central with previously peripheral or subordinate sectors. When this happens, a sustained ascent along the vertical rise–decline axis by one or several powers is conjoined with a substantial horizontal expansion of the action–reaction dynamic. The conjunction will mark, through major and often enduring alignments, the first major turning point in the longer-term evolution of the system.

It is through exuberant expansionism's effect on the system, as much as through the kind of internal resource development that has made the posture possible, that the post-consolidation differs from the earlier, objectless variety of expansive policy while incorporating some of its features. Thus when the newly disciplined chivalry of a revitalized French monarchy careered into Italy under Charles VIII, the drive conjugated the resources assembled by Louis XI with the older claims of the junior branches or offshoots of the dynasty, in pursuit of glory and greed inextricably commingled behind the screen of a rationalization (the crusade) borrowed from an earlier age. More substantial in both kind and consequence than the broadly resisted French continental foray was to be the overseas drive of the Elizabethans, only to gather additional momentum from territorial consolidation with Scotland and religious consolidation under the Protestant succession. It collided ever more successfully with the anterior expansion of an early Habsburg Spain that had carried the combined Aragonese Mediterranean and Castile's Atlantic vocations farther afield by the addition of the Low Countries and Portugal. The compounded result was to extend world-wide a European balance of power previously enlarged by absorbing the Italian theater and to be completed by adding fully operationalized systemic to the earlier economic incorporation of the northern or Baltic arena.

Central authority retains the monopoly of control over official policy in this phase, but ever more diversified (including private) agents function as exploratory spearheads of the government in compensation for being repressed or exerting self-restraint domestically. The central authority has the ability to either control or generate much of the material resource used for supporting non- or para-official initiatives, before taking over their products. However, this capacity is not yet matched by the means needed to absorb the extra-governmental energies in long-term tasks of internal development. And although domestic stability does rest on the expanding base of plural socio-political and economic-interest groups, it is critically reinforced by the multiplying of outlets for their energies. By the same token, the resources garnered at large complement usefully the increase in capabilities which, wrought internally, triggered the earlier transition to the exuberant foreign-policy posture. Thus, whereas the French magnates and princes of the blood who spearheaded France's descent into Italy in search of a feudal-type establishment had prefigured the crucial role of Genoese navigators, financiers, and traders in Spain's expansion across the Atlantic, England's chartered companies were to be more effective than either when succeeding to privateers in linking private pursuits to public purposes. However, in grafting speculation on statecraft, they also re-enacted the effort to marry rapine to religion pioneered by the crusading conquerors of independent dominions in the Near East and eastern Europe. Public control over private initiative fits at this stage the external setting of progressing crystallization and constraint at the center of the system and expanding openings into vacua of power or vulnerable would-be monopolies in the outer peripheral zone. Para-official parties or groups are socialized into the political system all the more easily, the more the larger system is segmented, and the more readily energies constrained at home or at the system's core can flow into areas of lower pressure and less resistance in response to manifest opportunity or in recoil from insurmountable repression.

Many factors contribute to the self-liquidating dynamism's subsidence into yet another opposite in the cyclical rhythm of expansion–consolidation–re-expansion. The very spontaneity of exuberant expansionism makes it difficult to orchestrate non-governmental initiative and governmental control more than precariously and adjust private resources to far-reaching enterprises indefinitely. But the significant changes attending evolution from the initial expansive to later exuberant patterns are again in evidence when consolidating individual actors gives way to an analogous objective for the arena, as an incident to preserving the actor's previous achievements. When the "conservative" foreign-policy posture marks the mid-life phase in the evolution of major actors, it completes the prior development of the balance-of-power mechanism on a system-wide basis before depending on it for support. This is so despite the fact that only insular Britain realized fully the norm of the pro-equilibrium policy phase in relatively smooth succession from the preceding policy orientation and in conformity with the simultaneously evolving structure of the state system; and that she did so only when the mid-eighteenth-century Hanoverian succession (building on the William-and-Mary interlude) welded once again politically critical domestic requirements with system-related incentives in forging ties to the continent, albeit in a form very different from the medieval-feudal link. As for the other and more authentically founding members of the European system, the Holy Roman Empire had never reached the phase; a succession of French regimes, beginning with the waning ancien regime as it approached financial bankruptcy, attempted the critical transition only inter-mittently and then half-heartedly (all the way to the interwar Third Republic); and Spain was only briefly and inconclusively poised on the verge of a conservative policy during the brief period of Philip III's "peace policy" between the first and the second hegemonial bids (under Philips II and IV, respectively).

One reason for the rarity is in the fact that for counterbalancing others for equilibrium to work on a sustained basis and from strength, an increasingly complex interplay of multiplying political factions or economic interest coalitions within a rapidly developing domestic pluralism, peculiar to an insular maritime-mercantile polity, is crucial. Domestic political stability is now more firmly rooted in the expanded sociopolitical breadth and depth, but requires increasingly delicate adjustments among the rival groups to shield its fruits. The paradox, if any, is replicated insofar as "national" capabilities have reached an overall peak on the rise–decline curve and can be but laboriously maintained there even as internal claims on resources grow at a higher rate than the resources continue to be generated, while the diversifying sociopolitical structure induces government to expand its functions conformably, if often reluctantly. It will accordingly require an overt foreign crisis to activate the requisite quota of the available resource potential for use abroad, revitalize any surviving ethos in favor of the primacy of foreign-policy concerns, and bring into the open the security mandate of a central authority that is normally subject to the increased complexity of the internal power structure, the prudential mind-set of policy makers, and the deadweight of foreign-policy traditions deriving from past dealings with often only seemingly identical or comparable conflict issues.

Likewise paradoxical is the fact that the increasing self-assertion of an ever greater range of social and political forces within a matured actor (e.g. Great Britain) due to their growing stronger, is apt to coincide at this stage perversely with the relative decline of a growing number of the system's founding or original members (e.g. Spain, France, Austria). Their waning will be attended by reactive self-assertion as they recede within the system core concurrently with the surfacing of previously peripheral actors into major-power status (e.g. Russia, Germany, pending Japan and the United States). If, in this setting, it has become necessary to uphold the inherited doctrine of foreign-policy primacy to reserve control over policy for an authority that has become internally too responsive even when not yet constitutionally responsible, previously saturated parties will propound new ideologies of "legitimacy" and "just equilibrium" as part of "concert" in order to both mute the natural propensities and supplement the slackening potencies at work in the actual balancing of raw capabilities. Formulating the balance-of-power universe ideologically will usefully enhance its role in saving face for actors that are increasingly inclined to compromise interests but have not yet forfeited the ability to exert and expend force. As the international system continues to crystallize at its own evolutionary mid-point within an expanding scope, the significance of peripheral vacua of power that have fostered outflows of excess energy will be exceeded by the impact of capabilities that erode at the original center and capabilities that only grow or also erupt operationally outside it: peripheral outlets will be overshadowed by outward diffusion of power from the center. A tightening connection between the center of the system and the regional arenas will match that between domestic pluralism and central authority: just as control by domestic authority is precarious but ultimately effective, so the results of inter-actor balancing will be uncertain from time to time. However, they will not be finally and fatally flawed in a system that is not only multipolar but also pluri-generational, not only regionally segmented within a broadly hierarchical structure but also organically layered in terms of uneven developmental stages.

Significant for the operation of the balance of power when it besets a growing number of parties, decline is critical for the foreign-policy posture of any one actor that is markedly receding, or is about to recede, in relation to ostensibly stationary or actually rising powers – and, therefore, to the aggregate fund or averaged-out mean of capabilities available in the system. The consequent, compulsively defensive–offensive effort is to have activity abroad compensate for only waning or severely depleted material capabilities and collective psychic energies. The effort will differ from previous forms of self-assertion, be it the unfocused pre-consolidation expansiveness, which can conduce to transient status parity at the most, or the more spontaneous post-consolidation exuberance, which can produce a more substantially resource-supported preeminence in role as well as status before being routinely institutionalized in the conservative phase. By contrast with both, and depending on the levels of supporting resources and incurred frustration, the compulsively induced and manifest last instance of aggressive expansionism will set off disturbances ranging from only local or regional turbulence to a final bid for system-wide dominance. If the pressures that propel the extreme bid and are exacerbated by it grow as the challenger's mobilizable potential becomes more precarious, the resulting confrontation will escalate as the challenger's desperation deepens concurrently with the rising determination of the opposing coalition to frustrate the bid.

Given its character, the compulsively expansionist policy will be all the more forceful the more the conservative posture of one or more contemporaries has solidified systemic constraints. And the revolt will occur earlier in the evolution of an actor, as well as being more intense, if his own conservative phase was brief and the posture had proved barren – thus, for the first but not last time in modern Europe, when the last stand of Counter-Reformation Spain under the *valido* of Philip IV followed upon the vain efforts of the preceding ruler's favorite to appease the system from waning strength. By contrast, compulsive self-assertion may alternate with returns to behavior more typical of the pro-equilibrium stance when the mature policy has been insufficiently sustained internally and sustaining externally. Such was France's case, only beginning with the revolutionary-to-Napoleonic reaction to the disappointing results of late ancien-regime equilibrium policy. And compulsive re-expansion will set in late and be relatively mild when the conservative phase was lengthy and successful enough to help the attendant diffusion of power ease the travail of descent from supremacy. This was the case of late nineteenth- and early twentieth-century British overseas imperialism, when prosecuted under the auspices of social-Darwinian ideology and with backing from internationally radical conservatives and reactionary liberals. The Spanish model was eventually to catch up with late-entering Germany in the guise of the policies of the Third Reich, when the severity of the World War I defeat and its consequences had definitively derailed what would have been the "correct" sequence, from no more than consolidation under Bismarck to moderately successful exuberance under Wilhelm and on to conditions conferring on the successor regime a fair chance to implement the conservative posture.

Compulsive self-assertion abroad will only coincide with attempts or will actually implement the urge to overcome internal checks on the use of diminishing resources. When the constraints are due to sociopolitical pluralism and managerial bureaucratic pragmatism – a condition typical of the later conservative phase – the internal reactions are apt to be relatively mild and so will be the locally confined external ones. When the maturity phase has been aborted or bypassed, attendant internal crises will tend to have contributed to only atomizing or also polarizing the popular base. The result will be to project to the top an authority that seeks in a socially mobilizing extremist ideology the support for more radical external remedies. Latent strains are then apt to be contained in a quasi-total or even totalitarian stability, just as material shortcomings are disguised by ostensibly total mobilization of human resources.

A similarly absolute governmental control is contingent on visible progress toward achieving objectives affirmed as vital in the face of alternatives perceived as life-threatening; it will begin to erode under the impact of setbacks and collapse quickly before the evidence of failure. The corresponding tension within the larger inter-actor system will be between irreducible reason-of-state norms and either conflictually slanted "irrational" or restraint-rationalizing liberal or pacific ideologies, each more potent rhetorically than motivationally at different stages of the unfolding drama, and both centering on the issue of the legitimate scope of forcefully pursued goals of policy. The extent of normative-ideological polarization will depend on the degree to which a system-dominant conflict has cleft in two the heterogeneous composite of diverse foreign policy postures while ever more peripheral powers are inching along their evolutionary trajectory toward the center stage in function of strife forms ranging from local and limited conflicts to hegemony-related confrontation. As the recurrently bemusing impression of a permissive setting is again and again belied in a constraining structure, an atmosphere of unpredictability pervades an arena visibly prone to chronic instability in the very midst of efforts to re-establish lastingly its opposite.

The compulsively expansionist posture represents an actor's effort to retain or recover a significant role in a system the structure of which still (and for the last time) influences the transition from one foreign policy phase to another critically. The next and terminal posture, of gradual withdrawal pointing toward self-isolation, signals acceptance of the fact that no substitute for effective self-help can lastingly pacify or fundamentally transform the system in its entirety. Common and natural for only briefly "major" lesser powers such as Portugal, Sweden, and the Netherlands, which had risen meteorically for mostly accidental reasons only to be felled precipitously when normalcy reasserted itself, the posture marks a traumatizing finis to a prolonged career for a major power. Thus Spain's regression into only sporadically or locally interrupted passivity in the eighteenth century, if not before, set the pattern for the declension of all of the other original members of the European system.

Although withdrawal is not induced by any particular situation or configuration overall, it will be made easier because less immediately costly if a stalemate between active powers or support by one such power constitutes a protective sanctuary for the deactivated party. A protecting power such as Britain for Portugal and Holland, or France for Bourbon Spain, will guarantee an irreducible measure of physical security; a stalemated equilibrium will add a residual significance to safety in that a small margin of difference between rival major powers' capabilities will magnify the diplomatic if no other weight of third parties, including a greatly reduced one. In the system at large, even a qualified withdrawal of a once major and operationally salient power will create a near-vacuum in or near the center to be competed over when it cannot be tacitly neutralized (an alternative available to the European system at its peak); when several contiguous powers are dwarfed and deactivated simultaneously or sequentially (as happened in Europe later), that which was the systemic center will be superseded by a re-centered and typically larger system, while the parties retired from leading roles may go on simulating "real-politics" among themselves and in relation to their successors.

No less than falling prey to authentic conflicts among others, only simulating competitive relations will dissipate the foreign-policy-making authority in regimes (and, by extension, states) increasingly dependent for legitimacy on welfare functions as a substitute for effectively performed security function. The ebbing authority will flow toward cliques or coalitions of extra- or sub-governmental actors as, in different political systems, royal favorites or political-party factions, bureaucratic or army cliques, or industrial and business corporations, pose as reformers of collective purpose when not restorers of national power and prestige. Residual stability will in fact rest largely on spreading mass apathy internally and deepening elite resignation internationally, as one or the other attitude provisionally defuses the effects of widening social or ethnic cleavages no less real for being latent or dormant. When ethnic diversity is the main issue, particularism verging on separatism will predominate over the patriotism or mere careerism that contained centrifugal tendencies during the great-power or imperial era. When social-class divisions are central, the political order comes now to overdepend on the economic conjuncture for a minimum of social peace, either because reducing the cost of foreign and military initiatives translates into greater or more evenly diffused prosperity (thus the Netherlands and the subsequently netherlandized west European democracies) or because extreme exhaustion and material impoverishment have progressively stilled all, including rebellious, energies (thus the Iberian powers for the remainder of Europe's ascendancy). Resources diverted reluctantly from internal use to more or less sporadic support of haphazard engagements or auxiliary commitments abroad will depend for real or only but prestige effect on the deployment of greater resources by more steadily and purposefully involved major powers.

DERANGEMENTS AND DISJUNCTIONS AMONG UNEVENLY EVOLVING POWERS

Inasmuch as few actors conform to the succession of foreign policy postures fully at all times, and no set of interacting powers moves through the sequence simultaneously, the implicit derangements are part of the complex matrix within which a system evolves. One such derangement takes place when the original or founding members of the system have deviated from the ideal congruence of domestic structures and foreign-policy posture as a result of having failed to keep pace internally with the evolutionary trends or tempo of the international system, notably in regard to its structure. Another and more conspicuous as well as critical derangement is due to the late-entering powers whose internal development, although accelerated and more deliberately managed because of outside impulsions or other-directed imitation, was nonetheless roughly coincident with the appropriate foreign-policy phase, but the latter was in conflict with the by-then attained developmental stage of the system, not least in regard to its declaratory norms. And yet another, most fundamental if elusive, derangement is latent in discrepancies among states unevenly invested with, and influenced by, their dual capacity as major actors in the territorial arena and leading factors in the world economy, each subject to a different evolutionary trajectory.

The most likely critical derangement for an original member will occur when the exuberantly expansionist is to pass into the conservative phase. Before that stage, the congruence between domestic political arrangements and either the foreign-policy posture or the structure of the state system is less vital, and less likely to be distorted with fatal consequences, for the system-founding members. Any political regime or order *can* engage in first-stage expansive foreign policies when an inchoate system permits objectless expansion, and any regime *must* engage in foreign policies keyed to consolidation if it is to survive similar efforts in an initially crystallizing and constraining system. And some form of or urge for exuberant expansionism *will* follow from consolidation. The inofficial or private agents of that expansion are normally the seminal constituents of sociopolitical pluralism. However, the extent to which they are such and, consequently, sustain the movement into the conservative pro-equilibrium stance is no more identical for all parties than a continuing articulation of societal pluralism is automatic. This is important because, unlike other basic foreign policy postures, a conservative policy keyed to or incidentally conducive to the maintenance of systemic equilibrium is not self-generating and -sustaining any more than it is imposed by the environment, but depends on coinciding with the pursuit of specific strategic objectives. No power outside a universal empire (which transcends the equilibrium mechanism outside only to reconstitute it within itself) is salient enough to be able to foster equilibrium independently of concern with narrower and more immediate interests. The conservative bias must, therefore, be lodged more integrally than any other policy in the dynamic of domestic interest groups, one that helps develop resources for a realistically conceptualized foreign policy while imposing restraints on its course and implementation. This means that a finitely elastic domestic base will in the last resort be more important than the fictional requirement of infinite flexibility in external alignments if a stable policy is to be incidentally stabilizing, and a moderate one moderating, abroad.

Neither Spain nor France developed in time the requisite sociopolitical pluralism out of its rudiments in either the foreign merchants or the feudal magnates who underpinned the foreign-policy exuberance of the two essentially continental Latin powers. Since the post-consolidation phase of the two most original members of the system set in correspondingly early in the transition from feudal chivalry to financial capitalism, it was not closely enough tied to objectives that were to foster sociopolitical and economic pluralism in the initially slower-developing as well as differently situated England. As a result, the conservative foreign-policy phase, nearly non-existent in Spain, expressed in France only inorganically the fact of declining capabilities relative to both the western maritime and the eastern continental powers. It mirrored then the fading royal regime's lack of a sustaining domestic base in terms of both efficacy (self-propelling augmentation of resources) and legitimacy (unenforced self-restraint). When the gradually radicalized domestic reaction had first carried over into revolutionary-and-Napoleonic expansionism, alternately assertive and conservative policies were a way for all of the following regimes to make up for their own as much as for the state's weakness. Internally as well as externally weak regimes (Bourbon restoration, last years of the succeeding Orleanist and the restored Bonapartist regime) inclined toward conservative foreign policies in search of societal as much as of systemic equilibrium, while sporadic self-assertion abroad was the compensatory recourse of regimes more adventurous than genuinely authoritative (early Louis-Philippe and, more consistently and longer, Napoleon III). A long period was marked by accelerated fluctuations between the diluted versions of the two modes (the Third Republic between

1871 and 1939), once the unification of Germany had made it more necessary than before, but also more difficult, to face the external environment offensively for a defensive purpose (late nineteenth-century overseas imperialism and the continental pseudo-hegemonism of the 1920s). The alternative was to see the internally immobilizing inter-factional deadlock, characteristic of failed maturity, spill over irrevocably into the country being immobilized, drawn or driven into de facto withdrawal, also abroad.

A mismatch between domestic structure and the external stimuli favoring a mature pro-equilibrium foreign policy posture will cause system-wide disturbance when the response to it, a compulsively self-assertive foreign policy, is out of keeping with the achieved crystallization in the system's structure (comprising the actor's relative capabilities). Such a radical derangement occurred when the Second (French) Empire's ambitious foreign policies in Europe and the western hemisphere (culminating in Mexico) were of a kind and scale more fitting for the phase of exuberant or even objectlessly expansive initiatives in a permissive international system. The would-be recrudescence in terms of position was actually a relapse in terms of policy phase. It only accelerated the descent from continental preeminence when the Napoleonic initiatives foundered on the still intact power of Britain worldwide, the emergent power potential of Prussia–Germany (and, secondarily, Italy) in Europe, and the about-to-be-affirmed hegemony of post-Civil War United States in the western hemisphere. The ensuing instabilities in the international system were commensurate with the insufficiency of the capabilities mobilized in support of the deviant policies and could not but create openings for stronger powers. However, most fundamentally upsetting for the system and its evolution was France's basic failure to enter upon the conservative foreign-policy phase in time and implement the posture in ways best suited to contain the disturbances attendant on the integration of late-entering (or also latter-generation) powers into the system. Instead of assorting the constraints to be imposed with the concessions from strength to be allowed, as a confident pre-established actor might and should, France's erratic hegemonism achieved the opposite. It induced a concerned Britain to first passively condone the emergence and later fitfully encourage the re-emergence of Germany to a destabilizingly prominent position. Moreover, French volatility had this effect after precluding sustained cooperation with the insular balancer in containing the rate at which late-entering Russia rose to diplomatic preeminence (before and after the Crimean War) and the United States progressed to regional and hemispheric supremacy (before and after the completion of America's continental expansion).

The weights of the different discrepancies that disrupt the stability and derange the evolution of the system are distributed inversely in the case of the late-entering powers. If, for the principal founding members, the primary discrepancy is between domestic structures and the normal progression of foreign-policy postures, while the discrepancy between actual foreign policy or diplomatic strategy and the system structure is in large part derivative from the primary one, the warped relationship between the foreign-policy phase and the evolutionary stage of the system is primarily significant for the late-comers and that of domestic structures to the foreign-policy posture is secondary.

Moreover, the transition to the conservative phase being critical for the older powers, the passage from anterior consolidation of a viable habitat to its extension by an exuberant foreign policy was critical in the case of later-emerging powers such as Germany and Russia.

No late-comer into an articulated system can effectively pursue vague and vast objectives with inadequate means, in the expansive fashion peculiar to the formative stage. It is for this reason that the foreign-policy schemes of the Frankfurt parliamentarians in 1848 on behalf of "greater" Germany, and the more extreme among the musings of the Russian pan-Slavs, were fantasies born of long-repressed frustrations, intent on validating historic fictions. Whereas the *grossdeutsch* scheme was crushed with help from a strong Russian regime committed to reaction at home and quiescence abroad, the pan-Slav design ceased being academic only when the tsarist government had lost firm control at home and could no longer afford prudence abroad. By contrast, Bismarck's diplomatic strategy for unification reproduced deliberately the external conditions proper to the consolidation phase. It adjusted the environing (central-systemic) structure of power and alignments so that it did no more than confine the achievement within bounds consistent with immediate system stability; and the foreign-policy monopoly of the central authority in Prussia (and its military core) had been maintained intact by extra-legal means pending decisive action abroad, only to be relaxed thereafter slightly in favor of an authoritative manipulation of socio- and party-political elements that were compatible with a similarly oriented and managed foreign policy.

The Bismarckian system of checks and balances through a network of complementary alliances was an attempt to overleap the phase of post-consolidation exuberance into a balance-of-power conservatism under the auspices of Germany's diplomatic preeminence on the continent. On the face of it, the strategy was consonant with the evolutionary stage and existing power structure of the narrowly European system as a whole. Replacing it with a *Weltpolitik* that retraced evolution back to the post-consolidation phase of exuberant expansionism signalled the anachronistic nature of an only continental policy in conditions of world-wide imperialism. It also revealed the artificiality of trying to bypass a stage in the normal evolutionary rhythm. However, the straining outward of a widening spectrum of newly emergent sociopolitical and -economic groups, which sustained the effort in basic conformity with the norm, could not but run up against the incongruously advanced preemption of the peripheral outlet areas, which had the effect of prior system crystallization. The resulting disjunction between the foreign-policy posture and the structure of the system was made worse by the ongoing revision of system norms past ideologizing the balance-of-power principle (with its corollary in favor of concert and legitimacy of possession) to delegitimizing the conflictual use of force for changing the status quo through new acquisitions. Britain's conservative stance had by then been radicalized in defense of her species of global hegemony through continental stalemate, and France's foreign policy-makers vacillated between only resisting and actually reversing the transfer of continental preeminence to Germany. But both western powers conceived similarly of the norms to govern state behavior, in keeping with their being withdrawal-prone if not yet -ready. The disjunction between surviving role and sustaining resource intrinsic to their position combined with the discrepancies between foreign-policy posture and system structure in Germany's to lay the basis for a systemic crisis.

Secondary in immediate effects was meanwhile the discrepancy between imperial Germany's dynamic foreign policy and her sociopolitical and -economic pluralism, which included too many pseudo- or quasi-feudal survivals to sustain contemporary forms of overseas activism with a minimum of direct governmental involvement. At the same time, the central authority itself was neither sufficiently self-assured to risk prolonging a foreign policy limited to the needs of continuing consolidation within the continent alone nor sufficiently rooted in a wide-ranging social pluralism to meet the requirements of a conservative posture. The difficulty to evolve a foreign policy that would fit the state of domestic politics surfaced fully when military defeat had unleashed a social revolution, and the ensuing spell of enforced withdrawal from a scale of foreign involvement commensurate with Germany's power potential contributed to preventing a conservative sequel to the exuberance, however aborted. The (Weimar) interlude ended in one more overleap of normal phasing, the compulsively expansionist policies of the Nazi era, after accumulating the underlying forces and frustrations. In fair conformity with the norm, that posture was internally sustained by a degraded pluralism propping up, before being terminally subverted from, its ideologically exalted authoritarian-to-totalitarian pinnacle. Internationally, the policy stance was a preemptive response to the diminishing opportunities for a power of Germany's size and potential within the central system (with respect to Russia) as well as globally (with respect to the United States, and secondarily, Japan). In part present and in part only projected, the context formed a structural link to the anticipatory Wilhelmine reaction to such foreclosure, focused then on the periphery and seeking there a reprieve from the consequences of backsliding at the center of the system, in either cooperation or competition with Britain and so long as Russia (and her French associate) could be kept in check.

Compared with France, a Russia that had experienced the Mongol interruption of the Kiev-centered development was not fully an original member of the European system. Nor was she, compared with Germany, fully a late-comer to the system considering the latter's evolutionary stage at the point of the Russian state's re-entry in the seventeenth century. She was instead a delayed participant and a crucial background factor. This being so, Russia's distorted evolution had its fullest impact only after the European system had given way to a global one – a fact also true, with complementary effects, of the genuinely late-entering United States.

Critical for Russia's development and its relationship to the system's has been a species of evolutionary arrest at the point of consolidation, with only ephemeral or episodic movement beyond. The crucial transition point was thus antecedent to that decisive for France (from exuberance to conservatism) and even, though closer to it, for imperial Germany's (from completed consolidation to exuberance). Moreover, neither the domestic nor the system structure has been clearly primary in the critical discrepancies. Domestic authoritarianism was congruent with the foreign policy of consolidation under both the pre- and the post-revolutionary regimes, and so was the foreign-policy posture with the state of the system as one sufficiently crystallized to exert constraint. However, if the central authority implementing foreign-policy monopoly under the tsarist and the Soviet regimes varied more in procedural forms than in basic character, what constituted a legitimate viable habitat for a power such as Russia – one half nation state and the other half multi-national empire – was always difficult to determine both in and of itself and from the viewpoint of third-power interests and concerns. This ambiguity led to problems whenever a Russian regime deviated inconclusively from the pattern of foreign policy consistent with the consolidation phase in ways that could be construed as disturbing either the regional or the system-wide balance of power.

Aggravating the difficulty were the unusually wide fluctuations in Russia's actual and, even more so, perceived position on the capability curve. Was Russia at any one time organically a still rising power, consolidating its orbit as a platform for indefinitely continuing expansion; a stationary as well as backward power interested in no more than cushioning her historically attained maximum against eventual decline; or, finally, an already declining state pursuing self-preservation coercively outside the boundaries of its legitimate orbit? Accordingly, was Russia to be offered a latitude apt to moderate compulsive reactions to external constraints (as might be preferable under the last hypothesis), or was she to be severely constrained as part of inflecting her course away from exuberance toward equilibrium-directed policy posture (as would be appropriate under the first hypothesis), or would an intermediate response be fitting (in keeping with the second hypothesis)? On the strength of precedents other major (continental) powers had created in their orbits, Russia's foreign policy could continue to be viewed and treated as one keyed to consolidation on one condition: that her initiatives within the usual concentric zones, of inner-core conquest and coercion, and the outer zone of indirect control or only influence, were required or at least justified by the vulnerable multi-ethnic structure of the Russian state and consistent with both the "size" of the state and the "scale" of containment-capable non-Russian power in Europe and Asia. It was (only) within such a framework of evaluation that the penetrations of military proconsuls into central and north-eastern Asia, drawn in by peripheral disorders and either following anterior or making the way for concurrent peasant migrations in the late nineteenth century, could still pertain to territorial consolidation. Subsequently, even more elaborate rationalization would be required to fit the mid-twentieth-century extension of coercive control in especially the European outfield of the Soviet state within this category.

Wholly spilling over from the consolidative into the exuberant posture were the foreign-policy forays inspired by Alexander I or his diplomatic agents toward western Europe after 1815, to be equaled in the Soviet replica by Khrushchev's initiative toward southern Asia and world-wide in the 1960s. Representing a wide-ranging forward defense of the measure of consolidation achieved by the defeat of Napoleon and affirmed by the victory under Stalin, the Soviet excursions were alternately pulled into the vacuum of power left behind by the retreat of the European overseas empires and provoked by the American bid for integral succession, just as the British pretension to monopoly of sea-control had stimulated Alexander's probings in the direction of a comparably dislocated and turbulent coastal-and-maritime Europe. Sub-delegating technical tasks in long-distance overseas probings to Soviet and client-state elites was a step toward realizing a normal attribute of the exuberant policy phase, on a par with the semi-independent initiatives by Alexander I's largely non-Russian ambassadors earlier. But the agents' lack of autonomy and the embryonic state of domestic pluralism overall made the congruence with domestic structure very limited in both phases, even as, in the Soviet instance, the sociopolitical turbulence following upon the relaxation of western controls in the peripheries reopened outlets beyond what they had been for imperial Germany.

Even less congruent with domestic structure (as distinct from regime concerns) were superficially "conservative" approaches to foreign policy such as the post-Alexander I mid-century policy of Nicholas I and the post-Khrushchev détente policy of Leonid Brezhnev. The primitive state of domestic pluralism withheld an internal base from a mature policy of equilibrium in both instances while the comparably but primitive state of systemic multipolarity compounded the limitations in the later case. And it could serve at the most as a possible precedent – and portent – for the Soviet era that the late-tsarist drive in the Far East and the Balkans at the turn of the century acquired aspects symptomatic of the compulsive phase. However, the decline the policy reacted to at the time was of the ruling regime's popular support and legitimacy and not of Russia as a power in terms of either potential or developing material capabilities. The state of the capabilities dictated instead a prudent or even passive foreign policy, keyed to gaining the time for translating growing resources into farther-reaching and more solidly sustained national policies abroad. Accordingly, in the absence of internal stimuli and supports, the deviant policies could serve more credibly as levers and bargaining counters employed to shield consolidation than as plausible initiatives to lift Russia to the next evolutionary phase.

If Russia as a developmentally delayed near-original member of the system was intermediate between France and Germany, the United States has been an authentic late entrant who, like Britain before, bestrode the evolutionary trajectory of a territorial state and the life cycle of a maritime-mercantile center of the world economy. The US successor has re-enacted Britain's duality in a more compressed timespan and a more relaxed spatial environment in its capacity as a territorial actor, and in alternately more favorable and more complexly crisis-prone circumstances in the other capacity as a lead-economy. A largely power-empty, highly permissive North American arena made it possible to very nearly collapse the first-stage expansive and the consolidation-oriented postures into one, under a central authority confined to coordinating a range of forces engaged on militant if not also military expansion. The consolidation within the continent and its closely adjacent offshore insular strategic outposts was predictably followed in the 1890s by exuberant overseas imperialism. Spearheaded by private and para-official internal elements, the posture was facilitated when Britain switched from trying to impede American expansion to dramatically conceding when not actively condoning it as one preferred to less congenial alternatives. A superficially auspicious environment obtained again after World War II when, conjointly with American re-expansion into positions vacated by the retreat of the European (including British) colonial powers, an economically revitalized pluralistic domestic combined with an extraordinarily fluid and ostensibly malleable systemic structure to favor a painless transition to the conservative policy posture, to be first implemented in the imperial mode of reconstructing a dislocated equilibrium.

However, although the policy was in line with domestic structure, it was also hemmed in by the well-developed pluralism lacking a configuration commonly arising out of a more stressful course of development. It is as a result of one that an experienced political class interacts with politically attentive and economically active sustaining groups in a dynamic equilibrium ordered hierarchically. Lacking experience in harmonizing control with consensus and flexibility with firmness, with a view to maximizing both resources and restraint, the US foreign policy elites were unable to reconcile a foreign-policy ideology committed to the restoration and maintenance of equilibrium with a deeper-seated if mostly unavowed actual bias in favor of maritime-continental predominance in the British manner. They could do this least within a systemic structure which, so long as it was bipolar, was not sufficiently diversified as to its range and the developmental stages of vital major actors to permit constraining an assertive continental power without transmuting the offshore insular balancer into world-wide hegemon. In such a setting the gap between politically immature society and the mandated maturity in foreign policy was not to be filled by projecting into an unready system, as a matter of mostly but formally posited principle, the national ethos of constitutionally entrenched legal and normative checks on inter-group conflict. In consequence, the conservative foreign-policy ideology was not patently enough capable of legitimating the *de facto* US hegemony while it lasted. Nor would the ideology be subsequently sufficient to shelter a deliberate dismantling of the ordering role and function in favor of a new-style world order capable of supplanting the traditional cycle of inter-hegemonial succession.

Since any such transformation lay beyond the policy-relevant horizon, the momentum of international-system evolution was critically deranged along with its matrix by a mere possibility. Were the hegemonial successor in the relatively short term to be Soviet Russia or, after Russia's demotion, China, it would be a power engaged in a precarious passage past the consolidation phase and subject to the historically evidenced unfitness of premier continental powers to either peaceably replace or functionally substitute for premier maritime-mercantile powers. The latent sources of instability were further enriched by the uncertainty as to whether, when, and to what extent the United States would incur the full measure of the predicament that had beset declining Britain as the territorial seat of world power and societal pivot of a globally ramifying economy. For such an actor, the costs of the military-security responsibilities incurred in one identity will initially stimulate, only to eventually overburden, performance in the other. As its national economy passes from emphasis on commerce or industry to financial and other services, the polity is liable to face a growing external challenge from a correspondingly weakened internal base and a narrowing capacity to orchestrate a both safe and stabilizing devolution of responsibilities for equilibrium maintenance.

POWER TRAJECTORIES AND ECONOMIC LEADERSHIP CYCLES

The fact that different actors deviate from the evolutionary norm at different points of transition from one foreign-policy posture to the next impedes a frictionless system evolution. Crises consequent on the derangements will stimulate the catastrophic variety of evolution until policy realignments have ceased being capable of redressing disequilibrium – ostensibly among actors but actually between the role and the supporting resources of the prominent one or ones – within the bounds of the existing system. Thus, discrepancies between (systemic or domestic) structures and (foreign policy) postures may well be most disruptive in connection with the exuberant type of the latter, and structure-posture congruence or concordance perturb the system most when the compulsive posture is salient. But the terminal disequilibrium will be precipitated when major actors have withdrawn from a balancing performance equally alert and prudent, one well-funded as well as solidly founded.

In addition to these generally valid factors, moreover, both the evolutionary rhythm and the stability of the system are deranged when a dissonance compounds discrepancies between original and late-entering members of the system *qua* territorial actors. Such a dissonance is implicit in the dual, territorial and functional-economic, character of the major maritime-mercantile power in particular. Critical for that actor is not so much the transition between phases as the tendency peculiar to a definite, conservative, foreign-policy posture at the mid-point climacteric in the evolutionary trajectory and the related capability curve. Even if the mature foreign-policy phase is in keeping with the domestic sociopolitical and the systemic structures, it will be vulnerable to the impact of an asymmetrically overmature national economy. Such over-ripeness spells declension within the cycle of economic surge, salience, and subsidence, a cycle discrete from if intermittently parallel with the evolutionary trajectory of the actor *qua* territorial state. A terminal crisis is likely when concerns about the security and power of the territorial state and the superiority and prosperity of the economic system, ostensibly disjoined at the apex of the economic growth cycle, are re-entangled during the latter's downturn in a relationship that is not so much perverse as it inverts their likewise close connection at the outset of the territorial actor's rise to mercantile-maritime supremacy.

Inasmuch as the complete life cycle of a lead-economy normally parallels the middle sector of the actor's total evolutionary trajectory, the curve will move upwards in the phase of (typically war-studded) foreign-policy exuberance and reach its climax, follow a plateau, and begin to move downward toward decline in the phase marked by conservative commitment to equilibrium. While the cycle of an actor's economic salience covers thus a briefer time span than his trajectory as a territorial state, the two qualitatively different processes are operationally entangled over a critical span. And just as the economic cycle takes up less time, it encompasses a narrower range of more specific and tangible determinants of rise, stabilization, and decline, manifestated in the uneven capacity to innovate, when compared with the complex material and moral, organic and operational, conditions that account for the rise and decline of an actor overall. Moreover, the critical activities will rest more directly and exclusively on the acquisitive drive than do significant undertakings in foreign policy, as often drawn into assertiveness by environing configuration as they are driven by straightforward ambition. The near-predatory competitive economic drives eventuate on the face of it in an economic *order* that connotes a harmony of interdependent needs under the aegis of a leader economy widely recognized and credibly posing as generally beneficial. The more often preclusively defensive foreign policy strategies animate a politico-military *system* that connotes conflict and climaxes in the issue of coercive hegemony. Actually, the cycle of economic leadership traces the incumbent's evolving capacity to impose the rules under which transactions and communications occur in a change-prone setting that expanded from trade routes to more varied trade and industrial routines. By contrast, the rules of the politico-military system are typically under no one's exclusive control and will constrain even the preeminent-to-hegemonial actor anxious to transcend the constraining rules even when not to abolish the attendant dynamics.

However, more important than any other difference is the fact that, unlike shorter-term fluctuations between boom and recession or depression, the longer-term cycle of growth, ascendancy, and decline of a lead-economy is apt to be irreversible. The sequence of development, dominance, and dissipation takes off from an innovative use of innate assets including mineral resources conferring manufacturing or industrial primacy; and it continues as the resulting advantages in commerce eventually narrow to dominance in international finance with support from a strong currency increasingly dependent on revenues from investments abroad (if not infusions from foreign investment) or internationally useful services. Such a course, first traversed in the modern European era by the Dutch, has yet to be reversed and a serious backsliding redressed by an incumbent. Conversely, repeating an attempt at diplomatic preeminence or continental military primacy is not only possible but normal, as are more or less successful relapses into an anterior foreign policy phase. The actor *qua* territorial state can draw on the greater resilience of his multi-faceted makeup and rely on the wider range of relevant assets and capabilities to underwrite a narrow range of priority concerns within a constantly reconfiguring arena. The critical assets being intrinsically identical with those of competing powers as well as relative to them in efficacy, they are *eo ipso* qualitatively unlike the original innovative constituents of economic primacy prone to induce imitative diffusion as a step to their dissipation. It both fits and confirms the differences that the onset of irreversible decline from world-economic leadership, due to the insufficiency of narrowly economic efforts to recharge faltering innovation and enterprise, will compel an attempt to prop up the faltering economy for a time by drawing on the actor's position in the politico-military arena as one easier to sustain longer. It follows from the characteristics of economic salience and subsidence that the cycle will not unfold separately from the total evolutionary trajectory of an incumbent. Whereas the faltering bases of economic leadership will require reinforcement from still-superior politico-military role and resource toward the end of the cycle, the innovative utilization of innate assets in its ascendant phase will be both cause and effect of the exceptionally dynamic, exuberant, phase in the overall evolutionary trajectory.

To be sure, economic-leadership cycle and territorial-actor trajectory are closely connected only when the leading economic power is also a protagonist in the interstate system over a significant period of time. Only enduringly major and thus maximally autonomous actors are subject to discernible evolutionary trajectories, and only intersections between specifically economic and more comprehensively underwritten rise–decline cycles will demarcate the evolutionary rhythm of the state system through major warlike crises. Thus, since neither declining Portugal nor Holland when rising was a major enough systemic actor, the intersection between their economic cycles caused mainly commercial rivalry. The related military encounters were too peripheral to have a significant effect on the European system outside an indirect one from the ensuing expansion of the economic arena proper eastward and worldwide. More intense in kind and central-systemic in location were the conflicts attendant on England's rising and the Netherlands' declining economic curves. But even the Anglo–Dutch wars were systemically significant mainly because they formed a part, if a rather subsidiary one, of the concurrent struggle between England and France over the allocation of continental preeminence and global hegemony.

The situation exhibited a recurrent pattern. The incumbent of leadership in the world economy will have to cope with the three-phase (industrial-mercantile-financial development–dominance–dissipation) economic cycle even as it is involved in three-cornered competition comprising the aspiring major land power on one plane and a more or less overtly upthrusting mercantile-maritime power on another, while the tendency for peripheral parties to alternately invite and resist economic contact determines the need for politico-administrative control. Thus Spain as the faltering would-be monopolist had to contend simultaneously with France and the associated so-called Maritime Powers, against the background of problems raised by her not always cooperative and rarely complementary transatlantic overseas dependencies. Similarly beset were to be the Dutch when facing France on one plane and England on the other against a transitional economic background extending from the Baltic to Brazil. And when Britain succeeded the Dutch in economic ascendancy, she completed her three-sided predicament when forced to add to the leading continental power of the day the United States (and/or Japan) as the maritime-mercantile competitor while overseas dominions preceded crown colonies in displaying increasingly competitive economic ambitions and separatist tendencies.

The only time the economic plane ever appears to function independently of the territorial plane will be when the apex of the economic cycle, registering the combination of industrial with commercial and financial leadership in one power's "liberal" economic posture and policy, coincides with a lull in (schism-related) politico-military competition. Yet, even at the climax of Britain's free-trade ascendancy in the post-mercantilist-and-Napoleonic period, the relation-ship between the balance of trade and the balance of power, between industrialization and imperialism, while relaxed, was – and was seen by keener observers to be – continuing. Schemes abounded to guarantee future markets by officially fostering emigration of and colonization by British subjects overseas (after failing to check the outflow of technology and expertise to the continent). They were intended to limit the effects of diffusion on foreign competition and tighten the link between foreign trade and national power without preventing Britain's initial headstart from fading, competition from augmenting the costs of defense, and erection of politico-strategic safeguards from inducing overextension. Just as the essentially politico-military earlier Roman and Spanish Empires, so the British maritime-mercantile one had to be defended where it had been won: on land as well as on sea, and be so defended at rising costs to be extracted from a materially shrinking even when monetarily inflated economy. The preeminent continental power must add maritime-mercantile assets as also militarily crucial in its ascendant period if it is to qualify for parity globally; the established global-economic hegemon (not least when colliding with a competitive thrust from a later-developing maritime-mercantile party) will have to revert to the continental theater in strength but as part of overall descent, after enjoying a brief and largely fictitious latitude for a measure of self-isolation. At that point, the resources drawn from the periphery will gain in value not only because they are contested, but because they had become crucially needed to support the reactivated politico-military role in the central system, where the contest over the peripheries is "finally" decided. Thus if Spain with help from American silver had to defend her overseas empire against the Dutch interlopers and their French backers in Germany, Britain, having won Canada there and secured the West Indies from France, was to defend her economic and imperial position against Germany in France and in Flanders at a crippling cost in overseas assets.

Just as the efficiently compact territorial state format had been eventually dispersed system-wide, from early Norman England and late Hohenstaufen Sicily, so the later British model of society and economy was generalized in a multi-industrial world system. More than any anti-diffusionist British measures, inefficacy of the promotional measures by continental governments, beginning with Colbertian France, retarded the full effect of the diffusion until the late nineteenth century. While the growing pains of the modern world economy were then merging with the onset of death throes for Britain's leadership, the coincidence highlighted the implications of economic policies interweaving with sequentially salient (industrial-commercial-financial) activities as part of yet another cycle: one that begins with mercantilist policies designed to protect and promote an early-rising economy (and embraced by the English as much as eventually the Americans and the Germans); peaks in liberal, non- and anti-regulatory, policies (originally adumbrated by the Dutch in the period of their dominance in carrying trade); and closes as "neo-mercantilistic" restraints become again attractive the moment free trade and enterprise have ceased perpetuating the full range of the earlier comparative advantage.

Britain never fully faced up in time to the option of such restrictive measures in defense against the industrial and commercial surge of the German and the American economies, solidified almost simultaneously by the outcomes of the wars of German unification and American reunification (the Civil War). Although the United States became a major recipient of British investments just as England had been of the Dutch, while Germany was developing into a major buyer of British goods, in economic terms alone the British could have identified either of the rising industrial powers as the main rival in a first politicized and eventually militarized competition. If Germany was the chosen prime adversary, it was because Britain's life cycle as the world economy leader could not be separated from her longer trajectory as a territorial actor and her foreign-policy posture was increasingly at variance with the continental European power's. By contrast, the disparate evolutionary trajectories of spatially widely separated Britain and the United States crossed only at the periphery of the system and did so at a time of Britain's greatest self-confidence. Her inclination was then to apply to North America from the base in Canada the equivalent of the Low Countries-based conservative balance of power strategy in Europe, with a view to confining the despised cousins' expansive drive across the continent. However, since the policy of containing US expansionism was not buttressed by cooperation with like-minded Napoleon III, it was as decisively impaired in the western hemisphere as the balance-of-power policy would be later in Europe when forgoing accommodation with imperial Germany.

America's post-consolidation exuberance converging subsequently with Britain's near-compulsively defensive expansionism in the Asian–Pacific theater caused only a potential for conflict once Britain's main concern began to shift to security in the home waters. Altogether, the both geostrategically and -economically conditioned Anglo–American contention was, after the mis-begotten war of 1812, only the functional equivalent of the mid-seventeenth-century Anglo–Dutch wars which, motivated economically, were stimulated by parallel (exuberant) foreign policy postures and more basically determined by the emergent (triangular) geopolitical configuration. Economic stakes caused the later Anglo–French conflict more directly in the mercantilistic than the Anglo–German in the comparatively liberal-capitalistic setting, despite the fact that, starting out from a more advantageous initial position, eighteenth- and early nineteenth-century France never managed to match Germany's economic challenge to Britain's position in the world economy. Thus it was the Anglo–German relationship's entanglement in a convergence of criss-crossing economic cycles with divergent foreign policy postures (i.e., Britain's economic decline combined with late-conservative and part-compulsive posture and Germany's economic rise combined with exuberant expansionism), attending the two powers' evolutionary trajectories, that set the stage for the terminal crisis of the European state system within a fully crystallized geopolitical triangle (including Russia).

As the two evolutionary cycles crossed at the point of crisis, they revealed one more asymmetry. In the economic life cycle, relatively short periods of steep spontaneous rise and irreversible decline flank the longer-lasting plateau of supremacy. In the territorial-actor trajectory by contrast, alternating spells of differently motivated and manifested expansion and consolidation climax in mostly two peak efforts, each presumed to be non-repeatable. The mind-set flowing from Britain's "sudden" economic decline collided with the mentality underlying two successive German attempts to seize a "unique" and "last" opportunity to secure past gains and safeguard future prospects. More than from any specific trade-industrial rivalry, the climactic military engagements ensued from a difference in perspectives engendered when Germany's economic growth coincided with foreign-policy exuberance in the first (Wilhelmine imperial) instance and consummated while a precariously contrived resurgence from economic depression went hand in hand with compulsive self-assertion in the (National–Socialist) second. The worsening German compounded deterioration in the British stance once the latter combined a faltering conservative foreign-policy posture, keyed to central-systemic equilibrium by henceforth near-permanent and increasingly provocative alignments, with growing pressures to prolong a both economically and sociopolitically flawed liberal *Pax Britannica* by means of compulsive re-expansion and correspondingly rigid denials of German ambitions at the peripheries. Implementing the combination meant reverting to the territorial principle and re-emphasizing tangible determinants of policies in ways typical also of economies shifting gears from an upward to a downward course.

At the start of ascent to economic leadership, forceful territorial conquest or direct control overseas augment home-based material resources and strengthen efficacy in the central balance of power, the operation of which is in turn instrumental in stimulating or safeguarding the peripheral gains. The early phase of overseas economic expansionism, studded with and stimulated by wars will evolve into climactic free-trading imperialism, materially less dependent on territorial occupation and territorially implanted controls. Once the British had passed the apex, after thus ascending, they followed the pattern and reverted to a preemptive approach to the periphery by participating in the terminal partition of Africa and ceasing to oppose the efforts to divide China. The late imperialist phase is less distinctly marked by protectionist economic policy than by employing institutionally formalized military-strategic supports to prop up a weakening economy. Entering upon it meant adapting the balancing principle to rival bids for access and control that were no longer manageable with the weapons of informal influence alone from a safe margin of also economic advantage. Increases in the specific costs of appropriating questionably valuable peripheries coincided then with Britain's growing dependence on the proceeds from overseas investments and colonial trade to bankroll deepening reinvolvement in the central balance of power. In the event, upgrading military security and fighting major wars was to entail cumulatively greater material losses than even substantial timely concessions to the adversary would have entailed. Moreover, military defeat failed to inhibit for long the growth of Germany's material and demographic advantages, to be turned to civilian purposes only after the defeat-related sociopolitical revolution had mobilized them once more and to the full.

As the capability curves of rising intersect with those of declining powers, their trajectories as territorial actors cross with cycles of economic leadership, and foreign-policy postures do or do not conform with domestic or systemic structures, frictions of greater or less intensity co-define the matrix within which parties interact and the system evolves. At any time critical for the impact of the frictions will be either assumptions or uncertainty as to the scope of the system, its expansion or contraction in several pertinent dimensions. Questions arise: What are the ranges of strategic options in geopolitical space, and the time spans available for correcting the incurred risks? Are the corresponding (spatial) latitudes and (temporal) longitudes such as to compress or decompress the perceptual environment within which competing actors adjust to one another and react to their disparate situations and divergent evolutionary stages with effects that will disrupt the stability of the system before it can recover equilibrium?

When measured against the tendency of wide-ranging if relatively objectless and radically resource-poor policies to expand the (proto-) system spatially, the onset of consolidation-related postures will incline system scope toward temporary stabilization. But it will initiate operational expansion in the rate of significant transactions, which will continue and accelerate when the balance of foreign-policy postures has moved on to favor post-consolidation exuberance. The tendency of declining actors to withdraw from active self-assertion will make the system contract in terms of operationally defined rates and spatially delimited ranges of interactions when the withdrawal has been uncompensated; or it will work toward displacing the system's center of gravity within only spatially or also operationally expanded boundaries when previously extraneous powers have become more active as a result. An increased incidence of the conservative foreign-policy posture will (re-) stabilize the system's scope as to the space it covers and the interactions it comprises, unless it helped provoke a compulsively intensified drive for hegemony apt to activate opposition from hitherto marginal or extraneous parties. An unsolicited impingement from such an actor (e.g. the Ottomans in sixteenth-century Europe) will constrict the system spatially even if reactions to that confinement intensify interactions not only within but also across its boundary. When deliberate alignment policies implement any one foreign-policy posture, this will tend to expand the system in one or both respects most when the alignments integrate a previously unrelated regional system or segment into the central one (by linking so far only parallel conflicts within each into one enlarged universe of action and policy). If the Italian sub-system was integrated into the core-European (or vice versa), and subsequently the so-called northern (Scandinavian–Baltic) into the all-European system, the still later waning of both the southern (Italian) and northern (Baltic) segments set the stage for the vacuum being filled from a renascent eastern Europe.

Although spatial expansion or contraction of the system is tied up with fluctuations in more or less physical, material and demographic, resources, equally or more significant are the perceptions of the corresponding latitudes for effective action. In an evolving system such perceptions will depend decreasingly on the relationship between an actor's basic foreign policy posture and the structure of the system, and will depend increasingly on the intensity of the attendant crises relative to the prospects for resolving them in a conflicted or an adaptative manner. That is to say, the critical factor will shift away from the distribution of variably dissolution-prone and dissolution-resistant capabilities, which makes the system more or less permissive or constraining (and expansion-oriented foreign policies unevenly attractive); and critical will become the configuration of the various foreign policy postures, which operationalize the current state of the rise–decline dynamics (and make equilibrium-oriented policies more or less feasible). When the escalation of cumulating crises foreshortens the longitude measured in the time apparently available for crisis resolution, emphasis will shift not only from "objective" actuality to "subjective" evaluations but also from space to time, and the two dimensions will not necessarily coincide in their effects on strategic decisions.

Thus the early-stage tendency for actors to regress developmentally after a false start, and for major-power aggregations to dissolve before spatial contiguity has intensified frictional contact, will extend the time spans requisite for reaction to adverse developments, in keeping with the precariousness of individual gains and the slow tempo of evolution. Subsequently, when foreign policies shift to consolidation of viable actors and evolution gets fully underway through locally intensified conflicts, tempo will pick up along with risks and both will shorten the disposable reaction time. The perceived universe will contract temporally even if the system expands spatially and the means of communication for the purpose of projecting power remain virtually static. The time dimension shrinks most when founders come to interact with second-wave late entrants, and when the foreshortened evolutionary trajectory of the late-comers confronts also the original members with the choice between hard-to-defer evils. Compared with the ten centuries (fifth to fifteenth) of the false starts in Europe, the crucial evolutionary period of the original members covered barely the four to five following centuries (to the nineteenth), while the telescoped trajectory of the most conspicuous late entrant (Germany) and its impact on the system encompassed no more than three quarters of a century.

In fostering crises and conflicts or relaxing them, expectations as to trends predominate until or unless belied by established "facts." This is true also in regard to material factors such as the volume of population or production, rate and range of innovations in productive and destructive technologies, and the expanding or contracting movement of either national or world economies. It will matter whether major actors operate (and the system as a result functions) on the "liberal" assumption of an infinitely expansible total environment, only including the economic one, or proceed on the "mercantilistic" assumption of a fixed or static fund of factors or features, decreasingly confined to territorial ones, to be divided contentiously. With respect to the economic dimension, it will be critical in this connection whether the policies of the leader in world economy are premised on the initial comparative advantage being indefinitely self-perpetuating (as a result of continuing innovation) and the assault on the leader's headstart by actual or potential rivals being automatically self-liquidating (as a result of continuously amplifying diffusion). Anticipating an indefinite continuance of favored or favorable trends, in economics as much as outside it, will expand the perceived latitudes for strategy and decompress the systemic universe of crisis and conflict management. However, when the positive assumptions having failed to materialize contracts the latitude for and compresses the environment of action more or less suddenly and dramatically, as will often be the case, the urge to roll back the revealed actuality and recover neglected options will exacerbate conflict and accelerate evolution. Whereas such evolution has previously tended toward being incremental and gradualist, it is then more likely to become discontinuously catastrophic.

The dialectic between anticipation and actuality, operative in regard to economic trends and cycles, will work also in transitions between foreign policy phases: less dramatically when initially formative expansive policies are thrown back upon the tasks of consolidating a viable habitat, or the perspectives of an indefinitely continuing exuberant expansionism have to be scaled down to cultivating balance; more disruptively when internal or external developments disprove a major actor's expectation of a long plateau of status-and-role salience (or eligibility for one) within a stable systemic setting. The consequence is for conflicts to intensify, and evolution to accelerate, as the system "ages." Moreover, the degree to which a system is beset by crises will depend, next to the ways and respects in which it does or is expected to expand or contract, on how its multi-cellular structure is split up or segmented. One basis of segmentation is the prevailing schism. It will underlie the alliances and alignments that, implementing more or less closely schism-related diplomatic strategies, only parcellate the arena or also, not least when the schism has imbued the dominant conflict with attributions of contrasting values, tend to polarize the actors. More even than such values, the functional or material features that differentiate actors will be part of the multi-faceted overlaps which distinguish a schism from polarity and one schism from another. All will segment the system in ways that may or may not coincide with its more elementary sub-divisions into unevenly crystallized or developed central and secondary regional theaters.

By the time the largely mytho-normative secular–spiritual schism was superseded by the territorially conditioned land–sea power schism, the latter had extended from western Europe to the world at large the impulse derived from a series of functional revolutions, spreading from early administrative through commercial and nautical to incipient industrial and, after enabling, impelling the secular authority to disengage from the indifferentiate feudal-monarchical-ecclesiastical universe of medieval Christendom. The subsequent eastward movement of consolidated power on the European continent, running initially parallel with the westward migration of maritime-mercantile centers before the two pathways would cross much later in the Asian–Pacific theater, was supported by the organizationally and technologically implemented revolutions in agricultural means of production and military means of destruction supplying the constructive resources and the coercive instruments for consummating an antecedent administrative revolution. All of these transformations were necessary to update the structural articulation of eastern Europe, extending from Prussia to Russia and shading off into Eurasia, and to lay the basis for evening out the terms of the region's strategic interlock with the Euro–Atlantic West. The integration itself was in turn necessary if the primarily cultural-institutional East–West schism (related directly or indirectly to the impact of Islam) was to link up operationally with the land–sea power schism in an all-European core of the global setting. While it did so as the latter cleavage's complicating corollary, old and new East–West value differences had first to deteriorate from perceptually original causes into emotionally aggravating effects of specific contentions. Only then could the laicized ideo-cultural and socio-ideological update of the East–West schism's early medieval theological variety (pitting Byzantine against Roman orthodoxy) settle into a middle position in cause–effect circularity, as mythical figments and material factors permeated one another while seeming to alternate in determinative primacy.

Since the sacral–secular schism pervaded actors more than it segregated them from one another, it entailed spatial segmentation least except when the camps or cliques supporting Pope or Emperor were fixed territorially. Articulation occurred instead mainly on the declaratory level, in function of concerns confounding transcendent with tangible facets of significant reality. Segmentation defined normatively was not to change decisively before the land–sea power schism delimited the materially increasingly favored Atlantic-oriented western part of Europe from the backsliding continental-military sector, and dominant but decline-prone parties to the maritime-mercantile segment had begun (in the guise of the Dutch) to propagate conflict-moderating or -regulating diplomatic and legal norms favoring arbitration in opposition to primitively antagonistic patterns. But only when Europe's east was being integrated with the west operationally (first via the auxiliary role of Prussia or Russia in the Anglo–French land–sea power conflict, to be followed by the two powers' more direct role in relation to England) would values-related behavioral segmentation resurface fully, soon to be compounded by the ensuing change in tone-setting actor generation. When the different behavior norms of the Sun King and of the Dutch burghers had impinged on alliance options and adversary relations, they did so as significantly as the more conspicuous socio-ideological or nationalist-cultural divisions were to do later. The implicit transition from first-generational medieval-type monarchy in eclipse to the second-generation actor-type to be more lastingly and prominently embodied in England prepared the ground for the attempt by a third generation, in continental east central and eastern Europe, to anchor an attempted synthesis of the predecessors' substantive traits morally in the principled rejection of the western insulars' efforts to restrict the range of legitimate behavior with irreversible finality.

Thus, a system will be compartmentalized by segments shading off into mere facets in several respects: organically, by virtue of uneven degrees or stages of politico-economic and related cultural or institutional development, as the basic given; operationally, when separate conflict theaters are subject to parallel balance-of-power mechanisms, each of them self-sustaining until or unless they merge when the better-articulated because spatially more clearly confined one draws in the only inchoate segment and stimulates its crystallization; and normatively with effects on professions or also practices as to behavior. Basic organic disparities can be lessened by mainly uni-directional diffusion of material or ideatal factors, a process that promotes an unevenly reciprocal assimilation; alliances across lines of segmentation bridge parallel operational dynamics more efficiently but with likewise conflict-stimulating and thus evolution-promoting effects, not least when they stimulate normative-behavioral discrepancies. The early modern history of the Atlantic-abutting (western) Europe shows that an expanding core system will impose upon less developed or more anarchic peripheral segments not only its distinctive material and immaterial culture through the process of value-functional diffusion, but also its dominant conflict or conflicts as part of inter-segmental system integration. Subsequent developments show that the expansion tends to decompress the central system in regard to conflictual tensions original to the core, but only so long as the previously exported pressures have not begun to feed back into the nucleus: peripherally located conflicts or counter-expansion of peripheral actors will then compress the perceptual environment of the central system, forcing the confined energies to explode into re-expansion or implode with auto-destructive effect.

Whatever the nature of the successive schisms and of the kinds of segmentation, they were a crucial part of the matrix of system evolution: when the secular-spiritual variety encompassed changes that propelled Europe from a near-polarized proto-system toward a crystallizing plural system; when the land–sea power schism encompassed changes that not only expanded but also differentiated the capability bases of actors (from rural-agricultural to commercial-industrial) and the effective scope of the arena (as a world-wide system of politico-strategic, as distinct from only quasi-systemic economic, and largely non-systemic cultural or missionary, relationships and activities); and when the East–West schism encompassed changes (operationally manifest in the mid-eighteenth-century diplomatic revolution if not before) that confirmed the European or Eurocentric system as an ongoing process, distinct from any fixed pattern of political alignments and specified location of the center of political gravity. Throughout, much as the counsels of economic rationality founded in the liberal perspectives might progressively secrete directives in favor of a parallel or consensual approach to the either expanding (extra-European) or segmented (intra-European) material resource sectors, they were being counteracted by those of strategic rationality responding competitively to structure- and capabilities-related disparities. However, the values-related ideological rationalization of the inter-segment competition (intensified at times by the conflict between the two "rational" directives) was being periodically subverted by the prevalence of the uniform tenets of real-politics, albeit unevenly: unevenly from one schism to the next, but also and mainly as each schism-defined conflict or conflict series outlived the early need for an ideologically formulated definition of the environment and the stakes it generated, under the erosive impact of more practical (strategic or economic) concerns.

Just as schisms have a cause–effect role in compartmentalizing the system spatio-operationally into segments, they shape the texture of the system's environment in terms of value-normative strands with behavioral consequences. However, if discrete segments of geopolitical space will not remain indefinitely isolated from one another over a long period of time (witness the eventual integration of even a Japan and China into the Eurocentric system), this is even truer for the strand of pragmatic real-politics that discloses structure (of system) through process (of conflict). It could be even less lastingly severed from the more varied and elusive strands of schism-related values and belief systems, or generationally defined behavior modes, that intermittently appear to transcend more specific interest-related determinants. Thus, despite appearances to the contrary, it had been no more difficult for the early (Papal–Imperial conflict-related) than for the later (religious wars-related) phase of the sacral–secular schism to integrate schism-related values into *realpolitik*; and, in keeping with expectations, it was less difficult to do this in the mercantilistic than the liberal-economic phase of the land–sea power schism. In each case, the *politiques* prevailed soon enough over the changing brand of mystics and, with them, pragmatic over "principled" policies. Similarly, the original and powerful mass-cultural and ideological diversity between West and East was unable to generate a dynamic that would lastingly demote *realpolitik* from ultimately determinative primacy in and past the late nineteenth century any more than the alleged uniformity of a universal aristocratic culture had done: it could not disestablish conflicting real-political concerns of late eighteenth-century regimes and limit their conflicts for reasons other than those of a generalized dearth of material resources coinciding with cyclically recurrent declension in the system's propensity to violent conflict. However, even if pragmatic *realpolitik* was constantly if variably predominant, varying perceptions of impact from the creedal strand or ideological layer did alternately contribute to compressing or decompressing the ambience of interstate relations in ways that did not fundamentally differ from the bearing of either the spatio-operational or the temporal constituents of the matrix of system evolution.

As an international system evolves and, severally contracting or expanding, grows at once more complex and more determinate while the perceived time-scale for reactions undergoes compression, it moves toward and past its state of maturity. At that climactic point the matrix meets a range of conditions. (1) The major original actors, after having reached the apex, and before declining sharply from the plateau, of their individual capabilities, cluster within a narrow band around the conservative foreign-policy posture. (2) The size of the major actors is congruent with the scope of the systemic arena. (3) The segmentation of the system is compatible with integrating subsidiary or regional systems into the central one, and co-opting marginal actors, without radically displacing the system's center of gravity. And (4) a single schism predominates over any subsidiary one or ones, defining clearly the stakes of the system-dominant conflict – while major-power strategies allow a degree of autonomy to local conflicts that are schism-indifferent or neutral. The mid-eighteenth- and, after the intervening convulsions, early nineteenth-century European system approximated the maturity norm, suggesting that maturity is not identical with a conflict-free, quiescent form of stability. It obtains so long as a disturbed system is capable of being re-equilibrated without recourse to major wars (and major extraneous powers), along lines consistent with prolonging the conditions that make up the maturity norm. For this to be the case, strategies will have to fit *grosso modo* the total structure of the system, one coterminous with the full matrix of system evolution: in regard to actors, their position on the rise–decline capability curves and corresponding foreign-policy posture along the evolutionary trajectory; in regard to the arena, the scope of the system in terms of its expansion-and-contraction and its schism-related segmentation; and in regard to actors and arena jointly, the configuration of contiguous powers and conflictually determined alignments that constitute structure in the narrower sense of the term and the most easily perceived and readily apprehended form.

As the matrix grows more complex because its constituents become more varied and disparate, correct strategies become ever harder to identify and apply. The system evolves past its maturity as its original major members in particular cling to more or less obsolete foreign-policy traditions that incorporate precedents spawned by what for even a long-lasting system will commonly be a small number of truly major, protracted conflicts. The awareness of space and time has grown substantially at that point and has correspondingly reduced the impact of reflexively instinctual responses to internal or external stimuli. But the enhanced strategic rationality does not necessarily match the more rapidly and steeply growing multiplicity of the conditioning factors. Nor does a sharpened awareness of precedents offset the bias to worst-case evaluations of the present. The urge to preempt putative dangers prevails in competitive reactions to an extent that prevents actors from incorporating the long or historical view; historical fails to correct for the limitations of politico-strategic intelligence by fitting either foreign-policy traditions born of antecedent conflicts or strategic responses to current pressures into an evolutionary perspective. The fact that sequences and stages materialize in more or less neat cycles is no warrant for such progression amounting to qualitatively superior progress. By the same token, motor energies generated by crises and the energy-processing conflictual mechanism can, while diversifying the matrix, propel evolution of the system. But they can also, as happened in Europe, erode the capacity to defer indefinitely a system's extinction as an autonomous field of forces.

Discourses 5–7
The Geopolitics of Political Economy

The political economy of world politics – unlike the science of economics applied to global scale – is secretly centered on and manifestly revolves around the politics' inner economy. In both positions the distinctive thrust of political economy as a set of phenomena and propositions about them is to concretize that which would otherwise remain conceptual, and make actual that which was previously real mainly by analogy. The inner extends into politicized economy and economically underpinned politics when the operation of the laws of (political) physics has been emplaced within geographically articulated and materially diversified physical space, the dilemmas of tragic collisions and insurgencies against them have been exteriorized in the problematic identity of unevenly proximate and ultimate determinants of policies provoking or precluding war, and the ideal resources of rationally informed intelligence were unwittingly instrumental in actualizing materially significant outcomes only unforeseen or wholly unintended.

Discourse 5   On Causation of Policies

Political physics actuating the poetics of tragedy so as to limit practicable progress constitutes the innermost economy of world politics. Nothing mediates its translation into the "political economy" of world politics more conspicuously than the enactment of a schism between land- and sea-oriented powers: it concretizes what is most elusive in the essential world politics and politicizes what is most tangible or material in it (the narrowly economic dimension). Moreover, whether only latent or fully operationalized at any one time, the land–sea power distinction permeates most or all facets of the most problematic quandary of interstate relations: one bearing on the determination of fundamental dispositions and policy orientations (as distinct from both specific-particular *ad hoc* policies and actually transpiring warlike conflicts) by internal-domestic, environmental-systemic, and economic, structures and/or dynamics. A basic distinction in connection with all of these is between a causation that implements the virtual tyranny of this or that factor and a mere conditioning of behavior by a range of interrelated factors or facets. Whereas one-factor causation suggests severely conflicted interactions with disruptively-to-catastrophically evolutionary effects, multi-factor conditioning implies compromise-effecting transactions conducive to eventual re-equilibration in an evolution that progresses continuously for the period in question.

Crucial in regard to domestic structures is the relationship between either central authority or the (supporting) ruling class and a range of vertically graduated (middle- and lower-class) sociopolitical groupings. The connection to the systemic environment is all the more continuous the more the domestic (inter-group) structure and dynamics conform in kind if not always in style with the systemic (inter-power) configuration and competition; and being qualitatively continuous with systemic structure (thus sociopolitical pluralism with equilibrium-prone multipolarity) will translate all the more directly into actually conditioning external behavior the closer is the connection between evolving domestic structures-or-dynamics and the sequential foreign-policy postures attending the rise, consolidation, and decline of (major) powers via a parallel sequence: from the crystallization of a central authority or ruling class implicitly entrusted with determining the direction of foreign policy in response to the environmental requisites of an ascent-assuring survival; through transactional interplays of the domestic power center with a widening range of increasingly articulated sociopolitical groups, which condition the actor's foreign policy at or near his developmental plateau; and, finally, to the traumatic lapse into a widening disconnection between central authority and the societal setting translated into a tyranny of the domestic factor, when a foreign policy preparing or attending decline becomes more of a projection of internal stresses outward than a reflection of externally focused strains. The land–sea power schism plays a role when the greater propensity of maritime-mercantile powers to respond to economically conditioned domestic pluralism in their less constraining international environment clashes with the more narrowly statist bias of continental powers. While the latter tend toward central authority and control in conditions of ascent or ascendancy, the bias will become even more exclusive of other concerns when a continental power declines in the more oppressive outward setting peculiar to it.

A species of one-factor causation, and a likewise tyrannical determination of policies, is implicit in perceiving the structure of the inter-actor system as limited to poles of manifest power in being and their configuration as the prime if not sole basis for reflexive behavioral responses. Ideally mediated through the ruling authority's decisional monopoly as a matter of internally non-accountable trusteeship, the simplified dynamic runs counter to the structure's qualitative differentiation. Thus differentiation in terms of unevenly crystallized core and periphery will condition foreign policy responses to attendant constraints and outlets, imperatives and opportunities, in one or the other segment; and it will do so in ways that, incorporating domestic-political and/or material-economic requirements or capabilities, will consolidate transition to inter-group transactions qualifying if not supplanting ruling-group trusteeship. And trauma is in the making for the actors and through them the system when strategies determined by the narrowly conceived (spatially distributed bi- to multi-polar) systemic structure have persistently failed to fit or match the differentiation of actors along the lines of the dominant schism and the developmental rise–decline curves with related foreign-policy postures.

Finally, the one-factor bias predominates in perceiving inter-actor relations as determined by either the structure of world economy, decomposed into divergently evolved core and peripheries within the relevant arena, or the salience of specific national economic policies and priorities within the life cycle of a major actor, unevenly free from or tied to territorially focused politico-administrative controls and consequent military conflicts.

Either emphasis fails to relate specific behavior-conditioning transactions prompted by economic factors to interactions among actors as they bestride a configuration both geostrategically and economically significant. One such configuration is the land–sea power spectrum of insular, central–amphibious, and rear-continental powers competing over primarily military-strategically significant stakes at the center and mainly or equally significant economic or prestige-related role status stakes at the periphery of the system in ways and by methods intertwining economic-development stages with only partially derivative foreign-policy phases. And to the extent that forms of foreign-policy behavior could be – or would be viewed as being – reflexive replicas of either actual medium-to-long cycles of expansion and contraction in world economy or a postulated longest cycle (or only trend) from territory- to trade-centered dynamic in world politics, the causally relevant disjunction would be (again) from other objectively present or subjectively affecting conditioning factors. Catastrophic disruptions that derouted an accelerated evolution would ensue insofar as actions reflecting the singularly biased perception were contrary to other likewise cyclically inclined processes – processes, that is, such as spatio-temporal expansion and contraction of a variously segmented interstate system; the near-autonomous alternations in the propensity to war and to peace in function of internally or externally accumulated stresses and crisis; and the role of alliances in aggregating and dispersing the incidence of warlike conflicts in time or space.

All in all, the economic factor *qua* surplus-creating productivity and surplus-derived capability is ultimately decisive in relation to administrative proficiency and military preparedness; and it is on that "organic" level determining in the same sense as are the internal domestic arrangements and aptitudes for linking power to prosperity and vice versa. This fact is conceptually significant. But it is not perceptually useful insofar as overemphasizing it downgrades the more readily ascertainable "operational" dynamics and incentives. Although emanating from the underlying organic plane, these are transposed onto the geostrategically articulated plane of action with uneven time lags through more or less extended and complex cause–effect chains, and arouse uneven degrees of actor understanding and capacity to integrate perception into strategic action. Conversely, the perception of the narrowly defined systemic structure as one that actually does determine behavior on the operational level (and more so as the systemic-strategic overtops the internally or economically generated crisis), is significant for actual behavior and its reduction to parsimoniously statable analysis and precepts. But it does not negate the conceptual importance of the additional facets or elements in the total structure or matrix which account for the consequences of behavior that has failed to take them into account because they were too difficult to ascertain or too unwelcome to assimilate. When these consequences crystallize into the more manifest features of the narrowly defined structure of an international system through cause-effect chains comparatively less complex or extended than those operationalizing the organic factors, they appear to confirm the structure's determinative primacy to the equal detriment of the crucial modifiers' conditioning role and the connection between actor intent and systemic outcome. However, just as an analysis or theory of interstate relations is irrelevant to practice when centered on factors or processes that are no less difficult to assess intellectually than to integrate into strategy (e.g. long-range economic cycles), so no actor need be held blameless for the consequences of ignoring theoretically identified actors and processes (e.g. broadly defined rise–decline or system-evolutionary trends-related features) that are understandable in principle and assimilable in practice.

That neither differences nor changes in domestic makeups and ideological orientations do in themselves determine patterns of strategic behavior is shown when the patterns reoccur among successive incumbents of positions and roles within the land–sea power schism and spectrum. And the determinative potency of the schism-related factors suggested by such recurrences of events is confirmed by the persistence of domestic institutional and ideological features: when superficial variations are duly abstracted to reveal essentials, the features and attributes will be seen to vary less over time as between comparably situated parties than they do across space between contrarily situated contemporaneous parties. This fact will show the institutional and ideological features and attributes to be largely derivative from the material – geo-economic – basic givens that underlie and constitute the schism. Whereas land powers have been predominantly agricultural with mainly local trades, insular-maritime powers exhibited long-distance commercial and large-scale industrial economies. The former have displayed a corresponding tendency to monolithic authoritarian if not despotic regimes propped up by conservative-hierarchical social systems, exhibiting emphasis on organic and corporate features and inclining toward romantic values; the latter have featured a contrary tendency to oligarchical or representative democratic regimes and liberal cum pluralistic social system, displaying emphasis on mechanistic and individualistic traits and pragmatic utilitarian values. The geo-economic and related constants are supplemented by, when not encompassed in, the geo-historical one inasmuch as the institutional-and-value makeup of the insular-maritime or maritime-mercantile power normally typifies a more advanced (or just later) stage of evolutionary development than the makeup of the land power, even when the latter is a co-founding member of the system.

However, the differences in geographically conditioned economic and related capability and institutional factors, adding up to the organic dimension, do no more than condition the both patterned and recurrent operational interplays. It is their momentum that "motivates" strategic behavior, which in turn implements the inseparability of land- and sea-based material and/or strategic assets. As the momentum accelerates, the interplays obscure the perception of the underlying factors comprised in the overall geo-historical, i.e., spatial-temporal, determinant. When operational transactions subordinate thus the basic givens to politico-military or geo-strategic concerns and complements, they elevate what are but second-degree derivatives from the actors' constituent attributes to a causally primary role in the making of decisions. And they introduce absolutized value judgments about rival actors and competing actions when they sever both acts and appreciations from the relativities that characterize the actors' disparate situations and developmental stages.

Circularities do not make it impossible to distinguish degrees of determinative influence when they are lopsided. The primacy of the land–sea power schism and related structures, when in evidence, and of evolutionary stages, as they become manifest, is corroborated when not only domestic institutions but also dominant ideologies are revealed as derived therefrom. Thus, when conditions peculiar to the land–sea power schism have begun to crystallize, ideologies related to foreign policy cease to be linked to cosmic or transcendent values that rationalize instrumental insufficiencies and become wedded to commercial and transactional or otherwise efficiency-maximizing values; essentially religious ideologies and religio-political conflicts give way to politico-economic ideologies and conflicts, with corresponding variations in domestic institutions and orders.

In the European–Atlantic, as also in the earlier Mesopotamian and Mediterranean, era and setting, religious beliefs and considerations shaped the continental–maritime disparity ever less after setting off the attendant conflicts and imparting to them the initial intensity, to be perpetuated by politico-economic ideologies polarized between progressive-liberal and protectionist-mercantilistic and defined still later in terms of capitalist and anti-capitalist or state-capitalist values and organizational principles of left- or right-wing coloration. Any attendant erosion of the contrast between (quasi-) religious organismic values and the secular individualist ones implicit in the materially charged schism was meanwhile more than undone by the correspondingly divergent cultural overtones and emphases peculiar to the East–West schism being reintroduced into the continental–maritime cleavage. In the era dominated by the religio-political ideologies, the difference critical for domestic regimes had been between ecclesiastico-dynastic monarchical and aristo-feudal republican polities ordered, respectively, by alliances of throne with altar and collusions between aristocratic Fronde and religious faction. When the critical opposition evolved into that between oligarchic-to-democratic and authoritarian-to-totalitarian tendencies in the era of politico- or socio-economic ideologies, stressing the latest differentiation at the expense of its historical antecedents and related continuities could not but encourage the attribution of determinative influence on foreign policy to the regimes' supposed essence, to the detriment of actually operative intra- and inter-actor structures.

When the determinative role of the land–sea power configuration is disclosed in actual operations, this confirms evidence from the derivative character of domestic and ideological features. The two indicators merge when the schism's effects on value-ideological concomitants of conflicts can be distinguished from what happens within schism-neutral -or indifferent multi-power structures. Foremost among such effects is the land–sea power schism's propensity to absolutize contrary value systems as it brings deeper-seated asymmetries to bear on the traumatizing issue of (imputed) hegemony, and does so by means that activate such equally anguishing diplomatic and politico-military states as "isolation" and "encirclement". By the same token, the values-exacerbating effect will taper off, and approximate the relativizing-to-eroding effect schism-indifferent multipolarity has on value differentials, when enacting the schism debases the ideological factor into rhetorical rationalization of otherwise motivated policies. Thus one of the available strategies may dictate stressing ideological affinities with a sought partner regardless of his contrary geo-economic situation while emphasizing ideological differences with the target state coincides with attempts to convert neutral parties. Ideological polarity or rigidity will be wholly defused in favor of geostrategic pragmatism when the special characteristics of the geo-functional spectrum induce a power to search for association with a third party that is ideologically closer to the power's key adversary in the triangle than to the power itself. Inasmuch as such a "third" party is likely to be the "second" land power, defusing ideological differences between the insular and the rear-continental power will also confuse ideological contrasts and affinities between the "first" (or central, would-be amphibious) land and the other two powers.

In any case it would be difficult to identify value-ideological and related domestic-institutional factors either internal to the actors or materially affecting their relations that were not directly or indirectly, proximately or ultimately, related either genetically (by their derivation) or operationally (in consequence of interactions) to either the dominant schism or to its strategic enactment – and could be viewed as important autonomous determinants of major policies as a result. Stressing instead the domestic or (related) ideological factors as policy-determining for theoretically unverifiable doctrinal reasons will mean in practice exacerbating conflicts the impugned factors have not really caused, just as similarities therein can only consolidate associations the same factors have not induced.

Major historical events confirm the primacy of system structure, as repeatedly modified by the land–sea power disparity, over both domestic institutions and belief systems. A close and enduring alliance was no more feasible or sustainable when both the land and the sea powers were theocratic systems (the Egyptian and Hittite Empires) or essentially secular (eighteenth-century France and England), were conservative (Cimon's Athens and Sparta) or liberal (Britain and France in early and middle nineteenth century), and when the ties were dynastic at the summit (Louis XIV and the late Stuarts, Victorian Britain and Wilhelmine Germany) or democratic at the base (France and Britain in the late nineteenth and early twentieth centuries) – than when the parties were of contrasting or opposing character in these respects. Neither did similarity of regimes and social philosophies suffice to speed up movement toward an overdue alliance between two land powers (Bourbon France and Habsburg Austria) or perpetuate the alliance past one party's initial dependence on the other's diplomatic support or material assistance (Prussia's diplomatic on Russia and Russia's economic on imperial Germany, as well as early Maoist China's on Soviet Russia in both respects). By the same token, ideological and regime differences could do no more than delay or superficially complicate the alliance of wing powers in a grand coalition against a central power in both respects closer to each of the wing powers than they were to one another (witness Anglo–Austrian alliance against France, and even more clearly, the Anglo–Russian one against Germany, with Britain and imperial Germany being also more complementary in commercial exchanges than England was with either Russia or France).

It follows that while the land–sea power schism originates in geographic and related material-economic givens, the strategic compulsions it has generated and the politico-military operational momentum it sustains will predominate over routinely competitive or cooperative economic transactions and interests. Close economic exchanges and complementarity between England and France in one era and Britain and Germany in another, each equal to or exceeding competition in foreign markets, did not produce political dividends in the form of lasting accommodation, let alone condominial association; nor did Anglo–Dutch rivalry in the earlier era and differences over colonial and commercial issues between Great Britain and France (and, also, the United States) in the later one prevent diplomatic or military cooperation, disproving in both instances the contrary expectations of unavoidable conflict on the part of the would-be amphibian powers. Economic factors and concerns will influence foreign policies on a par with (or, in specific connections, even more than) the geostrategic only when the land–sea power schism is either not (yet) fully crystallized or is temporarily dissociated from the global politico-military triangle (e.g. in the seventeenth-century Anglo–Dutch–French setting), or is in abeyance (e.g. in early to mid-nineteenth century).

No more will routine domestic transactions influence foreign policy so decisively or exclusively as to positively determine it on other than secondary issues in periods between acute international crises. A more substantial, if only conditioning, influence will in all circumstances flow from two aspects of internal structures: one relating to the material foundation of central authority and the other to its institutional and functional identity or character.

Pertinent in regard to the material foundation has been the reoccurring inner cleavage between discrete and mostly competitive land- and sea-ward turned geographic (inland versus coastal) and functional (agricultural versus commercial) sectors that characterized continental powers across time and space: seventeenth-century France no less than late nineteenth-century Germany and both no less than China at different periods in her long history. If the fragmentation in France was largely territorial (and confessional) and Germany's was more along social-class and professional-caste lines, China evinced a different combination of the lines of division at different times. By contrast, from Athens through Venice to Great Britain the sea powers displayed a relatively harmonious assortment of the two kinds of sectors and interests, with this difference:

Beginning with the eighteenth century England combined the two elements most harmoniously (in her pro-trade-and-industry landed ruling class), Athens least (as the progressive regression of the landed aristocracy was consummated in the class-annihilative Periclean maritime-only military strategy), and the Venice formula (of progressive continentalization of the original trading oligarchy and its replacement by a new breed of traders) was intermediate between the two in both kind and effect.

The internal structures were reflected in foreign policies in both categories of powers. In the continental powers the political primacy of the inland sectors or landed interests was in both France and Germany translated into when not due to the primacy of geostrategic concerns focusing on the continental balance of power in general and the adjoining rear-continental power in particular, represented in China by barbarian threats or invasions. The intermittently more dramatic entanglements with the leading (English) sea power, represented in China by first the Japanese and then the western interlopers from across the seas, was to an uncertain extent either a projection of the economic interests of the coastal-commercial sector or a compensation for its secondary political position and role internally. Conversely, the foreign policies of all insular powers were more fully and directly influenced by economic concerns, without it being possible to ignore the latter's dependence on dealing effectively with geostrategic requirements and preconditions – the obverse of the land powers' regard for the economic requisites of buttressing the critically important geostrategic position. Thus, if Athenian foreign policy reflected the mercantile interests of the Piraeus merchants, the economic costs of an expanded democracy, and the exigencies of extraneous food supplies, to extend the supporting military-strategic framework to the western Mediterranean was also a way of inflicting the disabling loss of the Corinthian alliance on Sparta's regional security system. Similarly, expanding into the Italian terra firma was for the Venetian oligarchy a way to secure access to the northern markets by politico-military means before the bridgehead became a self-justifying asset to protect and expand through deepening involvement in the Italian balance of power. And for England's Whig magnates to cultivate the European balance was a way to simultaneously underpin Atlantic and Indian Ocean monopoly and safeguard the link between equally continent-related insular security and internal stability (dependent on the Hanoverian confessional and constitutional settlement).

Although the internal structures as defined by economically differentiated regional sectors or social classes had an effect on foreign policy behavior by virtue of either projection (of dominant or minority interests) or compensation (for discrepancies between them) through inter-sector or -class transactions or efforts to transcend intractable divisions, they did not dictate the policy as either self-sufficient or paramount determinants. For one, the degree of continuity in foreign-policy behavior on the part of competing land and sea powers exceeded the degree of similarity in the internal (including regional-sectorial or social-class) components on both sides of the divide, pointing to an independent causal factor inhering in the external or environmental configuration. For another, while the diplomatic and military-strategic aspects of the land–sea power contention became increasingly definite as well as repetitive, the stakes of the contention became ever less markedly and overtly economic. Thus, the economic factor became increasingly salient as the Anglo–Dutch assault on Spain (or the Hispano–Genoese complex, nearest in kind to the Athenian assault on the Spartan–Corinthian complex) was freed of its initial association with the issue of political and religious self-determination. But it receded thereafter gradually in favor of an increasingly mythical "world power" concept by way of the mercantilistic hybrid of power-and-plenty in the Anglo–French contest through the privatized (if not de-politicized) liberal-economic environment of the Anglo–German competition to the virtual (if gradually decreasing) subordination of the economic to the military-strategic concerns in the Russo–American contest.

Likewise only conditioning foreign policy strategies are internal structures concerned with the organization of central authority as it relates to sociopolitical dynamics and a changing balance between internal and external functions of government. Such structures (not unlike inter-actor or systemic structures) will influence foreign policy mainly insofar as they have become supportive of or remain consistent with the alternately expansive and prior gains-conserving foreign policy postures which denote an actor's progression through stages of development. When the linked structures and postures succeed one another in a process that is in part autonomously self-propelling, they actualize in readily perceivable behavior the full range of the factors that account for the rise and decline of the major actors in terms of power potentials that only include the material-economic elements. And the (domestic) structures and (foreign-policy) postures will be so linked not least, if not only, as the actors qualify and then perform as principal parties to the land–sea power schism and spectrum. However, for the effect of internal transactions on external policies to be mediated through intricate linkages between (intra- and inter-actor) structures and processes will inevitably impede any direct and immediate bearing of the domestic factor on critical external strategies. This will tend to internationalize the domestic, just as the same mediation will politicize the impact of the narrowly economic, factor.

Transient or superficial domestic features will have an inordinate influence in periods when either the role of a particular country within the framework of the schism and its position in the geo-functional spectrum are in transitional flux, or the identity of the dominant schism itself is unclear. Thus it was when France was either only evolving toward or was already receding from the position of the main continental challenger to sea-dominating England (i.e., in periods after 1715 and 1830, respectively) that weak and insecure French regimes vacillated most between "liberal" alliance with England and a "conservative" one with Austria or Russia in search of a policy that would firm-up internal stability. In the case of Germany, if Bismarck heated up colonial demands on Britain in the mid-1880s also or mainly for domestic reasons (as a tactic to preemptively discredit the liberal-Anglophile heir-apparent), it was before Germany actually emerged as the principal would-be amphibian under the Iron Chancellor's navalist successors.

At the later point, foreign policy was not insulated from the swaying and shifting when not stalemated internal balance of power between the traditional element (the East–Elbian Junkers, preoccupied with Russia, the grain trade, and the army), the modernist element (the industrial and professional bourgeoisie, concerned primarily with navally supported "world policy" and England), and the potentially revolutionary social force (the urban-industrial proletariat, to be weaned from socialism to nationalism via imperialism). In Wilhelmine Germany's representative system, however primitive, the socio-politically fragmented forces may have impacted on foreign policy somewhat more than regionally defined particularisms with confessional overtones, and divergent continental and maritime orientations, had done in Spain (Castile versus Aragon or Portugal) or France (Paris versus Bordeaux or Marseilles). However, even then it was Germany's position within the geo-functional spectrum and her consequently felt needs along the survival–security–supremacy range, that determined the net thrust of the inter-group compromise in foreign affairs. Consequently, the foreign policy – including *Welt-* or *Weltmachtpolitik* – was less a mechanism for reconciling the different social interests than their reconciliation for societal concord was for successive governments an increasingly imperative prerequisite to implementing a foreign policy entailing the risk of war. The "primacy of foreign policy" had by then become an abstract code word for the determining role of the reactivated land–sea power schism in the re-ordered triangular setting.

Any ambiguity as to the proper thrust of foreign policy that remained after the land–sea power schism re-emerged in Europe was exceeded by earlier uncertainties. When, for instance, English policy had wavered (in sixteenth to early seventeenth century) whether to treat Spain rather than first France and subsequently the rising Dutch as the main rival and threat, the issue was caught up in the struggle of rival domestic interest groups motivated in about equal degree by considerations peculiar to the receding and terminally turbulent sacral–secular, and the only inchoate and indeterminately configurated land–sea power, schism: the Catholic landed aristocracy opposing war with Spain also in support of a royal absolutism threatened by increased dependence on the parliamentary power of the purse during a war, and the anti-Spanish trading and Protestant interest supportive of war with Spain and parliamentary supremacy on the same grounds. The issue continued undecided until the alternately pro-Spanish and pro-French Stuart autocracy and the variably anti-Dutch and anti-Spain Cromwellian interregnum had given way, under institutionally Protestant religious aegis, to mercantile-parliamentary ascendancy and under William III to a more settled and predictable English foreign policy. By the same token, unlike what was then to become the case within a settled Anglo–French–Germanic triangle, conservative-dynastic solidarities and radical (pan-) nationalist antagonisms, lodged in the re-emerging East–West schism exerted confusing influences on subsequent Anglo–German–Russian relations before they settled into patterns conforming to the continental–insular cleavage.

A fully crystallized land–sea power schism and spectrum will generate correspondingly specific stimuli in favor of a definite range of diplomatic strategies, to be drawn upon by both dynastic and doctrinally underpinned absolutisms as well as both authoritatively managed and democratically chaotic pluralisms. The attendant instabilities will originate in the risks and limitations peculiar to each of the alternative strategies. But instability will increase when internal political or sectarian-ideological considerations distort the application of the available strategies; and it will be at its highest when, as tended to be off and on the case in the twentieth century, the land–sea power schism is at the same time only partially operative because not yet or no longer sustained by its technological and material, functional and geo-economic, requisites to the full. The resulting slack in determinative impact will then be taken up by the East–West or updated sacral–secular schisms, each less firmly rooted in discrete positions and capabilities of actors and less conclusively subject to constraints from the structure of the system.

Discourse 6   On Causes of War and Precipitants

Correlating the incidence of major wars with cyclically unfolding states of expansion and contraction in the world economy is no more revealing of the essential political economy of interstate relations than is blaming contraction in the life cycle of a lead-economy on the economic leader's exposure, *qua* territorial actor, to a growing incidence of war in defending a deteriorating imperial position. Either approach is flawed analytically insofar as it tries to establish anything like a causal relation between war and economics alone or mainly; and it is flawed fundamentally insofar as it singles out war, its causes and effects, as the central problem of interstate relations. It serves analysis and conforms to actuality better to view war as just one factor – regulatory in the interactional dynamics and mediatory in the evolution – of a state system to be approached through its overall morphology rather than its supposed pathology. Like any other trait or attribute of inter-actor relations, war is just one particular manifestation of the competition over access to assets (only including material) among actors with rising and declining national capabilities (only including economic) taking place within geostrategically conditioned structures and configurations (including triangular continental–maritime) of an evolving international system.

In such a complex setting, the general impetus to war is reducible in the last resort to disparities between asserted roles and supporting resources of actors brought into the open by a range of specific crises (originating *inter alia* in strategies failing to match system structure or in schism-related upheavals), which could not be adjusted through peaceable transactions (including realignments) within the prevailing configuration of qualitatively differentiated and quantitatively disparate capabilities of actors (not least as parties to the geopolitical land–sea power triangle). Thus, for instance, a setting will favor warlike resolution wherein the central-amphibious power is fearful of the rising capabilities (only including economic) of a rear-continental power whose earlier internal or external weakness was a condition of the central power's preceding rise: such was the situation of Spain relative to then rear-continental France, France's to Germany, and Germany's to Russia in conjunction with major war–peace cycles, and would continue to be Soviet Russia's *vis-à-vis* China in a future that remained subject to projection from past trends. By the same token, although expanding capabilities have repeatedly propelled insular sea powers toward leadership in world economy, consolidating the salience would only follow upon the maritime-mercantile actor deriving geostrategic ascendancy from a standoff between unevenly rising-and-declining continental powers, one challenging and the other preparing to challenge the sea power: thus Spain and France engaging one another in a standoff favorable to the Netherlands and England, or Germany and Russia in one promoting US ascendancy, for reasons even more marginally tied up with economic rivalry than was the mainlanders' challenge to the economic would-be monopoly of the insulars. Nor was economic competition unfailingly sufficient to coincidentally induce a war between rival maritime-mercantile powers: it had "caused" the Anglo–Dutch wars in the earlier, but not an Anglo–American war in the later, setting; and it was more likely to produce a trade than a shooting war between the United States and Japan in any future second (post-Pearl Harbor and Hiroshima) round of US–Japanese rivalry.

No more clear-cut or determinate was the role of economic factors in triggering wars due to a wider range of reasons. Thus, even less than the Austrian conglomerate's basic weakness, it was its immediate weakening and prospect of an accelerated debilitation that were successively responsible for precipitating a major war in 1618 (over Bohemia) and another in 1914 (over the Balkans). But neither incentive was any more distinctively or primarily economic than was the impulse behind the decision of the preeminent continental power, imperial Spain in the earlier and Germany in the later instance, to back the declining ally unconditionally. Nor would any comparable war-triggering role of a meta-systemized western Europe be in the US–Soviet setting due to economic distress within the European Community mainly or only – any more than the fear of such distress was decisive for the choice between war and peace in the same part of Europe in the heavily economics-conscious mercantilistic era. Then, the British stake in and the French denial of uninhibited-to-privileged trading access to the continent was only one of the reasons for the failure of the strategy for the Anglo–French accommodation (Peace of Amiens, pointing to condominium). Similarly in the failed Franco–Russian strategy of cooperation (the Tilsit policy, pointing toward duopoly) the economic stake, ramifying into crucial inter-group political dynamics within all parties, was only supplemental to a range of geostrategic concerns (over the continental and naval-oceanic balances of power) that were at least as difficult to deal with to mutual satisfaction. For like reasons undecisive was the financial, technological, or other material dependence of an economically semi-peripheral and geostrategically rear-continental power on the would-be amphibious central power, be it Austria's or Prussia's on France, Russia's on Germany, or China's on Soviet Russia. The dependence did not prevent the rear-continental power from propelling the system toward war as, resisting a coercive or abandoning a consensual strategy for duopoly with the other continental state, it opted in favor of encircling the latter in alliance with the insular state – a decision on strategy only secondarily due to the latter's richer material offerings and only remotely to its competition with the would-be amphibian over peripheral geostrategic and -economic assets.

Especially when the distinction between sea-oriented and land-based powers has become clear and crucial, the maritime powers become the main conduit for the economic factors that propel crises in the direction of wars or revolutions, the continental states being then largely consigned to imitative reactions. Just as the formation of state-like actors, so strategically significant behavior is reducible to mutually stimulating and dependent fiscally relevant economic and force-related military factors. With the operational momentum set off and sustained by contending politico-military strategies being most conspicuously causal, basic material (including economic) conditions will *qua* capabilities ultimately determine what is possible or apparently necessary while more specific economic concerns or rivalries are more likely to merely create a conflict-prone atmosphere or only precipitate a conflict than actually or really cause it.

In the aggregate, the overall state of the "world" economy is basic to the economic factors shaping predispositions to conflict. However, the extreme states within the economy's cyclical movement – its expansion and contraction passing or not through consolidation – do not by themselves determine the presence or absence of politically significant crises. They will affect the nature and location of such crises, but even less definitely than they shape attitudes toward their management and resolution. In an expanding world economy – thus in most of the sixteenth and early seventeenth century, in much of the eighteenth and at the end of the nineteenth – the goals of the actors too should have been "logically," and were *grosso modo* actually, expansive as each party was bent upon securing a greater share. The result would be expansion outside the pre-existing system, producing clashes with or over societies or cultures outside its boundaries. When the world economy is stagnating or contracting – thus in the balance of the seventeenth, early eighteenth, and much of the last quarter of the nineteenth century – the goals of the actors would accordingly be defensively damage-limiting, each party being bent upon protecting if not enlarging its absolutely shrinking share of the diminished total assets relative to the others'. The resulting conflicts would be confined within the boundaries of the system as actors tried to deflect abroad the domestic distress and divisions ensuing from the contraction and compensate there for them. Thus the world-wide extra-European conflicts from the sixteenth to mid-seventeenth century can be seen as followed by the more limited Anglo–Dutch contest (somehow related to the English revolutions) in the period of economic contraction, and the eighteenth-century English and French military exertions in the western and eastern hemispheres (triggering the French Revolution) as coinciding with the eighteenth-century re-expansion of the world economy. By the same token, Bismarck's reluctant squabble with England over colonies in the mid-1880s would appear as a gambit to gain tactical advantage in central-systemic issues, and to divert the pressures of internal party conflicts intensified by the economic stagnation or indecisive fluctuation dating from the early 1870s. Conversely, the enthusiastic Wilhelmine naval-mercantile-colonial "world policy" was floated on the wave of the economic expansion begun in the mid-1890s, adding naval to the economic rivalry with Britain in the makeup of the mutually hostile psychoses which were to affect the perception of the geostrategic issues more directly responsible for the eventual detonation of successive crises in warlike conflict.

The expansion–contraction rhythm of the (world) economy has thus a role to play in the shaping or timing of crises. But it will matter – and may matter decisively – whether policies leading to war are due to spontaneously assertive or aggressively inflected defensive self-affirmation; and it will matter how the expansive relate to more restrained policies keyed to stabilizing the actor's role and status in the system, even if not the system as such. All are significant so long as both motivation and manifestation of superficially similar policies vary in function of the longest-term rise and decline of major actors or historic nations. In principle, then, major foreign policies will be at any one time a function of the actual state of at least two developmental patterns: the expansion–contraction cycles in world economy, loosely tied to the life cycles of major mercantile empires or lead-economies, and the evolutionary trajectories of all major powers, be they maritime or continental, reflected in sequences of alternately (but each time around differently) expansive, consolidative, re-expansive, and finally withdrawal-oriented basic foreign-policy orientations. Crises of war or revolution will be most explosive if one or more states on the verge of relative decline are being compulsively-defensively expansionist within a contracting or only stagnating world economy. Such an assortment describes, if only roughly, the antecedents to the late eighteenth- and early twentieth-century warlike-cum-revolutionary crises. In conditions of uncertainty about the future state of the capitalistic world economy, ancien-regime France (and Spain) were on the first and Habsburg Austria–Hungary (and Romanov Russia) on the second occasion the compulsively expansionist or just self-assertive decadent parties that pulled healthier polities into the crucible of crisis.

Specific economic concerns and contentions will then merely transmit the conditioning-to-causal impact of the attendant frictions to either more fundamental or operationally more influential factors, and may transmute combative predispositions into politically significant acts liable to precipitate military conflict. In either case, whether the immediate concern is primarily domestic (internal stability assured by security of ruling-class tenure, itself based on viable employment and consumption levels for the lower classes) or external ("national" security based on assured material capability), it will be viewed as reflecting basic needs. The needs can, and often will, bear on access to foreign trade (markets) and primary strategic commodities (raw materials), not least when revenues from foreign markets outstrip the efficacy of domestic fiscal and monetary mechanisms in averting economic depression – and so long as the "strategic" raw materials ranging from timber for naval stores in the seventeenth and eighteenth through coal and iron in the nineteenth to petroleum and a range of rare metals in the twentieth century are essential for the naval or military and the industrial or trade posture of a power. Such linkages suggest that, across their full range, the interplay between the requirements of "power" and "plenty" – of "defence" and "opulence" – within the determinants of crisis-type upheavals is as constant as it is circular. The comparative primacy of the "political" and the "economic" goals and stakes is not to be decisively clarified by the fact that sea powers tend to be more overtly concerned with plenty and continental states with power, and that mercantilist doctrines stress state power while liberal-capitalist dogma emphasizes societal plenty. Neither will the directions, the scope, and the motivation of the resulting conflicts be determined by the relative magnitudes or volumes of commodity exchanges within the central system (e.g. Europe, quantitatively more important most of the time) and in the peripheries (comparatively marginal even at the height of the eighteenth-century global trade wars). Nor is the recurrently greater complementarity in trade of politically hostile land and sea powers, conjoined with economic competition between politically allied maritime and amphibious powers, decisive in resolving the issue.

Ambiguities of this kind reside safely in the interlock between economic conditions, concerns, and contentions and the both strategically inspired and strategies-prompting politico-diplomatic operations and activities responding to the equally or more salient geopolitical structures and configurations. It will not matter in this connection whether the strategies are deliberately designed with an eye to satisfying specific needs (e.g. bases assuring economic or military access) or both strategies and ensuing conflict are the by-products of an operational entanglement that has bred its own momentum after it had been triggered by the pursuit of access to materially or strategically significant assets.

In such a closed circuit it is less easy to identify the degrees in which geographically conditioned material-economic structures or politico-military strategies, the basic or organic givens or the operational dynamics, were causally responsible for any one crisis or conflict than it is to calibrate their respective surface salience or visibility. And although it may in concrete instances be feasible to differentiate ultimate (or conditioning) determinants from proximate (or precipitating) stimuli among the levels of causation, it remains that either different or identical kinds of (short- or long-term transaction- versus resource-related) "economic" and (interaction- versus evolution-related) "political" factors can be the causally determining or the only contingently precipitating factors in a concrete situation.

The British concerns behind the eighteenth-century Anglo–French wars in the western hemisphere centering on Canada (as distinct from those focused on the West Indies) were primarily strategic, in defense of the English colonists in North America who had no significant economic frictions with the much fewer and differently specialized French colonists, while the Newfoundland fisheries were more crucial for training naval sailors than for fostering trade. However, the long-term interest in the colonies as markets and the colonists as customers for English produce implies the presence of an economic, just as the role overseas dominion played in the burgeoining inter-party politics suggests a domestic, stake in the "first" empire. Neither can a strategic rationale for the nineteenth-century Anglo–French competition over Egypt and Britain's seizure of the same ignore the British economic interest in India (the terminal point of the strategic passage through Suez Canal) and the triangular trade centered on India in the "second" empire. Similarly, imperial Germany's stake in a strong national navy could not be reduced to either trade-related economic or diplomacy- (and war-) related strategic considerations, since any would-be amphibious central power's concern to forestall or frustrate a military-strategic encirclement by the two wing powers on land will at all times be inseparable from its stake in eluding enmeshment in a world economy run on terms determined by the sea power.

It illuminates somewhat the issue of causation, without solving the problem, to reduce the ambiguities and circularities between economic and strategic factors – or, differently put, organic givens and operational dynamics – to two relationships, each suggesting a close connection between them. One relationship is between resource and risk, constituting a trade-off: it gives rise to a substitution whenever actors relatively weak or weaker in material resource (capability) compensate by assuming greater strategic risks (in or for conflict). The result has repeatedly been to shift focus from economic instruments to military ones, and economic determination to military-strategic, mainly on the part of materially weaker or economically less attractive land powers. The other and linked relationship is a matter of transformation rather than trade-off, and entails a species of sublimation rather than substitution. Because material capabilities distributed in space are the vital ingredients of an actor's position, a sublimation occurs when preoccupation with resources-supported role as an aspect of national power shades off into concern with role-supported status as the object of policy and a possible stake of conflict. From the Athenians' Megarian Decree before the Peloponnesian War to the German navy bills and consular trade promotion before World War I and on to comparable contentious issues since, refusing to revise or repeal such measures at the behest of the adversary was as much a matter of upholding equal or sovereign status internationally as it was of improving one's capabilities over the adversary's. In all such cases, considerations of formal status and material substance alternated in shaping operational transactions conducive to conflict. Nor was it typically possible to determine to what extent the material subjects of dispute were mere symptoms of deeper or wider, including structural, sources of conflict, making the resolution of the former in no way equivalent with the removal of the latter.

It will be largely a matter of perspective, and may be one of prejudice, which of the elements engaged in either the trade-off or the transformation process is isolated from its context and identified as determining. Moreover, a range of rationalizations will make it even less practical to differentiate and disentangle the "organic" from the "operational" factors or levels. One kind of rationalization is in evidence especially in a would-be realistic or self-consciously doctrinal retrospective analysis. Then, either economic or military-technological factors will be treated as determinant because they are more determinate in their makeup than the elusive and non-quantifiable political – interactions- or evolution-related – factors. A different kind of rationalization reverses the bias when seemingly more legitimate political or ideological rationales are invoked to conceal economic objectives. Such objectives can be external, thus when the politically liberal Girondin faction in the French Revolution was at bottom concerned with the continuing economic rivalry with England; or they can be internal, when the ideologically radical and purist Jacobin faction was anxious to compensate for economic deterioration or conceal financial corruption. An essentially non-ideological, diplomatic-strategic rationalization of more fundamental, including economic, interests can in turn reflect the fact or feeling that, over the same period of time critical for addressing a security or stability issue, the strategic or operational dimension is more readily responsive to prudently rational manipulation than any underlying "real" factors can be purposefully managed. Unlike any such rationalization, a rational – or just reasonable – approach will start from the recognition that all "international" crises have a domestic, and all "political" crises an economic, component. However, in most serious crises the second-named factors will be only partial determinants; and, what is more important, will be even that only provisionally until they have helped trigger the operational momentum which secretes its own requirements and necessities and, thus, motivation.

Even as ambiguities confound the possibility of truly rigorous analysis, and invade strategic actions unevenly autonomous in relation to domestic or economic conditioning factors, they cannot be resolved by the injection of doctrinally inspired certainties. One such certainty would substitute the supposedly aggression-prone "essence" of particular regimes for environing competition-prone "structures" as determinant. The result will be policies fraught with a conflict implicitly revolutionary on both the domestic and the interstate levels for reasons other than, and to a point exceeding, the unavoidably revolutionizing redefinition of the stakes of competition tied to the emergence of major maritime-mercantile powers. Thus the Peloponnesian War portended, and its sequelae consummated, the end of the Greek city-state system that had been revolutionized by the rise of Athenian sea power. Similarly, World War I and its likewise if differently unavoidable sequel terminated the Eurocentric nation state system, increasingly convulsed by continental responses to British sea power. The comparable consequences wrought by the climactic wars of the (pre-Greek) Babylonic and the (post-Greek) Hellenistic systems can all be traced to misconceived or mistimed strategies: of the primarily mercantile-maritime powers (initially Egypt and toward the end neo-Babylonia), would-be or actually amphibious central powers (initially Hatti and toward the end neo-Assyria), and rear-continental powers surging toward the sea from afar (first the early Assyria and eventually the Medans and Persians) in the earlier contests, and in the later ones to strategies of the amphibious central powers (Macedon and Syria) facing the Roman and the Greek wing powers.

In each case the progressively escalating conflicts focused sooner or later on the intersection of militarily enacted (population-migratory) pressures from the hinterland and (profit-seeking) drives in space toward the sea, beginning with the parts of the Mediterranean seaboard flanking the junction of Europe and Asia. When in each case the conflicts ended in the principal contestants and the plural system being superseded by a comparatively primitive and essentially continental power (Assyria and Persia, Macedon, and Rome prefiguring the later near-success of Nazi Germany), the brutal conquests expressed graphically the prior failure to bring land- and sea-oriented military capabilities and land- and sea-derived economic resources under closely enough unified control by other means and for a time sufficiently long to contain the pressures converging on the critical continental–maritime overlap and liable to set off disruptive ripples throughout the system. With half-hearted attempts at the condominial type of unified control in the Babylonic and Greek systems (Egyptian–Hatti and Atheno–Spartan, respectively) matched in the Hellenistic and the Italic–European arenas by the brevity of the Macedonia-centered Alexandrine and the insufficiency of the Spain-centered Philippine imperial combination of sway on land and sea, one or the other version of the failure set off a nearly automatic series of conflicts sufficiently self-perpetuating to be in effect self-caused.

The incidence of such conflicts is not incompatible with otherwise caused or constituted conflicts spawned by the plural structure of the self-help system, modified by no definite schism or one different from the continental–maritime. Yet again, the existence of other crises and conflicts does not negate the tendency for the continental–maritime division to reoccur and be critical in all known inter-unit systems at a point of development that displays a suitable combination of naval-technological, trading-industrial, and spatial-structural factors. When present, the incentives will plausibly impersonate instruments of fate as they impact a field of forces and wills, and point both toward war.

Discourse 7   On Cycles and Circularities

The expansion and contraction of the international system is an important constituent of its evolutionary matrix. So is, as part of it, the expansion and contraction of the world economy. However, it would construe too narrowly the political economy of international relations to concentrate on the economic factor, not least when viewing it in relation to the conflicts that channel into evolutionary outcomes the energy-generating crises which fuel the evolutionary process. The prime reason is that there are no assured coincidences between a system's economic and its spatial and operational (including temporal) expansion or contraction, each of which has implications for the generation as well as enactment of conflicts. And if it matters in what way a system expands or contracts, it matters also for what reasons: those internal or external to it.

Thus, when the emergent core of the European system contracted spatially in the ninth century due to renewed barbarian invasions and, later on, economically due to Ottoman interference with access to the Black Sea, the reasons were largely extraneous to it; they were even more markedly extrinsic when the system expanded spatially and economically in and following the seventeenth century into socially disrupted vacua of power in the peripheries, albeit with help from internally generated innovative techniques and technologies. Conversely, different strains within the system impelled both the early feudal crusades in the twelfth century and the later feudal expansion in the fifteenth and after; and if the innovations (classifiable as issuing from outside the conceptual, if within the physical, boundaries of an operative system) that supported the later expansion were triggered by the fourteenth-century depopulation from within, the demographic depletion originated in a plague imported from the outside and only aggravated by the antecedent excess of population over land in Europe. Economic contraction is most definitely endogenous when it follows an automatic downturn in the cycle; so is expansion due to an upturn. The same is true for spatio-operational contraction when a previously major power has ceased being actively involved without the withdrawal being compensated, while only operational expansion will be internally generated when a new major power is added from within the system and complicates the conflict map.

Although the particular effects of differently caused changes in system scale can be specified only in concrete instances, it is likely that intra-systemic reasons predominate as the system matures and that the balance moves once again toward extra-systemic impellents when it approaches its evolutionary terminus. It would seem that, insofar as the exogenous factors materialize quicker or are easier to discern than the endogenous ones, they should induce efforts to counteract their impact by strategies designed to mute conflict within a system when portending its (spatial) contraction, and to exploit them at limited cost in relaxed competition when pointing to (spatio-operational) expansion. Conversely, transformations induced from within a system will tend to flow from sources that are hard to identify when they do not inhere in competitive dynamics, and hard to control when they are part of such dynamics; and they will tend to emerge and pass away over protracted periods of time, instigate highly competitive search for elusive remedies or tentative exploitation, and greatly augment tensions in the maturing system.

However, neither set of reactions is certain and the effect of strategic responses on the incidence and distribution of conflicts becomes even more problematic when contraction and expansion combine intra- and extra-systemic sources in unequal proportions, as is common. Thus, in their mundane dimension, the crusades originated in intra-systemic strains only to be stimulated by discovery of power vacua, sociopolitical dislocations, and economic opportunities, in and around the Holy Land. Much the same applied in changed proportions to later overseas colonization. Conversely, the system contracted in the ninth century due to extraneous pressures on as well as from the Northmen, the Saracens, and the Magyars, while the state of sociopolitical organization in the exposed areas amplified the impact before containing it. However, ignoring the distinction between internal and external impellents to expansion and contraction will barely reduce the complexities built into the inherently ambiguous relationship between economic and spatio-operational expansion or contraction.

After the ninth-century contraction of the European system, economic depression from low productivity lasting until the eleventh century coincided with the system's spatial re-expansion due, next to the crusades, to accelerating agrarian colonization eastward inside Europe (the "drive to the east"). When economic expansion resumed between the eleventh and mid-fourteenth century, it initially favored spatial expansion as Italian merchants helped integrate Europe's south with north and German merchants east with west. But, by the end of the thirteenth century at the latest, spatial expansion had veered toward contraction by virtue of onslaughts from the east even as the economy continued to expand, while the economic and related demographic contraction from the 1360s to about 1500 was the seedbed of the re-expansion by a spatially reduced but richer Europe that was to reach maximum speed by the mid-eighteenth century, when the economic expansion had long given way (by the 1650s through the 1750s) to consolidation or even contraction. Whereas spatial re-expansion and operational expansion had continued past economic contraction, the rate of continuing occupation of overseas space was if anything slowing down after the mid-eighteenth-century re-expansion of the world economy. In the aftermath of the incongruously related spells and rates of economic and spatial expansion or contraction during the wars of the French Revolution and Napoleon, major economic expansion resumed from about 1847 and continued to 1873. It was as much (or as little) due to inflows of gold from overseas (California and Australia) as its analogue in the sixteenth and early seventeenth centuries had been to inflows of silver, and coincided with the mid-Victorian lull in overseas imperialism. Thereafter, the world economy contracted again, only to re-expand in the early 1890s, at which stage it became even harder than usual to identify the relationship between economic and spatio-operational contraction–expansion trends and rates. The last-stage expansionary momentum on the part of the major European powers gathered speed until it ran up against checks in Asia (the Russo–Japanese War and indigenous upheavals in China), while expansion overseas was ever more intricately tied up with the competitive equilibrium dynamics at the center of the system. Both the momentum of the related inter-actor conflicts and their entanglement in central-systemic or peripheral arenas are certain to make strictly economic conditions, or just atmospherics, in and of themselves less determining of what happens in and to the system.

Whereas economic cycles fail to mesh neatly with fluctuations in spatial (and related operational-strategic) magnitudes of the system, the relationship tends to be inverse with respect to the size of actors. Thus, in Italy, smaller city-states superseded larger kingdoms or duchies as the typical or optimum units conjointly with commercial revolution and economic expansion in the peninsula, translatable into overseas "empires" for some of the cities. In Europe, the economic expansion of the eleventh to fourteenth centuries coincided with "national" kingdoms being carved out of both imperial and papal universalisms. The still more extensive economic expansion during the so-called "long" sixteenth century, extending into the seventeenth, witnessed the consolidation of Britain (out of the feudal-dynastic Anglo–French and Franco–Scottish conglomerates) and of the Netherlands (out of the larger Burgundian realm). Economic expansion both before the 1870s and after the 1890s was attended by the *grossdeutch* being discarded for the *kleindeutsch* solution to the German problem.

There is, to be sure, no inherent contradiction between economic expansion and a contraction in the prevalent actor size, and there may even be an effective consonance between the two. However, the consequent increase in the plurality and internal solidity of the actors is apt to stimulate politically defined crises and conflicts, even if only temporarily. Especially in the earlier periods, the ordeal of implementing the internal consolidation of medium-sized actors by coercive constraints on either particularistic or trans-"national" anachronisms tended to counteract any psychological decompression consequent on economic expansion. And the growing disparity between actors reduced in size, as part of an unwitting search for its optimum, and an expanding area, responding to the deliberate parallel quest for maximum material substance, introduced additional strains into the environment of the system. By the end of the nineteenth century, like consequences followed from the quest for another optimum, as regards the balance of dependence on external and on internal markets, as the latter's attainable size under existing as compared with radically altered sociopolitical orders was a parallel source of tensions. Internal turmoils then cancelled out the effect of any lessening in the competition over how to allocate the last remaining overseas spoils (when compared with the climax of the "new" imperialism), and offset any improvement in the proportionality between the size of major-actor capabilities and the scope of the arena (when compared with the imperialism of the eighteenth century).

Potentially most asymmetrical is the relationship between economic or spatial contraction–expansion of the system, and its operational scope, defined by the range of strategically significant conflictual interactions and related actual or potential coalition-type links between strategically autonomous parties. Thus, before the European proto-system was in a position to expand either economically or (to any great extent) spatially, it had expanded operationally. The fractioning of Moslem power made it possible for Christian and Moslem parties to cooperate in mutually outflanking mixed alliances while, within Christendom, the Empire alone (pending the implications of its contest with the Papacy) was ready and able to enlarge its strategy-relevant options, thus when aligning with heathen Slavs against Christian Slavic Poland. Conversely, the post-eleventh-century economic expansion was paralleled, and the briefer spatial expansion was counteracted, by the failure of Christian efforts to forge a alliance with the Mongol Khans of Persia against the Sultan of Egypt in defense of the crusading Latin Kingdoms.

The attendant regression in the Near East and the Mongol invasion in south-eastern Europe reduced the system both spatially and operationally, until Ottoman occupation of both areas began to reintegrate them operationally within the European system while continuing to restrict it spatially. The subsequent economic and spatial expansion overseas compensated for the regression in the east while consummating the recession of the Italian–German dorsal spine of medieval Europe. However, both kinds of expansion coincided with a temporary contraction of strategic latitudes so long as the newly accented differentiation between continental and maritime parties coincided with the early intensity of Catholic–Protestant confessional differences, and the religiously formulated ideological inhibitions reduced Christian–Islamic alignments (between the Ottomans and either Catholic France or German and Dutch Protestants) to narrowly circumscribed collusion. The relationship was again inverted when the next-following economic consolidation-to-contraction in mid-seventeenth century was attended by fading of confessional constraints on alliances. The system re-expanded then spatio-operationally at the center as the northern European powers and balance of power were being fully integrated into the western European core; and re-expanded overall, as the European and North American theaters began to interstimulate in generating conflict and complement one another in facilitating peace settlements.

Changes in operational latitudes continued to exceed in importance both economically and spatially manifest fluctuations when, from the end of eighteenth into early nineteenth century, the Napoleonic and post-Napoleonic restoration of conventional diplomacy relaxed the alignment rigidities spawned by the French Revolution. The resources of statecraft were enlarged by the procedural innovations implicit in the so-called concert system, which expanded the modes of adjusting conflicts by emphasizing institutionalized diplomatic over against militarily implemented alignments and constraints in behalf of transacting traditional issues with largely traditional outcomes. If the enlargement of the operational range was only partially offset by the range of direct (great-power) participants being reduced simultaneously, the relaxing effect of the post-1840s and post-1890s spells of economic expansion was thereafter counteracted – in a mode reminiscent of the post-1750s – by the growing awareness of disparities in the rise–decline capability curves and evolutionary trajectories of the major actors. Moreover, spreading eastward from the French original, spontaneously reacting nationalisms or state-centered and -fostered patriotisms had by then begun to replace confessional differences, and exceeded emerging differences in sociopolitical ideologies, in gradually restricting alliance options; so did the simultaneous waning of the neo-universalism of free trade and the conflicts-muting diplomatic phantom hegemony of its foremost (British) proponent and beneficiary. And finally, compounding the reluctance of the late-entering major newcomers from outside Europe to be integrated into the Eurocentric system in conformity with the needs and mores of its established members, extreme left- and right-wing revolutions inside the old continent made certain that operational contraction would continue steadily after World War I, conjointly with an accelerating interplay between longer expansion–contraction and shorter boom–bust economic cycles. It was to reappear, after a brief reactivation surrounding World War II, in the spatially expanded global system for a number of reasons including socio-ideological, military-technological, and polarity-related rigidities. It required thereafter a steadily expanding world economy to contain politically counter-expansive self-assertion bids from the post-colonial periphery. These tended to reduce locally effective access by outsiders more frequently than they expanded the availability of coalition-type links among strategically autonomous parties for the sake of dealing with regional conflicts.

As a system reaches maturity and passes beyond it, the several dimensions of contraction and expansion will coincide ever less, complicating strategic calculations in a perceptually time-compressed setting. Both the "objective" conditions of multi-faceted contraction-and-expansion dynamics and its "subjective" side bearing on the perception of the environment as one that is compressed or decompressed in the range of options it offers and the length of reaction times it imposes, will play a role in shaping the crises that act as the motor of evolution and locating in space and time conflicts that are evolution's mediating mechanism. However, the less determinate is the effect of the different facets of the expansion–contraction dynamic on the incidence of conflicts, the more worth considering will it become that war and peace unfold, at least in part, autonomously in ways that are as much (or as little) self-propelling as are those responsible for the expansion–contraction cycles:

spatial, when contraction takes place in regression from prior extension that has exceeded (and expansion in recoil from contraction that failed to give sufficient scope to) the control potential of major actors; operational, when peripheral or marginal actors alternate between isolation and involvement, not least in function of the central-systemic actors oscillating between overcommitment and retrenchment; and, last but not least, economic, subject to mutually corrective overproduction and underconsumption.

War–peace cycles became discernible in Europe no later than in the late sixteenth century when they emerged out of an undifferentiated continuum of turbulence, subject mainly or only to nature's seasons. It may have been in keeping with change-overs between generations, but was more probably accidental in response to exhaustion and recovery, that relative appeasements occurred in the early and late decades of a century, while major conflicts resumed in the middle decades of a century only to bestride the passage from one century to the next or coincide with its onset. Thus formal peace or only lesser wars obtained from 1598 to 1618 and again from 1659 to the 1680s, from 1713 to 1740 and again from 1763 to 1790, from 1815 to 1853 and again from 1871 to 1904, and from 1919 to 1939 and again after the 1960s, while major wars (including the peak of the latest "Cold War") were taking place in the intervals. Within these alternations, the war–peace cycle accommodated significant distinctions: between the relatively moderate first-stage military engagements implementing the land–sea power schism and the more extreme second-stage belligerencies, as well as, with respect to the intervening peace periods, between mere truces separating the two stages involving the same and longer interludes between engagements by different contestants. Relatively shortest, but also least peace-like (averaging 24 years) were the truces between the end of a first-phase and onset of a second-phase engagement between the same protagonists: the Dutch versus Spain, 1609 to 1621, the Anglo–French 1763 to 1802 at the latest, and the Anglo–German 1918 to 1939. Longer than such truces (76 years on the average) were the intervals separating the end of a second-stage from the onset of the next-following first-stage confrontation: from the Dutch–Spanish in 1648 to the Anglo–French in 1701; from the Anglo–French in 1815 to the Anglo–German in 1914. And longest, averaging 139 years, was the span of time between the end of one second-stage and the onset of the next-following second-stage belligerency: the Dutch–Spanish in 1648 and the Anglo–French in 1802, the Anglo–French in 1815 and the Anglo–German in 1939.*

Insofar as the phases of expansion and contraction in the economic cycles were either longer or shorter than the phases in the war–peace cycles, movements within the two (semi-) autonomous cycles would overlap at times and the effect of one reinforce the other's without the economic being in any special way uniquely determinant. Instead, there is then a measure of "causal" interconnection, insofar as preparations attending the onset of the war-prone

---

* Projecting the time span differentials into the future would locate first-stage US–Soviet confrontation at the beginning of the twenty-first century (AD 2021: 1945 plus 76) and the second and final installment at the century's end (AD 2084: 1945 plus 139).

phase in the war–peace cycle help lift the economy out of depression and into the beginning of a re-expansion which reinforces warlike propensities due (also) to other reasons. The same applies when the range of conditions favoring peace after a period of warfare has reinforced any parallel tendency toward economic downturn, and its effects. Similarly, no more than it causes a war will the state of the economic cycle one-sidedly determine whether (hegemonial) interstate prevail over (revolutionary) intra-actor contentions, or vice versa. A major war may become more likely when economic contraction has ended and re-expansion begun; revolution, when economic expansion had given rise to expectations that appear unlikely to be satisfied in the existing sociopolitical order before the expansionist phase has drawn to its close. But, again, just as there is a (semi-) autonomous war–peace cycle, there is a revolution–restoration cycle subject to its own laws and momentum. The latter cycle is affected by events in the former when revolution from below follows defeat in war while revolution from above – intended to preempt violent social upheaval and obviate sterile political reaction – is keyed to the expectation of war and is legitimated by military victory.

War breeds peace by exhausting parties to it and eliminating the contentious issues that were or appeared to be susceptible of composition by the use of force. Moreover, war will generate domestic needs or at least highlight internal strains that require a pause of introversion as either an alternative or a sequel to revolutionary upheaval. By the same token, peace will give birth to war and, up to a point, the absence of war stimulate internal violence, by contrary processes. Operationally impelling the alternations will be self-consciously rational calculations of costs and benefits of engaging in conflicts and avoiding or at least deferring them, commonly related to the costs and benefits of embracing or avoiding particular alignments. The costs and benefits change, become more diverse and less determinate in kind, as a system evolves past crudely territorial criteria of gain and loss, success and failure. However, in an expanding system conflicts will take place at all stages of evolution because the net cost of contention over expected gains appears less than the costs of domestic adaptations that would make the inflows of tangible or intangible "goods" from the outside less necessary or their pursuit less contentious. Thus, at an early stage, spatial expansion through the crusades was attractive because of the prohibitive costs of internal adjustments (such as forcible concentration of authority) necessary to constrain widespread internal feuding and of external adjustments (such as separation of ecclesiastical and secular authorities within narrowed orbits for each) necessary for muting the secular–spiritual conflict.

It will be less easy to calculate the net costs of conflicts when spatial or operational expansion has an ambiguous effect on maintaining the dynamic of the system and its members' potential for economic growth. Thus on the eve of the sixteenth-century spatial expansion, the European economy could do with the additional assets and incentives from overseas, either so as to maintain its independently initiated growth momentum or to demonstrate its capacity to absorb the new assets productively. However, only if Europe's actual need of the extraneous inflows could be reliably established would it be possible to judge the net ultimate cost of the ensuing land–sea power conflicts, which were to eventually bring down the European system through a sequence of self-perpetuating conflicts. In the process, incurring the sociopolitical costs of diffusing purchasing power among the governed as part of fusing expanded social and economic with politico-military functions of government was the alternative to defraying the costs of conflicts attending colonial expansion. When expansion is also or primarily operational, this is not least because the alliances that have integrated so far peripheral actors into an equilibrium system were rated as costing less in the coin of diffused role and status than would be the cost of reallocating relative standing conflictually within the core system. When a system is in danger of contraction as the established actors weaken or drop out, conflicts will be more or less severe depending on how the immediate costs of concessions toward upgrading the role and status of a previously marginal late entrant are seen to compare with the less immediate cost of co-opting instead a more peripheral and not necessarily more assimilation-prone power, a cost enhanced by the choice arousing the spurned marginal's antagonism before intensifying the deferred conflict.

The ambiguity of the cost-benefit calculations surrounding alliances of all types – those designed to aggregate capabilities to contain an ascendant adversary or intended to constrain adventurous behavior by a declining ally – will be matched by the indeterminacy of the cause–effect relationship alliances have to the war–peace cycle. Thus, accelerated alliance making is, like economic (re-) expansion, typically but a concomitant of an imminent onset of the war-phase in the cycle, itself due to a range of reasons including interest-based contentions cohering around a dominant schism. This being so, as the system matures and the balance of power dynamic crystallizes, the alternately war-deterring and -precipitating autonomous effect of alliances will be increasingly confined to extending intervals between spells of violence and enhancing its scale and intensity when war has taken place. The consequence for the shape of the war–peace cycle has been no less definite insofar as the European wars occurring regularly from the sixteenth century on became more major and the intervening periods more integrally peaceful from the eighteenth century on. One reason was that explicitly offensive alliances, which had amplified the tendency for alliances to be the consequence of deliberate preparations for war, tended thereafter to give way also formally to not only nominally but also effectively defensive-deterrent ones. Whereas these have tended to delay the outbreak of violence, they augmented correspondingly the unresolved underlying tensions. The trade-off between the shrinkage of time occupied by warlike activities and the expanding scale of violence implies the existence of a constant sum of violent conflict over a period of time that perforce lengthens (to accommodate "peace" periods) as the system evolves. The hypothesis is all the more plausible when the oscillation of violence between inter- and intra-actor upheavals has been allowed for, and the constant sum is calculated so as to compound incidence of conflicts with their intensity and intensity is allowed to reflect variably destructive military technologies.*

* Taking into account different kinds and degrees of violence, culminating in actual fighting, some support for the hypothesis may be found in the finding that comparable assortments of violence covered (relatively long) periods which, grossly comparable in

Although a thus defined sum of inter- and intra-actor conflicts may be fairly constant over much of the life cycle of a system, and vary mainly in the level on which strife occurs and the degree of its centrally controlled orderliness, it is less certain that the aggregate energy available in the system remains constant over an equal period of time and is only being redistributed among unevenly maturing members. The available sum of energy fluctuating between internal and external upheavals is least of all processed at all times by clearly focused and inherently manageable conflicts best suited to restabilize the system within its existing boundaries. As a result, the sum of energy may be constant only in a particular (broadened or narrowed) sense: when the conflict mechanism is unable to combine periodic equilibration with incremental evolution within the boundary of a system or segment of system, the energy deficiency will be made up from outside it by means of activating so far extraneous, secondary or peripheral, actors. By the same token, energies will be condensed within a smaller physical compass in the form of coordinated defense efforts or intensified intramural conflicts when an earlier dissipation of energy has conduced to the arena being spatially contracted from the outside.

Meanwhile, a substantial measure of autonomy of the war–peace cycle will have been confirmed whenever it overrides or, at least, mutes the divergent effects on the propensity to conflict of differently polar structures in an either expanding or contracting system. Such was the case when the war–peace fluctuation was not fundamentally different in the sixteenth- to early seventeenth-century conditions of fading loose bipolarity (or parallel bipolarities) and the rapidly crystallizing multipolarity thereafter. Isolated from everything else, the logic of a two-power structure in an expanding system is to intensify conflict, since the

orders of magnitude, were decreasing overall and in actual fighting time as the intensity of violence rose. (1) Preliminaries to and first-stage confrontations attending the land–sea power schism: Dutch–Spanish, 1560s to 1609 (49 years, actual-dispersed fighting much of the time); Anglo–French, 1701–63 (62 years, but only 27 of actual fighting); Anglo–German, 1885/1901/1906–18 (12 years-plus, four years of fighting). (2) From onset of prior second-stage to end of next-following first-stage engagement: Dutch–Spanish, 1621–48, to Anglo–French, 1701–63 (142 years, with 27 plus 27, total of 54 years of fighting); Anglo–French, 1802–15, to Anglo–German 1914–18, (116 years, with 17 years of fighting). (3) From onset of previous second-stage to end of next-following second-stage confrontation: Dutch–Spanish, 1621–48, to Anglo–French, 1802–15 (194 years, with 67 years of fighting); Anglo–French, 1802–15, to Anglo–German, 1914–45 (143 years, with 23 years of fighting). The corresponding data (as projected on p. 331) for US–Soviet conflict would be with respect to data under (1) 1945–2021 (76 years, with less/more than one year of actual fighting?); under (2) 1939–2021 (82 years, with six plus unspecifiable number of fighting years); under (3) 1939–2084 (145 years – same as above). Where the projected total number of years exceeds the historically latest (under 3: 145 versus 143) and both the latest and the averaged number (under 1: 76 versus 12-plus and/or 41), this can be attributed (next to war-substitutes) to the deterrent effect of nuclear weapons, while the anomaly is offset by the intensity-related brevity of actual fighting increasing at a still faster rate if the weapons are used. Taken together, the deviations confirm the rule of the "constant sum" applying to ever longer periods as the system evolves over the long term, whenever the quantitative-qualitative dimensions of warfare have changed materially.

main concern of each party will be to acquire a share no less than equal to the adversary's in order to forestall an unfavorable turn in the balance. Every position will be a stake of contest even when different situations of (land- and sea-based; temporal and spiritual) actors do not make it more than usually difficult to define equality of gains and parity of outcomes. Conversely, in a setting of several coherently interacting powers, the expansion of a system should create new latitudes for ways out of deadlock or stalemate and a more open-ended fund of compensations for the inferiority of a key player or imbalance within the core system. Conflict ought to be moderated because central-systemic and peripheral assets and advantages can be traded off against one another and partial de-alignments or outright realignments make certain that no actor will profit from system expansion sufficiently to achieve an uncompensable and irreversible superiority. Whereas a loosely bipolar setting predominated in the sixteenth century when the Franco–Habsburg conflict paralleled the expansion of the system into Italy, conditions peculiar to a multi-polar system were most clearly in evidence in mid- to late nineteenth century when imperialist re-expansion helped tone down conflicts within the core of the system before its being repolarized by rival alliance and entente systems.

On the other hand, when the system contracts for reasons located in the periphery, a two-power structure ought to maximize pressures for accommodation, inasmuch as the avoidance of militarily enacted conflict would make it easier for both sides to coordinate responses to what in principle is a common threat. However, the requisite for forward-looking strategic rationality prevailing over short-term tactical reasoning is unlikely to be present, thus when sixteenth-century Ottoman inroads failed to induce powers such as France to rally around Spain as the pivotal western power pole. Likewise in a shrinking multipolar system, it will be as or more difficult to concert responses as to perceive an outside threat as one shared by all in the last resort. For at least some members it will be immediately opportune and appear to be rational to seek comfort in alignment or collusion with actors outside the boundary of a contracting (central) system, and to count on future events or outside powers for containing the extraneous actor before its impact has nullified any provisional advantage or reprieve. This propensity is likely to intensify conflict within the contracting system boundary: thus when the dwarfing of the European system in the twentieth century rather than rallying all, encouraged some powers to look for relief against others to hopefully costfree alignments with parties increasingly extraneous to the reactivated continental sector of the system.

However difficult it may be to quantify the factors relevant to the relative autonomy of the war–peace cycle, and verify its relation to the constant sum of conflict, the hypothesis or hypotheses are no more far-fetched than any that would correlate the outbreak of wars with only one facet of the total matrix of interaction and evolution, including the economic. The qualifying phenomena have, therefore, a place in the intricate political economy of interstate relations wherein issues of wealth, resource distribution, and prosperity matter most when they bear directly on those of war, revolution, and peace. When taken into account, the qualifiers complement worthily the quintessentially political physics and poetics of world politics, and do so at the very heart of the qualitative progress-resistant inner economy distinctive of such politics.

Part III

The Woof of Choice

Part III

The Book of Arda

7
Evolutionary Progression Short of Progress

Just as the motor and the mechanism of evolution pass imperceptibly into the constituents of its matrix, so the many-faceted framework of evolution assumes under a displaced perspective the simplified outline of its salient manifestations. The seamless web of the different strands in an intrinsically amorphous, if discernibly phased, process is an elusive, but integral, part of the total structure of the system around its more clearly articulated core of unequally distributed actor capabilities and unevenly responsive strategies. Amidst the subtly shaded distinctions that analytically separate interdependent givens and operations, one genuine difference stands out: between evolution as a progression in time which, interrupted by regressions, links the crests of cyclical fluctuations, and progress, as a straight line to and beyond the present that denotes a qualitative or categorical change of a kind which, if authentic, would consign formerly recurrent patterns to antiquarian interest.

Without prejudging the critical ratios or balances between progression and progress over time, or at any one particular time including a contemporary one seemingly replete with change and choice, isolating the pattern of secular progression is as necessarily antecedent to tentatively projecting the disclosed trends forward as such a projection is prior to speculative guesses about the prospects for only reforming or altogether revolutionizing traditional ways of power procedurally or also the ordeal of power substantively.

CONSECUTIVE STAGES AND CONTENTIOUS STRATEGIES IN CRYSTALLIZING STRUCTURES

There is a point at which a system will have evolved past its starting proto-systemic phase and becomes crystallized in structure and articulated as to status and roles of actors who are no longer prone to dissolution from within and have become subject to reciprocal countervailing – if not, yet, to either subversion or integration by parties from outside the system boundary. It is in terms such as these that a system graduates from an initial phase through and past the climactic phase of maturity as discrete changes cumulate into comparatively major structural transformations, while the actors meet a less substantially changing range of challenges by means of strategic transactions that periodically surface in conspicuous events. Both before and after the evolutionary mid-point – one which has displayed a basic congruence between actor and arena scales and resources with regard to structure, and between available means and pursued goals in regard to strategic behavior – the progression will in different systems deviate but slightly from a set pattern. Validated by recurrences as "normal," the patterned progression is uniformly due to conflict as the operationally conspicuous part, but not the efficient cause, of crises which surface a range of discrepancies between interdependent factors and fields of action before helping narrow them through the ensuing kinds of wars or revolutions.

When it circumscribes the range of strategies least at variance with the longer-term stability of the commonly action-determining configuration of power, the matrix denotes the state of a system's evolution at a particular point in time. Over any length of time, evolution is outwardly manifested only as particular outcomes, processed out of crises by the conflict mechanism, feed back into the conditioning matrix and alter it in the process. The process is mediated by consciously perceiving and performing actors responding to threats and opportunities, constraints and stimulants. They do so in an operational environment as the major part of which the matrix merges with structure in its broadest connotation and overlaps with process. Actors adapt to environing changes and challenges most creatively, if with transiently catastrophic effects, when they generate and assimilate radically novel revolutionary techniques for managing resources, institutions for coordinating transactions, and values for rationalizing policy goals or means, while the adaptive process itself will periodically activate established, when not also generate new, actors as one of the features manifesting an ongoing evolution.

As evolution progresses, ongoing redistribution of system-inherent resources is manifest in major events that surface the consequences of strategies commonly impelled or constrained by the perceived structure of actor capabilities in the arena. The actor–arena interplay begins as primitively organized units prone to dissolution have to relate to an arena wherein unfocused drives responsible for large-scale nebular formations ("empires"), original to an emergent system or surviving into it from the preceding one, coexist with the tendency to concentrate effective capabilities in smaller nuclear entities ("states"). In such conditions not all actors are finitely bounded organisms focused territorially. In consequence, heterogeneity in types of actor is of the primary kind and is apt to have a counterpart in the system being heteropolar: salient or polarized actors with universalist pretensions will coexist with intricate plurality of precariously particularistic actors within a (proto-) system still undefined in either structure or scope, wherein actor strategies are neither keyed to nor capable of making either kind of polarity prevail any more than a specific type of polity. Moreover, whenever a (proto-) system emerges out of a near-extinct pre-existing one, structural heterogeneity and heteropolarity will be combined with value-institutional hybridization. Europe around 800 AD exemplified the situation when the only emergent western (barbarian, Carolingian) and the pre-established eastern (civilized, Byzantine) empires were polarized by contest over parity of status, in the presence of and under pressure from a third (Islamic) power aggregation, while the nuclei of future territorial states were about to be exposed to territorially unfocused and unbounded migrants-invaders.

An inchoate structure will incrementally receive the impact of actions that are only loosely coordinated by the existence of the single stake – survival through self-affirmation – that the most diverse actors have in common. The impulse from this stake is sufficient for initial diffuseness to begin being articulated in favor of actors best able to contain violence internally and project it externally. Out of the situation obtaining around 800 AD there emerged thus by the end of the ninth century five areas of state-like entities, France (or Francia), Germany, Italy, Upper Burgundy and Lower Burgundy, as the core of the European proto-system. At that point the system begins to emerge as a body politic writ large that is capable of translating sporadic conflictual interaction into sustained and cumulating evolution. This happens as some actors relate elementary capabilities to more elaborate concerns, and start developing physical sinews, as they respond to the stimuli issuing from the nerve center of the system through the medium of a shared awareness of the major stake. Simultaneously, the skeletal frame of the systemic "body politic" only begins to flesh out into the discernible shape of a power configuration, and the responses of actors to outside stimuli only begin to fall under the control of their rational "souls," as instinctual drives blend with rationally guided will-to-power subsumed in a fluctuating balance between aspirations and restraints.

When, no later than the fifteenth century in Europe, actors have become differentiated, mainly as more or less viable and major, a rudimentary hierarchy of fundamentally uniform territorial powers will stratify an essentially homogeneous arena, tending toward a single dominant polarity. The boundary of the system will have been drawn simultaneously by segregating geopolitically motivated strategic interactions within, from only economic (trade) or religio-cultural (missionary) links with parties outside, the system. Thus sketched out, the scope of the system will comprise differently innovation- and adaptation-capable actors and areas as the arena's centers of gravity migrate in a traceable process – one that, in Europe, favored successively the Italian or southern, the north-western, and the eastern segment. As the uneven tempo of evolution resegments the system, early-developing actors and areas recede from central-systemic status to the advantage of a later-developing class of actors with greater intrinsic potential. Thus the fading of the Burgundian mini-actors was followed by that of the Italian micro-system in favor of the relatively more northern (i.e., west European) macro-system, before the latter's center of gravity shifted toward the Prussian and Russian parties to the more authentically northern (including east European) regional balance of power.

The process of system scope expanding around alternately dominant sub-divisions climaxed in twentieth-century Europe, exposing the historically prominent actors to the prospect of incurring the "Italian" mode of integration into a successor system taking shape around two world-class powers graduating from unevenly auxiliary roles in the earlier-developing arena.

Thus re-centered, the global arena has been displaying, in forms and ways modified by altered conditions, most of the defining features of a proto-system, including heterogeneity and heteropolarity, by comprising actors of widely uneven sizes and degrees of internal consolidation (including empire-like "nebular" entities), with highly uneven capacity to innovate and to adapt to the consequences of innovation. It did so within a setting wherein bare survival of actors was or seemed sufficiently assured by both the material and the moral environment to minimize the traditional role of survival-centered activities in identifying viable actors and constraining the irrationalizing potential of disparate values. Even as the center of gravity was provisionally located in mid-Atlantic, with a sub-center in the heart of Eurasia, and as the sheer magnitude of gross actor capabilities continued to grow relative to past standards, functionally more varied criteria of viability than the military-political were in the ascendant. They differentiated actors without major crises or decisive conflicts testing these as able to sustain an either assumed or attributed role and status in ways certifying coherence for the system as a whole.

PATTERNS IN EVOLUTION AND PROPENSITIES TOWARD EQUILIBRATION

Like other developmental cycles, that undergone by a system is divisible into three main phases subject to only marginal modifications, of which only the first has been fully manifest across the global system so far. Building upon an initial correction of actor propensity to internal dissolution, functional indifferentiation, and essential heterogeneity, the developmental plateau implements the congruence in scale and resource between (faster-crystallized) arena and (farther-developing) key actors ordered into the hierarchical variety of equilibrium, only to veer toward susceptibility to subversion from within and supersession from the outside. Within these parameters it becomes a matter of emphasis and/or terminology whether the overlapping sequences of evolutionary outcomes in first progression and then regression are viewed in terms of structuration (stratification, scope definition, core–periphery segmentation), gradual socialization of actors into rational behavior norms fostered by increasingly definite structures and conducive to stabilization of the system as predictably re-equilibration-capable, pending the supersession of system-founding actors and the displacement of the original system core by increasingly extraneous successors – or else whether, highlighting the role of crises as sources of process-fueling energy, the sequence is viewed as taking off from the crises-generated impulse to crystallization, climaxes in routinized containment of crises through effectively countervailing activities, and ends in the catastrophic cumulation of crises that are inassimilable and conflicts that prove unmanageable within the pre-established system boundary.

However formulated, the sequence is attended but also actuated, propelled as well as paralleled, by actors being formed as their military-economic-administrative circuits take shape under impulsion from either functional or sociopolitical–successorial revolutions, the transformations being reflected in changing (pre- to post-norm) basic modes of behavior and specific foreign-policy postures more or less coherently configurated system-wide. The ongoing interplay between actors and arena shifts concurrently from a paradox toward a predicament: paradox, insofar as the initially least firmly structured and thus relatively permissive arena does most to stimulate actor development while structuration of the international system is both increasingly and ultimately the result of actor formation; predicament, which starts out from the tendency for a constraining because already crystallized systemic environment to intensify internally disruptive-to-revolutionary adaptations to the expanding range of structures-related discrepancies, only to culminate in externally disruptive reactions to would-be revolutionizing normative emendations of traditional self-help norms, expressing disparate rates and modes of actor socialization.

As this happens, actors display individually a progression from mechanically assembling the functional elements of state-like power to integrating these in maturing societal organisms, before becoming vulnerable to idealized self-perceptions as a remedy to the progressive unraveling of the previously assembled and integrated constituents of actor identity. The arena itself is being simultaneously structured through partly uncompleted tendencies toward concentration-cum-polarization and dispersion-cum-pluralization of significant power units, as the procreative potential of early bipolarity (or sets of polar relationships) has been actualized in erosion- and late entry-prone multipolarity before the latter's growing propensity to systemic crisis starts fostering reduction in the number of major actors. Successive one-power bids for hegemonial unification may achieve such reduction from within as, typically, late-entering parties react to multiple discrepancies – between role and resources of previous incumbents, their recidivist or anticipatory foreign-policy postures and either domestic or systemic structures, and the traditional and melioristic norms and rules of conduct – or, alternately and more frequently than more or less open and forcible conquest by an outsider, competition between two extraneous powers will thus set the stage for the successor system's resumed multipolarization. The concurrent delineation of the system's scope is subject to likewise not necessarily fully realized tendencies to spatio-operational expansion and contraction. Actuated from within the system boundary by alternating responses to stalemate at the system's core or center (due to its having become too firmly structured) and to the exhaustion of peripheral outlets (when prior expansion has diffused assets to the point of congesting the outlets), the oscillation between expansion and contraction will exhibit a trend mainly at evolutionary extremes: in that early-stage vulnerability to spatial contraction (due to forcible preemption of space from outside the prior system boundary) will give way to late-stage vulnerability to only spatial or also spatio-operational expansion (as outsiders are co-opted to participate in an equilibrium resistant to redressal from within).

A concurrently progressing rationalization of the diplomatic-strategic initiatives that impelled, and the material-economic techniques and processes that underpinned, the initiatives converging in the balancing process will precede, only to merge with, the gravitation of the critical mass toward the outer boundary of an expanding balance-of-power theater. This essentially political dynamic will in turn roughly coincide with an accelerating diffusion of material-technological innovations from the center, while the diffusion intensifies an always asymmetrical mutual dependence between the (receding) core and the (resurgent) periphery, subject to shifting lines of substantively economic or operationally tactical-or-strategic "exploitation" of actors in one segment by actors in the other. However, once money has been introduced, no such evolutionary trend informs the politico-military economy, insofar as the purchase of military service from professionals is wont to alternate with the barter of such service for political participation by citizens for reasons mere internal to actors' development than peculiar to inter-actor dynamics.

Either mode of one actor countervailing another is inherent in the most inchoate structure of a (proto-) system whose expansionist members are no longer safely dissolution-prone. It represents an instinctual, reflexive response to threat from a superior capability suspect of persisting indefinitely. However, it will be always as crucial in practice as it is controversial retrospectively at what precise point in a system's evolution the more systematic – deliberate and plural – balancing has begun: when, that is, an inherently competitive structure has been transposed into routinely structured competition as much impelled as constrained by the existing configuration of usable power and clarified interests. The ambiguities surrounding the roles of the United States as counterpoise to Soviet "hegemony" – and of Russia in relation to the American one – and any future role of each or both in relation to any later third-party threat to the equilibrium of the global system, were prefigured in France's successive roles as one-power barrier (alternating with England) to the Habsburg hegemony and the focal point in multi-state coalition-type balancing (as its target first in Italy and then in Europe and subsequently its would-be beneficiary).

The socializing of actors into the basic behavior norm pertaining to equilibrium, and the consequent stabilizing of the system as one reliably capable of re-equilibration, take place as the potential for two kinds of consolidation is being actualized: more fully that for actors to grow into constantly interstimulating because territorially contiguous parties; less fully that of one-power territorial acquisitions to be so extensive as to trigger a cumulative disequilibrium. Once the balance-of-power system has developed thus far, the mid-term stage will compound incentives to countervailing due to the consolidation and expansion of actors on the spatial or horizontal plane with incentives due to capabilities rising and declining along a temporal or vertical axis; sequential countervailing of the strongest power by alternately fittest single parties yields at this point to unevenly robust and resolute parties, some ascending and others receding, coalescing in fragile defensive union. Finally, as divergences in rise and decline trends increase and intensify last-stage competition, the balancing process will register pressures from the original system members being incapable of generating adequate countervailing power. When realignments involving the original and the late-entering members can no longer be depended upon to contain ascending late-entering actors through either the countervailing impact of alliances opposing them or the restraining effect of those which include them, links to outside actors will expand the operational scope of the balance of power at the price of replacing the lopsided structure of the system with the system's effective demise.

Concurrently changing will be the alliances which, with alternately conflict-intensifying and system-stabilizing effects, implement and institutionalize the balance-of-power dynamic as it centralizes the energies-channeling and evolution-propelling conflict mechanism. The changes occur as the balancing process itself shifts from resting mainly on force-related reflexive impulses toward comprising more broadly power-related organismic imponderables. This will happen concurrently with the rise–decline factor becoming increasingly manifest and operationally relevant in a maturing-to-ageing system. Even before the balancing process has been invested with value-ideologically defined attributions (centered on differentiated legitimacy), let alone supplanted by normatively charged alternatives (implicit in egalitarian institutions), alliances themselves will have evolved: from two-power connections to multi-member coalitions, from typically offensive to effectively deterrent-defensive associations, and from aggregating assets and capabilities with respect to expansion-prone rivals to controlling compulsively self-assertive declining allies as well or primarily. Whereas the common denominator of such changes is a growing importance of inter-allied or intra-alliance distribution of initiatives, gains, and contributions, the stabilizing effects will be offset by actors being sufficiently differentiated to make the finite number and variety of alignment options less evenly attractive, without for all that expanding their range or substantially altering their underlying strategic purposes and uses.

The basic thrust of power-balancing is toward equalizing actors in weight and homogenizing them in kind: that is, it will foster a territorial state that grows to a manageable size around a nucleus, as compared with either an invertebrate nebular empire or atom-sized city-state, or any form of trans-territorial entity. This condition materializes past the earliest proto-systemic phase wherein actors are as diffusely diverse in kind (or degree of territoriality) as they are undifferentiated functionally within. Having disposed of the primary kind of inter-actor heterogeneity, the balance of power mechanism falters when the capacity of its near-automatic operations to homogenize most or all and equalize the major actors comes up against the nearly as natural tendency for actors to re-diversify within the limits of their basic (territorial-actor) uniformity. Either before or concurrently with the differentiation caused by virtue of unequal organic or organizational endowments governing ascent and decline, actors will be differentiated by functional and situational attributes expressing the unevenly developing capacity to derive principal resources from land (agriculture and mining) or the sea (long-distance commerce and traded manufactures). Whereas this second-level heterogeneity first stimulates the balance of power mechanism after the implied process has assimilated actors into one basic territorial kind, the equilibrium dynamic will be deranged and its system-maintaining effect subverted when the technological innovations responsible for the principal secondary re-differentiation have given rise to unevenly successful efforts to re-aggregate the discrete land- and sea-based and -oriented capabilities in a type of power and balance-threatening hegemony that combines both.

If an evolving system tends toward the salience of the land–sea power schism, it is because the latter is the one most potent in qualitatively differentiating the quantitatively construed structure of unevenly powerful but substantively interchangeable two or more key actors while being itself qualitatively closest to such structure. And whereas the schism is firmly rooted in different spatial location and divergent material endowment of parties, which encompass the efficient and the material causes of conflict-oriented conduct, these foundations are distilled into closely corresponding value-institutional differences which dramatize the formal causes implicit in role-status or parity–preeminence issues. The normal evolution from the sacral–secular schism, with center of gravity within actors, as the primary one to the distinctively inter-actor continental–maritime (and East–West) schism contrasts with an opposite, overall and longer-term evolution-manifesting, tendency: for governmental functions to veer progressively from mainly external to also or primarily internal ones. The contrast will obtain until the interstimulative sequence of schisms (thus when the sacral–secular stimulated the religio-politically defined East–West schism as its extension and moderator at the time of the crusades) has given way to their completed interlock or reciprocal conditioning (thus when the sacral–secular schism, transmuted into opposing transcendent state-sustaining to tangible society-shaping values and interests, permeates the land–sea power schism to the point of domesticating it in ways that parallel the value-institutional range along the East–West spectrum). The shift from inter-schism sequence to a species of synthesis tends then to redress, if not wholly reverse, the balance between external-systemic and internal-domestic crises and concerns in favor of the latter and makes it more concordant with the displacement in governmental functions.

Although notably the continental–maritime schism impedes the operation of conflict-implementing alliances and consensus-fostering concert on the inter-actor plane before conducing to the system's terminal collapse, its emergence and impact will exhibit a positive effect as well. It will counteract the more elusively destabilizing tendency for action in a primitive system or distinctive system phase to be initially informed by wide-ranging ideologies largely extraneous to geopolitical realities, drawn upon to help actors orient themselves in a still unformed or transitional and in either case perceptually opaque environment. As the schism takes shape conjointly with the system's structure it will accentuate the inclination of actors to be guided by more concrete-pragmatic concerns, before the real conditions of parties to the schism generate at a still later or last stage distinctive value-institutional extrapolations easier to integrate into strategically rational action than were the earlier-stage ideologies (e.g. twelfth-century Papal versus Imperial universalisms superseded by sixteenth-century Spanish–Catholic–continental versus Anglo/Dutch-mercantile-Protestant doctrines, just as communist versus capitalist ideologies by Russian-continental-authoritarian versus US-insular-pluralist values and belief systems).

When the sacral–secular and East–West schisms have preceded the land–sea power schism before mainly the East–West cleavage aggravates the latter's impact internationally or mainly the updated sacral–secular schism consummates it domestically, the pattern manifests the tendency for attributes peculiar to each of the several schisms, or in fact constituent of them, to alternate between separateness and near-fusion before tending toward the latter over the life cycle of a system. The tendency applies also to the embodiments of schisms-relevant factors or features in the successively tone-setting generations of actor-types. Thus in the sacral-monarchical-military first generation the interpenetration of the legitimating and/or propitiatory sacral dimension with the functionally propulsive and materially empowering secular elements will be very extensive, especially when compared with the primitive segregation between anxiously struggling humans and either disembodied spirits in early post-Roman Europe or anthropomorphically represented ruling or interfering gods in early Mesopotamia and Greece. Subsequently, the sacral and the secular facets were disjoined again when the more tangible individualist-to-societal secular values and material interests prevailed gradually in and in favor of the second-generation western-insular leading actor-type. Thus abridged, the transcendent principle was concurrently transposed into the statist cult distinctive of land-military powers, progressively depersonalized as divine-right absolutism receded before enlightened despotism. Only attempted or actually effected, re-fusing of secular with (pseudo-) sacral traits marked subsequently the reactive challenge of the third-generation actor-type as the eastern continental powers set out to merge state with society in a totalitarian polity and forge continental-military and naval-mercantile capabilities into a winning amphibious potential.

In all major systems, sporadic clashes between the differently situated and endowed land-tied and earth-tilling and purely seafaring-nomadic and coast-raiding societies developed eventually into attempts to combine the distinctive material resources and fiscal or commercial revenues into a salient politico-military capability and role. In the Mesopotamian system, Akkad or Babylon pushed in the direction of the Tigris-Euphrates delta cities just as did, in the larger Near East, Hatti and Mitanni and, especially, Assyria toward the Palestinian–Syrian coast – also Egypt's objective. Similarly, maritime Athens' foray into central Greece before the Peloponnesian War and Sparta's more hesitant probing in the Aegean after the war resembled the expansion of Venice into the Italian terra firma and continental Spain's across the Atlantic. In the wake of attendant upheavals among the autochthonous actors indigenous to the system, the latter's last phase was determined by an outside power combining the two kinds of capabilities more effectively. Whereas the Near Eastern system had been rolled up by Persia and the Greek prepared by Hellenistic Macedon (and Syria) for absorption by Rome, the Italian was pre-empted by Spain and the European has been contended over by the United States and Soviet Russia; and whereas the commotions prepared a fuller emergence of a differentiated insular maritime–continental spectrum, each of the superseding powers bridged the passage from a fading to the geographically close next-following core system: thus Persia from the Near Eastern to the Greek, Macedonia from the Hellenic to the Hellenistic or all-Mediterranean, Spain from the Italian to the European, America and Russia from the Eurocentric to an authentically global, only to falter when trying to dominate the succeeding system.

Whether temporarily successful or wholly futile, climactic attempts to forcefully reaggregate land- and sea-based and -oriented capabilities will cumulate crises and point the system to its terminal phase. A prolonged inability of primarily continental and primarily maritime actors to overcome the schism by means of diplomatic accommodation discloses then mutually reinforcing strategic failures. If these converge in policies that do not reflect the evolutionary stages and the situational differences between the principal parties, they are also likely to testify to the fact that the divergence between basic foreign policy postures of all of the major participants became such as not to be easily contained within a band conducive (via the postures' complementarity) to equilibrium or re-equilibration. The causes of all major, hegemonial, conflicts can be schematically reduced to generic categories grouped in an all-encompassing formula: a marked imbalance between resource (underpinning broader-based capability) and role (secreting more widely differentiated interests) will magnify (diplomatic strategies-attending) risks and tend to misallocate them between challengers and defenders of the status quo vying over ways how to compensate for deficiencies in either role or resource. The competition will engender war before the war can engender a correction to the imbalance. However, within the schematic resource–role–risk triad, the relative weight of its constituents will vary over the evolutionary trajectory of major actors and, conjointly, the system. And it will vary in function of phased, rise/decline-related sequences in the actors' basic foreign-policy postures and orientations performing as mediators between the three generic factors and the greater variety of specific controversies that have emerged as the precipitants (as distinct from "causes" or determinants) of a military confrontation.

Most elementary is the shift from concrete resource located in contiguous territory, as the primary stake of and stimulus to major conflict, to resources sited more remotely or peripherally. This transition will be set off as the basic foreign-policy posture of the major, system-founding actors evolves from the formative one attending consolidation of the habitat to one implementing post-consolidation exuberance. When, next, the core powers approach or have actually reached the conservative posture which implements a stake in rationalized power-balancing, the attendant routinization of the equilibrium dynamic tantamount to its institutionalization will have begun shifting emphasis from resource-rich horizontal space to competition over hierarchically ordered roles, and to the roles' congruence with supporting capability centered in material resource. The next key turning-point in the relationship between the primary and the subsidiary or derivative stimuli is reached when the risk incurred in provoking or resorting to war has reached its maximum. It will do so conjointly with the system-founding members graduating to the compulsively aggressive foreign-policy posture which reflects incipient decline in capability and growing fear of declension in sustainable role, both to be forcibly counteracted at even ultimate risk in transactions with later-developing or late-entering challengers. Moreover, to the extent that the successive shifts in emphasis overlap with the (re-) emergence of the land–sea power schism out of an antecedent interplay of qualitatively undifferentiated territorial entities intent on consolidating a viable habitat, the displacement of determinative weight from concrete resource-maximizing toward relatively intangible role- and status-centered stakes in a heightened-risk environment will parallel the situationally conditioned schism being (re-) connected with the more subjectively values-centered ones.

As the realignments in determinant concerns and stimuli unfold, equally subtle shifts in relative importance take place in the actors' readiness to engage in conflict. The shift is then away from concordance in the two facets of readiness: effective capability and psychopolitical disposition, toward their disjunction in favor of enhanced disposition compensating for deficits in capability. And with respect to the conflict's origination in, primarily, physical contact or protean concept, the evolution-attending realignments restore gradually the importance of concept (dominant in the objectlessly expansive sub-phase of the formative posture), to the detriment of friction-generating contact (paramount in the early posture's consolidation-related phase). Simultaneously revived will be the conceptual determinant's original form except that genuinely religious or theocratic themes concerned with individual or group salvation, typified by crusades, will have been reshaped into quasi-religiously statist concerns with corporate status, exemplified in "great" or "world" powers. The metamorphosis will also mean that the catalytic function of conflict, to reconfigure the systemic environment positively in a desired specific direction, will have receded in favor of its cathartic function: to relieve the tensions accumulated at large and redirect internal strains as equally or immediately more urgent than any power-politically favorable specific outcome. It is in keeping with this change that all the other shifts in relative weights are aggregated in one from openly offensive to ultimately defensive purposes and stimuli to major wars: from predatory acquisition of specific and concrete assets to anticipatory preemption of postulated threats to the more intangible of actor attributes – a change no less real for predation being at all times rationalized in terms of preclusion and effective preemption being contingent on effective performance with respect to acquisition.

The variably aligned or assorted causal determinants of major conflicts differ from the conditions responsible for moderating the conflictual enactment of the balance of power in and through a concert of powers. And the more they differ, the more clearly will the difference identify one set of factors as war-provoking. Thus the spread between postures critical for a particular war at any one stage of development can be quite wide: for example, when actors in pre-consolidation expansive or, more likely, post-consolidation exuberant posture compete with one another or with mature-conservative actors over succession to positions occupied by actors engaged in terminal withdrawal from an active role in the system. By contrast, a concert not only coordinates policies toward appeasing conflict but is in effect contingent on members occupying a but narrow band of foreign-policy predispositions weighted in favor of a particular, the conservative, posture. Moreover, the interplay that reflects the lesser divergences will lack the intensity which infuses the greater variety of more contrasting postures and is conducive to major conflicts polarizing the arena in terms of both issues, protagonists, and their associates. Such polarization is in marked contrast to the plurality of near-equal parties and multiplicity of intersecting lower-intensity conflicts which form the prerequisite to, before constituting the dynamic of, a concert.

It follows from the several attributes of a concert that the roles in making it work are distributed relatively evenly over time and across changing conflict issues; and that variations in role are contingent not so much problematically on an actor's material capability to back the role as paradoxically on how directly a particular member is engaged in advancing a specific claim: the less forward or venturesome the member, the greater and more decisive is its role. The dampening effect on conflict is reinforced by risks being reduced overall in a concert the defining characteristic of which is reliance on flexible diplomatic instruments and coalitions rather than forceful military ones for resolving differences and limiting individual ambitions and gains. Further reducing the risks already limited to abridgement of diplomatic prestige, options, and leverages for the party losing out on a pretension is the likewise concert-constituent and -perpetuating requirement for the *ad hoc* "winners" to offer the "loser" a face-saving compensation of a procedural or like formal kind for any material loss attending a setback in the quasi-parliamentary forum that marks a system's apogee.

CONTINUITIES WITHIN AND LINKS BETWEEN SYSTEMS

Commonly preceding the demise of a regressing system will be an inadvertent diffusion, or deliberate dissemination, of its dominant value-institutional norms and operational techniques among parties to the succeeding system. The spread may accelerate the demotion and only ideally compensate for it, regardless of whether the superseded system has been wholly suppressed by an outside unifier, only subjected to the supervision by an outside arbiter, or supplanted as central in an enlarged arena. Contentious interactions among parties to the demoted (meta-) system are in the milder instances merely sublimated as to mode (henceforth principally non-military and institutionalized diplomatic) and largely simulated in kind (as procedures are emptied of effective sanctions and stakes of geopolitical substance). They will revolve around concerns focused less on strategic security of the parties than on their internal political stability and economic prosperity, more on appearances of prestige and status than on realities of power and role – all in all, be governed less by external than by internal configurations of power and policy imperatives.

The terminally catastrophic disjunction between structure and strategies has been repeatedly due to the diplomatically premier power being unable to effectively lead from diminishing strength in a correspondingly weakened system. Egypt, post-Peloponnesian War Sparta, Hellenistic Macedon, late fifteenth-century Florence, and pre-World War I Britain were alike in failing to correctly identify in time the rising-or-declining and continental-or-maritime party most threatening to the autonomy of the system, to be neutralized at all costs including accommodation with the member of the endangered system perceived as most directly menacing to the premier power itself. Opting in favor of the extra- against the intra-systemic power, even when the latter has already passed its apogee, reduced sharply the extent to which the receding system could more than formally participate in the successor system through the agency of one of its members. Unlike Babylon that may have kept the Sumerian inter-city complex repeatedly participant in the larger Near Eastern system, no Greek city-state in the Hellenic and neither Macedon nor Syria in the Hellenistic system was both strong and self-restrained enough to implement such a role. Neither was Venice able, or allowed, to mediate effectively the integration of the Italian into the emergent European system before settling for the pretense of a balancer role between larger northern powers, nor Germany to perform the task for a decadent European system before too gross resource–role disparity made her react in ways destructive of a last chance for internal re-equilibration.

Insofar as the missing mediators were the powers mistakenly overcontained in the preceding phase, the strategies that had precipitated supersession of a system impeded also its meaningful integration into the next-following one. The consequences were likewise uniform. Not unlike what had been the case for the Sumerian micro-system, the increasingly crises-ridden Greek one was reduced under loose Persian and (in the wake of Philip II and Alexander) under tighter Macedonian and Syrian arbitral supervision to merely simulating a purposeful enactment of conflicts among decaying cities and rival leagues, pending final extinction by Rome. The Italian city-state system was comparably demoted during the Franco–Spanish contest, only to gradually forfeit under the Austrian Habsburgs even the elements of sublimation-and-simulation surviving into the era of Spanish predominance. And the Graeco–Italian developments have prefigured the consequences for the European system of its internal divisions subsiding only under the regionally distributed supervision by the United States and the Soviet Union, while overcontaining the latter by a weakening former entailed the possibility that the consequences of Britain's overcontainment of Germany would be re-enacted for the Europe-derived sector of the global system at the intersection of the westerners' late and the easterners' early stage of development.

When a system has reached its last stage, once-major actors are encompassed within an empire or constrained within the successor macro-system. In either case they lapse from acting as subjects into being at once the stage and the stake of decisive interstate transactions. No one actor can realistically aspire henceforth to a meaningfully aggrandizing conquest or preeminence-conferring influence or control in regard to another, since any such prize of success has become subject to confiscation by one or another outside agency. Any consequent increase in narrowly physical security will entail psychological debilitation of one sort or another; and either the debasing or the diluting of the stakes of contention that attend sublimation-to-simulation of competitive relations will preserve a superficial turbulence mainly as a result of trade-or-industrial transformations and transactions. For Greece, the declension was completed by 120 BC when Rome had defeated Antiochus the Great of Syria after disposing of a lesser among Macedon's Philips; for Italy, by the late sixteenth century with the weakening of both the French and the Ottoman challenges to Spanish predominance in the central Mediterranean. Even the economic significance of the Italy-centered Mediterranean was to be passing by mid-seventeenth century at the latest in favor of the Atlantic, to be challenged in the twentieth by the Pacific basin concurrently with the most authentic part of the European state system regressing into a (west-) European economic community and its members taking refuge within the Atlantic hybrid (part-empire, part-community) format of a meta-system.

For a once central and autonomous arena to recede into one subsidiary only politico-militarily or in due course also economically, and for once major actors to regress from concern with strategic security to preoccupation with sociopolitical stability and economic prosperity as the primary one, are the most dramatic sequences that manifest the evolution of a system. However, the sequence does no more point to any more generally revealing role of different successive economic systems as the manifestation of system evolution than economic contraction and expansion does in and by itself cause evolution-propelling crises or evolution-mediating military conflicts.

Command economies evolved even less often or reliably into mercantilistic-to-liberal capitalistic economic systems in the case of the agricultural empires of antiquity than in the case of more recent authoritarian continental powers, in contradistinction with the maritime empires in both eras. Beginning with those of insular Crete and Old-Kingdom (continental) Egypt, and proceeding through the many juxtapositions of agricultural hinterlands with commerce-plying coastal cities, the two types of economies tended instead to coexist at different stages of development for each. And when an economy would evolve (as did those of the modern maritime powers) from early promotional management and regulation, through mid-term deregulation and liberalization at peak efficiency, to late-stage remedial return to some kind of management, there was little likelihood that its course would coincide not only with the rise–decline trajectory of a single empire as territorial actor, but also with the evolutionary cycle of the politico-military balance-of-power dynamic – one ranging from promoting actor consolidation to being first activated and then deranged by accelerating differentiation of actors into rising and declining and/or primarily land- and sea-oriented powers before activating a previous outsider. A seeming coincidence or intersection of the two evolutionary strands – thus the mid-nineteenth-century one of British-led free trade and a moderated balance-of-power dynamic – was so rare as to be more probably than not accidental.

In elementary fact, the balance of power has been tied to the economic factor throughout in two ways: generally, in terms of the material capabilities to be mobilized and equalized; more specifically, in terms of the hard-to-equate distinctive land- and sea-based material endowments to be brought into elusive equilibrium. However, it did not fundamentally alter the overall dynamics of a system whether the key economic stake was control of land or of mineral deposits in mainly the continental sphere, and of the territorial termini of trade routes or the terms of trade governing commercial transactions in mainly the maritime sphere, any more than whether the prime actors were the agricultural-cum-mining empires of antiquity or the industrialized states of modernity. Nor did evolution within and across systems display a traceable trend from crudely territory- to purely trade-related stakes, rather than from less to more subtly and from more to less directly interrelating the two types of concerns and implied objectives.

In all cases and at all times, there will be economic incentives to expand by means of politico-military strategies and military-strategic incentives to seek influence by economic means, while the consequent conflicts surface the latent tension between the dynamics of equilibrium and the demonic drive for monolithic empire. In either case, too, the critical issue will be how to distribute the material resources created in one way or another among state-like actors and how to deal with the risks implicit in failing to secure an adequate share of resources available in the critical arena. Consequently, the main substantive (if not necessarily operational) difference will be in the nature and location of key stakes: "nature," as between direct control over territory or more indirect control over a wider range of strategic assets; "location," mainly at the center of the system adjoining the main actors or in the system's periphery. Within the bounds of such differences, the critical issues will revolve in all circumstances around access and denial of access. The range of implementing strategies and their implications for the system will remain roughly the same when at stake was the access of Athens to the Hellespont and past it to the Black Sea, overriding Sparta's capacity or disposition to deny it, or to the Corinthian isthmus and the western Mediterranean despite Corinth's opposition; and when the access critical for first Britain and subsequently the United States has shifted to either Persia itself or the Persian Gulf, despite any capacity or disposition of Russia to impede the access, or to the western Pacific, despite past opposition of Japan and possible future one of China as well. Moreover, if the ways of rationalizing the stakes and pursuing the access vary, the range of variations will narrow as the level of crisis rises. And, so long as there are geopolitical implications, the variations will be contingent more on an economic system's precipitates in the form of value-institutional frameworks of transactions than on such a system's productive or distributive modes.

That no particular economic system can by and of itself shape the fundamental political dispositions of actors any more than particular economic interests can safely determine policies over time, is confirmed when similar major events reoccur in economically variable settings. At the outset of the long developmental cycle – one that would end only when differently alien extraneous forces supplant an overmature core system – a key actor will repeatedly emerge into salience and be met by more or less sustained and coordinated resistance. Often only after the earliest waves of barbarians had been passively absorbed, one such formative event took place in the Near East, when Egypt expelled the Hyksos invaders; another in Greece, when Sparta and Athens headed successful resistance to Persia; and still others in Italy, when the Lombard communes led by Milan fought off the Holy Roman Empire in the figure of the Hohenstaufen Frederic I Barbarossa, and in Europe, when the key European actors-to-be, France, the Ottonian Germanic Empire, and, eventually, Spain, resisted successfully either the Saracens, or the Norsemen, or the

Magyars. The successful resister will subsequently occupy the storm center of a first sustained series of conflicts over balance of power and hegemony, as the strongest single territorial power to be reduced to the scale of other participants in a plural system. Thus post-Hyskos Egypt will expand imperially and evoke resistance before facing up to and repeatedly going down before a number of continental–barbarian "empires;" the inordinate power of Athens after the Persian Wars will be resented and resisted more than was and would be again Sparta's more traditionally legitimate hegemony; and opposition to the Milan of the Visconti dukes will focalize diffuse conflicts and trigger the emergence of the Italian five-power equilibrium system (including also Florence, Venice, Naples, and the Papal States) just as opposition to the Holy Roman Empire as a territorial bloc and to France's first of several ascendancies (preceding the more substantial one of Spain) will galvanize its European equivalent. Accordingly, it would be Russia's (or America's) successful resistance to the Nazi barbarians that identified her as the power to oppose by a coalition in the global setting.

Soon after the potentially hegemonial preeminent power to be contained has been identified, major events will center on early attempts to combine land-based agricultural and military with naval-mercantile resources. Long before it became the key issue whether this would result from the United States adding continental-military to its insular-mercantile, or Russia naval to her land-military, capabilities and resources more efficiently, such an effort had come from Egypt when bidding to add control of the Syrian–Palestinian coast to the riches of the Nile Valley; Athens, when advancing into central Greece (and attacking Egypt) in the interlude between the Persian and the Peloponnesian Wars; Venice or Naples, whenever it appeared they might absorb Milan as successors to the extinct Visconti line; and a France that would – and Spain that did – achieve control of the maritime resources of Genoa and of only Naples or also Sicily. The next critical events, still awaiting the global system while critical for its future evolution, will reveal the system of consolidated actors as being itself continuous: stable, because susceptible of re-equilibration; flexible, because capable of achieving a new equilibrium by means of transactions that adjusted seemingly permanent conflicts and constellations to altered conditions. When established major rivals facing new or even common threats strove then to remove themselves from servitude to the whims of secondary powers by a separate peace, this would restablize the system not least if the partial impelled the initially excluded parties toward a general settlement. Matching the separate peace between the Egyptians and the Hittites were the two largely separate peace settlements between Athens and Sparta prior to and in the middle of the Peloponnesian War, the separate peace between (Sforza) Milan and Venice initiating the mid-fifteenth century Peace of Lodi, and the separate peace arrangements of the Dutch with Spain and the English with France, the former triggering the Westphalian and the latter the Utrecht peace settlement. Often related to such transactions were conspicuous realignments, typically at or near evolutionary mid-points. They comprised, following upon ones including Egypt not least against or with (neo-) Assyria, the alignment of Sparta and Athens against rising Thebes, the shift of Florence from alliance with Venice against

Milan to one with Milan against a Venice moving inland and bidding for the Milanese succession, and that of France from alliance with Prussia against the House of Austria to one with the Habsburg monarchy against Prussia.

Likewise periodically recurrent were the more ambitious attempts to routinize balance of power conflicts through concert-type initiatives. The difficulty to convert the initiative into an accomplished concert of power encouraged efforts to place the effort under supernatural auspices. The earliest blendings of religio-mythical conclaves of tutelary gods of cities into pragmatic conciliation among territorial powers, which had made their appearance in Mesopotamia and Greece, were equaled in the Italian and European systems by allegedly holy leagues or alliances. Intended to sanctify the more prosaic goals of initiators and participants, the appeals to a higher power helped preserve the status quo only briefly or inconclusively at best: thus the early fifteenth-century Most Holy League in Italy and, enlarging in early nineteenth-century Europe upon earlier ambitious conciliation efforts at Cateau Cambrésis and Utrecht, the "sublimely mystical and nonsensical" Holy Alliance in competition with the wholly secular and pragmatic institution of concert-type consultations. The common denominator of such climactic efforts to pacify and consolidate, without fundamentally transforming, a still vigorous system among its original members included post-war exhaustion and rough equipoise, a momentary absence of an acutely polarizing conflict stake, internal disruptions calling for a period of introversion, an outside threat common to all (ranging in the more modern instances from Ottoman infidel through Protestant heretics to regicide revolutionaries), and some form of (crusading or colonial) outlet for reviving energies external to the central system.

Still less successful and also rarer than multi-power concerts were attempts at a two-power condominium or co-hegemony, such as Egypto–Hittite, Atheno–Spartan, Florentine–Venetian or -Milanese, and Anglo–French or Franco–Austrian. They were climactic mainly because their failure was followed by the center of gravity moving outward in a deteriorating system. Thus the main role in appeasement efforts migrated from would-be arbiters within to their analogues outside the system core, be it from the priests at Delphi to the king of Persia in Greece, or from a Medici of Florence to England's Cardinal Wolsey when arranging for yet another Holy League on matters Italian. In Europe, the process began when the still-births of designs for a Franco–Austrian duopoly (before the fall of the Bourbon and as an alternative to extinction of the short-lived Napoleonic dynasty) displaced leadership in the concert-type blend of demilitarized competition and institutionalized conciliation definitively to England. Likewise gravitating outward were the variably illegitimate-barbarian principal disruptive pressures on the core system, their agents ranging from the "sea peoples" to the Medans and the Persians in the Near East and from the Macedonians to the Syrians in Greece, and from the French in Italy to imperial Russia and unified Germany in Europe, while earlier-established powers, not only Egypt but also Sparta as much as Athens, Genoa and to a lesser extent Florence, Austria and more slowly France, would decline substantially.

The original members' compulsively self-assertive resistance to consummating relative demotion by complete withdrawal into passivity will, as it collides ineffectually with the more spontaneous expansionism of later or lateral entrants, announce the system's near-terminal stage. Its suppression will have been reached by stages from the earliest false starts, set afoot by objectlessly expansive nebular power aggregations, through only rudimentarily coordinated but initially system-crystallizing resistance to the first of the major powers capable of offensively consolidating an enlarged habitat, to the mid-term stage at which the differentiation of actors along rise–decline and situationally conditioned functional-institutional lines has triggered major realignments. Concert-type devices would subsequently institutionalize efforts to delay or moderate the effect of transfers of primacy from by then conservatively disposed or compulsively withdrawal-resistant system-founding members to still exuberantly expansionist late entrants.

Actors always succeed to leadership within a system contentiously, at definite points of decline of one power and ascent of another. By contrast, any one system will be linked to a succeeding one more or less consecutively in time and contiguously in space, at a less definite point of either system's progression from aggregating constituent elements (proto-system) through crises-propelled crystallization (the system's maturity norm) to some form of autonomy-terminating collapse and supersession (meta-system). Direct in time and space was the succession from the Sumerian micro-system to the (politico-culturally Babylonic) Near Eastern macro-system and on to the unifying Persian Empire. The sequence from the Greek micro-system through the eastern Mediterranean Hellenistic macro-system ended in Roman unification only when it converged with a near-parallel sequence from the Italo-western Mediterranean micro-system (centered on Rome, Syracuse, and Carthage) to the all-Mediterranean Hellenistic macro-system (initiated by Macedon's alliance with Carthage against Rome in the Second Punic War). The next-in-line Italian micro-system, which had evolved out of the remnants of the meta-system centered on the western Roman Empire beginning with the fifth century AD, was eventually superseded by the (culturally Italic) European macro-system – one that was itself to be micro-systemized relative to its world-wide expansion before the founding members of a still inchoate but genuinely global (proto-) system would divide it into two adjoining segments unevenly meta-systemized into community- and empire-types.

Before the contemporary world system could evolve toward either a world empire on the Persian and Roman model or an unprecedented community on a global scale (as distinct from a community-type regional meta-system), it had first to crystallize along lines familiar from earlier systems. If it did so in function of the US–Soviet polarity enhancing third parties (on the Papacy–Empire or Valois–Habsburg models), dealing with the polarity by means of conflict or concert would largely determine whether the next seminal micro-system (or its functional-structural equivalent, henceforth as likely or more so to amplify, than to be absorbed, into the global macro-system) clustered around the Atlantic–Northern seas region (in case of concert) or around the Pacific–Indian Ocean region (in case of conflict) – whether it was geo-culturally Euro- or Asia-centric. In either case, the enlargement would be in lie with the successive systems continuing to cluster around expanding bodies of water: from around river beds and delta estuaries (Sumerian and Near Eastern) or inland seas (Greek and Hellenistic and, subsequently, Italian in the southern, and later on the Baltic or Northern in the "northern," Mediterranean), all the way to surrounding or only adjoining major oceans (European and global).

Any such sequences are all the more cyclical the more one (micro-) system is contiguous in space and consecutive in time with the next-following (macro-) system, prefigures the next by its pattern of interactions, and helps shape it operationally by the values and institutions of its political culture. When this happens, the next-following system is not only unwittingly imitative of, but will have somehow been immanent in, the preceding one. Quasi-imitatively encompassed pattern recurrence is due to a succession of actors complying with elementary psychopolitical constants, acted out as both needs and urges persist in an environment that is fundamentally unchanging so long as it is defined by plurality of units and scarcity of assets. Immanence is by contrast a matter of more particular structural and strategic connections between systems, issuing from the contests of parties to a later (macro-) over an earlier (micro-) system and reinforced by the transmission of values and institutions from the earlier to the later system. The connection between linked systems will be consequently both operational and organic. And a significant interlock will do more than help raise mere sequences into a process of comparably staged evolutions; it will largely contribute to making the rhythm of the process genuinely cyclical in that developments in one phase co-produce the next and the complete span of evolution displays a beginning, a climax, and a terminus from which the next cycle takes off.

Structure and strategies conspire to make a macro-system most directly and immediately immanent in a micro-system wherein alliances polarize a multi-power structure, inhibiting consolidation from within and increasing incentives and opportunities for larger outside powers. The all-Mediterranean macro-system was shaped by the Greek, and the European one by the Italian, failure to group the mini-states firmly around an indigenous power capable of interacting with major outsiders on a basis approaching equality. Conversely, the gathering of the Sumerian micro-system under a relatively cognate power – Akkad and, later, Babylon – preserved for a time the area's centrality in the enlarged balance of power. Either way of the micro– yielding to a macro-system will affect the politico-cultural aspect of immanence. It does so either as the cultural reinforces the power-political impact of a unified micro-system – thus when the values, techniques, and institutions that make up a political civilization radiated from Hammurabi's Babylon into the Near Eastern macro-system – or as cultural diffusion partially compensates for a divided micro-system's power-political absorption – thus when the civilization of the Greek *poleis* spread into the Hellenistic macro-system. The difference between the two modes, and its different consequences, were most graphically conveyed by the Italian micro-system when, in the earlier instance, the Roman Law had been diffused throughout the Mediterranean in the wake of conquering Roman power and, in the later one, the Renaissance transmitted indigenous diplomatic and commercial techniques and values (along with rediscovered Roman Law institutions) to the superseding European macro-system.

The process of transmission continued and expanded when intangibles were being diffused along with tangibles to a succession of larger peripheral powers from Europe as she was being dwarfed to micro-systemic scale. At that point a growing number of local elites with broadening access to European intellectual and practical resources began to take over the function of a transmission belt previously performed by to-be-prominent future rulers more or less voluntarily apprenticed at a superior court or in a more advanced country: all the way from Sargon of Akkad, familiarized with strategically crucial innovations in Ladesh within the Sumerian, through Philip II of Macedon tutored in the Thebes of Empedocles within the Greek, to Peter I of Russia repeating the experience in Denmark and the Netherlands within Europe's Northern, microsystem. In all instances, values, techniques, and institutions will have begun to be diffused before thus energized and rationalized macro-actors did or could reduce the cultural models to the status of power-political inferiors – a process that pointed to different consequences for the global system depending on whether the continuing but not unresisted transmission of Europe-generated political culture paralleled an escalating conflict or a progressing concertation between its American and Russian recipients within the Euro-Atlantic sub-system.

The fermentation due to diffusion will foster a confluence approximating synthesis. The previously peripheral actors have repeatedly blended the received values, institutions, and techniques into native modes of thinking and doing, even as the imported ethos amplified their greater resource potential and activated latent energy. However, a cleavage will also open between the more assimilation-capable upper or ruling classes and unreceptive nativist masses, as well as between relatively easy-to-assimilate techniques and values easier to reduce to procedural or instrumental applications than to reproduce or improve upon substantively within the less intimate and possibly less stimulating atmosphere of the macro-system. Both kinds of cleavages were in evidence with regard to the Babylonic infusions into the Near East, while the societal cleavage, deep and deepening in post-Alexandrine Hellenistic successor states, obtained, with consequences for the chances of religious orthodoxy and reform, in Italianate Europe. Intra-actor cleavages extended into inter-actor schism insofar as the secular outlook transmitted from typically more urbanized micro-actors was alien to the typically more rural continental ones among the macro-states, prone to favor an explicit divine sanction for secular rule in the guise of the deified rulers in antiquity, the kingship by divine right in early modern times, and different forms of politicized religio-ideological dogmatism in the later modern era.

The imperfect synthesis sowed the seeds of eventual decay whenever inadequately assimilated foreign values worked as a dormant virus in the larger bodies social, producing fatal illness under stress from the attendant inter-actor schism. Consequently, as the "world" system grew in scope through a chain of sequences from smaller to larger-sized systems, the fact of the successor macro-systems devouring their micro-systemic progenitors only to be felled by the ingestion suggested that the resulting evolution was not only continuous, because the successive systems were linked in time and space, but also catastrophic, because the linkage was implemented through more or less concentrated violence and a more or less invasive value diffusion, in both of which the tendency to self-annihilation predominated over the capacity for assimilation and adaptation.

As distinct from the spatial contiguities and temporal continuities within the cycle from micro- to macro-systems (and, within each, from proto- to metasystemic phases) and beyond, less direct were links between successive seminal micro-systems: from the Sumerian to the Greek and from the "first" Italic (cum west Mediterranean) to the "second" (post-Roman Empire to Renaissance) Italian. Any existing currents of influence were weak from Sumeria to Greece by way of either Egypt or Crete, from the Greek to the Italic microsystem through Magna Graecia in Sicily, and through the rediscovered Roman Law principles from the earlier to the later Italian. Stronger in comparison and more direct were the connections between the early macro-systems: from the Near Eastern to the east Mediterranean Hellenistic, by way of Syria and Egypt, and from the east to the all-Mediterranean, by way of Macedon and the lesser Greek powers. The chain of transmission breaks with the Roman republic-centered Hellenistic system except for the thin thread of continuity detouring via the second Italian micro- to the post-Roman Empire European macro-system. As salience alternated meanwhile between micro- and macro-systems, the contact between an intervening macro- and the next-following micro-system was closer than the connection between the two micro-systems, if less close than the tie from a micro- to the macro-system that superseded it. Thus in the cycle from the Sumerian micro- through the Near Eastern macro- to the Greek micro-system the main connection between the latter two was through the operative impact of Persia–Phoenicia and Egypt on the maritime Greek states in particular, and less by way of Assyria serving as a presumptive model for early Sparta. Macedon linked not only the Greek micro- to the east Mediterranean macro-system, but (faintly) also the latter to the Italo–Hispanic–North African west Mediterranean micro-system as part of the process through which the all-Mediterranean macro-system was to be meta-systemized under Rome.

As the quintessential Europe of the founding members receded to micro-systemic scale relative to the global arena, she like her predecessors was being devoured by her progeny. Should the successors misapply imperfectly absorbed values and techniques during the macro-systemic interlude centered on the US–Soviet polarity, it would be in keeping with the pattern of discontinuities between micro-systems if, the next seminal one being Asian–Pacific rather than Euro-Atlantic, it was spatially and value-institutionally remote from Europe while occupying a larger space and clustering around a more important body of water than a preceding one. In such a case, any impact from the Eurocentric system would be substantially modified by being transmitted through the United States and the Soviet Union as henceforth mainly Pacific powers geostrategically as well as culturally.

Implicit in the phenomenon of transmission is the question whether successive systems – and, especially, discontinuous seminal micro-systems –

start each at a higher level of development than the preceding one and reach a higher stage of development within either the same or a shorter period of time. Unlike a micro-system being superseded by a macro-system as a matter of operational interlock and value-institutional transmission in space, are successive micro- (and macro-) systems linked through development acceleration over time? The question is easier to pose than to answer if only because the length of the proto-systemic phase is the most difficult to assess, with consequences for the duration of the crystallized norm-period before a system subsides and becomes extinct. Thus even if the evolution of the Greek system can be said to have started from a higher level and evolved farther quicker than the Sumerian analogue, if only because the latter lacked any discernible antecedents of a system-like character, a similar acceleration need not necessarily apply to the Italic micro-system relative to the Greek and to the Italian relative to the Italic any more than to any one of the macro-systems relative to the one preceding it. To the extent that development did accelerate, this would be due less to any precedents-assimilating imitation amounting to learning than to conditions in the last phase of the immediately antecedent (if not necessarily identically scaled) system as it were reproducing themselves while benefiting from rising levels of overall, but mainly the material-technical, civilization.

Whatever the reasons for it, the Near Eastern and the Hellenistic macro-systems would appear to have reached their climax at a level denoting an earlier (fifteenth- to sixteenth-century) stage of development of the European system. It is likewise no more than plausible that the Greek micro-system either started at or quickly proceeded to a higher level than had the Sumerian and, by resisting complete supersession longer, reached a higher developmental level at its climax. By the same token, the Italian micro-system was at its fifteenth-century height developmentally superior to the Greek (and more clearly to the first Italian) one at their respective peaks of structural crystallization and self-conscious strategic rationality; it may be held to have also evolved at an accelerated rate, provided the length of its incubation from the fifth to the fourteenth centuries is discounted because of the unusually severe disruptions and technological retrogressions wrought by the disintegrating Roman Empire. The obverse has been the case so far, for opposite reasons, for the incubation of at least the central core of the global system, whatever might prove to be true for its remainder. One reason is that, just as an antecedent system can not only anticipate the evolution of a later or emergent one in the sense of prefiguring it, but can also advance and accelerate such evolution, it can constrain or hinder it as well. It will do so by diffusing or imposing values and techniques inimical to the full deployment of the crises-processing motor and the conflicts-centered mechanism of evolution. Thus, transposing the conflict-inhibiting norms of the late Eurocentric system onto an unsuitable terrain has constrained the rudimentary formation of regional balance-of-power systems in the periphery of the global proto-system. This happened even as the competitive US–Soviet bipolarity promoted peripheral actors to levels of resource and projected them into roles well in excess of their innate capabilities and potential for self-governing conduct – while sheltering them from the attendant risks and sanctions that normally help identify viable and stimulate developing actors while ordering a system.

All in all, the evolution of more or less linked micro- and macro-systems is over very long periods of time a function of three overlapping cycles or quasi-cycles: (1) the life cycle of each system individually; (2) the longer cycle comprising two systems of unequal, micro- and macro-, scale linked in space through strategies that intertwine structures and foment value-institutional transmission at uneven points of transition in time from the proto- to the meta-systemic phase of each; and (3) the longest but also least continuous and internally reproductive quasi-cycle, relating one seminal micro-system to the next via an intervening macro-system. In consequence, the most inclusive manifestation of evolution encompassing discrete systems resides in a combination of gravitation and gradation: gravitation in space of salient systems attending the overall expansion of the boundary of any two linked systems; and, roughly parallel to the gravitation, a less determinate gradation in the levels of the climactic evolutionary stage attained by successive (micro- and macro-) systems and, least reliably, acceleration in the rate of their evolutionary tempo over the very long term if not uniformly over shorter time periods.

Tracing the broadly cyclical progression of evolution across successive systems reveals different traits and phenomena as the inspected periods lengthen. The focus shifts and the compass expands from individual recent events to more inclusive processes and tendencies that subsume them, from competitive interactions to cumulative evolution, and from precipitants or "causes" of particular actions to general patterns of continuities in regard to specifically changing actors and arenas. Thus, as the encompassed time-span lengthens, the fading of detail is compensated for by a sharpened outline, abstracted from unevenly remote events and capable of ordering the shapeless plethora of happenings at once too recent and too many.

Looking back to, say, the mid-nineteenth century (1848) reveals only the separate factors presumed to have led to the first of the two world wars that extinguished the European macro-system. The attention is focused on events such as the German unification and the consequent intensification of inter-great-power antagonisms and on such phenomena as rival nationalisms and imperialisms caught up in and exacerbating a resuscitated *realpolitik*. Pushing back the boundary of retrospection to 1815 – another commonplace conventional date for considering the "evolution" of the international system – brings into focus the remoter origins of the just-mentioned events and phenomena. They include the French Revolutionary and Napoleonic impetus to the chain-reacting spread of France-originated nationalism eastward, via Germany; the provisionally culminating gravitation of land-based power in the same direction toward briefly triumphant Russia, and the impulse urbanization and industrialism gave to the sociopolitical and -economic mass mobilization that underlay nationalism and imperialism and supplied the raw materials for rival sociopolitical ideologies as the putative challengers to more prosaically motivated rivalries. Beginning the inspection still further back, the mid-seventeenth century (1648), reveals the rise of the basic politico-administrative framework of the above-named events and processes, the modern territorial state. It also reveals the coincident differentiations, into land- and sea-oriented and ascending and declining powers, significant for the operation of a by-then clearly articulated balance of power as well as for the henceforth perceptible recurrent linkages between strategies and structures.

It will, however, be reserved for the view encompassing the "fall" of the Roman Empire and its sequelae, to identify the gradual and unevenly spaced crystallization of the actors and the arena critical for the European state system from earliest beginnings: the alternating contraction and expansion of both and the attendant actor–arena disparities; the hierarchical stratification of unevenly consolidated actors and the segmentation of the arena among unevenly developing central and subordinate theaters; and the passage of both the state-like actors and the systemic arena through the full range of evolutionary stages (from initial structuration to final supersession) and foreign-policy phases (between tentative adumbration and terminal simulation of self-affirmation or self-restraint), spanning the complete spectrum of overlapping schisms and actor generations. The longest possible view, finally, will reach past the empire and state systems of late antiquity to the beginnings of both western civilization and westward-gravitating complexes of power. Over that distance it becomes possible to combine two crucial and complementary perspectives: at one extreme to penetrate to the most elementary givens that make up the physical, the existentially operative, and the normatively charged, constituents of any and all "world politics"; at the other extreme to embrace the most elusive interlocks of particular systems in their either merely sequential or also cyclical, but almost always somehow linked, dynamic connections.

When the particular structures and specific strategies identified in the shorter perspectives are as it were retrojected upon more dimly seen remoter events, they reveal past analogues and substantiate the presumption of recurrence. Major developments appear then in a light that shifts emphasis from unique to uniform phenomena and from specific cases to comparable circumstances: it becomes possible to weigh the comparative significance of the particular and the general. A complementary gain accrues when the full range of factors affecting system evolution over the longest time span is brought to bear on the course of events within the shorter or shortest span of time still qualifying as historical. Thus validating structurally conditioned strategic options that were demonstrably essayed by the land and the sea powers of East and West prior to World War I by projecting them backward onto comparable past contingencies has the same, and a reinforcing, effect as projecting forward onto and beyond the twentieth-century supersession of the European system the patterns of like developments that can be derived only from the longer and the longest perspectives: both procedures reduce the causal significance of seemingly time-bound peculiar factors and idiosyncratic perversions of any one power's or policy-maker's strategy or tactics.

Within the converging perspectives the drama of the European system, only more vividly recorded than that of any other system, appears as merging with the destinies of the main actors as they and the arena underwent the processes of becoming, maturing, and yielding to the future. At the latter point, it became possible on the strength of precedents to project the near-term future of the global international system emerging out of World War II. Whereas the climactic conflict was implicit in the resource–role–risk triad that had shaped the relations between previously "victorious" and "defeated" European powers, before its outcome corrected the derangement in favor of the larger successor powers, the future has predictably exhibited features substantially short of the actually anticipated radical transformation in all of the highlighted areas. This has been the case inasmuch as the supposedly transforming revolutionary military technology was subject to historically amply evidenced tendency for it to be absorbed in and through conventional political routines even before the self-correcting dynamics of technological change did its part; the allegedly co-responsible impact of fundamentally contrary sociopolitical ideologies was pragmatized through the re-emergence of unevenly tangible territorial and role/status-related stakes peculiar to operationally manageable hegemony-and-equilibrium centered competition between parties pulled thus back to rediscovering traditional modes; and, finally, the postulated source of radical discontinuity in structural bipolarity was progressively dried up as the tendency to pluralization implicit in a two-power conflict made itself felt. By the same token, the remoter, medium-term future was likely to preserve – as it did at other apparently radical turning points – much of the patterns that enframed and manifested evolution in the past. It would do so even as the transient presents witnessed a softening of the harsher or only disguised the cruder particulars of the interactions that had historically impelled or mediated this progression.

Over the longest time, action constitutive of world politics has appeared to be prone, at perhaps an accelerating rate, to being diluted in kind as a result of the instantly manifest affects of operational transactions falling behind the consequences of longer-term organic transformations. If the gradual refinement of instinctual reflexes into the rigors of strategic rationality was being simultaneously infused with counsels from practical reasonableness, less primitively visceral reflexes than originally dominant or not-so-virtuously progressivist instincts as allegedly regnant were also being disguised within the contours of only deceptive or also self-deceiving rationalizations. Dilution and disguise merged into morally problematic actuality behind the façade of ethical progress as, in near parallel, the world political process stalled in its progression from gods-saturated mythological antecedents toward the high summit at which turbulent clashes of raw forces are invested with genuinely tragic collision of deeply felt values. Whereas the two confrontations have long contributed about equally to the doomed heroics of attempts to evade the compounded stress through the achievement of hegemony, a provisionally entrenched routine politics could record only lengthening spells of a contrary tendency: for the dramatic tension to slacken before subsiding into a parody of the primeval beginnings in melodramatized encounters of equally shallow civic or official myths.

8

From Progression to Projection

Historically evidenced continuities justify the initial presumption of their continuance. And the presumption can guide speculation about the emerging future of the contemporary global system, to begin with the system's structure as the setting within which actors are formed and their conflicts take shape.*

CORE AND PERIPHERY IN THE GLOBAL SYSTEM-TO-BE

That which has been hailed after World War II as the global system was initially far from deserving that label. It was at first global only operationally, in function of the inter-superpower conflict extending from the crystallized core into a periphery that was not yet articulated in structure and differentiated as to functions (i.e., was "proto-systemic"). By drawing in, as either passive or only responsive parties, a range of third countries, the competition supplied the crucial stimulus and supplement to intra- and inter-regional dynamics actuated by issues that were locally relevant. The consequent onset of the recurrent trend toward diffusion of power among partially self-sustaining and inner-oriented actors was arguably set off by the United States opposing Russia as the most assertive and threatening, or also by Soviet opposition to the United States as the initially dominant and overbearing, first salient power acting as the trigger to a polarized conflict apt to eventually disperse power more widely within the system.

Lastingly more important than which impulse was primary was the fact that it impinged from the outset directly or indirectly on both the European (or

---

* The following three sections apply to contemporary issues the evolving structure-relevant patterns developed in chapters 1, 2, and 3, respectively.

central-systemic) and the extra-European (or peripheral) sectors. Before the two would become part of a future system, they had been linked processually by virtue of the peripheral (or Third-World) segment being latent in the European colonial empires. To the debatable extent that those empires comprised pre-existing sociopolitical organisms which had approximated the attributes of a state within arenas approaching the quality of a structured system of states or quasi-states, the colonial arrangements represented one way of transcending or just moving beyond the condition of a mature, conflict-centered interstate system into that of a "meta-system" (of a particular, the imperial, kind). The subsequent lapse of (western) Europe into a different (community-type) variety of meta-system coincided with the center of the only emergent rudimentary global system (or "proto-system") being divided into two contrasting and competing imperial orders: on one side the two-tier Atlantic system, consisting of the European Community and the superimposed imperialized community of the Atlantic alliance under a hegemonial ally; on the other side a two-stage empire-type eastern European meta-system, slowly evolving from a coercive empire into more consensual relations of the commonwealth or community character.

Two main consequences followed from the overall process of system formation comprising once again unevenly evolved central-systemic and peripheral sectors. One consequence replicated the tendency to premature structuration in the peripheral segment, reminiscent of the abortive efforts in early Europe to "renovate" the Roman Empire. A restored Ghanaian empire-centered Pan–Africa and a colonial empire-seeking Indonesia were only the most conspicuous instances. Such false starts assumed nearly everywhere the form of non-viable actual or attempted, would-be authoritative or associational, aggregations of presumed power potentials for the generation of prompt prosperity. They conformed to type by displaying functional indifferentiation (mainly as to political-economic and policing-military functions or also secular and pseudo-sacral elements) within actors, and giving rise to radical hetero-geneity among them. Primarily responsible for the array of the substantially risk- and cost-free initiatives was an environment that was operationally permissive due to the partially stalemated inter-superpower competition being itself a relatively low-risk and low-tension affair in the last resort. The other, reinforcing consequence flowed from the largely effective efforts to impose central-systemic norms constraining the use of force on peripheral actors from the outside. This unprecedented brake on spontaneous dynamics, dictated by the desire to avoid direct superpower involvement on opposing sides to local-peripheral conflicts, confirmed the trend for force to be locally organized and used primarily for factional intra-actor contentions. The consequence of precipitation in ambitious initiatives and retardation in developing the means for backing them forcefully has been to slow down the identification of viable peripheral actors. Such were necessary to galvanize the development of largely self-contained, autonomous Third-World systems of relatively minor actors within a correspondingly constricted arena (i.e., "micro-systems"), capable of performing one of the roles available to micro-systems in the emergence of a system of larger actors (a "macro-system"), now on global scale.

Whereas the proto-systemic Third-World segment was manifestly latent in either the colonial or the pre-colonial antecedents, the global macro-system might eventually be recognized as having been immanent in a Third-World micro-system – in the sense that it was the latter that stimulated the larger powers into forms of organization and behavior constitutive of a system rather than the other way around. This was an alternative to several such micro-systems being gradually integrated (*qua* sub-systems) into a global system that confirmed its immanence, with respect to both operational dynamics and operative values, in a European system that had been dwarfed (was "micro-systemized") by outside actors being sporadically brought into, before helping supersede, the pre-existing core. The already achieved extent to which the global system was structured has been due to the sheer fact of inter-superpower competition projecting third parties into becoming. But it would be the specific strategies adopted by the two major powers with respect to one another and, implicitly, the third parties that would largely shape the link between particular micro-systems, evolving toward plurality or enforced unity, and the global macro-system-to-be.

The immanence of the Hellenistic macro- in the Greek micro-system and of the European in the Italian, materialized as a widening range of outside major parties became involved in the decreasingly autonomous contentions that had taken place or originated within the earlier developed smaller systems. The prior invitations to the United States and Russia to take part in intra-European conflicts having had a like consequence, the ensuing US–Soviet competition over the succession to Europe has already begun to induce or permit other extraneous powers to take part in specifically European matters (China) or matters affecting Europe directly (e.g. India in south-west Asia). The effects of the inter-superpower competition on the emergent macrosystem compared then with the consequences which the Papal–Imperial conflict, focused on the emergent periphery of Europe and preceding the Franco–Aragonese/Spanish–Imperial conflict targeting the farther-advanced Italy, had had for its European antecedent. Likewise comparable has been the infusion of religio- or social-political (then Papal and Imperial, now socialist and capitalist) and procedural-institutional (then Italian, now European) values into the larger system. If, moreover, the impact of New World American on Old World European values generated a western hybrid comparable to the Hispano–Italian synthesis, a question remained unresolved: Whose, if anyone's, would be the "barbarian" energy injected decisively into Europe's maturer culture from the east (or south) to either complement or offset the American?

So far, in conformity with earlier precedents, east European and even more extraneous Third-World actors impinged on the European core operationally and, in value terms, normatively only to the extent such actors' comparative development stage made possible. By the same token, it again depended on future developments toward or away from various forms of unity inside the generative micro-system – currently the nucleus of the one-time European system – what if any impact it would have on the macro-system-to-be. Reflecting precedents, a unity more or less enforced from within could be facilitated, as had been Italy's around Rome, by a triangularized (US–Soviet–

Chinese) competition that deflected the major powers' concerns elsewhere. It would then materialize around Germany or a Franco–German core. Or a markedly consensual coordination of polities by the core-European powers would result from inter-superpower accommodation in the peripheries having relaxed their competition at the system's center as well. Closer coordination on the small-European plane would then aim at protecting joint autonomy from the consequences of the superpowers' drift into co-hegemony.

The global effect of a united Western Europe of something like the Gaullist persuasion would differ from the diplomatic initiatives by de Gaulle himself, based on France alone. Thus also in the Hellenistic–Mediterranean setting the effect of the rebellion by a Perseus against Roman supremacy had differed from that of Greece being effectively unified around Macedon under one of his predecessors; similarly, in the Italo–European context, the impact of Venice as a would-be balancer between extra-Italian powers differed from what she could have accomplished as the effective unifier of Italy from within. Of critical importance was in either case the material potential, implicit in the amount of space from which to act. So was – and continued to be – the timing of the crucial interplay between unevenly developed actors and arenas. In this respect, the difference is one between the effect an Italy unified in the fifteenth century would have had on European developments and the much smaller impact the nineteenth-century unity actually did have. Both the spatial and the temporal aspects carried implications for the range of possible future roles classic Europe would play globally, within a range extending from a pivotal role in the formation of a system to the position of a passive object of policies and pressures originating from outside the boundary of indigenous civilization.

As regards the Third-World periphery, its parallel role in evolving the macro-system will be that of positional "barbarians," impacting from outside the boundaries of the (core-) system. And if the alternative was between the future macro-system being immanent in a Third-World micro-system and the regional micro-systems being integrated into a differently centered system of larger actors, the conduct of potential major Third-World powers and the strategies of the pre-established central-systemic powers would determine which alternative applies. For an eventual macro-system to grow out of, say, a Middle Eastern or one of the regional Asian micro-systems in being or becoming, certain developments would have to precede. One is the definitive displacement of US–Soviet (and third-power) competition, liable to aggrandize the local parties in one way or another, to such an area from a European arena that was frozen by terminal stalemate. Another, still more conclusive and in all probability consequent development, would be for both of the Europe-related contenders to be effectively eliminated as prime global actors through sudden cataclysms or gradual erosion. And a still other prerequisite, arising out of one or both of the other two, is for the regional Third-World micro-system to have become more firmly crystallized than either the decaying or the still-emergent other segments of the global arena. In such circumstances, what role the procreative micro-system would play in shaping the macro-system would again depend on whether a superior power indigenous to it did or did not unify it, more or less forcibly, from within.

A regional system comprising such major powers as China, Japan, and India, flanked or not by diminished Asia- or Pacific-oriented Russia and America, could functionally perform as one of the micro-type. But it would tend to resist both unification from within and an early loss of either identity or independence to a superseding larger system of the macro-type. By contrast, the same major powers would be the ones to respond actively to dynamics within a micro-system consisting of mini-states or mini-empires in south-east Asia or the Middle East. The micro-system's forcible unification from within would replicate a pattern historically common in the East, and China as the unifier from the outside would conform still more exactly to the model of rural hinterland pressing against coastal-commercial cities – currently Hong Kong and beyond. Conversely, were the micro-systems to remain plural and autonomous, they were apt to hinge in one region on the contemporary equivalents of past city-states such as Singapore, Taiwan, and South Korea asserting themselves relative to Indochina or China; and, in another, on Israel, core areas of Lebanon, and the Persian Gulf sheikdoms facing up to (Greater) Syria and Iraq or Iran.

Other things being equal, effective capability (including societal energy) will develop sooner in units of (territorially and demographically) small size than in larger units. Meeting the capability requisite of actor and system formation in either of the two regions before the larger actors have caught up would reflect the re-emergence of once-prevailing conditions: chief among them has been the restored significance of the capacity to finance state-of-art weaponry (rather than mobilize vast armies) as critical for determining both role and status. Moreover, the extent to which actor autonomy was favored over bids to unify either arena would then again reflect topography, assimilating a south-east Asia rich in natural divides to Greece and the obstacle-free desert of the Middle East to the alluvial Sumerian plain.

The difference between plural autonomy and empire-type unity in the Third World would affect not only the operational weight of the extra-European actors in the emergent macro-system. It would condition also the force of impact from indigenous values, raising the issue of succession to Europe also in normative and procedural terms. The countervailing diffusion of non-western political culture might not in either case differ all that much from a mere infiltration (and imperceptibly subversive hybridization) of core-systemic values by the mores communicated in earlier times through barbarian migrations escalating into or experienced as invasions. But it would create a more immediate or pressing problem for the previously dominant (Europeanist or Euro–Americanist) value system if the extraneous impact was backed by a major power arising out of empire-type unification than if it was mediated by plural micro-systems. In the former instance in particular, the values of hierarchical sub- and super-ordination would seriously challenge the (western) ideal of equality in status modified by inequality of role or function as the normative basis for the preservation of essential corporate autonomies through actual power-balancing; and any reduction of the high value placed on competitively safeguarded corporate autonomy, responsible for the catastrophically enacted incremental evolution in the West, would foster the resurgence of cyclically operative statics oriental-style. At the very least, the wider reception of the western values would remain, or become increasingly, only formal. It would replicate, if for opposite reasons, the only superficial reception of the values and practices of Italian statecraft in a Europe materially unready before the French invasions, were indigenous rituals (such as the Chinese one of "punishing expeditions" in behalf of unfocused intimidation of offending barbarians substituting for openly declared or enacted belligerency with a specific object) to continue to prevail over the alien western forms.

Contrary to the future global system originating from outside the West is the process of integrating previously peripheral areas into the pre-developed central-systemic core in ways that continued fostering the essential homogeneity of the enlarged system as one of near-uniformly constituted and motivated (territorial) actors. It was then up to issue-aware strategies to forge functional and/or political links between the current central system and what then would provisionally be its sub-systems in ways calculated to slow down the erosion and forestall a premature supersession of the core. As for the position of the sub-systems, it would follow the precedent of, say, the so-called Northern system in Europe at the turn of the seventeenth into the eighteenth century, as distinct from that of the Italian system in the late fifteenth and the sixteenth. The development would leave open the question which of the parties to the sub-system (on the model of the same issue arising between Denmark, Sweden, and Russia in the earlier instance), if any, would evolve into a major-power member in the enlarged central system; and which, therefore, would infuse the member's assimilable values into the presiding value synthesis, conjointly with the core system's center of gravity migrating across its expanding scope.

Since it is the course of competition among the major powers that will largely determine the locus of the impulse to shape the global macro-system, and its short- and long-term effects on the so far seminal micro-system, it has continued to be of note which particular cleavages, or schisms, conditioned the same powers' strategic postures and self-perceived identities.

It has been in keeping with historical antecedents that the US–Soviet conflict and, as its consequences, the beginnings of a major new phase in the development of the international system, began under the auspices of the sacral–secular schism, appropriately modified and updated from its manifestations in medieval Europe and still earlier. The peculiarly strong ideological content, characteristic of early phases of system evolution, resurfaced in the conflict being initially defined as one between (Marxist–Leninist) communism and (Keynesian or welfare) capitalism. It became a matter for the evolving balance, or overlap, between messianic-universalist (standing for "sacral") and pragmatic-particularist ("secular") values and mind-sets inherent in each party to shape its foreign-policy-relevant political culture and institutions, determining the two powers' strategic perceptions and actual conduct. When the eventual ascendancy of the more secular-pragmatic over the (pseudo-) sacral-aspirational element had once again made itself felt, the habitual trend set in. It was reflected in the conflict being redefined as one between the United States and the Soviet Union as great powers, while their being perceived as representing the liberal-democratic West and the authoritarian-to-totalitarian East highlighted the pertinence of the corresponding (East–West) schism. Just as, before, the schism-defining overlap has been between socialism and capitalism as rational techniques for dealing with material culture, so now it was one between the political-cultural values of East and West. The ambiguous mix of diversity and similarity would near-clandestinely intensify a conflict over geostrategic stakes, fanning out from east-central Europe into outlying peripheral areas as it escalated between parties mistakenly treated as polar opposites in every respect.

Once the shift of emphasis from the sacral–secular to the East–West schism had concretized the parties to conflict, the next step was to pragmatize the enactment of the conflict itself as it was being routinized in mode and amplified in the range of instruments and scope of the arena. The trend pointed to yet another, the land–sea power, schism emerging as objectively salient if not always consciously commanding strategically. The main schism-related consequence of the global expansion of the conflict was to shift two major eastern powers westward in strategy-relevant perception: first Japan, culturally only incipiently and superficially westernized; and, subsequently, an even less assimilated or assimilation-ready China. This confused both the character and the policy implications of the East–West schism, just as the intermittent strategic activation of some Third-World parties was blurring the boundary between center and periphery.

The re-emergence of the land–sea power schism, one focused on functions and supporting resources, was confirmed when revolutions aimed from above at improving managerial-economic efficacy set out belatedly, first in China (Deng) and then also in Soviet Russia (Gorbachev). To the extent that their bias was to imitate the US-orchestrated if not US-imposed post-World War II revolution in Japan, they differed from earlier revolutions more closely reflective of the East–West schism: the 1911 Sun Yat Sen and post-1949 Maoist revolutions following in China upon a Russian antecedent to each. The revolutionary upheavals in the Third World lagged by contrast appropriately behind, since for the underlying tension between modernist and traditionalist features to bear mainly on actor formation was in keeping with the more commonly intra- than inter-actor focus of the corresponding (secular–sacral) schism. It mattered then less whether the element doing duty for the sacral assumed formally religious characteristics (fundamentalism) or superficially secularized cultural ones (mythologizing nativism), because both were anti-western. The challenge of the autochthonous factor to western-secular elements could remain unresolved in a latently revolutionary situation (beginning with post-colonial India, among many others); or one or the other element might provisionally preside over only apparent fusion as part of an official, or as a result of a grass-roots, revolution (witness the sequence in Iran). In either case, the intra-actor varieties of the (quasi-) sacral–secular schism and its temporary resolutions did not engender a more definitive cleavage between West- and East-favoring actors within the periphery, nor did they unequivocally affect the enactment of the land–sea power schism by powers of the central system.

This fact could not but enhance the measure of schism-related indeterminacy in the more developed system segment, reinforcing the effect of the more conspicuously structure-related ambiguities. In reproducing the dilemmas of transition to a clearer differentiation between schisms and a more definite salience of one of them, the situation may have compounded the conditions following in earlier eras upon the dissolution of the Roman imperial order and subsequently of a medieval order formally if not otherwise centered on the Holy Roman Empire. On the plane of the corresponding schisms, the United States reproduced more closely Byzantium's alternately more maritime and continental orientation, whereas the Soviet Union matched the older Empire's ambiguously eastern and western character. And while both superpowers, *qua* continent-wide powers with (unequal) naval capabilities, approximated the amphibious character of Spain in the early modern setting, especially a Russia extending also physically into Asia shared Africa-facing Spain's inner turmoil as a not wholly European power. Finally, with regard to the sacral–secular schism, Byzantine caesaro-papism passed on one (synthesizing) way of dealing with the dualism to tsarist and, in radically secularized form, Soviet Russia, just as identifying Spain's secular interests with the cause of Catholicism (and the latter's cause with the interests of the West) was replicated by the United States when it assumed the mantle of selfless defender of the free world (and identified the latter's cause with that of free-market capitalism).

All such ambiguities would fade only gradually when the surfacing issue of hegemony invariably prevailed over everything else due to the attendant strategic stress. Only when West–East or East–East polarities were tied up with inter-sacral ones would the sobering issue of politico-military hegemony be temporarily overwhelmed by the inflammatory issue of doctrinal heresy: within Christianity between the (Eastern or Orthodox) Patriarch and the (Western or Catholic) Popes and then between Catholicism and Protestantism just as between Ottoman Sunni and Persian Shia within Islam – and, more recently, between Soviet and Chinese brands of Marxism or socialism, before real-politics resurfaced as determinant out of the resulting confusion.

In such (transitional, or only peripherally impinging) conditions, it will be the added task for deliberate strategy to dissipate the ambiguities in favor of a priority of conflict stakes reflecting the salience of one schism. In the contemporary setting, the deranging effects of schisms-related ambiguity have been aggravated on two counts. One has had to do with the extraordinary degree of value anarchy. It has consisted, next to the range of micro-systemic values potentially in line to shape an emergent global macro-system, and the hypertrophy of unevenly vital-or-eroded schism-related actor values, of divergent views on the legitimacy or expediency of the use of force. The operationally disruptive effect or consequence of this normative heterogeneity exceeded the impact a different heterogeneity, due to actors based and defined territorially coexisting with differently constituted and oriented actors (currently "transnational"), normally has had on nascent proto-systems (and, occasionally, meta-systems). The other, easier to identify, count was implicit in more specific, functional or instrumental, factors. They have impeded the emergence of the land–sea power schism, typical of a fully developed core-system, to objectively dominant and subjectively perceived salience.

The integral purity of the land–sea power schism has faded with the decreasing superiority of the leading sea power. Such superiority rested historically on a unique possession of skills in navigation and maneuver (and related exchanges of fire), at special premium in conditions of technological stability. And it was buttressed by privileged allocation of resource for naval construction and maintenance, equally crucial when the cost of the latter exceeds that of the former and the combined costs are high relative to overall country resources and to instantly achievable returns on investment. That superiority declined from its eighteenth-century peak in the Anglo–French period with the shift from sail-equipped to steam-propelled vessels in the Anglo–German and on to atomic-powered vessels in the US–Soviet era. Not only the mechanical skills became easier to acquire, but the leading powers have had to allocate limited resources more nearly equally between technologically more rapidly changing land- and sea-based military instruments. The constraints, growing for Britain as the German phase unfolded, have not been negligible for the United States. And although the resources the Soviet political system was able to allocate to the naval arm once it had been accorded priority were greater than those available to Admiral Tripitz, they were subject to definite limits from competing demands. In the circumstances, the United States could aspire to sufficient sea control to seriously inhibit Soviet naval action against key global bottlenecks. But it could not confidently assert naval supremacy, necessary for projecting naval power against the Soviet home base in ways affecting the military balance on land directly – a capacity Britain had possessed against Spain and France and could still envisage when formulating war-waging scenarios against Germany.

A diminished capacity of the leading maritime power to exercise supremacy does not automatically annul the salience of sea-power itself, *qua* capability, another defining condition of effective land–sea power schism. In this respect, the atomic variety of inanimate propulsion has gone far toward restoring the independence of naval craft from widely disseminated land-based facilities – an independence that was previously highest for the (wind-dependent) sailing ship and lowest in the (coal-dependent) steamship era. The effect of the military importance of the sea being thus heightened has been limited so long as land- and space-based nuclear instruments were needed to supplement sea-borne deterrents, as part of a complementarity that matched that of dreadnoughts or U-boats with army and tank corps. But the growing reliance on sea-borne instruments has nevertheless offset the diminished significance of commercially valuable colonial positions overseas, previously nourishing the schism. This meant that, if the seaborne part of the Soviet retaliatory capability matched the German High Sea Fleet in its military objective as a defense against preemptive assault by the maritime adversary, it matched no less the psychopolitical purpose of the capability as a source of pressure in support of peacetime geopolitical objectives. Meanwhile, the critical importance of deploying the age's ultimate weapon on both land and sea has not been nullified by the emergent third, outer-space, dimension (itself subject to the neutralizing effect of anti-satellite technology).

Likewise modified, if in essence preserved, were the related conditions of a land–sea power schism, such as the requirement that the continental and maritime arenas be inseparable. This requisite was only updated from its original basis in shared needs for economic and diplomatic-strategic access to both spheres when the early industrial was followed by the latest military-technological revolution and the worldwide scope of the demand-and-supply was supplemented by that of the deterrence-and-defense equation. If the latter reinforced the inseparability requisite, its military-technological and -strategic constituents weakened only temporarily and hypothetically the other requisite, demanding that the two (insular-maritime and continental) power types be invulnerable to one another when employing only the resources specific to them – a condition that forces each to invade the sphere of the other through alliances and other forms of penetration. The mutual vulnerability due to long-range strategic missiles, which seemed to nullify this condition, ceased to be controlling as soon as military-technological and other defense-oriented innovations favored a return to more conventional military strategies and their diplomatic and economic supports.

The overall result has been a marginally altered land–sea power relationship. The two core powers were less polar opposites and more mixed continental–maritime or amphibious powers: less different than England had been from France or Germany and more like Spain and the Ottomans or the Hellenistic powers among themselves – a situation somewhere between a pure or classic schism of seventeenth to twentieth-century Europe and near-complete separation or separability of land- and sea-based capabilities in medieval Europe (as well as in early or primitive antiquity). At the same time, key objective-operational and subjective-perceptual features associated with the schism persisted within the west-to-east spectrum of decreasingly maritime and increasingly continental powers extending to China. Moreover, the very narrowing of the difference between the two superpowers increased the land–sea power overlap with the result of intensifying the conflict at least provisionally. The anxiety of the principal sea power to preserve its narrowed lead has heightened, concurrently with the ambition of the navally still inferior power to extend parity to the oceans and overseas, while pressures from a protracted arms race exceeded cumulatively the concentrated impact of armed combat.

Two additional factors contributed meanwhile to the continuing psychological significance of the schism: one material and the other attitudinal. The former resided in a historically validated fact: even though naval battles were never militarily decisive unless confirmed by outcomes of fighting on land (a fact generating the maritime powers' interest in continental allies), superior naval capacity engendered the material preconditions of eventual success also in the territorial balance of military power (a fact sufficient in technological and otherwise varied conditions to nurture the interest of land powers in overseas assets). The other factor consists in a tendency peculiar to sea powers such as the Dutch and the English: to equate naval mastery with divine mandate, with the result of conferring a still higher sanction on the practice to identify naval power with defense of peace against its war- and aggression-biased land-based military counterpart. Asserting normative asymmetry where the facts pointed to functional complementarity of the two branches of militarily usable capabilities has continued to be provocative. It has done so even after naval superiority had ceased to confer a physical invulnerability more difficult to match on land, while being offensively usable (through blockade, transport of troops, coastal bombardment) against a land power attempting to even out the disparity.

Just as the material foundation of the psychology of the land–sea power schism in disparate geo-economic situations has thus survived to technological changes, so has its value-related normative extrapolation. It has been fully revived when the physical protection conferred on the insular power by nature has appeared capable of being raised by advanced technology from the maritime moat to outer space and justified by the uniquely defensive peaceableness of both the object of such protection and its means.

POLAR VARIETIES OF NEW AND NOT-SO-NEW ACTORS

Perhaps at no time prior to the latest (and last?) spell of the Atlantic era had the structure of the arena conditioned the early formation of actors as much as it has in the "less developed" periphery of the post-European global system. Surfacing from latent to manifest existence by virtue of system-wide pressures in favor of decolonization, the "new" states were stimulated by inter-superpower competition and initially socialized by membership in proliferating international institutions. The inflow of both tangible and intangible resources promoted the new-born actors materially, as recipients of competitive (US and Soviet) assistance for economic development and military defense; and, as either stakes or strategic supports in contentions between the greater powers, when not would-be mediators if not arbiters between them, the minor countries were projected into diplomatic roles far beyond their national capabilities. Both kinds of stimulants were at odds with parallel restraints, from the same source, on conflicts between the lesser states, impeding internally or intra-regionally fuelled resource consolidation. For the effects of system-wide normative restraints to commonly prevail over the inflow of material and other resources meant that conflictual stimulants would be blunted in favor of developmental stagnation. And since locally operative constraints on indigenous initiatives were weak, the preservation of weaker parties depended on the liability of would-be stronger or predominant states to dissipation of effort if not outright dissolution of the expansionist entity, while regime concern over internal challenges to incumbency equalled when it did not exceed preoccupation with external threats to "national" security.

In these conditions, it was only in rare instances (e.g. a consolidated Israel in a conflicted Middle East) that the articulation of actor capabilities and institutionalized policy-making matched, let alone surpassed, the extent to which the arena itself had been crystallized. The precise point of transition from arena to actor primacy in shaping the other is difficult to locate in all circumstances. For this reason alone, the Third-World actors could evolve at different rates in different areas without it being clear which particular segment has become developmentally contemporary with, say, mid-seventeenth-century

Europe (when the secularization and institutionalization of uniformly territorial states by the Peace of Westphalia brought their level of articulation up to that of the system itself), or has been only emerging from – unless, as independence took hold, regressing into – the equivalent of the (early) Middle Ages. Pointing to the latter alternative was the fairly long-lasting and widespread prevalence of the mythical over the material core factors in the peripheral polities. So was, in determining their identity, the predominance of the quasi-genealogically constituted nebular format (assembled haphazardly and lacking inner coherence) over the geopolitically conditioned nuclear one (growing incrementally out of a territorial core). One kind of the distinguishing features was present in the myths of a regionally original "way" of managing inter-actor political or intra-actor social relations; the other underlay the fact or fiction of cooperative organisms consensually arrived at, ranging from multi-state regional organizations through pluri-state constitutional unions or economic communities, to replicas of pre-colonial empires.

In either case, the scope of institutions clustering around the voluntaristic designs of dynastically oriented founding fathers or families exceeded the range of supporting instruments. The founders were to be only gradually supplanted by more pragmatically inclined successors, ostensibly committed to addressing geopolitical and -economic realities through a more gradualist construction of a more prosaic functional and limited territorial nucleus. Thus, when a Suharto replaced a Sukarno in Indonesia on the model of constructively despotic Louis XI succeeding to Charles VIII as the last of his crusading predecessors in France, the succession matched the medieval pattern and intimated its waning. The obverse was the case when economic integration was given priority over politico-military interactions in attempts at or plans for multi-state associations in East Africa, Central America, or south-east Asia. Substituting avoidance of conflict for its management and resolution would invert the sequence proven in the medieval model in favor of one-step overleap into the political mentality and material realizations of post-modern Europe. Putting economic sustenance before military security could work in a few instances of essentially city-state character. But in many or most others the inversion pointed to a pervasive inter-functional derangement in the material core of actor formation.

The consequences – inimical to a progressive, and only hypothetically capable of fostering a catastrophic, development – had to be dealt with by means of equally insufficient compensations and correctives. The compensations drew upon the normative plane when the political morality of post-colonial neutralism was formulated so as to underpin a resource-deficient rhetorical emphasis on external functions of government. Shifting thus effective power politics inward, toward inter-factional or -sectional warfare, became a substitute for the environmentally decreed but domestically impracticable model of the welfare state. Subsequently, a corrective was offered, if rarely delivered, by the military assuming politico-administrative functions in behalf of public morality and social peace. However, the military were unable to arrange for the kind of economic surge which, converted into internally decisive military-technological monopoly, had favored Italy's post-communal *signori* and the north European despots. As a result, the soldiers-become-politicians could not repair quickly enough the condition which had propelled them into an unfamiliar arena: the absence of a domestic productivity sufficient to trigger an upward spiral in military-economic relations – a spiral most conspicuously in evidence when adequately paid military personnel enforced the collection of additional public revenue while generating the critical mass of purchasing power for local manufactures.

Yet another, and often last-in-line, consequence of the abortive compensations and correctives was a peculiar form of conversion, if not outright subversion. Its object was the "modernizing" early stage in prospective actor formation, in favor of a recidivist transformation along traditional lines. The relapse got under way whenever the failure to offset material scarcities and functional deficiencies with at least an immaterial surplus, that of readily mobilizable collective energies, weakened a Third-World country's capacity to absorb either the material or the status-related intangible goods being funneled in from the outside. The casualty was institutional development (combining diffusion of capabilities with differentiation of functions) commensurate with material growth (conciliating agricultural with industrial development in a productive sequence) that would take place on a basis combining imitation of foreign models with indigenous adaptations if not innovations.

Liabilities due to faulty actor–arena and inter-functional relationships could be only aggravated by unfavorable material and physical factors pertaining to size and scale. This has been so not least because the excess of human procreation over the attainable levels of material production has spelled in many places a catastrophic land–population ratio. Responsible for social strains and physiological debilitation, the imbalance was denied a ready corrective other than localized equivalents of Europe's fourteenth-century plague. Likewise inhibiting was the size of many of the Third-World countries. When disproportionately vast relative to the size and substance of the nucleus fit for aggregating capabilities, it augmented inordinately the radius for projecting outward only central authority or also national power, perpetuating when not expanding the adverse consequences for elite dispositions and popular integration graphically prefigured in the first generation of decolonized countries (in Latin America). The weight of topography would compound the burden of size when the configuration of terrain was such as to seriously inhibit productive communication (e.g. in ancient Greece-like south-east Asia) while withholding the stimulus of physical conditions that facilitate hostile surprise (e.g. in the Middle Eastern replica of ancient Mesopotamia). The propensity of oversized areas to the nebular mode of actor formation was especially pronounced when the new states (e.g. the Congo, Nigeria) were artificial colonial-time creations. As such, they were particularly subject to centrifugal reactions to the centralizing core by tribally distinct regions (e.g. Katanga, Biafra) more advanced culturally or (recalling the critical role of a mineral resource-base in comparable entities in the past) better endowed materially. The resemblance of such entities to "personal" unions in dynastic Europe was increased whenever they depended on charismatic or repressive leaders for elementary cohesion. The rate of changeover among such leaders symbolized the migratory character of central authority typical of the format, manifested physically by capital cities being transplanted to a more central or tribally neutral location.

The strains and stresses were not absent in countries which either reproduced from the outset, or gradually evolved toward, uneven mixes of nuclear and nebular elements and formats, thus India as compared with Pakistan (especially while still comprising the eastern region). Such countries' prospects and achievements moved then uncertainly along a spectrum the opposite poles of which were illustrated in antiquity by Rome-in-Italy and (Pyrrhus') Syracuse-in-Sicily, and by France and the Holy Roman Empire in medieval to early modern Europe. Whatever may be the nature of the nuclei on the Indian sub-continent – more tribal-ethnic (Punjab) in Pakistan and more religio-dynastic in India (the Gandhi mystique, retreating before the Nehru–Gandhi dynasty) – neither has been reliably resistant, let alone immune, to ethnic or sectarian forces with separatist dispositions. A series of intra-regional military encounters has infused neither side with a religiously buttressed sense of indissoluble political nationhood (of the kind France had derived from the hundred years of conflict with the English). As for the larger global setting, it was more disruptive than productive. It was such especially for Pakistan, insofar as the materially profitable commitment on the East–West issue failed to preclude and may have accelerated the country's internal scission along the same lines. Nor did non-aligned India benefit unequivocally from doctrinal self-insulation from the East–West conflict: intended to create a species of protected sanctuary such as the one that the Papal–Imperial conflict had once unwittingly erected over an ascending France, the insulation conferred on India more of precarious psychopolitical than of solid real-political advantages, more status than role. And much the same rewards were to be forthcoming from diplomatic alignment with one, the Soviet, superpower (in a triangular situation involving China as India's regional rival and Pakistan's backer) in either the security–superiority or the role-status coin.

To the extent that internal threats to the unity were distributed unevenly, the nuclear element was stronger for India and the nebular for Pakistan, reflecting the Islamic state's origin in improvised resistance of incongruous constituents to a religiously defined alien (Hindi) element, itself taking off from a historically re-emergent core-entity. Moreover, insofar as forming a nation state from heterogeneous components depends on generating collective ego-satisfying external attributes, Pakistan's chances faded as India's prospects grew even if they would not (soon) match those of China as a continental or Japan as a mercantile-maritime power. Likewise, if only hypothetically, comparable with earlier French developments in this respect was the disparity between the New Delhi-centered political core, oriented toward overland security at the north-western frontier (immediately and avowedly against Pakistan, implicitly against Russia), and the coastal-maritime fringe oriented toward the Indian Ocean and centered on Bombay and Calcutta. An integration of the two sectors and related sensitivities would have to be more effective and speedier than had been France's if India was to fare better relative to Japan or South Korea than France did relative to England and Holland. Only then could she assume the position of one of the world's major amphibian powers that consolidated political nationhood along with regional supremacy and achieved global strategic relevance equal to the superpowers'.

As one of the two indisputably major powers, the United States, although essentially of the sea-power type, has been more markedly insular than mercantile-maritime in its determining characteristics. Consequently, it was reproducing the psychopolitical attitudes of the type more closely and fully than anything else, including the role of economics in shaping foreign policy. The sense of exceptionality manifest in moral superiority has underlain the tension between declaratory legalism and actual pragmatism in policy, reminiscent of the Dutch at their peak, once the tension had evolved out of a primitive combination: of high-principled proclamations with actual aloofness in regard to the twentieth-century continental conflicts, reminiscent of the Britain of James I in relation to an earlier conflict of likewise thirty years' duration. Just as Britain would not be effectively insular for diplomatic purposes before integrating Scotland with England, so the United States had first to achieve territorial consolidation as a virtual island by succeeding to the European implantations in the western hemisphere. Viewed as divinely preordained where that of the United Kingdom was near-accidentally dynastic, the consolidation set off the yet uncompleted three-phase sequence in the changing relationship of an insular realm to the continental sphere, only slightly dissimilar from that of more integrally offshore-insular earlier actors.

Insular identity and safe insulation materialized in two tempos, the first of which comprised overland expansion in North America. Opposed by Britain, it replicated in essence that of Muscovy in Russia, except for its being longer more markedly predatory than preclusive in character and implications: character, because of the mild nature of threats to the core, to be rolled back; implications, in that acquiring control over the lower Mississippi River toward New Orleans contrasted favorably with Russia's inability to break through the Straits to Constantinople. This contrast symbolized the difference, while substantially differentiating the positions, of the two polities on the geopolitically and economically crucial continental–maritime spectrum. The second tempo comprised the expansion of the fledgling United States in the western hemisphere by way of real economic ascendancy and intermittent pretensions to policing the area. Helping to overcome an only progressively subsiding British opposition were economic-policy instruments (Reciprocity Treaties) of the kind Germany essayed in the 1890s in Middle Europe as part of a liberal phase in the post-Bismarckian New Course.

Achieving a continent-wide scope for the (quasi-) insular base meant realizing the historical tendency of an insular power base to be enlarged spatially to its outermost limit. But the character of America's consequent continentalization was as unlike the only operational one of a Britain that has exchanged proprietary rights in Europe for managerial implantation in Egypt, as it differed from Japan's physical one via military conquests in China, until such time as strategic fixation on the Eurasian continent brought the US experience in line with the precedents. The involvement, while it conformed to the norm of the military and the diplomatic costs of policy increasing sequentially when compared with more stringently economizing strategies, implemented the initial phase in the developing foreign-policy orientation of an offshore-insular power. However, if the policy met the norm of expansion into an adjacent continental mass, it also telescoped two normally consecutive policies: initial assertion of control by conquest or otherwise, and subsequent subsidence into the role of a mere balancer. The two were fused in one declaratory policy, pending clarification as to which parties were to be balanced from an appropriate, relatively detached and impartial, posture: consolidated Western and Eastern ensembles inside Europe only, or Russia with China in Eurasia? Contentious engagement kept meanwhile in abeyance the normal third phase, one of strategic disengagement from the continent in favor of a free hand for military-politically low-cost if not cost-free world-wide trading activity. Although latent in a standing temptation to disengage strategically, the alternative may have been compromised by a contradiction before succeeding to a strategic contraction, insofar as dependence on foreign trade would grow in parallel with decline in the economic-technological leadership acquired coincidentally with politico-military salience.

At its climax, the American empire encompassed a leading insular sea power's habitual, near-indistinguishable and interdependent three zones of security and superiority: the North American (or western hemispheric) insular habitat as the inner, (western) Europe and Japan (plus the Persian Gulf?) as the outer, and the wider Third-World periphery as the outermost, zone. More or less coercive control shading off into more or less indirect influence was long facilitated by immunity to containment policies emanating from the continent, likewise typical for insular-maritime powers. The immunity (which had survived unabridged to mid- and late nineteenth-century English, French, and sporadic Anglo–French, efforts to curtail it in the western hemisphere) was to be only tangentially qualified by manifestations of European neutralism (laced with de Gaulle-like opposition to the "two hegemonies" just as elsewhere with Nehru-like anti-colonialism or -imperialism); and it was only potentially vulnerable to allied resentments of the privileges extracted from either the balancer or the alliance-leader role, should they exceed the fears inspired by the preeminent continental power. Either role might then be seen as abused by policies suspect of doing more to provoke the Russian adversary than protect America's allies; of implying self-immunization by "decoupling" defensive systems or strategies over against shielding the larger association; of entailing exchange of military protection against intrinsically unrelated economic and related concessions; and of combining an ultra-adversarial stance *vis-à-vis* the common adversary with the equivalent of separate-peacemaking in the guise of arms-control agreements. The latter abuses in particular would have to revive suspicions from an earlier era, as to the real US objectives when helping liquidate European colonialism in favor of an only superficially modified (neo-) colonialist or imperialist approach to Third-World needs and issues, before the later doubts could create more than only local and transient prerequisites for what, seen from the Soviet side, would be America's counter-containment.

More immediately limiting has been the quicker-than-normal erosion of the post-World War II initial US assets and advantages, compounded by their diffusion. And as the material and institutional limitations on policy-making expanded conjointly with the shrinkage of external latitudes, so did the inter- or intra-elite conflict over fundamental strategy options and directions, always apt to intensify at the climactic point in a power's trajectory. Whereas continuing self-assertion meant overexertion if not also overextension, accommodating with the principal adversary entailed ever more thoroughgoing détente while sharing the burden of conflict with third powers implied more or less far-reaching devolution. Much as the diplomatic quandary recalled Britain's hesitations at the turn of the nineteenth into the twentieth century between entente with Germany and devolution in favor of Japan, France, and Russia, the underlying geostrategic dilemma recalled a still more basic mid-eighteenth-century British policy debate over continental versus overseas priorities in combating ancien-regime France when the postulated choice was once more between a continentalist (now Europe-centered NATO) and an oceanic strategy (resting on offshore-insular positions, backed by restored naval supremacy). It did not appease the disputants that either debate was again likely to be resolved in favor of attempting to combine the alternatives if, currently, from diminishing overall advantage and within a more limited range of effective options. Only remotely but still significantly mirroring the British Tory versus Whig and King versus Parliament dialectic, the US debate was taking place amidst an intensifying sociopolitical and ethnic pluralization and institutional (executive–legislative) polarization. A consequence has been to displace primacy in foreign-policy-making from a prudently moderate Anglo–Saxon ruling class, undergirding an "imperial Presidency," to technically if not necessarily judgmentally better-equipped individuals who, marginal socio-culturally, were prone as such to seek proof of their authentic Americanism in ideological dogmatism.

The task confronting the US as a world power was the largely unprecedented one of relating competition with the prime land power deliberately to fostering evolution in the global periphery of the international system. The issue confronting it as a hegemonial ally was not unlike that facing Britain as a pretended intra-European balancer and center of an actual multi-racial world empire. It revolved around the choice between attempts to increase cohesion within a crucial association (Atlantic alliance, as before the white dominions) by either intensified integration of capabilities or controlled delegation of responsibilities, and a foreign policy for reducing the need for and the costs of such cohesion. A key decision, whether to have the lesser parties contribute their share in actual capabilities or help defray the costs of the principal's more exclusive defense expenditures and efforts instead, had been made differently in the early stage of the Athenian and in the late stage of the British Empire; it was eluded in the American case in favor of an intermediate or mixed approach. So was the still more important and fundamental foreign policy quandary concerning the development of the international system itself. It could evolve toward one resembling the post-Greek Hellenistic variety of several amphibian powers; or it could perpetuate the legacy of the post-Italian European one, polarized between land and sea powers, but be moved toward reducing the incidence of major wars that made the ascent of singular sea powers as sudden as their ascendancy (on the Athenian model) relatively short-lived.

If America's insular identity has been somewhat modified, Russia's situation conformed fully to the historically bequeathed land-power model. As outside constraints on the expanding territorial nucleus predominated over environmental latitudes, this favored central authority for collective survival over individual liberties for either self-realization or communally profitable innovation. Replacing the Mongol khans with Moscovite tsars and updating the latter into Marxist commissars has made for little change. The absence of favorable accidents as well as of the favors of nature made it incumbent on either ruthless or artful rulers to coercively contain internal divisions favoring defections, and to forcibly exploit external opportunities indistinguishable from threats. Natural limitations compelled the search for instrumental compensations, causing expansion to occur at all times with the assistance of military rather than any other – economic or cultural – methods and devices.

In the post-World War II Soviet phase of Russian defensive–offensive expansion into a continental empire, the result conformed closely to the model established by Sparta. Fool-proof control of potentially rebellious domestic groups (helot-like "class enemies" evolving into "dissidents of conscience") was assured through a belt of (perioecs-like) client states in Eastern Europe. These were in turn to be safeguarded by diplomacy toward Western Europe, Russia's outer security zone, alternating between intimidation and courtship before the long-range objective of a militarily "hegemonial" if politically latitudinous leadership in Europe, on a par with Sparta's in the Peloponnesian League, would become plausible. Within these interconnected – narrowly regional and continental – spheres, the trend was toward an essentially conservative (as distinct from passively defensive) strategy. More offensively assertive were attempts to extend influence-or-control to the outermost peripheral zone in the Third World. They reflected not so much economic opportunities (for trade) and needs (for raw materials) or material capabilities (for conquest) as military-strategic requirements and diplomatic-strategic incentives. This being so, any combination of pressures from within the Soviet political system – in the form of ideological rationales, regime-legitimation requisites, or diversionary responses to economic or other stress – was more than matched by a structurally conditioned external incentive: the urge to reciprocate, if not retaliate for, US-originated or -encouraged attempts to break away from the Soviet empire by extending support to similarly motivated forces and undertakings inside the US inner security zone in particular. The underlying urge, backed by a naval following a nuclear-strategic build-up, was to combine military deterrence with political compellence in the service of geostrategic parity – an objective to be approximated in the face of persisting situational and capability-related US–Soviet asymmetries, responsible for the popular appeal of US- or West-type material prosperity as much as for the military expenditures contravening its attainment in the East.

Accounting for policies in the inner and outer security spheres, the Sparta-like configuration and ethos made for weaknesses in the outermost, overseas zone. The limitation was only sufficiently remedied by the practical utility of the regime ideology as an instrument (as distinct from determinant) of policy. Insofar as considerable Soviet self-sufficiency in key raw materials made material incentives for overseas activities less than compelling, the analogy with France was suggestive, while shortcomings in Soviet agriculture have had an inhibiting effect not unlike that of imperial Spain's decaying pastoral economy. In contrast with the Spartan mode, of externally buttressed domestic regime supremacy, the Spanish model of empire was one of a sociopolitical system open to co-optation of dependent elites willing to collaborate. The format found a limited application in the opportunities and outlets Soviet global activities have been offering the Eastern European elites, even as the costs of Third-World-directed outlays antagonized the populace at large. However, if sharing nominal communism replaced common observance of the Catholic religion in camouflaging inherent inequalities, the alienating arrogance of the Spaniards also prefigured the Great Russians' *vis-à-vis* the lesser Slavic and other nationalities and perpetuated the inner flaw within the tsarist era's pan-Slavism. Only superficially overlaid by universalist ideological tenets, the psychological insularity of the Russians bred in continental depths and nurtured by feelings of cultural peculiarity, has thus replaced the German ideology of tribal-racialist exclusiveness, fatal to the initial appeal of Nazism for disaffected European elites, in outdoing the deleterious effect on policy of the Anglo–Saxon insulars' moralizing propensities.

The Stalinist revolution from above was designed to raise Soviet capabilities to the minimal requirements of intra-continental physical security. Being for the same reason insufficient to make Russia competitive on a global scale, it, if anything, compounded the handicaps which, innate to any land power, have been growing worse as the leading such power moved eastward. Yet, imbued as the Stalinist period was with features of oriental despotism, the regime differed significantly from the format's pure model inasmuch as the centrally managed forced-draft industrialization required only provisional self-isolation before economic and social development would generate the need for substantial change. Similarities with the despotic model could thus not continue intact for long, except for the state's proprietary claim curtailing private property and overshadowing other rights. While they lasted, the closest parallels with the Ottoman Empire, another imperfect example, included modalities of rulership succession (contingent on ready access to instruments of force and terror in the formative period prior to incremental institutionalization) and preferred methods of reform (to offset subsequent stagnation, through restored disciplines rather than structural change). Gradually loosening the autocracy were again Soviet analogues of the corporative sub-groupings in the Ottoman Empire and the widespread network of patron–client relations, apt to soften bureaucratic-authoritarian rigidities and reduce personal insecurities.

Likewise relaxing rigid structures over the longer run was the erosion of the dominant positions of key operatives, be they Christian converts to Islam or Communist Party apparatchiki. Wholly detached from the society at large, these had risen to the top at the peak of either despotism or totalitarianism, only to decay in favor of elements more religiously authentic (born Moslems) or provisionally qualified (technocrats) amidst a partial revival of the hereditary principle among the elites. The resurgence of the indigenous Turk element was to ultimately coincide with Ottoman decline, and the re-emphasis on

Russianism in war was to raise the issue of the empire's socio-ethnic cohesion. But appeals to either nationalism or larger patriotism in the face of any kind of threat, while fully consistent with authoritarianism, have proved incompatible with pristine despotism's basis in slave-like individual and collective self-effacement before an effectively or symbolically personalized ruling power. Meanwhile, the still evolving Soviet continued to be more comparable with the Islamic Empire in its climactic period of rivalry with imperial Spain than during the Ottomans' nineteenth-century decadence, with one crucial exception due to a fundamental difference: the built-in dependence of the quasi-feudal Ottoman (timar) system on continuing territorial expansion, peculiar to a primitive fiscality and force structure resting on services in exchange for land.

If Stalinist Russia was not fully, and Soviet Russia has been decreasingly, oriental-despotic when projected against a national norm that allowed for reformist interludes, has the type been more persistently present in the latest – Maoist and post-Mao – embodiment of the Chinese exemplar as it replicated historically evidenced cycles and alternations, was alternately self-isolating and opened to the outside, drew on the outside world materially while both fearing and despising it culturally? A conclusive answer had to await longer-term developments in a China that has unquestionably retained the principal characteristics of a farthest-eastern rear-continental power. As such, she directed her maritime aspirations and naval capabilities to limited military (coastal-defense) and economic (oil-exploitation) purposes, while her overseas political initiatives remained sporadic and selective rather than systematic in mode and system-wide in scope. Reflecting once again the tension between xenophobic nativism and imitative cosmopolitanism was meanwhile the customary oscillation between the Middle Kingdom model of self-isolation in imperial self-sufficiency in the Mao era and, after Mao, pragmatic-opportunistic involvement historically associated with the empire's weakness or dissolution and attempted reconstruction. The pattern continued to point to an instability which, fully compatible with the fixity of a fundamental pretension, exceeded variations between isolationism and involvement in the American and the oscillations between Europe and Asia in the traditional Russian postures.

Including as it does transitions between dynasties or dynasty-substitutes, the predominantly static cyclism that differentiates oriental from cyclically evolving occidental dynamics has contributed to China's failure to be fully integrated into the evolutionary stream of the world system. The related defining feature of despotism – isolation and both capacity and preference for self-isolation, notably from outer zones relevant for security – bore on the future of China's intra-regional relationships. It was historically that very condition of isolation, that permitted regional sway to be exercised in a highly permissive, only loosely suzerain, fashion in many if not all instances (thus relative to Korea, as distinct from Vietnam). Finally, only the future would tell which strategic orientation would continue to predominate: one centered on barbarians encroaching overland, apt to intensify the conflict with Russia and perpetuate despotic propensities; or one responsive to the pull from the mercantile port cities toward the ocean, pointing to a more problematic or ambiguous relationship with Japan, the United States, and the lesser countries of the area (including

Taiwan and Hong Kong) with modernizing if not necessarily democratizing consequences.

On balance, both external (power) and internal (population) pressures have made it impossible for China to continue reproducing all of the essential preconditions and characteristics of oriental despotism, any more than Soviet Russia was likely to reactivate her quota of some of the critical traits in western-style totalitarianism. However, if the waning of modern totalitarianism in both countries resurfaced indigenous features, they have tended to be more oriental-despotic in China and more authoritarian-traditionalist in Russia. There, an increasingly only nominal adherence to Marxist–Leninist ideological tenets had to be distinguished from the more deeply embedded ideology-related organizational practices; in China it coincided with the perpetuation of nativist cultural tenets (including those stressing peculiarity and superiority), while self-isolation was being repeatedly reduced to calculated aloofness (or equidistance) from both of the superpowers. The rapidly increasing proximity of both Eurasian land powers to the outside world made them invert the shift from mainly external to mainly internal functions of government, manifest over the long term in historic Europe. It remained to be seen what consequences would flow from a related difference: whereas the Europeans' shift to the domestic agenda had been at least initially inspired by the need to defray the growing cost of quantitatively increased armaments and armed men, the "socialist" powers' increased emphasis on the external arena and relations with it was linked this time in large part to qualitative changes in military and related civilian technology.

The dilution of prototypical traits of oriental despotism in an internationally engaged modern China, comprising the intrusion of the diplomatic culture of *realpolitik* behind the veneer of allegedly unique or uniquely rigorous and consistent principles of statecraft, did not invalidate an essential continuity in regard to the typology of actors and their strategies on the West–East axis and spectrum. It has done so no more than deviations from the maximalist characteristics of the continental and the insular powers and the land–sea power schism abrogated the latter's relevance in regard to US–Soviet relations. These deviations only included the fact that a continent-wide United States, continuously involved in the politico-military issues of the central system at costs that enhanced a leading sea power's normal susceptibility to late-stage economic stress, has in major respects been less intrinsically insular and mercantile than contemporary Japan. After failing at an experiment in continental expansionism, and while still unequipped and unwilling to play the balancer role among the larger continental powers, Japan shed the key attributes of oriental despotism as part of experimenting with the third phase of an insular polity's external posture, politico-military detachment in behalf of worldwide trade. However, the close alliance between governmental and corporate oligarchies has meanwhile resembled the political-economic regime of eighteenth-century oligarchical Britain to the same extent that it departed from the American liberal-democratic free-trading model, tentatively introduced by the post-war military occupation. At the same time, a Soviet Union that has only begun to experience the implications of a land empire continuously involved in overseas activities, was progressively less closely comparable with either the Spartan or the Assyrian land-empire prototypes, only briefly or inorganically affected by such activities' liberalizing influence.

Insofar as, with due differences, both the United States and Soviet Russia were becoming intermediate types seeking to enhance their capacity to compete, the key question was whether the more basic similarities would promote also typological convergence – or whether a parallel experience in major and minor wars (the Second World War and the lesser conflicts in Vietnam and Afghanistan) would serve only as a prelude to military collision of unprecedented magnitude, capable of facilitating the rise of new insular or continental powers and empires while weakening when not destroying the established ones.

STRUCTURED CONFLICTS AND CONTRASTING STRUCTURES

Coinciding with the German defeat and Britain's eclipse, the US–Soviet conflict set off the reconstruction of the international system in conditions of a still indeterminate schism. The vacuum of power intervening between the two powers prejudged the choice between antagonism and accommodation in favor of a conflict that would polarize lesser powers pending the adoption of first one-sided (US) and eventually mutual encirclement strategies. The inchoate nature of the stakes, due to schism indeterminacy, combined with the only progressively emergent structural polarity, due to the initial survival of west European colonial empires, to halt the formulation of strategy. The immediate consequence was to convert an existential ambiguity into a precipitately absolutized normativization of the contest. Interests had been defined in terms of ideologies before emphasis on values could serve to rationalize gradually disclosed interests and, ultimately, serve to revitalize an intermittently flagging adversary relationship.

Predictable as a matter of structure because of the post-war power vacuum, and propagated by strategies aimed at converting actual or potential clients ideologically, the US–Soviet conflict aggregated features of past two-power conflicts attendant on early, or critical intermediate, developmental states in any state system. Within the European system it resembled the early-stage Papal–Imperial conflict, as one defined doctrinally on the face of it and progressively pragmatized as it ramified into both intra- and inter-actor contentions of (Guelph and Ghibelline) partisans of either principal, with the result of projecting a range of "new" states into at least nominal independence at the nascent system's widening peripheries. Like the ensuing Spanish (or Habsburg)–Ottoman conflict, the US–Soviet was waged on the East–West axis over the ideologically camouflaged world-hegemony issue on three main fronts: western, expanding from Italy to Western Europe; eastern, in south-east and eventually eastern Europe; and southern, in and around the Red Sea and the Indian Ocean. And when, like in the conflict between France and the accidental Habsburg conglomerate, a differently fortuitous US-centered aggregation of power positions was investing ever more tightly the more compact actor, the question arose once more which of the dissimilar powers represented a greater departure from or also threat to systemic equilibrium – and, thus, to the autonomy of third countries.

As distinct from the investment of one party as a factual condition, all instances illustrated encirclement as the object or actual achievement of policy. And each conflict resulted invariably in the controlling schism changing to the detriment of the prime contestants and to third-party advantage: the sacral–spiritual schism of the Papal–Imperial contest yielding to the East–West schism governing the Ottoman–Spanish, and this and the related Franco–Spanish conflict being superseded by the land–sea power schism involving the Anglo–Dutch Maritime Powers. The ever more overtly material character of the stakes raised increasingly urgent questions of the *cui bono* type. Bequeathed to the US–Soviet conflict as it telescoped the sequence, the quandary has been rendered more acute by a difference: the more elastic enactment of the analogous three-front Ottoman–Habsburg conflict, due in large part to the contestants' keen and continuous preoccupation with threatening third parties (France for Spain, Persia for the Ottomans) as the ultimately primary concerns.

So long as the US–Soviet conflict has not been significantly moderated by such a concern, a question remained dormant: did the third-party factor offer the prospect of dispersing the two-power relationship structurally and defusing the conflict operationally (via the constraints any two parties can exercise on a changing third that has been left out), or did it conceal instead the probability of the original principals being superseded as dominant actors (before discarding the divisive conflict issues as the one critical agenda)? Meanwhile, the possibility to accommodate the conflict while the two superpowers were still salient was being pushed back by their prolonged dual failure: to clarify priorities as between pragmatic interests and value-ideological issues, unevenly prominent in the alternative schisms; and to assess the reciprocal concessions requisite for inter-superpower parity against the costs of uncontrollably expanding plurality of "major" actors. In a situation allowing for only temporary thaws or contrastingly construed détentes, it was more congenial as well as common for both sides to monitor the course of material preponderance (which side was "winning" the Cold War in terms of geopolitical gains and losses and/ or economic growth and regression rates) than to relate the issue of tangible assets to that of status and role (how to change from contentiously to complementarily exerted preeminence so as to avoid material decline relative to third parties). It was one thing, and easier, on the model of early Spanish–Ottoman expansionisms, to implement the divergence in ideas and interests through basically similar strategies, eventuating in spatially converging or overlapping courses of expansion; it was another and more difficult thing for security concerns and attendant strategic thrusts, after reaching the limits of underlying momentum, to be targeted in different-to-opposing directions. This had been the balance of later Spanish and Ottoman initiatives, with the subsidence of conflict advancing substantive convergence of evolving institutional or operational modes.

As for third parties, the lesser among them inside and outside Europe could act as would-be mediators in the US–Soviet conflict (e.g. through the United Nations in the Korean War, through more conventional diplomacy during and after the Vietnam War). They were as or more likely to perform – wittingly or not – the function of conflict multipliers, instigating contention as its highly prized stakes only to restimulate the conflict's increasingly but inertial momentum as they changed from valuable stakes into its material beneficiaries. However, the lesser powers' capacity to be rendered only more autonomous or also more influential by the contention's bias toward stalemate (somewhat like the Italian or infant "northern" European states between the Papacy and Empire and the middle-sized European powers, the Italians' true successors, between the Ottoman and the Habsburg Empires) had a reverse side in a risk: that their autonomy (like the Italian states' in the Franco–Spanish conflict) might be extinguished to the benefit of an even but temporarily prevailing major-power contestant after serving (like the same Italians in the Spanish–Ottoman conflict) as the more or less committed avant-garde or glacis for one side.

As for the superpowers, before they could re-enact, in lieu of a stalemate, a more than transient accord of the Cateau Cambrésis type (between France and Spain), they would have to respond to less than usually diffuse third-party threat, with armed terrorism or religious fundamentalism emerging as a substitute for insurgent heresy, or to more than transient economic lassitude. Even then, the impetus would have to be experienced by both parties equally and simultaneously enough to minimize any resulting disparities in gains and losses and inferences of victory and defeat; and it would have to be sufficiently compelling to offset the fear that external relaxation entailed internal dissolution (of the kind nearly fatal to France relative to Spain in the sixteenth-century context). Barring the concert, material benefit to third parties of the US–Soviet conflict not being composed in time was again certain to grow if they were of major-power caliber: e.g. China, equaling France's gains from first the Papal–Imperial and subsequently the Ottoman–Habsburg conflict, and Japan equaling England as the ultimate winner in the Franco–Spanish contention. Only when of such caliber were third parties capable of redefining the key schism to reflect their position, character, and capabilities.

The major-power threat to both of the superpowers was for long remote in terms of time (before China matured into an industrial and Japan was ready to reconvert into a military next to an economic great power) and not close enough in space (both Asian powers being located near an only emergent central Pacific basin and the critical coastal-insular complex bordering it); and – almost as much as the shared dangers for the global environment – the lesser-power threats including that from terrorism have been too diffuse in kind and, compared with the central conflict, peripheral in critical importance. But the fundamental relationship of the US–Soviet two-power conflict to third parties has been nonetheless valid. Conducted in the traditional ways, the contention either already did or was likely to accomplish in the future the following transformations: (1) articulate the international system in that it generated third powers up to a five-power-plus scale, constituting thus genuine multipolarity with respect to major parties (a process the Papal–Imperial contest had begun and its follow-ups consummated) and a still wider-ranging polycentrism in relation to lesser ones; (2) expand the arena of conflict globally and articulate it regionally in space while beginning to surface its economic-material dimension in kind (the peculiar contribution or side effect of the Dutch–English contentions with Spain); and (3) institutionalize the system as an ongoing one capable of major realignments (incidental to the Franco–Habsburg conflict in particular).

All these changes, good or less auspicious, were effected at a cost in upheavals analogous to Europe's religious wars and inter-cultural alienation, but in the provisional absence of recourse to a decisive military engagement: only symbolically decisive outcomes, comparable to that at Lepanto in the Ottoman–Habsburg contest, announced the conflict's gradual subsidence, in contradistinction to substantively decisive victories, such as France's at Rocroi over the Spanish tercios, which signalled a succession from one to another power's primacy. In the process, some cultural-ideological animosities could be lessened and divides lowered by changes in only diplomatic or also strategic alignments, such as the Franco–Soviet followed and outdone by the US–Chinese, which performed as separate-peace transactions within a structure dispersed thus from polar into tripartite. The compensating risk was that expanding thus the range of strategic options would prematurely promote one (China) and drastically demote another (Russia) of the Eurasian powers. The former might be enabled and the latter forced to dramatize its differences with the conventional West, thus by playing on the differences between such a West (excluding Russia) and the ex-colonial Third World to the point of reopening a politico-ideological if not-religious cleavage still harder to bridge than the one between the superpowers.

When a two-power conflict activates a third major party and increasingly peripheral, including overseas, stakes, a land–sea power triangle will have been latent in the original contention – somewhat as the macro-system was in a micro-system that has passed on its diplomatic norms to previously extraneous powers, about to supersede the anterior system's quarrels. The latency became manifest when the "new" China was drawn into a US–Soviet conflict that was expanding in scale and stakes. The future possibility had been largely unnoticed when, prior to the Soviet growth in global ambition and naval armaments, the United States was emerging as the seat of a world-wide empire geopolitically and becoming an insular polity increasingly engaged in – if not also dependent on – likewise wide-ranging "free trade" economically and societally. The emergence, which put the United States in Britain's place, was also similar to England's earlier surfacing insofar as America's cultural links to and dependence on (Western) Europe was the functional equivalent of the eighteenth-century English political system's ties to confessionally indispensable continental dynasts (William III and the Hanoverians). Moreover, the larger insular power's continental connection was again tightened by a succession of wars within a triangular pattern of unevenly maritime and continental powers (America's German wars in lieu of England's French ones, which had facilitated America's independence before sheltering her early isolation); and the insulars' growth was attended by an expanding range of economic ties and tensions (centering for both Anglo–Saxon powers in due course on, though not confined to, Germany).

While the US–Soviet conflict was evolving into the US–Soviet–Chinese triangle along the west-to-east insular–continental spectrum, the latest version of the smaller, western and politico-economic, triangle was crystallizing even before it did fully interlock with the global military-political one. It took shape around a United States that performed immediately after the Second German War as an amphibious mercantile-maritime monopolist, on the model of Spain at the outset of the modern European system. In that capacity America was exposed to the competitive challenge from a new set of Maritime Powers, pairing resurgent Western Europe and Japan in an ambivalent relationship reminiscent of that between England and the Netherlands, against the strategic-security background of a Soviet Russia salient, as had been France earlier, within the global-strategic triangle while relatively secondary in the politico-economic triangle. The intervening enlargement of the theater was betokened by Western Europe assuming the intermediate position and acting out the only qualifiedly allied role of Venice in the seminal Spanish–Ottoman conflict, of the vaster Netherlands in the first authentic (Anglo–French–Germanic), and of the still larger France in the second such (Anglo–German–Russian), global triangle.

However, the enlargement did not alter the effect of the overall setting on policies. The effect resurfaced whenever the West Europeans, capable of triggering operationally an intensification of the US–Soviet conflict on security grounds, would simultaneously attempt to stay aloof from the structural causes of the competition on social and economic grounds. They would thus inject into the basic stance of dependent alliance with the principal western power more or less solid elements or only intimations of independence, incidentally favoring the eastern power. Moreover, while serving as the effective pretext for US policy of military-political containment of the Soviet Union, Western Europe represented for Russia a potential geo-economic asset conducive to or substituting for effective inter-superpower parity overseas. This was reminiscent of the position the weakening Dutch had occupied between England and France and, in a modified fashion, receding France or her empire between Britain and Germany. The situation did not rule out the analogy being extended further, to encompass reactions to a second stage of continuing relative decline. In keeping with the same set of precedents, a Western Europe beset by political and economic crisis and facing a United States declining in politico-military capabilities or will, and/or diverting elsewhere its economics-centered strategic emphasis, would then turn economically and politically to Russia as part of a cost-benefit calculation counselling appeasement.

Neither basically different from the west Europeans' nor fundamentally novel have been the position and policy alternatives of a Japan that initially faced in the United States a Spain-like monopolist. The pattern for conflicting US and Japanese priorities and attendant strains had been set when the commercially emergent English had stayed aloof from the Dutch wars for independence from Spain only to see the economically matured Netherlands prefer investing in a by-then allied as well as navally ascendant England while trying to stay out of her wars. So also the Japanese have fostered trade with Communist China and experimented with engagement in joint development projects with Soviet Russia almost as eagerly as the Dutch traded with France without forgoing the insular ally's low-cost backing for their security. The relationship between the strategically interdependent economic partners-competitors was meanwhile hostage to the American priorities alternating between Atlantic- and Pacific-centered trading and security strategies within a "West" which, comprising Japan, was increasingly ill-defined in economic and strategic terms and decreasingly coherent in politico-cultural traits. Critical in this connection was not only or primarily Japan's propensity to reproduce the high finance- and foreign investments-centered sequel to the industry- and the trade-centered phases in the growth of a lead-economy. A related factor in the background was whether and how Japan's "high" policies would evolve within the three-stage evolutionary trajectory typical of offshore-insular states. The question was then between and in favor of which among the parties to the contemporary global triangle Japan would exert the normally second-stage balancer role, on the grounds of which (political-cultural, economic, or military-strategic) concern as primary. Following upon the aborted first-stage continental expansion in the 1930s, the balancer role would mark a step back from the ongoing third-stage posture of strategic disengagement in favor of apolitical world-wide trading. Consequently, should an enhanced strategic role prove operationally inconsistent with the economic priority, this would reveal the latter as having been premature in evolutionary terms with unsettling consequences.

Aggregating parties to the smaller with those to the larger triangle – and the western politico-economic with a comparatively eastern politico-strategic mini-triangle – will move a system toward a five-power-plus, or pentagonal, structure. The key incongruity in the western mini-triangle is between military-strategic cooperation and economic and trading competition among the parties, within a balance of power that interlocks with that of trade. By contrast, uneven development rates of the parties to the eastern mini-triangle relate critically to diplomatic isolation, and do so within a dynamic that interlocks mechanical balancing with organic rise-and-decline fluctuations. The dynamic's gradual shift eastward has been shown by the Soviet position relative to differently unstable or revisionist states on one side and reascendant China on the other equaling the position of ancien-regime France between allied Bourbon Spain in decline but unreconciled to the loss of Gibraltar and an either ascending or assertive Germanic power, before the French predicament was succeeded by Germany's between a decaying Austria–Hungary plagued by ethnic *irredentas* and a resurgent tsarist Russia. As the identity of the weakest party in the triangle passed from Bourbon Spain through residually Germanic Austria–Hungary to largely Slavic eastern Europe, kinship in political culture or ethnicity with the stronger partner did not exclude and may have contributed to the resentment of his superior status and domineering role. And while the variably decaying protégés were as ambivalent in relation to the dominant ally as the latter was toward the main adversary, they seemed also impervious to either far-reaching or stability-conferring reform. This did anything but guarantee the allied protector and embattled would-be amphibian against isolation in the face of the western insular rival and, even more important, the strategically primary farthest-eastern rear-continental threat.

The task of managing the rudimentary framework of a balance of five powers, one that consolidates a network of discrete if interlocking two-power competitions, began tentatively to pass from Britain to the United States when it and imperial Japan replaced France and Austria and joined Nazified Germany and Sovietized Russia in a pentagonal system expanded to global scope by the terminal travails of the Anglo–German–Russian triangle. For isolationist America to inherit both the assets and the ambiguities of the British balancer could be viewed as the natural extension of her offshore-insular position into the corresponding function. The problem with the logic was that, in a reversal from what had been the case for Great Britain, the requisite ability to commingle the universal interest (in orderly systemic development) with the balancer's particular interests (in superiority-based security), and to promote the two purposes intermittently but then simultaneously, had in the American case preceded the crystallization of a largely self-balancing multipolar system while an adequate margin of supporting US resources has been fading as the system was assuming discernible form. As a result, the balancer's continuing dilemma as to whom to check more or most between asymmetrical potential unbalancers (for the British, at first, sprawling-but-heterogeneous Spain or smaller-but-compact France, and, in due course, residually assertive France or incipiently ascendant Germany) was taking shape for the United States in a condition that had been Britain's when she was already losing her grip: that of a declining rather than rising capability. The choice lay then not only between differently asymmetrical Russia and China as more or less acute or hypothetical threats, unevenly immediate in time and proximate to present-and-future centers of US interests in space, but also between the two mainly politico-military threats and challenges to US economic preeminence from any one Asian or European competitor individually or in unwitting combination.

The ambiguity only highlighted the fact, and was enhanced by the fact, that neither in time nor in kind was the cycle of US career as the world's core economy coterminous with the life cycle of either of the potential carriers of the politico-military challenge. The interplay between the politico-military and the economic issues and assets would determine the shape of a future plural system. But an emergent plurality could be only prematurely certified as "pentagonal" so long as it comprised powers that were major only militarily or only economically, and the United States alone combined the two requisites of great-power status by contemporary standards.

As matters stood, they altered to the point of turning upside down the "normal" situation as it had tested mature Britain's performance in both of the critical arenas. The first change was from balancing, or pretending to hold the balance, among several powers on land to countervailing, in the guise of Soviet Russia, one specific power only. Resurfacing in the process has been a conflict of principles, one expressed in the opposition to anything that pointed to the unbalancing preponderance of one power on the continent, held on to by British statecraft; another underlying the premier continental power's pretension to diplomatic preeminence short of military dominance, only explicitly formulated by France's Louis XIV. Stressing the first principle to the exclusion of the second exacerbated the perception of Soviet self-assertion sufficiently to evoke comparisons, in relation to Western Europe, with physical assaults on lesser by larger powers all the way from Assyria and Macedon to Napoleonic France and Nazi Germany. The second change was from Britain's contending with only one major naval challenger at a time most of the time to confronting the no longer supreme and only superior US naval capability with a more dispersed challenge. A growing number of military-technologically denial- or resistance-capable minor coastal or insular parties had to be dealt with, either balanced reciprocally or neutralized individually, thus in the Persian Gulf, in tacit collusion or stealthy rivalry with a Soviet navy roaming along an ever widening perimeter.

The new conditions in navally relevant military technology, tending to reduce disparities, coincided with the new situation on land, implicit in the comparable size of US and Soviet metropolitan bases and resources. Taken together, the novelties mitigated the discrepancy between the continental and the maritime spheres, which had accounted for many of modern Europe's diplomatic dilemmas and caused the worst of her military disasters. However, since the changes did not abolish the inseparability between the two spheres any more than the exposure of both superpowers to long-range nuclear-tipped missiles cancelled out their conventional-military invulnerability to each other, the essential structural and operational constituents of the land–sea power schism were preserved. They survived sufficiently to continue confusing the distinction between offensive and defensive aims and conduct behind the national strategies of the two principal power types, a traditional impediment to converting complementary capabilities into coordinated policies.

So long as the prevailing conditions stood in the way of a genuinely multipolar flexible system of five or more (amphibious) powers, there was sufficient basis for a pattern of multi-tripartite, largely self-equilibrating or self-correcting, strategic interplays guided by the instinct to deny any undue advantage to, or cause irreversible alienation from, a third party as part of dealing with a second. Acting thus was impeded so long as any appearance of a separate peace-like accommodation between America and Russia was perceived in Western Europe as a collusive deal, and one between the United States and China could be reprobated in the Soviet Union as a hostile encirclement. Inhibited concurrently was both the maintenance and a deliberately staged movement out of an increasingly only phantom-like US hegemony, henceforth dependent on (1) reluctant European and Japanese economic financial concessions-to-contributions in exchange for arguably less necessary military protection and (2) a mostly passive military-political checking of Russia by China and China by Russia in a relationship largely immune to American influence. The consequently growing need to exhibit self-restraint while effectively leading the alliance, conspicuously missing when Western European empires were being urged to decolonize even as the allies were commercially reviving, has been met since due less to matured design than to domestic inhibitions on the capacity to act and to the perplexing character of multiplying external challenges. Whatever its source, the reduced scope for leadership was ever more difficult to coordinate with unchangingly rigorous demands for Soviet geopolitical self-denial, which blocked an even-handed approach to the two Eurasian giants as much as Soviet admission to or acceptance of a junior partnership in a cooperatively upheld "world order" US-style.

The circumstances were only complicated further by uncertainty as to which of the actual and potential major powers were absolutely and relatively rising and declining organically, a key factor in their stimulating the balancing process or being sustained by it and being either restrained, preserved, or even resurrected as a result. It remained uncertain in consequence which aspect of the balancer role would eventually predominate, and be implemented by whom. One possibility was that of a Britain-like military-political balancer identifying and then opposing the momentarily strongest land power in support of transiently weaker ones, to be replicated against a Soviet Russia that expanded coercively or by induced consent in or close to Europe and against a China or Japan (or India) that would seek to extend direct or indirect influence in Asia. Another possibility, modeled on Venice, was that of a primarily political and only marginally military moderator and, alternately, conflict-precipitating trigger. The role, carried out chiefly by denying political backing and more-than-defensive military support to a winning and potentially triumphant ally, could be replicated by Western Europe, China, or the two by means of tacitly combined passive equidistance or active neutralism relative to the United States and Soviet Union as the interchangeable (would-be) hegemons. And still another alternative was that of a largely diplomatic and political leaner (as distinct from balancer), a posture similar to Britain's relative to Bismarckian Germany. The object is then to restrain the preeminent continental power by delegating to it well-defined functions on the continent while the mandating insular power retains the sanction of withdrawing its conditional toleration when the continental actor's interests and performances exceeded the requisites of rough status-role parity. Such an arrangement might become replicable on the Eurasian continent by the United States in favor of either Soviet Russia or China, whether or not it was targeted at a geopolitically assertive because economically troubled Japan.

None of the options was clearly superior to any other or more readily feasible so long as the dispersion of capabilities in the global system was only in its initial phase, and the prospective candidates for major-power role and status covered as a result a wide range of basic foreign-policy postures and dispositions reflecting their particular stage of evolution. Such a situation was radically different from that which made a balancer role appear easy, and its performance impartially beneficial, in mid-nineteenth century. However, it resembled the next-following conditions when, conjointly with the late entry of additional powers into the system and Germany's move into the formerly French role of amphibious challenger, Britain became a directly endangered party to the larger balance of power. She was then reduced to a conflict-aggravating devolution of counterbalancing performance to formerly rival parties still capable of both self-assertion and self-defense. More recently, the United States was still – where Britain had been again – directly involved within an acute phase of the land–sea power contention and was already, like late nineteenth-century Britain, losing unmatched economic superiority. But its formal or informal allies were better equipped to offer economic competition than effective military-strategic cooperation resulting from far-reaching devolution. This situation pointed less clearly to the balancing of the continental theater by the United States than to the cooperation of the two action-capable and conservative insular and continental powers in stabilizing the evolutionary process world-wide, in the direction intimated by the existing band of disparate basic foreign-policy postures reflecting the uneven stages of development of key actors.

9
Between Development and Drift

If historical antecedents are suggestive for the conditions of both state systems and state-like actors that shape conflicts, they also supply intimations for the strategies to deal with such conflicts which, mirroring the crises within and among actors that impel the evolution of the international system, mediate the rise and decline of major powers in material capabilities and political standing via a succession of basic foreign-policy postures. It will depend, also in this respect, on the actual balance between the competing forms of change – progression and progress – to what extent projecting from the past can serve to intimate a future that has emerged from a present wherein events denoting patterned development are inevitably overlaid with incidents suggesting rudderless drift, if only because the realm of necessity is alternately narrowed by real and concealed by imaginary choices.*

REVISITED STRATEGIES AND RECENT ANOMALIES

The aftermath of World War II witnessed the narrowing of the disjunction between the actual capabilities and the assigned role and status of the victorious and the defeated powers that had ensued from World War I and cumulated the crises conducive to its sequel. The questions surrounding major-power strategies flowed henceforth from the conditions of the system's structure: its evolving nature and the incomplete or imperfect character of the land–sea power schism and/or triangle, reminiscent of the conditions prior to the

---

* The following three sections replay the strategies- and evolutionary stages-relevant themes developed on historical examples in chapters 4, 5, and 6 respectively.

European climax centered on Britain. The resulting problems, including the issue of what actually did or should determine policy, have been reflected in strategic drift (the operational dimension) pending a future clarification of developmental growth–decline tendencies (the organic dimension) in the relationship or segment critical for the evolving (proto-) system.

Once the course and outcome of World War II had projected the United States into a monopoly position similar to that of amphibious Spain at her peak, only a gradually reconstructed Western Europe and Japan were in a position to replicate the Anglo–Dutch challenge to Spain within the politico-economic small-western triangle. The consequences of the economic reconstruction for diplomatic strategies were, however, suppressed by the security implications of the Cold War – a progressively de-ideologized politico-military conflict which, by imposing a more effective check on US monopoly, combined for the incipient global international system the function performed by the Papal–Imperial, Habsburg–Valois, and Spain–Ottoman conflicts for the incipient European one. The conflict's unfolding along the West–East axis was consummated when it was extended to include China. The latter's subsequent diplomatic promotion implemented the tendency for the dynamic of a two-power conflict to substitute an equipotent third power for secondary-or-inferior partners in outflanking strategies. At the same time, US–European–Japanese economic competition over the "China trade" was a potentially growing factor in strengthening the farthest-eastern power materially and technologically. Moreover, supplementing a two-power West–East with a tripartite land–sea power dimension coincided with replacing the intitial impression of ideologically polarized "revolutionary" international politics with a plurality of sociopolitical upheavals or even revolutions within a world politics increasingly conventional at its center.

When the United States moved to follow up the disruption of the near-coercive Soviet strategy for quasi-duopoly, or co-hegemony, with China in Eurasia with a policy consummating the continental-coalition strategy based on NATO through an outflanking quasi-alliance with China, this near-instinctual customary response to stalemate in two-power rivalry was mirrored in Soviet attempts to reciprocate with counter-encircling diplomatic activity. Applied from time to time to a Western Europe only inconclusively tempted to relax a committed-allied in favor of a mediatory-if-not-neutralist posture, the Soviet effort was more consistently pursued through less conventionally diplomatic but more effective probings in the Third World. The tentative strategies reflected on both sides the unfinished makeup of the land–sea power schism and triangle, deferring a serious consideration of the respective merits of the historically tested alternative strategies that exhaust the range of possible combinations and oppositions among the insular sea power, the would-be amphibious central power, and the easternmost rear-continental power of the day. Whereas the ever more pragmatic motives behind the third-party-promoting outflanking strategy had numberless antecedents in conflicts of two major powers, only some of them (notably the Ottoman–Spanish) suggested a useful potential for moderation. And to the extent that the only emergent triangular land–sea power setting replicated imperfections in earlier analogues in either (Egypt-centered) antiquity or the (pre-British) early modern era, these had only ambiguous or largely hidden implications for the intensity of the conflict and its likely course.

Foremost among the anomalies has been the split personality of the United States. It was more akin to Egypt than to England as a party supremely insular in its emphasis on ideo-cultural uniqueness, but physically only semi-insular in relating a continent-wide space to a physically contiguous western hemisphere and many-sidedly close Western Europe. While one facet accounted for an unusually assertive posture reflecting a sense of moral-political superiority, the other encouraged a higher degree of defensiveness and a lesser one of detachment than either was historically or would be objectively normal for an integrally insular party. The combined effect of the deviations was not only to curtail the immunity of the leading sea power. It implicitly reduced also the advantage of the oceanic over the continental arena, if without bestowing on the latter the superiority once manifest operationally in easy conquests of coastal cities from the hinterland and a feasible seizure of mainland-adjoining maritime-mercantile outposts with the help of easy-to-match or neutralize naval technology. However, even but partially restored equivalence of the two arenas was a plausible hypothetical background for attributing to the Soviets the indisputable capability and imputing to them the settled intention to re-enact an Assyria-like military strategy *vis-à-vis* a materially and geo-strategically critical Western Europe. The latter's exposure to conventional-military conquest seemed to consummate, and might even substitute for the effects of, America's own vulnerability to nuclear technology.

The implied dangers and their perception were partially offset in strategic calculations by positive differences. Foremost among them was the vast territorial resource base of the (quasi-) insular United States relative to Soviet Russia's when compared with the size- and resource-related inferiority of Britain's insular metropole relative to either France or Germany – a land-related factor that reduced the bearing of adverse changes in naval technology and the requisite related skills, which pointed to the diminished US capacity to achieve and maintain a degree of maritime supremacy exceeding mere superiority. Moreover, the importance of any strengths and flaws in the US sea power's economic assets and performance was less so long as the geo-economic factor was secondary in the competition with the Soviet land power to the geo-strategic. It mattered in this connection that the schism-constituting overlap between land- and sea-power attributes and interests in the economic domain was henceforth a limited one. It was confined not so much by the traditional gap between agriculture and commerce – at its widest when hinterland empires faced coastal cities in relations of one-sided conquest or exploitation rather than of sustained competition – as by only slowly diminishing disjunction between capitalist and socialist economies within a consequently heterogeneous world economy.

Reflecting the deviations from the pure insular–continental model were operational ambiguities, revealed in two key relationships: between economic and geostrategic determinants of diplomatic strategies and strategy-implementing policies; and between the principal two powers and the critical third party, affecting the link between the global military-political triangle and either of the smaller (western or eastern) triangles.

Operational ambiguity has always been latent in conditions of military-strategic stalemate, only intensified by the character and the potential of nuclear- or outer space-related technologies; and the potential of the economic factor to attain actual or apparent determinative salience surfaced whenever it failed to be constrained by imperatives from system structures, not least as refined by a crystallized land–sea power schism and spectrum, favoring the geo-strategic determinant. So long as this could or did happen, the indecision in, say, earlier Dutch policies between trade-economic and military-strategic or security considerations (pointing to alliance against and with England, respectively) reappeared to a degree in US–European–Japanese relations. Either precariously contained economic competition or an overrated potential for economic cooperation in response to changing premises and perspectives in regard to military security differed then from the clear primacy of the geostrategic concern formerly prevailing in, say, the pre-World War I Anglo–German–French western triangle despite high-intensity cooperative and competitive economic transactions among the parties to it.

Overrating the economic factor expressed either a conceptual confusion or a mistaken attribution. Subject to being confused were the ultimately determinative role (of material factors, as part of the capabilities-determining organic makeup) and the proximately motivating role (of geopolitically conditioned concerns and intentions, as part of the operational momentum) in the making of policies. A greater-than-conditioning effect on strategies could be attributed to either the (expansion–contraction) dynamics of the world economy or its structural (core–periphery) differentiation, to the detriment of considerations rooted in overall power distribution and configuration. When emphasizing functional over structural determinants extended to narrowly military causes and effects, overemphasis on the arms-related dimension nurtured directly or indirectly the ideological values-laden East–West polarization. This obscured the asymmetries in US and Soviet situations inherent in the triangular insular–continental configuration and critical for evaluating the conditions of parity, and the commonality of interest in parity, between them. When the economic dimension was overemphasized, one of the indirect effects was to intensify US–Soviet geopolitical competition in the Third-World peripheries. This implied a re-emphasis on the south–north axis in critical issues of politics, pre-dating the westward shift of the global center of gravity and the concurrent crystallization of the land–sea power schism.

The resulting confusions were reinforced – or only kept in force – by ambiguities surrounding the third party to the global or politico-military triangle. So long as its inferiority was tantamount to the absence of a coequal third power, this reproduced the situation of the Spain–Ottoman conflict whenever France in particular was paralyzed, and of the Papal–Imperial conflict pending the rise of major secular-territorial powers. So long as, in the next stage, the identity of the critical third party wavered between China as a territorial power and insurgent peripheral forces (such as Islamic fundamentalism or Third-World revisionism in general), such party's only intermittent and indirect impact on the two principals recalled Persia's on the Atheno–Spartan conflict. The hard-to-identify and -manage impact of the peripheral forces was meanwhile reminiscent of the role pre-institutionalized migrant populations had played in the rear of the principal sea and land powers in the early Near Eastern and late eastern Roman context.

Either third party was at the root of one or another kind of systemic derangement. This was true despite the fact that China's role in the system was not yet sufficiently in excess of her national capability (although exceeding the capability–role disparity in evidence for either the United States or the Soviet Union) to elicit corrective responses on a par with the consequences of the radical disparity that had emerged out of World War I. Then the general problem, an overmature state of the European system, had been narrowed down to the specific one of the declining western-democratic role-status incumbents confronting rising and relatively role/status-deprived claimants (the Axis powers). Insofar as the critical pathology had resided in this marked hiatus inflaming normally competitive relations between fundamentally homogeneous established powers, it differed from that besetting the more heterogeneous post-World War II global (proto-) system comprising two distinct classes of actors: state and non-state and, among the former, states occupying a wide spectrum of military capabilities centered on the conventional variety. In the overmature European system, the pathology was expressed in the incumbents invoking normative constraints to deny the employment of conventional military force for the traditionally legitimate end of restoring the capability–role balance; in the global proto-system, the principal anomaly was expressed in two ways: (1) an excess of unconventional high-technology instruments of force over political ends traditional to the state system, with the superior forms of weaponry constraining the use of conventional military means among (major) nuclear-armed states; and (2) insufficiency on the part of some of the lesser states and all non-state actors of the conventional-military force required to accomplish their political objectives.

Whereas superior weaponry declassed conventional military tools in degrees proportionate to the state of the balance of (nuclear) terror, insufficiency of the conventional tools depressed the quality of employed force all the way to acts of terrorism in ways and degrees proportionate to the imbalance between available force and coveted goal. The problem of choosing appropriate strategy was made worse in the post-World War II period by uncertainty as to which aspect of the era's ideal-typically discrete, but actually overlapping, pathologies was to be primarily attended to – was operationally salient at any one time or potentially more seriously system-destabilizing in the future. In terms of the interwar kind of pathology, escalating contentions over the validity of traditional goals and an increasingly lopsided distribution of material and immaterial assets would make a major (and only potentially conventional) conflict increasingly probable; the weakness of the conventional-military middle between the nuclear and sub-conventional terror-laden extremes – the critical gap in the post-World War II type of pathology – has made it at least provisionally certain that traditionally legitimate goals could be achieved, if at all, only by means of either continuous and diffuse low-level or centralized highest-level violence, differently resistant to being molded and controlled rationally.

The attendant problems were complicated, and stability undermined further, by the diverse ways efficacy of means would relate to legitimacy of ends. Peculiar to the post-World War I situation was one extreme: the low efficacy of normative constraints on the use of eminently usable and efficacious conventional military force coexisting, in the absence of alternative adjustment mechanisms, with a high (if contested) level of legitimacy for pursuing forcefully the traditional objective of revising possession-based but power- or will-deficient roles to fit altered capabilities. Problematic has since become an intermediate contingency: the use by non-state actors of terrorist methods to achieve territorial or sociopolitical change, making up for conventional-military capability that was unavailable or inefficacious. The degree of legitimacy depended then on why and how traditionally acceptable goals were being resisted or denied by the conventionally stronger party. Roughly the same criteria and attendant dilemmas have applied to action by nuclear-armed states when it came to the use of the ultimate weapon in support of traditionally legitimate supreme interests. Least problematic, because grossly illegitimate, was action by states pursuing aggrandizing objectives through covert support of non-state terrorist agents and their activities in an effort to compensate for insufficient conventional-military capability, constrained by inadequate material or organizational resources.

In situations short of an ultimate challenge to the great-power status of either superpower, the dilemmas attending the relationship between the efficacity of means and the legitimacy of goals were in the nuclear-armed environment of an imperfect land–sea power schism overshadowed for both prime actors by two factors: (1) the tendency for the gap between available force and coveted goals to produce near-continuous low-level violence; and (2) for the turbulence to overlay the salience of the land–sea power conflict. Nuclear constraints induced then both powers to seek limited political goals by (traditionally less-than-fully-legitimate) competitive support for parties to, and exploitation of the opportunities from, such a low-level violence, in preference to reimposing individually or jointly a greater degree of congruence between disposable (conventional military) force and pursued (limited conventional) goals on the part of third or lesser parties. If resort to major war reflected in the interwar type of pathology the absence of effective provisions for peaceful change on the part of the weakened victorious democratic powers, absence of sanctions for small-actor deviance from the conventional norm of behavior has reflected the insufficiency of a sense of common threat on the part of the still-dominant superpowers that would counteract incentives to exploit grass-roots turmoil as part of higher-level competition.

The latest type of pathologies added impediments to a strategy for land–sea power condominium, the third variant on available strategies next to the insular power's for encircling coalition with the rear-continental power and the latter's for continental duopoly with the would-be amphibious central power. If, in the interwar variety, the (British) insular power was too weak relative to the

(German) claimant, in the post-World War II conditions both principals considered themselves strong enough to deal with the derangements on their own. Between the world wars, the situation was most critical when, along the insular-to-continental spectrum, the leading insular-maritime power (and its dependent ally and former rival, France) suffered from insufficient capability and the would-be amphibious central power experienced an acute role-deficit. The rear-continental state (Soviet Russia) registered in different contexts both of the shortfalls, making the de facto regulatory role a state thus positioned had historically exercised from either strength or weakness more than usually destabilizing. In the post-World War II situation (when the propensity for the major actors to use the period's ultimate force had been more-than-previously curtailed), degrees of major-actor tolerance for low-level violence ranged along the same insular-to-continental continuum, but in a different fashion.

Both the US insular and the Soviet central-continental power had a principled stake in opposing and/or penalizing non-state-actor terrorism which aimed at territorial revisions, and state support for terrorism which aimed at revising power- or access-distribution. They had such a stake by virtue of possessing – but also on the condition of exercising – a role- and status-based primacy in either effectuating or supervising significant transformations. When terorrism was keyed to sociopolitical change of a revolutionary character, US dispositions would be expected to reflect the tendency for the leading maritime-insular power to be essentially conservative in regard to the international, and only selectively and opportunistically liberal in regard to internal-societal, orders. Even less definite were likely to be the positions of either of the continental states. The Soviet Union might pose as a socially revolutionary power, but it could still be in principle opposed to terrorism as the typically extreme (and specifically left-adventurist?) means for promoting radical transformations that had not yet acquired or had already forfeited widespread popular support. Moreover, the internationally "revolutionary" (anti-status quo) nominal Soviet posture was tied to preference for conventional methods as a safeguard against generalized turmoil inherently dangerous for the stability of an authoritarian political system poised over a multi-ethnic social structure. As for China, her position as the rear-continental state would tend to be indeterminate and her choices wider with respect for either of the pathologies: such a power might support terrorist forms of radical (territorial or societal) change as a means of expanding its international role above conventional-capability levels (when weak or defensively minded in particular); or it might oppose low-level violence (when relatively strong and confident in particular) so as to inhibit reasons for cooperation between the insular and central-continental powers and shift the locus of conflict and determinants of strategies to the higher levels of capabilities and actor types.

For either form of pathology to compound the only retarding or also distorting effects of deviations from a pure land–sea power schism was but one more obstacle to the superpowers finalizing a definitive strategic posture. Yet another impediment was present in the two critical relationships along the functional maritime–continental spectrum: the operational-developmental distance between the insular and the would-be amphibious power and the organic-physical proximity between the latter and the rear-continental state. For long, the "distance" between the inherently disparate US and Soviet rates and states of materially significant development and operationally significant methods and procedures could be neither reliably measured as decisively widening or narrowing nor corrected for by appropriate adjustments in strategies; and neither was the "proximity" of the rear-continental Chinese power to the would-be amphibious Soviet state, in terms of existing and prospective capability-based immediate geostrategic pressures, yet sufficient to dictate compensating strategic necessities or opportunities for the Soviets in relation to either the insular sea power or the global arena, including the oceanic world, as a whole.

Although thus defined distance, one immediately economic if ultimately psychological, and proximity, one critical militarily and essentially physical, are always crucial for choices in a land–sea power triangle, they evolve into strategic compellents only in one instance: when the evolutionary trajectories in (material) capabilities and (phased) policy dispositions of the land and the sea powers intersect in a way that shifts the decisive role and impact to the rear-continental state. The only incipient development along these lines, amounting to underdevelopment, has so far mainly augmented the propensity repeatedly manifest in such a setting: to wit, for the relatively western interactions between the insular sea and the challenging land power, combining military strategic and economic concerns (and commonly centered on the sea power's propensity toward embracing the continental-coalition strategy), to be dramatically salient operationally; and for the relatively eastern interactions between the central-amphibian and the rear-continental power (revolving around the option of duopoly or co-hegemony by full consent or virtual coercion by the stronger partner) to mature into becoming decisive – in the sense of making the operational transactions in the west come to a head in the inescapable choice between (partial) condominium and (total) confrontation.

For this to happen, the west- and east-centered military-strategic interactions and arena structures must first have taken shape individually and produced the setting necessary for definite diplomatic strategies to materialize. The military-strategic interactions, exemplified in the eastern sector by the Ottoman–Persian and German–Russian dynamics, reappeared insofar as Soviet Russia engaged the western parties increasingly as a matter of tactical offense for the sake of strengthening her long-term strategic defense *vis-à-vis* China by means of thus updating Soviet military technologies and reinforcing Russia's overall posture. Similarly precedent-rich have been the organic character and the strategic implications of the small-eastern triangle which, consisting of unevenly rising–declining Eastern European–Soviet Russian–Chinese parties, replicated closely one composed previously of the Balkans, the Ottoman Empire, and Persia. In that it added for the central-amphibian power the prospect of diplomatically distressing isolation to the dread peril of military-strategic encirclement, the small-eastern triangle complicated the endangered power's choices further. Whereas the encirclement threat highlighted the option between the consensual and the coercive form of duopoly relative to the rear-continental state, diplomatic isolation was at all times latent in possible defection by the central power's lesser allies or dependants closest to the attractions from the small-western politico-economic triangle headed by the insular balancer and/or phantom-hegemon. As the unreliable allies in analogous triangles, Bourbon Spain for France, Austria–Hungary for Germany, and the Eastern Europeans for the Soviet Union, were all revisionist because dissatisfied and resentful because dependent, while a too close tie was paradoxically all the more galling because of the very kinship (institutional, cultural or ideological) existing between the unequal partners.

The attendant pushes and pulls between parties to the relatively more fully articulated smaller or regional triangles would create opportunities for some and ominous trends for others. Both recommended postponing ultimate decisions on strategy apt to arbitrate between war and peace among parties to the encompassing global triangle, not least so long as both the "distance" and the "proximity" facets of the geo-functional continuum favored drift. The situation had become critical for Germany, when, uncertain of Austria–Hungary, she was developmentally overtaking Britain, but unsure of lasting success in the face of still greater growth potentials of the United States and Japan, was fearful of being organically outscaled and militarily overwhelmed by tsarist Russia in a still nearer future. In comparison, during most of the Cold War era, the developmental distance between the United States and Soviet Russia was neither alarmingly narrowing from the US nor irreversibly widening or irreparably widened from the Soviet viewpoint, while China has not yet loomed so large and threatening in her organic mass and military might to match Germany's perception of the Tsardom. By the same token, Germany's danger of becoming completely isolated by the defection of Austria–Hungary was greater, and the consequence of this happening more far-reaching, than was, despite recurrent turbulence in Eastern Europe, either the probability or the peril facing Soviet Russia in this regard. The only latent state of the implied risks, and of pressures for resolving the attendant dilemmas, has thus provisionally pointed less to an impending major war along the Anglo–German (-Russian) lines than toward a relatively low-conflict drift and tentative exploration of both dangers and opportunities. They were reminiscent of the relatively moderate warlike conditions extending over a prolonged period of time within a configuration made up of less decision-compelling distance in the Anglo–French, and proximity in the Franco–Austrian/Prussian, relationship.

Inasmuch as the ultimate contingencies have not yet been acutely present, the choice among the alternative strategies has lent itself again to the tactical exploitation of real or apparent options. These included a Russo–Chinese, as previously a Germano–Russian, duopoly for the sake of achieving a strategic breakthrough toward insular–continental condominium, while a significant movement toward such a breakthrough was being impeded by US fears of its tactically damaging effects on the existing strategy for continental coalition. At the same time, the latter strategy, aimed at forestalling conflict (by deterring the central power from assault on any one of the coalition's continental members), has called increasingly for tactically nuanced implementation (insufficiently present in Britain's handling of the Franco–German and Russo–German sides of the two lesser triangles), lest the attendant encirclement of the targeted power actually provoke the undesired conflict. Reflecting the dilemmas as they became slowly appareant was apt to be a growing measure of vacillation between strategies. Combining the preferred core-strategy with deviations in favor of alternatives, and exploring them through diplomatic flirtations (involving at first mainly China as both seeking and sought party), was likely to aggregate into the appearance of strategic instability before encompassing the reality of strategic drift.

Meanwhile, America's split personality as both naval-insular and military-continental only began to be translated into opposing a more free-wheeling maritime strategy (centered on oceanic alliances) to the rigidities of (NATO-centered) continental military strategy. Insofar as such a reorientation reflected a growing gap between US capabilities and commitments, a consequently enforced trade-off between diminished resources and enhanced liability to risks would portend a measure of disengagement from a multilateral to less one-sidedly onerous bilateral pattern of relations on the European continent, tantamount to exchanging the rigors of a static perimeter for the risks and rewards of an elastic in-depth defense. Pending clarification, the implications of the alternative military-strategic emphases for diplomatic strategies were in no way self-consciously related to an equally fluid and problematic Soviet choice: between emphasis on central-systemic Eurasia as part of continuing territorial and inter-ethnic regime consolidation, and a multi-instrumentally implemented activism at the periphery promoting sociopolitical pluralism through functional diversification. Moreover, the implications could be only hypothetically related to the ambiguities in the essential makeup of China. These related immediately to the disparities between the hinterland and the coastal maritime periphery, affecting material development, and with greater if longer-term foreign-policy relevance to an equally traditional tension: between a quasi-insular bias in favor of basing regional influence on cultural and/or economic attraction and a continental power-like (counter-) offensive military self-assertion *vis-à-vis* territorially contiguous "barbarians."

So long as such conditions prevailed in US–Soviet–Chinese relations, they expressed a twin contrast if not outright contradiction: between mind-sets variably attuned to the land–sea power schism and triangle and inhibitions implicit in the only evolving empirical setting; and, as a result of this, between the risks of warlike confrontation inherent in a consistent adoption of the continental-coalition strategy and the dangers from indefinitely deferring a serious exploration of alternatives before arriving at the "final" strategic choice. Meanwhile, either drift or premature decisions could be rationalized in terms of either unprecedented indeterminacy or radical novelty in the structure and dynamic of international relations, due to either an ultimate weapon (nuclear) or an also proximately (as distinct from only ultimately) determining effect of either domestic politics or global economics. Postulating a fundamental transformation in the nature of international politics fostered the perception of the Soviet Russian self-assertion as the last, historically obsolete because ideologically misguided, hegemonial bid. Either the postulate or the perception were all the easier to arrive at, the more the tendency for intervals between major great-power wars or clusters of such wars to lengthen was overlooked, and the more the propensity for the wars to occur in response to "intolerable" pressures harboring irreparable loss rather than "unique and unrepeatable" opportunities offering decisive gain was ignored.

This being so, the century-long interval between the climactic Anglo–French and Anglo–German wars has not been sufficiently duplicated so far to disprove a medium-term tendency: one for not only ideological, but also novel military-technological, factors to veer toward conventionality and resurrect traditional courses and outcomes in the appropriate structural setting. A setting would become "appropriate" in function of two apparently contrasting developments: (1) the fading of provisional deficiencies in the functional and initial uncertainties in the structural makeup of the land–sea power relationship in its more western dimension; and (2) the actualizing of the potential for self-assertion of the rear-continental third party to the triangle in the eastern dimension. The climax of the first-mentioned development – especially if coinciding with America's relative decline – would tend to surface the ultimate concern of the insular sea power as one that rested with the security of the home base and its material prosperity: this would relativize the merits of forward defenses in the outer security zones, be it the global periphery or the continental balance of power. The second-mentioned change – especially if connected with Soviet economic or other crisis – would redirect the central-amphibian land power's unremitting concern with inner-zone security: it would shift from global-peripheral contention with the sea power to the rear-continental power as the more compelling threat or, at least, preliminary target.

When powerful tradition has prevailed over putative transformations because structure has crystallized into a clear guideline for assessing the fitness of a strategy, the always latent choice for the main insular and continental parties between confrontation and condiminum-like concert becomes imperative. And once the choice of the cooperative over the conflictual course has become theoretically possible for both sides, other and related issues become of only secondary interest. One is to determine which of the involved principal and dependent-secondary powers was actually as against ostensibly (more) responsible for warlike conflict, through which manner of implementing the war-inducing strategy; another, to decide which of the more objective determinants predominated among the war's causes or merely precipitants: a vacuum of power fostering convergent advance to fill the void or the (consequently) resurfaced disparity between the oceanic and the continental arenas on the structural plane – or, on a functional plane, discrepancies between actual capability (including economic) and asserted (diplomatic) role and (strategic) interests or else consequent parallelisms in reflexively rigid approaches to arms competition on complementary levels of military technology.

For it to nullify all precedents, an authentic transformation of world politics would have to consummate the developmental cycle through a virtual reversion to its earliest beginnings. These were to be found in the primary givens that had preceded the conflictually wrought crystallization of a "modern" interstate system, modified only superficially over time when functional equivalents of apparently altered features have been taken into account. In such hypothetical future conditions, as the restored ascendancy of organic over operational determinants climaxed within a world community, the conflict-impeding material self-sufficiency of the primeval Mesopotamian or Nilotic village community would have been replaced by wholly symmetric full-scale economic interdependence and interpenetration. Moreover, foolproof reciprocal deterrence would have taken over from the logistical obstacles to aggression implicit in the lack of contiguity and/or the impassable terrain interposed between primitive actors. And, finally, likewise replicated would have to be the effects of there being no material surplus over reproduction-permitting means of subsistence, to be profitably usurped by conquest. This presupposes the clear and compelling cost-benefit superiority of domestic production over inter-group predation in any form, and for all parties, as both the cause and the consequence of a definite shift of governmental functions inward – and, presumably, entails a concurrent transfer of duly moderated or only modified and institutionalized strategic competition from inter-state to intra-(world)-community levels.

CONTINUING TENDENCIES AND HALTING EVOLUTION

The rise and decline of actors and the parallel expansion and contraction of the arena have provided both the setting and the stimulus for major-to-hegemonial conflicts at all times. However, the conflicts' intensity and the complexity of the underlying determinants, including revolutionary upheavals, was increasing as the evolution mediated by the conflicts progressed. In early Europe, the part-accidental aggregations of power in the permeable space of a geographically uncharted low-pressure arena tended to dissolve under their own weight. Weak internal cohesion and the prevailing modes of rulership succession and sub-elites secession favored fragmentation, blunting hegemonial contests between either the Empire and the Papacy or the Empire and the nascent kingdoms. This tendency to self-dissolution in an insufficiently constraining permissive environment combined with a conception of time that blotted out the span (intermediate between the transient moment and eternity) critical for strategic reflection and planning. Moreover, the concept of space was as unformed as the instrumental means of mastering it were primitive.

The next, middle period of evolution witnessed nonetheless the slow rise of more nearly homogeneous, even if unevenly developing and innovating, powers consolidated by virtue of routine conflicts and capable of waging intensified hegemonial conflicts. The Italian prelude, centering first on predominant Milan, was followed by the contest of the "northern" monarchies over the pre-crystallized Italy shifting gradually northward toward the Low Countries and Germany, while the contest over a henceforth more substantive than merely nominal or symbolic preeminence between Spain and France was clearing the path for the maritime powers. With the rise of these powers, the entire process became more intricate and the increasingly worldwide conflicts more intense, as sociopolitical and economic groups became more widely differentiated within actors and the actors themselves differed more in their functional makeup and general situation. More upwardly mobile group pluralism and the more diversified (agricultural–industrial–commercial) and fluctuating (expanding–contracting) economic environment of politics complicated henceforth the offensive–defensive calculus of the regimes when compared with the agriculture-based political economy of the narrowly continental era and arena, wherein graduated increases in military force and fiscal revenues had aggregated into relatively simple if not necessarily more stable equilibrium relationships.

Coincidentally, the irritant from uneven rates of organic rise and decline was compounded by the main continental-military powers being more promptly and predictably exposed to containment strategies than the maritime-mercantile powers. This strategically critical divergence between the two types of power could not but act against a previously developing tendency: for the process of balancing resources and adjusting roles among essentially homogeneous parties to generate an operational consensus on procedural rules sufficiently pragmatic (if not opportunistic) to override rigidities and distortions due to specific value or any other differences among the parties. Thus procedurally enhanced, the prevailing limitations in material resources had a sufficiently restraining effect to routinize actor consolidation and arena crystallization until such time as (by the eighteenth century) growing fears for societal stability on the part of old-regime elites would begin to alter the balance of restraints and stimulants. However, only when the ideological value-differences between sea- and land-oriented powers became more pronounced in the following (nineteenth) century as part of accelerating social mobilization, did they fail to be absorbed into the autonomous momentum of the balancing process anywhere like other actor disparities. They acted thereafter more frequently as the critical multipliers than the only marginal modifiers of the "real" incentives to conflict; and their impact was felt even before the psychopolitical complexes attending decline crystallized into normative constraints on ascent, and completed the anarchy while confounding the hierarchy of guidelines for formally legitimate as contrasted with operationally effective or necessary conduct.

Consequently deranged was the system-sustaining because actor-stimulating mechanism for bringing role into line with resource at a risk commensurate with the to-be-corrected disparity. This could in the end only prolong, and in prolonging exacerbate, the consequences of the delays incurred by an ultimately self-regulating process before readjusting the resource–role–risk equation. The derangement peaked in the following (twentieth) century when a latter-day Britain, cheered on by a radically innovative America, embarked, in collusion with the more cynical and candid French, upon the experiment of shielding their special ways of institutionally sublimating or concealing domestic inter-group struggles by projecting the methods onto the external plane. The undertaking could not but seriously undermine further the procedural consensus generated by uninhibited power balancing. It could not but set in train an escalating collision with latter-day challengers, determined to disallow in fact while denouncing in principle an uncompensated modification of traditional means and ends of statecraft by one-time winners pretending to stop a losing game by amending its rules.

When, in her decline, late nineteenth-century Britain had sought to retard if not arrest spontaneous system evolution by reverting from weakness to her traditional (coalitions-building balancer) role in hegemonial conflicts, the contrary, mainly German but secondarily also Russian and Japanese, efforts were inevitably directed to impeding prematurely disabling domestic developments by external achievements whose scope or rate of realization would exceed even steeply growing capabilities. The result was to accelerate a grand-political revolution that had been gradually bringing separate and successive sociopolitical revolutions within the major countries into a unifying focus within the dynamic of the international system as a whole. After relatively moderate beginnings (in Britain's contentions with France as the continental pretender) the systemic revolution underwent a lull in most of the nineteenth century (busy with sorting out the succession to France on the continent before reopening the succession to England globally) only to escalate into the subsequent terror-stage, compounding increasingly severe sociopolitical upheavals with total-war cataclysms.

When the terror-stage was resumed in the guise of a Cold War-surrogate subject to a species of thermidorian relaxation in successive thaws and détentes, the situation could issue into either a "Bonapartist" recrudescence of massive but controlled violence or a traditionalist restoration of conventionally limited force and politics between a new maritime incumbent (the United States) and a renovated continental challenger (the Soviet Union). The classic contest was taking place within an extended time-perspective and from enlarged space-and-resource potentials. However, the geostrategically conditioned slackening of the time-space incentives toward a military enactment of the hegemonial contest neither insured nor implemented anything like a stabilized post-revolutionary system restoration. This was not the case not least because traditional incentives to conflict from frictions-generating contact and values-embodying concept continued to inter-stimulate so long as reciprocal (military- and geo-) strategic encirclements periodically revived both the sense of physical vulnerability and the stress on normative differences, while the inconclusive competition was imperceptibly eroding the economic-material substance of the principals. Meanwhile, however, the factors of time and space compelling decisive preemptive action by one or another party did appear to be on the wane in the triangular configuration (comprising China). The time-related compellents were provisionally relaxed by the presumption of greater regime control over internal developments. More rigorous theory and organization, advances in science and technology, made it seem easier to manage the economic processes affecting rise and decline in capabilities, while complementary reassurance against time running out seemed to be offered by advances in managing sociopolitical dynamics pragmatically through unevenly flexible mixes of induced consensus and imperative constraints. The factor of space was relaxed, next to the vastness of all of the main actors and related distances, by the combination of greater capacity to exert indirect control and diminished willingness of peripheral actors to be interfered with and influenced by the principal powers.

Just as the urge, so the capacity to consolidate territorial acquisitions at large had been at its highest in the mid-period of European system evolution, as was the need to deliberately counterbalance such aggrandizements. With the gradual fading of the capacity weakened also, if more slowly, the at first compensatorily growing latter-stage urge to perpetuate the relatively immaterial rewards of ascendancy. And as it became increasingly dangerous to seek decisive advantage in military undertakings, it became more difficult to find in other recourses a shield against adverse consequences of ostensibly spontaneous (more organically than conflictually shaped) evolution of the system or genuinely automatic diffusion of any one actor's functional or technological innovations. On all these grounds the latitudes in regard to available time and disposable space, characteristic of the early stage of evolution among dissolution-prone actors, began to re-emerge, if for almost diametrically opposed reasons. These were now implicit in superabundant theoretical knowledge and its technical applications, with the result that ever greater expectations were attaching to the uncoerced – if competitively induced – unraveling of the rival's power aggregation.

Even while the conflict mechanism remained in place as to its formal procedures and, thus, function in systemic evolution, the evolutionary tempo was likely to slow down when curtailing the effective (conflictual) method that implements the mechanism, and eroding the effective stakes that stimulated it previously, has reduced the salience of deliberately sought and forcibly wrought transformations. And although basic tendencies and propensities along traditional lines remained nonetheless in force, so long as internal developments continued to predominate over strategic operations in arbitrating the relative standing of actors in the short-to-medium as well as (like always) the long term, organic trends were increasingly likely to do more than activate major conflicts into mediating evolution: they were replacing such conflicts as also the proximate (while remaining, like always, the ultimate) regulator of evolutionary trends and directions.

However, the capacity of organic rise–decline trends to actually resolve an ongoing hegemonial competition without resort to force remained necessarily untested and contingent. In abeyance with it was the issue of a fundamental transformation of the system itself. If a more thorough alteration was to terminally displace a differently configured but intrinsically identical conflict superseding earlier contentions, this required strategic rationality, wedded to achieving an optimum in an actor's power and prestige, to be supplanted with "reasonable" submission to an evolutionary process controllable only from within the actors if at all. So long as strategic rationality overtopped sensible reasonableness, an inertial observance of traditional assumptions about statecraft and precepts of strategy implied acting as if no substantive change was great enough to abrogate the validity of historically formed style and certified stakes.

Meanwhile, a relative mildness of crises could be due to militarily only intermittently or inconclusively backed diplomatic transactions, to the unevenly localized impact of economic disruptions within a fairly well-functioning world economy, or to globally containable if locally stressful demographic explosion. Whatever its source, the crisis deficit was reflected in a rate of evolutionary change that was slow when compared with climactic past or currently anticipated rates. In consequence, the emergent global system was only inching toward a mid-term stage through such processes as the diffusion of power, consolidation of a range of key actors, and their differentiation as rising and declining and specifically continental or maritime. So long as the slow-down was manifested less through stagnation than a measure of indeterminacy as to evolution's tempo and direction, it reflected nothing worse than built-in ambiguities.

One such crucial ambiguity was implicit in the fact that the emergent system was at once expanding and contracting. It was expanding structurally and presumptively also operationally as the number of new or newly middle or even incipiently major powers grew, but also contracting as previously great (European) powers were regressing and many an early power aggregation in the decolonized parts of the world proved again subject to dissolution, denoting false starts when not also effective withdrawals from competition. And if the system was expanding functionally, in regard to instruments of both military destruction and material production techniques and technology, it was also operationally contracting insofar as the newly absolute weapons constrained interactions directly and the economically enriched and politically activated mass-industrial society tended to inhibit wide-ranging politico-military initiatives indirectly. As for the domestic turmoil of economic development in other and less developed parts, it failed to translate into globally upsetting political turmoil so long as the sporadic – and on balance decreasing – military encounters were efficaciously managed from within or without a region.

Another ambiguity beset the actor–arena relationship so long as the principal impulsions to and constraints on many or most less-developed parties originated with the major developed powers representative of the arena. The more such impingements from the arena preponderated over the material and motivational resources of the Third-World actors themselves, the more were they being challenged by nativist reactions to the conventional modes. When, arising out of indigenous frustration with superimposed alien patterns, the challenges conduced to only normative or also operational anarchy, the revolutionary style or substance of world politics gravitated from the ever more routinely conventional behavior at the superpower core to the periphery. The disruptive impact on system development was then racing ahead of the capacity to impress internally institutionalized modes of operation on interstate transactions. Yet if an equilibrium in the arena's impact on actors and the actors' on the arena was to take shape as part of the system's progression toward evolutionary mid-term, also the lesser or less developed radical-revisionist powers had to become more directly accountable. For this to happen, the near-automatic sanctions increasingly in force among conventional powers to make them coordinate strategies with supporting resources had to apply to all states, as an alternative to filling the gap between pursued goals and disposable means by the use of conventionally illegitimate means (e.g. state-supported terroristic, subversively propagandistic, or similar devices). Whereas the major powers would then veer toward the self-limitation of, say, the late eighteenth-century old-regime powers assimilating the perception of a revolutionary situation into actual policies, the less developed powers would move or be moved toward the pattern set by the fifteenth-century new "monarchies" as they set about internal consolidation in reaction to prior overextension abroad and/or disorganization at home.

The corresponding contraction of the arena would be operational, due to the superpowers reducing their competitive involvement in the Third-World or southern periphery; structural, as a result of the global system's subdividing into near-autonomous regional balance-of-power systems, preponderating over the system's earlier attribute and operation as global by virtue of nothing more substantial than the geographic range of relations among the major powers and/ or activities of multinational corporations; and functional, as adjusting locally or regionally practicable economic-development techniques downward coincided with upgrading the role of locally usable military technologies over land- and air- or space-based technology with theoretically planetary implications. This meant that a broadly based system evolution was contingent on the post-World War II pair of crises or revolutions – post-conventional military and post-colonial sociopolitical – forfeiting the capacity to inhibit the traditionally evolution-activating effect of crises. A slowing down was inherent in the differently stalemating or paralyzing impact of (1) mutual deterrence among the nuclearized powers and (2) one-sided devolution of power or authority to the decolonized by the colonial powers. Accelerating the rate of change depended among the less developed polities in particular on restoring limited war-fighting abilities in support of commensurate politico-diplomatic strategies. If the strategies had to be backed by the diffusion of production techniques and productivity rates susceptible of funding the capabilities, the requisite economic surpluses had to grow. They were most likely to be increased when self-preserving elites had compelling reasons to assume their responsibilities with respect to locally generated strategic threats and/or opportunities. This required conditions correspondingly different from those responsible for the developmental arrest in and of Latin America in the aftermath of nineteenth-century local wars over the regional balance(s) of power.

The same, and critical, link between economic surplus, the cost of deployments, and their strategic employment was of moment also in the central system insofar as arms-related preparations for total (nuclear) war had to be combined with efforts to develop innovative means for dealing with equally or more plausible (conventional-military and broadly political) threats. To proceed differently was prohibitive at a time when the disposable economic surplus was shrinking for both the United States and the Soviet Union, when pressures from rising aggregate material and fiscal costs and risks continued to predominate (at, perhaps, an increasing rate) over opportunities for net political or other gains, and when sustainable economic productivity lagged behind the postulated requisites of maximum military preparedness on the part of the strategically engaged major military powers. Ignoring such factors could not but heighten the long-term advantage of parties capable of managing the critical equation with greater concern for long-term basics (Japan's US-protected "free ride" or China's downgrading of military needs under the shield of US–Soviet stalemate).

However, the precise condition of the surplus–cost–employment triad and its impact on developmental alternatives for the international system itself would remain uncertain in any event so long as the conventional-military middle ground was bounded by the availability of (nuclear) weapons of destruction in excess of either legitimate or feasible geopolitical objectives, and the widespread use of sub-conventional (including terroristic) military force in pursuit of unevenly legitimate political (including territorial) goals that could not be attained by the conventional means available to the aspirants. Not least because the triad-related dilemmas, aggravated by the armed force-related pathologies, impacted on the problematic relationship of warfare to welfare and inter-nation stability to intra-nation consolidation, they raised in an updated form also a long-standing sociopolitically loaded issue: one of the choice and balance between the barter-type politico-military economy (adjusting individuals' political rights to their military performance, especially in major or general "defensive" war) and the money-based purchase-type politico-military economy (insulating foreign policy from popular moods by way of a professional force, mainly for minor interventionary if not "offensive" military action). The compounded dilemmas were especially acute within a system structure seriously unbalanced because significantly constraining on some (developed leading) powers and highly permissive for other (lesser and dependent) states, and so long as radically innovative offensive military technology was once more provisionally prevailing over defense-favoring counter-innovations.

Closely related to the other sources and symptoms of developmental indeterminacy were uncertainties as to the system's directional thrust in regard to the prospective ranking of individual powers and their optimum size. Given the wide-open channels of communication and diffusion and unusually effective societal and managerial/administrative adaptation, imitation was favored over innovation at least for a time. In such conditions, geostrategic stalemate and diplomatic-strategic drift could readily favor countries such as Japan (and some lesser Asian countries) over either of the more stressfully engaged superpowers and raise them to at first mainly economic prominence. By the same token, US–Soviet stalemate alone would suffice to lift others, such as China, on the scale of more narrowly diplomatic significance – and enhance the military-strategic utility of a wider range of countries. If the short- to medium-term result was a movement toward variously lopsided pentagonal economic and triangular diplomatico-strategic configurations, another was the longer-term uncertainty as to the optimum size for regionally or globally effective actors of the future and the regional segment or segments most likely to promote and exhibit such optimum. Would, for instance, middle- to mini-sized but compact, socially and organizationally coherent, powers begin to again acquire comparative advantage (as they did in sixteenth-century Europe) over larger but ethnically fragmented and managerially overextended power aggregations at the next turn of the cycle, signalling a crisis of empires? If so, what effect would an advance toward multipolarity globally and a reversion to micro-systemization regionally have on the location of the system's center of gravity? Moreover, if the trend were due primarily to the next surge forward in functional innovations, would the latter occur in the realm of destruction (counter-innovating in favor of defenses, apt to offset advantages accruing from spatial and demographic bigness) or production (adding state-of-art managerial and labor-saving manufacturing techniques to more traditional-conventional material improvements)? And finally, would differentiating the islands of unevenly fine-tuned efficacity in the first three worlds at an ever accelerating rate from the wasteland of Fourth-World destitution be among the problematic results?

It was inevitable that a pattern of even ostensibly peaceable de facto succession among actors or actor-types and arena segments, attended and fostered by functional revolutions, would be punctuated by more or less genuine sociopolitical upheavals (either qualifying-prepatory revolutions historically associated with proto-capitalist insular countries or reactively-defensive if not corrective ones of mainly pre-capitalist land powers). And it was likely for such upheavals to cut confusingly across the lines of more explicitly formulated and deliberately promoted successorial claims against either or both of the reigning major powers, advanced along either the east–west or the north–south axis on the plane of declaratory norms of legitimate conduct or actually achieved role and status. Successorial challenges have been so far more effective, and the outcomes more determinate, as between sociopolitical groups or ideological factions within states: in post-Vietnam United States as much or more than in post-Stalin Soviet Russia and post-Mao China as well as in Third-World countries shedding their "founding fathers," than between states. Thus it was unclear which if any of the relatively Eastern powers would eventually succeed to the Western "hegemon" or "monopolist." It was no more predictable whether the line of succession between dominant power types would amount to retrocession of sea-power to land-power dominance or the pendulum would only swing back half-way in favor of amphibious powers. And it was equally, or more, uncertain whether the succession-related dynamic would eventuate in a procedural-normative hybrid, blending classic western modes (keyed to controlled competition) and revamped traditional "Afro-Asian" modes (stressing consensual and coercive extremes of the range), or else would conduce to a more narrowly bounded synthesis of differently pragmatic-improvisational (American) and doctrinal-traditional (Soviet Russian) modes. Whereas the more inclusive synthesis would amount to a new inter-generic (civilized–barbarian) type of international relations, the more restrictive one would entail an only moderately revised inter-generational (insular–continental) style of diplomacy.

Two factors would meanwhile tend to moderate any attendant convulsions and keep a slower because less turbulent system evolution on a relatively even keel, for a modicum of "net" advance over the medium term. Both factors were apt to sustain for a time the already manifest and historically common regression of doctrinal in favor of pragmatic biases, rationales, and stakes in a no longer incipient world system of no longer wholly inexperienced prime actors: to wit, a situation when acting in an unfamiliar environment to be shaped conceptually (i.e., ideologically) has been edged out in a sufficiently pre-structured environment by the growing capacity to proceed experimentally with appropriately (i.e., instrumentally) reinforced effect.

One such factor has been the paucity of genuine sociopolitical revolutions in favor of what were mainly or only rebellions, represented by Third-World independence struggles, and statist revolutions from above. Whereas, in the two communist great powers, the latter were intended to forestall continued backsliding by isolating the viable from the non-viable features of earlier and more genuinely popular continental-type revolutions for centralized efficiency, the mode had previously blended in Japan with elements of a revolution of the oligarchical type peculiar to maritime-mercantile polities and prepatory to impending ascent. The uneven depth and impact of the two kinds of upheavals was due to the fact that the Soviet, Japanese, and the Chinese revolutions from above were more or less immediately related to the both positionally and historically articulated land–sea power and east–west schisms. By contrast, the Third-World upheavals were more or less genuinely linked to the more ambiguous cleavage between heterogeneous aggregates of capabilities and interests of North and South that invited mainly declaratory postures to be operationalized only gradually by reference to pragmatic concerns on both sides. However, the cleavage's connection with a geostrategically relevant schism faded further when would-be system-revolutionizing demands of the South on the North to produce panaceas for its economic development either linked up or collided with mainly North-centered radical reformist concerns over a decaying environment. With ecological globalism and radical Third-World economism matching the practical-political inadequacies of other schism-neutral or -indifferent isms, such as greater-German nationalism associated with 1848 and Frankfurt, the in part conflicting aspirations in South and North pointed to a radically novel liberal-utopian vision, opposing a qualitative transformation of the international system into a world community to the established norm of the system's graduated evolution.

Another on balance moderating (and not unrelated) factor has been the absence, in a no-longer-so-young but not yet middle-aged international system, of a clearly identifiable late-entering dissatisfied power. Such a power is liable to disrupt evolutionary progression because it applies a retrogressive mode of operations in support of a claim to be assimilated into a substantially revised hierarchy and/or equilibrium. The world system might well be in due course exposed to, and its inflexible power distribution be dislocated by, such a revisionist power in the guise of any one of the slowly developing, because broad-based, polities outside Europe (or even a resurgent European combination). Meanwhile, the initial, early-stage – as distinct from a terminal, late-stage – assault by functionally barbarian forces, in the shape of politico-religiously fundamentalist or state-employed and -deployed terrorist movements and methods, has failed to represent a sufficiently focalized crisis or direct and potent threat to more conventionally organized "civilized" states to impel reactions translating into discernible evolution. But the assaults were sufficiently disruptive to convert the norm of an essentially orderly anarchy, peculiar to the principle of self-help, into an intermittent incidence of de facto chaos, only nominally presided over by essentially helpless major powers.

The forces so far responsible for the chaos would have a different, and deeper, bearing if they were to be supported by indigenously developed or opportunistically allied substantial capabilities. They might then prove to have amounted not so much to prophylactic injections of distemper into an incipient system still to be defined ethno-culturally as to agents of a terminal blow to the world-wide extension of a system centered on or derived from Europe in its twilight. The effect would then be to propel the evolution of the global system backward, beyond what was in essence a segmentally differentiated movement out of its proto-stage, to a virtually pre-natal condition intervening between radically discrete systems.

Meanwhile, so far largely unfocused inflows of energy – from either structural disparities between actors and arena or sociopolitically triggered disruptions – were being only laggardly mediated into system-crystallizing outcomes by the conflict mechanism. Just as the category of limited local conflicts was being stalemated by resource inadequacy in the periphery after an initial spurt, so the contention over global hegemony was held in abeyance by the hypertrophy of means undercutting both motivation and usable capability margins while strategic drift was affecting momentum across the full range of conflicts. When taking place in the Third World – be it Africa or south or south-east Asia – interstate conflicts did exhibit the normal trend from origins in (ideological) concept, related to pre-colonial myths or post-colonial megalomania of the early nation- and would-be empire-builders, to sources in (territorially contiguous) contact and friction, attending initial balancing of power regionally. This was especially the case in the Middle East, as the issue of Zionism gave way before the fact of Israel. However, the conflicts decreased in incidence as soon as actual war-fighting capabilities began to lag behind psychopolitical dispositions, the other facet of overall readiness for conflict. Contentions migrated then inward into domestic arenas, in keeping with both the norm of a constant sum of conflict within a system over a finite period of time and the tendency for power-balancing to reflect at all times the different hierarchy of perceived threats in internally consolidated and faction-ridden polities reacting to either a constraining or a permissive external setting. Moreover, enacting the residual interstate conflicts increasingly in a manner keyed to promoting internal catharsis of pent up demands or resentments would not compensate for the failure to project military power effectively abroad, in ways apt to catalyze a fluid force field into an intended redistribution of assets.

While Third-World conflicts were subject to the only limited and selective disposition of the major or global powers to either foment or fund the lesser controversies, the USA and the USSR were themselves experiencing the usual fluctuation between externally directed conflicts (late 1940s to early 1960s and late 1970s to mid-1980s), and more internally focused tensions or preoccupations (late 1960s and 1980s). Both would jockey for advantage in the peripheries as they rebounded from the rapidly crystallized deadlock at the center of the system. But neither superpower was ready to set off the preliminaries of a system-convulsing hegemonial conflict by upgrading token or proxy confrontations into contentions of a more than exploratory kind. Initial signs and tentative symptoms of the climactic testing of power and will were not fully absent, and could be differently assessed within and between the principal players. However, neither the comparative rise–decline trends nor the interacting domestic forces for social change were of a kind and intensity to actualize the conflict potential implicit in America's position as the defending incumbent of preeminence and Russia's as the aspiring claimant to parity in the world system, so long as the ambitions of the latter and achievements of the former stopped short of irreversible hegemony over that system.

For the same reasons neither power was, as an alternative, prepared to offset potentially destabilizing military-technological innovations and attendant economic-managerial stresses with a counter-innovative grand strategy for a concerted transition to a revised pattern of conflicts with and among third parties. Only such a deliberate effort was likely to preempt the dominant US–Soviet conflict being resolved in the customary fashion through its uncontrolled supersession by independently emerging later conflicts, and to forestall thus both parties' eventual dependence on the configuration of successor powers for minimal security and position. Forgoing anticipatory responses to currently only hypothetical threats and developments in favor of a wait-and-see posture was encouraged by the absence of structural crisis in the world economy. The state of the latter made it easier for the directly concerned parties to continue perceiving the Soviet Union's developmental distance from the United States and China's geostrategic and -economic proximity to the Soviet Union – the two intersecting factors that determine the timetable of bringing competition along the land–sea power spectrum to a head – as either inconclusive or manageable, a perception applicable also to the US–Japanese relationship.

The upshot has been to extend the time-frame for fundamental decisions and radical responses. Such responses might either consummate the expansion of the area of contention (by virtue of mutually encircling strategies via outflanking alliances, compelling offensively-defensive breakouts) or constrict it instead (by consensually limited superpower involvement in peripheral contentions, permitting a conservative co-management of graduated change). Meanwhile, for the US incumbent to follow in the footsteps of earlier and kindred powers and supplement a flagging drive for consolidation-capable finite gains in disposable space with escalating pretension to a time-unlimited paramountcy in role and status carried with it the long-term danger of eventual Soviet overreaction. Pending either a turnaround or a climax, it was reserved for any significant future contraction in the world economy to only weaken or also upset existing political alignments and attitudes. An end to economic expansion might then not so much cause as bring to the surface, in major conflict-precipitating crises (or crises-focalizing conflict), previously latent pressures for either simplifying the many-faceted or re-ranking the unorthodox objectives and determinants of policy. The absence of such pressures has so far kept the international system in a state of suspended evolution. Or, at least, it made an apparently directionless evolution eschew both an unprecedented degree of transformation in procedures and an equally radical substantive alteration in the hierarchy of perceived threats and preponderant powers, rich in precedents.

PAST MISJUDGMENTS AND PROBLEMATIC IMPROVEMENTS

A pertinent, if not necessarily paramount, feature of the total matrix within which the only maturing post-European global system has been evolving was that the Soviet did not qualify as the next-in-line lead-economy. So long as this was the case, any unevenness in the superpowers' rates of economic growth and decline would continue to be interlocked with discrepancies in their respective foreign-policy postures much less directly and explosively than had been the case in the Anglo–German setting. Another and related reason for the deferral of a climactic crisis was the uncertainty whether the United States would continue being able to buttress a weakening foundation for economic leadership by policies that, while forgoing the politico-economic costs of self-protective tariffs, elicited from economically equally strong or stronger allies continuing tributes in the form of accommodating economic policies in exchange for military-strategic protection. This device for distributing some if not all of the costs of maintaining the military balance of power was the alternative, although an inferior one, to continued innovation and augmented capacity to save (and productively reinvest) lasting long enough for the economic leadership to survive into radically altered political conditions. These would set in when multipolar dispersion of politico-military capabilities became again sufficiently extensive, and economic rise- and decline-related foreign policy postures were redifferentiated within a band sufficiently narrow, to create once more a situation which, favorable to a relatively de-politicized (and de-militarized) exercise of a liberal (free-trading) economic leadership, would be also compatible with less-than-debilitating costs of a conservative (including balancer-type) foreign-policy posture.

The historical background offered the United States a questionably valid guideline in Britain's failure to accommodate imperial Germany's economic ascent-attending foreign policy exuberance. In lieu of a compulsively motivated re-expansion (a typically decline-resisting post-conservative foreign policy posture) at the colonial periphery, the British could have staged a gradual disengagement from the role of a central-systemic balancer into less conspicuous involvement, stopping short of no-longer-splendid isolation (amounting to the terminal withdrawal posture). Britain's preference was instead for a calculated cession of (colonial) interests and devolution of (central-systemic) responsibilities to France and Russia through ententes that, intended to deter and thus avoid collision with Germany, ended by precipitating if not wholly provoking such conflict. Regardless of its merits, the devolutionary method has not been available to the United States in any event so long as the world system did not contain powers as willing and able to play an active role in countervailing the perceived Soviet challenger as France and Russia had been with respect to the German one at their then stage of development. When reducing international engagement insufficiently or in the wrong direction, the British missed the opportunity to foster a systematic conversion of their national economy to the next generation of industries within an expanded home and a retainable empire market, to be coupled with a timely realignment in power balances and status-role hierarchies within an expanded Eurocentric international system. As things turned out, the twin failure merely postponed the necessary adjustments: the economic remedy being in the event attempted too late only after the first, and the political readjustment being initiated in favor of the United States under crisis conditions during the second, world war of the twentieth century.

The performance showed incidentally that weaknesses in the national economy of an advanced industrial (and insular) power would not necessarily have a correspondingly restraining effect on its foreign policies under conditions of a matured world economy. The late weakening would have such an effect no more than early economic shortcomings had for the barely consolidating territorial powers in an only emergent (capitalist) world economy, when limits on available lending by banking houses and intermittent bankruptcies of state treasuries long caused but temporary fiscal embarrassments with only ultimately catastrophic consequences for a declining hegemon such as (continental-amphibious) Spain. The pre-World War I scenario continued to unfold when the British, having actually expanded their empire through the war, set about refloating their economy and embraced belatedly Locarno-type concert with one kind of Germany pending "appeasement" of another kind. By that time, the intervening damage to the foundations of Britain's increasingly only phantom-like hegemony could not be contained, let alone repaired, sufficiently to withstand the ravages of the Great Depression. The final act was near when the attendant contraction of the world economy triggered the initial expansionary surge of imperial Japan even before unleashing the second hegemonial bid by post-imperial Germany.

In the succeeding context, it was only one of the critical issues whether US economic advantage would persist relative to the capacity of the Soviet Union – typical of an economically not fully efficient land power – to focus (scarce) resources on well-chosen priority sectors and efforts immediately pertinent to the critically important regime performance abroad even more than at home. So long as the material capabilities of the two major powers evolved in rough parallel – the gap between the differing inputs and outputs of the two disparate economic systems being maintained rather than sharply widening or narrowing to one power's accelerating disadvantage – the crisis potential in the matrix of evolution would be concentrated in other disparities. If a salient one was between basic foreign policy postures, the subjacent one was between these postures and the corresponding domestic and/or systemic structures. What this meant was also that the determinative role of the economic factor in regard to the organic facets – its role in shaping the material capabilities base and conditioning the latter's sociopolitical-to-institutional promoters and reflectors – was well in excess of its directly operational impact.

The United States and Soviet Russia were confronting one another through most of the Cold War in the technologically and otherwise modified land–sea power setting on the basis of foreign-policy postures historically normal for thus situated powers: American conservative, keyed to status quo maintenance, and Soviet consolidative-to-exuberant, keyed to moving outward after ensuring a viable and defendable core habitat. At the same time, the very irregularities that have been deferring a climactic collision were also of a kind that could aggravate the conflict if and when it finally came to a head. At least part of the problem resided in a basic ambiguity: the two superpowers were late entrants into a defunct Eurocentric international system, lagging unevenly behind the foreign-policy phases of its founding members. But they were also the original or constituent parties in a nascent global system, with foreign policy postures unevenly in advance of those of that system's only potential future full members.

The ambiguity has manifested itself by one set of anomalies in the case of the United States. As a late entrant long insulated from the Eurocentric system, its domestic pluralism had evolved faster and fuller than did the foreign policy ethos and dispositions required for undergirding the conservative posture externally. As the co-founder of the global system, it has been called upon to foster equilibrium in a systemic environment wherein domestic American pluralism was not matched by the requisite plurality of variously differentiated actors. In an insufficiently crystallized balance-of-power setting, the countervailing role is typically assumed by (a sequence of) singular powers. Conformably, US strategy has assumed a counter-offensive character in the form of either rigid denial or activist duplication of the targeted Soviet expansionism: the conservative posture became on the face of it indistinguishable from the exuberant one (reminiscent of the imperialism of the late 1890s), with the aggravating difference that it would preempt drives imputed to the adversary rather than projecting one's own spontaneously generated energies and initiatives.

The similarities and differences of the US with the earlier British posture were matched on the Russian side with conditions analogous to Spain's and France's. The parallels were most pronounced insofar as a smooth transition from the foreign policy of consolidation to one of exuberance has been hampered by the insufficiency of internally generated (semi-private to para-official) initiatives. The insufficiency originated in the revolutionary-to-totalitarian phase itself, due to Russia's shortcomings as a peculiarly exposed late-comer to the Eurocentric international system; and the external conditions at mainly the periphery, requisite for (and normally attending) the exuberant posture, have been in the emergent global system or proto-system at least as much impeded by US blocking operations in the bipolar setting as expanded in the primitively polycentric setting by the sociopolitical upheavals attendant on the liquidation of the colonialist attributes of the Eurocentric system. Just as the wholly centrally sponsored and executed Soviet policies in the Third World anticipated on domestic structure and processes, so the US-wrought denial strategies made it difficult to impossible for peripheral Soviet activism to feed back dynamically into the domestic arena as a condition of the posture's efficacy. This fact carried with it the risk, familiar from the Spanish and French antecedents, that Russia's movement toward conservative foreign policy might be stunted or the phase overleapt into a compulsively expansionist posture amidst internal economic and possibly also political distress, once the earlier gains attending and following the consolidation phase were revealed as vulnerable to roll back even before the country would safely achieve world power status.

Such long-term risks had their obverse in the potential rewards of the superpowers concerting policies for the management of the ongoing dispersion of power in the global system from a position of superior resource, ensuring a key role in the developing system, and responsibility, traceable back to association with the antecedent system. Meanwhile, the risks remained largely dormant so long as the characteristics of the proto-systemic Third-World actors and the meta-systemized European powers were making two key aspects of the matrix more than usually indeterminate: the interplay of the balancing process with rise-decline tendencies, and the effects of the interplay on the system's multi-faceted expansion and contraction. The ambivalent behavior of the west European powers ensured that, for the time being, the foreign policy posture of withdrawal from international prominence would match its earlier implementation by the Netherlands more than by the wholly passive Iberian powers. This meant that one distinguishing feature, the propensity to draw concurrently on the leading sea power for physical security and its competition with the principal land power for independence or, at least, latitude in policy, was compounded by another, the inclination to allocate the simulation of competitive real-politics in the politico-military and diplomatic dimensions primarily to geostrategically sheltered alliance and community frameworks, and to divert the sublimation of such politics to mainly economic and institutional transactions involving the Third World. Resting in the last resort upon the superimposition of the US–Soviet on traditional internecine conflict, the two simulacra substituted for the reintensified rivalry or outward expansion that would normally have followed for the West Europeans from the spatial contraction of the theater by the enforced withdrawal of non-Soviet Eastern Europe from participation in European politics.

In western Europe, the intervening domestic transformations have precluded resistance to the consequences of relative decline from being manifest in compulsively expansionist or otherwise assertive behavior other than token (thus France in Africa and Great Britain in the Falklands), in favor of mainly functionally or institutionally significant attempts at compensation. The more symbolic than substantive activities at the center of the global system after being set in train by the onset, were facilitated by the long-inconclusive state, of the clash between superpowers separated as much by their situationally and generationally defined contrasting identities, accounting for the land–sea power schism, as by the diversities in their basic foreign-policy postures, pertaining to the rise–decline dynamic. To the extent that the Europeans' withdrawal-attending attitudes and policies have been applied to the Third World periphery in an apparently more substantial manner, this was so because of the developmental arrest in much of that peripheral segment of the system and the compensatory responses to that arrest in evidence there. Both emerged out of competing East–West efforts at neo-colonizing conversion of an expanded periphery to one of the rival socio-ideologically formulated doctrines or practices of politico-economic development. The policies and the process were but a contemporary equivalent of the religious conversion which, sought competitively by Rome and Constantinople as part of the theologically shaped early medieval variety of the East–West division, coincided with the initial phase of politico-economic colonization in the then east European periphery before being extended overseas with the emergence of the land–sea power schism.

Insofar as the pattern of sequential foreign-policy postures can apply to minor powers lacking the irreducible scope of autonomy, the initiation of the sequence in the spate of objectlessly expansive tendencies and policies in the Third World was aimed at recreating more or less mythical pre-colonial empire-like aggregations. That initial stance was also in most instances at least provisionally terminal, when the propensity of false starts to dissipate was not followed by a foreign-policy posture keyed systematically to the conflictual consolidation of viable territorial units. This was because, in addition to India in south Asia, Vietnam in south-east Asia, and Israel in the Middle East, few actors were able or disposed to project a concurrently evolved domestic resource potential abroad so that internal development could be advanced further by the attendant feedback. Self-protection of precarious regimes preponderated elsewhere over either protection or promotion of territorial entities in dictating international alignments and determining domestic political attitudes. As a result, a dynamic of conflicts centering on a balance of power within the several regions would not foster operationally desirable, as part of constraining equilibrium-upsetting, increases in national capabilities. Nor would such a dynamic impose elementary disciplines on mal-performing regimes any more than it would provisionally prop up deficient actors. To the extent that balance-of-power politics was practiced, it was so less as a system-wide extension of a self-consciously assimilated European model than as a sporadic deviation from a supposedly distinctive, consensual, Afro-Asian model of inter-country relations, provisionally departed from when playing the major powers off against one another.

Gradually to articulate the emergent global system required semi-autonomous regional balance-of-power theaters to crystallize and be integrated by means of inter- or trans-regional alignments responding to locally relevant concerns. Failing that, the task of expanding the system would be consigned to the procreative potential of bipolar competition assisted by the willingness of a sufficient number of Third World actors to barter formal or informal alignment with, and nominal or effective allegiance to, one of the superpowers for variably effective if invariably material (including military) assistance. Such opportunistic alignments, and more or less principled opposition to them, linked the mostly but inchoate regional (sub-) systems to the central conflict in a but rudimentary fashion. But the effect on both the matrix and the momentum of evolution was still greater than was that of two extreme reactions to developmental arrests. At one extreme was a normatively formulated presumption implicit in the promulgation of a new type of international relations by and for the Third World. This presumption was coupled with the expansive foreign-policy posture of the first, post-colonial charismatic, generation of leadership, non-aligned or neutralist internationally and internally committed to political modes of nation-building. The aim was to constrict the area of traditional international politics in a system to be segmented into two discrete sectors: of Cold War competition and post-colonial construction. The other extreme, inspired by narrowly material acquisitiveness, was subsequently directed toward revising the international economic order and its regimes as part of a revolutionary reallocation of resources. It supplanted with differently visionary objectives the averred goals of the founding fathers, even as military or civilian economic development-oriented pragmatists were succeeding to internal authority. Effectively development-oriented domestic and consolidation-oriented foreign policies would ideally activate the cumulatively creative circuit of interstimulating politico-military, economic, and administrative functions, traditionally responsible for actor formation. Instead, the successive alternations or evasions aimed in one way or another at easing attendant stresses by transposing the dialectic to an expanded, hopefully more latitudinous and partially institutionalized, global-systemic plane.

Designed to revolutionize conventional international politics by expanding its scope in one (functional) respect and segmenting it in another (operational or normative) respect, the Third World initiatives produced a more traditional precipitate as they receded under the cover of a waning inter-great power competition over peripheral stakes and sympathies. The precipitate's basic component was an operationally discovered and delineated common sense on the part of the great powers, initially on matters such as the regime of the seas, pointing to simultaneously perceived limits of tolerance for radically innovative departures. The implicit tendency was to offset the spatio-operational expansion of the nascent global system, due to polarity-related overt competition, with checks on transforming the system procedurally, due to covertly re-emergent hierarchy-related consensus. However, the actual chances for affirming hierarchy at the expense of either normative or operational anarchy depended on the course of a more crucial interplay within the total world political process: between the mechanics of the core-systemic balance of power, operative on the horizontal plane, and the organics of rising and declining major power capabilities, fluctuating along the vertical axis. That interplay was inconclusive so long as capabilities were insufficiently dispersed and foreign policy postures differentiated at large, and growth-and-decline trends in the capabilities of the system-founding principal powers were insufficiently determinate.

The consequences were both direct and indirect. One direct consequence was to deflect the key dynamic from deliberately changing political alignments among several powers to reflexively matching military armaments between mainly two parties, diverting attention from the more critical role of more comprehensively construed national capabilities in stabilizing long-term equilibrium. This bias only encouraged the principal third power, China, to manipulate, behind the screen of an ostensibly unchanging principle, highly elastic dispositions toward the two principals by alternately imputing inordinate growth or sudden decline in capabilities or will to use them, measured in narrowly military and superficially attitudinal terms, to one or the other. Among the indirect consequences of the ambiguous growth–decline equations, but one fraught with the risk of causing severe disruptions, was uncertainty how to evaluate critical superpower policies or more fundamental policy postures. Thus, for instance, did the post-war Soviet expansion into east-central Europe express the last installment of a policy of consolidation from a gradually growing strength, likely to translate in the next phase into less coercively-expansionist activities father afield? Or was a decline of Soviet capability liable to translate eventually into a compulsively staged expansion on the continent beyond the regional empire, impelled by the effort to defend an endangered position? Or again, was the Soviet-dominated regional order wholly inherent in essentially static (and thus retrogression-prone) capability, generating an obligatory regime of controls susceptible to decomposing from within?

Either alternative posed different questions or dilemmas for policies related to the balance of power. A conservative US posture, implemented with the aid of encircling alliances, would be redundant under the last-mentioned possibility, because the Soviet empire if not also state would be self-liquidating over time. And it might be considered unnecessarily provocative under the other scenarios: inappropriate as to its method if Soviet policies, while expansive, were to become more flexible with gradually rising capabilities; premature in its timing, and meanwhile wasteful, if only continuing decline in Soviet capabilities could be expected to engender offensively defensive violent reactions at a later date.

Yet another indirect consequence of ambiguity as to organic trends was that the global system was being expanded in ways that were not necessarily most favorable to combining evolution with stability. Thus for either stalemate or deliberate one-party efforts to promote a third power such as China into a largely but declaratory kind of diplomatic prominence well in excess of sustaining capability did not facilitate a realistic adjustment of conflict between the principals. It did not do so in the contemporary setting any more than a similarly textured involvement by England's James I early in the Thirty Years War or by the United States in periods preceding the two world wars had done earlier. The alternative was for third powers to be effectively activated in regional balances of power with global relevance – thus India in relation to Pakistan with bearing on China and/or Russia. This would combine spatio-operational expansion of the system with increased stability if, as was likely, the third-party interposition defused the central US–Soviet conflict in south Asia and by extension globally. More instability would follow only if the interpositions merely locked out one or both of the superpowers from the region without also prompting them to shift gears from conflict to concert as a compensation for a shared reduction in role and status.

The fact that Japan figured prominently alongside China and India among the "third" major powers suggested that the expansion of the global system entailed the economic or also the politico-military center of gravity shifting eastward: from one centered on Europe and the Atlantic to one centered on Asia and the Pacific and Indian Oceans. When, in the earlier context, a late-entering Japan had allied with Britain and defeated Russia before assaulting China and challenging militarily a temporizing United States, she was merely a precipitant and mainly the exploiter of systemic crises – and was to become the beneficiary again in a different fashion when the politico-military stalemate on the continental land mass enabled her to pursue militarily nearly costs-free economic activities. A victimized China's impact had been secondary even longer before the restored Middle Kingdom was ready to draw selectively on interweaving strands in its historical antecedents and political traditions, including the manipulation of outsiders in periods of internal weakness or disunity. Communist China moved then past expansively revolutionary rhetoric addressed mainly to the Third World to experimenting with a foreign-policy stance more propitious to consolidating a regional and reserving for herself a global position.

Differing in other respects, the two main Asian powers have so far impacted on system stability and evolution most by way of representing hypothetical future developments. These related on the one hand to the global geostrategic triangle (with China the rear-continental regulator of either superpower's foreign policy stance) and on the other to the three-sided predicament of the United States as leader in world economy (facing Soviet Russia's politico-military, Japan's economic and technological, and the Third World's multi-dimensional, challenges against the background of an only precariously growing national and stable world economy). Whereas China remained an inscrutable quantity, Japan's secondary position in the immediately dominant triangular setting, as a US-allied party to Russia's China-based encirclement, was crucially supportive of her salient one in America's three-sided predicament. Were she to succeed to US role in world economy, possibly in combination with Chinese land power, it would more certainly be with help from America's overconcentration on the conflict with Russia, repeating the consequence of the Dutch fixation on France and Britain's on Germany.

Alternative scenarios could revolve around the greater plausibility of continuing transfers of economic or resurfaced bids for politico-military "hegemony." They concerned an only emergent global system wherein spatial and operational latitudes for policies were expanding more certainly than the temporal longitudes for evolutionary progression were being extended. Transposing the European into the global system had extended the time spans available for the evolution of the late-entering United States and Japan, a delayed Russia, and a but emergent modern China, into a future that was indefinite without being infinite. Moreover, the system's globalization has allowed for potential future major powers engaging in false starts, even as the record suggested a substantial takeoff of only a few consolidated powers. However, it was uncertain whether and how the actual and perceived time longitudes would be affected, be extended or shortened, by innovations in miliary technologies and economic management in particular. This was true despite the real possibility that the military-strategic devices reduced the operational latitudes for key competitions by constraining the traditional modes of initiating, enacting, and resolving conflicts. The same, evolution-decelerating, consequence could be looked for in the area of other than military-political crises. It would flow from the putative ability of sophisticated economic management to moderate the fluctuations in the leadership, and flatten the extremes of expansion and contraction in the life cycles, of the world economy conjointly with rise–decline trends in national economies.

Whether evolution could be combined with stability depended in the future (as it had in the past) on how readily the rate at which the system was expanding spatially and/or operationally meshed with that at which the conflictual mechanisms channeling the energy generated by crises into discernible evolutionary outcomes kept pace with materially changed conditions. So far, since the spatio-operational expansion of the global system had occurred mainly under impulsion from the expansively implemented conservative US and similarly biased consolidation-oriented Soviet foreign-policy postures, the enlargement proceeded beyond a corresponding diffusion of either disposable capabilities or ready disposition on the part of other parties to effectively engage in either conflict or its composition. Compounding this incongruence as to the scope of the system was the state of the core system-segmenting schism. It was increasingly ambiguous as the naval-technological factors and related skills that have qualified the maximalist conditions of a fully operative land–sea power schism were supplemented with the geostrategic, -cultural, and -economic factors that were raising questions about the configuration of the complicating East–West schism. Insofar as the eastern sector was being increasingly (or, again) relocated to the purely Asian powers, the related issues involved, conjointly with the issue of the global system's future center of gravity, the question how the Western segment consisting of European or Europe-derived powers would respond to the flowing back of pressures and strains previously exported eastward.

Would the once again westward-impacting stresses induce, as a precaution against a disruptive implosion within a compressed Atlantic West, a preemptive reassertion of pertinent (politico-economic-military) resources and energies in favor of an inter-civilizational equilibrium? And, if so, would this happen as part of what mixture of competition and cooperation with Russia? Either response affected not only the characteristics of the tone-setting power type of the future but also the nature of the distinctive values and behavior modes that would color the aftermath of the relatively easy repulse of the normatively formulated value preferences promulgated from the Third World and projected along the North–South axis – a repulse which was necessary to prepare the ground for a relatively value-neutral integration of sufficiently crystallized regional balance-of-power theaters into the present or an alternative future center of the world system.

An explosive clarification of the issues relating to both the scope of the system and its segmentation, to both geostrategically and politico-economically evinced changes in actor capabilities, could be held in abeyance so long as the rate of evolution was being slowed down – i.e., the extension of the temporal longitude made it possible for the liberal assumption of indefinite expansion and only moderately competitive allocation of the "goods" affecting security as well as stability and status to hold off, even if not reliably indefinitely prevail over, the mercantilistic fixed-sum postulates secreted by structural bipolarity. This could be so regardless of the specific character of the reasons for extending the period of permissible infantile disorders: the precarious character of particular gains and inconclusive consequences of particular losses in the geostrategic realm; innovations in military technologies that constrained the mode of enacting conflicts (by reducing operationally the relevant or radically displacing the decisive space) or innovations in the management of resources that moderated the unfolding of the life cycle of lead-economies (by flattening the pertinent if not nullifying the persistent rise–decline curves); or the continuing absence of clearly identifiable ascendant late-comers who would press the enlarged system's founding members into reopening the issue of hegemony in an active mode and acute fashion.

All of these conditions made certain that the emergent global system was still far removed from approximating the norm of system maturity. Equally far from being resolved was a question overhanging the others: the future of the state, as its transcendent value dimmed in the minds of men in delayed reaction (among other more practical reasons) to its perversely terminal totalitarian apotheosis, and the dimming eased the movement from ideologically permeated revolutionary interstate politics to intra-state reform as the controlling concern in a resumed search for a viable order of being. Just as state-centered power-balancing assumed its classic form within an action-constraining because crystallizing system when the enhanced capacity to consolidate external (territorial) gains had replaced actor dissolution from within, so the rise of new and re-emergence of older kinds of threat to internal orders have tended to defuse the urgency and diffuse the operation of the balance of power among differently vulnerable developing and developed states. If continuing to expand the range of influencing factors within the same actors reduced the predictability of the balancing process at the problematic cost-or-benefit of issues dissolving instead of actors amidst strategic drift, it was only an aspect of the drift that the shift from revolutionary international to reformist domestic politics, by reopening with the historically persistent question as to the nature of political reality also that of the makeup and purpose of strategic rationality, resurfaced the previously briefly dormant and apparently resolved issue of what constituted authentic realism in perception and policy.

10
Past Reform Into Utopia?

As the time span the strategist takes into account shortens, the range of options promoting choice over necessity (because separating strategic rationality from historical intelligence) seems to increase, conjointly with the enhanced concreteness of the sought immediate outcomes matching their contingent character. Whereas projection of likely mid-term courses from evolutionary progression yields then before the postulate of unrestricted short-term possibilities, the prescriptive urge preempts the prophetic temper even as tactics threatens to overwhelm strategy. When a plethora of transactions does more than distract attention from proven trends as a result, and misdirects energies toward the pursuit of transformations all the more preferred for being unprecedented, utopia challenges actuality in the name of a higher realism of its imagining, based on nothing more solid than extrapolation of a contemporaneous tendency, toward totalitarianism and war one day, democracy and peace another.

REALISM AND REFORM IN A POST-TOTALITARIAN ERA

When tragedy is understood as it should be, not as a matter of man's being heir to pain and suffering for a range of reasons including the most trivial, but as a distinctive predicament – one which, arising out of a clash of positive values, creates an entanglement the tragic hero attempts to break out of, on pain of being brought down as the heightened contact with the hidden fabric of the cosmos reveals the flaws inherent in his, the daring challenger's, own character – a major if contingent change has begun to be noticeable four decades after the onset of the Cold War, around the very time an apocalyptic extrapolation of an apparent trend had earmarked as consummating an unalterable coupling: of congealed totalitarianism with permanent globe-girding conflict. Obeying different laws of evolution, the change has originated in the prediction's radical reversal: into a near-universal fading of totalitarianism even as conflicts unready for militant resolution were subsiding in the world at large. Conjointly, the seat of tragic tension was shifting from between the major political systems to within them; from values attributed to the contending ideologies to asserted merits of contrasting realisms and utopias: their comparative ability to fit essential goals of policy and foster effective or enlightened politics; from different views of social order and justice to diverse emphases on actuality and aspiration: whether and how to uphold the extant or change it in the direction of the better.

While the tug of war between realism and utopia has been so far only an undercurrent in a democratic West uncertain whether to celebrate defeat of the eastern adversary or apprehend its own decline, it was acutely in evidence in the totalitarian East. As the latter was caught up in a crisis linked to stagnation, it experienced a contradiction between reform and stability: the more urgent the repair, the greater the threat to repose. And the urgency of choosing between the two desiderata posed with new intensity the issue of tragic heroism, as its location shifted inward and away from hegemonic defiance of an international order anchored in self-help while constraining its application. Was the moral hero one who undertakes, in behalf of ideal change indictable as utopian, the struggle with the tyranny of things as they are, in lucid awareness of such effort's propensity to translate into the least intended of results: the reimposition of tyranny by men? Or was the agent of such reimposition himself eligible for a heroic part in the tragedy when he sets out in vain to resist all, or only precipitate or premature, change: romantically, in behalf of permanent revolution; or would-be realistically, in defense of the revolution's early fruits, rotted as they may have been in a social order which, though deteriorating, appears for the time as one uniquely safe – only to provoke bureaucratic reaction in the first or popular rebellion in the second case?

Equally high will be the price of escape from one or the other pitfall and the attendant personal and corporate risks into an opportunistic groping for a safe middle ground, one prone to setting off a slide from the tragic into the farcical as inept coercion alternates with either insufficient or intemperate concessions. This denouement has been in sight for left-wing (Marxist-Leninist) totalitarian regimes when, precariously presiding over a dual society and parallel economies, they resuscitated the very forces, secular and spiritual, they had set out to repress and replace. Their descent from noon-time darkness pointed them toward a twilight strikingly different from the *götterdämmerung* the rival right-wing (National-Socialist) totalitarians had invited as the fit scenery for their final defiance. Leaning as they did toward the bio-organismic pole of the spectrum (resting on the leader's life expectancy), where their left-wing counterpart has occupied its socio-mechanistic end (institutionalized in a collective leadership), the mytho-normative practitioners of nostalgic utopia on the right were denied the time to mellow; but leaning on empirically unverifiable myths where the left-wing species pretended to the test of societally identifiable performance, they were also spared the interval during which to molder before failing. They hardened instead first as they ran up against the era's multiplying obstacles to authoritative (let alone authoritarian or totalitarian) government, traceable to modern man's liberation from the deepest of his immemorial fears. A part of the costly rewards of material progress, the condition disclosed the spring behind the destructive fury of late modernity's neo-medieval naysayers to progress, before inhibiting the capacity of all political systems to combine effective with enlightened governance.

Diminished as Soviet left-wing totalitarianism has been since it was breifly revitalized and relegitimated by surviving the onslaught from the right, it has not yet been as clearly differentiated from the still vital body of Russia as it has, perhaps, been from China's. The divorce has not proceeded far enough to make it impossible for the wounded communist beast to draw on communal strength for turning upon its triumphing pursuers, not least if the latter acted so as to reforge the union by denying viscerally embedded national aspirations in the name of completing the defeat of the ideology's cerebrally inflated utopian pretensions. It was this fact that remained a given for authentically realist world politics as the tension between realisms and utopias permeated both the latest of domestic Soviet revolutions and the United States' hesitant movement toward a foreign-policy revolution: the internal reform designed to foreclose a creeping deterioration of the modified left-authoritarian economic system, a positive US response to it subject to the charge from the American version of the political Right of incidentally forestalling the same system's cataclysmic disintegration.

Any reform of the actual by revolution from below or above will aim at narrowing the gap between current reality and futuristic utopia, and be suspect of insufficient realism or excessive utopianism. The attendant confusions – a comedy of mistaken identities and misattributed intentions with potentially tragic consequences – flow from the fact that both realism and utopianism conceal varieties of different, if overlapping kinds. The differences have not been least important, and the dialogue surrounding them least intense, in an America going through a latest spell of Hamiltonianism in reaction to an intolerant dominance of more deeply internalized Jeffersonian motifs in foreign policy as much as in domestic politics.

Within the first of two sub-categories of realism, "philosophical realism" is concerned with securing recognition for the role of power in politics so as to better control and contain its use. The philosopher's intention is different from the political actor's will to actualize and then employ national or state power for realizing conspicuous concrete objectives, characteristic of "power politics." Within the parallel sub-category, "progressivist realism" is committed to activating the supposedly new reality of widening interdependence through expansively practiced institutionalized multilateralism; it is different from *realpolitik*, oriented toward a prudent management of restrictively construed resources for manifestly practical and immediately practicable ends. Practicing power politics and *realpolitik* has traditionally suited best the votaries of the conservative persuasion, the former its defiant and the latter its more defeatist variety; proponents of the liberal creed have found progressivist realism most congenial and philosophical realism only occasionally convenient. The couplings become somewhat different when arranged by essential affinities. Then the genuinely conservative temper's bias in favor of patiently therapeutic nursing of trends links it to philosophical realism as the rationale for practical *realpolitik*, while liberalism's penchant for the institutional and other shortcuts to surgically encompassed societal transformations is wholly in harmony with progressivist realism but fully compatible with power politics.

Interweavings between the two strands of association have accounted for seemingly odd bedfellows when special circumstances gave rise to passing moods. Thus American liberals would on occasion be seized with fervor for power politics (thus in the early Cold War phase, compensating for pre-World War II dispositions), and would more commonly subscribe to *realpolitik* (thus when reacting to neo-conservative ideologies more recently, in support of détente or disengagement). The implied effort has been to evade the irrelevance spawned by the pursuit of ideatal coherence under the pure sign of the progressivist variety of realism; it was reinforced by the recognition of how vitally dependent an effective functioning of the institutional mechanisms continued to be on a supporting constellation of power- and interest-centered prerequisites.

If the insight warranted a respected place within the spectrum of authentic realisms, solidly founded in general doctrine, for the liberal school of thought, no such place could be assigned to ex-liberal converts to the conservative gospel. The progressive might occasionally mistake a successful institutional involvement in crisis management for the effective cause of a peaceful conflict resolution, when it was the consequence of an even but tentative convergence of US and Soviet interests. On his part, the American neo-conservative has fashioned what he claimed to be a general doctrine to fit one specific (desired) consequence of policy, diametrically opposed to such convergence. And he tended to submerge the unevenly avowable reasons for anti-Soviet commitment in professions of a cause no more universally pertinent or realistically attainable than the unimpeded diffusion of a peculiarly American version of individual freedoms. Most directly at variance with the ideologically militant perspective was a realism equally or more concerned about cultural values – one capable of taking into account the range of values which, in contemporary conditions, instead of dividing the superpowers by contrary sociopolitical doctrines, associated the United States and Russia within a Europe-derived cultural-civilizational entity western by global standards.

It was possible to dismiss liberally progressivist, just as the conservatively inspired romantic, versions of realism as the ultimate utopias, or defend both as transcendent realism: the liberal variety because it strained beyond the self-imposed limits of routine politics, the conservative because it translated insight into the demonstrated costs and consequences of adopting conventional policies at crucial times into a program for remedial initiatives of a different kind from the liberal. However, both of the two ostensibly utopian versions could serve to enhance reality in due course when the inter-civilizational equilibrium propounded by one had undergirded the institutionalized multilateral cooperation favored by the other. In that the premises and the program of romantic realism pushed beyond the prudential sterility of *realpolitik*, the analytic detachment and timidity in action characteristic of philosophical realism, and the unevolving revolutions of winners and losers in power politics, they portended confluence with the forward-looking thrust of the progressivist impulse. However, any potential future confluence did not abrogate, and would have to come to terms with alleviating, the underlying real difference between two kinds of utopias: one aimed at transforming reality in the direction of an ideal, identifiable with qualitative progress; another associated with merely redefining reality so as to make it keep in step with empirically verifiable evolutionary progression.

The pure utopianism standing for idealism postulates a radical change in the nature of reality, extending from human nature stripped of its conflict-generating social attributes to the character of international society to be altered from a conflict-centered system of powers into a consensual community of functions. Such a utopianism's association with progress has been denoted by emphases on institutionalized approaches to economic and functional inter-dependences within an ecologically endangered global environment, in separation from and as part of rejecting power politics equated with the use of military force. The contrasting, realistically modified form of utopianism is less an expression of normatively extreme idealism than a reaction to elementary textbook-like realism. It rejects both opposites when it re-evaluates historical antecedents in order to break the hold of the most recent precedents on the present, and reassesses the changing hierarchy of threats and configuration of powers within an expanded framework of both politics and economics: the former amplified beyond structurally conditioned mechanics to encompass more variegated dynamics, the latter extended beyond apolitical economism in the direction of a political economy that embodies the relevant facets of geopolitics. In terms of the inner economy of international politics, finally, to modify utopia realistically entails applying lessons from authentic tragedy, as opposed to melodramatic pathos, so as to correct for both strategic rationality and commonsense reasonableness with the resources of historical intelligence; and from political physics, supplementing one that imitates only force- and gravitation-centered dynamics with one that encompasses time-space-centered relativities and discrete systems-linking flows of energy.

As an intended link between unsatisfactory actual and preferred future conditions, and the alternative to unsustainable stagnation or uncontrollable upheaval, reform can be differently realistic or utopian. Whether an actual reform was closer to one or the other kind of utopias, the pure-idealist or the modified-realist, will depend on how respectful it was of philosophical realism (was guided by awareness of the role power plays in society and its politics) and where it stood in relation to progressivist realism (was guided by the same awareness as regards institutions). If this was true for both kinds of reforms or reform-oriented revolutions, from below and from above, the latter's specific character will depend on how potent was the ingredient of power politics in the adopted means and of *realpolitik* in the immediately pursued objectives. The more realistically conceived and executed reform was apt to be one elicited by specific crisis or crises. It will itself constitute a crisis releasing new energy to be channeled into the affected systems' evolutionary progression by controlled conflicts over the type and extent of the change to pursue. A more purely utopian reform effort will normally respond to a diffuse disaffection with the perceived character of actuality, and be borne up by largely unfocused energy. It will tend to produce generalized dislocation certain to elicit a frontally repressive reaction.

As it got underway, the Soviet reform effort initiated in the mid-1980s was a response to structural crisis of economy that generated diffuse dissatisfaction in the society and risked spilling over into a crisis of institutions. If the effort was internally slanted so as to correct a faltering socialist utopia with a dose of capitalist realism, internationally it was characterized by an inverse relationship between realism and utopia. The power politics of the preceding era of domestic stagnation was to be amended by a foreign policy which, with a view to saving resources at home and adding others thanks to improved perceptions from abroad, incorporated in a toned-down *realpolitik* at least partially utopian new emphases on international institutions, economic and ecological interdependence, and arms control-centered avoidance of military competition. Ideally co-ordinating the internal and international planes would be realistically reformed governing institutions capable of concentrating decision-making on the state level, containing the centrifugal effects of controlled devolution of political and more radical decentralization of economic functions, and amounting in the aggregate to a comparative demotion of the party organization. The character of the attempted revolution from above, its relation to and effect on foreign-policy behavior, and the international conditions and effects of its success or failure raised issues of principle that called for being tested against Russia's historical experience.

The need for Russia to readjust the state–society relationship was being addressed anew in conditions neither as propitious as had been America's when evolving her libertarian approach to the relation between man and state nor as ambiguous as has been the west Europeans' when following suit in the wake of a stressful fall from great power. To reinforce a revolution from above with resentments from below has required mobilizing hitherto dormant political forces; to keep the revolution from either deviating or dissipating called for seemingly overconcentrating authority at the top. The reasons were obvious: the deeper the crisis, the less it will be manageable by either divided or consensual leaderships; unlike factionalism, pluralism is the child of relative stability and prosperity before it can become the progenitor of growth and depth in either. In all other conditions the founding law-giver must, Solon-like, set the framework for relating particular interests to general will and common weal before retiring from the scene. As important as striking the right balance between power from above and participation from below in effectuating the transition was to distinguish between Communism, the Soviet system, and Russia (between ideology, sociopolitical system, and geopolitically conditioned historic identity) in judging the transition's inner character and external implications. Failure to draw the distinction sharply enough risked impeding an orderly exit out of the Cold War as surely as it had helped sweep the world into the conflict to begin with – not least because ignoring the principal conceals a secondary distinction, one which has evolved from that between aggressively and defensively inspired Soviet "expansionism" into that between structural-to-systemic crisis of the regime and secular decline of Russia herself.

Unless the distinction was made and observed, a terminal crisis of Communism was liable to be equated with the impending collapse of the Soviet system explicitly and the latter implicitly with Russia's as a power, on a par with the death throes of any number of historic empires. Observing the distinction allowed instead for less drastic outcomes and a more pertinent analogy – with Soviet Russia's contemporary imperial opponent, the United States, as likewise combining a socio-economic ideology, a sociopolitical system, and geopolitically conditioned and historically shaped power. Within such a perspective, the crisis of Communist-type socialism with disruptive consequences for the Soviet system is analogous to the crisis of capitalism in the Great Depression. Both crises occurred on top of a henceforth insufficient and unsustainable ground-floor accomplishment: one wrought by uncontrolled predation by the robber barons, the other a result of rigid control and planning by robot-like bureaucrats. Whereas one kind of crisis called for reform along "socialist" lines in the New Deal, the other has required inflection along "capitalist" lines according to the New Thinking: the former in order to meet the need for a more extensive foundation of social productivity (relaunching its intensive stage), the latter to satisfy the requirements of intensive goods-generation in the post-industrial mode (replacing extensive growth).

So stated, the parallel pointed to long-term convergence from both sides of the spectrum instead of implying implacable conflict or imminent catastrophe for one side. Much the same was true for the Soviet system within its core and as extended to east-central Europe. If the New Deal revolution entailed, as has Gorbachev's, the integration of so far excluded actors into fuller participation in the national political process, the Good Neighbor policy did likewise regionally when it set off the so far uncompleted transition away from an earlier Roosevelt's corollary to the Monroe Doctrine. No more than what has been or might be happening in east-central Europe, was less overt control and less frequent or habitual coercion tantamount to the regional caudillo" withdrawing in favor of unfettered license by the local "peons": mixing exploitation with preferential trade promotion in economics did not yield in either case to the privilege of cost-free defection toward an alternative material magnet or creedal ensemble; and penetrating into or interfering with the area from the outside has remained subject in the western hemisphere, as it would for some time continue to be in eastern Europe, to the interloper's restraint that was only in part imposed by the core-power's capacity to retaliate.

Whereas the derangements and disruptions affecting the two, US- and USSR-defining, isms and systems could be met by policies employing new instruments before reconsolidating valid elements of older institutions, there was less room for conciliation and compromise when national-imperial identities were at stake. The difference shifted the focus of comparison from Central America and the Caribbean to the relevance for any threat to the cohesion of the pre-1917 Russian empire of the line the North had drawn between the preservation of the Union and permissible denunciation of an inherited (if one-sidedly reinterpreted?) inter-sectional contract by the South.

In this as in other respects, the United States is not Russia as to historical existence, but there is enough of essential similarities in regard to earliest national origins and later growth-sustaining popular beliefs to make the ideatal self-definition of each entail an imperial one.

To hold otherwise would be as narrow-minded on ethnic grounds as to believe the creative and recuperative potentialities of US-type capitalism to be wholly absent from Soviet-type socialism was short-sighted on systemic grounds. Denying that fundamental processes lacked universality on any level was to make nonsense in logic of America as an exception and, more important, invalidate America's self-perception as a practical and practicable example. As for Russia, her future course depended on steering a course between both horns of a not quite unique but nonetheless distinctive dilemma: the fallacy of propelling the country as historically constituted into a cerebrally constructed democratic-cosmopolitan utopia, and the fantasy of returning a Russia evolving in real history to an imaginatively deformed autocratic embodiment of the tribal myth.

The incremental changes that had propelled traditional-rural Russia into and haltingly past the industrial age did not negate a central fact about the latest revolution. It was one of the periodically recurring sporadic efforts to radically transform the Russian polity so as to either preclude the chaos or terminate the stagnation that resulted from more frequent and less far-reaching efforts at liberal-conservative reform alternating with conservative-authoritarian reactions to such an effort's failure. At their most ambitious the most recent initiatives represented a high-risk attempt to both avoid the extreme methods of the historic transformers from Ivan through Peter to Stalin and exceed the goals without incurring the frustrations of the more numerous would-be reformers. Backed by the intervening socio-economic development, the effort exhibited the dual purpose and hybrid character of a revolution from above which was also a final step toward definitive post-revolutionary restoration of something akin to normalcy, even as the transition from the totalitarian- to a liberal-autocratic mode of governance was institutionalizing a difference: between enlightened and oriental despotisms, which located the Gorbachev undertaking closer to the great Catherine's than to either of the oriental-type transformers (and, as between them, closer to Peter's than to Stalin's) on Russia's rocky road to managed democracy socialist-style.

Both forms of despotism would do away with traditionally entrenched intermediaries between the popular base and the central power, inhibiting the sway or agenda of the ruler. But the enlightened despot differs from his opposite in this respect: he leans on the mobilizing potential of the intellectual elites and leaves it in part at least to the dynamic of change to fashion and mobilize the implementing agents. The oriental potentate relies instead for the execution of more or less clearly expressed sovereign will on deliberately molded executory instruments, locked into inherently slave-like obedience and dependence (Ivan's *oprichnina*, Peter's service nobility, and Stalin's bureaucratic apparatchiks, matching the Ottoman sultans' Christian converts to Islam from the grand viziers down). It both conforms to and confirms this difference that while the oriental despot traces the principle of unrestricted personal power to a precisely indefinable (heavenly, divine, or doctrinal) mandate, the enlightened despot's claim to authority is less latitudinous. It is held to derive from the ruler being the foremost servant of a superordinate state that is itself constrained by the law, procedurally if not otherwise. And finally, whereas the oriental despot aims at insulating his universe of rule from the environing world, enlightened despotism is both actuated and legitimated by the goal of integrating the state into the pre-articulated system. If this ambition may be pursued in ways that conform with the methods and conditions of the time, it will always aim at achieving equality of status and role with earlier-developed and thus tone-setting powers.

When anticipating the consequences either the success or the failure of the Gorbachev revolution was likely to have internationally, the general proposition to start from was that reform like all issues critical for high policy was a matter of space and time. When hurried through in the face of an adversarially shaped environment, and thus compressed in both available time and disposable geopolitical access, a reform or transformation effort will have harder-to-control disruptive effects at home as well as abroad than a reform undertaken in a setting that was both temporally and spatially extensible. Compared with this fundamental difference, it will matter less whether the undertaking has succeeded or failed: has given rise to heightened self-assertion abroad as the milder complement to success or the harsher compensation for failure. In a spatio-temporally compressed setting, both success and failure will set off relatively high-intensity assaults in or near the center of the international system. When successful, central authority will draw on the newly generated or activated (but still insecure) functional elites for restabilization; it will depend on the passionally mobilized mass for sheer survival in case of traumatizing failure – and will do one or the other under correspondingly different ideological or doctrinal auspices. Conversely, a latitudinously extended setting will foster lower-intensity efforts to expand the state's access to the system's periphery and enhance or only safeguard its status at the center. When the reform has failed, the central authority will be compelled to so appease the only frustrated or also antagonized military and economic elites (by engaging them in, or condoning their semi-independent, low-risk activism abroad); in case of a successful reform, both the methods and the objectives of an active but moderate foreign policy will transpose abroad the enhanced plurality of more diversified group interests and societal layers.

In Russia's case so far, the three successive transformation processes were compressed in both time and space. They were as much stimulated by the urge to consolidate state power in areas close to that power's core as the degree of the transformation's success first mirrored and then magnified the measure of the centrally guided military ability to achieve the consolidation. A less strenuous and mostly less centralized external activism, in areas ever more peripheral to the power center, attended conservative-authoritarian sequelae to failures of the comparatively less time- and space-compressed liberal-conservative reforms of Alexanders I and II, Stolypin and Witte, and Khrushchev. The compensating activism ranging from the Near East (Nicholas I) through central Asia (Alexander III) to the Far East (Nicholas II) before ramifying worldwide (Brezhnev) was still relatively harsh when compared with the external activity attending the liberal-conservative reforms themselves. Originating typically in military setbacks or reacting to forcible transformation, these reforms had given rise to relatively most moderate or benign active-to-exuberant diplomacy with strong financial-economic components, calculated to strengthen the reform's home base and secure a favorable external setting.

Throughout, the cyclically alternating rhythm of reform and reaction, punctuated by more radical transformations, was taking place in an international environment molded by two givens: a triangularized land–sea power spectrum, exposing Russia to a farther-developed western insular realm and materially-to-physically threatening amphibian central or rear-continental power; and a sequence of variably expansive and actor- or arena-consolidating basic foreign policy orientations of the critical powers, divergent from those of Russia herself. Even as the two givens interlocked repeatedly in ways tending to galvanize routine competition into major conflicts, and did so in patterns of alternation grossly paralleling domestic fluctuations between the turbulence of reform and the repose of reaction or restoration, Russia's principal contiguous neighbor which triggered the escalation of reform into transformation efforts grew larger and more threatening as its locale shifted from nordic West to Sinic East concurrently with tsarist-to-Soviet Russia assuming a focal position in the triangle. Gorbachev's effort to relaunch Khrushchev's liberalizing drive for greater efficacy, now more state- than party-centered, was only unwittingly linked to the full range of the enveloping dynamic, concealed as it was by socio-ideological residues alternately affirmed and renounced in the East and invariably arraigned and denounced in the West. Its more conscious because immediate object was to relieve the stagnation which had finally caught up with Brezhnev's initially successful effort to restabilize the post-Stalin ferment. But the attempt was also set off by the strains and stresses cumulatively engendered abroad by the defeated liberal reformer's exuberant, and the conservative restorer's only initially more cautious, strategies for implementing the Soviet land power's challenge to insular America's headstart in the central and peripheral, continental and oceanic, power balances.

Like the antecedent would-be transformers, the latest one acted ultimately in support of, if immediately also in formal or material opposition to, a myth: of competition-capable socialism, overlaying that of Holy Russia (Ivan and Peter) while discarding (like Stalin) that of permanent for that of controlled revolution. Each raised the issue of present and future, mutually reinforcing or exclusive, relationships between authoritative-to-coercive state and civil-to-autonomous society. However, where Gorbachev's predecessors' unqualifiedly external priority had required a strong state to alternately tame the society and dynamize it artificially, the cause of Russia's international position was now indissolubly joined with the cause of societal spontaneity as part of forging the historically ratified link between liberally released domestic pluralism and authoritatively entrenched conservative balance-of-power posture in foreign policy.

Despite the propitious evolutionary direction, if not yet irreversibly established trend, domestic strains and external pressures might easily converge into constituting the elements of a failure so sudden and thorough as to amount to Russia's non-military defeat in the first, and by historical precedent relatively moderate, phase of the leading land power's classic challenge. For the otherwise inconclusive outcome of the Cold War to be thus decided risked giving rise to a period of unrest comparable to the pre-revolutionary death throes of the ancien regime in France and to the post-revolutionary Weimar interlude between the imperial and the Nazi regimes in Germany – and, as such, liable to precede a final bid of the kind staged by the First (French) Empire and the Third Reich. Such a terminal, compulsive reaction would be carried out by a ruling group sufficiently traumatized to be no longer capable of acting as society's authoritative trustee. Nor could such a group enter into mutually rewarding transactions with aspiring middle-level elites prepared to support the regime in exchange for enlarged professional and other latitudes at home and abroad, on the model of economic outlets for a rising commercial-industrial middle class in a capitalistic setting. Instead, the diminished political class would be compelled to reach for backing past such elites to the popular mass, and pay the necessary price. Among the casualties would be the moribund ideology of internationalist socialism, no longer exportable world-wide as the developmental distance from the United States widened, in favor of a continentally focused nationalism, fearful of a more effectively developing and physically suddenly too proximate China, when not also a resurgent Germany. The implied risk after an isolationist spell was that of a final, and then military, surge defeated by the combined forces of traditional West and East, before a truncated Russia withdrew into a West-anathematizing xenophobia destabilizing globally in a different fashion but in no lesser degree than the westernizing ideology had been.

Meanwhile, unlike the previous attempts to transform or reform Russia, the latest one was taking place in a relatively non-conflicted international setting: globally, because the US–Soviet conflict has been receding; and on the continent, because Russia's reformist – westernizing and Europeanizing – side faced a western half less uncongenial in key values to the enduring spirit of Russia and less immediately hostile in policy to her power than had been the case when Western Europe was pretending to universally valid ideas and practicing a form of governance suspect of propagating moral decline. A Europe disposed henceforth to rely on no single ism or combination of isms for broadening the basis of her resurgence was making it possible to suspend historically alienating communications: possible for the eastward spread of military techniques and technologies to elicit western diplomatic and other efforts less one-sidedly targeted on confining the diffusion's equalizing effect on the recipient's role and status; and possible for the diffusion of adaptable non-military innovations – ranging currently from welfare- and consumer-type capitalism through executively tamed parliamentarianism to a post-"imperialist" supranationalism – to provoke less of the nativist Russian resistance which had often made nominally converging institutions and practices only deepen effective divergence between Europe's west and east in the past.

If, because of the developments intervening in the Soviet Union as well as in Western Europe, Russia's latest reform effort and the foreign policy program attached to it were in the future less prone to arousing anti-western reactions triggered by failure and fired by nostalgia, outside responses to the effort became only more crucial: they would retroactively determine which part of the attempted "restructuring" and "new thinking" had been realistic and which naively utopian – or, on the face of it, cynically calculating. However, the fact that the critical environment had a European and a global facet meant also that the (west) European and the American impacts on the Soviet experiment could be mutually reinforcing or disparate, with different consequences for the future development of Europe, the conventional West assembled in the Atlantic Alliance, and an Occident conforming in scope and content with the realities of a theater covering the globe and an era bestriding a millennium.

CRISIS OF DOCTRINES AND EMPIRES AND POSSIBLE REMEDIES

The confrontation of various kinds of realisms and utopias that shapes the outcome of reform efforts has a counterpart in the contrast between linear progress and cyclically unfolding progression. Where one promises escape from tragic collisions through the magic of melioristic hubris, the other is propelled by such collisions toward contingent improvements, while the opposition between the two kinds of advance derives its own tragic overtones from the spate of unintended outcomes revealing human errors. A thus aggravated tension between realism and utopia is permanent and pervasive in national policies. But it is at its highest when, the nature of reality itself being provisionally in question, because the superficial certainties bestowed by neatly polarizing competition over territory or ideology or just role and status are in abeyance, the issue of reform moves conspicuously to the fore.

Such a situation has been in evidence both internationally and internally. It was present internationally when the waning of rival sociopolitical ideologies and partially contrasting belief systems on the East–West divide was not compensated for by a conclusive articulation of the functional schism, along the land–sea power divide. This gave unavoidably rise to uncertainties in regard to national strategies, systemic structures, and evolutionary rates and trends. And it also left open the exact relative weight of historical antecedents and the intervening modifiers, accounting for real changes that have emerged out of evolutionary progression. All these ambiguities were bound to moderate polarization around one or more specific stakes, just as the erosion of one or both of the competing ideologies would facilitate a habitual convergence of modalities for managing a protracted conflict over real stakes. Less directly responsible for the subsidence of ideological polarization than for the surfacing of the tension between realism and utopianism were meanwhile two factors critical internally: the ethically mixed character of the competing ideologies, and the difficulty of arriving at an ethically less equivocal and operationally equally or more effective synthesis.

The socialist alternative communist-style has been shown to depend on totalitarian constraints and coercion in politics to offset gaps in the utopian presuppositions about human nature, applied to economics: the assumption that man's good side was sufficiently dominant to ensure individually self-effacing and satisfaction-deferring dedication to optimizing the social product (as a complement to the central planner's perfect information and rationality). No sooner had the totalitarian potential begun to atrophy because the growth of social needs and the rate of societal mobilization exceeded the limited degree of industrialization achievable in this manner, than the system's performance began to fall decisively behind the efficacy of the rival system's generous democratic-liberal latitudes in politics. These have been safely affordable within the broad margin for inter-group adjustments created by an economy productively functioning on the strength of essentially negative human characteristics: greed (behind the drive for acquisitions) and fear (of the consequences of either individual or collective inability to meet the system's rigorous conditions of survival). So long as the socialist formula has not found a substitute for the psychologically driving motor behind materially creative competition (euphemistically described as incentives and showing their harsher side whenever the capitalist engine stalled or seemed on the point of stalling), it would remain on trial. And no more proven will be the premise of the advocates of democratized socialism in Eastern Europe or fulfilled the promise of its practitioners in Western Europe, that a genuinely plural democracy and sufficiently collectivist socialism could, in drawing on both (politics- and economics-related) aspects of man's potential for goodness, engender a superior blend: a sufficiently dynamic economy and vibrant enough polity to improve on both of the ethically mixed systems.

The second reason for the resurgence of reform or the spirit of reform and one closely related to the first – an ambiguous reality – becomes operative when traditional systems of action for dealing with reality are in question. Prominently belonging to this category has been the ongoing phase of a historically recurrent crisis of empires, detrimental to vertically or hierarchically arranged relationships of power and authority. If such a crisis, which has not spared the US-centered order in Western Europe after subsiding somewhat in the Third World, was most prominently in evidence in the Soviet empire in Middle Europe, it was generalized by extending to Israel's mini-empire in the Middle East. In both areas, the questionably continuing realism of similar basic doctrines was challenged by actually emergent parallel dynamics that could serve as the point of departure for corrective diplomacy and remedial domestic strategies.

The doctrines keyed to empire preservation postulated the necessity and, more important, the possibility to hold on to peripheral buffers of the imperial core polity long enough to transform effective possession into presumptive right. Associated with Soviet response to turmoil in east-central Europe, the doctrine's Middle Eastern equivalent was implicit in the Israeli approach to the West Bank and Lebanon. Though the presuppositions underlying both the Brezhnev and the Begin doctrines were largely valid when judged by the maxims and achievements of traditional power politics, they have been proven near-impossible to transpose into lastingly practical politics in the surrounding climate. The dynamics of subverting such empires as the first step toward reforming them were likewise similar when near-simultaneous uprising of

Palestinian youth and wildcat strikes of young Polish workers armed older leaders and organizations – a Yasser Arafat and the Palestinian Liberation Organization, a Lech Walesa and Poland's Solidarity – with a fresh mass base for experimenting with unprecedented moderation. The prospect for repression engendering explosions unless relief followed from conciliation highlighted the third and last factor critical for reform: uncertainty about the kind or scope of the arena best suited to effective diplomacy between states and politic strategies within states. Incentives to reform increase when deadlocked conflicts have ceased to be resoluble locally and pressures have built up to shift decisive action to larger scope or higher levels, to be reconfigured so as to generate a creative tension between traditionally realistic modes and a novel way, in some fashion utopian. The critical choice lay between local and global arenas for both sets of regional issues. Whereas the Middle Eastern dynamics called primarily for a diplomacy capable of linking the alternative arenas, the problems of east-central Europe required first of all domestic strategies for bridging alternative perceptions of sociopolitical reality – while deadlocks peculiar to both pointed to the utility of revising the global agenda.

In east-central Europe, initial reform efforts under the auspices of "market socialism" in Hungary and "socialist pluralism" in Poland started by pitting a sterile because too narrow realism of the regimes, intent on precluding the unraveling of the political systems, against the ostensibly unrealistic because too radical demands of the political oppositions, arguing with the zest of converts for political practices and institutional panaceas unrealized in full, still unproven, or already discarded in their native western habitat. Whenever the iron laws of power were expected to melt in fires stoked by reformist fervor, utopianism seemed to migrate from the proponents of Marxism-Leninism to its opponents. And the more the regime's poor record of past attempts at reform isolated it from both the radical-utopian reformers and an equally reform- and repression-weary public, the more would the regime confront the question whether and how long to remain paralyzed by vacillation between concessions and coercion. By the same token, the more would the reformers be inclined to forgo efficacy for the sake of the legitimacy seeming to flow from close alliance with the working class. As a result, illusionism combined with consumerism to hinder the system's breaking out of inefficiency masked by insidious oppression into greater liberty.

The implicit ironies threatened to do more than reflect the essence of tragedy and begin enacting it existentially whenever the collision between conflicting assumptions about what was feasible and contrary agendas for undertaking it surfaced the emotionally charged dispute over the possession of authentic patriotism, overshadowing once again the ethic of socialism. In regard to the latter, if the alliance between workers and intellectuals obscured the difference between the political and the economic values and purposes of desired reform, the deadlock the alliance helped consolidate limited the extent of sustainable reform. Genuine realism and reformed socialism had in common that the liberalization of economics and politics had to proceed in tandem (the reformers' demand), if a reform concentrating on economics (the self-styled conservatives' preference) was not to either bog down (Poland) or degenerate

(Hungary). Throughout, actual compromises could not but run foul of a stubborn incompatibility: between the requisite range of quasi-capitalistic measures and policies, materially necessary to deal with inefficient production and monetary inflation, and such socialist basics as full employment and low cost of essentials guaranteed under central planning even after such societal luxuries have ceased to be materially affordable.

Besetting reform efforts in Poland and Hungary, and only emerging to challenge *perestroika* and *glasnost* in the Soviet Union, the problems overshadowed the psychological malignancy while highlighting the refurbished political and economic magic of Marxism-Leninism's liberal-capitalist opposite. All of the problems had been manifest earlier in Czechoslovakia, before post-1968 "normalization" gave a bad name to political realism on both sides of the divide: a repressive regime fearful of a politically alert population, and a gradually de-politicized population resigning itself to a corrupt social contract with the militarily imposed regime. However, as the dialectic between the Prague and the Moscow "springs" unfolded, a more exalted historical reality would emerge as part of which the Czech reform-suppressing Soviet invasion was a major, but not necessarily a concluding, event in two converging dramas: Russia's alternations of reform with reaction, as she moved from the outside toward the center of the land–sea power triangle, and the likewise cyclical alternance between freedom or struggle for freedom and oppression or submission to it in the centrally located Czech lands always exposed to peripheral tremors from the eastward-moving triangular great-power dynamics.

In the shorter run, the differences between the revolutionary Prague and Moscow events were at bottom a matter of the contrast between the dominant and a dependent socialist country, reflected in a different mix of utopianism and realism in the programs of a Gorbachev and a Dubček. And the difference between the outlook for ideas promoted since under the label of socialist pluralism (intended to institutionalize socialism with a human face) and the actual outcome of the pre-1948 Czechoslovak experiment with a qualified multi-party system was primarily a reflection of the distance between a Cold War in the making and one that was waning. By 1948, Soviet Russia had been hunkering down in eastern Europe after the failure of the communist parties in France and Italy to dominate the local scenes and the inception of the Marshall Plan – an isolation US foreign policy was in 1968 still trying to perpetuate by means of a "peaceful engagement" with differentially treated Soviet satellites; at the later date, the local aspirations were predicated on the prospects for a cumulative (Euro-) détente.

Yet the same, not to be neatly resolved, problem that had existed in 1948 was still in being: how to preserve the "leading" – or any significant – role of the Communist Party while conceding more than nominal influence to non-communist political or functional organizations without raising Soviet doubts about the regime being friendly and the alliance firm. So long as the location of effective authority or ultimate power remained unresolved in principle or became ambiguous in practice, even tentative cooperation among rival domestic forces would continue to depend on an ephemeral sense of crisis. Either disruptive jockeying for post-crisis positions or stultifying immobilism were certain to set in, in ways familiar from experiences with National Government in Britain, *union sacrée* in France, and the Great Coalition in West Germany, once the crisis appeared to be over or was shown to be endemic. There being no ready-made devices to transplant from abroad for the purpose of spiriting away the key issue of political science and practical governance, failure to distribute or locate authority decisively would continue to produce either deadlock or disarray, both of which reopened the prospect for decisive power migrating outside the smaller country and reverting to one or another regional hegemon, with rising costs for all concerned.

Although its constituents differed, the parallel deadlock among indigenous forces was not fundamentally dissimilar in the Middle East. The stalemate resided as much in inter-Arab as in intra-Israel political dynamics, and its link to contrasting utopias was being at one and the same time forged and deformed so long as the controversial Palestinian issue was serviceable as a metaphor for avoiding other problems on both sides. Just as the moral and ideological aspirations that make up the Zionist utopia were increasingly on a collision course with the practical conditions of maximum short-term security for the Jewish state, so the myth of pan-Arabism was waging an even more troubled rearguard action against the operatively prior conditions of the several Arab regimes' immediate survival. So long as the realistic concerns of national security and regime survival were strong enough to prevail over the utopian aspirations in determining behavior, but were not sufficiently flexible to be adjusted among the local parties to a sluggish "peace process," they would unfailingly bring in forces and interests from outside the region. However, the residual force of the ideals was sufficient to help rationalize opposition to kinds and degrees of extraneous involvements that did not meet the test of pragmatically calculated local costs and benefits. This being so, the limited scope and impact of the outsiders' interference could occasionally loosen, but was unable to override, the indigenous stalemate.

For the hiatus between pluralism and one-party paramountcy in Middle Europe and between self-defense for Israel and self-respect for the Arabs in the Middle East to be transcended, the chasm between pragmatic *realpolitik* and the sundry utopias had to be narrowed by virtue of mutually reinforcing patterns of reassurance and restraint within wider – European and global – settings. At the outset, it was still utopian, but in a realistically modified fashion, to insist on the right of non-communist political actors in Eastern Europe to be gradually imbricated with comparable tendencies in Western Europe for reassurance, in exchange for the restraint implicit in the west Europeans, although sympathetic to individual aspirations, being solicitous of the Soviet residual interest in the region and developing stake in a pan-European framework. By the same token, to minimize Soviet alarms at the reduced capacity of the non-Soviet communist parties to guarantee Russia's national security by exerting local hegemonies, the United States had to engage the Soviets in a reassuring cooperative relationship globally. If taking part in consolidating an all-European framework entailed for the United States practical co-stewardship with Russia and the West Europeans in east-central Europe, it pointed also to a species of US–Soviet condominium in key peripheral areas outside Europe, including the Middle East, underpinned by joint guarantee of the co-sponsored conflict settlements.

A concerted approach to Europe would provide an initial impulse toward European reunification before serving as the ultimate safeguard for unity remaining viable. Conversely, a continuing US refusal to engage in the effort might eventually tip the scales in favor of Gorbachev's "common European house" without or even against the United States. At the back of the alternatives was the historically ratified norm of a working European order. For that order to invariably aggregate a multilateral balance of power with the diplomatic preeminence of a leading state did not mean that the particular structure and relative weight of the first constituent and the incumbency and centrality of the second could not change. They were likely to change subtly and shift flexibly as the old continent's reintegration got underway and the two Europe-derived superpowers matured both individually and in their relationship. Especially if allowing for emergent sub-regional groupings also in eastern Europe, the restored European order, intricate in itself, would be only part of a complex self-enforcing global equilibrium: one more complex than the traditional military-political balance of power, because consisting of a network of varied intersecting impulses and inhibitions; and self-enforcing, because any two parties that had advanced too far too fast toward cooperation or competition would automatically incur costly estrangement from an adversely affected party.

For the conventional West to participate in disaggregating the world balance of power in this direction was not without immediate costs. But it was a more feasible, and might well be a more attractive, option than to attempt to decompose the Soviet empire without regard for the unsettling geopolitical consequences of such an accomplishment. And to interlock restraints with reassurance in ways minimizing the inevitable mishaps on the road to reform would make it practical for reform-minded east-central European regimes to search for a complementary kind of working balance: between societal discipline and political latitude, between economic austerities and residually necessary authority. The measure of individual freedom and national independence to be realistically sought and immediately attained was bound to be limited initially by the degree and kind of regional predominance all premier continental great powers have always found necessary to assure them a security and standing equal to the insular counterpart's in its sphere. However, if substantial change in conditions lastingly non-viable for all parties was to be achieved, a matching limitation on Soviet control would follow almost automatically as the previously dominated parties demonstrated self-restraint in utilizing the expanding latitudes. In compensation, solid new non-ideological ties had to ensure the elementary cohesion of a Russia-centered regional order over the next phase of global politics, supplementing the eroded doctrinal and organizational ties and displacing for good the coercive mechanisms of the preceding era. As the seat of vital responsibility shifted consequently from Moscow to places such as Warsaw, the key question would no longer be whether the former let up on demands for doctrinal conformity by the lesser countries; it would be increasingly up to the latter to rein in nationalist animosities against Russia if the evolution was to proceed.

A way to mute the local resentments and neutralize their disruptive effects was for the Soviet Union to abrogate Stalin's veto of subregional inter-nation associations on its borders, conducive to Tito's defection in the late 1940s. Extending thus *perestroika* regionally and complementing the movement toward pluralism inside the east-central European countries has followed the lines of development sketched out for the several border nationalities within the Soviet Union, deemed beneficial for the Soviet national economy. On a larger scale, such a pattern and tendency, parallel to China's approach to Hong Kong and Taiwan, denoted a return to pre-nation-state imperial as much as progress toward post-empire structures and priorities. Incrementally, as east-central Europe was being transformed from military-strategic glacis and politico-ideological buffer into a zone of transition and mediation between Russia and Europe, from insulating to intertwining East and West, the importance of Soviet-style orthodoxy as the immaterial nimbus around the military-strategic nucleus could not but fade in pragmatic Russian calculations.

The most promising theater for proceeding with this reorientation was the northern tier of Middle Europe comprising key lesser power parties to the organic small eastern triangle: East Germany, Poland and Czechoslovakia. On the one hand, a post-Stalinst eastern half of Germany that matched in the adjoining Slavic areas West Germany's involvement with the Latins would recover the lost sense of identity and reason for existence by reconciling the German vocation in the East with a larger cause. On the other hand, the consequences of the failure of the Czechs and the Poles to act in common in the 1930s against German revisionism were such as to encourage coordinating their attitudes toward Russian reformism. This meant offsetting the Russophobe Poles' self-destructive political romanticism with the traditionally Russophile Czechs' greater realism. Although in different ways, both strove to ground spiritual freedom in political independence and national in individual autonomy.

The efforts of the Czechs faltered then repeatedly under the heavy weight of monotonously recurrent pressures from greater states competing along the spectrum of insular, amphibious, and continental power types. As the fulcrum of the attendant balancing moved from west to east, and the earliest (Anglo/Dutch–Spanish–French) triangle was replicated by the terminal (US–Soviet–Chinese) configuration in the wake of the world wars enframing the two phases of the intermediate (Anglo–German–Russian) triangle, the smaller nation was caught on no less than three occasions – in 1618, 1938, and 1948/1968 – in the middle of the web alternately spun by and entangling the larger players. In the process, equally absolutist-dogmatic and amphibious-imperial Spain and Russia impacted on exposed Middle Europe from the spatial and temporal extremities of modern Europe. With the Soviet phase following upon the intermediate German one and its climax in the Munich crisis, the two contemporary instances served to reveal by 1938, confirm in 1948, and reconfirm in 1968, a long-ignored impossibility: for either liberal-nationalist or totalitarian-ideological shortcuts or panaceas to fill the formal shell of sovereign independence with enduring substance before the regional dialectic between Germany and Russia had played itself out to the full.

It was but an aspect of the dilemma and its implementing dialectic that communist rule would be the shape history assigned to the price to pay for achieving a future freed of the internal German problem bequeathed by the self-same history. Since Soviet backing for the removal of the border Germans from Bohemia was even more indispensable for overcoming Western reluctance than it was for Poland's territorial relocation between her larger neighbors, and the achievement was on the face of it more lastingly secure, the Czechs have had to pay a harsher price longer than the Poles. However, it was a likewise time-limited aspect of the Russian problem that the burden would ease and could finally lift for both only when the Czechs' pre-1948 aspiration to serve as the bridge between West and East, just as the Poles' more recently reactivated ambition to realize a West-East synthesis within, have given way to something more fruitful as well as feasible: for Russia to use relations with the two western Slavic countries to demonstrate her entitlement to be considered an integral part of Europe and the larger West.

Central to relieving the other, the Middle Eastern, stalemate and indirectly supportive of a new all-European order was a US–Soviet concert with condominial attributes globally. A more consistent parallel-to-cooperative superpower involvement in the Middle Eastern peace process meant that all local parties would incur limitations matching those requisite for a European settlement. Thus Israel had to advance toward a more modest view of sufficient security and learn to live with the degree of immunity historically achievable by territorial states and, *a fortiori*, small or newly created states. A matching limitation on the autonomy of the Palestinians would be the nearly automatic corollary to redefining Israel's essential security through a multilaterally revised peacemaking procedure. It would meanwhile be purely utopian to demand, and naive to expect, acts of self-denial by parties to the regional dilemmas to take place for altruistic reasons in the Middle East, out of a shared feeling of outrage at the absurdity of the interests of so few keeping so many in a state of turbulence for so long, any more than in Middle Europe for the sake of making the expansion of freedoms there safe for only Europe or the world as a whole. Constraints could be imposed, and might be accepted, only as the necessary condition for combining internationally guaranteed progress toward peace with regionally generated enhancement of common prosperity. Manifest economic complementarities could then underwrite the latently growing socio-cultural convergence between Arabs as they were westernized and an Israel that was being orientalized at a comparable rate.

The realism of having the superpowers co-guarantee the results of a concerted conflict resolution was testable by first applying the formula beneficially to more fluid regional situations such as south-west Asia (Afghanistan) and Central America (Nicaragua). If proven, the realism might overcome an actuality that, contravening both effective interposition and attempts at disarmed mediation from the outside, has consisted of nearly all of the Middle Eastern actors, headed by Israel, being opposed to superpower concertation of a regional peace settlement that entailed a concession of diplomatic parity to the Soviet Union. So have also the west Europeans been against an approach to the European settlement entailing the prospect of Russia's diplomatic preeminence. Missing was the recognition that both the parity and the preeminence would be reduced to a largely symbolic, status-related expression by the Soviets' economic weakness relative to the United States in the Middle East and to the erstwhile western preeminents in Europe.

The local parties preferred that US protection continued so long as it did not substantially curtail their diplomatic options. An Israel still in its prime exercised such options in an imperial manner *vis-à-vis* the still weaker parties intra-regionally, and in an imperious mode *vis-à-vis* the US patron inter- and intra-nationally. On the part of the only slowly recovering west Europeans, procedural intransigence within the Atlantic Alliance and demonstrative diplomatic independence in the Third World compensated for America'a political dominance being endured in preference to Soviet military domination. As that particular threat receded, the Europeans were reluctant to activate the potential of US–Soviet entente to stimulate them into incurring the costs of politico-military self-dependence, as one of the preconditions to the old continent reasserting itself globally in a fashion consummating its material rebirth. Meanwhile, although decreasingly ready to shoulder the other than monetary offset payments for America's military protection, the west Europeans were equally reluctant to make a downpayment on a "common European house" matching Gorbachev's in that they accepted all of the implications of Russia's Europeanization in ways signalling a belated recognition that the predicaments bequeathed to Eastern Europe by a troubled past constituted a burden to be shared and a legacy to dispose of in common.

How much and how long would inertial actuality weigh against revising strategies so as to transpose outmoded stalemates into future stability? The prospects depended also on how valid supposedly realistic earlier approaches had been or have continued to be. Among these was the project for a "Year of Europe," embraced by a US administration avid, on a rebound from military frustrations in Asia, to integrate a western Europe further detached from the eastern half even more fully into the US-led side of the global balance of power. Ostensibly realistic, the design was profoundly utopian in that it ran counter to a more deep-seated desire of the West Europeans: to reaffirm their common identity by at least procedural acts of self-differentiation from the United States. In the Middle East, the balance between realism and utopianism was harder to assess with respect to local peace initiatives, depending on whether they were aimed at a separate peace or also a general settlement on the Egyptian side and whether an international conference was backed by some Israelis as a cover for the superpowers to mediate, or a forum for the local parties to spontaneously concert, a settlement. Equally ambiguous were US efforts in the region, beginning with a hectic shuttle diplomacy after misjudging the psychological reality of Sadat's repeated threats of war and followed by summitry at Camp David after abandoning a token effort to include the Soviets in peacemaking diplomacy: whereas the former embodied the questionable realism of an incremental step-by-step approach that lacked the barest outline of a substantive final settlement, the latter could do no better when trying to sidestep an ultimately unavoidable procedural requirement.

The American architects of the European initiative postulated as unlikely to change any time soon a Soviet military threat that proved to be in its current form but a phase growing out of World War II-related dislocations, and was subject to the gradually moderating rhythm of a revolution born of World War I. The case for excluding Soviet Russia from a Middle Eastern settlement was predicated on the immutability of Soviet support for maximum Arab demands. In fact, the support was near-certain to be modified in keeping with perennial diplomatic practice once the Soviets have been admitted to a meaningful part in negotiations. Basing policy on Soviet reiteration of impractical terms in one area and recitation of outworn dogma in the other was unconvincing on the part of a diplomacy intelligent enough to be able to discount the latter and be aware, in relation to the former, of the difference between a party's initial maximum and its real conditions for terminating a conflict. To the extent that the same statecraft was less than alert to the psychopolitical needs and consequent operational compulsions at work in *all* of the parties, the discrepancy between skill and sensitivity could not but cast doubt on the authenticity of the motivating realism and its superiority over seemingly utopian schemes for widening the exits out of regional stalemates.

THE MERGING OF EAST AND WEST

The balance between realism and utopia can be assessed on the strength of expectations from alternatives to past approaches only as tentatively as on the evidence of such approaches' actual results. Nor can either empirical inquiry or enthusiastic advocacy reliably address the related questions: Was ostensible realism in any one case marred by unwitting misapprehension of psychopolitical realities that shape the overt behavior routine diplomacy is best or solely equipped to address? Or has authentic realism been subverted by, or sacrificed to, deliberate concealment of ulterior motives and immediate objectives that would not stand the test of exposure to strategic rationality subserving the national interest? Has then, in either case, the practitioner's diplomatic virtuosity outstripped its ultimately validating basis in either insight or integrity? For such reasons alone the realist–utopist mix or balance was not least conclusively deducible from background factors of a conceptual character: one set bearing on policies, the other concerning the character of politics.

To begin with, how utopian was a policy for a US–Soviet condominium that would create a global basis for redefining the boundaries of the West on a likewise global scale? An assessment required that "condominium" be defined realistically and a "larger" West be compared with fundamental alternatives. Just as in the past a concert among several great powers did not in the best of times imply spontaneous harmony, but merely a substitution of diplomatic for military coalitions in resolving conflicts, so condominium neither does nor can mean a preconcerted diktat by two powers. Rather, condominium reflected in contemporary conditions a disposition shared by the two greatest powers to attenuate conflict where such competition provided little clear benefit to either side but yielded disproportionate economic, military, and diplomatic rewards to third parties. Once the behavior of the two superpowers has been adjusted to reflect an understanding of the shared plight, an operationally significant paradox became manifest. Just as the effective scope of de facto condominium expands when local contestants are without sufficient material means both to continue their conflict and to compose it unaided, so its price for others will shrink when the superpowers' move to concert positions on regional issues has prompted viable third parties, in and out of Europe, to improve their individual or collective standing as an alternative to finding themselves (worse than defenseless) irrelevant.

A different kind of irrelevance lurked for the condominial principles in a conflict which to continue describing as one between East and West betrayed an obsolete deference to the increasingly parochial and ethnocentric world-view confined to the Euro-Atlantic. The alternative was to embrace the goal of cooperatively enacted commonality of fate within an area extending from the Pacific shores of the United States to Russia's Ural Mountains and the predominantly Russian-populated areas beyond, with a view to consolidating an enlarged but still authentic West spiritually centered on Europe and internally balanced among its sub-groupings. The Soviets' desire to hold on to the ethnically Asian territorial acquisitions of the tsars was dictated by the economic and world power assets the areas represent. However, it was impossible to doubt Russia's ultimate priority and choice (the conventional West permitting) when confronted with the growing power and reactivated pressure from China's land and population mass, despite Moscow's intermittent efforts to step up its Asian diplomacy for immediate bargaining and somewhat more substantive longer-term purposes.

Leaving the final terms of the relationship between the European and the Asian parts of the Soviet Union to be resolved late in the next century and beyond was not the same as discounting the possibility of a resolution that would ease the issue of intra-European and -Western equilibrium. But it did mean that the latent problem was just one aspect of an evolving intercultural equilibrium that would ideally, and could for the first time in history practically, take shape on the plane of genuine equality among the leading civilizations of West and East. A decisive setback for such an evolution would produce only a short-lived triumph for some of the West's most vocal defenders, were a Pacific–Asian orientation of US foreign policy finally to drive Russia into re-accentuating the anti-Western features of a special kind of nationalism – one its reformers, including the latest one, have been struggling to overcome so as to leave its oriental-despotic accompaniments safely behind.

When thought through, a culturally aware long-term strategy for replacing reciprocal enfeeblement with mutual reinforcement within a greater West was no more utopian than were attempts to repair military insufficiencies by playing the China "card" geostrategically against Russia, only to see the gambit employed, at first only diplomatically, against the United States. Another alternative would seek to halt economic backsliding in a deepening integration with Japan that barely concealed America's loss of leadership to a Nippon precariously poised between smug self-satisfaction *vis-à-vis* the western patron and anxious contemplation of newly emergent eastern competitors. In such conditions only a US–Soviet entente downgrading the role of military alliances could create an even playing field with Japan in the economics of foreign trade and investments as well as with China in regional and global diplomacy, just as a sustained movement toward such entente could alone consolidate military-strategic readjustments and ease the impediments to a new order of political economy for socialism today and capitalism tomorrow.

Even if not unqualifiedly utopian in itself, could a condominial approach to a greater West and its specific features emerge out of an actual interplay of interstate with intra-state dynamics? To wit, could the United States influence internal Soviet developments in a correspondingly positive direction, and would it have reasons for doing so? Whether the United States was able to turn Soviet behavior toward concert gradually exceeding competition was a query that could not be answered simply and, even less, simplistically. It was one thing to micro-manage the particulars of internal dynamics from the outside, and quite another to influence the other side's range and ranking of options and inhibitions by reshaping the environment. The former engages the perspective of the career diplomat and leads invariably to a negative conclusion; the latter engages that of a creative statesman and is consistent with a positive finding. This is so although the attempt to imitate a Bismarck combining the two approaches *vis-à-vis* crisis-prone France was certain to be even less completely successful. In such circumstances, all that could be confidently asserted was this: it would be inconsistent to hypothesize that an only marginal domestic reform was bound to peter out, and to deny that a substantial transformation of the international setting alone could affect a radical reform effort materially. And it would be unconvincing to argue that the (US-wrought) international setting could not significantly affect a reform effort while ascribing the effort's origins in large part to the (Soviet) domestic system's declining ability to cope with the external setting effectively.

The interplay between internal and external environments – and the difference between micro-management and macro-conditioning – had a special bearing for a political system such as the Soviet. Its lodgement in an official ideology will make basic foreign policy orientation subject to the shifting source or focus of regime legitimacy, but will neither dictate nor even imply any particular foreign policy tactic or even strategy. When the system suffered from doctrinal erosion and operational malfunction, the regime shifted to rhetorically militant or (in most instances) indirect military means in support of ostensibly revolutionary movements in the Third World. The hope was that external outlets for individual energies and occasions for regime prestige might correct for immobilism at home at least marginally. The succeeding drive to revitalize the home front has been attended by changing to a conventionally diplomatic approach to the same Third World, out of necessity to reduce the material outlays and political costs implicit in the more militant strategy. The hope was then one of releasing individual and collective energies for reciprocal stimulation internally until such time as the augmented and, more significantly, diversified resources could be redeployed abroad.

A plausible presumption was that the resources would be deployed to back the conventionalized diplomacy, provided the response to it and its results were such as to warrant linking the reformed regime's wider range of methods with its material achievements in an internally coherent structure of reconstituted domestic legitimacy. Anticipating a contrary foreign policy orientation, toward an assertiveness that was re-radicalized after being reinforced materially, presupposed a possibility and a probability: the possibility that a regime could only pretend to change its stripes for a time before rechanneling reform-induced increases of societal energy into a pre-reform kind of foreign policy and objectives; and the probability that this would happen for reasons other than as a reluctant response to the rival side obstructing even the benignly altered methods of projecting the reform's results abroad, pending the reformed power's subsidence into a conservative foreign-policy stance on an expanded basis of parity.

The West could live with the expectation of a socially more pluralist and economically more productive Soviet Union displaying an enhanced dynamism abroad, albeit one implemented less by direct and military means than by means of a kind that attenuated competition while qualifying Russia for a widening range of cooperation. For the West to opt instead for the pessimistic variant made sense only against the background of an inadmissible fear or a hidden ambition. Both required the reformed Soviet regime to adopt a completely passive foreign policy, adhering in full to the declaratory principles of a supposedly reformed international politics perpetuating in effect the pre-established positions of its beneficiaries. Merely to contemplate the suspicion of this being so raised immediately critical questions: What international position was the conventional West, and the United States in particular, prepared to concede to a successfully reformed Soviet Union? And was it the governing assumption when formulating an answer that a foreign policy, including the Soviet, was fully the reflection of domestic conditions which, if positively reformed, would or should automatically produce likewise "progressive" policy abroad?

To reply in the affirmative required ignoring a positive fact: whatever might be the condition and evolution of its society, the Soviet polity was also – or still – either preeminently or residually a state and a power. It continued to be subject as such to laws of necessary self-expression and self-assertion at different stages of evolution that did not exactly coincide in either time or tenor with societal developments. The additional fact was that a continental Russia and the insular United States weighted the respective claims and rights of the state and the society somewhat differently. This contrast had a counterpart in a parallel distinction and difference, giving rise to a policy-relevant dialectic between a manifest crisis, affecting the Russian state in the last resort, and a real or apparent decline, of concern to the American society in the first instance.

The Soviet crisis consisted mainly in material and organizational shortcomings with clear implications for definite operations. Identifying the trouble rendered correction possible at least in principle, whatever might prove to be the case in practice. It has, by contrast, proved much more difficult to diagnose the United States' liability to a condition affected by morale-related as much as by material factors and considerations. The very notion of decline remains ambiguous: it can signify re-ordering within a hierarchy and refer then to the loss of power concentrated in a state, or suggest diffusion of comparative prosperity in a society, indicating progress toward equality. Whereas one connotation implies inevitable demotion, the other opens up the compensating possibility of development and, when the latter has softened the urge to undo the former, makes real the fiction of liberal-democratic peaceableness. Conspicuously true for continental France (and so far) Germany, this applied also to insular Britain when her loss of primacy in Europe and of empire overseas made internal changes – thanks to which the comman man "never had it so good" – coincide with a but harmlessly contentious approach to the continent and a largely pacific subsidence into a commonwealth. Internationally significant decline is always relative to other actors. But this did not necessarily mean – any more than it conclusively differentiated America's weakening position from Britain's earlier plight – that decline was not in evidence when no other power was either pressing or manifestly prepared to replace the receding "hegemon." Nor was the issue of decline irrelevant so long as friendly or allied states were provisionally ready to subsidize the faltering leader's capacity, and prop up his will, to continue performing a useful function (so long as the capability-role gap could be filled by the subsidy). The international system could function in an orderly fashion when one-power leadership had yielded to equality among several powers; and the system could also lapse into transitional chaos until one-power ascendancy or a revised hierarchy has been forcibly reasserted as a testimony to the system's capacity to be regenerated exceeding that of its leading members to eschew eventual regression. The United States could not but decline from the peak it had occupied after World War II; and it did develop toward maturity as material wealth and other goods were being more equitably dispersed at home. But the country's condition could be none the less plausibly diagnosed as one of decline so long as economic weakening (reflecting the public's rejection of traditional mores expressed in savings) and the faltering of will or vision on the part of its political elites (reflected in the surrender of empire, uncompensated by adoption of equilibrium) continued.

If economic aspects of imperial decline, tediously repetitive over the ages and across forms of government, have been clearly present in the American experiment, so too, despite compensating resurgences of demonstrative patriotism, has been the latent disposition of public morale to collapse under stress. The fact that democratic pluralism prevented the United States from prosecuting an imperial war in Asia to either a sweet or the bitter end did not validate the national presumption that the body politic was thus immunized to fall. Likewise, the special potential for regeneration, implicit in ready absorption of new ethnic groups into American society, was at least a two-edged sword. Just as receptivity did not guarantee assimilation of all newcomers, so it did not safeguard against dilution of the constituent culture with unpredictable consequences for the creativity of a national polity. Insofar as the continuing dilution could be included among the reasons for America's susceptibility to decline on a par at least with the infusions being a source of limitless resilience, a diametrically opposite standard of evaluation was questionably valid when applied to the resurgence of non-Russian nationalities as an aspect of the Soviet systemic crisis. In the last resort, it was the stress lines in the European core identity of both major powers that pointed most emphatically to the geopolitical and cultural goal of a concerted global strategy. Like the Soviet Union, so also the United States had a lesson to learn from the Europeans: that the consequences of world power were most bitter when the ebbing of that power had revealed its price in the loss of communal and cultural homogeneity.

WAR AND PEACE IN PAST AND FUTURE

At all times, but especially when a turning-point in world affairs activates the delicate balance between realism and utopia, specific policy choices – as well as their advocacy – presuppose the asking of antecedent questions of both conceptual and substantive character. At the latest turning-point, a key conceptual quandary had to do with the choice between surrendering the reformist initiative to local parties as it were from below, and assuming it from above at the major-power level. Subsidiary to this was the related choice between an open-ended gradualist, incrementally unfolding process and a predetermination of the goals or terminal states aimed at. Consistent with culturally ingrained and institutionally reinforced pragmatism, US official preference was apt to be in favor of the gradualist-from-below approach to both critical areas, also because any temptation to anticipate on process by outlining its intended product was certain to elicit less-than-friendly domestic fire lethal to any possible external advantage. Prominent on Middle Eastern issues, the attendant risk was one of stalemate- and/or confusion-generating tentativeness, accentuating the impression of drift not least in the reforming parts of Middle Europe; the danger, that either stalemate or confusion made all parties miss the optimum conditions for a remedial superpower contribution. Pressures to move beyond intercession to imposition were then likely to concern more critically the outcome than the procedure, as local parties had either lost control (Middle Europe) or entrenched themselves in only procedural or also substantive intransigence (Middle East).

The more mandatory or acceptable superpower interposition became, the more would the previously but latent option, between a minimalist and a maximalist turning away from the Cold War, move to the fore. Deliberately latitudinous objectives, such as replacing containment of the Soviet Union with its integration into (the US conception of) the world order, appealed meanwhile as both positive and progressive while leaving specific choices open and the ultimate strategic direction in limbo. Yet if, as was probable, local frictions inhibited settlements of local-regional conflicts in the way technical problems impeded adjustments of nuclear and conventional arms issues, self-consciously prudent realism was likely to prove insufficient to achieve enough soon enough. Structures bequeathed by the Cold War and including the western alliance system would then erode and might dissipate while an alternative order was only inconclusively struggling to be born – and risked being stillborn. The genuinely prudent and realistic choice would then prove to have been the ostensibly utopian maximalist one: a turnaround from containment to properly understood condominium, on the premise that to be integrated into a still inchoate community of nations was not primarily the Soviet Union by a unilateral act of grace, but the post-Cold War international (proto-) system itself, propelled toward an eventual world order by a multilateral effort headed provisionally by the two major powers.

A technically defensive military posture is not politically dependable, and the requisite deployments and strength levels may not be precisely identifiable, unless the military planners have been instructed to consider war between two former rivals as highly unlikely if not impossible. Between two still viable powers such a condition arises only when they have become in effect allied against a third party or against dangers jointly perceived as exceeding their remaining disagreements. That which is self-evident on the military-strategic plane, a dimension that helps clarify when it is not employed to conceal the more basic geopolitical givens, is likewise true for the latter in the last resort. The kind of issues raised in Middle Europe and the Middle East – and around the global perimeter of crisis and confusion, development and drift – might well be impossible to deal with productively by the minimalist technique: painstakingly calibrated concessions and counter-concessions that reserve or only grudgingly surrender cherished positions, unless a prior fundamental accord in the form of a global bargain has prevented divergent appreciations of "vital" interests and biased assessments of successes and failures from escalating into a renewal of across-the-board antagonism between the major players.

Critical for the determination was not so much the more or less self-serving appraisal of the (provisional) outcome of the Cold War as identifying the present stage of the US–Soviet conflict. The outcome was more favorable to the West in the essentialist perspective pitting freedom/free market against totalitarianism/planned economy than in the structuralist perspective highlighting the relative global standing of the United States and the Soviet Union in 1945 and, say, 1985; the conflict's phase could be intuited only against the longer background of hegemonial land–sea power contentions. Have we reached an intermediate lull before the climactic second-stage confrontation, following the first comparatively mild contest round on the continental land mass and overseas, a lull that replicated the Lerma (or Philip III) era in Spain's contention with the Anglo–Dutch combine, the immediately pre-revolutionary stance in old-regime France's struggle with England and the Weimar interlude in Germany's? Or are we witnessing only the end of the initial skirmish devoted to efforts to elude even the moderate first round, marked by the marriage of Philip (II to be) of Spain with Mary of England and Elizabeth's ensuing tractations with the latter's Spain-supported Scottish namesake, the Orleanist–Hanoverian entente, and Caprivi's liberal New-Course era respectively? In either case, can the world avoid a catastrophic lapse into the second and decisive round previously engineered by Olivares, Napoleon, and Hitler?

Only one thing was certain: the 45-year-long peace after World War II, whether owed to nuclear weapons or not (as was more likely), has not been the longest in recent history when projected against past such intervals in general and the surcease from a hegemonial conflict between 1815 and 1914 (separating the second French from the first German bid) in particular. That century-long spell moves the next critical conjuncture into the middle of the twenty-first century – a deferral plausible also on empirical grounds supplied by the still-developing organic growth–decline trend (and relaxed operational tempo) as well as the (land–sea power schism-related) war–peace cycles.*

Much or all was likely to depend henceforth on how US–Soviet relationship was managed (a thought-stopping word, when denied substance) directly and its setting via operationally salient issues indirectly. Becoming critical in and for Europe with respect to politico-economic reform by individual countries and their prospective sub-groupings were West Germany's relations with east-central Europe, bearing directly on Russo–German equations and the place and role East Germany would occupy in the area. Critical for Eurasia were the comparative rates of growth of the Soviet Union and China secreted by their different approaches to reform. And critical for the Pacific theater as well as globally was the impact of Japan's increasing economic salience on America's world role and Sino–Soviet competition or conciliation. Whereas all these issues had a prominent economic surface, they pointed directly to politico-military and diplomatic-strategic implications by raising questions such as these: What would or could serve as a counterpoise to West Germany's (or the Germanys') economic engagement in east-central Europe, one sufficient to contain a neo-imperial reincarnation of the "drive to the east" while regulating the extent and tempo of continuing intra-German rapprochement? What was likely to be the effect of a no longer pivotal America's position and performance in the henceforth equal but volatile geostrategic triangle on the course of the Sino–Soviet development race, and what the more explosively crisis-laden (if delayed) effect of the race's outcome on peace or war in Asia and globally? Finally, what about the crucial if incidental effect of the geostrategically triangular transactions on Japan's trade- and technology-related advantages over the United States and her emergent opportunities to manipulate the Sino–

---

* Roughly corresponding to AD 2045 identified as the time for the next hegemonial confrontation by transposing the 100 years separating 1815 from 1914 onto the period following 1945 is the date (AD 2021) intimated by the average 76 years that had historically separated the end of a second-stage confrontation from the onset of the first stage of the next-following war series (see p. 331). More conformably still, 2045 is close to the midpoint between 2021 and 2084 projected on the same principle for the second-stage climax and applicable if the Cold War is viewed as a substitute for the initial mixed-moderate engagement.

More important for general projections than any such overly precise futurological forecasts are the ambiguous effects of nuclear weapons (alongside the other factors alleged to transform world politics). They were not "required" to defer overt US–Soviet belligerency so long as it was not "due" on the strength of the multiple precedents. Instead, the currently ultimate weapon's real impact was of greater interest in regard to a related hypothesis regarding a constant sum of violence over periods of time (see p. 333). Closely related to the effect of weapons on war-making is the opportunity for peacemaking implicit in another qualified coincidence. The interval between the end of the Cold War (1988, dated from the signing of the INF Treaty) and the putative onset of first-stage belligerency (2021) amounting to roughly three decades becomes, as the time allowing for final US–Soviet accommodation, a symbolic counterpart to the 30-year-long war series in the seventeenth and twentieth centuries critical for the initial and so far climactic development of the insular–continental geo-functional spectrum and -strategic triangle.

Soviet balance as part of, or an alternative to, reactivating Nippon's pre-war ambitions in the region by the more efficient novel means?

All such issues harbored an equal potential for restructuring a rigid bipolar into a genuinely global and self-equilibrating multipolar (and pluri-amphibious?) international system or they might lead up to a thunderously dissonant finale for a re-polarized (or re-triangularized?) international system's slippage into crisis and conflict of a war-threatening character. Meanwhile, attendant transactions would denote the latest interlude between major crises while ostensibly salient economic preoccupations precariously submerging security and rolestatus concerns had one of two possible effects: mute and counteract for a time at least the instabilities peculiar to three-power relationships, or bemuse superficial observers and improvident policy-makers into overlooking the subterranean deterioration of the politico-military equations.

Meanwhile, both the procedural and the substantive choices – who was to exert primary initiative toward what aim in how perceived and construed a setting – were as always contingent on the actors' willingness to envision in a philosophico-historical and ability to implement in a grand-strategic framework an option that eschewed utopia without foreclosing real change essential for stability. Utopianism has been in evidence so long as the focus was on some of the more far-fetched reversals in official Soviet rhetoric; realism has been only skin-deep so long as it was largely a function of US efforts not to unsettle actual change in the making and fight off the rhetoric's appeal at the same time. Among the directly concerned, change-precipitating upheavals in one part of east-central Europe (Poland and Hungary) left wide open the reformers' capacity to realize in action what they were proclaiming, before being overwhelmed by aspirations they had awakened and could neither moderate nor satisfy, while greater realism was briefly an option for regimes in the initially lagging countries (East Germany, Czechoslovakia) that, comparatively solvent economically, would in the end decisively test the feasibility of sustainable political reform, provided they used reactionaly language to conceal radical thoughts.

The missing middle, enlightened conservatism, could alone determine what kind of economic and political reform was compatible in eastern Europe including Russia, and in China, with a government that was both legitimate (because popularly supported) and capable of governing (because functionally authoritative): a combination imperfectly enough achieved in the western democracies to foreclose declarations of final and total victory in a competition that exceeded the Cold War in both time and space. Much depended on the evolving relationship between the intellectual and professional elites and the laboring masses (and, in consequence, between the two and the regimes). Would the elites, after using the masses' material aspirations to batter down the gates to reform closed by unproductively entrenched communist regimes, unwittingly guide the proletariat back into the arms of a reformed and no longer monopolistically leading party by fostering the kind of change that reawakened class-based resentments? And, if this reversal of alliances was necessary to assure the communist parties of a continuing role in a multi-party system, radical recasting of the alliance structures in Europe had to take place before it became clear what legitimate place an irreversibly altered Soviet Union could beneficially occupy in world politics. Functionally equivalent with the Eastern European proletariat's relationship to pluralism was then that of organic capability to operational latitudes: could or would activating the transactional plane cooperatively by Gorbachev, as part of an effort to shore up the Soviets' role and status internationally, serve as a concomitant to restoring their organic base as effectively as truculence had concealed the Soviets' radical weakness after World War II and tumultuous competition screened an increasingly sluggish growth later on?

Related questions arose about basic dispositions and manifest attitudes. Was it more productive to welcome Russia back into the community of nations as a repentant pariah, or make room for her on the flexible principle of parity on the grounds of past deserts in war and anticipated future performance in peace? Was containment to be replaced by condescension or in-depth conciliation? Was it reasonable or prudent to assume that the Soviets' embarrassingly hyperbolic ideological abjuration was tantamount to geopolitical abdication – and that making the recantation credible depended on its being followed by wholesale territorial and strategic contraction? Just as the US–Soviet conflict had not been an emanation of a class war Soviet-style, so it had not been the US-favored collision of integrally just causes with their perversion. The ideological and perceptual fog would begin to lift only when the Soviets have begun to apply a touch of the dialectic of historical determinism to their internal development before, during, and after Stalin; have achieved a constructive equanimity internationally as they extricated themselves from the complex-ridden residua of an immediate past. Feeding alternately into abject confession and arrogant compensation for a sense of inferiority *vis-à-vis* the Atlantic West, the alternation-cum-ambivalence matched too closely its German analogue, disastrous before 1945 and reappearing mutedly as part of an urge to shed the flagellant's garb for one yet to be fashioned. The air would begin to clear only when westerners stopped acting as if their libertarian approach to man and state was an innate virtue rather than the dividend of sheltered growth on the part of the United States and the accoutrement adopted by fall from stressful great power in the case of the West Europeans.

It has become the no more clearly avowable goal of many West Europeans, encouraged from the USA, to move matters toward a "united Europe" which, extending from the Polish–Soviet border to the Atlantic, would have expanded the reach while consolidating the bases of democratic cum capitalist institutions at the cost of consigning Russia to the no man's land between a Europe so defined and an Asia in ferment. Such an agglomerate would be "Europe" only within an extent that Britain (let alone the United States) was not part of, and be "united" only in the sense that Eastern Europe minus Russia would have become the economic colony of a European community that supplied the camouflage for unified Germany. So enlarged a Western Europe, or so truncated a Europe, would be a political entity only in the new-fangled communitarian (historically meta-systemic) mode, without a substantial geo-strategic role in Eurasia and the world at large. If half-way successful economically, such a Europe would exert a sufficiently strong disruptive attraction on the non-Great Russian parts of the Soviet Union to be compelled to either surrender to Russian retaliatory threats, rearm to the teeth, or flee back into the American fold; she would have ceased being a "European" Europe in the process of becoming all that was to Europe by dint of inner conceit and outsiders' courtesy.

The belief that, as part of the package, the West could offer the Soviets reassuring guarantees of politico-military security against western interference in east-central Europe was the crypto-legalist's utopia hiding behind the eager would-be negotiator's seductive agenda. The reality that such a guarantee was not formally negotiable so as to cover the full range of possible contingencies is safely embedded in fruitless efforts to define "intervention" before repeating the experience with "aggression;" and the assurance could not be negotiated for substantive reasons, because if Soviet Russia was (held to be) too strong to be included in Europe, she could not also (be judged to) be so weak as to require – and be willing to accept – unilateral assurances of security from only Western Europe or the West at large.

The alternative to a contractually united rump Europe was a gradually reconstructed all-European order that required only a diminishing military-strategic engagement by the US (or Anglo–American) segment of the total Occident. A negotiated lowering of arms levels would have made it easier for the west Europeans to match the Soviet military capability as an alternative to inviting Russian political interference or relapsing under American protection, while trial and error evolved a west-to-east spectrum of indigenously appropriate because viable regimes.

If for the retrenching or only energies-redirecting United States to become the latest New World's balance wheel, and for an enlarged Europe to become again its genuinely real-political next to only economic constituent, entailed a measure of Russia's preeminence in a Europe for whose revival as a collective personality the United States would have made its finest contribution, such preeminence need be no more frightening on the regional than was condominium on the global plane. All it meant was that while the "greatest power" led in setting the diplomatic agenda, its initiatives did not automatically elicit a flight to outside help so long as the less "great" powers were not manifestly threatened in their substantive autonomy. Should such a condition, one currently further contained by the contrarily slanted economic-technological balance, continue to be regionally unacceptable even as the Soviet Union was Europeanized in depth, this would merely confirm the suspicion that the West Europeans have definitively opted out of politics as their forbears more than anyone else had historically defined it. Having opted instead for the utopia of the "new" politics at an incalculable cost in received national traits and the region's global relevance, they would refuse realism by giving up on what was at once do-able and power-politically restorative. The stakes were higher still for the smaller east-central European countries recoiling from any and all association with Russia, in hopes of a successful Prague super-spring with Euro-communitarian trimmings. They risked, when the winter chill had again set in as a consequence, to wake up to a massive Munich as the western democracies either withdrew once more into self-protective shells before a power play from the East or their Anglo–French nucleus proved unable to stem the manifold consequences of a German surge into the power vacuum without assistance from the same quarter.

A mere possibility of such calamities points to a question. Will it be necessary or just prudent to take a few steps back from the post-World War II organization of Europe so as to release diplomatic if no other resources for appeasing national if no wider anxieties reaching through the interwar period back to before World War I? Answers must be looked for in three areas critical for the Occident's restructuring: western Europe, east-central Europe, and the American and Russian wing powers.

A crucial step in the first arena was to slow down the rush into a community that continued to be made tighter within and vaster abroad, poised to expand eastward after having been enlarged southeast- and westward. Neither in the shape of an only economic, including monetary, union nor as a repoliticized super-state could the western complex durably deflect the Germans from the East: not by means of solidified prosperity and even less in the face of any future economic distress. Perhaps least of all when drowning in opulence would the Germans be forever willing or able to live by bread alone. Nor will the materially deprived East Europeans, when moderately sated, heed best-intentioned denials. Assurances to the contrary will only feed suspicions that associating east-central Europe with the Common Market will not only dilute it further but also make the political absorption of East in West Germany easier, before serving as a cloak for colonizing Middle Europe economically.

Loosening up the west European structure instead need neither devalue its past achievements nor impede their diffusion. It was unlikely to bar Middle Europe's involvement with the Community while upgrading the quality of the region's links with a Russia more comparable in economic development and complementary in trade. In the west, the Federal Republic would be liberated for its re-equilibrating ties to the West with interests in the East without having to make a choice as difficult to make in the immediate present as it is impossible to divine its thrust for the day after. A French diplomacy that gave up on the idea to make the Germans' choice for them would be freer to legitimize qualms aroused by Germany's precipitous resurgence. And Britain too would be released, from the wrenchingly contrary pulls of the land mass across the water and the blue yonder, for revitalizing trans-Atlantic links as the United States shifted its attention to the Pacific, the center of future world politics. Such a displacement alone could provide a solid place for an Albion retooling from an aircraft carrier off Europe into a major floating support for the pontoon bridge spanning the northern seas between the former colony and its future partner in the Far East.

A Russo–American partnership could serve, alongside a reorganized European and Atlantic community, as the second pillar of a future order. It would then accomplish that which England repeatedly tried, and invariably thwarted, first and foremost in relations with France. All US statecraft had to do was to take counsel with Britain's arrangement with Bismarckian Germany before, combining indecision with intransigence, the British furthered the Wilhelmine era's escalating bid for world power. Just as the strategies with a continental focus – for an encircling coalition against a supposed aspirant to hegemony or his co-hegemonial duopoly with a still farther–eastern land power – produced invariably war, so the stabilizing potential of the sea power's partnership with the premier land power was commonly undone by the former's arrogance and the latter's pride. The continentals would refuse to endure the unrewarding status of a junior partner, atoning forever for the one setback that brought them into the second-best variety of an otherwise coveted relationship with the insulars in the first place.

The latest opportunity to reverse course arose from the outcome of the Cold War and the internal Soviet crisis, even if the former was not so triumphantly in the West's favor as has been claimed and the latter was as incomparably deeper than America's own problems as appeared on the surface. As to any other junior party, unequal partnership will be acceptable to the Soviet Union only if its position, to be expressed again in initiatives that safeguard US vital interests on the continent and in Russia's self-restraint if not abstention overseas, could be safely expected to progressively yield to an equality in status and parity in role no strong continental state will or can willingly renounce. Thus the United States had to signal in advance its acquiescence in the Soviets garnering, in due course and in the world at large, a dividend from successful domestic reform, albeit through the gentler methods the success will have made not only possible but also necessary. Absent such tacit or explicit understanding, cumulating material costs of continued rivalry threatened converting the particular crises of each into secular decline for both, as the convergence that inevitably attends an inconclusively protracted conflict exhibited its darker over its positive side.

Reviving the junior-partner formula in US–Soviet relations meant for Russia, taking the place of Bismarckian Germany in relation to Britain, to assume the posture of a continentally satiated and globally self-restrained premier land power that is actually leaned upon by the insular state as the main factor for maintaining European stability rather than counterbalanced as a threatening force. In return the Soviet Union, as Germany before, is conceded the status of the preeminent continental state, a position contingent on doing nothing that provoked potentially revisionist powers, now Germany and China, into policies threatening to duplicate revanchist France's encircling alliance with tsarist Russia. If this implied condoning German outlets in east-central Europe as an alternative to territorial revision (the equivalent of French colonial compensations for Alsace-Lorraine), it meant also, and importantly, maintaining good relations with the United States as an insurance equal to Bismarck's diplomatic "wire" to London (read Washington) matching one to Russia (read China).

The costs of a Soviet special relationship with America for the previously preeminent European powers, minimized by Russia's economic weakness in the short run, were further reduced by her stake in a reorganized Europe for geostrategic protection against China in the long run. Moreover, making a prominent European role comfortable for the others was Russia's only available diplomatic foundation for equality of status with the United States in the medium term. The generally applicable principle is that of a complex equilibrium, maintained near-automatically by neither party moving impetuously in any one direction for fear of triggering prohibitively adverse reactions.

Disaggregating thus the military-political balance of power into acts of only residually armed policy replaces attempts to dissolve Soviet power further or finally, the henceforth only remaining aim of pressing on with the military kind of balancing.

Like all parties to strategic triangles – thus France with her choice between a Germanic, an east European, and a western-insular power as the principal prop or partner – Germany, too, disposes of a limited range of foreign policy orientations modifiable in technique only. Applying the Bismarckian model to Germany directly rather than by analogy to the Soviet Union, highlights Bismarck's effort to foster stability, once Germany had been unified, through a balanced relationship with the wing powers. Rather than playing one off against the other for specific gains, the policy stopped as much short of close alignment with either as of using one relationship to injure significant interests of the other party. If this meant for the Federal Republic calibrating carefully its engagements in the west, it meant also for it to allow the eastern part of Germany perform an internationally useful role acceptable to the Soviet Union and congenial to the smaller states in the east.

A but loosely confederal unity would permit the Germans achieving the essentials of Bismarck's post-unification contribution to European stability. They might even do better in that deferring thus indefinitely any possibility of forceful change in Eastern Europe would improve on the original taint of violence in the Franco–Prussian war, which ultimately doomed Bismarck's constructive achievement. Differently disruptive were the two other basic German policies, adopted by Bismarck's successors. One, more immediately applicable, is the liberal trading approach to a German-dominated "Mitteleuropa" under the auspices of amicable relations with the insular power and at best indifferent ones with Russia, identified with the so-called "new course." It is expected to achieve peacefully, if over a longer period of time, the objectives of the harsher third policy, embraced, in light of the intervening disappointment with the western-liberal, English, option by Caprivi's eventual successor, von Bülow. The objective is to exploit Germany's uncommitted position between the feuding wing powers for a more tangible and larger advantage to be won in deferred, but then dictated, alliance with a Russia unable to avoid setbacks in her confrontation with the Anglo-Saxon sea power.

In the post-Cold War era, combining the continental and the global facets, the direct and the analogous applications, of the Bismarckian formula permitted replacing both the Atlantic and the Warsaw alliances as protection either for or against Germany: against her oscillating between West and East diplomatically as a neutralist, or turning east militantly as revisionist, but detaching herself in either case from the West to appease Russian strength or fish in Russia's sea of troubles. The partnership formula combined in a unique fashion America's potential as a brake with Russia's as a ballast against either calamity, while France extended the blessing of classic Europe and the two Germanies narrowed gradually in peace and stability the gulf war and defeat had opened between them. Containing thus German power for the foreseeable future in a rebuilt all-Europe was the opposite to dulling the rich Germans forever by promise of ever greater prosperity. It also screened them from inner demons and their new-found democracy from threats kept in abeyance by the very division that gave it birth. Replacing partition with fusion would remove the still indispensable time-and-space cushion between acquiescing in the post-World War II territorial settlement and being driven by turbulent domestic politics to repudiate it.

For the Federal Republic not to reprise the Mitteleuropa-centered imperialism of the Second Reich at its most liberal and pacific was, paradoxically, the inferior alternative to the recidivist medievalism of the Third Reich, to be revised in a Middle Europe stabilized around three Germanic components: western Germany, eastern Germany, and Austria. Ottonian is the historically resonant designation for a structure that matches the Franco–German nucleus of reconciliation in the neo-Carolingian European Community with a Germano–Slavic one, and complements Bismarckian policies. It refers in the northern, east German–Polish–Czech, tier to the short-lived Saxon Emperor, Otto III, who embarked almost to a day one thousand years ago on a "renovation" of the Empire through cooperatively established consensual links with the neighboring Slavs among others.

Fostering a regional entente in the north as a counterpart to one centered on Hungary and Austria in the south required tying western, including West German, aid to joint action for economic recovery and political reconstruction. Even if such an ensemble combined revised military-strategic links to Russia with reviving diplomatic links to France, it would undoubtedly be a but porous buffer against and a ready-made medium for Germany's involvement in the East. But, if knit closely enough, it would hamper the engagement's momentum eventuating once again in enforced migrations of people in the area, now in the opposite direction from that taken after World War II, while painful memories still lingered.

In the meantime, the inherited conflict of Slav and German could be laid to rest in an area that was the home to successive "national" empires and cross-currents of ethnic cultures. Once the East Germans discovered, under the code name of "socialism," their distinctively German values as setting them apart from the materialism of the western co-nationals, they only needed a valid international role to buttress restored civic pride with a post-Stalinist legitimacy for the "other Germany." In tempering the anarchic libertarianism of the Poles, the traditional German sense of discipline would usefully mesh with the practical sense of the Czechs which, lampooned in the literary figure of Good Soldier Schweik, was sufficiently leavened by the spiritual striving epitomized by Jan Hus to form a middle ground between the Germans' protestant ethic and the Poles' many-sided catholicity. Taken together, the regional mix would mediate between Western rationalism and Russian "soul" on the plane of values, and span the gap between stages of economic development and differentials in strategic needs. No single country could individually and separately build such a bridge, willing and anxious as more than one of them was. Last but not least, there was enough complementarity to underpin the political mission with economic integration and help overcome differences in shared national crisis, as shown by the mass exodus of Poles seeking work into East Germany.

German national unity will be safe when bringing together Czech and Slovak with Pole in a reshaped relationship to Russia has fitted a Slavic community of nations into the organic foundation of an institutionalized European equilibrium. Until then, preliminary goals similar to those of the Ottonian north could be pursued in the Austro–Hungarian south (the object of special solicitude of another Otto, von Habsburg, as part of a democratically adjusted dynastic ambition). To reconstruct the Occident around the three main pillars (United States, Germany, Russia – Latins, Germans, Slavs – along the geographic spectrum) and principles of organization (Carolingian, Ottonian, and Bismarckian along the temporal trajectory) was a way to dispose of the unfinished business of Europe before her history, at long last at peace with itself, could definitively merge with world history.

The immediate task was for the west Europeans to help repair the hurts Eastern Europe suffered when absorbing the shocks Asia had repeatedly aimed at the West; for Germany in particular, the duty was to undo the consequences of her failed last bid for world power, which propelled the last oriental-despotic manifestation of Russia's dual personality into the heart of Europe. In each case the emergency freed western Europe for a materially profitable Atlantic diversion. Not to be ignored indefinitely was the related imperative to equip the Occident for facing an already reviving farther East with confident serenity. This required the westward ties from the all-European structure of stability to the Atlantic realm (United States and United Kingdom) to continue, linked up with the historically transmitted connection to the Eurasian realm (Russia).

One challenge from the farther East could persist in the milder form of Japan's economic ascendancy. Or it might assume, in conjunction with any future crisis of the world or only Japanese economy, the more directly threatening physiognomy of more widely impacting regional imperialism. Another test will come from a China that, emerging out of stressful economic development, either imposed on herself and her smaller neighbors the burden of imperial restoration or advanced the claim for moral-political reparation on ex-imperialistic West. In either case the consequence, already in the making as the perception of Soviet threat waned, was for the critical East–West spectrum, if not necessarily schism, to re-extend globally.

In either case also, the United States will have to have readied itself for shifting the energies and resources saved in Europe to the henceforth crucial Pacific theater, even as it retained a sufficient European foothold to guard against an isolated Russia being tempted to repair by an act of force the otherwise stabilizing discrepancy between the fiction of diplomatic preeminence and the material fact of economic debility if not dependence. Thus reinsured against plausible risks, US priorities will change from counterbalancing Russia via integrating western Europe ever more tightly into the Atlantic sphere to conditionally sustaining Russia's bid for full re-entry into the house of Europe. If a full re-entry had to eventually reflect Russia's status as the last remaining European great power capable militarily in both physical and psychological terms, its immediate purpose was to implement a role centered inevitably on preventing that a neatly polarizing (and thus manageable) East–West cleavage subside, only to be replaced by a jigsaw puzzle-like fragmentation of first Europe and then the West in its entirety around the German issue, unappeased by the spread of economic well-being.

As the past recedes into history, her lessons are learned only by reinterpreting what has transpired in light of present imperatives and future opportunities. To place different facets of a complex past into ever-changing relief is not the same as to rewrite history by suppressing one and glorifying another fact or person so as to control the present and constrain the future all the more arbitrarily. It is, rather, to allow that which might be done more wisely to avoid earlier misjudgments and mitigate past misfortunes. This, a presentist, way of deciphering the past is also the most realistic way of approaching the future. To proceed differently when revolution yielded, or has been yielding, to restoration is to have learned nothing and forgotten nothing; to be unmindful of the fact that, unlike domestic politics, the relationship among sovereign states has always been a record of non-recurring opportunities which, when missed, would not have another day in parliament. The opportunity, at a time when the chain of materially destructive but also miraculously generative Europe-centered conflicts seemed to be transmuted into links of more certainly materially than otherwise productive cooperation in and beyond Europe, was to complete in regard to Russia the task already far advanced with respect to Germany; the purpose, to heal definitively with respect to the former the post-war ills that originated in the distempers unleashed on Europe by the latter. As the passage of time transformed the record of past transgressions into a potentially redeeming perspective on the present, it became all the more important that certain events not be forgotten. Yet the deeper the real crimes – against branches of humanity conspicuously including the Slavic – were forever impressed upon mind and memory, the more room will have been freed for appreciating the features in Germany's tortured past that made the country heed the call to revolt in war against despair over a politically imperfect and both materially and morally debilitating peace. And the more that ordeal by power has been purged of that which was not integrally part of it despite ominous precedents, the more compellingly did it secrete a duty to act so that such resentments and the recourses they give rise to were not replicated for Germany's eastern conqueror.

Discourses 8–10
The Essence of World Politics

The conceptually constant inner economy and the conjuncturally changing political economy of world politics confront and complement one another in processes of interaction and evolution that engender the uneven compound of continuity and change. The operational and functional facets of either make manifest the subjacent relations of state to society and of spirit to structures. They do so within a universe of action and perception wherein the limitations of prudent reason and strategic rationality are disclosed by their works before they can be corrected by historical intelligence, just as interests have to be elevated by principle and purpose heightened by passion if they are to point the actor to highest undertakings and the observer to deeper understanding, each partaking of prophecy.

Discourse 8   On the Primacy of Politics and Its Enemies

It is a symptom of a power's decline – although no less elusive than are its causes – that national policies predicated on the continuation of past capability and performance have ceased to be realistic and became in effect utopian, with only development-distorting or also deterioration-accelerating consequences. Such national policies reflect then a tendency declining actors share with only initially ascending ones: to overemphasize the tangible functional – economic and military – features and instruments of policy to the detriment of the intangibles at work in world politics; and to restlessly rearrange priorities among the economic and military factors in light of changing contingencies or capabilities over against steadfastly adhering to the primacy of politics over both.

Basic to implementing the primacy of politics is a strategy that, keyed to reconciling the military-strategic requirements of physical security with the society's material needs, relates the pursuit of both to domestic political and external geopolitical contexts recognized as not only independently changing but also deliberately – actively or perceptually – changeable. Such a practice differs from a pragmatic approach to solving specific problems that is fixated on the given geopolitical setting, while changes are confined to instrumental requirements of sufficient security assessed in light of moderately waxing and waning tensions only. If the more broadly political approach was congenial to a statist bias permeating the (Soviet) approach to acute internal and external crises, the more narrowly pragmatic orientation has been a reflection of the (US) national style or political culture born of a less crises-prone existential situation and historical experience. Downgrading the importance of political stimuli to the US–Soviet arms race as much as of political foundations for stabilizing East–West arms control preceded a similar approach to the possibility of restructuring deployed forces and revising strategic doctrines to fit a lowered level of military balance and threat. For the United States to have defined the relationship with the Soviet Union in military-strategic and -technological terms at the conflict's beginnings (witness the NSC-68 document), and for both sides to redefine it in like manner at a potentially critical turning point (the INF Treaty), was a fitting backdrop for debating the respective merits of "offensive defense" and "defensive defense" amidst questions about good faith on one or both sides. It was easy to overlook in such a climate the extent to which the military issues merely operationalized a pervasive uncertainty: as to which act or initiative within a long chain of events has been offensive and which defensive – a facet of political action and reaction that accounts for the ethical neutrality characteristic of genuinely tragic collisions.

Similarly, if a realistically modified utopia was to have a chance, economic measures – such as western credits, joint ventures, and institutional or other ways of integrating the Soviet into the world economy – had also to be founded politically in the intention to mute the conflict by facilitating domestic Soviet reform, on the assumption that the combined political benefits of backing the reform's success would exceed the costs *vis-à-vis* third parties (e.g. China) while the risks implicit in a failure that could not be attributed to western obstruction remained manageable. A commonplace in both Leninist theory and actual practice, the primacy of politics has coexisted easily in the Soviet Union with Marxian tenets of economic determinism. In western Europe, the principle was tacitly challenged by a practice slanted in favor of the new religion of this-worldly economic well-being, dispensed as an opiate to the materially exacting masses by managers of public policy as hesitant about using at home the powers of government they technically possessed as they were aware of lacking real power to employ abroad. And both principle and practice were in a state of flux in a United States half-heartedly groping (while emphasis fluctuated between competition for and control of arms) for a way to correct, by a return to (geo-) politics, the arms-centered overreaction to but the latest of infatuations with only nominally "political" economy, spawned by the coupling of oil shortage generated in the Middle East with a military fiasco incurred in Asia.

Within the larger West as a whole, the principle of *politique d'abord* has divided parties to it less as a matter of doctrine than of practical awareness and its application. The high cards western Europe was holding in the foreign-trade-and-aid dimension of the Soviet economic crisis set definite limits to Soviet diplomatic preeminence to be exerted in the foreign policy arena; but the narrower West could draw upon its economic assets for political returns only to a point as definite as was that beyond which economic reform could not proceed internally without having a counterpart in political institutions. Within the global context, the letter principle seemed to have been understood better in Gorbachev's Russia than in Deng's China when the two were deciding whether to fear more the economic advance bogging down eventually (when the political scene had been frozen) or the political arena exploding prematurely (when it was unfrozen). The controlling factor may then well have been a cultural one: the classical West's preoccupation – prominently surviving in continental European Russia – with clarifying goals conceptually before exploring experimentally the means to achieve them, a bias which favored action on a plane of (political) reality easier to impress (than the economic) by thus informed will.

Reducing political economy to specific economic policies and strategies within frameworks more administrative than political was part of elevating a supposedly ever more complex economic interdependence to a central role in the change away from the supposedly traditional mode of international politics, reduced to narrowly military competition. Either emphasis evaded the more critical complexity of the circular relationship between politics and economics. The evasion, fostered by the liberal notion of foreign policy as a mere projection of domestic politics, encouraged the fragmenting of reality into discrete functional or inter-functional sectors operative in relations between equally segregated sets of only two powers (specifically, of the United States with discrete allied or adversary parties). Although the sectorial approach was easier to articulate descriptively, it was less accurately reflective of the more intricately articulated actuality than a genuinely systemic – dialectical rather than dyadic – perspective.

A systemic perspective on the primacy of politics over isolated or crudely interlinked economics and military strategics allows for both constants and effective changes operative in world politics. Within the latter's inner economy, a broadly construed political economy coexists with features pertaining to political physics and tragic poetics, while their interrelations are mediated by a strategic rationality variably informed by historical intelligence.

Whereas the link between economics and politics is equally circular in the formation of individual actors and in the relations among actors already formed, the link is unevenly direct in regard to diversely tangible givens and intangible processes. The most direct relation is between an actor's physical and material-resource base in geography and the economic system or orientation most germane to the base. The concrete assets and liabilities behind the connection, differentiating most clearly the land- from sea-based-or-oriented powers, are of interest to the narrowly resource-centered variety of geopolitics concerned with relations among such organisms. The connection between politics and economics is less direct to the extent that quantitatively and qualitatively differentiated material-economic capabilities influence interstate dynamics more distinctly and less equivocally, even if only ultimately, than specific economic interests or transactions or objectives do proximately. This is so not least because not only different economic systems (liberal free-trading as much as mercantilist, keyed to interdependence or imperialism) but also economically defined types of power (industrially diverse insular-mercantile and continental-agricultural) are equally if unevenly permeated and actuated by power-political concerns. Finally, the connection is most indirect, but most significant over time, when domestic markets have become more important than material assets (including territory and trade) sought or achievable abroad, and the reversal has contributed to one of the real changes in world politics: the secular shift of governmental functions and political priorities from external acquisitions to internal accomplishments (favoring reform) – i.e., the gradual displacement of focus away from the systemic arena outside the state and toward the society within the state.

For the more indirect connections between economics and politics to have become increasingly significant conformed with the growing tendency for the organic factor to predominate over the operational, a related real – functionally significant rather than formally spectacular – change. However, diminished as its ranking among the determinants and concurrently enhanced the quota of *as if* simulation of traditional modes may have been, the operational facet remained critically important. It would continue to matter so long as mismanaging it produced misallocation of either material or immaterial resources, thus when the existing hierarchy of threats has been wrongly perceived or policy was influenced less by the geopolitical configuration than by the institutional and ideo-cultural manifestations of the competing powers' geographically defined basic situations. And transactions would matter so long as the ultimate resort of world politics, war, was preserved by the shift in incentives from opportunities for tangible gain to defiance against even but hypothetical threat to an established position or the future potential and prospects of a major actor.

Closely related to the political economy of world politics, the real changes were fully in keeping with a political physics expanding its scope from interacting forces differentiated *qua* powers, by space- and time-conditioned relativities, to encompass flows of energy translated into involvement and influence among linked systems and sub-systems. The latter kind of communications was crucial in a strategy that would transpose contentions insoluble locally onto a larger, all-European or global plane. The image is then of a field of forces sufficiently enlarged to expand the range of attractions and repulsions. But the image is also that of a pattern of interactions which, de-emphasizing a mechanical-quantitative balance of militarily defined capabilities implemented through fixed and exclusive alliances as power-aggregating devices, extends into a more complex equilibrium expressing fluid politico-diplomatic attitudes and relations for combining reassurance with restraint between, within, and outside alliances.

In principle, expanding the arena and range of attractions and revulsions has advantages similar to those from diversifying assets and liabilities in

economic equations and adding non-material to money issues in the universe of
labor-management bargaining. In practice, the attractions would include the
economic or cultural ones exerted from the West on the east Europeans,
and by the fellow-regional society on both the Arabs and the Israelis in
conditions of extraneously underwritten peaceable communication and convergence. And if at least some of the east Europeans would rediscover in a
revised pan-European framework the danger of resurgent Germany moving
into a power vacuum, while others might detect previously unsuspected vices in
the sociopolitical mores and practices of a demythologized West, the Middle
Easterners would in a depolarized global and regional setting recoil from a
henceforth expendable dependence on outside parties and arrangements
among them. As the intensified flows of energies between the formerly
deadlocked and the less change-resistant larger systems destabilized the built-
in regional stalemates, sustainable change became possible: it would be the
systems-re-equilibrating product of local responses to the impulses issuing
from outside an East European arena caught up in controlled turmoil from
cumulative reform and a Middle Eastern arena stirred by a managed transition
from the state of war to that of peace. Not the least important consequence
would be to brake, even if not forever block, the tendency for unused –
stalemated or atrophied – energy to migrate elsewhere: eastward toward the
Asian East from the larger Atlantic–Pacific West; westward toward the Jewish-
and Arab-American backers and would-be mentors of their embattled brethren
in the Middle East.

Such a state of things had a long-term potential superior to that of a strategic
alternative with a different analogue in physics. Equally preferred by the
American political right for Middle Europe and its Israeli equivalent for the
Middle East, the strategy would apply to the inertial adversary system a
sufficiently potent force or pressure so as to, by slowing down any potentially
threatening advance on its part, accelerate its descent into terminal decay.
Failing which result, or absent the means of promoting it, the preferred second
best was to implement (in the power-balancing mode) the tendency of contrary
forces to strain toward equalization, if at presumably unequal and unevenly
burdensome costs.

A strategy will be best suited to implement the laws of political physics in
such a way as to convert morally intuited tragic predicaments into processes
with regionally and globally beneficial outcomes when it has been informed by
historical intelligence. Such intelligence, distilled from an understanding of
past precedents projected against present realities, will prompt either the
replication or the revision of traditional modes in light of crucial relativities: the
uneven (time-bound) developmental stage and (space-dependent) situation of
actors competing within inter-communicating larger and smaller segments of
the system. The object is then to refine and, if need be, reverse instructions
from a strategic rationality responsive to immediate stimulations only. Confined
to available means, pressing needs, and presumptively attainable short-term
ends, such stimuli predominate in the comparatively narrow universe of a
political physics focused on mechanically interacting forces. Consequently, an
intended rationality of the narrower kind will implement the primacy of politics

most markedly, and often dramatically, in conditions of manifest crisis of security or survival.

Although energies thus mobilized and released fuel the evolution of the state system and its members, without necessarily reforming either, the routine crisis itself will have originated in the existing configuration of power, roles and status, among actors or sociopolitical groups within actors. Only when the crisis embraces all of the facets of the inner economy of politics at major turning points in the evolution of the state system, will strategic rationality operating through the agency of *realpolitik* or, in more extreme cases, power politics, be clearly inadequate: the resources of philosophical realism will then be on call for basic insight, allowing for counsel from the romantic strain peculiar to such realism to introduce culture-related factors into action-preceding conceptual analysis. As history's tribunal pronounces its verdict in due course, the judgment will have disclosed whether and how aptly the politics and the policies brought to bear on the extraordinary crisis related the power employed by strategy to passionately aroused spirit, and cerebrally evolved concepts to viscerally experienced compulsions.

At a time when the larger crisis was apparently present, practicing the more exalted kind of politics was far from contravening the already manifest real changes, much as these tended to depress the level of intensity of world politics. If a real change consisted of statecraft being conducted *as if* its traditional modes continued to apply in full, either a subtle change or a transparently crude simulation was reflected in the watered-down formats of old stand-bys, such as multipower concert and two-power condominium on a par with one-power empire or hegemony. Like consequences flowed from the growing importance of organic transformations, biased toward a power's rise or decline, over operational transactions supported readily by force; and from both trans-formations and transactions stopping short of completed states of being in favor of no more than corresponding tendencies. To substitute incentives to self-restraint in policy implicit in a complex equilibrium for the balancing of power backed by war would revitalize the operational dimension in these conditions by reincluding it within the bounds of the feasible, without markedly diminishing the primacy of the organic dimension. However, conducive as the alterations might be to realizing a still longer-term prospect, they were still far from shifting the balance to a form of activities so radically novel in their principles and priorities as to transmute world politics into the quasi-domestic politics of a world community raising unanswerable questions about the future site and shape of ineradicable tragedy.

Pending further progression toward the far-off contingency, traditional predicaments would permeate world politics long after essential continuity had incorporated significant change. So far, in contrast with a progress predicated on the possibility to transform the nature of man, the state, and politics, feasible progress pointed only to a widened range of plausible objectives for a statecraft disposed to implement realistically modified utopias – utopias which themselves gave expression to the demonstrable real changes in world politics. Such objectives being available in principle made it possible in practice to relax – or even resolve – the polarizing standoff between narrow realism and unbounded utopia: the former aimed at achieving a power-related end with equally circumscribed means for either diffusely ideological or discreetly camouflaged specific reasons; the latter inspired by the vision of generalized harmony around a focal value of supposedly pan-human significance. In concretely historical terms, the realistically modified utopia was thus equally distinct from and contrary to the extreme form of progressist utopia in left-wing totalitarianism and the nostalgic utopia of a reversed evolutionary progression in right-wing totalitarianism: the former postulating the definitive erosion of the territorial state and with it of interstate conflict; the latter committed to broadening the territorial base of the appropriated state as part of repressing the free play of interstate equilibrium. In the process, each of the totalitarianisms helped in its way discredit the primacy of politics among territorial states by exalting a quintessentially conflictual politics, but one stripped of its functionally or normatively moderating attributes within inter-class or inter-racial frameworks disruptive of community, state, or both.

If it was to avoid both extremes but retain the necessary contact with reality a practicably utopian strategic scheme had to do more than be consistent with the subtly modified constants in the inner economy of world politics. It had to correct as much as possible for the ambiguities and interdeterminacies that the assortment of continuity with change has introduced into contemporary world politics: structures pertaining to actors, the emergent global (proto-) system itself, and alternate schisms, as well as the resulting tendency for strategic choices to be indecisively adrift with still obscure consequences for the rate and the direction of the system's evolution. Ostensibly utopian policies which took into account both innate attributes and transitional ambiguities of world politics were the most likely ones to mitigate the disruptive potential of the uncertainties taken together. However, in the best of cases, the ensuing progress was unlikely to be far-reaching enough to release parties to the turmoils of world politics – or its transition to a world community – from the web of tragedy so long as its interweaving filaments continued to be spun on the warp of change deputizing for fate.

Discourse 9   *On Meaning in History and for Politics*

Where the factual data of world politics provide a but tenuous basis for predictions other than linear extrapolations of presently existing conditions and trends, the constant constituents of the politics' inner economy supply a firm foundation for prophecy so long as it confines itself to projecting traditional quandaries into a future precariously poised between re-enacting the dilemmas in only superficially altered shapes and transcending them without radically altering the factors and forces that shape them. This being so, amorphousness is to prophecy concerned with policy-relevant future happenings what the ambiguity of all past and present action and circumstance is to tragedy. Prophecy blends empirical with transcendent data within a design that is confusedly predictive and preemptive. The intent to predict the future by extrapolating from the past is bound up with the desire to prevent future from integrally repeating the past. Prophecy paints darkly the experience of a tribe in strife with other tribes, in hopes of lightening the lot of one or all in future existence. By announcing the future in tones of dismay over past or present, it would bar the future from being no more than the past deferred beyond the present, just as when it dwells on the unfolding of necessity it would help realize the slender potentiality of choice realizing the freedom to escape doom and alter destiny.

In the process of amorphously bringing together past, present, and future, prophecy engages all the main facets of the reality it addresses. It implicitly negates the affirmation of progress in interstate relations as either automatic or autonomous qualitative change, because holding otherwise would make nonsense of projecting from the past into the future and would defeat, among other things, tragedy. And it draws equally on the insights of physics and poetics transposed into politics, both of which support the premonition of unalterable conflict implementing the laws of either the political or the moral order. But, if the impulsions and constraints that are the stuff of political physics can be relaxed, the defining terms of poetics leave room for an informed struggle against the unalterable repetition of ordeal; both offer the promise of possible exemption from the predicaments that, deriving from one, are at the source of the other. This is so because tragedy is a matter of will and spirit realized in dramatics and not of instinct and impulse manifested in mechanics; and because ordeal can be slanted toward concord between any two parties if not instantly among all by the judicious application of concepts and precepts from a physics that transcends mechanics.

Although prophecy inevitably propounds or implies the lessons of history, soliciting lessons from history has to be informed by cognizance of the laws of political physics and of the special dilemmas it introduces into the already slender latitude for free endeavor allowed by poetics. By drawing on all of the components for sources of imaginative intuition, prophecy seeks to turn into a real force in the world that which history conveys through information, poetics highlights by and for imitation, and physics elucidates by means of analogy. History informs about sequences and recurrences in an evolution punctuated by a range of revolutions from social to functional; physics permits analogies from gravitational revolutions of bodies held together in regular motions that constitute elementary order; and poetics dramatizes the consequences of acute rivalry within, and of arrogant revolt against, such order. Thus armed, prophetics holds out a warning against the several processes converging into an ever deeper predicament; and it offers a prospect and defines the conditions of reprieve from the predicament deepening into irreversible catastrophe.

Prophetic warning points to the consequences of inertial momentum in both motion (physics) and emotions (poetics); the promise of reprieve is tied to the freedom of preparing the future in a perspective refracted by insight into both. The would-be prophet is a seeker for truth bestriding presentiment of doom and promise of deliverance, willingly tied with one hand to the chain of necessity but pointing with the other to the possibility of release through choice. His is a quest for a temporal-historical dimension of human experience that, together with and beyond the ahistorical-extratemporal striving and suffering emblematic of tragedy, would impart a meaning to the narrowly factual-empirical propellants and the austerely schematic patterns of change amounting to evolution. The added meaning that combines temporality and transcendence is to be looked for in a central event toward which history moves through not wholly secret rhythms: rhythms that combine contradiction and concordance in ways discernible to a philosophy of history – or meta-history. The intuited central event in the progressing and regressing movement of time is a conceptual counterpart to the intangible center of gravity in space: the bodies politic of unequal mass revolving around that center do so in a constant sum of motion that corresponds to the historically enacted momentum which, in keeping with the postulate of a constant sum of conflictually channeled energy in a particular system over a definite period of time, is both sufficient and necessary to sustain prophetic premonitions.

Relating prophecy to its components reduces the amorphousness which is its most conspicuous feature when it is viewed as impressionistic in nature and arbitrary in direction and destination. The shapelessness is still less when the several components are seen as linked unevenly to the discrete facets of prophecy. Thus the necessitarian laws of physics suit best prophecy as the premonition of doom, based on the projection of continuing tendencies in interstate dynamics into future contingencies within an unchanging arena of action and motivation of actors. Poetics as the summation of and abstraction from plots that are only probable in keeping with the qualified laws of moral necessity, enlarges the scope for more benign prophecy: it holds out a promise of even but contingent deliverance for actors who deliberately will themselves into shaping the arena as protagonists lucidly grappling with fortune, instead of being swayed by a narrowed focus on the structure of power in the arena as helpless puppets of fate. And, finally, history as the record of all that was or seemed to be possible expands the alternatives further to include developments capable of sidestepping not only doom but also false deliverance in an order that did better than pile up grounds for redeeming catharsis by postponing terminal catastrophe. A mere simulation of genuine impulses (political physics) will have replaced in the deficient order active imitation of tragic drama (poetics). It will continue to deteriorate in keeping with yet another analogy-capable law of physics, suggesting deterioration for any system that has been left too long to the play of unconsummated tendencies and debilitated energies.

A prophecy keyed to averting doom by avoiding the perpetuation of past patterns growing out of mechanical and moral compulsions, must point to a middle ground from which to mediate between utopia and myth, progress and regression, so that ingrained tendencies may be redirected toward opening up auspicious new possibilities. And if the mediatory middle ground is to be more than illusion and stimulate imagination, it will have to have a significant relationship to a central event in history: one that imparts to the flow of events a substantive meaning and fits into, while it complements, the ethical meaning implicit in tragedy. The two kinds of meaning merge when they converge in, and sustain a prophecy focused on, an originating curse that overhangs protagonists and plot in the dramatic universe of tragedy, and must be lifted before the tragic cycle can be closed.

The fact that the most pervasive curse of interstate relations resides in the very structure of the system inviting competitive search for the means of self-preservation by acts construable as provocation is the cardinal reason for the tragic mode of international politics. It also attenuates the shared guilt, or only responsibility, implicit in the inevitable error of pursuing greater security than is consistent with the structure and nature of the system and with the human condition overall. An effort to attenuate the working of the fundamental curse in the actual history of particular states must address the curse's more particular manifestation, one which converts the inevitable error into a redeemable original crime. In the modern Eurocentric system, such a "crime" can be traced to the murderous assault on that system's late medieval Spanish progenitor by jealous early modern rivals, condemned to enact the ensuing schisms within a henceforth too deeply divided common house. Since Spain uniquely fused the secular and the sacral, the continental and the maritime, and the western and the eastern (Islamic) elements, disrupting the unity meant setting the paired phenomena against each other in sharpened conflict: the secular against the sacral within societies, land- and sea-based power among states, and East and West between cultures. Being the main assailants, France and England (or the Dutch and English so-called Maritime Powers) with the German Protestants in the background were fittingly the first to bear, struggling, the burden of the contested inheritance.

In the concluding enactment of the struggle that was to unfold in three sequential parts within a strategically crucial triangle among actors embodying different types of power and ethos, Russia or America were the last Europe-derived powers that could, by replicating the synthesis achieved by imperial Spain, bring the globally ramifying Europe-centered international system back to its starting point either unilaterally or jointly. In the Aeschylean tragic drama which convention confined to three actors, action depicting the crescendo of terror extended over a trilogy before the original curse could be lifted in the concluding play. Just as in theatrical drama so in the real world of politics a curse can be lifted only as the conflict is resolved and passions are appeased by one of two kinds of denouement: through reconciliation entailing absolution for the incurred guilt (*The Eumenides* in the *Oresteia* and/or *Oedipus at Colonus* in the Sophoclean variant on the Theban trilogy); or through sacrifice, when the last surviving generation of the doomed race of protagonists perishes in fratricidal contest (*Seven Against Thebes* in Aeschylus' Theban trilogy).

Were the cycle of land–sea power conflicts to end through the self-annihilation of America and Russia in fratricidal *agon*, it would mean that the ambiguities flowing from their being linked by essential identity (as imperial powers) and opposed by situational disparity (as primarily insular and continental powers) made both equally self-deceived about the nature of the stakes: the threats as well as opportunities. The greater weight of the error would fall on the challenging land power, the prime tragic hero, as its greater (love–hate) ambivalence toward the adversary injected a more deeply frustrated passion into the appearance of aggression. The incumbent sea power on its part would have increased its share of responsibility because it had failed to act in ways mandated by its psychological and material advantage. The different kinds of hubris and the shared *hamartia* would work in favor of actors not necessarily subject to either of the schisms and almost certainly not cast in the cultural mode of the West, shaped by the very ambition to relate the mundane to the ideal that is the heart of tragedy. For the two Europe-derived powers to close instead the conflict cycle by restoring the lost synthesis in concert would entail first loosening tragedy's tightening knot. For this to happen, a strategy keyed to continuing system evolution had to address both sides of a twin menace: diffuse anarchy, engendered by too sudden and uncompensated relaxation of the collision between great powers which imposes elementary disciplines on lesser states; and concentrated hubris, displayed by any one great power impelled by acts of the other or others to seek exit from the tragic nexus through a door to be forced open by the acquisition of sole mastery.

Genuine progress toward a truly new world order that was more than "new diplomacy" could be wrought only by taming primeval mythological–demonic urges and forces (the pre-Olympian Furies of Aeschylus' *Eumenides*) even while conceding them a place in realizing feasibly utopian precepts and perspectives. Were such innovation to preside over appeasement in the West expressing revulsion from common threats, this would reflect both the impulsions and the reactions peculiar to political physics, bequeathed by history, being augmented by futuristic technology as well as illuminated by an enhanced sense of timeless poetics in the newly favorable conditions in space and time. Consisting of the enlarged continental expanse of the United States (as compared with Britain's) and the less immediate pressure on Russia from China (as compared with that from Russia on Germany), the relaxed setting allowed the existential space-time relativity of the higher kind of political physics and the ethical relativity implicit in the poetics of politics to be combined in a three-step dialectical thinking about policy, one that incorporates into each party's reactions to the other's action an anticipatory awareness of the reaction's conflict- or crisis-aggravating secondary effects.

Both individual and collective destiny, disclosed through evolution, can be affected by tragedy mainly through learning from the striving-and-suffering that supplies the clear ethical meaning to politics; the grasp of the more shadowy meaning conveyed by history supplies an understanding of the peripeties through which learning can occur and its product become history. The meta-physics of poetics is thus the vital complement of philosophical meta-history, and the other way round. They converge in a complete historical intelligence, supplemental to the strategic rationality that impels the daily drama of politics.

Prophecy entails history as something both lower and higher than political physics and transposed poetics. History is lower as a story that narrates (Homer-like) in the epic mode a sequence of extraordinary events – thus the "rise" of the Anglo-American peoples to providentially decreed ascendancy – rather than refining the events (Thucydides-like) into a tragic plot – thus the escalating embroilment of the two Anglo-Saxon maritime actors with their continental counterparts, portending the "fall" of the West after encompassing the decline of Europe. Whereas the epic narrative deals discursively with what is particular in actuality, poeticized history addresses (as does politicized physics) the universal in a sufficiently concentrated manner to permit inferring from the facts the fatally necessary reasons behind them. Yet history is also higher than either transposed physics or applied poetics when the object is to distill the record of accomplished evolution into transcendent rhythms of meta-history. The needed intelligence must then infuse instrumental rationality with tragic knowledge as it seeks to understand both the compulsions inhering in the natural-physical and the imperatives peculiar to the moral order. As the supply arsenal of such intelligence, the data of history import indispensable concreteness into the laws of political physics and the entanglements that are the stuff of poetics. History injects thus through them a needed specificity into prophecy that would transpose evidence from both completed and ongoing present drama into a disciplined divination of destiny. History as a past–present–future continuum stands thus for the greatest of theaters and highest of tribunals. It discloses the rules of drama and the action of players while acting as the high court for finally arbitrating individual misjudgments.

Being both lower and higher than transposed physics and poetics, facts-transcending history is complementary with both. It is complementary with political physics because it illustrates the operation of quasi-physical laws of power of which it is not the sole or even the main source, and because the operation of these laws propels history forward without being its sole stimulus. If political dynamics supplies a major key to comprehending theoretically the fundamental underpinnings and the core mechanism of interstate relations, its classic formulation provides an incomplete understanding because an only partial explanation of these relations. Poetics contributes to further understanding through its association with histrionic sensibility, which projects interstate relations graphically onto a dramatic stage by a feat of imaginative imitation. Duly transposed and transmuted, physics and poetics subserve historical intelligence in its task of tracing interstate relations through structures conditioning strategies and cyclical stages of evolution in the real world. History and tragedy produce each a distinct form of knowledge from the contemplation of a continuous past strung together by a repetitive plot; the compounded knowledge ideally informs without disarming the instinctually driven pursuit of inherently unlimited near-physical needs (to be appeased by a surplus) within a circumscribed universe (marked by scarcity).

Both the insights and the instincts are encompassed in the exemplary kind of vision that inspirits disciplined prophecy keyed to expanding choices. The ability to draw on such prophecy presupposes the capacity to moderate conflict by exploiting any real change in the nature of politics and exhibiting the highest form of maturity. If actors are to make productive use of real change, they must first come to terms with their differential time-space reference systems expressing unequal situations and stages of evolution. This is especially crucial for unevenly evolved land- and sea-oriented powers whose inability to disengage by each withdrawing into its prime element ties the tragic knot all the more tightly. And if the actors are to consummate their maturation, they must have ascended, through intellectual comprehension of the shared entanglement, from achieving internal consolidation to experiencing mutual compassion. That kind of maturity runs deeper than one that qualifies for rationally implemented conservative balance-of-power foreign policy; it will more commonly, but then futilely, follow upon decline from a climactic drive introducing withdrawal from active engagement in world politics. However, when achieved in time, tragic insight is the most genuinely normative force in interstate relations, surpassing legal-institutional codifications of conventional morality. Although the insight does not foster the onset of progressist utopia of a vastly expanded freedom to cultivate the harmonies, it does militate against mytho-normative exaltation of conflictual necessities. By enlarging ever so little the exit from automatic recurrence of conflicts in a self-perpetuating series, tragic insight is the surest antidote to rationalizing instinctual reflexes in either the progressive or the regressive mode.

Fostered by learning from past tragedies, the insight is sustained by a sense of awe at the consequences of entanglement that remains after the immediate feeling of terror has passed through purifying catharsis. Awe is felt all the more intensely the more the tragic plot has unfolded in a context (systemic setting) and process (interaction and evolution) that assume the character of impersonal fate by ordaining catastrophic results no one has fully intended. A calamitous issue of the discrepancy between intentions and results is the malignant obverse of equilibrium emerging unintended from moderately competing assertions of individual self-interests. If the more benign outcome is undramatic and achieved incrementally, the discrepancy peculiar to tragedy will be brought to light by the reversal from auspicious to ominous trends and from favorable to adverse outcomes: for the would-be hegemon suddenly and for the other major-power contenders more gradually and in succession. To the extent that the deeds, rooted in misapprehension of either the extent of achievable security or the level of actual threat from the adversary, were founded in error, the measure of the ensuing doom is all the more awesome for being on the face of it undeserved. As the tragic plot ascends towards its climax, to avert catastrophe will demand reducing passions and relieving emotions by reasoned recognition of the true character of the crisis. Only then can a chain of events initiated by flawed purposes and forged stronger by rising passions be broken by acts expressing righted perception. However, for the actors to see things plainly in time, the fear and pity aroused by the near-certain consequences of persisting in the error must come before missing the last occasion for a liberating choice has begun the unstoppable onrush of fatality.

Discourse 10   On Structure and Spirit in Complete Politics

A realistic philosophy of history is the infrastructure supporting plausible, portentous or redemptive, prophecy and pointing toward enlightened policy. In the light of such philosophy the sixteenth- to seventeenth-century Spanish Empire stands out as the central event toward which post-Roman Empire Europe had evolved before the Euro-Atlantic world began to unravel in a series of land–sea power conflicts liable to culminate in terminal catastrophe. The saving alternative is for that same empire to be seen as but the first and, because premature, abortive high point, significant mainly as a model for reconstituting a comparable focus of order in circumstances that are more enlarged than fundamentally altered. At the moment of transition from high Middle Ages to early modernity, the Spanish Empire with its absorbed Portuguese and co-opted Italian adjuncts linked the twilight of feudalism's inner genius to the first dawn of maritime-mercantile capitalism on a global scale. Thus also the present age marks the passage beyond a late stage of traditional industrialism and classic liberalism in conditions that have turned upside down the medieval combination of spiritual universalism and material or economic localism. If order spreading out from a core will as ever have to rest on a central synthesis, embodied in an identifiable political phenomenon, it could not derive from either a desiccated official ideology such as the Soviet or a ritualized civic myth such as the American. It can derive better or only from a synthesizing confluence of power and values of the two still-viable polities that represent the main contemporary varieties of geo-historically shaped political experience and types of power in existence – as it happens, at the extreme outposts of the West in its largest scope.

The main difference between conventional domestic politics and crises-prone foreign affairs is the same as that between comedy and tragedy. Whereas mistakes committed in the second-named settings are grave, and once made cannot be easily undone past a definite point in time, events in the first-named settings, or when the two are combined in the routines of domestic politicking, revolve around relatively benign confusions of mistaken purposes or identities. They will eventually be in most instances brought under control in a comparatively painless resolution of a plot that is commonly no more than tragicomical at its most serious. The intricate cross-purposes that make up the stuff of routine domestic politics become stark crossroads when the dramatic focus shifts to foreign statecraft and national survival.

The gravity of periodically arising major choices imposes an equally grave responsibility upon alternative ways of thinking about international politics. Such thinking has a social value only insofar as it aids the making of policy by rising above tactical reflection and instant gain–loss calculations and, in doing so, expands its frame of reference to processes transcending the immediately pressing contingency. Academic standards of valid theory must be relaxed, in favor of conceptually informed mere understanding, if such is the condition of making comprehensive thought formulate the bases for the higher kind of policy. This will mean complementing analytic penetration of ongoing interactions with contemplative perspective on their background in factors and features pertaining to evolution. And to penetration and perspective will have to be added compassionate probing into the moral-psychological sources and stresses of conduct. Insofar as these differentiate the driving passion behind ultimate purpose from the calculating deliberations sustaining the surfaces of policy, they set the role of spirit apart from that of structure in swaying policy and molding process through policies. Better to understand methods and estimate motives rightly requires delving into the historically shaped intimate moods of societies that propel states through the agency of daring statesman toward the peaks of effort and risk. No amount of scientific rigor or sophisticated rumination can fill the void created by absence of sympathy when acts and actors strain at the leash of prudence in their vaulting leap into ordeal. To participate instead feelingly in the dramas through which the actors' dilemmas are transmuted into their destinies enriches the historical sense with histrionic sensibility. Each is and both are at the antipodes from the cheap theatricality of an ahistorically melodramatic, Manichean conception of relations among "good" and bad" states at one extreme and from the facile rigorism of the but covertly moralizing, mechanistic conception of the actions of states as "offensive" and "defensive" at another extreme.

It follows that political realism cannot be divorced from a realistic philosophy of history that imitates in the real world the theater of tragedy, and be reduced instead to the cold directives of *realpolitik*. The equilibrium internal to political realism can be only deranged by placing all of the analytic weight upon the dictates emanating from balance-of-power mechanics; its external setting in culture be only debased by reducing cultural differences to institutionally channeled managerial aptitudes. The expanded variety of realism will be guardedly romantic in an effort to encompass the Machiavellian dialectic of strong manly will, capricious chance, and compelling necessity – a dialectic that sums up the themes of tragic poetry for practicing statecraft. And the outlook that suits best a philosophy of history that romanticizes realism by reuniting it with the feelings aroused by tragedy and crystallized in culture will be one genuinely conservative. To transpose the predilection for nursing extant if latent trends and for organic healing of viable bodies politic into the international arena is the opposite of both utopian blueprints for and surgical shortcuts to stress-free national existence. In politics this will mean promoting continuities in ways that contain upheavals and avert catastrophes without blocking long-maturing changes in the configuration of power and hierarchy of values. In eschewing the cult of the ostensibly rational as much as of the seemingly pragmatic, conservatively biased policy thinking will opt for implementing the reason of state in ways that respect and seek to realize statecraft's still higher reason for existence.

Exploring the growth and decline of alternately westward- and eastward-moving centers of equilibrium and the conditions of evolution as they affect the West in its largest compass in a thus delimited philosophical perspective is bound to be imcomplete. It is more than necessarily so when it leaves in shadowy background the schematically comparable structures and processes within the global East, only uncertainly different in its governing substantive values, and when it downplays the instrumentally crucial arms-centered equations, controversially connected to the political ones in terms of action-determinant priorities. However, even as divided, the globally defined West was still the center of the world system; even when most threatening, a nuclear disaster has not been the most likely cause of the West's premature demise. The latter was more likely to ensue from divisions having been deepened by concentrating ingenuity on adjusting nuclear-strategic equations in the context of esoterically technical arms-related speculation, and perpetuated by confining the approach to political issues to half-assimilated traditional canons of prudently staged diplomatic negotiations. Separating military strategics from comprehensively construed politics, and decomposing the political whole into negotiable particles, in an effort to be also scientific or only pragmatic, meant fragmenting reality perceptually into separate pieces as part of a methodological pluralism prefiguring real-world anarchy. The alternative was to break up reality analytically into facets of a composite held together by internal coherence, and do this at a level of abstraction and schematization that did not prevent reassembling the facets into a sense of the total structure and process that could inspire attempts at policy-wrought synthesis.

The relevance of schematized history for synthesizing policy rests on a wager that projecting contemporary ambiguities against a range of structures and patterns of transformation abstracted from the record of the past has utility, if only to reduce confusions engendered by viewing the present in terms of itself alone. The procedure implements the perception of the nature of world politics as if continuous, rooted in the enduring possibility of major war; and both, perception and procedure, confer jointly a warrant on the objective of foreclosing a particular major war by virtue of a diplomatic strategy selected as if the historically disclosed structures were fully operative and their problematic becoming was tantamount to accomplished being. The apparent contradiction implicit in imputing a definite and determining structure to an actuality in transition from one partly indeterminate to one unpredictable in specific parts (and in thus resuscitating historically validated patterns that invariably led to wars for the purpose of avoiding the incidence of a particular one) is resolved through the agency of two temporalities within a fundamentally unchanged continental–oceanic space: if the ambiguities are largely due to the brevity of the time during which the global system has so far been able to assume definite shape through either interactions or evolution, the practical object of evading the principal penalty inexorably attached to patterns more firmly articulated in the past is made in principle feasible by the new latitudes owed to the expanding length of available future time. The reason for it is lodged, more deeply than in the explosive potential of military technology, in the limited intensity and confused identity of traditionally evolution-accelerating crises and conflicts – a respite that, due not least to the existential attributes of the powers flanking the West-to-East geo-functional spectrum, offered a transitory chance to avoid repeating one facet of history by virtue of apprehending its structure-conditioned processes as a whole.

Distinctly structuralist will be any approach that favors the role of configuration in conditioning-to-determining events, as an alternative to searching for cause–effect interlocks reducible to correlations between any two factors. However, the structures to be identified are not sufficiently defined and differentiated quantitatively, in terms of either the number of poles of power (making a system uni- through bi- to multi-polar) or magnitudes of the polarity-constituting actors (as big or small), and must be defined also qualitatively, encompassing uneven rise and decline of actors set apart as mainly continental (agro-military) and insular (maritime-mercantile) in substance or situation and either western and eastern or secular and (quasi-) sacralized in values and institutions. A thus differentiated portrayal ramifies naturally from significant power relationships between actors into distinctive authority and inter-group structures within them, the two being linked through sequential foreign-policy postures in the overall setting of an evolution that is itself structured (i.e., differentiated by discernible stages or phases).

Refusing to reduce conditioning-to-determining factors to either functionally-instrumentally or quantitatively specific ones is made easier by their being subsumed in the qualitatively biased multi-structural framework. Thus the polar structure model is implicit in the triangular insular–amphibious continental–rear-continental configuration; the economically defined structures (e.g. in terms of core, semi-periphery, periphery) are comprised in the conception of the land–sea power contest as one actually taking place over both economically and geostrategically peripheral areas in either association or competition with a rear-continental power typically semi-peripheral economically as well as relatively eastern culturally-institutionally; the military-technological and -strategic factor is accounted for through the reliance of land- and sea-oriented powers on qualitatively distinct military technologies and/or strategies in unevenly prized battleground arenas, as part of quantitatively disparate reliance on the military relative to other instruments of policy; and, finally, the domestic-institutional factor is subsumed, next to the different internal concomitants of successive foreign-policy postures, through the different types of (continental and insular, western and eastern, and to an extent narrowly secular and diffusely sacralized) actors. Each entails different (and generationally changing) ways of organizing and asserting authority for dealing with either distinctive or shared tasks of societal consolidation, as these tasks relate to interstate conflict at different stages of development.

Encompassing the various facets within an inclusively total structure augments the complexity of the analysis and permits only suggestive portrayals of the interconnections. The same is the case when a cyclical perspective is not confined to any one single factor or relation and is integrated instead into an inclusive model of evolutionary progression. Compensating for the complexity of a cyclically slanted multi-structural approach is that it helps avoid alternative pitfalls. One is the attraction of functionally or instrumentally biased utopias: next to a presentist utopia, in terms of which traditional international relations are seen as transformed by currently dominant military technologies, is a futurist one which posits the fast-approaching possibility to replace territory- (or interests-) based with trade- (or institutional norms-) determined patterns of policy priorities and, thus, strategies. Another is the difficulty, or reluctance, to differentiate clearly between the number and the magnitude of actors as they relate to presumptive conditions of system stability – a pitfall peculiar to the quantitatively biased structuralist approach; and yet another is the tendency, in the functionally-instrumentally biased such approach, to attribute proximately determinative force to a particular (economic, military-technological, or other) factor, one better relegated to only ultimately causative role in keeping with the crucial distinction between a structure's organic attributes and its operational manifestation.

Were only narrowly and quantitatively defined structures to determine policies, established structures would not change because policies thus determined would indefinitely sustain the dominant structure. On the other hand, were givens intrinsically distinct from the operational dynamic and the considerations it prompts to determine major events (such as conflict and its containment or avoidance) proximately, rather than only ultimately, power-politically relevant configurations could change constantly for reasons having little or nothing to do with the strategic precepts as traditionally understood and applied by diplomatic actors. Accounting instead for both stability and change, for decisional latitudes and environmentally imposed limitations, requires relating the finite range of diplomatic strategies that implement basic foreign-policy postures to a multi-faceted, qualitatively differentiated total structure – i.e, the operational to the organic dimensions of actor makeup and motivation – with a view to disclosing the uneven (and unevenly re-equilibration-prone or - resistant) "fits" between structure, strategies, and stages of evolution in a given time and place.

Organizing historically validated facts in this fashion means adjusting the requisite of analytical parsimony to the higher one of interpretative potency for the sake of approximating two objectives. One is to explicate the innermost economy of essential politics as it manifests itself in political physics (standing for motion) and poetics (incorporating emotions). Doing this will implicitly reveal the limitations the inner economy imposes, through the medium of rational strategies and strategies-vindicating rationalizations, on achieving through commonsensically reasonable policies a measure of progress sufficient to transform such politics' essence. The other objective is to politicize mere economics within an expanded concept of the political economy of interstate relations. A way of doing this is to subsume the economic factor in the politics of the land–sea power schism whenever this most materially conditioned and pragmatically enacted of schisms was operative and its geo-historically conditioned manifestations acted as the medium for injecting value-institutional differences peculiar to the other two key (sacral–secular and East–West) schisms into the complex web of world politics.

For the effort to unravel the attendant complexities while linking theory to praxis in ways that allow a philosophically deepened and historically informed realism to assist pragmatic *realpolitik*, the reality of (great-) power politics has first to be disclosed by complexity-simplifying crises: conjunctures which reduce alternatives to the austere choice between a prolonged conflict of rival purposes, relieved only by the prospect of eventual convergence as part of unevenly timed mutual enfeeblement, and a bid for solitary predominance, portending the certainty of immediate defeat or eventual dissolution. The resulting predicaments remained in force even though the high-tension politics would repeatedly lapse into a self-correcting comedy of errors between crises or as part of inane responses to misjudged crisis, whenever more-than-commonplace ambiguities pervaded dominant polarities and greater-than-usual ambivalence informed the ensuing actor propensities. When this happens, structure is depleted of heightened spirit and world politics mutates from an absorbing public theater into the backdrop for gradually reassembling the elements of dramatic action.

So far, the intervening pause has always ended in the rationale of policy escalating from less-than-vital national interests to fundamental public values when the territorial state was reinstated in its full status: as the central repository of the values, because the indispensable shelter of last resort from manifold individual anxieties and multi-layered environing uncertainties. It was in function of its role in serving basic human needs that the territorial state reached this status by a process of devolution wherein periodic surrogation mediated an uncompleted secularization: a long process, which had begun in the cities-owning gods of Mesopotamia believed to act quasi-politically among themselves in behalf of inchoate social organisms in lieu of worldly authorities; was continued via the anthropomorphic gods of the Greeks only interfering, but then personally, in mundane inter-city conflicts, pending the divine power's reduction in medieval to early modern Europe to being vicariously represented on earth by lay monarchical agents displacing priestly ones; and climaxed when the state-like organization of ever more broadly based societal management became itself the object of politically expressed quasi-religious worship. It was in keeping with this process of surrogation that viewing the political process through the prism of an epic saga of the god-favored, which incarnated the early-stage protean social organism's susceptibility to inordinate expansion on pain of likewise sudden collapse, gave repeatedly way at critical turning points to impressing relations among territorially fixed state-like organisms with the tragic form of sustained and ultimately unwinnable confrontations.

Restoring a thus underpinned reason of state again and again to ideal dominance, and the principles implementing it to practical observance, from first intermittent and then cumulative erosions of physical insecurity, mundane authority, and transcendent myth meant reactivating each time around the pattern of operations that fuel evolution by being both essentially orderly and inherently dramatic: orderly, because predictable as to the kinds of reactions apt to follow upon status-quo-disturbing actions as well as types of penalties to be imposed upon pretensions to means-deficient ends; and dramatic, as the dynamics of balancing power was infused with the poetics vested in colliding values to compound mechanical equilibrium with tragic entanglement.

The recurrence of crises which restore tradition and accelerate evolution militates thus against even real changes debouching into a definitive trans- formation of world politics within a span of time relevant for either grand theory or high policy. For world politics to be altered irreversibly in kind will require that man be transformed first: not in his "nature," as confusedly social and asocial, but in his relation to and valuation of the state and *its* nature, as also emotionally significant or only instrumentally convenient. Evidencing such fundamental mutation as one that has taken place, the organic factor – the actual distribution of fluctuating actor capabilities – must have definitively prevailed over the operational process, implementing the capability–role congruence and resource–risk trade-off, with the result that disparities between the two (organic and operational) planes will have ceased triggering major wars. If this meant that politico-militarily manifested or, at least, relevant primacy (amounting to or stopping somewhat short of hegemony) had to be at least once peaceably relinquished by one and assumed by another major power, it also meant that any future derangement on the organic plane amounting to a crisis in the world economy must have failed to reactivate the traditional modalities of the operational dimension. For the latter change to materialize, the representative actors must not so much impede the transfer of outward primacy away from themselves as they must renounce shifting internal problems onto others and avoid falling back themselves on remedial crisis-type domestic governance.

It is ironic that the blameable remedy was in the future most likely to tempt and the relapse tarnish polities that, sidestepping key stages of evolution by favor of an abnormally peaceful and prosperous global environment, will have missed the progression's tempering effects. This prospective liability reinforced doubts based on the fragility of evidence for the supposedly benign effects of economic priorities extracted from the past, insofar as the exemplary collectives were by contrast those that had traversed the main developmental stages, and have since entered into corporate decline and incurred systemic marginality. This being so, a militant reversion to traditional world politics has remained more than possible; it became probable when previous fading of traditional concerns transposed the dialectic between ostensibly offensive initiatives and allegedly defensive responses from the realm of military-strategic self-protection onto one susceptible to economic protectionism. For politico-military alliances to cease moderating economic rivalry among some (the allied) states placed the alliance of apolitical economism with societal pluralism in jeopardy. The formula risked foundering on the revival of remedial authoritarianism and diversionary militarism on the part of some or all (previously de-aligned) parties, such revival being the shape of the revenge a prematurely discarded statecraft wrought on its detractors and replacements. An all to casually indicted culprit, a belatedly redeployed interstate system could become the principal casualty. With it would disappear an existential framework wherein formal anarchy imposes conduct that is rigorously ordered even when not superficially orderly and occasional disarray is contained short of chaos, a dynamic invigorated at all times by the survival-related necessity for actors to anchor corporate autonomy in self-help, but also moderated by encouraging them to implement necessity in ways that did not frustrate means, defeat interests, and pervert values through excesses in their application.

In conditions that might pass for an unprecedented era of radical change in styles and stakes of action denoting a henceforth irreversible progress, the different varieties of realism embraced and practiced by individual actors reflected more markedly than ever the parties' positions within the several schisms and on the rise–decline curve: one location conditioning the value-institutional makeups to be related to their contrasting-overlapping near-opposites, the other determining the disposable resource to be matched with incurred or invited risks. So long as a conventional method of inquiry was stretched to the outer boundaries of its interpretative potential, it could diagnose next to the authenticity of the purported transformation also the acceptability of what the change implied and did thus portend to differently situated and evolved actors. Moreover, the traditional method remained indispensable not only if progression was to be monitored and deviation from familiar patterns measured ever so crudely, but also if utopia was to be shielded from the nemesis lurking in any headlong rush toward overfulfilling a wish and collecting too soon on the overhanging promise. In world politics the wish and the promise meet in the uncertain chance of choosing rightly when renouncing cyclically unfolding progression in favor of circular return to an original myth: the laborious quietude of the prehistoric rural village, reborn in the industriously vibrant global village exempt from the predators preying on pacific villagers from the environing hills.

Conclusion
Toward a Phenomenology of World Politics

Regardless of whether the sanguine predicter of progress emplaces the Golden Age in a mythical past or a beckoning future, he risks seeing the postulated best realize the gloomy prophet's premonition of the worst. In world politics a descent from community to calamity was latent in post-modern man's crowning arrogance, itself rooted in an error: the presumption of being freed at no vitiating cost of the compulsions and the commitments that, even when scaled down from the civic cult of the state to a sobered *sens de l'Etat*, made historic man no less proudly individual and responsibly social for enabling him to remain residually – but, then, authentically – spiritual. When such cardinal options loom in a widely envisioned future, the task of scholarly inquiry is correspondingly enhanced. In relation to the practicing statesman, the task was henceforth to help seek for ways to relax the bond between power politics and tragedy in ways that did not abrogate along with the politics of power the positive, alternately stimulating and disciplining, tension contained in the tragic knot; in relation to the participant society, the task was to supply less a theory than an understanding, one that provoked a wiser response to the predicaments that make up the tragic poetry of power than facile indignation at the policy-maker's unreasonable stubbornness in defeating enlightenment by cultivating senseless turbulence.

The search for understanding with the help of, but also past and beyond, surface phenomena does not point to rigorously demonstrating either the specifics or the immutably valid characteristics of world politics. Truths of this kind are not germane to a reality wherein problems susceptible of rationally guided solution (implicit in the crisis-driven operational dynamic) are surrounded by a residuum of inexplicable mystery (present beyond identifiable causes or determinants of action and peculiar to especially the decline side of evolution). To reduce the scope of mystery without obscuring its site and prejudicing efforts at easing attendant predicaments is the paramount objective of a method intended to do more than abstract recurrent patterns from observable phenomena: to also disclose the more continuous underlying processes and help intuit the relatively most constant essence of world politics. Compounding all of these are the ways of power that bring into the open contending expressions of the will to power; and do so in a manner which permits reaching beyond the ostensible patterns of evolving interactions for potentialities that convey or imply a meaning – or a hierarchy of meanings.

<h2 style="text-align:center">THE FIRST LEVEL OF MEANING</h2>

Within the hierarchy, a meaning of world politics to be guessed at from the vantage point of the state system at any present moment in its progression through historical time is different from, and in the last resort subsidiary to, the ultimate meaning of man's active political engagement in the world that transcends the historically evolved inter-actor system. Beyond either progress or mere progression, at issue is then a categorical mutation; past the particular transformations or mere tendencies mediating real existential change, an essentially altered reality.

Identifying the lower kind of meaning as one to be consummated in Russo–American accommodation and concert flows directly from the ways past triangularized schismatic conflicts had been taking shape over the longest term before climaxing in modern European history and, in it, in the Anglo–German conflict; after which, relaxation of the conditions impelling conflict could conspire with full revelation of past causes and consequences of the contentions to prompt a remedial response – lest the expanded range of choices be again undone through even the fragile past restraints being abolished in a fresh series of conflicts converging in space along an inverted, east-to-west, axis in lieu of a mutually enriching inter-civilizational dialectic unfolding in time. It will advance the latter alternative if, to begin with, the age's Rome and Macedon, America and Russia, were to meet in Europe as something else than rivals. To do so was more meaningful than for them to clash to third-party advantage or for modern Rome, orientalized prematurely in strategic priorities and de-Europeanized in dominant cultural personality, to relinquish the place to an increasingly occidentalized and Europeanized modern Macedon alone. By the same token, the direct heirs to classic Europe had to build on the inheritance something superior to the institutional fabric of economic self-aggrandizement. Outperforming the Hellenes' role in the Hellen*istic* meant doing more than prosper ever more materially and predominate ever less culturally within a European*istic* component of a reshaped world balance of power.

Such a balance sustaining henceforth an evolving multi-civilizational world order was the far-from-assured alternative to its degenerating again, once bereft of the scrambling effect of Russian "expansionism" on alliances, into wildly see-sawing or rigidly frozen inter-civilizational (if not -racial) polarization. Consequently, if the West was to retain a role and preserve relevance in either, the balance or the order, grafting psychologically "younger" offshoots on "old" Europe was history's counsel in a world which had ceased to be Europe-centered in powers of decision and remained only contingently Europeanist in its procedural norms and value hierarchies. The heroic era of classic Europe as a power – symbol and proof of human potency to sow the seeds but look beyond the fruits of prosperity – spanned the centuries from Charlemagne to Charles de Gaulle: from an achievement that had been premature to an effort to revive it in full that came too late. Henceforth, only a Europe expanded beyond the "Frankish" core could reinfuse some of the old spirit into a new kind of material substance if, improving in sufficient time on the Greeks, she adjusted to enlarged scale and heightened complexity the responses her medieval founders offered to the extraneous challenges from east to north that had engulfed the fragile Carolingian renaissance. This meant that the western engaged with the eastern half of Europe untouched by Rome so that the latter might attempt more, while being expected to endure less, than merely absorb unaided the shocks emanating from a more driven and better organized East. It meant also that, the two halves having successively absorbed some of the outward-thrusting energy that had twice brought to Europe's western shores the raw seafarers from across the northern sea, they helped renovate that energy and through it Europe herself.

For Europe to be enlarged and in the process transfigured, she could be neither squeezed between America and Russia as before nor could she try to squeeze out first one and then the other so as to ground successful economism in rediscovered neutralism. To continue instead her immediate antecedent's productive role in systemic evolution on a global basis was to add one more link to a chain connecting the Greek (if not still earlier) to the Italian and the latter to the classic core-European state system. And for the continuing quantitative enlargement in the territorial scope of each of the successive systems' meta-systemization to coincide with accentuating any prior shift from the terminal stage's empire to its communal genre implied the long-range possibility of qualitative change world-wide. However, for an updated "Europe" to recover a full part in releasing and directing the motor energy behind the crises attending transformation, the core of historic Europe had to re-examine the prematurely assumed (or imputed) role of a "transnational" model. Immediately irrelevant because irreproducible on a wider basis, the model was inherently imperfect so long as, "community" remaining mainly economic and institutional, it represented the highest stage in the conquest of the state (in its attributes and functions) by society (and its material foundations and aspirations) to the detriment of spirit (capable of integrating the two only when mobilizing the immaterial aura of power for its mundane affirmation).

This being so, before the western part of Europe could advance meaningful evolution globally beyond the residually still proto-systemic stage, it had to pause first, regress from the point of meta-systemization it had already achieved in values and attitudes, and halt if not push back some of the anticipated progressive steps in institutions and functions, so as to enable the west European polities to address individually as well as in combination two interconnected tasks: position themselves for the transfer of the transformation-attending crises from East–West divisions in Europe to the East–West dynamic globally and the East–East dialectic in Asia; and rebuild, as part of the transition, ties with the relatively retrograde cultures in Europe's eastern half, which have not yet adopted fully the de-politicized post-norm behavior mode and where the region's native great power has stalled at an earlier, unequivocally pre-withdrawal, phase in foreign policy posture.

In the heart of Europe, to regress part of the way from the economics of the market to the politics of power, from fomenting societal pluralism to facing up to the plurality of states, was mandated by the persistence of the German question: keeping Germany's options open was as mandatory as to keep the capacity of the intra-European balance of power to adapt elastically to the question's evolution intact. The theoretical alternative in re-politicizing the European community by advancing it toward a unitary super-state, was not a practical one. It was not such so long as, were the Leviathan to take shape before West Germany absorbed East Germany, this would bring to a head the former's choice between obligations in western and opportunities in eastern Europe across the full range of concerns, from inter-nation trade to national tradition. The necessity to choose would overburden internal cohesion, and an unequivocal choice would not necessarily favor equally recent and fragile links to the West, as barriers to unification were being lowered in the East. Nor were the prospects brighter should dramatic advances toward western European consolidation coincide with like moves toward German unification. A nascent super-state would then be as much subject to dissolution as Europe as a whole would be to multiple re-division, if not outright repolarization: a unified Germany, though overly strong only economically to begin with, would be no easier to assimilate than was the Germany emerging out of economic collapse – least of all in a Europe bereft of the Russian weight.

If this meant that Russian presence in Europe west of the Soviet–Polish border was the necessary safeguard against all eventualities, and that mediating the presence through continued Russian involvement in east-central Europe was preferable to Russo–German confrontation across an intervening power vacuum, it also meant that the US–Soviet relationship had to be reshaped. The process of reconstructing the Occident engaged inevitably, directly or by proxy, all of the five historic European great powers in their remaining or reviving strength.

First France, a *grande nation* not least because the model European state through its successive stages and thus the indispensable fountainhead of legitimacy for any future order, from comparative weakness as before from strength. She will continue experimenting, through the Common Market, with one more platform for her nearly two centuries-long refusal to accept the consequences of decline relative to Germany compounding an even more bitter demotion at the hands of the longer-lasting British enemy which had initiated, at her peak, the backsliding from the pride and power of an eastern connection into the softening embrace of a viscerally repugnant Anglo–Saxon-dominated alliance.

Second Great Britain, as she continued to hesitate between a European and an Atlantic future. No longer able to exploit either political divisions on the continent or the material boon from her lead in the first Industrial Revolution, she will continue to resist falling back into her pre-modern position of a strategically redundant offshore island, not needed by a self-sufficient Europe and unwanted by America in conditions short of a US-affecting threat to the global balance. She will thus make up for any diminution in the upheavals France's defiance of the fate common to all powers has long been causing in Europe.

Third West Germany, as she saw reopening, past the failure of Weimar and its Nazi sequelae, the issues last confronted in relative peace and stability by the Second German Reich, and searched anew for identity outside the Atlantic cocoon. She is the troubled heir to the Prussia-centered Bismarckian–Wilhelmine entity that proved too weak to prevail on the seas and too strong to fit into a viable balance on land. The dilemmas Germany will continue posing from a posture of economic exuberance were only superficially different from the dangers her successive imperial incarnations had occasioned in response to different forms of economic frailty.

Fourth Russia, the eastern giant repeatedly causing panic in the West before disclosing its earthen feet. She was caught up once again in the tsarist era's see-saw between regional dominance and regime decadence. Again and again serviceable in redressing the balance of the West in her own depths, many would again expel her from Europe to Asia once she had done her work.

Fifth, deputizing for first the Ottoman and then the Habsburg Empires, the small states located between Russia and Germany. They were again poised between repairing and re-enacting their lot as more victim than agent of Europe's decay between the two world wars. Some of them will again look back nostalgically to the Habsburg formation which, after fulfilling its historic mission *vis-à-vis* the Ottoman East, proved unable to assimilate Slav on an equal basis with Magyar so as to withstand either the weight or the pull of the Germanic north.

And, last but not least, the shadows cast back by Hitler's Third Reich. After brutally terminating the small-state experiment, it propelled into existence the no less brutal totalitarian-collectivist substitute for the liberal-nationalist shortcut to a visionary (Wilsonian) order, to be fashioned between the wars from the formal independence of materially inadequate states. Being an integral part of the era's pathology, the Third Reich's violent solutions prefigured more benign future application of at least some. Wartime integration of west European resources into the Nazi machine was by common consent the model for the European community. Less self-evident was the possibility that Hitler's bid for continental mastery as a springboard for wider dominion did more than enact the decisive phase in the chain of land powers' conflicts with the sea powers. The unconvincing attempt to legitimate continental conquest in the heart of Europe by invoking the medieval Holy Roman Empire suggested a possible blueprint for avoiding the larger conflict's repetition.

The question has since become how to absorb the past, and the present, into the foundations of a viable future order: the wholly defunct or eclipsed elements of the classic modern European variety; the European Community and the pseudo-communal Soviet-centered Comecon, the crypto-hegemonial Atlantic Alliance and the openly imperialistic Warsaw Pact, all unevenly moribund in their original conception if not otherwise; and, finally, Middle Europe's earliest formations openly confessing to being empires and capable of reformed revival. Such future order would mark an end to something more than the Cold War as a mere episode in history and less than the continuing historical drama shaping man's secular destiny. What might – but only might – terminate was the modern era in world politics shaped by the recovery, from the amphibious power of Rome and naval impotence of earlymedieval Europe, of the contentions that were to raise insular Britain to unchallengeable dominion overseas and both disguised and denied hegemony on the continent; all this before the cumulative costs of the attendant exertions brought England to her knees in a "special relationship" and Europe to her demise as the world's power center once the escalating war series had propelled first Russia and then the United States into a decisive role in and the struggle for Europe and the world.

For the modern era shaped by contests between the dominant insular state and the successively leading continental ones to end peacefully inside the Occident would be without precedent, much as it was commonplace for the geopolitical bases of the underlying schism to be concealed by differences in ideologies and sociopolitical systems. Could the western-insular and eastern-continental wings of the Occident utilize novel features of military technology and material capabilities, their socio-economic bases in industrial society and -political expression in democratic polity, to address common concerns in a concerted policy comprising updated elements of also the medieval approach to pluralistic unity?

Were the history of the Eurocentric state system to end in the blaze of conspicuous liberal-capitalist triumph, such a finale would actually mark the victory of materialism as the co-progenitor of liberal ideals and institutions and the principal impetus and temptation behind their self-destructive surge to fulfillment in the materially deprived parts of Europe and the world at large, under the aegis of liberty. This would amount to the final betrayal of an Occident that had been brought to life and was sustained through its formative ordeals by grappling creatively with the never fully bridgeable tension between the actual and the ideal, the material and the spiritual – between the discordant if potentially complementary ambiguities of realism and utopia.

A true dialectic of history does neither produce nor should it postulate the end of history at the time of its fleeting beneficiary's triumph: a liberal French Revolutionary-Napoleonic state one day, a reactively rationalized authoritarianism of the Prussian state the next – and the liberal-capitalist West down the road to euphoria. Proceeding dialectically meant achieving temporary reconciliations of a remoter past with more recent reactions to it in a new departure embodying the best or just survival-worthy in both.

Thus out of the adversities and achievements of the modern age's response to the insufficiently funded aspirations of Europe's Middle Ages could yet arise a unity that combined the material and institutional legacy of one age with the high spiritual content of the other. It can do so by allowing the major reversals, of medieval localism into transnational proto-universalism in economics and of the earlier age's near-genuine universalism into dislocating parochialism in culturally shaped ethics, which define the difference between the two eras, to correct one another in infusing pan-European and -occidental structures with residually vital and still necessary national sources of spirit.

To believe this possible and act accordingly is not to affirm that the ways of power manifested in history are equal in essence and for the purposes of existence to the march of God – call it Spirit – through History. But it does suggest that the dialectic that shapes mundane history is not necessarily forever implemented through the struggle of the separate parts of the Europe-centered and -derived Occident, and of its principal counterpart, among themselves and of the two with each other. But it can only possibly, if helped along by historically informed conscious effort, eventuate in the Mazzinian utopia of mutually complementing national cultures of Europe being transposed onto a larger, first all-occidental and then global, plane as state-forming nations are comprised without being extinguished in culturally distinct and politically integration-capable civilizations.

THE SECOND LEVEL OF MEANING

Precipitating divisive solutions in Europe was least desirable if a reshaped West was in its restored entirety to confront with success and to mutual profit the increasingly state-like polities located still farther afield and occupying still earlier evolutionary states in respect of both manifest behavioral norms and more or less latent psychopolitical drives. To consolidate instead the Occident, however gradually, as a political civilization capable of holding its own against rapidly materializing pressures from the outside was to lay the indispensable initial bases for a more far-reaching eventual transformation that, engaging two discrete levels, might offer relief from traditional predicaments even as it secreted novel challenges.

On the level of process, the emergence of a world community bringing to an end the alternating ascendance of East and West, Europe and Asia, would impart a redemptive meaning to the conflictual dialectic of world politics. It would do so as two interlocking sets of antecedent developments were being incorporated and upgraded in a movement relating European reconstruction to a gradual reduction of differentials in the rates of actor formation (and reformation) and sub-system evolution (or transformation) in the world at large. The longest-term development is represented by the meta-systemization of successive state systems. It pointed to a global future that consummated prior intimations of a secular shift from the empire to the community type of this terminal evolutionary stage, and did so on a spatial basis that continued to expand while the involvement of the superseded system segment grew progressively more active (exceeding the extent to which the part Italy of the Renaissance had in the formation of the European, and that of the Risorgimento in the Eurocentric global, system surpassed the Greek part in the Hellenistic system). The other, medium-term development, covering the so far climactic and thus representative European system of states up to the late symptoms of meta-systemic decay, was bounded by two contrary types of renaissance, enframing intermediate ones. It pointed to a future wherein extraneous challenges following upon a rebirth would again offer the opportunity to correct the imbalance responsible for the restorations being but partial or apparent: by equipping the incremental articulation of Europe's material and organizational foundation, grossly deficient in the predominantly intellectual-cultural Carolingian renaissance, with a political-spiritual foundation so far lacking within the largely but material-organizational infrastructure of the Communitarian renaissance.

In principle at least, greater west European self-assertion that continued and consummated the Gaullist correction of Monnetist principles was compatible with the sublimation of power drives characteristic of meta-systemization in the same, contingent, manner that US–Soviet accommodation in and over Europe as well as globally was with the land–sea power schism. In that context, the relation between an internally lopsided renaissance and broad-based resurgence in response to challenges from the outside implied, next to the mode of implementing the self-assertion, its direction. Accordingly, if the mode consisted of lifting western Europe from mere simulation of high policy by means of energies-stimulating incorporation of a proximate East that performed the function traditional for socio-cultural and territorial marginals in historic states and empires and helped revitalize the West by reformulating its ethos, the direction was indicated by the need of facing up to the remoter East. Represented in (so far) different ways by China and Japan, its rising challenge was being shaped by Asian and global developments within an ambiguous setting made up equally of suppressed competition and superficial consensus, latent antagonisms and proclaimed affinities, and liable to be revolutionized as the salient threat or threats migrated away from Russia.

Managing the change so as to inflect it from confrontation between military or re-militarized powers toward interstimulation among political cultures was favored by having an internally balanced all-European renaissance take place within a power configuration comprising both of the Europe-derived polities in ways and for purposes creative of the presently widest possible concrete and organic community because fostering the appearance of a guiding idea: one that would supplement the infusion of energy, of fresh passion reactivating traditional power, from outside the narrow Europe with an energy-sustaining and -directing ideology. For such a new creed to be capable of moving the system beyond the state of evolution encompassed by religio-confessional and sociopolitical doctrines in succession or alternately, it would have to meet two requirements: fit the pattern and fuel the completion of European history concurrently with the continuance and consummation of evolution globally; and, to this end, define or redefine the great composite civilizations, including the western, in ways sufficiently broad to encompass their constituent elements but also sufficiently focused to differentiate each distinctive civilization from the other. It was in the nature of things – the fact that the main material responsibility for intra-Western reformation had to be borne by the extreme-western parts, and the historically incurred liabilities establishing the claim to equalization exceeding prompt satiation of material appetites lay in the proximate eastern half – that the seeds of the ideology were more likely to be planted, if anywhere, in Europe's East as part of it performing the historically recurrent lead of more primitive sectors in contriving a larger unity, from the upper-Nilotic tribesmen in Old-Kingdom Egypt on.

From so reconstructed a basis the West could contemplate with confidence, and help crystallize with authority, a new "system" of the five-plus major political civilizations, each of them culturally composite but coherent, continent-wide or continents-bridging in scope but amphibious in endowment and vocation, interacting with the others competitively in the inherited multi-tripartite mode but in ways capable of advancing universal accord as the works of hubris gave way in some measure before the ancient dream of *homonoia*.

On the level that parallels before converging with that of process, the level of institutions, any development beyond the evolution of the conflictual state system impelled by the assimilation of partial innovations entailed a transformation wrought by wholesale absorptions. In this perspective on meaning, the key factor is not a possibly but provisional relaxation of compulsions from secular (land–sea and East–West) schisms, but the apparently irreversible fading of a numinous power pertaining to the sacral-secular schism. Generically close to the awe elicited by phenomena perceived as holy, such power had historically come to be vested in the territorial state; but as the secular-institutional embodiment of a quality that frightens as much as it fascinates, the state has continued to combine numinous with mundane power only so long as the latter encompassed effectively its near-physical kernel in the kind of force that repels before it can attract.

In one way or another, across a continuum extending from the Mesopotamian temple community to the post-Roman Empire Roman Church, the territorial state (or its equivalent) had disengaged from the chrysalis of a religious setting in the primitive shape of a predatory military organization, before itself attaining to a quasi-sacral apotheosis. By the same token, after devouring the Church, the State was being absorbed by society. The absorption was in both instances effected instrumentally, by the previously or originally dominant and eventually "reformed" institution being reduced to an auxiliary mechanism servicing the succeeding one; and it was in due course consummated integrally, when the institutional procreator had been demythologized in favor of a mystique half-usurped and half-updated by the successor. However, just as the primitive state (*qua* military organization) had been capable of attaining the more august attributes and exalted status only when invested with functions and feelings close to the confessional, so society as a mechanism for managing material needs and moderating acquisitive instincts (next to sheltering individual rights at the very moment the state was losing either the power or the purpose for endangering them) could realize a higher potential only as it became communal: was endowed on a transterritorial cultural basis with the functions and was capable of eliciting the feelings historically vested in Church and State. This would happen as, though unevenly secularized, the two ideal-organic frameworks of existence helped reabsorb the mechanistic-materialistic features into an at once respiritualized and concretely organic foundation – and this in a manner which, realistically utopian in inspiration, matched a likewise dialectically (competitively-cooperatively) implemented gradual expansion in the community's scale.

An institutional alteration propelled by impulses from the similarly operative processual level, before being completed by the last-stage resultant encompassing the antecedent ones, is fully consummated when it has disclosed an inferable meaning. In groping for such meaning one option is to stay within the secular realm of science and morals, or their equivalents. Located beyond the phenomenal world of provisionally rehabilitated states could then be dimly perceived a distant reality which, born of the political analogue to Newtonian mechanics and capable of incorporating the space-and-time qualifiers purloined from Einsteinian relativity, reaffirmed the purposive endeavor posited in the pre-scientific physics of Aristotle. However imbued with creative potential, an Aristotelian physical world is no less subject to the potential for catastrophe in a moral world governed by the tenets of Aristotle's poetics. For the two disparate potentials to fuse in genuinely progressive statecraft required that tragedy, recognized as ineradicable on the plane of power politics, be not so much relocated from competing territorial states to contending civilizations as reconsigned to its original, private human, sphere; be reclaimed as both a man-defining right and a testing burden by individuals who have relinked tragedy-resistant prosaic concerns to more pristine values in respiritualized community.

A different, if complementary, mode of inferring meaning is to imitate the scholastic theologian's resort to analogy with a better-known or more readily apprehensible actuality, for the sake of a rational grasp of a profounder reality. The imitation can be confined to the method, implicit in the limitations of the relevant branch of knowledge; or it can reflect the substance of the subject matters, implicit in the arcane quality shared with the sacred by a secular statecraft the operations of which are not fully explicable through either systemic or economic determinants as it mediates the stresses of rise and decline that are not fully accounted for by either material or morale factors.

Exploring the meaning confined to the state system was assisted by treating the contemporary one, with its propensity to the organic, as analogous nonetheless to traditionally operative classic world politics by virtue of the "as if" hypothesis; doing so exposes the intimations the analogy affords to methodologically or judgmentally inspired anathema. More deeply suspect is analogy from the history of religion when suggesting parallel progressions: one from tribal-national associations to a world community as only reflecting or also consummating the development from tribal or ethnic into universal or world religions, largely coterminous with the principal civilizations.

Any future meshing together of politico-cultural with religio-confessional civilizations in a radically novel world order, immediately antecedent to a culturally differentiated but politically integrated world community, would be rooted in and bring to fruition developments suggestive of more specific analogies: between magic power vested originally in a variety of physical objects and likewise diffuse mundane power inhering in radically heterogeneous inchoate actors in the transition from the prehistoric era to the earliest recorded and subsequently re-emerging proto-systems; and between a multiplicity of ambiguously disposed and unpredictably behaving spirits or demons, marking the next developmental phase, and ever more uniformly constituted personalist-dynastic actors drawing for anarchic power on resources more commonly innate to the arena than constrained by the arena's structure. The obverse was to be the case in the systemic setting peculiar to the diminished number of fully developed statehoods of major actors when they coalesced, in the historically last (or, possibly, only penultimate) stage, from their antecedents on a par with the few surviving, syncretically evolved, godhoods. Both were part of an order which, originated in either of the two spheres by its founders' faculties, was capable of continuing consolidation as to numbers and of further development as to its foundation and normative efficacy.

Undergirding the supposition of an ultimate meaning suggested by analogy is the dialectic of historically traceable reactions to the nucleus-centered state's vulnerability to dispersion into atomized society. It was most recently manifest in the attempts of the totalitarian religion-substitutes of Right and Left to orchestrate such opposition. If the former's tribal variety failed because its racial exclusiveness condemned it to the necessity to conquer all by renouncing the potential to convert a sufficient number, the latter's would-be universalist version was condemned to coercion by its failure to divert a growing number from pre-established folk-religious practices and loyalties, of the material-acquisitive individualist kind, from its vantage point idolatrously pagan. Although the failures have not estopped the ongoing hidden struggle between progress past the conflictual state system to institutionalized economic cooperation, and regression to tradition for the sake of resuming evolutionary progression, they dramatized the *agon*'s costs.

The ensuing tension continued meanwhile to be centered on the perennial war-peace cycle as one that mirrors the imbrication of mainly inter-state politico-military with mainly intra-state politico-economic factors and processes. For the prediction of impending progress to overwhelm the prophetic insistence on the predicament continuing in the absence of fundamental mutation, it was necessary that the salience of externally focused military-political concerns cease definitively to alternate with - i.e., that it be permanently supplanted by - the salience of domestically focused economic preoccupations. So far, the two alternated as overinvolvement on the military-political plane beyond actor capabilities produced primarily internal economic dislocation, or as underachievement of the politico-militarily pursued objectives promoted intra- or inter-actor economic transactions into the preferred method for combining role-status with stability goals – until like malfunctioning in the economic sphere reversed the operational emphasis and directional thrust once more. The reciprocal compensation for alternate overinvolvements and/or underperformances in the interrelated spheres has been all the more compelling psychopolitically in action because the precipitating discrete conditions have been more easily discernible by the actors than other, largely but retrospectively (and then tentatively) identifiable, interconnections. So long as the compensations continued, they removed progress defined in economic-institutional terms from the realm of impending certainty to the domain of contingent possibility, and depressed its thus defined attributes from the main instigating feature into an implementing incident of the more fundamental mutation.

When treading the path toward an understanding that leads past patterns to meaning, it has been useful to articulate empirically accessible phenomena (making their appearance in function of situations and schisms conditioned spatially and stages of evolution manifest temporally, all fully if often imperfectly externalized in strategies) with the help of an approach, the geo-historical, that aggregates a general perspective with particular principles of analysis. However, a thus disclosed actuality merely represents a deeper reality; the surface facts only reveal subjacent facets consisting, in the first degree of regression from the observable phenomena, of the processes that dynamize world politics and, in regression's second degree, of the latter's defining essence.

One set of the processual facet, comprising rational-strategically shaped interactions, is best apprehensible analogically from principles governing better-articulated universes, physical (political physics) and moral (poetics of politics). The missed features are identifiable inductively from traceable, or inferentially from postulated, relationships of material to immaterial factors and domestic to systemic or geographical determinants (political economy). A closely related set concerned with the evolutionary development that ensues from the interactional dynamic is most approachable speculatively, by virtue of hypotheses aided by the empathy peculiar to historical intelligence.

A thus conducted exploration of the processual features exposes the essential form of world politics, which shapes the ostensibly ever-changing matter of world affairs. The form is then revealed as made up of the primacy of politics, which, residing in the opposite extremes of only proximate motivation and of profoundest inspiration of action, is consistent with actions's ultimate causation by either material capability or domestic authority structures and concerns. And the primacy is more than consistent with, because it is sustained by, the infusion of quantifiable constituents and structures of power with situationally and developmentally conditioned qualifiers of attitudes and purposes. Reducible to spirit, the values and norms emanating from an actor's location in space (situation), time (evolutionary stage), and culture (schisms) are as conspicuously active in operations as they are secretly guiding evolution.

With respect specifically to the temporal-evolutionary dimension, one that confounds operational with organic features, the form is imparted through an overall thrust – a finality implied in the process working itself out through structures invaded by spirit, and doing so, in ways that invest momentum with a possible meaning or meanings approachable by quasi-prophetic intuition. When assisted by projection from proven trends, that kind of divination is neither less nor more reliable than predictions of future events extrapolated quasi-inductively from ostensibly manifest but typically but transient tendencies. All that can be affirmed is that the possibility of inferring meaning from manifest patterns is as much, or as little, implicit in conceiving of politics as an activity assimilating to itself all others in the process of ordering or coordinating them – a faculty of the political warranting its primacy – as it is in viewing the ubiquitous presence of properly construed spirit as an active quality that, by permeating structures, assimilates them to process. The interrelationships do not disappear when they are extended from the several features that inform action to the discrete facets of analysis. Ascending from cyclical recurrences via correspondingly evolving progression to postulated meaning – from discerning the decreasingly manifest to guessing at the ever more problematic if not mysterious – supplements then the likewise three-layered descent from phenomena via process to essence.

Since insight deepens with every step of descent from the superficially extant and problematic features through the subjacent process to the essential attributes of world politics, inquisition into the deeper layers is necessary for fullest possible understanding. Conversely, the decreasing degree to which statements about thus layered features can be empirically verified and the perception of them actually directs strategic behavior makes a dissection of the phenomenal surface into the indispensable preliminary to such understanding. Adopting to this end the geo-historical perspective is to think about world politics in terms of space and time as a corrective to an optic that blots out the former and obscures most of the latter. Treating time as equally important as space means focusing on phases of evolution of states or empires and corresponding plural systems as critical for interactions in physical space. The immediate consequence of including the evolutionary dynamic is to withhold the monopoly of interpretative significance from the instant operations of the balance of power or equilibrium. Downgrading thus the only powerful concept and significant theory of world politics ever devised in favor of a process that cannot be reduced to a theoretical construct of comparable simplicity and power has a larger consequence. It implies renouncing the quest for a parsimonious theory of interstate relations in favor of only loosely structured thinking about these relations in a part-systematic and part-speculative fashion.

Achieving the historical perspective is not a matter of looking down a valley with events arrayed in a straight line of evolution identified with progress. It is rather a matter of climbing successive ranges of mountains ascending to ever higher peaks, each vantage point revealing a vaster horizon in diminishing detail. An effort at thinking about international relations within the temporal-historical dimension will usefully distinguish three unevenly large slices of evolutionary time: from the beginning of recorded history in the ancient Near East; from the beginnings of the European state system in the dissolution of the Roman Empire; and from the onset of the modern era with the global expansion of world politics consequent on the overseas discoveries. Embracing the longest time span from the highest vantage point makes for looking farthest and seeing most, in least detail: it reveals salient subjects, structures, and sequences of actions and conditions not to be encompassed in a shorter view and apt to be buried under the growing mass of data about increasingly recent times; the intermediate time span, surveyed from the middle ranges of the imaginary mountain chain, favors as well as permits a more elaborate delineation and illustration of the stages in continuous evolution of a major state system and its key members; and the relatively shortest view, from the lowest hill above the plain stretching from past toward future, makes it possible to identify and illustrate most precisely the basic strategies implementing the dynamics of balance-of-power interactions: action can now define actors and both merge with the arena.

Thus, the variety and richness of comprised phenomena grow as the contemplated time span shrinks in length and moves forward in historical time, while the clarity of the outline and the proof of continuity diminish and come to depend on the longer perspectives. Much the same is true for the dimension of space as the arena of relationships defined by the two basic physical constituents, land and water. The two were invariably intermeshed, albeit in ever widening orbits of primarily water- and primarily land-based and -oriented actors, expanding in the three uneven periods progressively from local arenas around a river flow through regional ones focused on a closed sea to global scope and demarcated by continents and oceans. Differentiating and combining the three scales of time and space reveals continuity of issues through recurrences. It makes it possible to articulate with some precision the ways of enacting the related conflicts, in acute strife and attempts at accommodation.

Implied in the spatial-temporal complex is the breaking down of world politics into its basic constituents: structures of both state-like actors and system-like arenas; stages in the evolution or development of both; and strategies of interaction around conflictually enacted schisms. Within an environment changing in particulars more than in essentials, structure and stages condition strategies as the most concentrated form of action that feeds back into the conditioning framework of action. However, breaking down complex space-time reality into the main patterns, phases, and policies is only the preliminary to reconfiguring these interdependent units into composite pictures of recurrent systems and situations. Insofar as these, though not conformable in every detail, are still comparable, they delimit the range of practicable possibilities and, while revealing the intricacies of particular patterns, safeguard the essential continuity.

Expanding thus the inquiry in several directions rules out a confident quest for precise correlations and confines the find to clusters or configurations of factors and processes. Nor will isolating comparables as part of making meaningful composites issue in rigorous comparisons, and identifying manifest constraints and presumed imperatives unfailingly reveal specific causality. Only generally construed determinants can be inferred from the interplay between material or organic givens and operational dynamics, one that crystallizes in the behavioral tendencies of state-like actors and helps structure the systemic arenas. The same is true for the broadly cyclical patterns of actor development and system evolution that articulate continuities. Manifest recurrences of actions and configurations cast an only oblique light on the reasons why these take place, but do this in ways that always supplement and often improve upon insights afforded by investigations of supposedly hidden roots or proclamations of ostensible rationales.

A geo-historically articulated dissection of phenomenal world politics is not as readily satisfying as is analysis of interactions by virtue of an abstract-general concept such as "power" or "value" or narrowly defined "structure," and as are explanations of evolution by means of a concrete-specific factor such as trade routes or military technologies. Comprising a range of determinants rules out any single one surfacing as routinely determining; compiling a set of patterns creates the need for circumscribing their permutations; renouncing a rigorous theory and an exact science of international politics augments the obligation to understand it sympathetically. The search for such an understanding that is not only intuitive will perforce be armed with arid schemata, just as these have to be buoyed up with adventurous speculation; imperfect models will serve as the starting point for informed meditation.

There is no assurance that the analytic quality of the product will faithfully mirror the practices of statecraft, any more than its esthetic quality will validate the conception of statecraft as high art. Nor is it certain that a sense of what can be encompassed and what is certain to be missed by self-consciously rigorous theory – a sense that constitutes indispensable theoretical wisdom – can inspirit a valid supplement to such theory in the domain of scholarship; any more than that, for the purposes of enlightened statecraft, a practical intelligence nourished by regard for findings distilled from a purposively dissected past, and chastened by insights from tragic poetry, can usefully revise the imperatives issuing from a strategic rationality biased in favor of immediately accessible perceptions and instruments.

Implied in the query is the question whether anything valid can be built upon the reduction of international relations to the powerfully simplifying realist view of power politics; whether the next step toward understanding can relieve the austerities and redeem the self-imposed simplicity of the balance-of-power paradigm within a larger setting and a longer perspective. The power-balancing appears then as but the core, if a vital one, of a more amorphous whole with a more profound meaning, wherein the oscillations of a more complex equilibrium in geopolitical space are but so many ripples on the less clearly charted currents of time. The related puzzle is whether the understanding of states and empires in their relations that reaches beyond elementary diagnosis can help arm praxis with policy-relevant prognosis; whether such a raising of sights will match in its results the capacity of actors and systems of actors themselves to mature past elemental urges, albeit with comparable costs to the drives' narrow-gauged specificity. The wager taken up in the attempt is that trying for more has not from the outset been doomed to achieving less, as the later stumbling disturbed the impression left by the earlier steps; that the attempt to discern potentially fruitful meaning in a customarily fateful momentum did better than disclose the search's inevitably sterile end.

Select Bibliography

Adams, Brooks, *The New Empire*, MacMillan, New York, 1902.
—— *The Law of Civilization and Decay*, Knopf, New York, 1943.
Anderson, M. S. *Britain's Discovery of Russia, 1553–1815*, MacMillan, London, 1958.
—— *The Eastern Question 1774–1923*, St Martin's, New York, 1966.
—— *Europe in the Eighteenth Century 1713–1783*, Longman, New York, 1976.
—— *The Ascendancy of Europe 1815–1914*, Longman, London, 1972.
Anderson, Perry, *Lineages of the Absolutist State*, Humanities Press, Atlantic Highlands, 1974.
Andrewes, Antony, *The Greeks*, Hutchinson, London, 1967.
Aston, Margaret, *The Fifteenth Century: The Prospect of Europe*, Harcourt, Brace & World, New York, 1968.
Aston, T. H. (ed.), *Crisis in Europe 1560–1660*, Basic Books, New York, 1965.
Badian, Emil, *Roman Imperialism in the Late Republic*, Cornell University Press, Ithaca, 1968.
Barraclough, Geoffrey, *The Medieval Empire: Idea and Reality*, G. Philip, London, 1950.
—— *History in A Changing World*, Blackwell, Oxford, 1955.
—— *The Medieval Papacy*, Harcourt, Brace and World, New York, 1968.
—— *The Crucible of Europe*, University of California Press, Berkeley, 1976.
Bartlett, C. J. (ed.), *Britain Pre-Eminent*, St Martin's, New York, 1969.
Baynes, N. H., *Byzantine Studies and Other Essays*, Athlone Press, London, 1955.
Berghahn, V. R., *Germany and the Approach of War in 1914*, St Martin's, New York, 1973.
Berlin, Isaiah, *The Hedgehog and the Fox: An Essay on Tolstoy's View of History*, Simon & Schuster, New York, 1953.
Billington, James H., *The Icon and the Axe: An Intepretive History of Russian Culture*, Knopf, New York, 1966.
Borst, Arno, *Lebensformen in Mittelalter*, Propylän, Frankfurt a. Main, 1973.
Bourne, Kenneth, *Britain and the Balance of Power in North America 1815–1908*, University of California Press, Berkeley, 1967.

—— *The Foreign Policy of Victorian England 1830–1902*, Clarendon, Oxford, 1970.

Bouwsma, William James, *Venice and the Defense of Republican Liberty*, University of California Press, Berkeley, 1968.

Bozeman, Adda, *Politics and Culture in International History*, Princeton University Press, Princeton, 1960.

Braudel, Fernand, *The Mediterranean and the Mediterranean World in the Age of Philip II*, Harper & Row, New York, 1972.

—— *Afterthoughts on Material Civilization and Capitalism*, Johns Hopkins University Press, Baltimore, 1977.

Bromley, J. S., and E. H. Kossmann, (eds), *Britain and the Netherlands in Europe and Asia*, St Martin's, New York, 1968.

Brucker, Gene, *Florentine Politics and Society 1343–1378*, Princeton University Press, Princeton, 1962.

—— *Renaissance Florence*, University of California Press, Berkeley, 1969.

Butterfield, Herbert, *The Origins of Modern Science 1300–1800*, G. Bell, London, 1949.

Carsten, F.L., *The Origins of Prussia*, Oxford University Press, New York, 1954.

Carter, C.H., *The Secret Diplomacy of the Habsburgs 1598–1625*, Columbia University Press, New York, 1964.

Cherniavsky, Michael (ed.), *The Structure of Russian History*, Random House, New York, 1970.

Cipolla, Carlo M., *Guns and Sails in the Early Phase of European Expansion 1400–1700*, Pantheon Books, New York, 1966.

—— (ed.), *The Economic Decline of Empires, Methuen*, London, 1970.

Clark, G. N., *War and Society in the Seventeenth Century*, University Press, Cambridge (Eng.), 1958.

Cohen, Saul B., *Geography and Politics in a World Divided*, Random House, New York, 1963.

Coles, Paul, *The Ottoman Impact on Europe*, Thames & Hudson, London, 1968.

Collingwood, R. G., *The Idea of History*, Clarendon House, Oxford, 1948.

Cook, Albert S. (ed.), *Oedipus Rex: A Mirror for Greek Drama*, Wadsworth Publishing Co., Belmont, CA, 1963.

Cooper, J. P., "Sea Power," *New Cambridge Modern History*, Vol. IV, University Press, Cambridge, (Eng.), 1970.

Daniel, Norman, *Islam, Europe and Empire*, Edinburgh University Press, Edinburgh, 1966.

—— *The Arabs and Medieval Europe*, Longman, London, 1979.

Davis, Ralph, *The Rise of Atlantic Economies*, Cornell University Press, Ithaca, 1977.

Dehio, Ludwig, *The Precarious Balance*, Knopf, New York, 1962.

DeMolen, Richard L. (ed.), *One Thousand Years: Western Europe in the Middle Ages*, Houghton Mifflin, Boston, 1974.

Dvornik, Francis, *Slavs in European History and Civilization*, Rutgers University Press, New Brunswick, 1962.

Earle, Peter (ed.), *Essays in European Economic History 1500–1800*, Clarendon Press, Oxford, 1974.

Elliott, J. H. *Imperial Spain 1469–1716*, St. Martin's, New York, 1963.

—— *Europe Divided 1559–1598*, Harper & Row, New York, 1969.

—— *The Old World and the New 1492–1650*, University Press, Cambridge (Eng.)., 1970.

Elvin, Mark, *The Patterns of Chinese Past*, Stanford University Press, Stanford, 1973.

Fadner, Frank, L., *Seventy Years of Pan-Slavism in Russia*, Georgetown University Press, Washington, DC, 1962.

Fergusson, Francis, *The Idea of a Theater*, Princeton University Press, Princeton, 1949.
Finley, John H., Jr., *Three Essays on Thucydides*, Harvard University Press, Cambridge (MA), 1967.
Fischer-Galati, S. A., *Ottoman Imperialism and the German Protestants*, Harvard University Press, Cambridge MA, 1959.
Fliess, Peter J., *Thucydides and the Politics of Bipolarity*, Louisiana State University Press, Baton Rouge, 1966.
Fox, Edward W., *History in Geographic Perspective*, Norton, New York, 1971.
Gamow, George, and John M. Cleveland, *Physics: Foundations and Frontiers*, 3rd edn, Prentice-Hall, Englewood Cliffs, 1976.
Gilbert, Felix, "The 'New Diplomacy' of the 18th Century", World Politics 4 (1951).
—— *Machiavelli and Guicciardini: Politics and History in Sixteenth Century Florence*, Princeton University Press, Princeton, 1965.
Gollwitzer, Heinz, *Europe in the Age of Imperialism 1880–1914*, Harcourt, Brace and World, New York, 1969.
Graham, Gerald S., *The Politics of Naval Supremacy*, Cambridge University Press, London, 1965.
Grenville, Johns A. S., and George Berkeley Young, *Politics, Strategy and American Diplomacy* Yale University Press, New Haven, 1966.
Grundy, George B., *Thucydides and the History of His Age*, Blackwell, Oxford, 1948.
Hale, J. R. (ed.), *Renaissance Venice*, Rowman and Littlefield, Totowa, NJ, 1973.
Halecki, Oskar, *The Limits and Divisions of European History*, Sheed and Ward, New York, 1950.
—— *The Millennium of Europe*, University of Notre Dame Press, Notre Dame, 1963.
Heer, Friedrich, *The Holy Roman Empire*, Praeger, New York, 1968.
Hellie, Richard, *Enserfment and Military Change in Muscovy*, University of Chicago Press, Chicago, 1971.
Herlihy, David, *The History of Feudalism*, Harper and Row, New York, 1970.
Hill, Christopher, *The Century of Revolution 1603–1714*, T. Nelson, Edinburgh, 1961.
Hillgruber, Andreas, *Germany and the Two World Wars*, Harvard University Press, Cambridge MA, 1981.
Hobsbawm, E. J., *The Age of Revolution 1789–1848*, New American Library, New York, 1962.
—— *Industry and Empire*, Weidenfeld and Nicolson, London, 1968.
Hoetzsch, Otto, *The Evolution of Russia*, Harcourt, Brace and World, New York, 1966.
Howard, Michael, *War in European History*, Oxford University Press, New York, 1976.
Hyde, John K., *Society and Politics in Medieval Italy*, St. Martin's, New York, 1973.
Issawi, Charles Philip, *The Arab World's Legacy*, Darwin Press, Princeton, 1981.
Itzkowitz, Norman, *Ottoman Empire and Islamic Tradition*, University of Chicago Press, Chicago, 1972.
Jensen, DeLamar, *Diplomacy and Dogmatism*, Harvard University Press, Cambridge MA, 1964.
Kagan, Donald, *The Outbreak of the Peloponnesian War*, Cornell University Press, Ithaca, 1969.
Kantorowicz, E. H., *The King's Two Bodies*, Princeton University Press, Princeton, 1957.
Karpat, Kemal H. (ed.), *The Ottoman State and Its Place in World History*, E. J. Brill, Leiden, 1974.
Kasperson, Roger E., and Julian V. Minghi (eds), *The Structure of Political Geography*, Aldine Publishing Co., Chicago, 1969.
Katz, Solomon, *The Decline of Rome and the Rise of Medieval Europe*, Cornell University Press, Ithaca, 1955.

Kennedy, Paul, *The Rise of Anglo-American Antagonism 1860–1914*, Allen & Unwin, London, 1980.

Kerner, Robert J., *The Urge to the Sea: The Course of Russian History*, University of California Press, Berkeley, 1942.

Kitto, H. D. F., *Greek Tragedy: A Literary Study*, Methuen, London, 1976.

Knox, Bernard McG. W., *Oedipus at Thebes*, Yale University Press, New Haven, 1957.

Kortepeter, C. Max, *Ottoman Imperialism During the Reformation*, New York University Press, New York, 1972.

Koyré, Alexandre, *From the Closed World to the Infinite Universe*, Harper, New York, 1958.

Krook, Dorothea, *Elements of Tragedy*, Yale University Press, New Haven, 1969.

Kuntz, Paul G. (ed.), *The Concept of Order*, University of Washington Press, Seattle, 1968.

Labande, E. R., *L'Italie de la Renaissance*, Payot, Paris, 1954.

Landes, David S., *The Unbound Prometheus*, Cambridge University Press, London 1969.

Lane, Frederic C., *Venice and History*, Johns Hopkins University Press, Baltimore, 1966.

Leech, Clifford, *Tragedy*, Methuen, London, 1969.

Levenson, Joseph R. (ed.), *European Expansion and the Counter-Example of Asia 1300–1600*, Prentice-Hall, Englewood Cliffs, 1967.

Li, Dun J., *The Ageless Chinese: A History*, Scribner, New York, 1965.

Lobanov-Rostovsky, Andrei, *Russia and Asia*, MacMillan, New York, 1933.

Loewe, Michael, *Imperial China*, Allen & Unwin, London, 1966.

Lopez, Robert S., *The Birth of Europe*, M. Evans, New York, 1967.

—— *The Three Ages of the Italian Renaissance*, University Press of Virginia, Charlottesville, 1970.

Löwith, Karl, *Meaning in History: The Theological Implications of the Philosophy of History*, University of Chicago Press, Chicago, 1949.

Lublinskaya, A. D., *French Absolutism: The Crucial Phase 1620–1629*, Cambridge University Press, London, 1968.

Lynch, John, *Spain Under the Habsburgs*, vol. I, Oxford University Press, New York, 1965.

McCall, Marsh H. (ed.), *Aeschylus: A Collection of Critical Essays*, Prentice-Hall, Englewood Cliffs, 1972.

Mackinder, Halford, *Democratic Ideals and Reality*, Holt, New York, 1950.

MacMaster, Robert E., *Danilevsky: A Russian Totalitarian Philosopher*, Harvard University Press, Cambridge MA, 1967.

McNeill, William H., *The Rise of the West*, University of Chicago Prerss, Chicago, 1963.

—— *Europe's Steppe Frontier 1500–1800*, University of Chicago Press, Chicago, 1964.

—— *The Shape of European History*, Oxford University Press, New York, 1974.

—— *The Pursuit of Power*, University of Chicago Press, Chicago, 1982.

March, A., and I. M. Freeman, *The New World of Physics*, Random House, New York, 1962.

Martines, Lauro, *Power and Imagination: City-States in Renaissance Italy*, Knopf, New York, 1979.

Mattingly, Garrett, *Renaissance Diplomacy*, J. Cape, London, 1955.

Mensching, Gustav, *Structures and Patterns of Religion*, Motilal Banarsidass, Delhi, 1976.

Meyerhoff, Hans (ed.), *The Philosophy of History in Our Time*, Doubleday, Garden City, 1959.

Modelski, George, "The Long Cycle of Global Politics and the Nation-State," *Comparative Studies in Society and History*, vol. 20, no. 2, April 1978.

Mundy, John H., *Europe in the High Middle Ages 1150–1309*, Longman, London, 1973.

New Cambridge Modern History, vols. *I–VI*, University Press, Cambridge (Eng.), 1967–70.

Oates, Joan, *Babylon*, Thames & Hudson, London, 1979.

Otis, Brooks, *Cosmos and Tragedy: An Essay on the Meaning of Aeschylus*, University of North Carolina Press, Chapel Hill, 1981.

Painter, Sidney, *Medieval Society*, Cornell University Press, Ithaca, 1957.

Parker, Geoffrey, *Spain and the Netherlands 1559–1659*, Enslow Publishers, Short Hills, NJ, 1979.

Pipes, Richard, *Russia Under the Old Regime*, Scribner, New York, 1974.

Pirenne, Jacques, *The Tides of History*, 2 vols., Allen & Unwin, London, 1962.

Pois, Robert A., *Friedrich Meinecke and German Politics in the Twentieth Century*, University of California Press, Berkeley, 1972.

Pokrovskii, M. N., *Russia in World History*, University of Michigan Press, Ann Arbor, 1970.

Porter, Bernard, *Britain, Europe and the World 1850–1982*, Allen & Unwin, London, 1983.

Postan, Michael M., *Medieval Trade and Finance*, University Press, Cambridge (Eng.), 1973,

Preston, Richard A. et al., *Men in Arms*, Praeger, New York, 1962.

Quester, George H., *Offense and Defense in the International System*, J. Wiley, New York, 1977.

Raeff, Marc, *Understanding Imperial Russia*, Columbia University Press, New York, 1984.

Randall, John H., *Aristotle*, Columbia University Press, New York, 1960.

Reichen, Charles Albert, *A History of Physics*, Hawthorn Books, New York, 1963.

Ritter, Gerhard, *The Sword and the Scepter: The Problem of Militarism in Germany*, 4 vols., University of Miami Press, Coral Gables, 1969–1973.

Rohl, J. C. G. and N. Sombart (eds), *Kaiser Wilhelm II: New Interpretations*, Cambridge University Press, New York, 1982.

Romilly, Jacqueline de *Thucydide et l'impérialisme Athénien*, Société d'Edition "Les Belles Lettres," Paris, 1947.

—— *The Rise and Fall of States According to Greek Authors*, University of Michigan Press, Ann Arbor, 1977.

Ropp, Theodore, *War in the Modern World*, Duke University Press, Durham, 1959.

Rosecrance, Richard N., *The Rise of the Trading State: Commerce and Conquest in the Modern World*, Basic Books, New York, 1985.

Scheler, Max, "On the Tragic,'" in Michel Laurence and Richard B. Sewall (eds), *Tragedy: Modern Essays in Criticism*, Prentice-Hall, Englewood Cliffs, 1963.

Segal, Gerald (ed.), *The China Factor: Peking and the Superpowers*, Holmes & Meier, New York, 1982.

Semmel, Bernard, *The Rise of Free Trade Imperialism*, Cambridge University Press, New York, 1970.

Shaw, Stanford, *History of the Ottoman Empire and Modern Turkey*, vol. 1, Cambridge University Press, New York, 1976.

Sheehan, James J. (ed.), *Imperial Germany*, New Viewpoints, New York, 1976.

Skocpol, Theda, *States and Social Revolutions*, Cambridge University Press, New York, 1979.

Smith, Morton, *The Greeks*, Cornell University Press, Ithaca, 1960.

Spuler, Bertold, *The Mongols in History*, Praeger, New York, 1971.

Steiner, George, *The Death of Tragedy*, Knopf, New York, 1961.

Steiner, Zara S., *Britain and the Origins of the First World War*, St. Martin's, New York, 1977.

Stern, Fritz, *The Politics of Cultural Despair: A Study in the Rise of the German Ideology*, University of California Press, Berkeley, 1974.

Stradling, R. A., *Europe and the Decline of Spain*, Allen & Unwin, London, 1981.

Sumner, B. H., *Tsardom and Imperialism in the Far East and Middle East 1880–1914*, H. Milford, London, 1942.

Tilly, Charles (ed.), *The Formation of National States in Western Europe*, Princeton University Press, Princeton, 1975.

Vaughan, Dorothy M., *Europe and the Turk: A Pattern of Alliances 1350–1700*, Liverpool University Press, Liverpool, 1954.

Von Laue, Theodore, *Theodore Ranke: The Formative Years*, Princeton University Press, Princeton, 1950.

Waley, Arthur, *Three Ways of Thought in Ancient China*, Doubleday, Garden City, 1956.

Walker, Richard L., *The Multi-State System of Ancient China*, Shoe String Press, Hamden CT, 1953.

Wallace-Hadrill, J. M., *The Barbarian West 400–1000*, Harper & Row, New York, 1962.

Wallerstein, Immanuel, *The Modern World System, vols. I, II*, Academic Press, New York, 1974, 1980.

Wesson, Robert G., *The Russian Dilemma*, Rutgers University Press, New Brunswick, 1974.

Westfall, Richard S., *Never at Rest: A Biography of Isaac Newton*, Cambridge University Press, New York, 1980.

White, Lynn T., *Medieval Technology and Social Change*, Clarendon Press, Oxford, 1962.

Wilson, Charles H., *Transformation of Europe 1558–1648*, University of California Press, Berkeley, 1976.

—— *Profit and Power*, Longman Green, London, 1957.

Wilson, John A., *The Culture of Ancient Egypt*, University of Chicago Press, Chicago, 1963.

Winzen, Peter, *Bülows Weltmachtkonzept*, H. Boldt, Boppard am Rhein, 1977.

Wittfogel, Karl August, *Oriental Despotism: A Comparative Study of Total Power*, Yale University Press, New Haven, 1957.

Woodbridge, F. J. E. (ed.), *Aristotle's Vision of Nature*, Columbia University Press, New York, 1965.

Index